This series of interlinked essays takes the form of historical 'voyages' around the Victorian intellectual John Henry Newman, and Newman's classic work *The Idea of a University*, as well as changes in the structure and culture of universities which occurred in Newman's lifetime.

The voyages connect nineteenth- and twentieth-century university history, mainly in Britain and the United States but with side excursions to Continental Europe. Among the many important topics discussed are the history of student communities in Oxford and Cambridge, the growth of a modern examinations culture, university architecture and the use of space in connection with educational ideals, urbanism and universities, and the competition of states, markets and academic guilds for the control of universities and the right to define the missions of university professors.

The modern university and its discontents

THE MODERN UNIVERSITY AND ITS DISCONTENTS

THE FATE OF NEWMAN'S LEGACIES IN BRITAIN AND AMERICA

SHELDON ROTHBLATT

CAMBRIDGE
UNIVERSITY PRESS

PUBLISHED BY THE PRESS SYNDICATE OF THE UNIVERSITY OF CAMBRIDGE
The Pitt Building, Trumpington Street, Cambridge CB2 1RP, United Kingdom

CAMBRIDGE UNIVERSITY PRESS
The Edinburgh Building, Cambridge CB2 2RU, United Kingdom
40 West 20th Street, New York, NY 10011–4211, USA
10 Stamford Road, Oakleigh, Melbourne 3166, Australia

First published 1997

Printed in the United Kingdom at the University Press, Cambridge

Typeset in Granjon 11/13 pt

*A catalogue record for this book is available from
the British Library*

Library of Congress cataloguing in publication data

Rothblatt, Sheldon.
The modern university and its discontents: the fate of Newman's
legacies in Britain and America / Sheldon Rothblatt.
p.   cm.
ISBN 0 521 45331 3 (hc)
1. Education, Higher – Great Britain – History. 2. Education,
Higher – United States – History. 3. Education, Higher – Aims and
objectives – Great Britain. 4. Education, Higher – Aims and
objectives – United States. 5. Newman, John Henry, 1801–1890.
LA636.R67   1997
378.41 – dc20   96–2950   CIP

ISBN 0 521 45331 3

For Barbara
more precious than rubies

Having therefore consulted with my Wife, and some of my Acquaintance, I determined to go again to Sea . . . My Hours of Leisure I spent in reading the best Authors, ancient and modern; being always provided with a good Number of Books; and when I was ashore, in observing the Manners and Dispositions of the People, as well as learning their Language.

Jonathan Swift, *Gulliver's Travels*

CONTENTS

CONTENTS

PREFACE

History is about origins, transformations and outcomes. But the outcomes are always temporary or even false. Historians who write on topics of contemporary concern consequently face obvious dangers when they assume that a trend is over, granting them a licence to pontificate. It is therefore best to admit at the outset that I fell prey to a minuscule amount of moralising possibly excusable in light of the intense and to me disturbing political and ideological academic exchanges of the last thirty years. But in general I hope readers will agree that I am primarily interested in understanding events in accordance with the conventional rules of historical practice.

In composing this work, drawing together materials from many locations, revisiting arguments in the light of recent developments, comparing early and later thoughts and trying to absorb the insights and learning of valued colleagues from many countries, I was pleasantly surprised to discover that I had more origins than I at first imagined. The chapters tell all, but a short list can be added here. I am clearly concerned about the origins of a way of thinking about universities that is, even in its denial, permanent; about a species of creature called an 'undergraduate'; about market discipline as a concept, a fact and a method of historical inquiry; about failure, not just the absence of success but a lingering sense of inadequacy and how universities have contributed to both. I share an interest with others in the beginnings of competitive examinations, how they became institutionalised and led to the formation of different academic cultures. The fabrication of new types of universities, exactly why they were new, how they compared to other universities and what happened to them over time are main themes. So are changes in how university spaces, buildings, iconography and emblems are understood as they become necessary parts of a university education. Cities and universities are an obvious interest, but cities and universities as intersecting entities whose propensity for continual rebirth always produces fresh and interesting problems.

Relationships between parenting, the life cycle and higher education frame another set of inquiries. Most historical and sociological attention has been directed to families and schooling, but the stress here (because universities are the subject) is on patterns of child-rearing as they intertwine with the occasionally parallel but often contradictory educational programmes maintained by academic guilds. And the academic guild itself, the origins of a guild outlook in competition with other possible or rejected outlooks, is also a subject that appears in the following pages. Each of these origins and developments has ironical and certainly problematical dimensions.

This is not a work about John Henry Newman, the subject of more expert attention, but that his name should be mentioned in the title is not in doubt. He is the grand master of the subject of origins. *The Idea of a University* remains the greatest work on the etiology of a 'university' in the English language. Newman identified many of the central issues regarding the functions of a university on any occasion and gave lasting literary form to an argument that still mesmerises scholars, inspiring innumerable reflections on what a university is and ought to be.[1] That he was able to exert such extraordinary influence is of course attributable to his gigantic talents as an intellect, but also, as his reappearance at key points in the following chapters indicates, because he participated in so many of the transformations and departures noticed in this book. He himself was one of the first undergraduates, 'recognizable as such'. He understood the relationship of college to university and of teaching to personal development, of the importance of new knowledge and its limitations as a factor in the formation of human understanding. And he knew who the enemies were to his way of envisioning the good life, saw them being born and turned his anger against them. He was not an easy nor a simple man. His conclusions are hardly beyond dispute, and they are not the last word, but that is irrelevant to these studies. He is an important part of the history being discussed, and that is sufficient reason for giving him prominent billing.

As the epigraph indicates, the format adopted in this book is that of a number of 'voyages' around Newman, with some of the digressions, intrusions and surprises that come with travels, even when the destination

---

[1] E.g. *The Idea of a Modern University*, ed. Sidney Hook, Paul Kurtz and Miro Tudorovich (Buffalo, NY, 1974). I regret that a new work, *The Idea of a University, John Henry Newman,* ed. Frank M. Turner (New Haven and London, 1996), appeared too late for me to use.

is approximately known. If that were not true, neither the Bible nor the *Odyssey* would be interesting.

The notes indicate particular debts, but I want to reserve space for very special obligations, professional, intellectual, personal. Martin Trow and Neil Smelser at the University of California, Berkeley; Burton R. Clark at the University of California, Los Angeles; A. H. Halsey at Oxford University; Noël Gilroy, Lord Annan of Cambridge and London – old and cherished friends all – have been lasting influences. Their names appear and reappear in this volume, but even where citations are absent, their presence is apparent. Norma Landau of the University of California at Davis has been a stimulating colleague for thirty years, as well as a formidable critic. She is always right. President Emeritus Clark Kerr of the University of California has been and continues to be an indispensable example. I also want to record a particular tribute to the late Edward Shils of the University of Chicago and Cambridge University, to his memory, for debts incurred many years ago.

Roger Hahn and John Heilbron, colleagues in the Department of History at Berkeley, have always been ready with intellectual assistance. Rowland Eustace of the Society for Research into Higher Education has maintained a running correspondence with me on the 'federal principle' in higher education. He makes a very good Socratic daemon. Guy Neave of the International Association of Universities in Paris, Graeme Moodie of York, Roy Lowe of Birmingham (and now Swansea), Donald Withrington of King's College, Aberdeen, Svante Lindqvist of the Royal Swedish Institute of Technology, Thorsten Nybom of Linköping University and Director of the Swedish Council for Studies in Higher Education, colleagues at the universities of Uppsala, Göteborg, Umeå and at the Swedish Collegium for Advanced Studies in the Social Sciences, Uppsala, have been unfailingly supportive in every way for a long time now. I greatly admire their learning and, what is more, their integrity, a word favoured by Newman.

I want to thank Elizabeth Morse (now living in Oxford) for assisting me in some parts of the research. Closer to home, staff members at the Center for Studies in Higher Education – Valerie Guzman, Diane Terry, Barbara Briscoe, Carroll Brentano and Marian Gade – were stalwarts. Edna and Louis Martin, consummate Londoners, also deserve a special tribute: the best of guides, the best of friends.

For the use of original material and other courtesies, I am indebted to the late Dame Lucy Sutherland who provided me with access to the transcripts of John Cooke's Corpus Christi College, Oxford, correspondence. For the use of their collections, I want to thank the Warden and

Fellows of Nuffield College; the Provost and Fellows of Oriel College; the Dean and Students of Christ Church; the President and Fellows of Magdalen College; the Principal and Fellows of Brasenose College; and David Vaisey of the Bodleian Library.

An earlier version of Chapter 1 appeared in *Conversazione* (1989), published by La Trobe University, Melbourne, Australia, and in Swedish translation as 'Tesen om universitetets idé och dess antites', in *Tvärsnitt* (1994). I wish to thank Claudio Véliz, now of Boston University, for suggesting the subject and allowing me to do it, and for granting permission to build on the original platform. Permission to use parts of Chapter 3, then called 'The Student Sub-culture and the Examination System in Early Nineteenth-Century Oxbridge' appearing in *The University in Society,* ed. Lawrence Stone, I (Princeton, 1974), has been granted by the Princeton University Press. An Italian translation was published by Società editrice il Mulino, Bologna, in 1980. Sections of Chapter 4 were published as 'Failure in Early Nineteenth-Century Oxford and Cambridge' in *History of Education*, 11 (March 1982), and of Chapter 5 under the same title in *History of Education*, 16 (1987). Taylor & Francis, publishers of the journal, have granted reproduction rights. Chapter 7 first appeared as 'London: A Metropolitan University?' It has been adapted from *The City and the University: From Medieval Origins to the Present,* ed. Thomas Bender, copyright 1989 by Oxford University Press, and has been reprinted by permission. Chapter 8 is reprinted in part from *History of European Ideas*, 7, 'George Eliot as a Type of European Intellectual', pages 46–66, copyright (1986), with kind permission from Elsevier Science Ltd., The Boulevard, Langford Lane, Kidlington OX5 1GB. Chapter 9 but with a different purport was first published as 'The Notion of an Open Scientific Community in Historical Perspective' in *Science as a Commodity*, eds. Michael Gibbons and Björn Wittrock (London, 1985). Addison Wesley Longman Ltd. has granted permission for the publication of a different version.

I am eternally indebted to the Swedish Council for Studies of Higher Education for sponsoring publication of this work. The Council's breathtaking support of international scholarship sets a standard difficult – I am inclined to say impossible – for any other country to match.

Extensive new material and drastic alterations have been undertaken throughout this book. New voyages have provided second thoughts. Nevertheless, unlike Lemuel Gulliver, I did not forswear the company of Yahoos nor pretend to admire Houyhnhnms when completing the last voyage.

CHAPTER ONE

THE IDEA OF THE IDEA OF A UNIVERSITY
AND ITS ANTITHESIS

INTRODUCTION: IDEAS OF A UNIVERSITY

The subject of this chapter is the history of the 'idea of a university', or rather, it is the history of the idea that a university derives its identity from an idea. The subject is puzzling. Why does a university require an 'idea'? Quite simply, it does not. The historical answer, however, is more interesting. Whether or not a university needs an 'idea', it has been assigned one, more than one, in fact. For two centuries a particular kind of debate has gone on, revived in every generation, concerning the role and purpose of a university and the education it provides. The debate has been inconclusive. Yet what is significant about the history of the idea of a university is the search for one, the striving after an ideal that must satisfy two conditions: it must be pure, like a platonic ideal, and it must be lasting, superior to all apparent transformations.

By 'idea', then, is meant an inherent purpose, embedded, as it were, into the university and possibly its history – but this is not always clear from debate. An 'idea' is also a genetic code that dictates the subsequent development of a university; but like all such inheritances, the signals are not always recognised.

Metaphors such as these come readily to mind, for the history of the idea of the idea of a university lacks precision. There is no clear linear development such as intellectual historians prefer, no Darwinian evolution from one idea to another. A single idea of a university has never truly existed, although in some periods fewer alternatives were available. There have been emphases. In approximately 800 years of history, the university as an institution has served many different cultures and societies. Its transmogrifications are nearly as numerous as the historical changes occurring in western society; but because there appears to be continuity between past and present – costumes, rituals and ways of self-government and the organisation of studies seem recognisable – it is convenient to deduce that universities have always shared an essential element.

It is both natural and unnatural to discuss institutions as if they embody an abiding, single purpose that provides a compass for decision-making. It is natural because complex institutions are otherwise unmanageable, adrift and open to all competing pressures. But it is unnatural for precisely the same reason. Highly differentiated organisations can be limited to key objectives only if they are inherently stable and unchanging. Universities are neither, which is why discussions today are more likely to focus on 'changing roles' and 'future challenges', categories that bypass the question of an institutional essence.[1] Yet any discussion of 'changing roles' inevitably invites a backward look. That look always encounters two stubborn traditions of idealising universities, the first English and the second German. Critics of universities appeal to both traditions. Those who believe universities are resistant to innovation point to bottlenecks created by the 'idea of a university'. Those who are saddened, or angered, by twentieth-century trends towards diversification and differentiation, appeal for help to the same source. This being the case, the history of a way of thinking about institutions is worth examining.

Quite probably those who live and work in universities, churches, governments or corporations carry with them some everyday conception of institutional purpose. Intermixed with an obvious career interest is a reference to a higher objective, often moral or at least elevating, self-justifying in some cases, but also uplifting. Ordinary occupational service is raised to a superior level. It is possible to speak about the idea of public service, the idea of corporate loyalty and cooperative effort, the idea of self-sacrifice and honour (as in military service), but few of these ideas, except for those associated with the history of religions, have as clear an historiography and available reference manual as do universities. The 'idea of a university' is a signature immediately recognisable.

A distinction can be made between 'idea' as a thing in itself and particular kinds of 'ideas'. For the sake of argument we might say that the idea of a university is education, but what kind should it be? Liberal, vocational, technical, research-related? Is the object culture, citizenship, leadership or career? Are the recipients young men, young men and women, 'mature' students, postgraduates? Do they attend full or part time? The idea of a university can be negative. A university is not the place for this or that purpose because it is the place for something else.

---

[1] E.g., *The Role of the University: a Global Perspective*, ed. Torsten Husén (The United Nations University and UNESCO, Tokyo, 1994).

In the absence of an idea of a university, there would exist no reason to dispute its nature. A university would simply be another institution, changing as circumstances allow, assuming new identities as easily as actors on the stage, with no particular aggregate commitment to any of a large number of easily assumed roles. We cannot deny that this occurs often in the history of universities. It seems to be the situation today. But such continuities as universities enjoy, such aspirations as they have to be a moral force in modern society, or at least a unique voice, are attributable to the odd and special history of the idea of the idea of a university. Even when that idea can no longer be discerned, it remains an intrusion, a method for organising thoughts about the essential purpose of higher education. It is consequently both inspiring and mischievous. An idea can elevate routine life to a higher realm, transposing mere occupations into callings; but its seductions can also channel energy into what appears to be hackneyed and sterile debate.

'Idea' is a useful but elusive word. Ambidextrous, it is of Greek origin and ranges in meaning from 'thought', 'opinion' or 'belief' to 'scheme' and 'project'. It descends into murkier depths yet to find itself only an 'inkling'. In short, 'idea' rivals 'thing', to which Dr Samuel Johnson, in his celebrated *Dictionary*, gave priority of place as the 'vaguest of all words'. Yet no matter how hazy or imprecise, or possibly because it is genuinely flaccid, no other word in the English language has had a comparable influence on discussions of what a university is, could or ought to be. And although other institutions have from time to time also been examined for their underlying 'idea' – the idea of a national Church, the idea of the State, the idea of an intelligentsia – no one of them has inspired a literature that continually builds upon itself, repeats itself almost desperately and is itself an inextricable and living part of the institution to which it refers. Futhermore, the 'idea of a university' is not merely a method for analysing the basic functions or missions of a university as if their fundamental utility is simply a matter of going down a list. The 'idea' of a university is invariably, one might say inevitably, a moral one, so that departures from it, or modifications of it, are a form of betrayal to be repented or an act of treason to be punished. Thus Julien Benda, in an argument parallel to that used to discuss universities, invoked the idea of an intellectual when he denounced activist ideology as *traison* in his famous book on the betrayal of intellectuals.

We need to begin the history of the idea of the idea of a university with a summary of the different if overlapping ways in which the university as an institution has been both defined and typified:

1   according to its forms of internal governance, in which case it is often
    referred to as a self-governing guild or corporation of junior and senior
    members, or masters and students;

2   according to its broadest existing social characteristics or identifi-
    cations, in which case it can be called, *inter alia*, aristocratic;

3   according to its principles of entry, which bear upon its funding and
    staffing ratios, in which case it is elitist, meritocratic, or mass-access or
    open;

4   according to its geographic location or outlook, so that it is civic or
    municipal, provincial, metropolitan, urban, suburban or exurban,
    local, regional or national;

5   according to its legal or constitutional status or principal source of
    financial support, in which case it is state-supported, or publicly main-
    tained, or private or quasi-private (as in the case of Cornell University
    in New York State), although, being one or the other, it sometimes
    simulates its opposite in part or full, as Berkeley is said to behave like a
    private university or the inner-city Roman Catholic universities of
    America act like public institutions;

6   according to its missions or functions, such as graduate research,
    undergraduate or collegiate instruction, professional education,
    vocational training, or, more vaguely, 'service';

7   more recently, according to the educational tier or sector to which it
    belongs, whether, for example, it is an autonomous campus or a federal
    component of a larger system, linked in a number of different ways to
    a central administrative authority.

These are largely convenient bureaucratic or sociological descriptions,
categories and organisational matrices. None of them evokes the majesty
or nobility of universities as does the simple reference 'idea'. For that
reason it is now necessary to trace the process by which the idea of a
university having an idea first emerged and became a significant feature of
university history.

ORIGINS OF THE 'IDEA' OF A UNIVERSITY

Nothing can be known unless it has a name. According to a *midrashic*
commentary on the Book of Genesis, Adam was commanded to name the
plants and beasts in Eden to bring into the world an order subject to
human speech and comprehensible to human agency. This was a primal
act. Naming things, as naming demons, is necessary for exorcising them.
Consequently it appears almost natural for us to speak about institutions

as if they have a primal identity, or incorporate some essential truth, purpose or essence. In this way, institutions are hypostatised. They are assigned the power of thinking because they have an 'idea'.[2] Furthermore, the casualness with which institutions are assigned an identity and made to think disguises the point that what truly requires explanation is not just the idea that may lie at the back of an institution but the very idea of an institution having an idea. And precisely because one of the characteristics of ideas is the ease with which they are manipulated once abstracted from their original historical contexts, it is astonishingly simple to forget that the process of assigning an idea to an institution usually implies a pre-history.

The pre-history of the idea of an idea of a university properly begins in the English-speaking world with the writings of the philosopher Edmund Burke. His principal successor is commonly and quite properly regarded as Samuel Taylor Coleridge, poet, littérateur, thinker and opium-eater. Burke is commonly associated with his denunciation of the French Revolution and those aspects of Enlightenment thought which he associated with revolution, but prior to 1789 he was a significant reformer and also a supporter of the 'English liberties' of American subjects of the Crown. After 1789 he saw his special problem as defending ancient institutions like the Church and ancient estates like the aristocracy but without at the same time becoming merely an apologist for inherited and illegitimate privilege. To do this Burke spoke more about the spirit of institutions, the spirit of religion, for example, or the religious idea of which the Church of England itself was merely an embodiment. For Coleridge, educated under the influence of Cambridge rationalism in the 1790s, against which he rebelled, and living on into the nineteenth century when the first major challenge to aristocratic leadership was being politically organised, the intellectual problem was similar: not to defend an older world against all criticism nor to forestall change, but to find a middle way that allowed for both continuity and reform. In practical terms this entailed finding an institutional structure that would be sufficiently independent to resist the inherent instability and unpredictability of social and economic change. This in turn led to a clear educational challenge, the desirability of educating leaders who would be able to steer between outmoded practices and passing fads and fancies.

The idea of an institution having an idea therefore came into being as a means of stabilising establishments at a revolutionary moment in European history, defending them against arguments that all existing institutions served narrow vested interests. The enemies were the

---

[2] On this note, see the lectures by Mary Douglas, *How Institutions Think* (Syracuse, 1986).

advocates of revolutionary institutional change – Unitarian radicals, Paineites and Philosophical Radicals, the last being the followers of the Utilitarian philosopher, Jeremy Bentham, whose articulated but clothed skeleton surmounted by a wax head is still imprisoned in a cabinet outside the office of the Provost of University College London.

As a functionalist critique, Utilitarianism was a powerful ally of radicals and detractors. For Utilitarians, the test of any institution's worth was whether it served the general interest or satisfied public opinion, conditions illustrated by the successful overthrow of imperial rule in North America. Neither Burke nor Coleridge could accept Utilitarianism as a philosophical justification for change. Neither believed with the Benthamites that the measure of the success of an institution was whether it provided happiness for the greatest number of people or met some criterion of the general interest. Yet both were utilitarians in another sense, in that they believed that institutions were and had to be functional, and therefore could be dysfunctional, and, if so, needed to be changed and reformed. For Burke, the basis upon which reform could be undertaken was not in reference to some abstract eighteenth-century theory, such as natural rights, or the happiness of the generality of mankind, but rather in relation to something far more fundamental and, we might say, anthropological, which he called human wants or needs – the need to be loved, the need to be sheltered, the need for security. Reform was clearly not revolution, since it was not necessary to demolish an institution in order to make it functional. For Romantics like Burke and Coleridge - for now we must label them as such – Utilitarianism was willy-nilly change. The 'general interest', 'public opinion', 'happiness' were crude terms, and no more firmly established as intellectual categories than 'spirit' or 'needs'.

After the French Revolution, particularly the Terror and the adventures of the famous Corsair, revolutionary alternatives did not seem so attractive, even to those small numbers of the intelligentsia (to use an anachronism) who had looked with favour upon the dawning of a new age in France. The English national course was set in the direction of gradual change, ultimately revolutionary but assimilable in the short run, allowing room for a great variety of opinion on how change was to be conducted, at what pace and with what consequences and with due but not slavish regard for what might be designated 'traditional', itself a word that would require continual definition.

As a middle way, Coleridge's method, to examine institutions with regard to their essence, was perfectly conceived for the historical circumstances of the 1820s. So great were its attractions that John Stuart Mill, carefully groomed by his lugubrious father James Mill as a Utilitarian and follower of Bentham, was deeply attracted to it almost from the moment of its publication in the seminal work *On the Constitution of Church and State* (1829). Across the Atlantic, where the Jacksonian populist trans-formation of American society was in full cry, an alarmed New Haven circle of scholars at Yale University also saw in Coleridge an opportunity to introduce purposeful reforms into the college curriculum without compromising what they regarded as the essential weight and mission of a university.[3]

It is not necessary to review in detail the intricacies and ultimate philo-sophical sources of Coleridge's thinking. A short presentation could scarcely do justice to it in any case, and only a few emphases are required to bring us to that point in the 1850s when John Henry, Cardinal New-man, adopted Coleridge's method for analysing the function of institu-tions to universities and wrote what remains the singlemost influential book on the meaning of a university in the English language. It was Newman who transformed the inherited legalistic description of a university as a corporate body possessing endowments and privileges pertaining to learning into a thrilling emotion-laden, higher order conception of education.

Coleridge was born into the clerical establishment, was sent, *inter alia*, to one of the great boarding schools, Christ's Hospital, and went up to Jesus College, Cambridge in 1791 as a sizar or poor scholar. He reacted strongly to Cambridge rationalism with its heavy dose of mathematics, classical philology and William Paley's Utilitarian theology. Most of his career was spent as a poet and man of letters. His interests in philosophy developed early. He read the neo-platonist Plotinus while at school and visited Germany with borrowed money as early as 1798, publishing a translation of Schiller's *Wallenstein* in 1800.

He began his philosophical search for an 'idea' by a convoluted, rambling and one suspects opiated investigation and refutation of John Locke's epistemology, which, he was suggesting, was responsible for Utilitarianism. He began discussion with a rather perverse reading of Locke, arguing that he could not be taken seriously because his philosophy was derived from Descartes. Locke was hardly a Cartesian, although his epistemology certainly fell into the broad category of materialism. Locke and his disciples on the Continent had produced a theory of knowing which, eventually elaborated and refined into the doctrine of the

---

[3] Louise Stevenson, *Scholarly Means to Evangelical Ends: The New Haven Scholars and the Transformation of Higher Learning in America, 1830–1890* (Baltimore, 1986).

association of ideas, had managed to find its way into all the major controversies of the Enlightenment.

At the core of any theory of change, when philosophers discuss change, lies an epistemology, an explanation of how we learn or know which subsequently serves as a basis for advocating social and institutional change. Epistemologies also have the advantage of furnishing educators with formidable pedagogical tools. This is the case whether we discuss phrenology or Piaget. But epistemologies can benefit more than one master at the same time. This was no less true for Locke. His ideas served either reformist or conservative ends. Thus the doctrine of the association of ideas became an article of faith to the Utilitarians because it justified radical change by rendering all knowledge, all establishments, all accepted and conventional ways of believing, merely relative to environment. Alter environment, and one alters belief. Tradition was only an excuse for inherited privilege. All religiously sanctioned systems of morality were but the power of the few over the timidity of the many. Even the appeal to self-sacrifice was a hypocritical justification for the status quo, for only those who protested against injustice were expected to desist. There was only one test of the value of an institution, or a social class, or a religious system, and that was a democratic but also a totalitarian principle: did the institution or moral system currently in vogue support the general public interest, creating the greatest good for the greatest number?

Although he had flirted with all manner of radical thought, joining other Romantics like the poet Robert Southey in a pantisocratic communitarian scheme for Pennsylvania, or becoming for a time a Unitarian minister, Coleridge ultimately gave up freethinking. He turned towards Platonism and the various traditions of idealist philosophy in a search for an alternative epistemology to Locke's. Where the associationists and Utilitarians made ideas subordinate to external stimuli received through the senses even when transformed in or by the mind, the Platonists or intuitionists made them independent of time and circumstances. Ideas about things were not relative. On the contrary, because they existed *a priori*, ideas possessed their own reality. It was no more evident that our mind was passive than that it was active. There were, Coleridge reasoned, according to the philosophical tradition he followed, pre-existing ideas of the world in the mind that could influence the interpretation of sensory data. The idealists could draw on the investigations of Bishop George Berkeley who had once demonstrated in his writings on vision that the senses were easily fooled. Does a paddle bend when inserted into water? It appears to do so. Nevertheless, in the context of revolutionary Europe a theory of knowing based on what we see, hear, taste, feel or smell was more immediately persuasive than its opponent doctrine. It does not matter, as a practical consideration, whether an object is ultimately real if it is contingently so, as Dr Johnson demonstrated by kicking a chair in a famous anecdote. If a chair can be kicked, it hardly matters whether it disappears when our backs are turned. It only matters when we want the Invisible to be actual.

Coleridge himself had great difficulty with the theory of pre-existing knowledge. In a notebook entry for 1808 he wrote 'of that abominable word, Idea / how have I been struggling to get rid of it, & to find some exact word for each exact meaning'. In yet another place he confessed to a 'mad metaphysician's Soliloquy', and in yet another, reviewing his wandering thoughts, he noticed that 'they may be thought to resemble the overflow of an earnest mind rather than an orderly premeditated composition',[4] to which even the most dedicated Coleridgean must immediately assent. Some years later Cardinal Newman, in his own effort to define the idea of an institution, interrupted the writing of his second lecture on 'Theology a Branch of Knowledge' by admitting that he too had plunged into a 'maze of metaphysics, from which I may be unable to heave myself'.[5]

Coleridge's particular version of the doctrine of innate ideas is close to and may have owed much to Kant. Ideas, Coleridge appeared to say, are certainly not dependent upon external stimuli as received through our senses, but neither are they strictly speaking innate. Rather ideas exist in the mind, to be recovered whenever awakened by stimuli or experiences received from the outer world. He distinguished between an idea and a conception (a distinction he attributed to Richard Hooker). The latter was a deduction from history and from circumstances. Because it was posterior, we tend to mistake the present 'form, construction, or model' of an institution for its original appearance. An idea was quite different. It was antecedent to history and circumstances and, unlike a conception, could not be 'abstracted from any particular state, form, or mode, in which the thing may happen to exist at this or at that time, not yet generalised from any number of succession of such forms or modes'.[6] Occasionally he used 'principle' as a synonym for 'idea'. A conception might follow

[4] Samuel Taylor Coleridge, *Lay Sermons*, ed. R. J. White, VI (Princeton, 1972), 100n, 101n, 43; *Collected Letters of Samuel Taylor Coleridge,* ed. Earl Leslie Briggs, II (Oxford, 1956), 677–704, 708–10.
[5] John Henry Newman, *The Letters and Diaries*, ed. Charles Stephen Dessain, XV (London, 1964), 90.
[6] Samuel Taylor Coleridge, *On the Constitution of the Church and State,* ed. John Colmer (Princeton, 1976), 12; John Stuart Mill, *On Bentham and Coleridge*, intro. F. R. Leavis (New York, 1962), 110–12.

from an idea without being coterminous with it, as the conception of a heliocentric universe was made possible by the idea or principle of gravity, which in the language of Plato was a 'law'. From the realm of social thought, Coleridge cited the example of an original social contract. No less than Bentham, he was scornful of the historical existence of a compact between governing and governed and called it an 'operatical farce . . . acted by the Illuminati and Constitution-manufacturers' of the late eighteenth century. As a theory Coleridge described the social contract as senseless and as a conception impossible. Yet as an 'idea' he pronounced it certain, and even more than certain, as indispensable, for without it no fundamental distinction between a servile polity and a commonwealth could have ever evolved. The idea of a social contract, therefore, was quite separate from the theory and conception of it. The first captured its essence, which was liberty, while the latter two tried to elaborate its essence into a working constitution, which was demonstrably false. Furthermore, while the existence of an original social contract was inacessible to proof, the existence of an idea of liberty of which its exponents might not even be conscious could be found in discussions of any number of issues, such as the question of labourers' wages and poor rates.

Introducing yet another term, Coleridge maintained that an idea was a 'power' that constituted its own reality and was known when we have learned to recognise the 'ultimate aim' of a given institution.[7] But how does one discover that an institution has an 'ultimate aim'? Coleridge rejected pure functionalism as proof of the existence of an ultimate aim, calling functionalism a conception not an idea. He rejected historical reasoning, at least in one form, by refusing to admit that an institution's idea could be derived from its particular manifestation in the past. Of course he was correct in one respect. How, from amidst the welter of facts and details pertaining to the history of a given institution or situation could we ever spot the precise essential idea, the one thing needful, that clearly exposed its ultimate purpose?

Coleridge answered that we know the antecedent idea buried in an institution from the conduct of those associated with it, by the actions that they take or refuse to take, by the beliefs they hold or reject, by the institutional forms they adopt or oppose. He cited labour conflicts over wage and poor rates as evidence for the existence of the idea of liberty, a conclusion that historians might find dubious. He turned to history after all and argued that we can grasp the antecedent idea by the gradual

[7] Coleridge, *Constitution*, 20.

realisation of related objectives over time, the past record containing a thread or consistency. Here we see why, in these borrowings from Hegel and Kant, John Stuart Mill in a famous discussion called this mode of understanding the Germano-Coleridgean school.[8]

Enter Confusion. We gather the purpose of an institution from its antecedent idea, we know its antecedent idea from its ultimate aim, we deduce its ultimate aim from a great many pieces of historical information, but the method requires us to maintain at all times a careful distinction between an idea, sometimes called a principle, and a conception. Ideas may be embedded in certain institutions – liberty in the social contract – but the latter is false, only the former true. For most readers this is casuistry, at best tautology, but in any case hardly the grounds upon which to argue today. We would not find the method useful for explaining how universities ought to function. Yet the young renegade philosophical radical, John Mill, found the method an enormous help in understanding how institutions could be accommodated to change, and in the Coleridgean habit of asking, 'What is the meaning of it?' he found a vast improvement over the Benthamite practice of saying, 'What is the use of it?' And is the Coleridgean mode of questioning really so alien today? It may not be far in spirit from the present social science method of looking beneath the obvious for a more general underlying principle or pattern, or from Freudian psychology with its stress on the unconscious, or from modern physics where ideal laboratory conditions are created in order to study natural phenomena, or from economic forecasting that also incorporates a teleological aspect and inevitably evaluates the present according to an ultimate aim.

But these rhetorical questions are not meant as a defence of Coleridge. They are intended to be an assist in explaining, if briefly, the rise of a habit of thinking about institutions as if they embodied an idea, whether we wish to call that idea a 'power' antecedent to history but understood through it, or a 'conception' deducible from the appearance of institutions and the actions of individuals in particular contexts. Both ideas and conceptions have informed the subsequent history of the method, even if Coleridge's distinction between them has not been customarily preserved. What has lasted is the persistent utility of his approach – the seductive influence of the inclination to see ideas existing at the heart of institutions.

His was the approach that received such remarkable application from Newman in the work that is the palladium of all such methods of reasoning and has inspired analyses about the role and purposes of

8 Mill, *Bentham and Coleridge*.

universities for over a hundred years, mainly in English-speaking countries but occasionally elsewhere in a minor way as in France.[9] Since Newman the belief that universities possess a core idea or have an historical undertaking or a special responsibility and trust beyond the moment – we can state this essence in any number of ways – has remained a constant part of the process of institutional self-evaluation and internal debate.

Newman employed Coleridge's method for summarising the purposes of a university. He wrote his *Idea of a University* in the 1850s as a programme for a proposed new Roman Catholic university in Ireland; and the expanded book version, consisting of the original addresses, or as he called them 'discourses', and additional materials appeared in the 1870s. He also produced another work, much less well known than the *Idea*, which contains an analysis of a second kind of higher education institution denoted a 'college'.[10] In his view they were complementary not antagonistic institutions, and they were of course exactly the pairing existing at the ancient universities of Oxford and Cambridge. Newman was an undergraduate at Oxford, and was elected Fellow of Oriel, a college that in the 1820s led the way in revitalising a university that was not, by comparison to the old and new universities of Germany, intellectually distinguished; but intellectual distinction, as measured by the standard of original inquiry, was not the primary mission of an English university in Newman's formative years. Many of the great names of Victorian scholarship, Richard Porson in classical philology, for example, or Charles Darwin in biology, his cousin Francis Galton in genetics or Thomas Babington Macaulay were not regular members of the university despite other kinds of affiliations and relationships.

Newman loved Oxford. In his letters, as well as in the letters of other undergraduates of his generation, we find an intense personal identification with the physical beauty of the ancient quadrangles and courts and the beginning of that romantic mystique that takes us from the moonlit courts of Oxford and Cambridge in the first third of the nineteenth century to the cultivation of ivy in America in the first third of the twentieth century.[11]

In formulating his idea of a university, Newman incorporated what he considered to be the finest features of the Oxford of his day, and it is

[9] Jacques Dreze and Jean Debelle, *Conceptions de l'université* (Paris, 1968).
[10] John Henry Newman, *Historical Sketches*, III (London, 1881).
[11] See John Thelin, *The Cultivation of Ivy: a Saga of the College in America* (Cambridge, MA, 1976).

correct to say that Newman's idea is also, at least in inspiration, both the Oxford and the English idea of a university. That is the positive side of his thinking. There is also a negative side. If Newman loved what he wanted Oxford to stand for, he also passionately disliked a new and rival conception of a university that had arisen in the metropolis in the late 1820s, the University of London.[12] We must bear this situation in mind as we proceed to understand just what the Cardinal meant when he said that a university – and he meant all universities – contained, that is *should* contain, an idea.

The famous definition of the *Idea* as stated in Newman's Preface is that a university is a place for teaching universal knowledge – 'Such is a University in its *essence*'.[13] The function of a university is teaching, or, as it was called in the middle decades of the nineteenth century, the dissemination of knowledge.

Newman was not the first of Oxford's devotees to speculate on the basic purpose of a university. He had heard or read some of the arguments before, never so wonderfully elongated as in his own prose, but certain points were part of the Oxford apology. We need go no farther back than to Edward Tatham's remarks on the creation of the Oxford Honours examination at the turn of the century. The Rector of Lincoln maintained that 'An University is . . . the place of *Universal Teaching*, which is its first and most important duty'. However, there is a twist to the argument, for Tatham also asserted that,

> An University is the seat of *Universal Learning* increasing and to be increased, from the nature of men and things, with the lapse of time . . . *Its Discipline should, accordingly, be adapted to the Increase or Advancement of Learning improving and to be improved according to the times.*

Why? Because, 'otherwise it may occupy young-men in studies that are obsolete and in errors that are exploded'. Yet to admit that previous teaching and learning may have contained serious errors is dangerous doctrine in times of war and ideological disagreement, when the work of the *philosophes* was so evident in revolutionary Europe. And so Tatham takes another step in his argument on the proper relationship between knowledge and teaching that brings him closer to the mainline view. Both must 'be in the *Right or Initiative Method*; otherwise [studies] will lead [undergraduates] *from* instead of *to* the Truth, into Sophistry instead of

---

[12] John Henry Newman, 'The Tamworth Reading Room', in *The Evangelical and Oxford Movements,* ed. Elisabeth Jay (Cambridge, 1983).

[13] John Henry Newman, *The Idea of a University*, ed. I. T. Ker (Oxford, 1976), 5.

Science'.[14] Clearly, then, while 'the times' may require some additions or alterations to what is known, there are right and wrong ways of learning, *a fortiori*, there is truth. A university exists to sort this out.

Many years later another Oxford don, on this occasion Newman's contemporary and sometime associate in the Oxford Movement, Edward Pusey, was less equivocal in announcing what should be taught:

> The object of Universities is . . . not how to advance science, not how to make discoveries, not to form new schools of mental philosophy, nor to invent new modes of analysis, not to produce works in Medicine, Jurisprudence or even Theology, but to form minds religiously, morally, intellectually, which shall discharge aright whatever duties God, in his Providence, shall appoint to them.

And to drive the point home, Pusey answered those who believed that a university ought to develop 'acute and subtle intellects'. They are not needed 'for most offices in the body politic . . . It would be a perversion of our institutions to turn the University into a forcing-house for intellect.'[15]

When Newman spoke about the idea of a university being a place where the teaching of universal knowledge took place, he was not talking about what the Germans would call *Lehrfreiheit*, the right to teach one's competence, or *Lernfreiheit,* the right of students to have open access to knowledge. Since teaching was the function of a university, it was important to teach the right things. Why should this even be an issue in a free society? Why not allow young adults the privilege – in America, with its natural rights traditions, one is almost always tempted to say 'right' – of reading and studying virtually whatever stimulates curiosity? Isn't the best kind of undergraduate education that which one chooses for oneself?

This is the rationale of today. It is the natural justification for mass education where the vast majority of undergraduates cannot enjoy the luxury of tutorial or small class instruction in the company of senior members of the university. It is the rationale required of research and public service universities where undergraduates are not the only community being served. Newman did not experience this kind of education at first hand, although he anticipated its future. His university had long existed for members of an elite whose lives were to be spent as public leaders in Church and State, in the military and at the bar. A handful of

[14] Edward Tatham (Rector of Lincoln College, Oxford), *An Address to the Members of Convocation at Large, on the Proposed New Statutes Respecting Public Examination in the University of Oxford*, 2nd ed. (London, 1807), 1.

[15] E. B. Pusey, *Collegiate and Professorial Teaching and Discipline* (Oxford and London, 1854), 215–16.

undergraduates were socialised to their future roles by exposure to those ideas and values that contributed to the maintenance of political stability. In the later eighteenth century the schoolmaster Vicesimus Knox, whose writings went through many editions, put the issue this way: 'Men of the world, who follow the opinions of Machiavel and Mandeville, laugh at all schemes of reformation, palliate vice, and justify folly; but it was the design of *universities* to counteract the prevalence of such principles.'[16] How Knox knew what the 'design' of universities was is undiscoverable. The basis is uncertain, but the context is clear. There are times in the life of a nation when the existence of a marketplace of competing ideas is unwise, and from an educational perspective, unsettling.

Newman was aware of the fact that English society was dynamic and changing, but at the top, at least, where the State was to offer guidance, it was essential that educated leaders be loyal. He agreed that ideas could be right or wrong, or, as he was to argue in the *Idea,* incomplete. Young people must not be led astray, particularly in times when values are in contention, religion competes with freethinking, and no consensus exists on moral questions. It should be said in Newman's defence (if it is a defence) that he was less authoritarian than his Roman Catholic superiors, but he did not hesitate to place limits on what ought to be exchanged in classrooms. He was by no means a nineteenth-century liberal individualist. In the famous passages of his remarkable autobiography, *Apologia pro Vita Sua,* he denounced the 'liberal heresy' of the age, its bland toleration and intellectual relativism, and his characterisation of Victorian liberalism is sufficiently vivid to remain a possible way of viewing nineteenth-century transformations. He had been driven from Oxford because of it, as explained in the autobiography. Absolute freedom of thought led to anarchy, to each man doing as he liked, as Matthew Arnold, another Coleridgean, was to state it.

When Newman prepared his discourses, the view that a university was more than a place for teaching universal knowledge, that it was also a place for professional education and primarily a place for the 'endowment of learning' or research, was prevalent enough for him to reassert the older Oxford position. He was aware of the pressure being exerted on Oxford and Cambridge to provide greater opportunities for teaching that was related to investigation and not to character formation. For centuries scholars and scientists had sought openings within universities for work that was not necessarily directly related to the teaching of young persons,

---

[16] Vicesimus Knox, *Liberal Education; or, a Practical Treatise on the Methods of Acquiring Useful and Polite Learning*, 11th ed., II (London, 1795), 113n.

or at least teaching dominated by literary, theological and mathematical subjects. There were some successes, and new histories of Oxford and Cambridge universities are uncovering more.[17] Even within the collegiate system, where teaching tutors rather than research professors predominated, research was never altogether out of the question for universities. A life spent in teaching will at some point shade over into research, or perhaps it is better to say 'study', since research is systematic study in a given area of knowledge and its subsequent dissemination, although not necessarily through the medium of the lecture hall. But although university professors wrote books, some of them original treatises and not texts, and learned papers were produced by classicists, philosophers and scientists, the overall intellectual environment was as Newman wished, whether in England or Scotland. The research function had not been raised to the level of an ideology. There was no strong culture of research that put a premium on originality and stressed the importance of discovery and a division of intellectual labour. It was not an era of Ph.D. candidates and graduate schools, extra-mural grants and contract research. University appointments were not made because potential fellows and chairholders were evaluated for their original contributions to knowledge or could be praised for being on the cutting edge of intellectual life. Learned, yes; but that most often meant an impressive command of existing knowledge with no expectation that scholarly work of seminal importance to a particular field of inquiry was some day likely to emerge and – most importantly – be systematically diffused. The principal institutional victories of Victorian researchers and their predecessors lay elsewhere, in the creation of learned societies, botanical gardens, museums, libraries and specialised institutions.

If the 'object' of a university 'was . . . scientific and philosophical discovery, I do not see why a university should have students', wrote Newman.[18] The teaching of students had assumed new importance during Newman's lifetime. In arguing for the traditional view that research, while a possible function for universities, should always be secondary, Newman was reflecting important internal transformations that had occurred in his youth. The new examinations culture introduced at Oxford by the reforms of 1800 and developed earlier at Cambridge had reinforced teaching and strengthened the hold of colleges on the university's pedagogical mission, and a new generation of students, of

---

[17] E.g., *The History of the University of Oxford,* V, *The Eighteenth Century,* ed. L. S. Sutherland and L. G. Mitchell (Oxford, 1986), Chapters 15–25.
[18] *Idea,* 5.

which Newman was one, had in effect demanded more attention from dons and stimulated many of the changes that improved the intellectual standing of the ancient universities of England.

But pressure from the advocates of original inquiry was not limited to England. Influences were arriving from Germany. The model for the scholar and scientist was the German professor. Shortly after Newman delivered his discourses in Ireland, Yale, a university in another corner of the English-speaking world, instituted the first Ph.D. degree in North America, a half century before a similar degree was introduced into the United Kingdom (although the 'research student' appeared in the 1890s).

There is, admittedly, a serious difficulty in understanding Newman on the question of research and teaching. He often reads as if he is supporting pure investigation. His statements about freedom of inquiry and knowledge its own reward are so compelling that virtually all subsequent commentators stress the intellectual argument to the exclusion of all others and use the authority of Newman's name to justify the importance of university based research. Giving testimony before the Royal Commission on the University of London before the First World War, a professor of medicine at University College Hospital distinguished between a university medical school and 'trade school' medicine. The 'main ideal' of a university is 'the acquisition and making of knowledge for its own sake and not for the sake of the money which may be gained by knowing how to do certain things'.[19] Alfred North Whitehead, Trinity College, Cambridge and Harvard University, repeats the grand senti-ments in 'Universities and Their Functions' while adding the strong, appealing and dangerous word 'imaginative': 'Thus the proper function of a university is the imaginative acquisition of knowledge ... A university is imaginative or it is nothing – at least nothing useful ... Imagination is a contagious disease.'[20] Indeed, which is why one form of it, 'genius', was so long considered to be tantamount to madness.

But we cannot confuse Newman with German influences, nor with the sort of Victorian liberalism of mind that prompted John Stuart Mill to assert the promiscuous obligation of an educated man to follow the argument withersoever it goes. Newman's own discourses run to some 560 pages in a recent edition, and they are precisely that, discursive and sometimes wandering statements about the relative merits of various disciplines, interspersed with lapidary remarks about knowledge and

---

[19] Royal Commission on London 1912–1913. Cd. 6312 xxii, 793. Evidence of Professor Starling.
[20] Alfred North Whitehead, 'Universities and Their Functions', in *The Aims of Education and Other Essays* (New York, 1957), 145.

culture that are suitable for framing and are often lifted from context
to adorn American college catalogues and university bulletins. Every
apparently straightforward statement in Newman about open investigation is followed by hard, complicated phrasing and unfamiliar diction,
so that his mode of reasoning resembles that of Pusey's acute and subtle
intellect. For examples we need only turn to the lecture he wrote on
'Christianity and Scientific Investigations'. In it he observes that,

> it is a matter of primary importance in the cultivation of those sciences, in
> which truth is discoverable by the human intellect, that the investigator
> should be free, independent, unshackled in his movements; that he should
> be allowed and enabled, without impediment, to fix his mind intently, nay
> exclusively, on his special project, without the risk of being distracted . . .
> by charges of temerariousness, or by warnings against extravagance or
> scandal.

This seems clear enough except for the qualifiers 'those sciences' and the
clause 'in which truth is discoverable by the human intellect'. Presumably
there are other kinds of sciences in which truth is not discovered by human
intellect. The mitigated word 'distracted' also gives pause. Another
paragraph is puzzling. While discussing 'what are called the *dogmas* of
faith', Newman announces that 'we, none of us, should say that it is any
shackle at all upon the intellect to maintain these inviolate'. Further on he
rejects the position that university based scientists should be allowed
to contradict [religious] dogma, and relatedly, he announces that the
'independence of philosophical thought' does not apply to '*formal teaching*'
but to 'investigations, speculations, and discussions'. And finally he
explains why this must be so, because 'there must be great care taken to
avoid scandal, or shocking the popular mind, or unsettling the weak'. So
having once told his auditors and readers that the inquiring mind
should not be distracted by scandal, he concludes with scandal as a
constraint.[21] One hears the cranky voice of Edward Tatham and Oxford's
past.

The teaching function of universities is the controlling force in all of
Newman's argument. After all, he announced this at the outset. Thus
while the 'idea' is that of a university, the teaching emphasis implied the
importance of colleges. Newman said very little about colleges in the *Idea*.
Because he appears only to be talking about knowledge, its different forms
and rankings, with theology at the top, it is easy to see why discussions of
a university that take the *Idea* as starting point fail to notice how much

---

[21] Newman, *Idea*, 379–80.

Newman takes for granted.[22] The intellectual life is only one kind of life led in universities. Equally important is the human dimension in which personal relationships matter, friendships count, and success is measured not by examinations, however necessary these may be for determining a certain level of competence, but by growth and maturation, by what, in a memorable passage on the qualities of a gentleman, Newman described as civilised behaviour. The pursuit of knowledge, in and for itself, by and for itself, cannot produce similar results. The pursuit of knowledge begets egotism. It is asocial, removing scholars from the world, and it is servile not liberating because it encourages concentration and specialisation.

Newman's emphasis on the college recalls the Greek idea of a liberal education wherein specialisation is illiberal because the skill or proficiency is rated above wholeness or completeness. An additional danger is the governing passion. One's character is subordinated to some task or achievement. The idea of a university is that it must ultimately produce emotionally whole and balanced people, no single part of the personality disproportionate to another.[23]

The English idea of a university was created by thinkers such as Newman associated with literary and philosophical traditions of learning, trained in classical languages, aesthetic in disposition and nurtured within the structure of an Established Church. Romantics all, they valued the personal and regarded universities as places to make friends. To use a difficult word, they were 'humanists', meaning that they favoured knowledge directed towards explicating personal and moral relationships. Hence although the English idea of a university broadened in time to include science, its primary association was with subjects that can be described as literary. It should not therefore be surprising that literary critics like F. R. Leavis have carried the tradition forward into our own century.[24] For a number of reasons – German and Scottish influences among them – the American version of the English idea of a university is

---

[22] E.g., in Jaroslav Pelikan's inspiring book, *The Idea of the University, A Reexamination* (New Haven and London, 1992), 181, research and publication are given central importance, and other passages suggest that Newman would approve. But perhaps in light of the fact that Pelikan's book is a 'reexamination', my point is too finicky.

[23] See Sheldon Rothblatt, 'The Limbs of Osiris', in *The European and American University since 1800, Historical and Sociological Essays*, ed. Sheldon Rothblatt and Björn Wittrock (Cambridge, 1993), 19–73.

[24] An unflattering but interesting account of how Oxbridge 'humanism' has dominated fiction to the detriment of viewpoints arising from non-literary perspectives appears in Ian Carter, *Ancient Cultures of Conceit, British University Fiction in the Post-War Years* (London and New York, 1990).

less restricted, but the bias is nonetheless present in the writings of recent critics.

The humanistic and aesthetic preconceptions of Newman are discernible in an essay he wrote when the University of London was founded. The new institution in Gower street, renamed University College in 1836, did not embody the idea of a university. How could it? Among its founders were the leading Utilitarians of the day, still pushing the mechanistic philosophy of the eighteenth century. Liberal Anglicans, Dissenting Protestants, Unitarians and Jews were also important players in the foundation of the new institution. To be sure, London was founded to be a teaching institution, but its pride and glory soon became the medical school not the undergraduate college. Newman was not absolutely opposed to university affiliated professional schools. His Irish university included preparation for the professions. In view of the pressures exerted upon him by his Irish Roman Catholic sponsors, he had little choice, but professional education was not his primary concern. The difficulty Newman encountered with London was that it was not an English, that is to say, an Oxford university. It was formed on existing Scottish models. The professorial lecture not the collegiate tutorial was the primary means of instruction, and the student as consumer exercised decisive influence over time-tabling and course provisions, just as in Scotland. The new university was also non-denominational, as well as secular, and for Newman the notion that a university could support a programme of studies where religion was not central was apostasy. One of London's 'spiritual' founders – the Scot Thomas Campbell – had visited the new city-state universities of Bonn and Berlin, and other supporters had taken an interest in Thomas Jefferson's new University of Virginia, another 'godless university', just opening its doors. Low fees, flexible scheduling, professorial lecturing, a certain amount of student choice in what to study, implying the relative worth of knowledge, no compulsory chapel or even instruction in religion – where were the principles of authority, beauty and steadiness of purpose essential to the idea of a university? Furthermore, London was 'Minerva under gaslights', an urban institution, set among streets, some of them dangerous or full of temptations. Students lived at home or in lodgings, and the institution did not concern itself with nurturing and did not worry whether friends were made. The unity of knowledge, as one commentator remarked, was abandoned as a university ideal.[25] In London only the intellectual life

[25] George B. Jeffery, *The Unity of Knowledge: Some Reflections on the Universities of Cambridge and London* (Cambridge, 1950).

mattered, and any wider objective was the responsibility of the urban not the university environment. The lines between university and city were confused, and because of that very confusion and absence of internal cohesion, the 'idea' of a university began to fade.

If the *Idea of a University* was meant to be more than a series of discussions about a Roman Catholic university for Ireland (the bishops sensed that it was an apology for Anglican Oxford), Newman's grand plan was a failure. All the new universities and university colleges of Ireland and the civic universities of England as well as the new University of Wales were like London, inspired by Scottish rather than English examples. Durham was the only exception, and Durham was wrongly conceived for the north of England. All the other new institutions were cost-conscious establishments. They were, to begin with, market-driven, fee-sensitive, vulnerable to changes in demand and willing to take students with weaker preparation than mid-Victorian Oxford and Cambridge. They had no choice. The civics possessed neither the independence nor the teaching resources of Oxford and Cambridge and could not, while they were young, adopt an elitist or meritocratic mission.

I have been describing the beginnings of a new way of looking at institutions by defining their essence, or rather, by claiming in the first instance that they possessed an essence. I have mentioned the philosophical difficulties in defining an idea encountered by Coleridge, and the intellectual problems facing Newman when he tried to turn the idea of a university into a clear statement of goals. Contradictions and semantic confusion arose with every attempt to clarify the question of just what made universities special. Now it should be stressed that what is truly significant about their efforts is not any particular idea of a university, however interesting it may appear, but the very idea of an idea of a university. The genius of Coleridge and Newman lies not in their efforts to isolate the precise functions of a university. It lies in their desire to elevate the university to the moral centre of modern culture and to do so by freeing the university from the grip of utilitarian and hedonistic schools of thought so influential in their own day.

The emotional appeal of thinking of universities as embodying an idea cannot be overestimated in the age of the multiversity, continually bombarded by wide and contradictory demands and commitments. The multiversity is the university of the Benthamites. Its utility is established on the basis of the calculus of pleasure, its capacity to satisfy the greatest number, to provide the greatest number of positional goods for the greatest number of people. However elusive the idea of a university, the conception of a basic thrust or mission is a relief, an attractive alternative to the accurate perhaps but also shapeless, relativistic and uninspiring descriptions of the contemporary university as one-stop shopping.

In countries influenced by German philosophy, which means in one way or another most of northern, central and eastern Europe but also modern countries like Israel, the idea of the idea of a university has a different history, if a similar purpose. In these nations, universities were regarded as the home of the highest and best form of scholarship and science, so rare and even spiritual that they required vigilant protection from the commercial and vulgar tendencies of modern culture. The line of argument runs back through many thinkers, from the Von Humboldt brothers to Kant and Moses Mendelssohn.[26] In time, a reasonably short time, this special claim, known under various headings such as *Bildung* in German or *bildning* in Swedish, broadened to encompass a research mission. It is consequently often ambiguously referred to as 'Humboldtianism'. In time too the research mission broadened to include a very high level of technological application, so that in Germany (and in Copenhagen, Stockholm, Vienna and Zurich) *technische universitäten* and institutes of technology, excluded from the English idea of a university, entered the lawful penumbra. Nevertheless, the disciplinary crown of the German idea of a university was philosophy (and philology), as incorporated into the faculty organisational structure of the Continental university. Philosophy was the means for unifying the disciplines. The search for a single discipline capable of achieving such an end has never actually ceased. Mathematics, for example, has been suggested as one possibility in discussions over curricular reform in Dutch universities today.[27]

German influence spread outward in several forms. First, it was disseminated as *Bildung*, often translated as self-formation or self-realisation, a conception of education possibly originating in German pietism and having less to do with institutions than with individuals. However, individualism *per se*, at least initially, was not the aim. Rather *Bildung* was the process, the methods, the continual reflection, self-

[26] Sven-Eric Liedman, 'In Search of Isis: General Education in Germany and Sweden', in Rothblatt and Wittrock, 74–106.
[27] Information communicated to me by Louis Vos of Leuven University in connection with the Standing Conference of European Rectors' project on the history of the university in Europe.

examination and study through which individuals reached and internalised the highest values of national culture. Second, German influence was disseminated as science or *Wissenschaft* (knowledge), but both conceptions shared a common purpose. Such German ideas of the proper aim of a university could be contrasted with the pastoral conception of teaching at Oxford and Cambridge, student-related, centred on the transmission of received values from teacher to disciple and embodied in such forms as college and tutorial.

German conceptions of *Bildung* did not penetrate very deeply into British universities until the end of the nineteenth century with the appearance of a neo-Hellenic aestheticism such as we find in writers like Walter Pater at Oxford and Goldsworthy Lowes Dickinson at Cambridge. The reasons were fundamentally political. In Britain, with its long history of civic humanism as embodied in aristocratic leadership, students were initiated into a world of institutional politics. This had not come easily, it must be admitted. During the period of the French Revolution, Oxbridge dons attempted to suppress student debating societies, driving some of them underground (as indeed also happened in America).[28] Yet the basic point remains. In Britain, undergraduates, few in number in proportion to the relevant age group, were expected to one day participate in public affairs as responsible citizens, exercising a self-discipline learned at home, in chapel or Church, in school and in university. The price of good citizenship was prolonged adolescence. Foreign visitors were alternately attracted to and repelled by what in their view was the schoolboyish quality of the British and American undergraduate.[29] There is a paradox. German universities were hardly 'free' in any absolute sense. They were far more closely attached to the State than were English institutions, although Scottish universities had long received subsidies from the Crown. The professoriate was annexed to the civil service, as was and remains common in Continental countries. English visitors to mid-nineteenth-century Germany remarked on the generally apolitical character of the professors and their detachment from worldly life. Yet students, unlike their British counterparts, were political activists. The Left Hegelians of the universites were the inspiration of Karl Marx, who was driven out of Germany into exile in Britain. The difference between countries is that in Germany undergraduates were allowed to drift into confrontational politics. There was no institutional tradition of *in loco parentis*, no or little concern with the private or personal lives of

---

[28] See Chapters 3, 5 and 6.
[29] Jacques Bardoux, *Memories of Oxford* (London, 1899), 9, 12, 13, 34–5, 40.

undergraduates, no need or desire or opportunity, certainly, to develop in young people that sense of wider civic responsibility, aristocratic in the English case, republican in the American, that are such conspicuous features of the inner academic life of nineteenth-century English-speaking universities. It was therefore possible to allow to German students the kind of intellectual (and spatial) freedom which on the whole dons were reluctant to furnish their own students or colleagues and to leave to the State the task of coping with the political consequences of open speculation.

There is some disagreement in the scholarly literature on the extent to which early proponents of *Bildung*, such as Wilhelm von Humboldt, were also interested in western traditions of civic humanism and attempted to unite German Enlightenment considerations of service to the State or possibly nation with self-formation, but the general outcome of this particular educational mission is not in doubt.[30] *Bildung* developed as an essentially apolitical educational theory, centring on the individual's efforts to achieve intellectual or spiritual perfection through *Wissenschaft*. Such conceptions, writes Fritz Ringer, protected (psychologically) the German professoriate from pressures for immediately applicable knowledge. At the turn of the twentieth century, *Wissenschaft* as well as *Bildung* had become deeply emplaced justifications for withdrawal from the actual world of affairs. The desire to avoid contaminating the intellect through contact with everyday life did not, however, spare the German universities from paternalistic control by the State and its bureaucracy.[31] Still, wherever individualism exists, either as a strong feature of culture, as in nineteenth-century America, or as an expression of artistic revolt, *Bildung* is likely to have appeal.[32]

The intellectual ideals of *Bildung, Wissenschaft, Lehrfreiheit* and *Lernfreiheit* were hothouse attractions for British and American scholars

[30] See David Sorkin, 'Wilhelm von Humboldt: The Theory and Practice of Self-Formation (*Bildung*), 1791–1810', *Journal of the History of Ideas*, 44 (January–March 1983), 55–74.
[31] Fritz Ringer, 'Comparing Two Academic Cultures: The University in Germany and France around 1900', in *History of Education*, 16 (September 1987), 181–5. Knowledge as the process by which the mind comes to understand itself also contains the notion of wholeness, the personality as a totality. Therefore at another level *Wissenschaft* and *Bildung* are part of the larger western tradition of liberal education, which in highly attenuated form resurfaces in American concerns for undergraduate general education. It is also as general education that *Bildung* has recently re-emerged in Sweden – in Swedish as *bildning* and *allmänbildning*. My source is Sven-Eric Liedman and Lennart Olausson, 'General Education, Culture, and Specialization', *Studies of Higher Education and Research* (1987), 6.
[32] The Yale scholars, however, believed they could attach German ideas of self-development to a wider sense of public responsibility, thus, evidently, pursuing a goal that seems to have eluded Humboldt. See Stevenson, *Scholarly Means*, Chapter 4.

more accustomed to colleges than to universities, that is to say, to dealing with undergraduates who still behaved, and were treated, as if they were at school and whose moral superintendence was a critical aspect of the university's inherited functions. They were bored and resented the schoolboy atmosphere of American and British institutions, the poor preparation of students (especially in the United States and the new English civic universities) and the necessity to teach subjects at routine or introductory levels. While *in loco parentis* made sense in earlier centuries when undergraduates were actually of secondary school age, the increase in age of entry in England throughout the eighteenth century, and in Scotland in the nineteenth century, lessened its universal appeal. Academic career-building was possible in nineteenth-century Germany, to a greater degree than in England, where the professor was still for the most part a clergyman usually bent on a clerical career and where research played only a limited part, so that the best place to be intellectually creative was outside rather than inside the universities. The appeal of the German idea of a university consequently grew. British and American scholars visiting or studying in Germany were impressed by the intellectual ethos of Leipzig, Frankfurt and Berlin, and the dons began to divide into two broad categories: the good college man, devoted to the welfare of his (and after 1860 her) charges; and the scholar and scientist who took Germany as an example. 'I only hope you will not copy Oxford and Cambridge too closely,' wrote the new type of post-1860s Cambridge don, John Robert Seeley, to Emily Davies, Mistress of Girton College. 'The German Universities seem to me to be the right model, not the English ones.'[33]

Many consequences follow from the research idea, amongst them the gradual subordination of the past to the future, of old knowledge to new knowledge, of tradition and the accumulation of knowledge in a form known as 'wisdom' to the excitement of making daringly new formulations. But the new German idea of a university did not replace the older Anglo-American idea of a university. Rather, in different ways in the different countries, the two ideas coexisted; and whereas theoretically they are difficult to reconcile if we attempt to draw out the ramifications of each, in practice accommodations between the ideas have of necessity occurred.

Bildung, because it was primarily an intellectual, or in a special sense a 'spiritual' educational ideal, placed teaching in tight proximity to scholarship and especially to the methods for acquiring knowledge, the *wissenschaftliche Methoden* that gave German science its particular

---

[33] Barbara Stephen, *Emily Davies and Girton College* (London, 1927), 155.

eminence.[34] The sober German professor in his seminar or institute expounding his theories and methods could be contrasted to the walk in the park, the socratic tutorial, the personal bonding, however strained or peculiar, between English tutor and undergraduate. Despite the importance of the seminar room with its specialised library, or the carefully arranged scientific laboratory, *Bildung* did not depend upon communal living, or the famous staircase of Oxford and Cambridge. Once the methods had been acquired, they could almost be developed away from the world at large. The literally disembodied discourses of Thomas Mann's novel *The Magic Mountain* take place in a sanitarium in isolated mountains. In Hermann Hesse's *The Glass Bead Game*, that most extraordinary depiction of a life devoted to the cultivation of mind in and for itself, the pursuit of self-knowledge is centred in an unworldly community. The ideal is neither British nor American. Willa Cather's 1920s novel, *The Professor's House*, specifically contrasts Continental-derived scholarship and the benefits of the lonely life with teaching at a midwestern university full of Yahoos.

Historically the university came to be the favoured environment of academics, at least in a number of western European and certainly American universities, precisely because in time it proved to be the institution most congenial to independent research. Before that could happen, however, the numerous State Churches and religious denominations had to accept the principle of free inquiry,[35] the States and various supporting publics had to recognise the value or utility of research in its different forms, undergraduate teaching was no longer to be considered the sole or primary function of universities, the parietal responsibilites of academics in English-speaking countries were no longer to be insisted upon, and professors had to consent to a social contract,[36] an implicit agreement to place objectivity before advocacy and truth before ideology in the pursuit of knowledge.

These conditions were not reached overnight, nor were they achieved in every country nor in the same degree or permanently, nor do they exist in every university even today. The argument has been made that in Latin America the universities are so intensely politicised that free research can

---

[34] Lorraine Daston, 'Wissenschaft, Research and the Institute', in *Universities and the Sciences*, ed. Guiliano Pancaldi (Bologna, 1993), 76.

[35] A serious problem, however, from the standpoint of maintaining the integrity and cohesion of a religious vision. Nor did the abolition of one form of dogmatism prevent the arrival of another.

[36] Sheldon Rothblatt, 'The Last Thing Said in Germany', *The London Review of Books* (19 May 1988), 12–18.

only be undertaken in special institutes without an undergraduate teaching mission.[37] The degree to which research is a protected and open-ended form of intellectual inquiry depends on much wider considerations. These are the nature of the research undertaking, whether it is 'pure', 'applied' or technical, whether it is conducted in secret or forms part of the inheritance of public knowledge, how it is funded, whether peer review is respected in the allocation of resources, whether grants are awarded competitively, and the general value placed by a society on educational activity whose results and consequences are difficult to measure, especially in the short run. Political traditions are the most important of all considerations, for it is not the university that ultimately guarantees freedom of inquiry, but the tolerance of government and publics. Universities themselves, in their long history, have no reason to boast of their freedom from the idols of the mind. Towards ideas, towards groups, towards religions and towards open thought, they have very often opposed rigid orthodoxies. They have also been guilty of racial and ethnic exclusion. Their collective record is, alas, far from pretty, but the universities of some nations have fared better in these regards than those of others.

AMERICAN DEPARTURES

The American inheritance from Europe is manifold and continuous, and the American use of it highly adaptive and flexible. What makes the American case so interesting is the strong connection between American colleges and universities and the characteristics of American social life, principally its religious pluralism and ethnic diversity, its immigrant composition, and its preference for market discipline interspersed with governmental efforts, many half-hearted or contradictory or unsystematic, to legislate or regulate.

The history of American higher education is characterised by the growth of multi-purpose institutions which continue to add functions and responsibilities without disregarding older commitments. New constituencies and new tasks are absorbed comparatively readily. American higher education institutions have been expansion-minded since the War for Independence and have generally shown a willingness to stretch existing resources to support new ventures. Market discipline

---

[37] See Simon Schwartzman, 'The Focus on Scientific Activity', in *Perspectives on Higher Education, Eight Disciplinary and Comparative Views,* ed. Burton R. Clark (Berkeley and Los Angeles, 1984), 199–232.

has certainly contributed to the comparative openness and flexibility of American institutions as a condition of survival in the public as well as private sector. Market decisions were also a prominent feature of the deliberations leading up to the establishment of the first English university to be founded since the thirteenth century. Some of the founders of the University of London spoke about enrolling at least 2000 students at a time when neither Oxford nor Cambridge could claim more than about 1200. Market-responsive institutions are usually forced to consider student numbers when setting curricula and allocating resources.

The American idea of a university was, in the earliest colonial period, derived from England's before it was common to speak of universities as incorporating an idea or essence. The original American universities were no more than university colleges for the training of clergy and political leaders, each separate colony regarding its college as a public institution, interfering spasmodically in its internal affairs until an extraordinary legal decision known as the Dartmouth case settled the issue of ownership. The decision came in the early nineteenth century, and henceforth the colonial colleges were regarded as private institutions under non-State management but with continued State aid of some kind.

The presence of many distinguished Scottish educators in the colonies in the eighteenth century brought Scottish and Scots-Irish influence into American higher education, leading to two new developments. First, medical and professional education generally were regarded as appropriate university responsibilities, whereas in England training in the law and medicine had devolved upon separate institutions; and second, the teaching of classical languages, mathematics and theology, the backbone of the English curriculum, was broadened into a Scottish humanistic curriculum which included social science, the new Enlightenment Philosophy of Man, and modern subjects, such as non-classical languages and natural science. Scottish influence also reinforced the democratic conceptions spreading throughout the colonies, stressing the notion that education was a national responsibility to be undertaken in the interests and well-being of the many. Without too much fuss, Americans adopted the philosophical Utilitarianism being advocated by the Benthamites, and utility meant, among other things, that education should, depending upon markets, also be low-cost.

One of the most extraordinary differences between American and British higher education was the care taken in the United States to secure the moral, political and financial support of graduates and their attachment to *alma mater*. Indeed, there is an interesting paradox here. The older universities of England had convocations or senates, legislative houses where MAs were entitled to vote, and as these, at least the interested parties, were largely clergy, one feature in the evolution of a secular university in the United Kingdom was neutralising the constitutional power of the graduates. The change occurred at Oxford and Cambridge in the early twentieth century. The newer civic universities, being small and undercapitalised, never really produced sufficient numbers of graduates to provide strong alumni support organisations. By contrast, the American colleges and universities cultivated their alumni without giving them a major governmental role in the life of the institution, apart from representation on lay boards of trustees. In this strategy American institutions were doubtless assisted by the absence of strong competing centres of loyalty, except religious ones, a class system weaker in its boundaries than in Europe, few forms of derived high status, and the importance therefore of institutional identification in providing some form of recognisable status or distinction. To be a graduate or near-graduate was sufficient and, in a continent-sized country, employment opportunities did not always depend upon where the degree had been obtained. The American university or college could not on the whole 'charter' its graduates by guaranteeing employment or career.[38]

After Independence, the Scottish notion of education for a national citizenry received special American emphasis, as colleges and new state universities, which began to spring up at the end of the eighteenth century, adopted republicanism and neo-republicanism as the special purpose of an undergraduate education. This emphasis, centred on the responsibilities of citizenship, is a perennial concern, especially during periods of heavy immigration (and particularly with regard to the flow from eastern or south-eastern Europe and the Far East or Latin America) or when social issues split the nation. These are not the sole reasons, however, for the recurrent interest in national morality and patriotism. The religious divisions of the country, family values, the condition of public schooling, military and political involvement abroad and the national preference for private behaviour and self-aggrandisement are contributing causes.

In 1963 Clark Kerr, then president of the University of California, delivered the Godkin lectures at Harvard. Published in book form, his remarkable analysis is now in a fourth edition and is a landmark contribution to the tradition discussed in this chapter. One of his principal conclusions was that American universities could not be said to be

---

[38] John W. Meyer, 'The Charter: Conditions of Diffuse Socialization in Schools', in *Social Process and Social Structures: an Introduction to Sociology*, ed. W. R. Scott (New York, 1970), 564–78.

animated by a single idea, that is, by an inherited referent serving as a touchstone or guide, a reminder of the university's true purposes and historical destiny, and as a means of sorting out and deciding between competing missions and rival claims. In place of an idea, there was in time a multiversity containing many ideas and very little unity, except whatever might be imposed upon it from above by a central administrative system and board of trustees, or outside in the form of public opinion or legislative pressure. In historical perspective it is certain that Americans abandoned or failed to adopt the Coleridge–Newman premise that institutions embodied an essential idea in the late nineteenth century, at least, after some initial attempts on the part of a number of institutions – I mentioned the New Haven scholars at Yale – to consider universities as centres of culture, regional but also national, from which the best or the highest or the most noteworthy ideas would be disseminated. The most senior institutions flirted with English ideas, but Harvard, the oldest of them, actually resisted the temptation. Instead, Harvard did the opposite and lent its prestige toward a movement that led away from the idea of a university. It was also Harvard, however, that issued a famous report on general education in 1946 attempting to define something approaching a common curriculum, one of many such on-going efforts in the history of American colleges and universities and one destined to continue – with only limited results the sceptic might conclude.

Harvard's contribution to institutional pluralism was the adoption of the elective system of course-taking which supplemented and later replaced the common degree programme wherein students remained in cohorts throughout their residence. Electives were the forerunner of teaching modules (there is actually no American name for this system) which, by the end of the nineteenth century or the beginning of the twentieth, had become standard educational practice.

In the American version, a degree curriculum was divided into modules that were nearly all self-contained, each taught by a single instructor who also examined and assigned a final mark or grade. A degree was awarded on the basis of a certain number of modules distributed among a large number of different subject areas, customarily with concentration in one subject in the last two years of the undergraduate curriculum. This remains the basic situation, although there are and have been any number of variations on the theme, at the University of Chicago for example, or in the core western civilisation programme at Columbia. In nearly every case, however, some element of student course choice is recognised.

The precise origins of modules and credits may be obscure but not in any way that need detain us. As noted, they first appeared as subject

electives at Harvard – or the University of Virginia earlier. Some writers
attribute their genesis to German conceptions of freedom of teaching and
freedom of learning brought to the United States by an early generation
of Americans studying overseas. Others, with pardonable loyalty, find
elective modules homegrown and attribute their birth to Thomas
Jefferson's belief in the ability of the common man to determine his own
educational needs. The University of Virginia experiments broke down
because of the poor preparation of entering students. Another version
unconvincingly attributes electives to eighteenth-century Scottish
sources.[39] Whatever the ultimate derivation, the course structure
embodying it is distinctly American. In its earliest American guise, that
is, in the middle of the nineteenth century, modularity was mainly an
'elective system'. It represented a complete and decisive break with the
old-time college curriculum of classical languages and mathematics, or
with the newer Scottish Enlightenment import of moral philosophy in its
several forms. Virtually all specified requirements were thrown out in
favour of free choice. To begin with the movement went furthest at
Harvard under the leadership of President Eliot. Other institutions
followed but slowly, waiting upon events. A partial reaction set in towards
the end of the century when it was discovered that undergradutes were
poorly prepared for university work (which the University of Virginia
discovered at the outset), let alone equipped to make choices between
competing fields of knowledge. The result was the quadripartite undergraduate curriculum of the present, composed of proficiency requirements, breadth requirements, electives and majors. However, a vast
amount of choice still remains within each category, with the independent
module as the central feature. The modular system can be contrasted with
the historic English honours degree which evolved at Cambridge sometime in the later eighteenth century and at Oxford after 1800. High
specialisation was a feature of English undergraduate education while in
Scotland greater scope was allowed. In both cases, a final examination
occurred at the end of a three- or four-year period of study, but teaching
and examining were separated. Exceptions could be found from time to
time, as in the somewhat more general undergraduate curriculum of
Keele after 1945. But American-style modules were not typical of British
higher education until the second half of the present century when
numerous versions started to appear at British polytechnics and some

[39] Sheldon Rothblatt, 'The American Modular System', in *Quality and Access in Higher
Education, Comparing Britain and the United States,* ed. Robert O. Berdahl, Graeme C. Moodie
and Irving J. Spitzberg, Jr. (Ballmoor, Buckingham, 1991), 130–2.

universities. Integration through the European Union and the development of mass-access institutions, with a need for greater flexibility in admissions and time-tabling, were causes of an increased interest throughout the 1980s and 1990s.[40]

Several important traits of the present American course structure were added in the late nineteenth or early twentieth centuries. The first was the assignment of unit credits to each module in order to increase flexibility in the curriculum. There could now be half and partial modules. This supported another trend, student transfer from one institution to another without loss of credit. A new national currency had been created capable of being traded almost anywhere in the American higher education system. A third trait of the system led in a wholly different direction, more European one might say and less American, an effort at classroom quality control through the assignment of marks or grades per unit. This began in the last decades of the nineteenth century but seems to have been the subject of more widespread debate in the Progressive Era, a period of concern about national efficiency and common standards, whether of weights and measures or of student achievement.

Modularity addressed and solved an ancient educational problem: how to alter the undergraduate curriculum and admit new subjects into it. Modularity made this relatively simple, since there was virtually no limit to the number of modules that could be added to a curriculum provided resources were available. Resources were stretched through the wide adoption of the lecture method of teaching, replacing the more labour-intensive tutorial or small group instruction. Changes could be introduced merely by having a single instructor alter the methods, scope and content of a course. This was more difficult to achieve in systems where terminal examinations and the separation of teaching and examining existed, if for no other reason than that these curricula were based on syllabi requiring committee approval, or because curricula and examination were set and administered from the outside by State agencies, as on the Continent.

Yet modules had their own drawbacks. Since academic standards varied from teacher to teacher, uniform quality control was awkward,

---

[40] Oliver Fulton, 'Modular Systems in Britain', in *Quality and Access in Higher Education, Comparing Britain and the United States*, ed. Robert O. Berdahl, Graeme C. Moodie and Irving J. Spitzberg, Jr. (Ballmoor, Buckingham, 1991), 142–51. By 1995 modular schemes had spread throughout the United Kingdom and Northern Ireland, taking several main forms. A summary appears in *The Times Higher Education Supplement* (29 September 1995), in the section called 'Synthesis'. British modules are more complex than American versions, since many of them are linked or shared between departments and programmes, do not allow for student choice in every instance and often feature centrally managed assessment.

requiring other regulatory devices: hearsay, student evaluations, peer review. The most effective quality control occurred in advance, as it were, in the hiring of faculty, followed by periodic review of the professional record at regular intervals. A further drawback was the vulnerability of the hybrid classroom instructor, both teacher and examiner, to student pressure or outside pressure for higher marks or lenient treatment. There was also an embarrassment of riches. The number of course choices in American institutions multiplied and continued to multiply; and even movements for the reform of the curriculum, for example, the introduction of core courses or interdisciplinary programmes, added to rather than subtracted from the existing body of options.

Despite such departures from European conceptions of proper teaching structure, modularity was perfectly suited to the changing characteristics of American culture. American federalism and localism produced many experiments in higher education, not all of them illustrious when measured by developments abroad. The American belief in market discipline made universities and colleges extremely vulnerable to fluctuations in educational opinion and taste. Wherever possible, American universities and colleges tried to ameliorate or mitigate pressure from outside by attempting to multiply the sources of income and especially to attract unrestricted endowment income, for the mark of a great institution became its ability to resist external demands. For the same reason, a national and even international constituency was preferable to one more purely local and parochial.

Therefore, while in Europe the 'problem' of adapting the university structure to an urban, technological, professional civilisation was often viewed intellectually as finding the correct 'idea' of a university, in the United States a single 'idea' of a university was increasingly impossible. Even the idea of a university having an idea, real but elusive, was doubted. To be sure, many American scholars, scientists, writers and artists found the plural environment of the United States unappealing. They were attracted to the privileges, the State subsidies, the intellectual and artistic culture of settled European capitals. They preferred to live and work abroad, or favoured European standards of artistic and literary taste at home. The most Euro-centred academics were invariably attracted to essentialism either in English or German form, but the German one was easier to assimilate since it was not based on the expensive institutional arrangements of Oxford and Cambridge. Abraham Flexner for one favoured German models as holding out the promise of a higher calling that would insulate universities from the vulgarities and commonplaces of a rather free-wheeling, expansive and aggressive participatory democracy,

often populist and certainly individualist. But such partisans of the idea
of a university were in the minority among academics for whom the
modular teaching system was a liberation from the tedium of undergraduate teaching. Furthermore, the advocates of essentialism did not
control American colleges and universities like the faculties of the
Continental university, the self-governing societies of Oxford and
Cambridge or the senates and courts of other British universities. In
America lay boards of trustees delegated authority to presidents. From
time to time some academic malcontents took refuge in wholly new
institutions, backed by eccentric financiers. Black Mountain College
situated in the foothills of North Carolina and lasting only from 1933 to
1956 was one such sanctuary from the world's dross. There, far from the
madding crowd, professors could embrace their conception of the good,
the true and the beautiful.[41] But these experiments customarily lasted only
as long as charismatic leaders were active. They were campuses under
one-man rule, unable to develop a constitution assuring longevity in the
volatile American educational market.

The modular system, that great antithesis to the very idea of a
university having an idea, did not come upon Americans overnight. It
took a long time to develop. It proceeded by fits and starts, a response to
the decentralised character of American political life and culture, a distant
and constantly expanding geographical frontier, and the continual
renewal of population through emigration from abroad. Each institution
watched the other, borrowing ideas from the market leaders, adjusting
them to find a particular niche of its own in order to secure even a tiny
competitive advantage, while continuing to dream of an upward drift
along a remarkable continuum of educational status hierarchies.

Competition and emulation drove old and new institutions to
continued exertion in a search for success or distinction as measured in
every possible manner, by income, by wider influence, by status and
numbers, by size of plant and extent of acreage, by location and pulling
power, even by 'mission'. It is difficult, however, for Americans to use
quality as a measure of distinctiveness, although the word springs
immediately to the lips of British (or Australian and European) academics.
Of course 'quality' is desired, but democratic propensities force Americans
to speak in euphemisms. Quality is therefore assessed mainly in relation to
an institution's self-declared 'programme' as measured in resources or

---

[41] See Martin Duberman, *Black Mountain, An Exploration in Community* (Garden City, New
York, 1973). For other experiments, see Gerald Grant and David Riesman, *The Perpetual
Dream* (Chicago, 1978).

institutional objectives, language that avoids giving offence to students, faculty, administrators and supporting publics. Six regional educational accrediting agencies exist as voluntary associations of universities and colleges, with some public representatives. Their function is to assess colleges and universities on the basis of their published objectives. Normally only minimum standards are assessed. The question of a Rolls Royce degree rarely enters into the equation.

Neither competition nor emulation would have succeeded in America had there not existed an extraordinary diversity of population, made even more diverse by the great emigrations of the post-Civil War period and the relative absence of central government constraints. I stress both the diversity of the population and the absence of central direction because it is certainly possible to have a diverse population without plural educational aims and structures. And it is quite clear to an American considering the end-of-century role of the Australian Commonwealth Government in the governance and support of Australian universities that a federal constitution is by itself no guarantee of institutional autonomy. Federalism embraces any number of authority arrangements and combinations of central and local decision-making. Until the 1980s federalism in Australia was more likely to reinforce the English idea of a university. The federal constitution of present-day Germany gives Bonn and the *Länder* far more authority over higher education than Washington can claim, and student examinations are primarily a governmental rather than an institutional responsibility. Swiss higher education, however, resembles the American in several ways, most notably in the different systems sponsored by individual cantons. But languages may be a factor.

Attempts to create central universities at public expense occurred early in the history of the American Republic. Shortly after the War for Independence followers of Alexander Hamilton debated with Jefferson on the issue of whether a national university should be established at Washington. The federated states, fearing a government monopoly over intellectual capital, defeated the Hamiltonian proposal. We can contrast this defeat of centralism with what was happening abroad. In Germany, universities were attached to the State, to the purposes of the State and to the very idea of a State, to the great consternation of Max Weber, who a century later wrote a classic essay on the question of university–state relations. We can find nothing in the American experience that corresponds to the systematic reform of Oxford and Cambridge by successive waves of royal and parliamentary commissions of inquiry in the thirty years from about 1850 to 1882, or the establishment of another kind of central institution, the examining University of London of 1836, created to protect the quality of the degree and in time to regulate the growth of new universities in the Midlands and northern cities of England, in Ireland and the Dominions and empire.

No American university could literally be at the centre or possess a monopoly of the nation's resources, not even Ivy with its historic advantages. The absence of an established set of institutions or favoured intelligentsia gave encouragement to new institutions and stimulated rivalries, so that even the oldest and most distinguished universities had to meet the continual competition of upstarts and innovations emanating from elsewhere. Remaining atop the prestige hierarchy required energy and resourcefulness, on-going appeals to donors and a watchful eye for potential growth opportunities. Harvard constantly redefined itself in an effort to stay current. It was overtaken as a birthplace of initiative at certain times by new universities like Chicago, or the Germanophile Johns Hopkins or Cornell or Clark. The next oldest American institution, William and Mary in Virginia, was hardly in the running at all. For a time Columbia University, the colonial King's College, led the pack. New state universities, Michigan or California, the latter enjoying generous gifts of land from the federal government, became instant universities, mixing Latin and the mechanical arts without bothering too much about their compatibility with an historic idea of a university. As Walter Metzger puts it:

> Military science was taught by all land-grant colleges, where it was legally required, and also by Baylor, Georgetown, Brown, and Yale, where it was not; domestic science was offered by state universities known for their 'low' utilitarianism, and also by Clark and Chicago, reputed to seek the most exalted knowledge the fortunes of their founders could buy.[42]

Whatever the fortunes of Oxford and Cambridge in the seminal nineteenth century, they never lost their traditional advantages, their ties to the governing elite, their ability to attract new talent, their close assocation with Church and State. New institutions arose: the London university colleges, Durham, the Federal University of Victoria. The Scottish universities were reformed and flourished; indeed, their intellectual distinction earlier could not be denied. Yet no university ever succeeded in posing a permanent challenge to the prestige of the ancient universities, which itself was an effective means of meeting such competition as from time to time appeared.

[42] Walter P. Metzger. 'Academic Profession in the United States', in *The Academic Profession*, ed. Burton R. Clark (Berkeley and Los Angeles, 1987), 132.

Many different ideas of a university contested for supremacy in America, and each institution contained all of these ideas at once, just as the modular system itself incorporated and permitted all forms of teaching at all levels of instruction. But if an historic justification for modules was needed, it could certainly be found in nineteenth-century German ideas of *Lehrfreiheit* and *Lernfreiheit*. Modularity permitted the teacher to teach what he liked, and allowed specialisation an easy entry into the curriculum. Electives permitted the student to choose from among a great array of educational goods. Over decades the principle of *Lernfreiheit* was extended still further with the appearance of student-initiated (and student-funded) courses in the 1960s.

Modules and electives are essential for mass-access institutions in a plural society and perhaps also a justification after the fact for the type of institution that American universities became. In order to make room for knowledge and for the process of specialisation and sub-specialisation and professionalism characteristic of urban societies, there must exist a high degree of curricular flexibility. In order to accommodate a multiplicity of interests, which is both a cause and an effect of the proliferation of course modules, resources must be concentrated on certain functions to the relative exclusion of others. Thus certain standbys of the Newman idea of a university, such as collegiate education and the tutorial system, the 'close action of the . . . matured character on the unformed', as another Oxford don said in the last century,[43] are luxuries barely possible. Students, particularly undergraduates, are presumed to know their own interests and to care for themselves. This assumption is necessary to legitimise poor staffing ratios and the weakening of the faculty role in advising and counselling. Yet American institutions are not altogether comfortable with the assumption that students are sufficiently mature to design their own educational programme. Proof of unease lies in the enormous investment in advising, counselling, psychological testing and health services. The complexity of the modular and unit credit systems requires employment of non-academic administrative staffs, interpenetrated by part-time deans drawn from the faculty. Altogether student services comprise a substantial addition to the costs of running a contemporary university. While long, idyllic walks, leisured conversation between students and teachers in protected islands of discourse are not unheard of in liberal arts colleges and in even the most populous state universities,

---

[43] Sheldon Rothblatt, *The Revolution of the Dons: Cambridge and Society in Victorian England* (London and New York, 1968, reissued Cambridge, 1981), 194–5.

they are an exception or anomaly and not really a part of the idea of an American university.

   Is there really no single idea of an American university? 'Knowledge' comes closest, but knowledge in every conceivable form and application, knowledge abstract and knowledge applied, from simple vocationalism to the most abstruse kind of inquiry. Knowledge as a thing in itself, as its own reward, is for the most part an abstract and impersonal conception, now assuredly, but can we claim that it was ever the dominant conception of a university? Despite the fact that many of Newman's most famous statements are about knowledge, it is all too easy to forget that as a teacher motivated by a pastoral conception of pedagogy, as a theologian concerned with sin and redemption, as a moralist bothered by the dissolution of authority in Liberal England, and as an educational thinker still operating within older notions of the possibility of ranking the arts, he is not talking about a universe of education similar to what obtains in most western universities today. That an undergraduate would attend the university and take away from it a list of courses certified by a degree or credential was exactly what horrified him about the new University of London. Had Newman's idea of a university prevailed, there would have been no London granting huge numbers of external degrees to undergraduates in remote colonial territories, no Manchester or Liverpool where the interests of manufacturers and shipowners had to be considered, no Keele or Sussex experimenting with different styles of curricula, no Cal Tech in Pasadena, no Oregon University of the Health Sciences, no Wirtschafts Universität in Vienna. The educational world would have been easier to define. Perhaps, possessing a beguiling clarity, it might have been more satisfying than what exists today, but it is not for the scientific historian to entertain such careless thoughts.

MULTIVERSITY NOT UNIVERSITY

In any case, we must be cautious in how we apply the idea of a university to contemporary or even nineteenth-century American higher education. To say that the governing conception of the American university is the pursuit of knowledge is to falsely suggest that Americans adopted German ideas of a university in more or less pure form. American university teachers did not control their universities through a system of professorial chairs grouped into 'faculties' that could effectively restrict curricular innovation, nor could they adopt and disseminate a conception of education resting on *Bildung* or self-mastery according to the highest aesthetic models. At best a few of them could advocate *Bildung*, which could then be absorbed by a handful of undergraduates of individualist or aesthetic temper. This rarely happened precisely because American universities and colleges, however they might at times resent the intrusion of the market, were forced to respond to it simply to exist. I am not speaking about passive responses, as in certain Marxist theories of social conflict, but about active and creative responses, about efforts to mitigate or mediate or persuade, to deflect and to play off one set of pressures against another, to summon up new worlds to redress the balance of the old, or old worlds to redress the balance of the new. Such strategies necessitated the creation of full-time university administrators and managers, leaders and staff who would negotiate on behalf of the faculty. The result was the rise of the multi-purpose university, incorporating in single institutions and later in systems all of the ideas of a university that had appeared in the nineteenth century, carrying out on a single campus the functions of a polytechnic, a normal school, a college of arts and crafts, a technological college, law and medical schools, a business school, research institutes and departments, an American community college (even an American upper secondary school) and a sprawling catch-all for undergraduates known variously as a College of Letters and Science or a College of Arts and Sciences, that is, the attenuated descendant of university colleges. Tucked away in the interstices of departments and laboratories were honours programmes for those who qualified by the test of merit. Even whole honours colleges within universities were created here and there, notably at Michigan, performing classic elite-training functions. Nevertheless, programmes for the meritorious coexisted with instruction that in Europe would surely be disdained as remedial and outside the definition of a true university.

The blurring of the boundaries between types of institutions, programmes and categories, the intermixture of liberal, vocational, professional and graduate research functions is perfectly captured in the way Americans confuse the words 'school', 'college', and 'university'. Originally, confusion between 'college' and 'university' was Scottish; but the addition of 'school' to mean higher education without a reference to 'schools of study' (as in the 'Old Schools' at Oxford) is, I believe, purely American. 'It would help', wrote one exasperated critic in 1911 of the American propensity to avoid careful distinctions,

> For the states to adopt a fairly uniform and severe restriction on the use of the terms 'university' and 'college' . . . it would eliminate some weaklings; though it is true that 'the college that is least worthy of the name, that is in every way inferior to such academies as Exeter and Andover, is the very one

which would cling most desperately to the title, would be most reluctant to relinquish its right to confer worthless degrees.'[44]

Universities that are simultaneously regarded as a school, a college or a university envelope structures and traditions that are contradictory, confusing and ambiguous. At one moment in a typical academic senate debate we are told that a university exists to promote knowledge, while at another we are informed that it is a place for self-cultivation. Some speakers denounce the 'worldly university', yet others have contempt for the ivory tower. Other speakers note that the cardinal object of an under-graduate education is citizenship, only to be answered that it is the higher learning that defines a university 'in the true sense of the word'. But the higher learning can also be described as professional education, the oldest of all university functions, and that too is a debate with a nineteenth-century history. Newman himself recognised the validity of professional education but more as a necessity than a priority. Still other voices inform us that a university in a democracy must place itself utterly at the service of society, as if there existed a single voice speaking for 'society'. And once again, in language filled with passion and disarming conviction, we are told that 'liberal education' is the ultimate reason for the existence of universities even though the American definition of a liberal education bears almost no resemblance to that sophistic-Italic humanist tradition that created the notion in the first place. Contradictions can be sustained at the level of ideas because the several disciplines speak from the standpoint of different inheritances and functions, and they can be sustained organ-isationally because of the many divisions of universities into autonomous or semi-autonomous schools, colleges, departments, programmes, research institutes and centres; student services, public relations, legal staffs and planning offices.

Meanwhile, reports and books are produced from inside the academy by presidents and professors, or from the outside by expatriates now with philanthropic foundations or academic associations, urging the great American university flamingo, its legs, neck and head already sprawling in every conceivable direction, to reconsider past options or new assign-ments. A sensitively written report from the Association of American Colleges takes up the vexed theme of a common core of undergraduate learning, as does Ernest Boyer of the Carnegie Foundation for the Advancement of Teaching, whose report is also a review of what he called

---

[44] William T. Foster, *Administration of the College Curriculum* (New York, 1911), 316. The odd punctuation appears in the original.

'best practice' in the existing curriculum. One former Secretary of Education, William Bennett, returns to the Battle of the Books, recommending that all students be exposed to authors and works that put them in the company of 'great souls' (he includes sceptical or cynical Machiavelli and Hobbes). Allan Bloom, who once looked out upon the world from the cosy corner of the tiny Committee on Social Thought of the private University of Chicago, tells us that only certain subjects and certain authors are genuinely worth studying. The former president of Harvard, Derek Bok, examines the service role of American universities in relation to traditional considerations like academic freedom, the pursuit of intellect and high standards of teaching. He questions whether great research universities ought to provide research and consulting facilities to city officials, or establish schools of hotel management, doctoral programmes in physical studies, radio and television communications 'and other doubtful enterprises' – all of which are in existence somewhere, including leading places. Yet he is solidly in favour of a service function for private research universities, which, after all, as he says, receive one-fifth to two-thirds of their income from a combination of government grants for research and student aid, as well as relief from taxes and other assessments. For such institutions, social problems cannot be off-limits. Yet other authors emphasise the importance of moral education (but whose set of morals?). Individual professors may dissent from, but university presidents ordinarily assent to, the multiversity conception, since it is their task to connect universities to the rest of American society in response to consumer demand and political pressure and in the understandable interests of longevity.[45] No idea of a university, past or present, escapes discussion at some level, but can a single university contain every one?

From the standpoint of the idea of an idea of a university, American forms of higher education represent a development that Newman and his successors in spirit could only deplore. Newman called the new London University a 'pantechnicon', and also a 'bazaar', and since then

---

[45] *A New Vitality in General Education* (Association of American Colleges, 1988); William Bennett, *To Reclaim a Legacy* (November, 1984), 11; Allan Bloom, *The Closing of the American Mind: How Higher Education has Failed Democracy and Impoverished the Souls of Today's Students* (New York, 1987); Ernest L. Boyer, *College, The Undergraduate Experience in America* (New York, 1987); Derek Bok, *Beyond the Ivory Tower, Social Responsibilites of the Modern University* (Cambridge, MA, 1982), 62, 64, 77, 88. See also *The Future of State Universities*, ed. Leslie W. Koepplin and David Wilson (New Brunswick, NJ, 1985); Frank Newman, *Choosing Quality, Reducing the Conflict between the State and the University* (Education Commission of the States, September, 1987); and *Higher Education and the American Resurgence* (Carnegie Foundation for the Advancement of Teaching, 1985).

descriptions like 'supermarket', 'smorgasbord' and other references to education as a commodity or item of consumption have been common.

For those familiar with this line of criticism, Allan Bloom's best-seller, *The Closing of the American Mind*, is not a departure but yet another restatement of the position that a university ought to stand for the highest and the best, that a university education ought to be exclusive, that it should not be vulgarly utilitarian, or utilitarian *tout court*, that it should deal with great and proven works, and that it should pose an alternative to whatever is popular, trendy or currently in vogue. It should nourish imagination and creativity and a love for knowledge as a thing in itself. The idea of a university demands that a true university should never succumb to the dictum that more is better and should fight vigorously against any crude market measure of success, such as classroom head-counts or value-added accountability or citation indices or productivity standards of research or any other attempt to apply cost-benefit analysis to universities as if they were banks and manufacturing firms. What makes Bloom's position somewhat different from the typical complaint is that, paradoxically, he attached a commercial title to his surprising best-seller, so that the very market that was the cause of his irritation was simultaneously the source of his success.

It is hardly evident that higher education has failed democracy in the United States, although definition of the word 'democracy' is critical to the argument. But if we take the historical perspective I have offered and consider the demographic and political pressures brought to bear on American higher education during and since the nineteenth century, we may well conclude that far from failing American democracy, American colleges and universities have served it well, providing widespread access, diversity and flexibility. One criticism that can be made is that they have served a particular conception of democracy all too well. Such criticism, however, must ultimately apply to the American political tradition and American consumerism which created higher education, and that is a completely different kind of critique.

Ironically, it is not the grand tradition of criticising American higher education from the standpoint of an idea of a university that produces consternation in the American academic environment. What makes American university administrators wince and orders public relations staffs into the field is the criticism that American higher education does not do enough of what in fact, comparatively speaking, it does extremely well. The persistent complaint is that it does not provide *enough* access, diversity and flexibility. Open admissions, a policy adopted in the City University of New York in the 1970s, a cry for greater breadth and choice in a curriculum already disconnected and incoherent, more part-time degrees in institutions as yet committed to some notion of the full-time student, credit for employment in certain occupations – these have been the louder and stronger demands, the demands which politicians heed. Even private institutions, great as well as small, are not immune from these pressures to make educational opportunity widespread and virtually universal. Meritocracy, an idea implicit in the English idea of a university, is difficult to defend in a society where young people do not begin life with the same social or natural advantages. While such may be true of all societies, not all societies have been politically committed to equality of opportunity. But the desire to expand access to universities (or other higher education institutions) is spreading rapidly everywhere at the end of the twentieth century.

LESSER IDEAS

The idea of an idea of a university is important. Without it, a university is utterly shapeless and possesses no means of distinguishing itself from any other kind of educational institution, the corporate classrooms, for example, appearing in giant firms. Even the promoters of corporate classrooms have seized upon the understanding that a university has a special history and appeal. Writing in 1990 about the lack of literacy and numeracy at the giant telecommunications firm, Motorola, its corporate vice-president for training and education and president of 'Motorola University' explained that the word 'university' seemed to reconcile 'public educators' to the $120 million investment in in-house education. 'The word university is undeniably ambitious . . . but will raise the expectations of the work force.' Who would have been 'electrified' by the term 'educational resource facility'?[46] Indeed! And the author knows his Newman, 'which, after 150 years, is still the cornerstone of liberal education'.

> But what *was* a university. And more to the point, what was a Motorola University? What kind of model should we work from? Newman's ideal university had no place for vocational training, so in that sense he and we part ways. But in another sense, we're in complete agreement. Newman wanted his university to mold the kind of individual who can 'fill any post with credit' and 'master any subject with facility' – an excellent description of what we wanted Motorola University to do.[47]

[46] William Wiggenhorn, 'Motorola U: When Training Becomes an Education', *Harvard Business Review* (July–August 1990), 83.
[47] *Ibid.*, 81.

What's in a name? Or idea? The idea of the idea of a university is talismanic. Yet Newman had little or nothing to say about the issues agitating university communities at the end of the twentieth century: affirmative action, competition, the transfer function, retention rates, binary systems, the role of planning, State–university relations, peer-review in the awarding of grants and contracts, flexibility and diversity, formula-funding, academic self-government, tenure, the ratio of professorial chairs to total faculty appointments, value-added learning, the use of Scholastic Aptitude Test scores in admissions (US) and 'useful knowledge'. For some of these, useful knowledge, for example, we can deduce his possible response. On others, student support and housing, he had fixed views, since he was founding a new university and had to involve himself in such matters. But we are rarely interested in what Newman thought about these 'lesser' issues.

Nevertheless, it is precisely the lesser issues that determine how an idea is to be carried out and that in time supplant any discernible idea of a university. As current American debates indicate, and the present strained central government–university relations in Britain and Australia prove, it is not so much the primary idea of a university that is producing controversy as the secondary ideas, the subsidiary ideas of a university, or rather, the other defining characteristics listed at the outset of this chapter.

Thus in the context of present-day tensions, the English idea of a university means a certain expensive staffing ratio, a high degree of self-government (so that even the lay councils of new universities like Essex include faculty),[48] students largely in residence, tutorials or small classes, a 'national' in preference to a 'local' mission,[49] the single honours degree or a linked 'curriculum' (in the spirit of 'Greats' or 'Modern Greats') with few options or modules. Students, wrote the first vice-chancellor of Essex, may have *table d'hôte* courses, but no *à la carte*.[50] The English idea of a university has meant devising machinery for the maintenance of a more or less common standard of excellence across different universities and 'places' for undergraduates gaining admission by competitive entry, with tuition payments and maintenance grants supplied as needed by local and central government.[51] It means, again in the interests of common

---

[48] Albert E. Sloman, *A University in the Making* (1964), 80, the BBC Reith Lectures for 1963.

[49] I noticed with interest that some participants in the 1980s Australian debate over the federal government's Green Paper reconsidered the advantages of local over central control with respect to academic freedom.

[50] Sloman, *University*, 41–2.

[51] Loan schemes, however, have become important in the 1990s as higher education expenses increase more rapidly than government expenditure.

standards and equity, a degree of supervision from Westminster, by no means as systematically severe or Cartesian as in the French higher education system; but the presence of the centre, whether of Crown, Privy Council, Parliament or Whitehall, was always noticeable. In the building of the new University of Essex more than thirty years ago, the University Grants Committee specified the amount of square footage per lecture hall per student, the maximum price of an office chair, required prior approval for the expenditure of public money on buildings and set salary scales and ranges. The vice-chancellor, while expressing a wish for greater flexibility, nevertheless remarked upon the freedom he enjoyed to plan a new university![52]

American academics have had to live without an idea of a university for at least a century. Its relative absence has also been an advantage. It means that there is very little prior restraint on experiment. It means that Americans have not created a privileged academic class that arrogates to itself the right to speak on behalf of the higher culture (the distinguished Oxonian historian-civil servant G. M. Young of another generation once spoke of the 'terrorists of the higher culture' whom he contrasted with proponents of Liberal Curiosity).[53] It means, in the words of a 1930s president of a land grant university, that the 'state universities hold that there is no intellectual service too undignified for them to perform'.[54] It means that if the academic community cannot reach a consensus on the idea of a university, then neither can the State, the general public, alumni and benefactors. And in view of the attacks on Australian universities as represented in the Dawkins Green Paper and Mrs Thatcher's attack on British universities in the 1980s, this may well be a relief. It also means that the terms of debate are fuzzy and indistinct, and potentially divisive issues concerning academic matters are transformed into side issues and details.[55] It means that a 'binary policy' such as arose in post-Robbins Britain and a similar policy in Australia, equal but separate segments of higher education, is only acceptable if student mobility across the dividing lines is guaranteed. In the United States the segments have been separate and unequal but also, in educational jargon, 'articulated', interconnected

[52] Sloman, *University*, 12–15.
[53] George Malcolm Young, 'The New Cortegiano', in *Victorian Essays* (London, 1962), 210.
[54] Quoted in Bok, *A New Vitality*, 62.
[55] There are major exceptions to this general observation. Controversial issues arising from larger American conflicts inevitably force their way into universities. This is especially damaging wherever no strong consensual 'idea' exists to provide guidance. McCarthy era restrictions on academic freedom are one example, affirmative action hiring and admission policies are another. These continue to divide the academy.

through modularity and the transfer function. Movement from one segment to another is possible, indeed, is essential to the maintenance of the legitimacy of higher education institutions in the eyes of the public and its legislative representatives.

I have stated the American problem as one of survival, but I hardly think the situation has been that desperate. The interconnections of an institution with society and culture through market discipline are complex and intricate. At any one time numerous markets are in existence, some soft and some stable, and there never can be a perfect fit between supply and demand. Markets are not always rigid. Some of them create slack, which provides openings for inspired selling and innovation, as well as opportunities to protect less popular but valued teaching. Historically, supply in higher education has often led demand, especially in providing for curricula, and we may even notice developments that seem to bear no direct relationship to market pressures at all, subjects that are taught because the faculty believes it is fitting they should be taught even if only the few are interested.

Market response is not passive, since the market is an arena for negotiation. American universities have been active participants in the elaborate and creative process of accommodation that enables Plato and courses in film-making to exist side by side, that provides a half-unit credit for classes in handball and four units for working in the laboratory of an internationally famous scientist and credit towards graduation for courses taken by advanced placement examinations while in high school, in the United States Army, in a community college over the summer, in extra-mural courses and by correspondence or during a year abroad learning the maxims of La Rochefoucauld in Grenoble. Historically, American universities and colleges, their presidents and deans and their faculties have reached out to the society, actively seeking the entanglements and compromises that are so fully captured in the modular system. The search for patrons, markets, supporters and funding has gone on for 200 years. Far from continually resenting the participation of the outside world, colleges and universities have often sought it, reacting adversely, of course, whenever that participation seemed to be restrictive rather than collaborative, or whenever the professorial guild was in danger of losing control.

Nevertheless, there are deep cultural and institutional problems associated with markets. The subject has its share of inherent tensions, paradoxes and ironies.[56] No university can survive without a high degree

[56] For a start, Sheldon Rothblatt, '"Standing Antagonisms": the Relationship of Under-graduate to Graduate Education', in Koepplin and Wilson, 39–66.

of external support, but the question is the nature and terms of that support. One of the more interesting findings of the first three volumes of the new Oxford *History of Oxford University* is the degree to which medieval Oxford willingly connected itself to the Crown in an effort to detach itself from the control of bishops, using its graduates to reach the ears and purse of the royal court, and ultimately enabling the Renaissance State to bludgeon and bribe the university into compliance with its goals of religious and ideological uniformity. The successful efforts of the aristocracy to control the instruments of monarchy allowed the universities a high measure of autonomy by the eighteenth century, yet it was nineteenth-century liberalism – the same liberalism against which Newman railed – that established the principle that universities must be independent of State authority. Until the early twentieth century the British State was reluctant to assist the universities old and new to any great extent. State reluctance was eventually overcome by pressure from the universities themselves, which, having lost the capacity to mobilise large amounts of private giving, found their income insufficient to undertake research in science and applied science.[57]

The search for patrons is common to all university systems in all ages and countries. The difference between Britain and Progressive Era America is that in Britain the academics (once) preferred the State to the public, the centre to the periphery, the metropolis to the province. For the State, like the Church and the universities, was staffed by the same sort of person, the product of the same kind of elite schooling and conceptions of liberal education, holder of the same belief in the idea of the idea of a university. But in the United States, the State was one source among many, one patron among several, one alternative among a number of them, sometimes a welcome partner in the grand exercise of higher education, on other occasions a necessary evil. And since Americans, because of their federal constitution, did not establish a Ministry of Higher Education or a Department of Education and Science with authority to control the destinies of the higher education community, income for higher education was remarkably diverse and uncoordinated, divided between feepayers and scholarship donors, private and public, state and national sources. Government support itself was distributed through a number of different civil service departments and national research institutes, each with

---

[57] For this story see Sheldon Rothblatt and Martin Trow, 'Government Policies and Higher Education: a Comparison of Britain and the United States from about 1630 to 1860', in *Social Research and Social Reform: Essays in Honour of A. H. Halsey*, ed. Colin Crouch and Anthony Heath (Oxford, 1992), 173–216.

separate policy-making authority, each exposed to a great number of educational lobbying organisations, the famous acronyms clustered for warmth in the vicinity of One Dupont Circle in Washington, DC.

THE ANTITHESIS OF THE IDEA OF A UNIVERSITY

If the American university is so fractured that it cannot organise itself around a distinct idea, it nevertheless exists in a recognisable container. Shared decision-making between trustees, administrators and professors creates bondings of sorts, as does the organisation of the institution around disciplines, which escape their perimeters and join allied fields and projects.[58] The allocation of resources is mainly a home affair, although multicampus systems impose a mega-university level of administration on top of the subordinate structures.

The American university attempts to incorporate all ideas of a university, so that the long shadow of the idea of the idea of a university is still discernible, however faint. It is not in the United States but in France that the anti- or non-essentialist idea of a university has in fact received its greatest expression. The most highly centralised of all western European systems, in theory as well as practice, French higher education institutions are virtually disembodied. Different government ministries, external councils, agencies and disciplinary boards, regional as well as national, prescribe and regulate teaching, research, curricula, examinations and degrees. Budgets are handled discretely. Research and teaching are separated and placed in separate institutional structures, with a few crossovers. Individual universities tend towards high specialisation. The university as a distinct institution, as a living organism, to use a biological metaphor, has disintegrated into many independent lines of bureaucratic management.[59]

Such a conception of a university can never inspire a masterpiece of literature capable of competing with Newman. Even the far more

---

[58] As explained by Burton R. Clark, 'The Problem of Complexity in Modern Higher Education', in Rothblatt and Wittrock, 263–79. But 'Shared decision-making' may be a cliche. It certainly begs the question of how much or just what is shared: admissions, curricula, research, appointments, grantsmanship? An analysis would require a separate chapter.

[59] Christine Musselin, 'Steering Higher Education in France: 1981–1991', *Higher Education in Europe*, 17 (1992), 70; Guy Neave, 'Séparation de Corps: The Training of Advanced Students and the Organization of Research in France', in *The Research Foundations of Graduate Education, Germany, Britain, France, the United States, Japan*, ed. Burton R. Clark (Berkeley and Los Angeles, 1993), 159–91, and Guy Neave and Richard Edelstein, 'The Research Training System in France: Microstudy of Three Academic Disciplines', in Clark, *ibid.*, 192–220.

integrated American university has the same difficulty according to Clark Kerr:

> The Idea of a Multiversity has no bard to sing its praises; no prophet to proclaim its vision; no guardian to protect its sanctity. It has its critics, its detractors, its transgressors. It also has its reality rooted in the logic of history. It is an imperative rather than a reasoned choice among elegant alternatives.[60]

A university whose borders are so penetrable will have Romans and barbarians mixing freely on campus streets. The American Puritans wanted to establish a city on the hill, an outpost of spiritual dedication and devotion, but the American university of today is more like a city of the plain, culturally and ethnically heterogenous, full of milling crowds, jugglers and tumblers. It has suburbs and subcultures, separate neighbourhoods, even local government, and sometimes the campus is so dispersed that a transport system is required to convey inhabitants to one location or another. Of course it has a parking problem. The division of labour prevails – one of the defining characteristics of a city. Elite functions jostle with popular ones, and a huge service organisation of counselling, housing and financial services coexists with an academic sector. The large American university is properly an urban conception, in fact a functional substitute for cities in areas of the continent where metropolises do not exist, providing galleries, concert halls and museums for the local population, not to mention highly commercial sporting events. It is a creation that has grown up in time and adjusted to its culture, not smoothly but inevitably. Like the city, it is forever pushing at its boundaries, always pointing beyond itself, inviting inhabitants to consider a long list of available opportunities and choices without guaranteeing that they will be experienced or used by everyone.

In asking what binds such an institution and keeps its parts together, we might well ask what holds a city together. For some the bonding is an 'idea'. For others it is a conception. Still others accept the challenge of the campus-city, focusing on the more immediate task of getting on, of coping with the exigencies of daily life and finding a niche for themselves. Therefore we can say that while it is often impossible to live in a city, so is it also impossible to live elsewhere.

---

[60] Clark Kerr, *The Uses of the University* (Cambridge, MA, 1963), 6.

CHAPTER TWO

'CONSULT THE *GENIUS* OF THE PLACE'[1]

INTRODUCTION: THE UNIVERSITY AS MILIEU

In Chapter 1 Newman's idea of a university was explored (yet again) in relation to the famous definition of his lasting work. A university was (is) 'a place of *teaching* universal *knowledge*'. The emphasis falls on the word 'teaching'. This was opposed to several other conceptions of a university but specifically to what eventually became the dominant transatlantic idea, at least in the view of an international community of researchers, that is to say, the German idea of original inquiry.

This opposite idea focuses on *wissenschaftliches Methoden*, the methods or process needed to convert information into knowledge. The stress falls on the process of conceptualisation, analysis and the organisation of facts into connected hypotheses and theories, to be added and corrected as an on-going scientific commitment. Whether that process is absolutely value-free, or relatively so, whether it is teleological and biased is an indissoluble part of the knowledge enterprise, provoking further reflections and debate and a vast literature on evidence and proof, the sociology of theory manufacture or the historiography of disciplinary specialisation. At issue are certainty not authority and the modes of inquiry best suited to representing actuality. Furthermore, the German idea of a university

To build, to plant, whatever you intend,
To rear the Column, or the Arch to bend,
To swell the Terras, or to sink the Grot;
In all, let *Nature* never be forgot.
Consult the *Genius* of the Place in all,
That tells the Waters or to rise, or fall,
Or helps th'ambitious Hill the Heav'ns to scale,
Or scoops in circling Theatres the Vale,
Calls in the Country, catches opening Glades,
Joins willing Woods, and varies Shades from Shades,
Now breaks, or now directs, th'intending Lines;
Paints as you plant, and as you work, *Designs*.
Alexander Pope, from *An Epistle to Lord Burlington* (1731)

implies that certain fields of knowledge may become obsolete, in which case the careers of their practitioners can be in jeopardy. (This pleasing thought actually occurred to the royal commissioners inquiring into the finances and organisation of Oxford and Cambridge in the later 1850s. Facing what they took to be entrenched but outmoded fields of inquiry, as well as professors, they suggested in private correspondence 'that it would be extremely beneficial to the University if powers were also given to it to alter or modify the subject matter of any Professorship which through lapse of time and change of circumstances should appear to be unnecessary or less necessary than some other'.)[2] Merely stating the commonplaces of scholarly discourse today describes a set of positions familiar enough to Newman in most respects but one that could never be expected to engage his fundamental sympathy.

The researcher has a professional career interest in a subject. Teaching is important, or may be important, but teaching in relation to the subject rather than the student. This sharp distinction becomes confused in practice, but it still has analytical value. Upon a research identity extramural scholarly associations arise, requirements for disseminating knowledge are devised, opportunities for collaborative research and peer review are created and career entry qualifications such as higher degrees are created. Rules and regulations regarding the conduct of scholarship are an important part of the career apparatus since they modulate relationships within the profession and define its elements of success.

There is a third form of teaching in universities close in spirit to the research model except that its special focus is a specific occupational path which itself may have a liberal, that is to say, characterological ingredient. The third form is teaching as professional training, and the liberal component is concerned with the specific norms and traditions of a given occupation. The professional teaching model was referred to in Hastings Rashdall's historic depiction of the medieval university as founded to train students for the liberal professions of law, medicine and divinity. When he wrote his great work at the conclusion of the nineteenth century, the common English view of universities was that they originated as liberal arts institutions. 'It behoves us not to lose or lower the idea of the University as the place *par excellence* for professional and properly trained students, not for amateurs or dilettantes', he wrote.[3] But even much earlier in the nineteenth century the case for a university as primarily the home of

2 S. W. Wayte to the Secretary of State for the Home Department (25 June 1858), Home Office papers 73/39.
3 Quoted in P. E. Matheson, *The Life of Hastings Rashdall, D.D.* (Oxford, 1928), 74–5.

professional education appeared in an American review of the *Statement by the Council of the University of London, explanatory of the Nature and Object of that Institution* [1827] and the *Report of a Committee of the Overseers of Harvard College* (1825). The review discussed the origins of universities not according to their essence but from the perspective of their legal and corporate status, their powers, function and organisation. The reviewer concluded that the 'very nature of a university requires, that the study of the professions should form its basis and its principal object, to which all other pursuits ought to be placed in remote or immediate relation, as contributing to the liberal education, or to the ornamental accomplishments of a professional student'. In other words, the reviewer agreed with the Statement of the Council of the University of London that liberal education was to be valued specifically in proximity to professional instruction rather than as an end in itself.[4]

If a university is a place for the dissemination of universal knowledge, most of the structural features of the professional academic's career do not apply. The teaching relationship has an utterly different thrust, not towards the promulgation of knowledge but towards one of several forms of self-mastery. Newman's version appears in his extraordinary portrait of the liberally educated gentleman who 'knows the weakness of human reason as well as its strength, its province and its limits'.[5] Another form is *Bildung,* where the boundaries of self-development are not determined so much by personal limitations as by the nature of a national culture. It would be a mistake to conclude that tensions never arose between individual self-expression and national ideas of appropriate aesthetic or intellectual concern. They did; but the tensions reinforced the idea of *Bildung* as an on-going process aiming towards a state of perfection.

In Britain liberal education was often a static conception. It required university graduates to have the right 'character',[6] but no consensus emerged as to the exact meaning of character. For some commentators, the vigorous life was evidence of having achieved the necessary end. For others, the correct route was intellectual or aesthetic. Both were assumed equivalent for reaching the same goal. Whether an undergraduate engaged in play or study, an energetic personality, strong-willed and courageous, was desirable. The outcome was particularly well-suited to an imperial power, especially if the empire were a jaggedly constructed affair

---

4 [Anon], *North American Review,* 27 (1828), 67–89, 72.

5 John Henry Newman, *The Idea of a University,* ed. I. T. Ker (Oxford, 1976), 180.

6 See Stefan Collini, *Public Moralists, Political Thought and Intellectual Life in Britain, 1850–1930* (Oxford, 1991); and Sheldon Rothblatt, *The Revolution of the Dons: Cambridge and Society in Victorian England* (London and New York, 1968; reissued Cambridge, 1981).

without firm central steering. Such it was and therefore heavily dependent upon local initiative and self-reliance.

A caveat. The independent personality was not, as we might imagine, necessarily unique, one of a kind, lost in some personal world. John Stuart Mill complained that the English 'character' was actually narrower or more one-sided than in the Humboldtian tradition.[7] Since idiosyncratic personalities were produced in abundance in Victorian Britain, we can understand why conformity to a type was generally believed to be more desirable than wholly self-contained personalities. Too much idiosyncracy led inevitably to alienation or withdrawal, too Bohème or what would later be called the world of the avant-garde. The primary object of a university education therefore was to inculcate the right kind of independence, of a sort that would permit leaders to stand up to public opinion in a period when a democratic electorate was coming into existence. There was an implicit distrust of 'public opinion' in the universities. Hence the conventional talk about the necessity to produce 'manly' and 'masculine' characters, but this was not exactly Newman's own position. His university educated character was self-disciplined certainly, but in some critical respects feminine, his mind finer and more sensitive.[8]

Because Anglo-American conceptions of a university depart from Continental versions in several critical respects, the differences are often stressed in comparisons. Writing thirty years ago, two French authors, Jacques Drèze and Jean Debelle, warned that when English or American academics adopt 'un titre quasi-germanique' (the idea of a university), readers must not for a second assume that the reference is to the existence of a community of researchers and students. The scholar teaches,

> non pour faire avancer la science, mais pour affermir une éducation; cette éducation est libérale, non pas faire sans contrainte, mais parce que l'exercice de l'intelligence, poursivi sans idée de profit, contribue à former une personalité indépendante, maîtresse d'elle-même.[9]

A fortiori, 'Voilà une discordance importante jusque dans l'idée de l'Université.'

To view this *discordance* in a fuller light, another emphasis needs to be put on Newman's definition. We need to shift the accent from *teaching* to *place*. A university is a *place* for the dissemination of universal learning. In the lucky translation of Drèze and Debelle, an English university is above

---

[7] Collini, *Public Moralists*, 101–2.   [8] Newman, *Idea*, 174, 179–81.
[9] Jacques Drèze and Jean Debelle, *Conceptions de l'université* (Paris, 1968), 14.

all 'un milieu d'éducation; milieu plutôt qu'institution, d'éducation plutôt
que de recherche; ce milieu est de préferénce résidential, l'éducation de
préférence "liberale et générale"'.[10]

For a different understanding of the teaching process which in the
English tradition assists students in achieving maturity and self-
understanding, we need now to explore the notion of *milieu* referred to
above. We shall see that Newman was intimately concerned with the
location where liberal education occurred. Because in his writings milieu
seems to be subordinated to the idea of a university, its reality is often
disguised or suppressed. But the right kind of character could only be
shaped under the right kind of spatial conditions. If the 'idea' was the
mind of an institution, what was the body? The answer requires us
to examine a strange but interesting cultural development connected to
changing ways of viewing personal experiences in relation to environment
and setting.

THE DESCENT FROM ON HIGH

Newman was heir to the remarkable concern for *topos* that developed in
the course of the eighteenth century. That development was itself rooted
in concrete historical circumstances, namely, the attachment to family,
house and estate so characteristic of the British aristocracy. These primary
affiliations were reinforced by conspicuous consumption resulting from
the diffusion of wealth and standards of taste. The combination of
political power, money and land made identification with place especially
potent and attractive. Contrast with newer landscaping practices in France
reinforces the point. There the association between land, politics and
economic patriotism was far less certain in the final decades of the old
regime. Gardens symbolised the individual's retreat from organised
institutions into free Rousseauesque space.[11] Because the British territorial
aristocracy managed to gather into its hands extensive local and
central government patronage, it became a magnet for the arts and other
professional services. The scarcity of major cities in the British Isles, unlike
Italy, Germany, the Netherlands or Switzerland, accentuated the
importance of field, hill, valley, stream and woods. The 'improving
landlords' of the eighteenth century, proud of their country seats whether
large or small, used every available commercial, legal or political
opportunity to enhance the beauty and appeal of their properties. The

---

[10] *Ibid.*, 46.
[11] Dora Wiebenson, *The Picturesque Garden in France* (Princeton, 1978), 3.

outcome, from the standpoint of a conception of place, was a succession of experiments with the English garden or 'landskip', recorded in rich and complex detail by innumerable writers, poets and painters obsessed with the transformation of the English countryside occurring in their own lifetimes.

A standard conclusion of the history of English landscape garden design is a convenient starting point for grasping the importance of surroundings in English education. A widespread concern for reshaping terrain is said to have originated in a painterly conception of countryside, a habit of arranging vistas and topographical features in conformity with popular pictures. Any number of European painters were regarded as suitable instructors, but the favourites were seventeenth-century artists like Salvator Rosa, whose wild landscapes were really better suited to a later, more avowedly romantic period, and Nicholas Poussin and Claude Lorraine, particularly the last.

Claude's paintings were highly composed landscapes, generalised rather than particular. Such landscapes could be wholly imaginary studio productions not particularly faithful to any actual location. Their artificiality in this respect was the outcome of a conflict within eighteenth-century elite culture between Nature and Art, or the natural world in its true condition versus the constructions of civilisation, with self-regulation being the supreme form of civilised behaviour. Being 'natural' was a problem for eighteenth-century men and women, who were continually tempted by the freedoms provided by the actor's opportunity to assume innumerable identities.[12] The attractions of theatrical locations were irresistible in an age of popular play-going. Venice with its masked balls and exotic scenery was the favourite visit on the Grand Tour, an excellent foreign spot in which to celebrate the abandonment of a conventional identity. An arcadian painter like Claude, whose landscapes drew the eye to the vast space and area of light far off and above the horizon, with mythological or other improbable scenes crowded into the darker bottom half, pronounced the triumph of Art over Nature, or, as stated by one recent scholar, art 'improved and selected nature'.[13]

Nature, says the same author, kept its distance in Claude's paintings. A parallel strategy was adopted by James Thomson for his poetry. The practice was in fact common. Nature must somehow be managed and not allowed to wander out of an assigned location. Consequently poets speak

---

[12] See *inter alia* Sheldon Rothblatt, *Tradition and Change in English Liberal Education, An Essay in History and Culture* (London, 1976), 102–4, 111–12.

[13] John Barrell, *The Idea of Landscape and the Sense of Place, 1730–1840* (Cambridge, 1972), 11.

of Nature as viewed from a 'commanding height' (a military borrowing).
If Nature keeps her distance, so do we the viewers since a closer engagement will lead to conflict and threaten civilisation, here correctly
interpreted as the poet's control over his emotions and destiny. 'Stretch'd
upon these banks of broom, We command the Landscape round,' is John
Cunningham's statement of position in 'The Landscape'. William Cowper
expresses similar sentiments:

> Now roves the eye;
> and, posted on this speculative height,
> Exhults in its command.[14]

The preoccupation with, but also disengagement from Nature provides
the kind of passive response that easily lends itself to reflective moralising.
The disengaged observer is moved, with classical restraint, to draw lessons
and analogies from the scene surveyed. And the since the scenes studied in
these poetic manifestations of Claude's rules are universalised – not any
special spot but just a spot, or a spot that invites broad reflections – no
promise of a tailor-made experience is on offer.[15]

The basic aspect of this way of viewing, whether it is an actual distant
prospect or the prospect captured in words and paint, was the imposition
of a controlling idea on the scene. The economic counterpart was, as John
Barrell interestingly observes, the land enclosure movement of the second
half of the eighteenth century wherein Nature was imprisoned within
walls, hedges, fences and ditches.[16] Wandering fields, fuzzy perimeters,
alternating strips of independently owned territory were chastened and
regimented.

Such in one sense was the culmination or triumph of what in shorthand
can be denominated a classical habit of viewing landscape and structures
as if they contained an essential lesson or message. In garden iconography
in the first half of the eighteenth century, these same classical sources
were frequently consulted. The Temple of Worthies at Stowe in
Buckinghamshire prominently displayed the political ideas and
sympathies of its Whig owner by associating Whig triumphalism with
sixteen past exemplars of English liberty, which included King Alfred,
Queen Elizabeth, William III and John Locke. Deliberately organised
ruins – collapsing stone archways, broken columns lying asunder – forced
the mind to reflect upon vanished supremacies and the transience of
earthly life, and either its vanity or a reminder that opportunities yet

---

[14] Quoted in Barrell, *ibid.*, 24–5.
[15] *Ibid.*, 35.   [16] *Ibid.*, 32.

remained to redeem a misspent life. Shards of the past were 'follies', sham creations, amusing but hardly replacements for authentic experience. In any event, all such architectural, emblematic and iconographical features familiarly displayed in the landscapes of stately homes were the result of rigorously contrived and guided visual effects, so that the moral importance of what was being noticed could not be lost on viewers instructed in the pertinent codes.

But such effects were only possible if romantic propensities were restrained. What was therefore sought was a fixed point of perceiving that guaranteed universality, permanence and reliability. Sight lines needed to be imprisoned so that landscapes (or paintings) could be properly viewed as exemplifications of single moral values: dignity and nobility, political and religious authority, beauty and scientific order, patriotism and self-sacrifice, courage, chastity, maternity and duty and so on. A landscape or building in motion could not achieve the same end, and eighteenth-century writers could point to the example of the baroque, whose use of deception and conception made the pursuit of clearly-sought moral goals more problematical. Trompe-l'oeil interiors, undulating façades, a promiscuous mix of orders and fenestration made the building not the viewer the controlling partner in a subject-object alignment.

Nevertheless, the stricter classicism of this position began to erode towards the end of the eighteenth century when other ancient traditions of aestheticism were recorded and invoked, especially with respect to architecture. Buildings, as well as landscapes and paintings, represented ideas intended to inspire thoughts that were moral and edifying, but they could also possess genuine human shapes and attributes. Structures or parts of structures were actually alive. Vitruvius's divisions of orders into masculine and feminine were well known, the doric signifying the former, the ionic the latter. French architects of the later eighteenth century were particularly enamoured of the sexuality of structural features. Right angles were male, suggesting firmness and quiet strength. Curved stairways and fountains were female. Cognitive and moral traits were said to be abstract, therefore male. Female ones were ornamental and erotic,[17] and each gendered feature contained further references to Greek myths or the mystery religions. Maidenly columns, to give one example, recalled the fertility myths connected to the stories of Demeter and Persephone, and the ionic may have also paraphrased conceptions such as the immortality of the individual soul. During the Counter-Reformation

---

[17] George L. Hersey, *High Victorian Gothic, a Study in Associationism* (Baltimore and London, 1972), 4–5.

this last possibility was drawn upon to link columns with Biblical sources.[18]

By the beginning of the nineteenth century, therefore, an extra-ordinarily large range of intellectual and emotive possibilities were intertwined with theories of perception and the experiences engendered by visiting places. The Victorian Age could and did draw upon a rich syntax for assigning signficant values to the built environment in order to humanise stone, steel and glass, or the spaces they enclosed, in a variety of interesting ways. These traditions of seeing were probably an important counter-thrust to urban sprawl, railway slums and low-cost, mass-produced housing threatening always to depersonalise the environment or awaken fears of the dangers of city life. Great public or private structures situated in industrial and urban locations would nevertheless be invested with proven certainties and authorities. 'Neoclassicism' was heavily used, especially at the beginning and end of the nineteenth centuries, for its established record of conveying nobility and grandeur. Museums, universities (e.g., University College, London), the London Stock Exchange and late nineteenth-century imperial banks were constructed in neoclassical variations, their revivalist façades and vaulted interiors declaring continuity with the past. But the word 'neoclassical' was also loosely applied to other 'neo' styles; virtually any one them could be made into a carrier of uplifting ideas. The obvious example was the combination of Barrie's pile of endless rooms and corridors and Pugin's perpendicular gothic façades and ornamentations in the Palace of Westminster. Through the symbolism of the gothic style, the Houses of Parliament were made the straight-line outcome of the origins of representative institutions in the middle ages. (Across the broad avenue rose up Westminster Abbey, the authentic perpendicular gothic article itself, signifying the spiritual rather than the political.) The inherent idea was the restraint of arbitrary authority. This was precisely the kind of example that inspired Coleridge's own use of 'idea', suggesting, as he said, the antonyms 'permanence' and 'progress'.

THE GENIUS LOCI

Before moving further into the nineteenth century to capture yet another conception of the meaning of place, and the objects gathered into a place, we need to review one other major feature of the preceding culture of

[18] Joseph Rykwert, 'The Orders: Doric, Ionic, Corinthian, Etruscan Composite' (Public lecture given at Princeton University on 3 December 1969).

seeing. Also inherited from classical antiquity and filtered into England
from Italian traditions was an affectation for populating spaces with a
spirit or demigod. Gardens contained statues identifying spaces with
particular deities whose attributes were somehow manifested in the
surroundings. Poetry utilised the same conceits. Virgil showed Aeneas
being greeted at Rome by Father Tiber. Thomas Gray in his ode on seeing
Eton substituted Father Thames. A Victorian like John Ruskin, looking
back on these conventions, found them empty of meaning and content.
They had, he said, degenerated into 'a witty allegory, or a graceful lie', at
best merely a pretty statue amongst shrubs.[19]

The practice had become greatly formalised. Before Claude, Nature
was not supposed to be kept at a distance, and the viewer was not intended
to be a prisoner of the tableaux and arrangements of a particular setting
but could expect a more direct experience, perhaps not always wholly
agreeable, emanating from the genius inhabiting a place. The controlling
element was always the god in the grove (Minerva with her quiver of
arrows), or the deity causing the waters to fall (Neptune and friends). Still
other presences beckoned from the bottom of walks. Since spaces were
populated with many kinds of presences, many different kinds of personal
experiences were possible within them.

The artificiality of the experience was of course apparent. Yet the fiction
of a god being present lent intrigue and moment to a location. An ordinary
stroll or visit might provide a number of encounters that awakened
curiosity and lent some special quality to an outing. Dedicated space might
be animated and challenging, even, in some odd way, transforming. If the
device of jumping the centuries for a moment will be allowed, we have a
perfect example of how the phenomenon of supervised space was intended
to work in a short tale by E. M. Forster, 'The Story of a Panic', published
in 1904. A group of English travellers pausing in Ravello decide to picnic
in the chestnut woods above the town. Conversation ensues about the
merits of tamed and wild nature, during which a disagreeable painter,
fancying himself an authority on the subject, sententiously remarks that
the violation of nature has left modern culture 'hopelessly steeped in
vulgarity . . . It is through us, and to our shame, that the Nereids have left
the waters and the Oreads the mountains, that the woods no longer give
shelter to Pan.' Some time afterwards he announces that 'The great God
Pan is dead.'

The mountains and valleys grow still, and the travellers fall silent,

---

[19] John Dixon Hunt, *Gardens and the Picturesque, Studies in the History of Landscape Architecture*
(Cambridge, MA and London, 1992), 223.

overcome by feelings of mounting alarm interrupted and then reinforced by the sudden 'excruciating noise' of the home-made whistle of an accompanying, normally sullen boy, the nephew of one of the hikers. The party suddenly bolts but return to the ominous spot when they notice the boy's absence. Turning back, the narrator notices some 'goat's footmarks'. The boy is safe but has undergone a mood change. His behaviour is odd and incomprehensible, for he who hated outings, soon, in a wild moment, salutes, praises and blesses 'the great forces and manifestations of Nature'. The unseen Pan has reclaimed his territory and taken possession of the boy by bestowing upon him the god's gift (or curse) of madness. The story ends with the death of an Italian waiter in unfathomable circumstances. The once-lugubrious boy escapes towards the sea (Nature) with shouts and laughter, liberated from the banalities and pedantries of the Edwardian polite classes, the underlying cause of his initial melancholy.[20]

Now let us notice how at the end of the eighteenth century the two ways of experiencing physical space and their overlapping elements, the one the genius of the place, the other Claudian, combined to produce a new sensibility that played a central part in defining the meaning of a university whose principal object was the dissemination of universal learning.

In the case of the genius of the place, the spirit's powers to electrify were restored. The statue in the garden more or less disappeared, but this lent an even more magical quality to place, for imagination was drawn into the act. Radical romantic painters also attempted to banish human representation from their compositions in the hope that landscape could carry an essential message unaided, or operate upon our senses like music.[21] We can hear and feel even when we cannot always see. The incorporeal god still retained the power to work through our minds. Indeed, unseen, the deity's influence was all the more effective. In landscaping, poetry and painting, the observer began to descend from the commanding heights, to lose rigid control over the composition and to be personally drawn forward into what had once been carefully managed territory. The safety of distance was in the process of being relinquished.

---

[20] E. M. Forster, 'The Story of a Panic', in *New Collected Short Stories* (London, 1985), 18–39. Forster often used references to the great Nature god Pan. He does so in *Howards End* when contrasting city and country. In *The Longest Journey* the protagonist writes a story about Pan. Forster's use of panic phenomena occurs most famously in *A Passage to India* in the episode of the inexplicable experiences of the Marabar caves.

[21] Charles Rosen and Henri Zerner, *Romanticism and Realism, The Mythology of Nineteenth-Century Art* (New York, 1984), 51–2.

Changes in garden design reached a new plateau in the work of Capability Brown who provided more 'natural' adventures in the landscape. The path whose curve was concealed by shrubbery was one important change. What lay beyond the bend? Another was the rougher detail associated with picturesque innovations which provided a less settled viewpoint. Now, as John Dixon Hunt notices, the landscape kept moving, since viewing was possible from a number of different locations. Its varieties and perturbations could be indulged. Humphrey Repton, bringing the newer landscaping forms into a different century, interpreted Alexander Pope's advice to 'consult the genius of the place' by recommending respect for existing terrain. It should not be invaded by the assorted icons and emblems of earlier gardening practices, a 'mouldering castle', for example, 'whose ruined turrets threaten destruction, and revive the horrors of feudal strife'.[22] Yet Repton found it necessary to apologise for interfering with a natural setting by making 'a road where nature never intended the foot of man to tread, much less that he should be conveyed in the vehicles of modern luxury'. Still, not wishing to be utterly captured by the passions certain to be released by a rude landscape, Repton recovered his Georgian balance. '[Where] man resides', he adds didactically, 'Nature must be conquered by Art, and it is only the ostentation of her triumph, and not her victory, that ought never to offend the correct Eye of Taste.'[23]

THE ASSOCIATIONS OF PLACE

One further step was required to merge the picturesque landscape – unpredictable, now free of the tutelage represented by presiding classical statuary – with the conventions derived from the abiding genius of the place. For that we turn to the influential theory of seeing as developed by the epistemologists and literary critics who adopted Locke's psychology of association. Included amongst them were representatives of the Scottish School of Common Sense Philosophy.

The philosophy of perception known as 'associationist psychology' was theoretically antithetical to the notion of places possessing an idea. Coleridge's search for an ideal mission for an institution was occasioned by the same desire to avoid plural meanings. Associations were personal to the beholder, and therefore no objective or universal experience was likely.

---

[22] Hunt, *Gardens and the Picturesque*, 237; John Dixon Hunt and Peter Willis, eds., *The English Landscape Garden 1620–1820* (London, 1975), 361.
[23] Hunt and Willis, *English Landscape Garden*, 361.

Yet associationism proved to have a peculiar affinity with the notion of the genius of a place, principally in support of the tendency to impart to locations a special virtue or quality which could then be transferred to the beholder. Associationism added a major element that has had a permanent influence on the tradition of 'reading' the university campus in Britain and the United States. Spaces not only possessed an in-dwelling spirit, a genius of the place in need of consulting. They were distinctive by virtue of history. They were witnesses to past events. They had been inhabited by great personalities, perhaps only lesser ones, but that hardly mattered. What mattered was that history added length and breadth to a place and filled it with memory, with tradition, with connections and with responsibilities that the sojourner must not ignore. To do so was to violate the integrity of the spot. As in the case of the idea of a university, to fail to heed the sensations and impressions of the place was to betray the heritage incorporated into the space. What was lost was the effect of the transforming power of the hidden but unmistakably vivid influences inhabiting location, and to lose that effect was to jeopardise personality development, heavily dependent upon the educative potentialities of place. At Oxford and Cambridge – or in any setting where the influence of the past can be systematically offered through a selection of appropriate icons and symbols – innumerable opportunities for creating associations existed. The gallery of portraits in the college hall is a particularly good example. The eye moves around the large common space over which dignitaries from the college's history preside from their commanding heights. Each picture recalls a different era, a different set of possible mental and imaginative awakenings, but the collection adds up to the history of the collegiate society, suggesting an institution greater than any one moment or person.

Archibald Alison of the Scottish School of Common Sense was probably the most influential theorist of aesthetics in the associationist pantheon, publishing his *Essays on the Nature and Principles of Taste* in 1790. His writings exercised great influence over Victorian critics and architects. He sometimes maintained that objects had intrinsic values, although unlike the French he made these affective rather than intellectual. Interior spaces, depending upon shape and size, projected emotional qualities like gaiety and gravity. But it was on the subjective side of perception that he centred, and for that effort one needed associations. Why, he asked, did the 'first prospect of Rome' excite so much 'sublime delight'? After all, the Rome of his day was filled with signs of destruction and disorder, the Tiber 'diminished to a paltry stream'. Rome today was 'the triumph of superstition over the wreck of human greatness'. (A conclusion similar to, or drawn from, Edward Gibbon?) Alison answered his own rhetorical questions by explaining that the sight of present-day Rome started the process of associational reflections that led back to a memory of the grandeur of antique Rome. 'All that the labours of . . . youth, or the studies of . . . [a] maturer age have acquired, with regard to the history of this great people, open at once.' And the denouement: without such associations, without a memory of Caesar, Cicero and Virgil and 'how different would be . . . [the] emotion'.[24]

Later authors like Payne Knight added another important element to the history of aesthetic associationism. Buildings did not have to be constructed in a pure style in order to be effective conveyors of associations. Eclectic architecture was equally useful for stirring the emotions and enriching the imagination. A mix of Grecian and gothic (the paintings of Claude), Romans and Goths (temples and battlements standing together) were fine assists to the imagination if they were naturalised to their surroundings. They too led and extended the 'chain of ideas . . . in the pleasantest manner through different ages and successive revolutions in tastes, arts and sciences'.[25] Finally we can count on Ruskin to devise a way for greatly enhancing the emotional, associational possibilities of place. Most Victorian critics and architects still assumed that whatever set of associations a location might contain, the effect in some way should be stylistically beautiful. Ruskin said otherwise. Beauty does not have to be the main aesthetic concern of the artist. Associations have other messages to reveal, and it might be useful to employ a melange of crude details as an opening and guide to these. Consequently spikes, rough-hewn stones or reptilian forms did not have to be overlooked in arranging areas for contemplation.[26] In truth there was virtually no limit to the number of different memories that could be stirred through the medium of associations.

In Ruskin we notice the fullest flowering of a shift in sensibility regarding external and internal space, landscapes and buildings and lesser structures, ornaments and virtually all features of a built-up environment. Whereas disagreement occurred over details such as beauty, or how best to provoke and invoke a desired effect, several critical assumptions were widely shared. Spaces and structures possessed significance. That significance was no longer as likely to be inherent as in the earlier readings of spaces. The subject-viewer was superior to the object, expressive experiences were superior to static messages.

---

[24] Hersey, *High Victorian Gothic*, 11. [25] *Ibid.*, 13. [26] *Ibid.*, 31.

The new aesthetic was less restricted, more adventurous and better able to release a fuller and complicated array of sensations, which then combined in the mind to awaken imagination. The new and developed aesthetic, long in the making as we have seen, and reinforced by a number of distinct but also differently employed traditions of perception, was perfectly suited to the nineteenth-century revolution in education. The number of schools and colleges increased, and these were institutions with widely diverse features and supporters. The expansion of educational markets involved greater participation by families underserved by formal institutions of learning. Students in the universities, of which there were new versions, were taken from a greater mix of social backgrounds, although more to the point, from a greater mix of upbringings. Associationism was the perfect theory for the times. It justified the proximity of old and new types of buildings, of which Britain was full. In any cathedral close a succession of historical styles was evident, as in any collegiate quadrangle. Early nineteenth-century architects like Nash exploited the possibilities of eclecticism in his designs for Park Village West on the edge of Regent's park. Villas and terraces of radically different domestic styles were juxtaposed along a semicircle, but as all of them were painted an identical cream colour, they blended into one effect. Associationism solved a problem arising during the reform movements of the 1830s when subscription to the 39 Articles was attacked in Parliament. A well-placed observer noted that associations were a far more effective means of ensuring an undergraduate's college loyalty than the assorted obsolete and impracticable oaths inherited from the past. He referred to the 'innumerable recollections of social and intellectual pleasures and of affectionate and abiding friendships which rarely fail to attach him to the place of his education'.[27]

Associationism also provided a class of educators with a potent pedagogical rationale for resolving a traditional problem within the history of liberal education, how to carry out the ideal of the whole and wholly rounded person in an era when the curriculum was likely to become more specialised. Associations of the kind mentioned here were not, we must remember, the random or free associations favoured by twentieth-century writers. Associationism, as its philosophical roots so well indicated, was first and foremost a theory of education with a moral referent. There were right and wrong ways of learning, and right and wrong outcomes.

[27] George Peacock, *Observations on the Statutes of Cambridge* (London and Cambridge, 1841), 76–7.

SEEING CORRECTLY

No arrangement of space, its enclosure and furniture, its allegory and symbolism, its style and layout is ever wholly natural. All are contrived in response to ways of seeing, or include a vision or potential realising principle that German organisational theorists call *Leitbild*.[28] All manipulations of topography require observers or wanderers to prepare themselves for the experience if they are to reap its optimal advantages. And to understand the 'fullest genius'[29] of a place, even merely to yield to the omnipresent, awful and sacred presence of the spot, the neophyte must be instructed in the ways of its guardian. This is particularly true if the experience is to be made unforgettable, lasting and transforming.

The willingness to submit to the experience of space represented the victory of Nature over Art, of what is regarded as natural over the artificial. This theme occurs often in the history of aesthetic choice, and neither 'nature' nor 'art' can ever be taken literally. The words must always be taken in the contexts in which they were used. For a romantic generation, 'Nature' was a word for experiences that were presumed to be truthful, free of artifice and theatricality, 'ordinary' and 'familiar'. One notable scholar, concerned with the unresolvable issue of defining 'romantic', has traced its essence to precisely the tension arising from the opposition of the two sets of meaning, which break down into the well-known antagonisms of subject and object, conscious and unconscious states of mind, man and nature.[30] We can be delighted by the victory of Nature over Art because it led in a wholly fortuitous direction with respect to the argument being advanced here. Nature, for William Wordsworth, Percy Bysshe Shelley and other romantic poets, was the educator and legislator of mankind. The new convention was to apostrophise Nature with the popular refrain, 'lead me', 'teach me', 'let me be thine'.[31] Once the viewer had descended from on high, the reading of space had become accessible, democratised, but now it had become subject to a new authority, no less than the educative process itself.[32]

The new apostrophe to Nature can be elaborated by returning to

---

[28] Meinolf Dierkes *et al.*, *Leitbild und Technik* (Berlin, 1992).

[29] Hunt, *Gardens and the Picturesque*, 237.

[30] René Wellek, 'Romanticism Re-examined', in *Romanticism Reconsidered*, ed. Northrop Frye (New York, 1963), 129.

[31] Hunt, *Gardens and the Picturesque*, 238.

[32] James S. Malek, 'The Influence of Empirical Psychology on Aesthetic Discourse: Two Eighteenth-Century Theories of Art', in *Enlightenment Essays*, I (Spring, 1970), 15, makes the point that experiential philosophy opened aesthetic theory to general inquiry, allowing a greater percentage of amateur writers to pronounce on questions of taste.

Newman's discussion of a university education. A university was
primarily a collection of teaching subjects; but if a university was to
become a *place* for teaching, it needed to have another kind of focus as
well, and that would be a 'college'. A college, Newman said, completed the
work of universities by providing them with a wholeness. The college was
the architectural or spatial counterpart of the liberal education theory
of breadth. We can now see why the idea of a university must be
complemented with place if the goal of rounded and integrated personalities was to be obtained.

The first point to recognise in discussing Newman's ideas about spatial
significance is that teaching requires such a setting but intellectual
discovery does not. The teacher leads a public life, 'dispensing his existing
knowledge to all comers', but the researcher requires seclusion and quiet.
'The greatest thinkers have been too intent on their subject to admit of
interruption; they have been men of absent minds and idiosyncratic habits,
and have, more or less, shunned the lecture room and the public school.'[33]
The 'strict idea' of a university Newman noted in the essays collected in
volumes entitled *Historical Sketches* was sufficient to give the university its
being, but, as the idea of a university was an abstraction called knowledge,
another type of institution with a more physical presence was required to
round out 'being' with 'well-being'. That institution was a college which
stands for the principle of 'integrity', which is Aristotle's word for a gift
or addition external to the primary thing itself. Colleges add ballast to a
university,[34] specifically, in the instance of a Roman Catholic university in
Ireland, by being a surrogate for the Church itself.[35] Without ballast or
integrity, a university became 'a set of examiners . . . who are teaching
or questioning a set of youths who do not know them, and do not know
each other . . . three times a week, or three times a year, or once in three
years, in chill lecture-rooms or on a pompous anniversary'. Newman
continued to use metaphors of glacial rigidity to describe the absence of
communication in teaching relationships as he remembered them. 'An
academical system without the personal influence of teachers upon pupils,
is an arctic winter; it will create an ice-bound, petrified, cast-iron
university'.[36] Newman excoriated college fellows for being 'cut off from
the taught as by an insurmountable barrier . . . [A] stiff manner, a pompous
voice, coldness and condescension were the teacher's attributes.'[37] Earlier
Wordsworth had adopted similar metaphors when he used the image

[33] *Idea*, 8.
[34] John Henry Newman, *Historical Sketches*, III (London, 1881), 182–228.
[35] *Ibid.*, 182.   [36] *Ibid.*, 74.   [37] *Ibid.*, 75.

of Isaac Newton's stone statue in the ante-chapel at Trinity College, Cambridge to symbolise eighteenth-century intellectualism at its most frozen and dehumanised, writing in *The Prelude* of 'The marble index of a mind for ever Voyaging through strange seas of Thought, alone.'[38] It hardly mattered how often teacher and taught assembled, or on what occasions, or for what purposes since no connections were made.

In the *Apologia*, Newman spoke about 'states of mind', predispositions towards various categories of emotion that include 'indefinite, vague and withall subtle feelings which quite pierce the soul and make it sick'.[39] States of mind have the rhetorical and logical efficacy of facts and reasons, and they are the silent engines of Newman's thinking in *The Idea of a University* and elsewhere. Drawing an important distinction, Walter Houghton emphasises Newman's art of composition by comparing his autobiography with J. S. Mill's. One is the record of a mind as developed under the influence of an eighteenth-century set of philosophical premises and doctrines, but the other is the story of a person.[40] One employs artifice to manage feelings, which are then intellectualised and distanced from the subject; the other regards mind and feelings as inseparable. No effort at objectification is attempted. Each autobiography is the story of education. The first is a narration of how the subject attempts to overcome a one-sided upbringing. The other is an effort to clarify a lifelong quest for assurance.

Even within the intellectual integuments of the *Idea,* Newman could not suppress the feelings engendered by his collegiate experiences. Quite suddenly in the middle of Discourse VI he burst forth with an explanation of the special power of England to 'subdue the earth ... and domineer over Catholics'. The colleges (and he included public schools with collegiate spaces like Eton and Winchester) possessed:

> a self-perpetuating tradition, or a *genius loci* . . . which haunts the home where it has been born, and which imbues and forms more or less, and one by one, every indvidual who is successfully brought under its shadow.

And the point is driven home in these telling lines: 'Thus it is that, independent of direct instruction on the part of Superiors, there is a sort of self-education in the academic institutions of Protestant England.' Even

---

[38] William Wordsworth, *The Prelude,* Book III, lines 61–3. See also Rothblatt, *Dons,* Chapter 6, on the portrait of the don as an uncaring snob, a favourite undergraduate stereotype of the pre-reform period.

[39] Walter E. Houghton, *The Art of Newman's Apologia* (New Haven, 1945), 28–34, esp. 32.

[40] *Ibid.,* 51–3.

Newman's icy tutors are not immune from the magical effects of the genius of the place, 'for they themselves have been educated in it, and at all times are exposed to the influence of its ethical atmosphere'.[41]

In 1832 Newman saw Cambridge University for the first time and wrote that 'there is a genius loci here, as in my own dear home – and the nearer I came to it the more I felt its power'. Not only the in-dwelling spirit was comprehensible, but through associations Newman's memory was stimulated. He reviewed in his mind the tactile pleasures of historical sites and beautiful scenes, as, after leaving Oxford and never returning, he remembered seeing the spires from his seat on a passing train and suddenly recalled the snapdragons visible through the window of the rooms in Trinity College in which he lived during his freshman year. The image lingered and was incorporated into *Verses on Various Occasions*. The simple flowers grow from the crevices 'Of buttress'd tower or ancient hall'. Prisoners of the stone, they are little valued compared to roses, ivy, dahlias, lordly oaks and fair lilies, all of which can claim one or more emblems, such as 'Pleasure, wealth, birth, knowledge, power'. The poem is subtitled 'A Riddle', and the riddle is solved when we are told just what the snapdragon represents. Its presence reveals the 'Unseen':

> In the crowded public way
> where life's busy arts combine
> To shut out the Hand Divine.

The insignificant flower has qualities beyond our first apprehension. Apparently without scent, its leaves actually exhale the fragrance of a Syrian gale, and Heaven responds with its own breath. The cloister where the crimson snapdragon blossoms, sharing its gloom as 'Brother of the lifeless stone', is made sensual and holy by its presence. All senses are stirred. The bloom brings colour, breath (movement), sweetness, life itself to the otherwise dead cloister. Newman's space is now full – has acquired integrity – as the place where another riddle is solved, that of the purpose and meaning of existence as preparation for Eternity.

> May it be! Then well might I
> In College cloister live and die.[42]

The interpenetration of flower and space are a perfect lesson in the power of associationism as later explicated by Ruskin. The recollection of

---

[41] *Idea*, 130–1.
[42] John Henry Newman, *Verses on Various Occasions* (New York, Bombay and London, 1912), 16–18. The poem was written in 1827.

the flower also demonstrates the working upon Newman's mind of what one critic calls St Paul's Doctrine of Analogy whereby the immediate becomes a reference to the Eternal. (Newman's epitaph was *ex umbris et imaginibus in veritatem* – from shadow and images to truth.)[43] A humble, oblique sighting of a flower starts a process of reconstruction that leads to an unexpected summary of life and death and their meanings. In the *Apologia* Newman wrote that the snapdragons were the 'emblem of my own perpetual residence even unto death in my University'.[44] An identical thought occurred to him when discussing the idea of a college. It possessed the structure and associations that developed states of mind and drew out from them the predispositions that influenced and transformed the participant. 'It is the shrine of our best affections, the bosom of our fondest recollections, a spell upon our afterlife, a stay for world-weary mind and soul, wherever we are cast, til the end comes.'[45]

Newman's sentiments were not his exclusive possession but very much the view of many of his contemporaries coming of age in collegiate settings in the first two or three decades of the nineteenth century. They were amongst a new generation of undergraduates who wanted more from Oxford and Cambridge than the dry and cool environment of unfeeling dons and eighteenth-century rationalism to which Coleridge and Wordsworth reacted. It hardly matters for our purpose at the moment whether the perception of dons as wholly without feelings was accurate. The historical record admits of many exceptions. But that was the perception of the time, reinforced by the tightening of internal discipline and the inauguration of a culture of examinations. Students went on reading parties to Scotland and other locations still unfamiliar to the English, adopted a form of political activism and in general sought out a richer, more imaginative and more complete collegiate experience.[46] Newman himself was the editor of England's first student-initiated and managed publication, *The Undergraduate,* which he and a friend founded in 1819. Characteristically, such publications did not generally last very long, and this was no exception. Newman has the additional distinction of authoring the first of the genre of university novels, the first one to directly connect the protagonist's personal growth to a university experience. University slang and unfamiliar colloquialisms were employed to

---

[43] George B. Tennyson, 'Removing the Veil: Newman as a Literary Artist', in *Critical Essays on John Henry Newman, English Literary Studies,* 55 (1992), ed. Ed Block, 11ff.
[44] *Apologia,* 274.
[45] *Historical Sketches,* 215.   [46] See Chapter 3.

construct a picture of a self-contained (and self-absorbed) learning environment.[47]

The undergraduates of the first third of the nineteenth century preferred to experience the college as a milieu or place. The historian, George Babington Macaulay, who had failed the mathematical honours examination (tripos) at Trinity College in the early 1820s, nevertheless loved his Cambridge college and according to his nephew always remembered the 'plashing' of the off-centre fountain in Trinity Great Court. Moonlight transforming the courts by night was also part of his attachment to Trinity, and moonlight was a recurring theme for a generation of romantics, taught to understand place in the new environmental sensibility as literally moving experiences, no two points offering the same kind of perspective. As an undergraduate Newman wandered about the quadrangles of Oxford at night, peering down from roofs 'into the deep, gas-lit, dark-shadowed' spaces wondering how his attachment could be made permanent, wondering, to be precise, if he would ever be elected to a college fellowship.[48]

It is generally useful to point up the responses of one culture to the phenomena of another by comparison. Alexis de Tocqueville, as sharp-eyed a traveller as history knows (Herodotus being another), visited Oxford one year after Newman's visit to see Cambridge. Instantly he appeared to fall under its physical spell. He saw beauty in the colour of stones, poppies and snapdragons (yes), the rich green of lawn, the picturesque arrangements of structures, the encircling spaces. 'One's first feeling in visiting Oxford is of unforced admiration for the men of old who founded such immense establishments to aid the development of the human spirit.'

So far so good: the ancient spaces and sensuosities work their sorcery. The associations line up in proper reverse order, the mind 'unforced' yet moving correctly in reverse. Any second thoughts? The rationalist, practical mind demands to know the underlying truth of the situation. 'When one examines things closely and gets below the surface of this imposing show, admiration almost vanishes and one sees a host of abuses

---

[47] Alan D. Hill, 'Originality and Realism in Newman's Novels', in *Newman after a Hundred Years*, ed. Ian Ker and Alan D. Hill (Oxford, 1990), 27. Some critics name *Reginald Dalton* by John Gibson Lockhart, Sir Walter Scott's son-in-law and biographer, as the first of the genre. Jane Austen has several of her undergraduates speak in the racy patois of the sporting set in *Northanger Abbey*, but the events are incidental to the overall story, and the characters do not appear in a university setting.

[48] *Autobiographical Writings of John Henry Newman*, ed. Henry Tristram (London and New York, 1956), 50. The passage appears in his novel, *Loss and Gain*.

which are not at first sight obvious.' The bells of Christ Church rang to summon residents before the gates closed, a meaningless announcement in that day and age Tocqueville thought. Latin and Greek studies were narrowly pursued, the natural sciences scarcely represented in the curriculum, rich students were indolent and the luxurious endowments were squandered. The place was show.[49] Possibly the system of socialisation and enculturation that Oxford had developed was suited to England (although it was antiquated), but it was certainly unsuited to post-revolutionary France. A theorist of our own century uses a different word to explain how a sentimental adherence to place manages to resist scientific dissection. He calls the preference 'habit'.[50]

Newman's underlying conceptions of education paralleled the complicated and mixed alterations in ways of noticing space that had been developing in art since his birth in 1801. He shared a number of fundamental assumptions with many of his generation. The first was that spaces had special meaning. The second was that meaning was sometimes inherent in location but more often operated through the medium of associations. Newman's variation on that theme was that the material world was helpful in knowing the eternal world, since the Divine Presence could be apprehended through signs and symbols. A third assumption was that associations in and of themselves were not a sufficient guarantee of the efficacy of a learning experience. All potential participants had in some way to be formally or emotionally ready in advance, and this caution was applied by Newman to teachers as well as students. In associational theory, inanimate objects are alive but only if life is breathed into them. Hence the participant needed to be active in taking advantage of available opportunities. Finally, as indicated in the preceding chapter, Newman believed in authority. He did not accept the extreme view of some romantic artists of the primacy and autonomy of art in defining experiences, especially religious experiences to which it was subordinate. The danger was quite apparent in Victorian aestheticism. Tennyson explored a palace of art, and Matthew Arnold substituted culture for religion as the highest expression of civilised values. However open to sensations Newman appeared to be, and no matter how quick he was to apprehend the genius of a place, he adopted more of a middle way. Some limits had to be put on how far individual experience could go in defining education. Boundaries were needed, much as the walls of a college were

---

[49] Marvin R. O'Connell, *The Oxford Conspirators, a History of the Oxford Movement 1833–1845* (Toronto and London, 1969), 50–1.
[50] Walter Benjamin, *Illuminations* (New York, 1969), 240.

a boundary rather than an absolute denial of freedom. Training and discipline rather than spontaneity in and for itself were his preferences. He was also careful to avoid equating the logic of an argument or the seductions of intellectual systems of reasoning with truth itself. That warning was particularly aimed at Utilitarianism.[51]

THE OPEN AND SHUT CAMPUS

This summary of an intricate cultural development is meant to help explain the powerful appeal of the early Victorian conception of a university as an institution embodying an idea. Unaided, Coleridge's wandering philosophical thoughts could never have strengthened Oxford and Cambridge's hold on elite conceptions of education. They were too abstract. And it is not altogether absurd to suggest that Newman's discourses on the idea of a university did not impress the Irish Roman Catholic bishops (or possibly Scottish educators) as much as it thrilled English supporters of the ancient colleges who understood the context of his remarks. Newman wanted Ireland to have an English collegiate university, and that is not exactly what the Catholic hierarchy had in mind.

We can also appreciate from this summary why it has so often been difficult for new institutions to gain an important foothold in the pantheon of university hierarchies in England and America. Either they lacked a genius of the place, or the surrounding associations were wrong, not without significant references perhaps, but wrong. A statement about the importance of urban settings for educational institutions such as Lord Dahrendorf has recently been able to make about the London School of Economics and Political Science was less convincing when more or less first tried out in the 1820s. Here is his list of LSE neighbours and associations:

> Westminster and Whitehall, Fleet Street and the City, the Law Courts, Theatreland and Bloomsbury, and much else besides. The names stand for institutions for politics and public administration, for the media, the world of finance, the law, for the cultural centres from the South Bank to the British Museum. Nowhere else in the world is there such a concentration of excellence in all major fields of human ingenuity in a handful of square miles.[52]

---

[51] John Barrie, 'Bantock on Newman: A Nineteenth-Century Perspective on Contemporary Educational Theory', *British Journal of Educational Studies*, 34 (February 1986), 66–78.

[52] Ralf Dahrendorf, *LSE, A History of the London School of Economics and Political Science 1895–1995* (Oxford, 1995), 518.

Most of these places and institutions existed when what became
University College, London, was first proposed (the British Museum
opened at more or less the same time; the South Bank awaited our
own time, and Bloomsbury had yet to acquire its literary distinction).
University College, London, was criticised on the basis of a number of
historical criteria. One of them was the absence of any identification with
the Church (and no such identification occurs in Dahrendorf's secular list),
and another was scorn for the belief that an English university could thrive
in a metropolis. The sharing of city space meant that the institution could
not develop its own spatial integrity where a suitable tutelary spirit might
dwell. Its history would become identical with the metropolis, and its
associations would be those developed and belonging to the city and not to
the university. Aware of such criticisms, eager to avoid them and anxious
to establish a religious presence in a London-based university college, the
founders of the rival King's College in the Strand built their institution
to resemble the archtypal college quadrangle entered through a narrow
gatehouse. The length of the college axis was altered because the site was
deep with a narrow frontage. The cloistered environment was more in
keeping with the traditional attempts by collegiate authorities to separate
gown from town, at least a symbol of the desire on the part of King's
College to prevent undergraduates from being on the razzle. Otherwise
the undergraduate was prematurely exposed to the temptations and evils
of the late Georgian/early Victorian city, its turmoil, overcrowding, crime
and vices. In such circumstances the normal process of overseeing and
guiding students to adulthood which was the particular responsibility of
the university was interfered with. How could self-management be
learned in such an environment? The same difficulty haunted the later
university colleges of the redbrick genre, for they too were considered to
be 'civic' institutions where municipal interests and concerns were certain
to overwhelm efforts by university authorities to pursue the proper ends of
a university. An additional drawback was the drab beginnings of some
new institutions. Liverpool University started in a lunatic asylum,
Durham-Newcastle in the attics and cellars of the Coal Chambers.[53] No
genius dwelling there. The 'campus' idea, the fortuitous use of space to
promote identity, was by and large absent in the case of new foundations
in Victorian Britain until the establishment of Birmingham University
after 1900. Birmingham very self-consciously sought out the American
planning model. But not perhaps until the creation of the new universities

---

[53] Sophie Forgan, 'The Architecture of Science and the Idea of a University', *Studies in History
and Philosophy of Science,* 20 (December 1989), 411.

of the post-Second World War era was the Birmingham example systematically emulated and the American university campus adopted as the model for combining different kinds of spatial educational experiences. Also, postwar British campus planning efforts favoured locations that were in or near small towns, particularly towns with historic identities and associations, or, as the Birmingham example of Edgbaston showed, the leafy neighbourhoods chosen by Victorian builders of garden suburbs (and their American counterparts).

But urban settings were probably the correct choices for universities like London that needed an identity closer to their mission. Professional education was at home in cities, since cities were homes for professions, the environment in which service occupations best flourished. Hospitals and law schools were appropriate institutions for the city, but liberal education required its separate space where the sacred groves of academe could be planted and the genius of the place find a suitable resting spot.

The history of institution building in an American context provides good examples for understanding how many obstacles new institutions face wherever the pull of the English idea of a university with a college at its core remains seductive. As an introduction to the subject, we can for a while follow Paul Venable Turner's fascinating analysis of collegiate architecture in the United States, the story of successive generations of academic and political leaders searching for suitable settings in which to educate the future statesmen of a democratic republic.

Americans inherited the English idea of a university through the form of the colonial university college. The first such college, Harvard, derived its spatial architecture from the Cambridge Puritan foundation of the seventeenth century, Emmanuel College, itself influenced by the example of Caius whose main court had only three sides. Its physician founder believed that an open front was necessary for ventilation and health.[54] Emmanuel's builders introduced a slight modification on the traditional college perimeter by replacing the buildings and rooms on the fourth side of the enclosed court with a wall and gate, thus hinting at a more amicable relationship with the street.[55] The American colleges took this modest introduction even further. The quadrangular form was eventually loosened again, buildings becoming solitary units in a grassland park, itself influenced by English landscaping innovations of the eighteenth century.

[54] Robert Willis and John Willis Clark, *The Architectural History of the University of Cambridge and of the Colleges of Cambridge and Eton*, II (New York and Cambridge, 1988), 275–7.
[55] My colleague Robert Brentano makes the point that despite appearance the medieval quadrangle did not necessarily imply the separation of college and town. I suggest that such implications are later and especially Romantic.

Thus was created the suburban collegiate style, the college facing the city or potential city, greeting its presumed ally 'confidently', says Turner,[56] but perhaps only hesitantly, preferring to be sited on the border. An alternative style associated with Yale College in New Haven allowed for a longitudinal building scheme – the Old Brick Row – with fronts parallel to the axis of the city street, but this arrangement never quite acquired the popularity of the open quadrangle (and Yale itself developed into a university with colleges and courts). Neo-historical styles, the 'cottage' or 'domestic' style and the gothic[57] rounded out a phase of collegiate architecture and planning centred around youth in need of moral instruction, in which the structural correspondent to tutorial teaching is a properly managed setting that encourages sentimental attachments to and respect for the genius of the place. The word 'campus' was introduced in the later eighteenth century at Princeton to reflect American use of space, replacing the English word 'yard' more descriptive of subordinated space (e.g., 'churchyard', 'farmyard').[58] Later the open quadrangle or 'E-shaped' plan (as viewed from above), with its separate and increasingly inorganic assemblage of buildings, was justified as an expression of American individualism.[59] In a memorable phrase, the Georgian dilettante Horace Walpole described how the garden, thanks to the invention of the ha-ha, had leaped the former border of the eighteenth-century country house to become the famed English park. The image was that of liberty, a favourite

---

[56] Paul Venable Turner, 'Some Thoughts on History and Campus Planning', *Planning for Higher Education*, 13 (1987–1988), 2.

[57] In an important manifesto on the gothic, the English architect Sir Thomas G. Jackson argued that gothic should not be revived for its own sake. However, its present popularity could elevate architecture to the status of art, thus paving the way for new architectural possibilities. Thomas G. Jackson, *Modern Gothic Architecture* (London, 1873). The gothic was considered 'modern' in the nineteenth century as a reaction to neoclassicism, which had itself once carried a modern message. For some observers, associations with religion and with the earliest periods of university history were the paramount consideration in accepting the gothic style. Hundreds of American colleges were affiliated with, or founded by, religious sects and denominations. But the gothic style was also 'picturesque' in the lexicon of the eighteenth century. It was an 'irregular' not a perfect form like the 'beautiful'. The picturesque thus gained a functional quality absent from the beautiful. Buildings could be arranged flexibly without concern for symmetry or integration of the whole. Just about any jumble could in the course of time be inhabited by a genius of the place.

 Such considerations, as well as the medieval symbolism of gothic, led directly to its adoption by the founders of the University of Chicago. Jean F. Block, *The Uses of Gothic, Planning and Building the Campus of the University of Chicago 1892–1932* (Chicago, 1983), 13.

[58] Paul Venable Turner, *Campus: an American Planning Tradition* (Cambridge, MA, 1984), Chapter 1.

[59] Charles F. Thwing, *A History of Higher Education in America* (New York, 1906), 404. The separate and detached building became a useful strategy for attracting donors anxious to perpetuate their names.

conceit of Whig gentry and aristocracy. Likewise American colleges tore down the walls separating their educational institutions from built-up surroundings and opened their park, the campus, to the wider public in a democratic gesture often attached to the name of Thomas Jefferson. But the university college style long antedated him. In an American context, the open sign of welcome was inevitable; but colleges remained nervous about extending the olive branch, unsure of the kinds of encounters the rapidly changing and unpredictable American population might invite.

The combination of open house and edgy concern is exemplified in the campus planning ideas of one of the greatest of all American landscape architects, Frederick Law Olmsted. His designs and handiwork extend from Central Park in New York City through the midwest and onto the campuses of Stanford University and the University of California at Berkeley. Turner notes his hand everywhere, from small college to land grant university.[60] A New Englander, he knew village life and respected the countryside, finding the big business environment (and the corresponding counter-attack by big labour) of the last part of the nineteenth century a threat to his attachment to 'free air, space and abundant vegetation'.[61] Travelling in Britain in 1850, he came away impressed by the public parks movement. American cities were in need of new medicine. They were full of social failures: criminals, mentally ill, alcoholics, prostitutes and the poor. Elected officials he found corrupt and self-serving, and he believed that one remedy was the creation of educational settings in which a future political elite would receive the instruction essential to the correct exercise of democratic responsibilities.

While interested in all forms of education, Olmsted took special notice of universities as the ultimate source of the values he espoused. He took a bold leap by placing more emphasis on the educational virtues of a planned environment than on the teacher, but the strength of this tradition was well-established before his day. The tradition was reinforced by native sources of idealism, as in the New England Transcendental movement with which Olmsted was acquainted. Ralph Waldo Emerson had expressed Transcendentalist ideas about American education in his address at Harvard in 1837. He defined the 'American scholar' as open to the influences of Nature, history and public life. The first of the trilogy was the most important.[62] Olmsted's opportunity to translate his planning theories

---

[60] Turner, 'Thoughts', 23.

[61] Albert Fein, *Frederick Law Olmsted and the American Environmental Tradition* (New York, 1972), 22.

[62] Joseph L. Blau, *American Philosophic Addresses* (New York, 1946), 155, 153–70.

into bricks, wood, plaster and mortar first occurred in the later 1860s with a number of projects at either end of the United States. In 1866 and 1867 he was involved with designs for the building of a new University of Maine and a new agricultural college at Amherst. Writing about the level of campus planning such institutions required, Olmsted consulted the collegiate manual and grafted traditions of liberal education onto multi-purpose and specialised foundations (in keeping, as a matter of fact, with the letter and spirit of the Congressional land grant university act of Justin Morrill, 1861). He noted that colleges needed to directly influence 'certain tastes, inclinations and habits'. This could be achieved through campus planning. Failure to do so meant that the college fell short of accomplishing 'the sole end had in view in its endowment'.[63]

Architecturally, Olmsted did not employ the Oxbridge style of formal courts and quadrangles. American opinion had long ago inclined to the view that similar spatial features were monastic and out of keeping with American symbols of accessibility and opportunity. (Enclosed perimeters, however, were to return to American campus planning with a vengeance in later periods when the democratic heritage of open access became more problematical.) He referred instead to the picturesque style of small, distinct structures offering continuity with American domestic ideals, 'models of healthy, cheerful, convenient family homes'.[64] For his 1886 design for Gallaudet College in the District of Columbia, Olmsted sketched a sensuous landscape where he again drew upon American images of cosy, intimate and agreeable surroundings, like 'a well-regulated garden the senses of sight and smell are gratified in a most complete and innocent way'. In this setting 'due importance is attached to that influential automatic education which depends certainly upon a habitual daily contemplation of good examples'.[65]

For the sometime governor of California, Leland Stanford, Jr, a multi-millionaire seeking a monument to his fame on the peninsula south of San Francisco, Olmsted had to relax his grip on the small-town conventions of his upbringing that, in opposition to the brash and vulgar transformations of industrialising America, had resulted in campus planning involving collegiate design and values. The site that Stanford provided for a university to bear his name was a vast 7000 acres. The region was mild in climate and semi-arid, and Olmsted was willing to forgo his preference for plant materials typical of the eastern United States by landscaping with the plentiful species of Californian flowers, shrubs and trees which

[63] Fein, *Olmsted*, 37.
[64] *Ibid.*, 38.   [65] *Ibid.*, Figure 23.

presumably could fulfil the requirements for an 'automatic education'.[66] But to his surprise Stanford was conservative in taste and preferred the use of New England trees and grass, although eventually yielding on both points.

Ultimately Olmsted withdrew from the planning of the new university, but before doing so he again modified his own principles by designing a series of low courts,[67] although with more open access points than existed at Oxford and Cambridge. And the whole campus itself was unbordered, so that the cloistered areas, functioning as Mediterranean gardens do to provide intimacy, privacy and shade, were merely one of many features and not the essential inspiration of the plan. But Olmsted's inheritance, and that of his closest associates, was very much in the grand tradition of architectural anthropomorphism. Buildings and landscapes were alive, they displayed and evoked emotional responses, and their carefully arranged structures, grounds and ornaments were as educationally functional as outright attendance at lectures and recitations.

Olmsted's very early plan of 1866 for the College of California on the eastern side of San Francisco Bay, a private New England style liberal arts institution founded by Congregationalists and New School Presbyterians, the great college builders of America, was typical of him. The 'Yale of the West' in the 'New Haven of the Pacific' (then thought of as Oakland and not Berkeley) consisted of curves that followed the fall and flow of the topography and were meant to be partnered with small-scaled structures and plentiful foliage. This plan was never carried out, and the assets of the college were eventually handed over to the new state University of California founded at Berkeley in 1869. (The town was named after the eighteenth-century Irish philosopher and Anglican bishop, George Berkeley, who had once given Yale a significant gift.) There Olmsted's hand can still be seen in the design of a street that partly runs across the top of the Berkeley campus. The quadrant of Piedmont Avenue leads away

---

[66] The preference of great American campus landscapers for indigenous plantings shows up often in the work of Beatrix Farrand, who was particularly influenced by the Anglo-American Arts and Crafts Movement. For midwestern universities she chose crabapples and hawthornes because their horizontal branching habits symbolised the flat terrain of the prairie. She also enjoyed wall plantings, likening them to the carved stone found on gothic structures. Gothic she thought of as the work of anonymous and humble craftsmen. By contrast classical buildings were financed by merchant princes and were more suited to an imperial or urban fabric. On this note, Farrand did not like rose parterres in quadrangles. They were too glaring, noisy. Diana Balmori, 'Campus Work and Public landscapes', in *Beatrix Farrand's American Landscapes, Her Garden and Campuses*, Diana Balmori *et al.* (New York, 1985), 127–33, 173.

[67] Fein, *Olmsted*, 62.

from the university towards a swish residential area to the south. The avenue itself is lined with villas (now fraternities and sororities) in the English garden suburb style, and landscaped areas of trees and grass accompany and divide the thoroughfare. The central campus axis that today lines up with the gap in the Marin headlands is also his.[68]

THE CAMPUS HAS A STORY TO TELL

We can follow the history of the American college as it struggled to maintain a heritage in yet another way, calling upon the superb empirical work of Burton Clark, who studied three famous American liberal arts colleges some two decades ago: Antioch in Ohio, Swarthmore in Pennsylvania and Reed in Oregon.[69] Each of these institutions has a national reputation. Clark explains how that national reputation has been carefully built up and tended, and how the task of maintaining the institution's drawing power is a permanent part of the governing strategy of the institution's leaders.

The first element in the strategy was to create a theme for a college that functioned as its essential identity: academic excellence in the case of Swarthmore, a Quaker foundation to begin with; a community-academic work-study programme in the case of Antioch, appealing to an American model of citizenship and public responsibility, suggesting at the same time that Antioch was not a typical ivory tower institution whose pampered students were permitted to lead lives of self-indulgence; a special set of 'junior qualifying examinations' in the case of Reed (and perhaps implicitly an indentification with the territories of the Pacific Northwest and an appeal to the simple and solid life of the region's nature-loving populations). The college's theme is all pervasive and needs to be incorporated into the active consciousness of all students, faculty and alumni. Any student subculture should be identified with the theme and reinforce it, since rival or plural objectives are an obvious distraction. The students should not, for example, be allowed to develop a rival counter-culture. The faculty should not be members of trade unions, and there should be low turnover only, otherwise the capacity of the institution to build upon and transmit its identity to incoming generations of students is substantially compromised. The pattern to be avoided is that of the

---

[68] *Ibid.*, Figure 4; George Marsden, *The Soul of the American University* (Oxford and New York, 1994), 134–5.

[69] Burton R. Clark, *The Distinctive College* (New Brunswick, NJ and London, 1992), first published 1970.

large state universities where research, academic professionalism and
competitive bidding for talent leave little space for establishing and maintaining tradition. As Clark says in other writings, organisationally the
research university is a 'conglomerate'.[70] While a research university is
woven around a 'college of letters and science', its multiple missions
prevent the emergence of a simple, immediately available identity. State
universities in particular fall into this category. Travelling around the
United States in search of great universities in the first decade of this
century, a reporter contrasted Yale students with those from the
University of Kansas, his own institution. The difference was that Kansas
had only one custom: disregarding the customs previously established.[71]
The weakness of tradition in multi-campus systems is a common
observation (or complaint). Clark Kerr bluntly states that systems have no
heritage.[72]

Other factors that protected the thematic identity of the college were
geographical location and careful cultivation of the theme in the wider
American culture, taking advantage of commercial methods for attracting
public attention to the college's existence. A further and crucial step was to
rapidly extend the institution's antiquity, to give it an instant and usable
past into which could be poured the associations that history provided in
vast abundance. The inventing of traditions being important, a college
needed to have or acquire a story to tell, a 'saga'. The saga – Clark also uses
the happy word 'epic' – cannot, however, be a narrative of unbounded
success. In an American, but not British, context this would be fatal, for
the institution lives by the annual donations of its alumni and the fees of
its students, unless it is also fortunate enough to have a substantial
endowment. Therefore the epic story was exactly that: an account of the
adventures of the college as hero, the wanderings, trials and temptations,
the retelling of those occasions when the college, beset by monsters or
sirens, nearly yielded its identity by taking the easy way out – giving up its
academic excellence, its special community oriented programmes, its
unique system of student evaluation because market conditions appeared
to warrant a change. An epic must have a hero whose life was and never

[70] As explained in Burton R. Clark, 'The Problem of Complexity in Modern Higher
Education', in *The European and American University since 1800, Historical and Sociological
Essays*, ed. Sheldon Rothblatt and Björn Wittrock (Cambridge, 1973), 263–74.
[71] Helen Lefkowitz Horowitz, *Campus Life, Undergraduate Cultures from the End of the
Eighteenth Century to the Present* (New York, 1987), 67. She also notes on page 205 that cliques
and subgroups in the form of fraternal organisations are more important to students than
campuswide customs.
[72] Clark Kerr, *Higher Education Cannot Escape History: Issues for the Twenty-first Century*
(Albany, NY, 1994), 48.

ceased to be a series of ordeals, challenges, temptations and impending seductions. Life and death, glory and humiliation hang in the balance. An epic must also have a *deus ex machina*. These are the donors, parents, supporters and loyal alumni whose patient hard work and willingness to respond to crisis saved the college from adversity. The American liberal arts college – but the same is true for many other kinds of market-dependent institutions (and all of them are to some degree) – constructs a gallery of epic heroes. Their names are commemorated on buildings, benches, doors, walls. They are the history of the college, reminders of the struggles through which the college passed in order to achieve its distinct place in higher education. They are also examples for future emulation.

The college will also create lore and fiction or fictionalised accounts of college celebrities, the stereotypes that will amuse future generations and rouse them to sentimental recollections. These can be crusty but tenacious members of the board of trustees, eccentric but utterly devoted former presidents and deans, or unworldly professors whose mismatched shirts and ties, charming inefficiencies and indifference to the dross of everyday life were evidence of their love for higher values. Students could also be part of the college's saga, especially those who distinguished themselves in some unforgettable fashion, ordinarily positive, but pranks do come into the process of legend manufacture.

Colleges and universities also may have peculiar traditions that serve to strengthen affiliations and enhance self-identity. How this occurs is well exemplified by student activities at Carleton College (founded in 1867) in Minnesota. The undergraduates play baseball while drinking beer, and in this enterprise they are sometimes joined by college faculty and administrators. The rationale behind the game, named after an inept professional pitcher for a Chicago team who was jeered into unsought notoriety almost before his career began, underscores the college's distinction as a place for serious students not jocks. Expectations are low. Tipsy students are not expected to hit, catch or run with much panache. The same joke was once carried out through the invention of 'metric football' in the 1970s when eliminating the inherited English system of weights and measures was of some national interest. The playing field was laid out in metres not yards, and cheerleaders became 'cheerliters'. Carleton's students were saying perversely that they too, like their counterparts in the commercial-minded athletics programmes of giant midwestern universities, understood the importance of a sound body. But as after all they were still Carleton students, they added mathematics, a sound mind, to games.

A third Carleton reminder of the college's self-conscious intellectual ideals involves the comic use of a plaster bust of the German poet and philosopher J. C. F. Schiller. The bust, mysteriously filched from the classics department, turns up when least expected. Once it was sighted dangling from a helicopter and at another time sentries claimed to have spotted it on the back of a pickup truck. On another occasion Schiller's unannounced appearance occurred in the middle of a commencement ceremony when the apparition raced through the audience, disrupting ceremonies while pleasing onlookers, who were reminded of the college's academic mascot in yet another way. Some institutions may have bears, cougars, wolverines and lions as mascots. Carleton has a world-famous *Gelehrter* whose genius periodically returns to repossess the spaces rightfully his.

Thus Carleton students, in a number of carefully staged episodes passed on from one generation to another, remind themselves of the essential goals of the college, its easy intellectuality, wit and invention, and its distinct place within a gallery of famous American liberal arts colleges. They have the full approval of college authorities and alumni, whose own feelings of attachment are stimulated by events familiar to them and associated with their own experiences.[73]

A saga without challenges does not hold the attention of the faithful alumni on the point of drowsing in the shade of leafy elms at annual commencement ceremonies. Success means they are not needed. Therefore the epic is a dramatic tale, even if, like the genre upon which it is modelled, familiar and repetitive. Martin Trow has several times noted that American higher education institutions always behave – and always must behave – as if they were on the point of financial collapse no matter how solid their resources.[74] The guard must never be let down. But the struggle for survival is often real enough to lend credibility to an appeal for support. In the early 1990s the trustees of Mills College, a long-established private college for women on a wooded site in Oakland, California, voted to admit men students on the grounds that women were not attending in sufficient numbers to make the historic single-sex admissions policy viable. The women protested, and parents took a pledge to raise whatever additional capital might be required. The trustees then reversed themselves.

In these ways colleges (and other institutions) make themselves 'distinctive'. Collegiate spaces are personalised and given names: the Oval at Michigan State, the Heart at Earlham, the Yard at Harvard, the Pasture

---

[73] I am greatly indebted to a graduate of Carleton College, Robert Rothblatt, for a typically insightful and stylish account of his alma mater's special ethos.
[74] In conversation with me as well as in essays.

at the University of Wyoming, the Horseshoe at the University of South Carolina, the Lawn at the University of Virginia, the Meadow at Mills College, Faculty Glade at Berkeley.[75] Colleges and universities fill their groves and history with associations unique to the institution and find different ways of awakening the elusive genius who inhabits the place. An environment is fashioned in which undergraduates expect to find an experience absolutely *sui generis*, an experience that they expect will ultimately transform them, so that they are not the same person coming out as going in. An historian recalled her own undergraduate years at the famous women's college Wellesley in these words: 'I never got over the sense that when I entered Wellesley [1959] I stepped on special ground.'[76] A novelist wrote of Radcliffe College in 1981 (when Harvard still had a separate women's college) that she went there 'to have my life changed'. She claimed that it indeed happened.[77] This has been the habitual American response to 'college'.

It is also the central point, the purpose of the *genius loci*. The particular experience of the location is anticipated, since the college has marketed its ethos in order to strengthen recruitment. And the more ambitious the college, the more it aspires to a national or regional reputation over a local one, the more the drama of the epic and the unique qualities of the institution need to be elaborated. The making of ivy, according to one source, was precisely of this nature. The whole notion of 'Ivy League' was systematically created in the early decades of the twentieth century when competition from state and other newer institutions became keen.[78]

The Oxford and Cambridge college, by virtue of its different history and privileges, does not depend so greatly upon the notion of an epic struggle. In the first place it is not detached since it is organic to a supporting university whose general glory it can share. The English college derives its prestige through association with elite or aristocratic culture, a clerical establishment and a system of distinguished feeder schools, public and grammar schools (the last now largely replaced by comprehensives). These were support networks long in place with their own associations and demiurges. The American college achieves its

---

[75] Thomas A. Gaines, *The Campus as a Work of Art* (New York, 1991), 2. The practice is also English: the Meadow at Christ Church, the Great Court at Trinity College, Cambridge, etc.

[76] Helen Lefkowitz Horowitz, *Alma Mater, Design and Experience in the Women's Colleges from their Nineteenth-Century Beginnings to the 1930s* (New York, 1984), xv.

[77] John R. Thelin and James Yankovich, '"Bricks and Mortar", Architects and the Study of Higher Education', in *Higher Education: Handbook of Theory and Research*, 3 (1987), 57.

[78] John R. Thelin, *The Cultivation of Ivy: a Saga of the College in America* (Cambridge, MA, 1976). The term was borrowed from a Chicago sports writer.

reputation through typically American methods of actively creating
support networks and by personalising the history of the institution to
make it into a legend of upward achievement. All such efforts combine
to provide the institution with a certain prominence and current relevance
and build a college mystique, or what Clark calls a cult-like attachment to
the institution.

WISSENSCHAFTLICHE METHODEN

The appeal of the collegiate style had many sources, as we have noticed,
ideational, functional and social,[79] and over time changing theories of
perception provided expressive and emotional understandings of the ties
between individuals and surroundings.

Yet continual challenges to that understanding arose. We have noted
the city ideal, and that will shortly be discussed again, but for the moment
it is essential to explain how the German conception of a university based
on knowledge rather than on the edification of the young presented
formidable obstacles to the maintenance of collegiate forms of spatial
employment. The growth of laboratory sciences provides a good
illustration.

The physical sciences had no or little space within the traditional
university or university college with its belle-lettrist inheritance. Science
space was customarily outside the boundaried space (if in some cases
adjacent), in museums, observatories, botanical gardens, lighthouses,
anatomy theatres and academies. Within a university, science would
naturally require space suitable for its own disciplinary development. The
laboratory experiment, the demonstration table, special considerations of
ventilation and room for equipment, cabinets, display cases and in some
instances special fenestration and height requirements could not be
accommodated within existing collegiate structures. At Oxford and
Cambridge early nineteenth-century laboratories were often personal, as
libraries could be personal, attached to private homes or located in
subterranean areas within colleges. Needless to say, moonlight did not
penetrate to these regions. New universities in England could of course
plan for science necessities, and Sophie Forgan has noted that the building
plans of the new provincial universities allocated proportionately more
space for science than for other subjects.[80]

[79] See also Sheldon Rothblatt, 'The Limbs of Osiris: Liberal Education in the English-Speaking World', in Rothblatt and Wittrock (Cambridge, 1973), 19–73.
[80] Forgan, 'Architecture of Science', 411.

Many science structures were built as quadrangles, or at least resembled the court of the 'Old Schools' at Oxford's Bodleian Library. These were useful for certain types of experiments only possible out of doors. Style in itself was less important in that either gothic or neoclassical forms were satisfactory. The point was that these, as well as other 'neo' designs, contained the necessary range of familiar associations that bestowed legitimacy on new science buildings. The famous Science Museum at Oxford, influenced by John Ruskin's ideas, incorporated classificatory schemes in the very arrangement of the parts of the building. In general, many of the associational devices used in colleges could be re-employed in science buildings. For the portraits in hall, there were the portraits of illustrious scientists or donors, or iconography and sculpture – busts, for example, of great scientists. The symbolic use of time, especially the American practice of creating a mythos of struggle, was also employed in England. Science was a struggle against superstition and ignorance, against the irrational and atavistic forces of the past continually threatening to undo moral and material progress. Sophie Forgan makes the special point that the new civics, being essentially non-residential, could not really duplicate the communal features of collegiate life, but some kind of compensation was found in a repeated emphasis on 'discipline', meaning both the discipline of the subject itself and the discipline symbolised by the physical arrangement of scientific space: the demonstration tables carefully laid out in parallel lines (a practice borrowed from German laboratories), and the precautions necessary in a location where overturning chemicals or turning on gas jets had far greater consequences than dropping books.[81]

Countries accepting Humboldtian conceptions of a university were not so *rétardataire*. They developed completely different ways of handling the problem of knowledge in space because they started with different conceptions of the place of students in higher education. Sven Widmalm has examined the architecture of Knut Ångström's physics institute constructed at Uppsala University in the years 1906–8. The growth of Swedish research science had produced a schism between the teaching of undergraduates and research. The two activities were considered distinct (as in today's French university system), and it was the intention of Uppsala at that time to insulate advanced from routine learning. One architectural expression of the dichotomy was a series of working and office spaces separated by floors. The laboratories of undergraduates and researchers shared a bottom floor, however, since classical physics's

---

[81] *Ibid.*, 423.

experimental rooms required stable footings to protect measurements from vibrations, but the laboratories were quite distinct. Passage from one to the other was only indirectly possible from an adjacent corridor. The whole of the building was considered to be a self-operating machine. Critics who were not in sympathy with this solution of how to design space for scientific activity found Continental innovations such as Uppsala too isolating and from their perspective actually detrimental to discovery.[82]

In the United States, the necessary adaptations proved easier in some instances, less so in others. Land was plentiful, and the solitary building in a landscape had long ago been accepted as a legitimate planning element. Indeed, the English country house, once described as a building grazing by itself like a solitary cow in a bucolic setting, was a fixture of eighteenth-century domestic architecture. All the other features of a college could be appropriated, as in the British case, preserving the trinity of place, time and youth.

Science, therefore, while it had to force its way into the American university curriculum – as did newer subjects generally – did not have to compete for space in quite the same way as in collegiate structures such as Oxford and Cambridge. True, science – and all university subjects were becoming science – could no longer so easily maintain its status as part of the liberal arts, nor, indeed, could virtually any subject lay simple claim to that heritage. But at least the American campus solved the problem of location.

Nevertheless, in another respect collegiate planning traditions as they had evolved in an American context still faced several crises.

MASS EDUCATION AND CITIES

Mass education, for which the open American campus appeared to have been created, still does not in principle sit easily with the values and institutional arrangements, the ethos, vocabulary and syntax of the collegiate legacy. Mass education does not imply intimacy or special experiences. Even when it boasts of a curricular cornucopia with something for everyone, it does so in a manner intended to preempt the accusation of 'exclusive'. There are choices rather than experiences, course offerings but not snapdragons growing against the opposite wall. The range of imagery changes. The symbols are often those of a Roman circus.

---

[82] Sven Widmalm, 'Vetenskapens korridorer: Experimentalfysikens institutionalisering i Uppsala 1858–1910', *Lychnos* (1993). I am grateful to Widmalm for bringing his work to my attention.

Mass education demands less ambivalence. It allows for but does not insist upon the personal experiences to be derived from an encounter with spaces that teach. Mass education also implies city-like campuses with monumental, or at least huge structures, large lecture halls, boulevards, plazas, symbolic towers and other such competing landmarks. Since the arrival of mass education in the United States virtually coincided with the mass production of the automobile, acres of parking and access roads were also necessary, not to mention additional space for recreational grounds and buildings. So the city issue was also a college issue, putting collegiate ideals in jeopardy.

American colleges stood in a problematical relationship to city culture even where no city existed. Educators, drawing on a long literary tradition of opposing rustic virtue (the Roman Cincinnatus, the American Jefferson) to the corruption of cities, had embraced the English college ideal of distancing undergraduates from urban locations. The Yale architectural example had not been typical except in suggesting the possibility of external alliances while maintaining the profile of a solitary sentinel. Yet in 1828 even the Yale faculty, in their famous report answering criticisms that the institution needed to be 'new-modelled' in order to accommodate the 'business character of the nation', argued the traditional case of *in loco parentis* in return. Young undergraduates, being in need of 'parental superintendence', required the familar substitute guardianship that was the function of colleges with Yale's educational inheritance. This in turn implied separating undergraduates from alien influences.[83]

The Yale Report (as it has been called) also mentioned the 'unexampled multiplication' of educational institutions of many different types, patterns and standards, and what was discernible in the late 1820s was already typical after the end of the Civil War. Just as American colleges, universities, academies and technical institutes had awaited the coming of the city, so now they awaited the enrolment increases that no one doubted would be a major aspect of American further and higher education. The structures and internal differentiation were in place to receive the massive student populations that came in the twentieth century.

The movement to urbanise the American campus began at approximately the same time as the public university expanded, shortly after the conclusion of the Civil War and during a period of industrialisation. The City Beautiful and Beaux Arts campus planning strategies occurred

---

[83] Excerpted in 'Original Papers in Relation to a Course of Liberal Education', *The American Journal of Science and Arts*, 15 (January 1829), 300, 303, 306, 309.

towards the end of the century, challenging inherited notions of land use. Berkeley's first encounter with urban ideas had nevertheless led to a campus plan that reproduced the main topographical features of the New England college. Various other plans followed in the picturesque style, but in the mid-1890s a break occurred. Stimulated in part by rivalries with Stanford University, an international competition to design the campus resulted in the selection of a French architect, Emile Bénard. The choice of a Beaux Arts plan was predetermined. The great urban influence of the style in the United States, as well as the fact that so many notable American architects were trained in Paris, meant there was virtually no competition. The grandeur of the French style, its monumentality and rational sense of order, were suited to planners who favoured a bold, attention-getting layout. The prospectus announcing the competition could scarcely have been plainer:

> [T]he advantages of the site, whose bold slope will enable the entire mass of buildings to be taken in at a single *coup d'oeil*, will permit the production of an effect unique in the world, and . . . the architect who can seize the opportunity it offers, will immortalize himself.[84]

Not a New Haven but yet another Athens was to arise in a remote corner of the world, saluting Edinburgh in one direction and Hellas in another.

Bénard designed a monumental campus in the Beaux Arts manner, urban in scale, feel and meaning. Boulevards, orthogonal streets, obelisks, neoclassical temples, squares, flagpoles cascaded down the Berkeley hills towards the bay; vistas towards San Francisco Bay enhance the sense of distance and grandeur so well developed in the Cartesian patterns of the great French landscapers of the seventeenth century. Sycamores, the American cousin of the plane tree of European cities, marched alongside the broad avenues or adorned formal terraces, their branches hard pruned in the French pollarded style. The campus pointed well beyond itself. Nothing could be further from the sentimental, inward-looking plan of the collegiate format, whether in its boundaried English character or greatly modified American colonial version. It has been said that the glass and steel high-rise building offers few ledges for pigeons to rest – the revenge of the city on one of its most tenacious invaders. It can therefore be said that Bénard's designs provided no sequestered grove, quiet pool of water or solitary enclave for a tutelary genius. The campus belonged to a city as yet to be born. The campus was therefore the North American

---

[84] Loren W. Partridge, *John Galen Howard and the Berkeley Campus: Beaux-Arts Architecture in the 'Athens of the West'* (Berkeley, CA, 1978), 11.

turn-of-the-century French city incarnate, a Washington DC on the other side of the continent.

Bénard never saw the Berkeley site. He worked from photographs and topographical maps. There were inevitable disagreements, and he abandoned the project, although a successor, John Galen Howard, who had unsuccessfully entered the competition, was brought in to carry out the French vision. Parts of it were indeed built. The central axis of the campus provides the view of the Golden Gate foreseen in the original design. A great Venetian belltower stands at the centre of the campus, and Beaux Arts buildings in materials more appropriate to earthquake territory do march along an avenue of sorts, and the avenue is indeed lined with regimented sycamores.

But once again the picturesque style intruded, and French styles of urban design encountered the persistent demand of the Anglo-American idea of a college wanting to be heard. Not far from the centrepiece of Beaux Arts styling, a curving path leads over a stream into a glade where a curious eclectic structure stands, an amalgam of various low-rise European domestic styles in plaster and wood, introduced by trellises covered in vines. More recent neighbours are undistinguished in style but their low elevations obey the rules of the place. The glade is partitioned from the central campus by water, rhododendrons, redwoods, native oaks and California bays, and most subsequent landscaping on the campus favours a curvilinear and not a rectilinear pattern.

New buildings have gone up at Berkeley as elsewhere in every conceivable post-Second World War style, a number of them regrettable by nearly universal consent, others more controversial; but the collegiate style continually asserts itself in one form or another, even in the newest outsize residence halls and schools of business that feature cloisters, arches and the elements of surprise offered by a sloping terrain and more than one hint of 'domestic' architecture. Every now and then, in early morning or quiet dusk, a guardian spirit can nearly be glimpsed.

The International Movement of the twentieth century did not respect traditions. Unsentimental and forthright in its vision of a high-speed, streamlined functionalist society, its adherents reduced the university college to little more than an urban village in an urban conurbation, just another garden suburb (perhaps) for middle and upper income commuters. After 1946 planners were eager to introduce educational shopping streets or malls, the skyscraper, buildings separated from one another not only by style – this had happened largely as a consequence of time – but also by function. The trend towards partitioning buildings from one another was not just a practical consideration (colonial builders found that they could reduce the damage by fire to wooden buildings by separating them) but a deliberate planning feature to make a given amount of space as usable as possible without having to consider classical architectural elements such as balance and symmetry. Ornament was eschewed as fussy, dishonest and needlessly expensive. Budget-conscious trustees or oversight civil servants vetoed such superfluous details wherever specified by architects.[85] Departments – the characteristic division of the modern university – were not colleges, and most departments did not have much 'hanging around' space for students and teachers, a prime feature of colleges. The professors have offices not rooms. Student unions and similar dedicated spaces are generally tangential to the academic experience of undergraduates, separated from the areas where formal and informal teaching take place.

Yet in a curious way the crisis of mass education gave new life to traditional conceptions of collegiate space, and the urban campus did not overwhelm inherited views of the idea of a college. The approach of science and the spread of scientific method to all disciplines actually strengthened the value accorded to traditions of location. A differentiation of functions took place corresponding to the differences between knowing and living. If the curriculum could not cooperate as fully in carrying out the responsibilities connected to liberal education as once expected, the environment would accept a greater share of the task. The knowledge-centred university put the meaning of milieu into proper perspective. It was understood that curriculum might not be the only means of endowing undergraduate careers with a wider set of references. Turner remarks how often the collegiate programme returned to claim its rightful place within the history of university building.[86] Associations have also remained as a means of providing meaning. It is in any case impossible to keep the mind from making leaps and connections, only they can no longer be systematically directed towards a set of prepared meanings. Private institutions may attempt to keep their histories, even as they also diversify their academic programmes of study in emulation of the large research universities and professional schools which their leading graduates will attend, but the possibility of arranging historical associations for public campuses is problematical. The remarkable number of bureaucratic agencies and offices, the mix of state and federal legislation regarding physical access for the handicapped, safety environmental impact reports and policies regarding the hiring of minority workers and contracts, seriously deter those architects still influenced by collegiate

---

[85] Thelin and Yankovich, '"Bricks and Mortar"', 74–5.   [86] Turner, 'Thoughts', 16.

traditions of building. The regulations do not originate with civil servants. They themselves are responding to legislation, which in turn results from public pressure and lobbying interests, although they do retain a certain latitude in the interpretation of rules and guidelines. The high mobility of the faculty and student transfer do not easily permit the maintenance of a theme or lend themselves to deuteronomic tellings of the institution's glorious but imperilled history. The new hero is Demos or Urbanus, and the extreme expressions of the disappearing campus are the symbols and architecture of the airport hub, a transit point essential for taking off in different directions. The stay is short, at least the traveller hopes so.

The third element of the Anglo-American conception of a college after place and time is that it exists for youth. This conception has also suffered at the hands of history. The changing distribution of the age of student populations has produced a situation in which the definition of 'young' is highly problematical, since freshmen mingle with 'mature' students and postgraduates. The model of the student is sometimes assumed to be the unattached city dweller. The student is regarded as autonomous and self-reliant, free to decide where to live and what to study, and free as well – it is in fact a duty – to challenge all vestiges of parietal rules and paternal protections inherent in collegiate education. But then it must also be admitted that the Anglo-American concern for the moral superin-tendence of youth is unique among western countries. *In loco parentis* has never played an important part in Continental universities beyond the German practice of grouping the *Ordinarius* together with his students and assistants in the seminar room or laboratory. The French style of university has been anti-campus altogether; and when, following the Second World War, the first wave of French campus planning occurred around Paris, the American model was so unfamiliar that it was mis-applied to French students accustomed to the free life of Left Bank cafés and bookstalls.[87]

British campus planning of the 1950s and 1960s was not so handicapped by problems arising from mass education. The wave of campus building and expansion occurring in the 1950s and 1960s in Britain made use of planning traditions closer in most respects to the collegiate or suburban inheritance than the urban constructions of the Victorian university. The Lionel Robbins era of expansion of higher education was concentrated on the building or upgrading of smallish campuses of about 5000 students,

---

[87] I am indebted to Nicole Fardet Carrié for her analysis of French campus planning as examined in her *thèse de doctorat* of the University of Paris VIII, 'Les universités américaines: de la genèse à la planification des campus' (11 May 1995).

'greenfields' universities generally sited adjacent to small towns or above them, and a number even chose to create college-like arrangements for teaching.

The fury with which some critics assail the persistent attachment to collegiate styles in British life is one indication of their tenacity. One author writing in 1972 complained that university architecture was based on an historical, backward-looking 'bourgeois' model which should be replaced by straightforward rectangular designs, uniform and 'monotonous'.[88] The reference to 'bourgeois' reveals the ideological source of the author's attack, but he is also representative of certain aspects of a modernist critique. As the defining characteristic of the modern world is flux, all structures ought to be temporary and flexible. Universities should abandon their long-standing commitment to history, continuity and permanence, as embodied in monumental and 'noble' architecture bespeaking the solidity of the ages and the strength of the past. Present-day students need to be accepted for what they are: 'free-ranging, mobile, metropolitan'. The required example is London University.

The author's recipe for today ends as follows. We must, he says, come to terms with an 'irrepressible romanticism'. The consequences for failing to do so are an irrational habit of thought inhibiting a 'materialist, utilitarian society' from 'consciously engaging in an international competitive struggle for survival'.[89]

This is not a pretty picture of contemporary civilisations, but similar sentiments were expressed at the turn of the century during the birth of what Nicole Carrié defines as the modern planning movement in America. While not a planner, that great academic *enfant terrible* and hammer of universities, Thorsten Veblen, scornfully attacked conventional architectural designs in an article appearing in 1918, 'Academic Prestige and the Material Equipment'. Donors, he maintained, only cared about celebrating their own success in 'curious façades and perplexing feats of architecture' and 'the architectural mannerisms in present vogue'. He named these as a 'fictitious winding stair' for a fake medieval keep 'surmounted with embrasured battlements and a . . . loopholed turret'. On the ground, space was wasted in 'heavy-ceilinged, ill-lighted lobbies, which might once have served as a mustering place for a body of unruly men-at-arms but which mean nothing more to the point today'. Warming to his argument, his colour rising, Veblen continued his parody of neo-historicism:

---

[88] Ian Brown, 'The Irrelevance of University Architecture', in *The Shape of Higher Education*, ed. Tyrell Burgess (London, 1972), 183–6, esp. 185.
[89] *Ibid.*

Out of the past comes the conventional preconception that these scholastic edifices should show something of the revered traits of ecclesiastical and monastic real estate; while out of the present comes an ingrained predilection for the more sprightly and exuberant effects of decoration and magnificence to which the modern concert hall, the more expensive cafés and clubrooms and the Pullman coaches have given a degree of authentication.[90]

In sum, fidelity to the academic enterprise was the mainspring of architectural design, and anything else was personal vanity and irresponsibility. In Europe the Viennese architect Alfred Loos was also burying the historical grammar governing the arrangement of architectural diction but with some understanding of how the spirit of location was supposed to function. In so far as buildings and spatial qualities stimulate the beholder to produce desirable character traits, the wrong environment produces false traits. Historical allusions, he observed, 'inculcate in the student a spirit of disingenuousness'.[91]

Veblen maintained that benefactors should be principally concerned about the real conditions of learning, which required equipping laboratories and stocking libraries. One consequence of what he denounced as wasteful expenditure on poor quality decoration and stage effects were buildings deficient in the simple technical requirements for study and instruction. Interiors were inadequately illuminated or acoustically unsatisfactory.

The ostentation and vanity of new money were not the only sources of critical anger. Progressive Era critics, journalists and reformers were the first generation of Americans to embrace a cult of efficiency and to proclaim the rule of the expert, the scientist or engineer trained in relevant methods of analysis. Planning was on their list as a means to reordering the institutions and fabric of American society. They not only disliked the meddling amateurish millionaires bent on acquiring European culture and presuming through their manipulation of markets to make judgements about serious aesthetic and organisational matters. They were also

---

[90] Quoted in Joseph Bilello, 'Deciding to Build: University Organization and the Design of Academic Buildings' (unpublished Ph.D dissertation, University of Maryland, 1993), 40–3. I want to thank Dr Bilello for kindly sending me his dissertation to read. The dislike of the irregular appears from time to time as part of the on-going modernist critique of neo-historicism. Writing in 1991, Thomas Gaines calls the average American university 'an architectural mess' and declares omnipotently that 'We . . . like well proportioned areas bounded with grace and consistent style.' The criticism of gothic is also an implicit denial of the authority of associations. Thomas Gaines, *The Campus as a Work of Art* (New York, 1991), x, 2.

[91] Bilello, 'Deciding to Build', 42.

suspicious of spontaneity, romance and the symbols of romance available in so much abundance. From their point of view, the availability of such sensuosities interfered with their custodial responsibilities, which required such public policies as zoning, the regulation of land use and a large number of regulatory and review agencies.[92]

We need to acknowledge the justice of many of the criticisms. Old buildings and styles are not always suited to the technical changes occurring in time. New building materials and new modes of communication require alterations in the layout of structures and grounds. The grand façade, visible and commemorative, does attract donors and contributors, while the more private face of the classroom is less appealing.

There is an undeniable tendency for any accepted artistic genre to deteriorate into copybook imitation devoid of invention, a slavish hearkening back to familiar associations and comfortable allegories no longer easily read by the changing generations. Tocqueville said this, but so did many Victorian critics when examining their own inheritances and wondering how to marry permanence and progress. From a severely critical perspective, traditions of neo-historical construction have not always been successful. A review of unbuilt as well as completed designs for Oxford University in the last two centuries finds plentiful examples of architectural mismanagement and sheer incompetence.[93] But that is another kind of tale and only marginally relevant to this one.

Newer criticisms of past planning decisions have been made. Helen Horowitz, in her study of the history of a number of famous American women's colleges, has explained how gender stereotypes were architecturally implemented. Late nineteenth-century women's colleges were generally less open and more restricted than men's. Care was taken to build in structural forms that allowed for adult supervision and watchfulness. Less scope was provided for the development of personal or intimate relationships, either with men or women. The atmosphere was one of suspicion and protection. Large single buildings were erected containing all the divisions of space necessary for study, teaching, dining, entertaining, sleeping and supervising. Order, regularity, hierarchy, tightly observed schedules of work, study and play – such was the conception at colleges like Mount Holyoke. In the case of Smith College in the small New England town of Northampton, cottages were laid out on campus grounds to allow for groupings of women as families. The practice

---

[92] Lowdon Wingo, Jr, *Cities and Space: the Future Use of Urban Land* (Baltimore, MD, 1963), 5–6.
[93] Howard Colvin, *Unbuilt Oxford* (New Haven and London, 1983), 104.

was meant to reinforce their potential role as homemakers, but it often backfired, providing exactly the environment for friendships that the colder, more asylum-like campus was designed to thwart.

Barnard (1889), however, located in Manhattan as an annex to Columbia University, simply yielded to the city. Women lived outside the college, commuted and had the freedom of bookshops, cafés and the cosmopolitan world inhabited by male students. At Bryn Mawr in Pennsylvania, meant to be draped in Quaker Lady Dress, the feminists triumphed. The system of cottage architecture in existence elsewhere was rejected, and the college borrowed the familiar lineaments of neo-gothic because it was common to male institutions.[94] Yet neo-gothic had other critical functions at the end of the century, whether for women or men. Irregularity continued to symbolise the freedom of associations within the confinements or suggestions of quadrangular space, but in the age of great cities gothic courts also separated the special experience of gown from the less secure pleasures of the town. Gothic was chosen at the University of Chicago for precisely this reason – 'a sense of protection . . . essential for an urban university'.[95]

Occasionally there came into Egypt a pharaoh who knew not what the original planners of many women's colleges intended, who contemplated the architectural orderings and directions designed to shelter and guide women students and who understood that the inhabitants would create their own embrasures in college fortifications. A strange pharaoh to think in such ways, but President John Raymond of Vassar was one of them. In 1873 he explained why the Vassar trustees had been wrong: 'The shell should be *grown* by, that it may be *fitted to*, the animal. It is an awkward thing, as I have learned by much & trying experience, to fit a live & vigorous animal to a shell manufactured to order, in advance.'[96]

THE COLLEGE AS THEATRE AND ILLUSION

From their inception universities have employed two kinds of ritual to invest the educational experience with unique significance and value.[97] The first separates the sacred from the profane. The great public ceremonies of the university – matriculation and Encenea (or its equivalents) in Britain, Charter Day and Commencement in the United

---

[94] Horowitz, *Alma Mater*, 6.
[95] Block, *Uses of Gothic*, 13.
[96] Horowitz, *Alma Mater*, 41, and for other information noted, Introduction, 3–6, 21, 302–9.
[97] The two forms are discussed in relation to cities in *Urban Rituals in Italy and the Netherlands*, ed. Heidi de Mare and Anna Vos (Assen, The Netherlands, 1993), 12.

States, direct attention to special moments or turning points. Participants are attached to the university as it prefers to see itself. The use of ancient language, references to the great personages and periods of academic life or to distinguished graduates, music, university hymns, processions, banners, academic costume and rhetoric or the dispensation of honours and the awarding of degrees enhance the occasion, make it general and personal at one and the same time. But ritual of a second kind, although far less grand, functions similarly by assigning importance to locations that are routine and even trivial, as when spaces are named and designated and thereby become distinct from other sites, acquiring their own lore and specificity, historical associations and literary importance. Scripture records a number of episodes where nondescript, unidentified locations are raised to the level of the sacred because of a revealing dream, or, in the most notable of all the stories, because Jacob wrestled through the night with a mysterious figure. The experience is marked by a change in his name, and the place, which had no designation, is now to be called Peniel.

But more homely examples should be cited. To meet 'under the clock' at Waterloo Station in London has bestowed upon the suspended time-piece, the space beneath and the train station itself an importance well beyond a convenient rendezvous. The very familiarity of the place, indeed its fame as a traditional spot, immediately distinguishes it from other possible meeting points. Universities are full of trivial locations that acquire significance through the repetition of experiences that have occurred at them or by commemorating an event. Special benches and walks, Speaker's Corners, pergolas where a first kiss is exchanged (Indiana in Bloomington), spots commemorated by historic events (one of the plazas at Berkeley where protesting students surrounded a police car in the 1960s), the corner at Trinity College, Cambridge, where Lord Byron chained his bear – these trivial places have been elevated to higher status through repetition, the ritual observance of an archetypal experience. The genius of the association principle therefore reveals itself once again. The picturesque aesthetic, the eighteenth-century version of the ordinary rendered extraordinary, was always confronted by the threat of oblivion. Investing the accidental, or what one writer calls the 'found object', with significance was no small task.[98] Ruskin understood that a tiny reference acquired importance when juxtaposed to a larger aesthetic cause to produce the magical spells cast by properly endowed space.

---

[98] Raimonda Modiano, 'The Legacy of the Picturesque: Landscape, Property and the Ruin', in *The Politics of the Picturesque*, ed. Stephen Copley and Peter Garside (Cambridge, 1995), 213–14.

What better ironic example of the rediscovery of the importance of 'milieu' can we find today than the renaming of the universities of Paris? Anonymously designated Paris 1, Paris 2 and so on to 13, possibly in homage to an egalitarian principle stretched out of all due proportion by a rationalising bureaucratic mentality, the universities of the capital have become Université Pantheon, Université de la Sorbonne Nouvelle, Université René Descartes, Université Pierre et Marie Curie, Université Denis Diderot. Several have acquired more pedestrian names; but all, from the perspective of an educational tradition that respects tactility, now contain references and allusions, memories and continuities, and are, as places, alive.

Enchantment succeeds where reason is suspended. The legacy of attributing vitality to space was based on a universal willingness to discard doubt. The dangers of doing so were sometimes noticed, especially where ritual, symbolism and belief were closely united in theology. The British neo-gothic revival, to give but one example, posed serious problems for English Nonconformists. They were troubled by the possibility that Protestant denominationalism would be confused with Anglicanism if 'symbolic mysteries' were taken seriously and supported by 'those ornaments which we know have been prostrated to purposes of super-stition'.[99] The fear drives home the efficacy of illusion in suggesting experiences.

Illusion, perhaps even deception, was regarded as a human need in the spirit of play (*homo ludens*) and as a pedagogical principle. Academic life could be legitimately understood as a species of theatre, with its own conventions, ceremonies and pageantries, a play in three or four years if not five acts. William Turnbull, Jr and Charles W. Moore, the distinguished designers of the Mediterranean village of Kresge College at the University of California at Santa Cruz, unabashedly adopted stage-craft in designing one of the retreats atop the Santa Cruz mountains. They maintained that such planning and design were wholly within the American tradition of reproducing foreign and exotic locations as a means of stretching the imagination, and they separated Kresge College from Disneyland by drawing a distinction between traditions that are patently fake and those which are an authentic reworking of symbolic genres with a proven history.[100]

The clarity demanded by the modernists of the American planning

---

[99] Dale A. Johnson, 'The Oxford Movement and English Nonconformity', *Anglican and Episcopal History*, 59 (March 1990), 86.
[100] Sally Woodbridge, 'How to Make a Place', *Progressive Architecture*, 5 (1974), 80.

tradition depended upon straight lines as pronounced in the urban design schools of Paris. The oldest traditions of seeing and understanding through experience rejected clarity when they embraced the principles of the picturesque and rejected a strict interpretation of neoclassical principles. Irregularity and asymmetry were preferred because they permitted peculiar variations in elevations and layouts, surprise exits and gates, hidden territories, walled gardens, corridors leading – where? Hence all college design was in some sense 'gothic', whether buildings were in Greek, Saracen, Spanish, Italian or Mayan designs (the platter of alternatives served up by the last of the generation of American neo-historical architects). New foundations of nineteenth-century England embraced a similar range of stylistic options. Manchester featured a building in the 'muted' gothic style, while at Liverpool perpendicular and decorated versions were used. French Renaissance was the chosen ornament for Leeds, French gothic for Nottingham, with flanking turrets, a spire and a loggia of three arches set below a stained glass window. At Newcastle the favourite was Elizabethan. Mock Tudor was in evidence at Bristol and Sheffield, and for the latter there was also room for a science block in the neo-Georgian fashion. Queen Anne reappeared in the Edwardian period, and the architect Aston Webb was especially pleased with his choice of Byzantine for Birmingham.[101]

The 'gothicising' of a collegiate education, consisting of associations and intimacy, was an important discovery in the rounding of personality and shaping of character required by the architecture of a college. The Australian Keith Hancock, arriving as a student at Balliol in the early 1920s, was at first taken aback by the staircase arrangement of rooms in college, which limited the number of students who could be grouped together. He unfavourably compared the 'gothic' staircase to the corridors at Melbourne University. The first encouraged the formation of cliques, while the latter was suited to the natural gregariousness of his native land. In time, however, he altered his views as the secrets of the place revealed themselves. The cliques were open not closed, but they were undeniably self-contained. He succumbed. His 'life was . . . so crowded and various at Balliol that he had neither time nor inclination to seek additional entertainment outside'.[102]

---

[101] Roy Lowe, '"A Western Acropolis of Learning": the University of California in 1897', in *Chapters in the History of the University of California,* eds. Carroll Brentano and Sheldon Rothblatt (Center for Studies in Higher Education and Institute for Governmental Studies, University of California, Berkeley, 1996); and 'Anglo-Americanism and the Planning of Universities in the United States', *History of Education,* 15 (December 1986), 247–60.

[102] Richard Symonds, *Oxford and Empire, The Last Lost Cause?* (New York, 1986), 275.

UNINHABITED SPACE

How many Nereids are left in the waters and how many Oreads in the mountains? Are they packing up to go, and is it actually the case that the woods no longer give shelter to Pan? We have seen how problematical the story of guardian spirits has been, but also how tenacious. The old history of associations has contemporary advocates in certain pockets of the amorphous environmentalist movements where a concern for the conscious experience adhering to space and place is expressed. These advocates go beyond the anti-urbanism of the back-to-nature senti-mentalists who have been pecking away at (first) commercial and (second) industrial civilisation since their genesis. Urban spaces are in fact being praised for their capacity to incorporate mystery and surprise. Even the lexicon of the picturesque is employed, if not necessarily by that name. One writer speaks about a 'host of small pictures' (rather than space *per se*) or even the 'tremendous trifles' important for connecting location to person, window shopping, for example, which is one of the pleasures of urban life. He also notes that time is required for exploring the experiential capacities of sites and for acquiring a relevant 'mental geography'.[103]

An accurate statement about the fate of the guardians of place requires some further mention of the continual efforts to restore spatial significance and personal experience to American, as well as British campuses.[104] Innumerable experiments in university construction have taken place in many corners of the earth in the last three to four decades. Many attractive adaptations of ingenious meldings of site, space and structure exist, as well as blendings of urban and collegiate models: campus streets, squares, cloisters, educational shopping malls, sculpture and monuments, vast stadia – the vocabulary is extensive. Since about 1900 campus planning efforts have oscillated between college and urban ideals.[105] The two conceptions of how life is to be lived are in constant tension. The Santa Cruz campus of the University of California was designed as a chain of six or more villages set amongst redwoods on a site overlooking the Pacific Ocean. Stockholm University is a collection of glass palaces set in grassland suburbs just on the edge of the capital and serviced by its own

103 Tony Hiss, *The Experience of Place* (New York, 1990), 28, 167, 168.
104 Swedish colleagues at Uppsala University, acknowledging the strength of Anglo-American custodial and tutorial inheritances, point to tiny innovations as evidence of some university concern for the extra-academic well-being of students. One such is the Café Alma in the cellars of the Great Aula, meant to be a student and teacher gathering place.
105 Turner, 'Thoughts', 26; Carrié, 'Les universités américaines', 225–35.

underground train stop. The Autonomous University of Madrid has a similar situation, if more distant from the centre. Louvain in Belgium goes even further. The university is said to have provided Newman's new Irish foundation with its constitution,[106] but it was then a very different place in a very different location. Today its successor is no less than a sparkling new city, having its own train station, shops, restaurants and residential districts constructed on two levels.

Neither college nor university ideal appears to have the uppermost hand in contemporary campus design, although presumably the trends favour the city over the village in mass education cultures. The university, suggests Turner, is in so many ways a laboratory for urban design.[107] Yet the further Britain and America architecturally travel towards an urban ideal, the stronger becomes the reaction to it, especially in the last decades of our own century when cities have lost a major portion of their glamour. Crime, drugs, the homeless, ghettos, overcrowding and traffic congestion – all of the terrors against which Olmsted reacted – have made the city unattractive. Hence there have been periodic revivals of collegiate thinking, efforts to make large universities appear small, intimate and safe by using 'domestic' styles of building (some post-modern work lends itself to this), attempts to build residential college teaching programmes, provide small classes, honours tutorials, better advising systems and an array of student-related support services.[108]

These are desirable, but their existence is another aspect of the accumulative approach to higher education that appears to prevail today, the incorporation of many 'ideas' into a multiversity mission and the grafting of many 'places' onto a campus. Variety has been labelled a 'collector's choice to enlivening the public realm'; and while appreciated, the resulting stylish finish is found wanting, lacking the authority and definition of what were once individual pieces.[109] Other observers seek a campus architecture that is boldly irregular and unpredictable and above all unafraid, even at the risk of confusion. The enemy is an overarching bureaucratic form of 'globalized and sterile imagery':

[106] For this and other features of Newman's Irish university, see Fergal McGrath, *Newman's University, Idea and Reality* (London, 1951).

[107] Turner, 'Thoughts', 267.

[108] See David Riesman and Gerald Grant, *The Perpetual Dream, Reform and Experiment in the American College* (Chicago and London, 1978).

[109] Charles W. Moore, 'You Have to Pay for the Public Life', in *The Public Face of Architecture, Civic Culture and Public Spaces*, ed. Nathan Glazer and Mark Lilla ((New York and London, 1987), 399–400.

Instead of opting for a cut-rate version of corporate design . . . universities
– especially public ones – ought to engage in exactly the same efforts that
have been diagnosed for business in general: unorthodox experimentation
along imaginative instead of schematic patterns of thinking, individualized
rather than corporate goals, and above all an engagement with playful, even
puzzling, subcurrents.[110]

Old yearnings are alive, if not exactly well, but reproducing the precise
social and educational conditions that formed the culture of Georgian and
Victorian environmentalism is clearly out of the question. Nostalgia in
these respects is no more helpful than the longing for self-contained
English villages, now turned into commuter dormitory suburbs, or small-
town midwestern America, although both are in fact part of the same
problem of reconfining people to agreeable locations.

The college experience, as it went through successive alterations and
corrections in the theory of vision, was far more open-ended and in
keeping with the relaxed, elite presuppositions of bygone eras respecting
the use of space for meandering, introspection and coming of age. Spaces
designed for separation and lingering, for the gradual awakening of
perceptions and self-development, a room of one's own and a room with a
view – whether of snapdragons or fountains - these were primary only in
another phase in the history of undergraduate education. Where students
must rush from one building to another to fulfil course breadth requirements, or where teaching and learning are subject to almost daily
assessment, evaluation and auditing 'exercises' (as they are presently called
in the United Kingdom), the magic of space vanishes. In civilisations
where leisure is not incorporated into teaching and learning activities,
education and location are incidental to one another. The 'empty' colleges
of Leuven in Flanders, St Andrews or King's College, Aberdeen in
Scotland, empty in the sense that the spaces fulfil university administrative
and lecturing purposes rather than house collegiate communities, are
additional evidence of the skittish temperament of tutelary spirits. The
spaces remain but the ruins are not inhabited. Education in the very
broadest sense created the spaces and encoded them, and in return the
spaces offered a unique kind of education.

Spaces require sharp definition. The boundaries may be irregular, but
the irregularity is itself understood to be integral to the experiences of

---

[110] Kurt W. Forster, 'From Catechism to Calisthenics: *Cliff Notes* on the History of the
American Campus', *Architecture California* (May, 1993), 74–5.

place. The absence of such conditions is increasingly a feature of contemporary higher education institutions, especially where the pressures for access and student and programme diversity are very strong. The blurring of boundaries, of mission, programme and place is very noticeable. A recent 'roundtable' discussion of how best to achieve 'particularity of place' leads away from the heritage discussed here. The roundtable authors define particularity as a close fit between educational services and student demand or type, invoking memories of the heyday of American women's and church-related colleges and historically black colleges. However, the arena they have in mind is considerably broader. Institutions should not attempt to follow a common academic pattern, but then the authors go on to suggest that even the most particularistic institutions are or will be heavily dependent upon a network of other higher education institutions, needing to share resources and classrooms, research objectives and 'outsourcing work to one another'.[111] Since what is being proposed is already a feature of American higher education viewed as a system, through student transfer mechanisms and intercampus research projects, as well as intra-university teaching via electronic means in multicampus systems, the outcome is actually an intensification of the process of erasing perimeters.

The largest group of American higher education institutions, placed in the Carnegie classification scheme as 'comprehensives', has long experienced the effects of ragged demarcations. According to one account, these institutions are 'misfits' (a self-description) falling somewhere between the well-established liberal arts college and the great research university. They are private colleges and universities – they are not themselves certain which label to adopt – and include places like Hamline University in Minnesota, Hood College in Maryland, Rollins College in Florida, Valparaiso University in Indiana and the University of the Pacific in California. Relatively small, some 1500 to 6000 students, generally suburban, tuition-dependent and serving local or regional markets, they offer liberal arts programmes and professional and vocational courses for a wide variety of student clients of all ages and social backgrounds. But while the mix is exactly that of the multiversity, the misfits have no central idea, no 'governing institutional metaphor' such as *wissenschaftliche Methoden* dominating the whole. The parts are uncertain about which academic standards to adopt. Administrative structures are problematic, organisational styles hesitant and unclear. Rituals and

---

[111] 'The Pew Higher Education Roundtable', *Policy Perspectives,* 6 (April 1995), 7A–8A.

ceremonies are undertaken from force of habit rather than in commemoration of past success.

Yet these institutions have been attempting to reinterpret their drawbacks as potential strengths and to seek rebirth under the new designation of the 'New American College'. Now proud of their hybrid character, they realise that the absence of a firm organisational structure means that they can avoid being taken over by managerial and bureaucratic ideas. The absence of a central idea means that they can be unashamedly aggressive in trying to meet the demands of multiple markets. The weak internal boundaries mean that liberal, professional, vocational and even research ideals can be combined in new, less exclusive academic programmes and fields of study, and the absence of tradition leaves room for innovation.[112]

What is missing from these accounts of how higher education can serve present and future generations of students – what must perforce be missing given the nature of mass education opportunities – is a sense of tactile place as important to a single institution, or to the students who would resort to it. Having no *genius loci*, and no real practical possibility of coaxing one back, the consortia and new American colleges of the future are unencumbered by a heritage heavily laden with past assumptions about pedagogy and self-fulfilment. Whether that constitutes freedom is problematical.

Campus design today is part of a highly professionalised activity called 'planning', which, *inter alia,* attempts to impose a set of solutions onto territory. It was once really only 'architecture' and 'landskip', additions to the existing university fabric or an extension to the genre of university occupied space. The resulting piles were presumed to be the alluvial deposits of the centuries, naturalised to small group scale and needs. Like the Hellenic and the gothic, whose proximity once filled certain observers with alarm but others with pleasure, old and new grew slowly together in comfortable fusion.

Curiously enough, one set of university locations suggests a habitat for the in-dwelling *genius loci*. They are those havens of *wissenschaftliche Methoden*, the postgraduate schools. Staffing ratios are better, socialisation albeit into professional life and not as preparation for citizenship prevails. In the sciences the research team, cooperative in spirit and sharing in space, retains an echo, however faint, of the collegiate ideal, and undergraduates fortunate enough to be part of laboratory teams receive a taste

---

[112] Daniel R. DeNicola, 'The Emergence of the New American College', *Liberal Education* (Winter, 1995), 63–78.

of what it means to be bonded together in shared space. Indeed, the laboratory sciences and the archaeological dig, or the dance company and campus orchestra may be the few places on or off campus where the ancient deities preside.

Nevertheless, while overlapping elements exist, a distinction between these organised academic employments sharing space and the history of spiritual precincts needs to be made. The first is still Humboldtian, which is to say that knowledge or activity centred on the training of intellect and intended for professional use is primary. The focus is on discipleship, increasingly on teamwork. Furthermore, recent speculation on the nature of future collaborative research suggests a scenario quite radically removed from shared space. For researchers, the College Invisible is becoming more important professionally than the College Visible. We are reminded repeatedly of how today's significant research derives from the work of teams and networks that function across specific institutional boundaries, so that the 'idea' of a university is not coterminous with the 'space' that it occupies. These teams, it is foreseen, will not be permanent aggregations of researchers and students but project groups assembled for specific investigations, disbanded when the task is completed, and regrouped with a different research configuration when the next assignment is received.[113] The German Humboldtian university was built upon an 'idea' about knowledge, but 'place', the campus as identifiable bounded space, could be more easily grasped. That probably remains the case, which is why the American campus has been described by visitors from abroad as a centre for tourists. Visiting the American campus is like visiting a chateau and its park in France.[114] Yet tourist sites are not *milieux*. The campus itself sometimes appears to be a museum: fixed, expensive, a reminder of the past and a drag on the future. Spatially boundless, the other incorporeal campus exists in an utterly different and revolutionary location that is electronic not-tactile, composed of images no longer captured in hard and lasting form.

It is difficult, with a subject like the *genius loci*, which rears columns and bends arches, catches opening glades and tells the waters to fall, to avoid the habit of hypostatisation. Pathetic fallacy or not, the ancient practice of attributing personality to structures and precincts is irresistible as a means for explaining the attractions of space. The personal possession of space in the sense of investing it with emotion and significance is a fundamental

[113] Michael Gibbons *et al., The New Production of Knowledge: The Dynamics of Science and Research in Contemporary Societies* (London, Thousand Oaks, CA, and New Delhi, 1994).
[114] Carrié, 'Les universités américaines', 229.

aspect of culture. The arch-typal act is Jacob struggling with the angel and coming away from the encounter changed in body and name, the spot itself now special and identified. That is how attachments are made. The problem is how to bequeath the inheritance, and it is an institutional problem as well as a wider one of culture and history.

The reader, having been indulgent thus far, may be persuaded to allow one or two additional closing thoughts. For a Victorian such as Cardinal Newman, heir to romanticism, all of life was a form of struggle, a series of losses and gains (the title of his university novel): a struggle to know the Unknowable, a struggle to know one's own mind, a struggle to establish oneself between competing authorities, a struggle to balance Truth with knowing, a struggle to reconcile friendship with personal authenticity, a struggle to balance the meaning of life with the meaning of the afterlife. In Newman's remarkable writings, university and college were complementary but also in tension since they embodied quite distinct aspects of mental authority and growth. University 'ideas' competed with college 'places', but neither was ever supposed to dominate the other. 'Place' held its own, since place was as deeply positioned in English and subsequently American civilisation as was the idea of a university. In fact, it was more strongly positioned when Newman wrote. The first consideration for founding a university, he himself said, was to consider the site, 'for that site should be a liberal one'.[115] In the incorporeal space of the age of computers and the relentless drive for additions to knowledge, is it conceivable that at long last the disembodied 'idea' of a university – and we have seen how many there can be – will triumph over the university as 'place'?

[115] *Historical Sketches*, 24.

CHAPTER THREE

'THE FIRST UNDERGRADUATES, RECOGNIZABLE AS SUCH'

PROLOGUE

G. M. Young remarks in a footnote in passing, that the poet P. B. Shelley and his friend and biographer, T. J. Hogg, 'seem to me the first under-graduates, recognizable as such, on record'.[1] We cannot know exactly what he meant, but we can surmise from Hogg's *Life of Shelley* and the facts of Shelley's residence at Oxford that he spotted in the circumstances of the poet's rebellion and expulsion a set of attitudes towards a university experience that approximated a style of response more typical afterwards. He could not have meant that subsequently all undergraduates would recapitulate the direct experiences of the two friends. But he probably meant that in and around Shelley, just before and after, a university education became a more significant, even a defining experience in the lives of those whose institutional connections earlier were more tenuous, less problematical or emotional and who were not so personally identified with the institutions, the routines and the history of the universities. They hardly shared in its 'idea' or experienced its 'place'.

We can therefore attempt to fill in the spaces that Young provides us by examining the emergence of a student estate and condition in which the university became a stage in the life cycle of the undergraduate, a necessary step on the path to adulthood and maturity. We can also notice the gradual appearance of a literature that purported to explore the meaning of that estate in story and novel. We can begin by demonstrating how the dominant influences on the lives of undergraduates originated outside the university and were never fully integrated into an academic culture before some paradigmatic point in the later eighteenth century. Afterwards changes in the structure and organisation of learning helped define a student subculture; but even more, that student subculture,

---

[1] George Malcolm Young, *Victorian England, Portrait of An Age*, 2nd ed. (London, 1957), 92n.

developing from its own sources of inspiration, helped define the structure and organisation of teaching and learning.

A perennial observation, implicit if not always explicit, that the besetting difficulty of Georgian Oxbridge was excessive leisure can be suggestively elaborated. For most of the eighteenth century undergraduates and collegiate fellows were bored. This was the inevitable consequence of social and historical conditions which turned a university education into one of the least desirable alternatives for a student making the transition from adolescence to maturity. The social history of the period contains the fullest evidence of the consequences of too much time. The slightest diversion was escalated into a boisterous and often violent adventure. University authorities quite rightly feared any situation which allowed students to gather in sufficient numbers to create a riot or demonstration. Strolling companies of actors, public games, sessions of county courts, street scenes occasioned by political or religious controversy were situations of potential disturbance. Festivals, holidays and any break in the daily routine that could be manufactured into a celebration assumed a special importance for individuals with nothing to do. Late rising, long walks, lengthened periods of dining, evenings spent in drink, pranks and practical jokes – often of the most primitive kind, played by bullying students on weaker classmates – are evidence of a situation in which learning and study were secondary and casually treated.

The tedium of life in Hanoverian Oxbridge was recognised by students and their parents. Matriculation levels for the century were consistently lower than at any point before and since the English Civil War; and this meant that for certain small colleges – e.g., St Catharine's at Cambridge – there were only two or three students in residence in any given term. At Gonville and Caius at most a dozen came up from 1790 to 1810.[2] At other colleges – Corpus Christi, Oxford, for example – the statutes themselves limited the number of students carried on the foundation and made no provision for commoners (fee-paying students) except for a half dozen wealthy bloods. Furthermore, as it was not even the practice for colleges to enforce residence in term, numerous matriculated students spent only the briefest part of every academic year in courts and quadrangles. Others simply left the universities after a year or two without taking a degree.

---

[2] Christopher Brooke, *A History of Gonville and Caius College* (Bury St Edmunds, 1985), 207.

Those *in statu pupillari* who remained in residence with every intention of observing the statutes of the universities learned that dons were not similarly scrupulous. In the early part of the eighteenth century residence ceased to be a condition for the award of fellowships, an interpretation not usually warranted by statute, and senior members of the universities, unless their career prospects were particularly dim, left the colleges for more lucrative or entertaining employment elsewhere. Besides wasting the resources of the colleges (at least by modern standards), exit also depressed the ratio of senior to junior members and weakened the arm of university authority.

A difficult situation was complicated further by a certain outmoded fidelity to the letter if not the spirit of the Elizabethan Statutes governing Cambridge and the Laudian ones in force at Oxford. Both sets of statutes assumed that undergraduates were of school age – the sort of under-graduate still in evidence at the Scottish universities as late as the first part of the nineteenth century. But as the age of entry had risen, university authorities had the frustrating task of enforcing the disciplinary provisions of an irrelevant set of ordinances. The age at entry had actually been lengthening throughout the seventeenth century, especially after the Civil War. College historians have long been struck by this development but they have been reluctant to draw conclusions from it. One historian has noticed that half the students entering Brasenose College, Oxford, in 1710–11 were 17 years of age and a quarter more were 18; while at Pembroke, another Oxford college, it has been estimated that students were about 18 years old in Dr Johnson's time two decades later. For Trinity College, Cambridge Rouse Ball has suggested that students were coming into residence at 18½ in the period 1721–32.[3] These casual observations and limited estimates are supplemented by Lawrence Stone's statistical evidence for the median age of entry of Oxford matriculants. He calculated the median at 17 years of age in 1590–2; 17.4 years in 1686; 17.7 years in 1711; 18.2 years in 1735–6; 18.3 years in 1785–6; and 18.5 years in 1810 and 1835. As the mean gradually rose, the numbers and percentage of students in the lowest quartile fell. The proportion of students under age 17 dropped substantially from 37 per cent of all Oxford matriculants in 1686 to 16 per cent at the end of the eighteenth century, rose slightly to

[3] Walter William Rouse Ball, *Notes on the History of Trinity College, Cambridge* (London, 1899), 129; Leonard Whibley, 'Dr. Johnson and the Universities', *Blackwood's Magazine*, 226 (1929), 371; Reginald W. Jeffrey, 'History of the College, 1690–1803', in Monograph XIII, *Brasenose Quatercentenary Monographs*, Oxford Historical Society (hereafter cited as *Brasenose Monographs*), LIII (Oxford, 1909), 46.

19 percent by 1810, and then virtually disappeared in the 1830s.[4] But a figure of just under one-fifth does provide some explanation of why college authorities were still concerned about the age of undergraduates. My own calculations based on information in J. A. Venn, *Alumni Cantabrigiensis*, but for a smaller population of Cambridge tripos students, show a similar trend, a decline in the number of students 16 years of age or younger from about 12 per cent in the mid-eighteenth century to about 2 per cent in the 1820s.

The older student of the Georgian period arrived in an age of great affluence and relative confidence. A new code of manners, far-reaching in its implications, was in effect. The Georgians placed immense value on conspicuous consumption, on following the rules of style and taste; and the call for a reformation of manners by the great Augustan publicist Joseph Addison was heard in the simple market towns of Oxford and Cambridge. The age was enlightened. Dr Johnson noted the decline of feudalism in once barbarous Scotland, the replacement of a warrior class by men of commerce. The vulgarities and indecencies of everyday life were no longer to be tolerated by those who aspired to the role of leaders of opinion. Polite behaviour, the cultivation of men and manners was evidence of self-mastery and civility. The satirists and compilers of gossip took pleasure in pointing out that the ancient universities had not kept pace. Critics maintained that the ancient foundations were still essentially monastic in character and austere in habits. Addison said that a better education could be obtained in cities, the universities of the world, but the situation had in fact changed. The dilettanti had summoned Wren, Hawksmoor and Gibbs to reshape the façades of their universities and thereby gave an unmistakable signal to new generations that a different standard now prevailed. At every level of university life elegance of style became the necessary sign of a civilised man.

Accordingly, a new set of themes appeared in undergraduate guides and handbooks and letters of advice. How not to be fleeced, how to keep the fool and his money together, was one favourite theme. Money and manners were indissoluble. No one disagreed on that point. Disagreement occurred over the different kinds of money that could make manners, old or new, land or commerce or the 'invisible' transactions associated with banking and securities. There can be no doubt that the advice and caution were necessary while so many temptations flourished. Students had to learn how to protect themselves from a new breed of rapacious tradesmen

---

[4] Lawrence Stone, 'The Size and Composition of the Oxford Student Body, 1580–1910', in *The University in Society*, ed. Lawrence Stone, I (Princeton, 1974), Table 6.

who exploited the new taste for fashion and goods and were only too willing to grant credit. College tutors tried to exercise some control over student expenditures, with what results we cannot be certain, since the concern for extravagance echoes through the entire century.[5] There was, however, a definite note of ambivalence in all warnings, proving that the universities had left behind them the material simplicities of an earlier day. While it is true that undergraduates were advised to spend their money with care, it is equally true that money had to be spent. 'If you work . . . you must play', recited the young writer of a guide to freshmen, 'But let that play consist, not in the low and degrading pleasures of an hostler; but in the amusements of a man of a liberal and enlarged understanding.' Rooms must be well furnished, redecorated if necessary, silver laid out, costly the habit as the purse can afford. Other less pleasurable expenditures were also required: the college bedmaker must have her half-a-crown, the shoe cleaner his pittance; Christmas boxes and Sunday gratuities for the hairdresser, and so on. College servants in attendance on their young superiors expected to dine on the remains of a wine or supper party. In fact, every cringing villain in wait on the staircase was to have his portion. Waste was justified as largesse. No matter what the cost, it was necessary to avoid the reputation of being a 'stingy dirty fellow'.[6]

Direct from the rough but forthright north country, the provincial freshman was virtually ordered to replace his coarse homespun with silks, frills and ruffles. Even a student of comfortable background with the best connections, like the future bishop of Calcutta, Reginald Heber, was surprised by the required standard of dress when he arrived in Brasenose in 1800. It was 'surely a luxurious age when a boy of seventeen requires so much fuss to fit him out', he wrote home to his parents.[7] Modest habits of consumption once praised as virtues were now deplored as the absence of generosity. 'By endeavouring to suppress the youthful Ardour of Extravagance [starts one of the many university pamphlets of the period], which is generally superseded by the Prudence of Manhood [or so the reader is reassured], we should infuse into the tender mind a cold and deadly Poison, which would extinguish every liberal and elevated sentiment, and degrade its future actions below the Rules of Honour and of Justice.'[8]

---

[5] L. S. Sutherland, 'The Curriculum', in *The History of the University of Oxford*, ed. L. S. Sutherland and L. G. Mitchell, V (Oxford, 1986), 480.

[6] *Ten Minutes Advice to Freshmen* (Cambridge, 1785).

[7] Amelia Shipley Heber, *The Life of Reginald Heber*, I (London, 1830), 22.

[8] *A Letter to the Rev. Vicesimus Knox on the Subject of his Animadversions on the University of Oxford . . .* [signed Philalethes] (Oxford, 1790), 19.

Augustan revisions of notions of taste and pleasure, the explosion in fashion and the decorative arts, the emphasis on surface appearance (on the grounds that it catches an underlying truth), the proliferation of courtesy books, manuals of etiquette and guides to behaviour – the instruments of civility in the age of illumination – produced a mixture of styles and values within the universities that further strained conventional discipline. To be gracious, to be open, to be cosmopolitan, to cut a good figure in society, to be a man of affairs – these were the values that the urbane revolution of Georgian London sent into the universities to challenge and conquer the drier, more provincial, slower-moving and once undeniably cruder life of the colleges. 'You are to be a gentleman of such learning and qualifications as may distinguish you in the service of your country hereafter; not a pedant, who reads only to be called learned, instead of considering learning as an instrument only for action.'[9] The new manners left little room for the ideal of a scholar's life of self-denial and dedication to learning.

Among the first manifestations of the urbane revolution were the coffee, tea and chocolate houses of the earlier Hanoverian period. The inspiration for these new public meeting places was no less than the social life of the capital. The influence of London, as E. A. Wrigley suggestively remarked, spread far beyond its pulsing boundaries to touch in some significant way perhaps one-sixth of the population of England on the eve of industrialism.[10] Places of common refreshment and conviviality suggested an advanced town culture as an alternative to college life. They opened up under the walls of the universities and attracted both under-graduates and fellows. Throughout the first half of the eighteenth century the highest university authorities regarded the coffee shops as their first object of regulation, but as long as dons themselves preferred the inns and coffee shops, students could not be prevented from showing up. In some respects the coffee house was a more appealing social centre than the traditional collegiate societies. The colleges had their halls, libraries and gardens, but so did the coffee houses of the period. They served hot beverages, laid on warm fires – a particular attraction for the poor student occupying a freezing garret room in college. They had occasional musical performances, newspapers that were rarely available in college, perhaps a collection of books and the light talk that passed for worldly and

[9] *Letters Written by the Late Earl of Chatham to His Nephew Thomas Pitt, Esq . . . Then at Cambridge*, ed. Lord Grenville (London, 1804), 13.
[10] E. A. Wrigley, 'A Simple Model of London's Importance in Changing English Society and Economy, 1650–1750', *Past and Present,* 37 (July 1967), 49.

informed discussion. 'At five I sometimes go to a Coffeehouse,' wrote a
freshman in 1767 who was whiling away some time at Gonville and
Caius in the summer before Michaelmas. '[You] meet with all the new
pamphlets, magazines, newspapers, &c., and drink a dish of tea, coffee or
chocolate.'[11] It is even possible that the very earliest coffee houses inspired
the origin of college junior combination and common rooms. Otherwise
students piled into one another's college rooms, leaving the serious student
with little opportunity for personal study. The success of the coffee house
sharpened the contrast between London city life and county town life,
between the urban *beau monde* and the quaint country dons. Its London
inspiration and ties to the world of gossip and fashion made the coffee
house the representative of cosmopolitanism; by contrast the ancient
universities with their antiquated regulations and remnants of
scholasticism appeared to stand for provincialism, even – had the word
been invented (it almost was) – philistinism.

CLUB LIFE AND STUDENT SOCIETIES

The coffee houses represented the first institutional phase of the new
emphasis on sociability radiating outwards from Hanoverian London.
The first phase detracted from university life and values, drawing
both students and dons away from the colleges to the pleasanter, less
constrained social life outside. After the middle of the century a second
phase occurred. Salons and private dining clubs replaced coffee shops as
the centre of London's social life. Similarly, clubs and societies supplanted
coffee shops in the market towns of Oxford and Cambridge. We enter a
distinctly new period of university history, both more positive and more
permanent in its influence.

The foregoing generalisation must be qualified to this extent: some
form of club life had existed in the towns of Oxford and Cambridge since
at least the Cromwellian Protectorate. A substantial list of the names of
clubs and societies survives. Although these titles and occasional anecdotes
indicate a certain amount of variety, it is apparent that dining, political,
and pleasure clubs form the majority. At the Restoration, or at least in
1633, there existed an Oxford society known as the Chemical Club, whose
activities are a matter for speculation, and in the next decade a Banterers'
Club appeared. In the reign of the later Stuarts party politics formed the
basis for club organisation. We know of the existence of two important
Oxford political clubs, the Constitution, a whig association of 1714 or 1715,

---

[11] Brooke, *Gonville and Caius*, 181.

and its famous rival, tory and Jacobite, the High Borlace, which lasted for several decades. In Cambridge the tory members of the True Blue wore blue coats, drank hard and opposed William of Orange. A compiler of Cambridge anecdotes mentioned the formation in 1726 of a Zodiac Club of twelve members which grew to eighteen a few years later – and he labelled it a literary society. Other names survive: the Free-cynics, a semi-secret philosophical society of 1737, the Nonsense Club, the Arcadian Society, the Poetical Club and the Jelly-bag Club. The last two appear around 1721 and 1750 in that order. They were secret literary clubs that met in pubs to write witty verses rather more of a burlesque than a satirical sort (satire was serious business in the first part of the century).[12] It is unclear why they wished to preserve their secrecy, since their doggerel was apolitical, but conceivably it was either to avoid drawing attention to their gaity when the colleges did not officially approve of public houses or simply to have their fun in private.

The surviving titles do not adequately identify the purpose of most associations. It is not always apparent who belonged to clubs, what the basis of their association was, how often or where they met, even how long they lasted. From various hints and sources it can be deduced that they differed from the clubs and societies of the later Georgian period in several important respects. Only a few of them were closely connected to the universities or had anything to do with the purposes of the universities, and undoubtedly most of the clubs met in taverns or coffee shops rather than in colleges. This is definitely the case with the Nonsense and Poetical Clubs but not exactly correct of the True Blue, whose members were drawn entirely from Trinity College, Cambridge, although they did not necessarily meet there. The High Borlace was almost certainly involved in county politics, enjoyed the support of leading Oxfordshire families and probably had no direct connection with Oxford University. It is said to have met only once a year.[13]

Another important difference between the clubs of the first and second halves of the eighteenth century is that the earliest societies were not usually undergraduate associations. The Zodiac Society of Cambridge was composed of fellows and BAs. The Hyson Club, another Cambridge society, was formed in the year 1758 by wranglers, students who had already taken an honours degree in mathematics, and was therefore composed of distinguished bachelors and fellows. For this reason alone it deserves special mention as an exception to the rule that club life had

12 David Fairer, 'Oxford and the Literary World', in Sutherland and Mitchell, 793–95.
13 Falconer Madan, *A Century of the Phoenix Common Room, 1786–1886* (Oxford, 1888), 9–10.

little correspondence to university culture. The controversialist, Gilbert Wakefield, joined the Hyson Club after becoming second wrangler in 1776. He listed an impressive number of Cambridge leading lights, such as the university's public orator, the professor of mathematics, a future dean of Ely and another who became bishop of Lincoln.[14] The Banterers of Oxford were probably MAs, although some undergraduates, perhaps scholarship holders, were allowed to join.

Of the Red Herring Club, an Oxford association, there are odd contradictory accounts, making it difficult to assign the society to its correct place in university history. One source maintains that it was a dining club for Welsh students, who were at one point very numerous in Oxford, comprising 15 per cent of the matriculants in the second third of the eighteenth century.[15] Another describes it as a political club for senior members of the university who met frequently in the rooms of individual members but celebrated the anniversary of the founding of the club in local taverns. Both accounts agree that fines were levied.[16]

It is probable that these departed associations and others like them – names that drift through notebooks, annals, periodicals and memories of the Hanoverian period – were not a very important part of student life in the later Stuart and early Georgian reigns, nor were they closely identified with the colleges. They seem to have little to do with career preparation, scholarship or avocations and were likely to have been formed for pleasure. Their main activities were eating and drinking rather than edification, especially in periods of low political interest. It seems unlikely that the early societies and clubs were successful in bringing together students from different backgrounds and colleges (probably this was not their purpose). Very likely they brought together persons in some manner already connected. A final point which deserves special emphasis is their instability. Continuity is not a feature of their history. The early clubs disbanded or rapidly faded when their principal organisers ceased to be active or left the universities, or when the circumstances that gave rise to them changed. The Holy Club of the Oxford Wesley brothers fits this

[14] *Memoirs of the Life of Gilbert Wakefield*, I, ed. John Towill Rutt and Arnold Wainewright (London, 1854), 132–3.

[15] Stone, 'Student Body', 60.

[16] For clubs and societies see, *inter alia*, Falconer Madan, *The Club, 1790–1917* (Oxford, 1917); Christopher Wordsworth, *The Undergraduate*, ed. R. Brimley Johnson (London, 1928), Chapter 4; W. N. Hargreaves-Mawdsley, *Woodforde at Oxford, 1759–1776* (Oxford, 1969), xvi; John Venn, *Early Collegiate Life* (Cambridge, 1913), 249; L. M. Quiller Couch, *Reminiscences of Oxford by Oxford Men* (Oxford, 1892), 281; John Nichols, *Literary Anecdotes of the Eighteenth Century*, VI (London, 1812), 228; A. D. Godley, *Oxford in the Eighteenth Century* (London and New York, 1908), 136; *Brasenose Monographs*, LIII, 29.

category. The great exception is the Red Herring Club which lasted from 1694 to 1773, but otherwise clubs disappeared shortly after their formation.

The pattern of club formation established in the early eighteenth century continued well into the next century. A disillusioned chronicler of Cambridge social customs mentioned the existence in 1790 of a wealthy group of card players who wore uniforms and were drawn mainly from King's College, although the founder was a rich student from Christ's. The club dined monthly but gambled weekly.[17] Several hell-fire clubs, hard-drinking imitators of the notorious Medmenham Monks, inevitably put in an appearance in the age of bucks and blasphemy. One existed when a very young Jeremy Bentham was at Queen's College, Oxford, in the early 1760s. It was composed of well-heeled dissolutes, 'Unbelievers, Atheists, and Deists, who professed that, as they had a knowledge of their future destiny, it became them to prepare for it; and they used, it was said, to strip naked, and turn themselves round before a huge fire.'[18] Another such club was formed in the late 1820s when the hell-fire style was on the point of going out of fashion and appears to have found a centre in Brasenose College.[19] Also in this period prominent individuals continued the practice of forming societies around themselves. Thomas Dyke Acland of Christ Church started a group called Grillon's Club in the early nineteenth century with politics the chief interest,[20] and in 1829 Gladstone founded an essay society which he named W. E. G. after himself. Attendance was poor and disputes frequent. The club does not appear to have been successful.[21]

While clubs of what may be called the traditional variety continued to be founded in Oxford and Cambridge in the Regency and later Georgian period with all the characteristics of the early associations, there is nevertheless an important departure. A new kind of student association also emerged, more permanent in character or more serious in tone, and in one way or another more closely identified with the universities or the colleges, at least more than nominally. The new societies did not replace the older forms but provided alternatives to them. It was possible, indeed common, to find the same student in both kinds of clubs.

[17] Henry Gunning, *Reminiscences of the University, Town, and County of Cambridge*, II (London, 1854), 152–4.
[18] Quoted in *The Correspondence of Jeremy Bentham*, ed. Timothy L. S. Sprigge, I (London, 1968), 17n.
[19] John Buchan, *Brasenose College* (London, 1898), 66.   [20] Acland, in DNB.
[21] John Morley, *The Life of William Ewart Gladstone*, I (London, 1903), 59. Peter Allen, *The Cambridge Apostles, The Early Years* (Cambridge, 1978), 84–5.

The first of the new societies – and it still exists – dates back to the early 1780s. This was the Phoenix Club, the oldest social club in Oxford. In origin and purpose it was entirely Georgian and probably took as its model Dr Johnson's famous dining and literary club; certainly the toasts were identical. In size it was originally limited to twelve – the apostolic prototype for so many Oxbridge associations – and its members adopted a uniform in 1823. Members of the Phoenix dined together every evening until 1840 when the time was changed to once per week. Besides antiquity and continuity the principal claim to distinction of the Phoenix Club is that in the course of the nineteenth century it was transformed into the Junior Common Room of Brasenose College (BNC). The club was highly select to begin with. Half of its founding members were from landed families, and after 1805 the membership grew even more exclusive as sons from landed and titled families increased. Recollecting the 1830s, one former member noted that 'we were a very gentlemanly and very jovial set during my time, when a certain amount of hard drinking was not considered derogatory, unless it led to ungentlemanly conduct in other respects'. High fees were charged, as well as supplementary charges for newspapers, magazines, wine, decanters and glasses and club attendants. The rules were elaborate. Penalties and fines were extracted from those whose dues were in arrears. Members were elected, and the blackball was used to keep out undesirables. The exclusiveness of the club was underscored by the wearing of a distinct and expensive uniform consisting of a claret-coloured coat with velvet collar and white kerseymere waistcoat with matching buttons. An interesting comment on the quality of its first members is that five of the original nine organisers were elected to BNC fellowships.[22]

In the next decade a second Junior Common Room appeared. The nephew of the President of Corpus Christi College, Oxford, formed a club for the small number of scholars carried on the foundation of Corpus. From all accounts it remained an important social focus for undergraduates until disbanded over half a century later when the social composition of the college changed.[23]

The most important Oxford and Cambridge student societies of the later Georgian period are three, the two famous debating unions, which

[22] Falconer Madan, 'A Short Account of the Phoenix Common Room, 1782–1900', *Brasenose Monographs*, LIV (Oxford, 1909), 91–135. The calculations of social backgrounds are based on the biographical entries provided on pages 47–126 of Madan, *A Century of the Phoenix Common Room.*
[23] Arthur Sidgwick, 'The Junior Common Room', *The Pelican Record* [Corpus Christi College Magazine], I (Oxford, 1893), 86–9.

were preceded by a number of similar but unsuccessful experiments, and
the most intellectual of all Oxbridge undergraduate associations, the
esoteric Cambridge Apostles, another famous 'Twelve'. The success of the
unions prompted several imitations, like the Rambler Society at Oxford,
and the Apostles were the spiritual ancestors and actual model for a
number of other famous societies of the Victorian period, including
several which were not part of the university. Even the W. E. G. Club took
its inspiration from the poets and idealists of Cambridge, and F. D.
Maurice, who had inspired the Cambridge Apostles, actually was
president of the W. E. G. in 1832 when up at Oxford.[24]

THE SEARCH FOR DISTINCTION

The search for like-minded friends, the tendency to form more permanent
associations, hold regular meetings and establish detailed rules and
regulations for conducting meetings, even fining members in order to
guarantee the survival and prosperity of clubs, were also features of the
history of Oxbridge games, sports, physical exercise and recreation. Here,
too, striking changes in the mode of recreation and in the use of leisure
time occurred in the second half of the eighteenth century, particularly
toward the end. Some of the changes appear to anticipate developments
of the games-conscious Victorian and Edwardian periods, but the fundamental differences are more interesting.

In the universities of the early eighteenth century dancing, fencing and
tennis were characteristic forms of exercise. The earl of Chatham spoke
well of the tradition of courtly arts when he urged his nephew at
Cambridge to fence, dance and ride, the young man's likelihood of
acquiring a stoop because of his height no doubt having something to do
with the counsel.[25] Other young aristocrats of the mid-eighteenth century
were civilised abroad on the Grand Tour, a substitute for a university
education. A young man of high family but provincial upbringing learned
his dancing and fencing in France, where also at the hands of a famous
equestrian he learned to ride the great horse. Graceful body movement,
however, was not an accomplishment generally valued in Oxford and

[24] Allen, *Apostles*, 84–5. For information on the Apostles and unions see Francis M. Brookfield,
The Cambridge Apostles (New York, 1906); Julia Wedgwood, *Nineteenth-Century Teachers*
(London, 1909); Allen Willard Brown, *The Metaphysical Society* (New York, 1947);
Christopher Hollis, *The Oxford Union* (London, 1965); Herbert Arthur Morrah, *The Oxford
Union, 1823–1923* (London, 1923); Percy Cradock, *Recollections of the Cambridge Union,
1815–1939* (Cambridge, 1953).
[25] *Letters Written by the Late Earl of Chatham*, 34.

Cambridge where county recreations were mainly indulged. If wealthy, a young man rode to hounds, and as late as 1834 hunting twice a week in season was still an accepted routine.[26] Hunting had the disadvantage, however, of being a seasonal activity, so other recreations were sought. Riding was certainly a common and almost equally expensive pastime. If a 'very capital hunter' cost 45 guineas in the 1790s, a riding mare might require from 30 to 50 guineas depending upon the quality of the animal or the sobriety of the buyer. In Cambridge, undergraduates rode out to the Gog Magog hills and in Oxford into the surrounding valleys. An innovation which appears to have entered about 1800 was the 'match against time'. Relay horses were spotted at regular intervals between Oxford and London, and undergraduates galloped both ways, some 108 miles, against the clock. The goal was to cover the distance in no more than twelve hours, and one talented equestrian set a record at less than nine. 'Betting was, no doubt, the first and chief motive; a foolish vanity the second.' But the most interesting cause 'was the absence at that time in the University of a better mode of proving pluck and taming down the animal spirits of non-reading youngsters'.[27] Until early into the nineteenth century young horsemen out for a canter often armed themselves with pistols or travelled in groups as a defence against highwaymen. Because of this danger, many undergraduates preferred to bet on horses rather than ride them; hence the Cambridge doggerel:

> Gownsmen with Jockeys hold an equal pace
> Learn'd in the Turf, and Students of the Race.[28]

Rope-swinging was popular up to the middle of the century, and throughout the period battledore, billiards, bowls, even leapfrog are described as typical amusements. Skating in the winter whenever ice formed on the Cam or Isis, swimming in the summer at Grantchester in Cambridge, Iffley, Medley or Godstow at Oxford when the weather was fine, are mentioned as undergraduate recreations, as are such less strenuous indoor games as cards and draughts. Also mentioned from time to time in accounts of student activities is a collection of very juvenile amusements, such as putting monkeys on the backs of asses. The prevalence of this diversion cannot even be guessed.

Both the Laudian Statutes of Oxford and Elizabethan Statutes of

---

[26] 'Life in Oxford', *The Oxford University Magazine*, 1 (1 March 1834), 101.
[27] G. V. Cox, *Recollections of Oxford* (London, 1868), 30–1; *The Loiterer* (Oxford, 1790), nos. 3, 7.
[28] *An Undergraduate's Letter of 1754* (London, 1886), 3.

Cambridge forbade or discouraged dangerous games: crossbows, gladiatorial combat, fighting with staves, duelling and swordplay. Forbidden also were popular brutal blood sports such as cock-fighting, goose-riding, badger-baiting and dog-hanging. Hunting with hounds was specifically prohibited, as were gambling activities, dice, cards and horses; but enforcement of these regulations was obviously lax in the extreme, and some of the banned activities lasted until well into the next century.[29]

Boxing, a modern version of gladiatorial combat, put in an appearance at Oxford in the mid-1820s, to the great chagrin of the vice-chancellor, then the master of Balliol, and the chancellor, Lord Grenville. Both expressed their deepest abhorrence of these new encouragements to undergraduate dissipation. As the subject is not referred to again, it may be concluded that Oxford did not allow pugilism to survive, or that it was no longer perceived as a difficulty.[30]

In the course of the eighteenth century recreations inspired by courtly traditions declined and were replaced by country sports. These were romanticised in the nineteenth century into the 'bare-chested hero pacing the open moors, knowing, loving and fighting the natural elements and, through his closeness to them and to his own essential nature, achieving a nobler being than ever the artificial life of towns could offer'.[31]

The vigorous outdoor sports of the eighteenth century were mainly pursued by the landed classes or were confined to students of means. Hunting was possible because both universities were still small market towns close to wild country. The undrained fens of Cambridge teemed with fowl, and there was shooting in the woods around Oxford.

It is worth pausing a moment to consider fox-hunting, for this is one country sport whose popularity actually increased in the nineteenth century. The systematic hunting of animals for sport and not food was actually fairly recent. To be sure, Oxford youths had hunted the fox in the late seventeenth century. In 1688 the principal of St Edmund's Hall had written satirically of the sickly youth scarce able to rise to prayers who was nevertheless up 'at four of the clock to a fox-chase'.[32] But hunting mainly involved hares and wild deer, and fox-hunting was a relatively minor

[29] Student recreations are mentioned in miscellaneous writings and also in Dennis Brailsford, *Sport and Society* (London, 1969); Christopher Wordsworth, *The Undergraduate*; Ball, *Trinity Notes*; Godley, *Oxford*; Ben Ross Schneider, Jr, *Wordsworth's Cambridge Education* (Cambridge, 1957).

[30] Draft of a letter by the Master of Balliol College, Oxford, to Lord Grenville, Chancellor [c. February 1825], and Grenville to the Master of Balliol College, 18 February 1825. Balliol College Library.

[31] Brailsford, *Sport and Society* (London, 1969), 250.

[32] Jan Morris, *The Oxford Book of Oxford* (Oxford, 1978), 109.

recreation, restricted to a few country squires of boorish reputation. In the course of the eighteenth century the herds of wild deer decreased in size. The subsequent transformation of the landscape because of enclosure, clearing and land reclamation resulted in a terrain more suitable for the hunting of foxes and hares, but hare-hunting became less popular with the breeding of fast hounds attributed to Hugo Meynell of Leicestershire after 1753. The pace of the hunt and the excitement of the chase were now increased. The balance tipped towards the hunter instead of the hunted. As an added bonus, the hunt could take place later in the morning since it no longer mattered whether the fox was gorged with food after a night of feeding or lighter and fleet. From the 1780s onwards, reaching a high point in the 1820s and 1830s, fox-hunting became the preeminent rural sport. Spread by the new sporting journalism and columns of the journalist 'Nimrod' (the Biblical hunter), the myth grew that pursuit of the fox was a true national pastime, the embodiment of the values of the country and English life, a genuine marriage of body and mind, and, incidentally, useful as preparation for war. The effect of this symbolic elevation of the hunt on undergraduate student life was immediate. No longer was the hunt merely the amusement of rustic squires. After Meynell, 'hunting was first of all a young man's sport'.[33] Fashionable undergraduates were no longer required to be up at the crack of dawn to run down the wily animal, and in defence of their pleasure could cite reasons of health, the mystique of the countryside, national approval and the welfare of the nation. When the season started, the colleges knew that term attendance would fall.

In the surviving accounts of student recreation there is almost no mention of team sports, especially competitive sports. The one famous school and university sport that makes its appearance in the middle of the century is cricket. By origins a Restoration game played in the downlands of the south-east, cricket became a favourite gentry sport, was professionalised at an early date, and then spread slowly to other regions. Before cricket reached the universities, it took hold in the schools, and as the landed classes were its principal promoters, the game appealed mainly to wealthy young men in the most exclusive foundations of Eton and Winchester. From there it travelled to the Oxbridge colleges with the strongest Etonian and Wykehamist ties, Trinity and King's at Cambridge, where it was being played at the end of the eighteenth century. At Oxford students formed the exclusive Bullingdon Club to support cricket.[34]

[33] David C. Itzkowitz, *Peculiar Privilege* (Hassocks, Sussex, 1977), 1–21, esp. 12.
[34] Brailsford, *Sport and Society*, 209–10; Ball, *Trinity Notes*, 159–60; Cox, *Recollections*, 54.

It is in the 1820s, the period of the unions and the Apostles, that we find competitive team sports firmly established in the fabric of undergraduate social life, their survival guaranteed. Regular rowing may have started in 1825. At Trinity College, Cambridge, in 1827, there were no less than four rowing clubs with boats on the river; the distinction between them seems to have been the school to which their members had belonged. Johnians started their famous Lady Margaret Boat Club about the same time, naming it after Henry VIII's mother who founded the college. The *Lady Margaret* was the first eight-oared boat on the Cam, and Trinity shortly put out a ten-oar. The students of Jesus College had a six-oar and invited students from other colleges to join them. By 1828 all colleges were represented, and bump races had started (on a river as narrow as the Cam, bumping could hardly be avoided). A similar development occurred at Oxford, and the first inter-university race was held in 1828, arranged partly by the son of the master of Trinity College, Cambridge who had attended Christ Church. The same person also claimed credit for arranging the first inter-university cricket match, which had taken place two years before.[35]

In the accounts of sports and games, strong expressions of the moral or character-formation virtues of physical exercise or games are conspicuously absent. Perhaps bell-ringing, in vogue in the 1770s, is a slight exception to this rule, but the lonely voices that deplored the decline of a joyous and vigorous tradition scorned as ungentlemanly in the 1790s were no doubt troubled most by the loss of an incentive to churchgoing.

On the whole, the pre-Romantic eighteenth century did not assign a higher purpose to exercise and organised games. Competitive sports or activities resembling military drill were not confused with patriotism, national virtue and masculinity. It is a familiar enough explanation that as England was not overrun by the armies of Napoleon there was no loss of national pride to be redeemed through gymnastics. Perhaps the closest we come to an expression of interest in the new kinds of exercises emanating from Sweden is Lord Grenville's letter to the vice-chancellor of Oxford in 1825. He forwarded a proposal originating with an army officer who wanted the university to licence a gymnastics school in the vicinity of the colleges. The vice-chancellor replied that however excellent the scheme

---

[35] Charles Wordsworth, 'A Chapter of Autobiography', *Fortnightly Review,* 40 (1883), 689; Ball, *Trinity Notes,* 155–9; Roger Baines, '150 Years of Cambridge College Rowing', *Country Life* (27 November 1975), 1463.

might be, it would invite low company and inevitably lead to gambling. Moreover, it would be a distraction.[36]

It is interesting that Grenville's faint support for gymnastics was based on the analogy of his own experiences in a fencing academy when he was an Oxford undergraduate in the late 1770s. Fencing then, he said, received the enthusiastic approval of dons. He thought of the new exercise as a revival of the old courtly recreations. The new hellenism so strongly backed on the Continent by government propaganda did not influence the way in which physical exercise was regarded in England. Winckelmann notwithstanding, there does not seem to have been any of the aesthetic spirit of Greek gymnastics, nor any desire to celebrate the naked torso à la Hamilton, nor throw the discus in the confined courts and muddy streets of Oxford and Cambridge. For the true platonic celebration of sound mind and body, and for homosexual verse linked to heroic rugger captains, we must wait for the later Victorians. The nearly professional athletics masters and gymnast specialists that appear in the public schools after 1860 were unknown half a century earlier, and the pride that Victorian and Edwardian dons took in the sporting achievements and reputations of their colleges would have seemed strange in a less principled age. 'When all has been said', begins the typical encomium of a modern Oxonian, 'it [success in sports] means that the life within [the college] . . . walls is manly and wholesome, and that, if the minor moralities get scant respect, there is abundant reverence for the greater virtues of pluck, endurance and good temper.'[37] We do not recognise a Georgian voice here.

The moral significance of success in games and sports is not self-evident. Physical activities are morally neutral. If they are considered useful for character improving purposes, such as pluck, endurance and good temper, it is the participants and observers who single out the benefits and judge them. They can then be called superior qualities, and a reward can be given for success. The victors are congratulated. Their exploits are written down as examples for a next generation, and they become part of the saga of a school or college. The celebration of the successful athlete is a later nineteenth-century development and was possible only after a major shift in the educational structure and objectives of the university had taken place. It can confidently be said that the first stage of such a shift was made possible by the emergence of competitive team sports in the third decade of the nineteenth century; and it needs to be stressed that the shift also

---

[36] Grenville to the Master of Balliol, 15 February 1825, and draft reply [c. February 1825], Balliol College Library.
[37] Buchan, *Brasenose College*, 76.

included an important new element, the association of games with the public life of the universities rather than with the private life of the clubs and independent societies. Virtually from the start university rowing was centred on the colleges, and boats were identified with particular houses. The second stage of the shift occurred in the mid-century period of the Victorian reforms when dons accepted the boat club as a genuine embodiment of college spirit and outlet for youthful enthusiasms, the same enthusiasms that were so troubling to university authorities in the earlier period. It was at a later date that dons borrowed from beaks in public schools the successful strategy that games, when sanctioned by college authority and legitimised by the actual participation of teachers themselves, are an invaluable educational incentive, an aid to discipline and a means for ensuring corporate identity.

I have discussed this development elsewhere, pointing out the combination of institutional changes, the widespread role conflict and psychological strain preceding and accompanying the promotion of competitive games to the extraordinary position they enjoyed in the Victorian and Edwardian public schools and universities.[38] Once elevated to a primary place in the educational functions and purposes of the university, competitive games ceased to be merely exercises and recreations. Just as courtly recreations were once indissolubly linked to the production of an ideal type of aristocrat, so competitive games were given a special justification. One difference – and there are many – between the courtly exercises of the eighteenth century and the demonstrations of manliness encountered repeatedly in Victorian sources is the pedagogical and moral utility of games-playing in the nineteenth century. The authority possessed by a Victorian housemaster, headmaster or don exceeded the influence wielded by a dancing or fencing master. Victorian dons took an active interest in student physical recreations, lent undergraduates their support as coaches and in every way encouraged competitive sports by emphasising character-building qualities. The situation was appreciably different in the earlier centuries, even right up to the eve of the mid-Victorian period. The dons of the first forty years of the nineteenth century left the development of team sports largely to the initiative of students, especially as the lesson from the past that meant most to them was that whether students participated in a horse race or a foot race, some form of betting was certain to be involved, and they would eventually have to answer to the remonstrances of parents angered by the

[38] Sheldon Rothblatt, *The Revolution of the Dons: Cambridge and Society in Victorian England* (London and New York, 1968), Chapter 7.

debts incurred away from home. At best their attitude towards games appears to have been indifference.

It cannot be an accident that the appearance of competitive games at Oxford and Cambridge coincides with the formation of the new kind of club and society. In both instances the same phenomenon was represented: the wish for companionship, the desire to have an organised and reliable routine, the search for a group identity. Members of clubs and societies submitted to a voluntary system of discipline, established a schedule of fines and started keeping detailed bookkeeping records of club expenditures. Uniforms, a major aspect of club formation, crop up repeatedly. The uniforms adopted by the Phoenix Club have already been noted. The members of a debating club founded by George Canning wore a special brown coat, velvet cuffs and collar and buttons stamped with the initials of Demosthenes, Cicero, Pitt and Fox. Official dress codes for undergraduates were specified in the Laudian Statutes at Oxford, replaced in 1770 by a new dress code, and in the revised orders and regulations at Cambridge dating from 1750. Both codes tried to reduce student expenditures on clothing by specifying simpler clothing or sombre hues, but the traditional correlation between costume and rank was upheld as a reminder of status and responsibilities. A considerable variety of dress remained even after revisions in the dress code. The Westminster scholars at Trinity College, Cambridge, continued to wear distinctive dress consisting of an unusual cut and a violet button with a silk loop attached to each sleeve until the early nineteenth century. This costume was phased out when the Cambridge colleges introduced a system of college gowns.[39] Uniform college dress suggests an attempt to substitute college loyalty for club or even status loyalty. However, distinctions in academic dress remained for wealthier students, and servitors at Christ Church, although long ago elevated into the ranks of minor scholarship holders, continued to wear a special gown until 1855.[40]

Team members participating in the new strenuous games and sports adopted different colours and placed markings on their equipment. That fines and other penalties were imposed on team members failing to show up for practice or races indicates the lengths to which students were now going to ensure the longevity and success of their enterprises. Money from fines, various kinds of subscriptions and fees were how rowing was

[39] Godley, *Oxford*, 166–7; W. W. Rouse Ball, *Cambridge Papers* (London, 1918), 69; Wordsworth, *The Undergraduate*, 160; Charles Edward Mallet, *A History of the University of Oxford*, III (New York, 1928), 174.

[40] 'The Last of the Servitors', Annual Report on Christ Church for 1975, Supplement (1976), 38.

financed in its earliest days. Initially boats were rented, but increasingly they were purchased. And the greater the investment in equipment, the greater was the necessity to protect the investment, find a permanent home and establish an on-going tradition. Gradually but unmistakably the more individualist recreations of the eighteenth century were superseded by activities in which group affiliation was the key feature. Social activities once undertaken out of boredom and for pleasure were still pursued from that perspective, but with one essential addition. They were a serious part of the undergraduate experience and helped to produce the memories of people and places with which the biographies of the Victorian age are replete.

A SOBERING EXPERIENCE

Sociability went hand in hand with Enlightenment values. The belief in the progressive improvement of men and manners meant that the cultivation of friendships was important for a rounded and satisfying life. Addison's university of the world took place in the open where people congregated and shared common space. Taverns were highly useful from this standpoint even if the price was a drunken brawl or a rap on the skull with a quart pot. Many of the messages to undergraduates from home were double-edged. For example, the same author who urged students to be gracious in spirit and generous with their purses also cautioned them against long hours spent in lonely study. Withdrawal from the company of others only produced crabbed and asocial behaviour. Addington sent his son to Christ Church in 1803 with the firm reminder that he was 'going to a place of study, and not of amusement', but unsure of how a young and inexperienced student was likely to interpret the advice, he became more explicit. 'I am far from wishing you, on that account, to be recluse and unsocial.'[41]

So strong was the theme of sociability and equally strong the fear that isolation was a threat to the well-being of the community that the famous master of St John's College, Cambridge, William Samuel Powell, made them the subjects of his discourses written in the 1770s. In a fascinating discussion, rooted in some of the assumptions of one of the many versions of faculty psychology then current, he addressed himself to the vices arising from a life 'abstracted in a great degree from the pleasures, the business, and the conversation of the world'. He concluded that the

---

[41] George Pellew, *The Life and Correspondence of the Right Hon. Henry Addington, First Viscount Sidmouth*, I (London, 1847), 388.

academic life made the unexceptional individual without internalised goals (as they are now called) especially prone to 'the dull and phlegmatic passions', melancholia, paranoia, pride – those characteristics, in fact, that would later be satirised as typically 'donnish'. 'Hear then the character of an idle monk, collected from all that has been observed. He is weak, obstinate, conceited, bigoted, unfriendly to man, ungrateful to God, melancholic, fretful, timid, cruel.'[42]

Powell was speaking of dons, but the lesson was absorbed by under-graduates and their parents who continually urged their sons to study but not excessively and never to forget their duty to others, hoping at the same time that they would wisely choose companions with whom to spend their plentiful leisure. For a sociable man – respectful and modest before his superiors, generous and frank with his equals, condescending and affable to inferiors – was by proven conduct a liberal man. Liberality implied comradeship and a life in public. The lonely man could never be liberal. The call for withdrawal from the vanities of society, the Virgilian return to the country so often voiced in Augustan poetry, is not to be taken at face value. The retirement ideal is more a mood than a manifesto, and the mood does not preclude having friends in the country. Dr Johnson, who more than once felt the urge to retire, remarked in *Rasselas* on the misery of isolation and warned his readers of its ill effects and dangers, at the extreme, madness. In general the eighteenth century possessed a deep suspicion of alienated or anti-social behaviour, which it associated with reformers and idealists. The preoccupation with the ridiculous in Georgian literature expressed the feelings of the century quite adequately on this point. Laurence Sterne tells us that he has no objection to the eccentric (he was one himself) provided he does not ride his hobby horse onto the king's highway; and a later writer, Edmund Burke, makes a sim-ilar point with greater malice by his scorn of his century's favourite demented figure, Don Quixote, the studious knight who pored over many old books. He calls him the heroic deliverer of criminals and anarchists. The importance attached to sociability as an ideal and the emphasis placed on getting along with others explain why university authorities were not comfortable with the Romantic student who showed up in the 1780s and afterwards. The student who asked to be left alone to reflect or brood was not making the effort to fit into communal life. Was he concealing a secret, perhaps scheming, or maybe sinking?

---

[42] Thomas Smart Hughes, *Discourses by William Samuel Powell, D.D., and James Fawcett* . . . (London, 1832), 5–6, 12–13. For 'donnishness' see the chapter by that name in Rothblatt, *Dons*.

In view of these widely circulated values – social, moral, educational – it is only logical to expect that in the later Georgian history of under-graduates the search for friends became one of the first requirements for freshmen, especially but not only if they needed influential career contacts. Writing to his son at Christ Church in 1847 and recalling his own residence, Lord Monson said that the purpose of college life was to 'make a select acquaintance, as much in your own rank as possible'. Become, he said, a 'subscriber to the concerts. The musical set, though I did not belong to it, I will own as the most gentlemanlike in my time at Christ Church.' Otherwise, as was commonly known, the tedium was dangerous. '[The] society of women is wanting, men grow splenetick; positive occupation is also wanting' is how the situation was described in 1805.[43] If the new student arrived without friends from school or introductions from a maternal aunt and failed to locate suitable companions, he could easily become despairing. 'I was so thoroughly lonely', recalled a Christ Church graduate who went up in 1820, 'that I caught at the first hand of fellowship held out to me.' The result was unfortunate. 'A freshman who does not at once drop into a respectable set is in imminent danger of finding himself a bad one. This was soon my case'. Withdrawing from a poor choice was painful and unsuccessful. '[It] was . . . too late to get into another set, and accordingly I hovered over the society of Christ Church for the remainder of my undergraduate life without ever again penetrating into it.'[44]

Without friends there was almost no university to enjoy. William Whewell, who was later to become one of the most famous masters in the history of Cambridge, found it hard to adjust when his friends went down.[45] Undergraduates soon discovered that the majority of senior dons were unlikely to be personal friends or even serious counsellors and that the key to a satisfying collegiate life was entry to the right set. Junior dons fresh from the BA and close to undergraduates in age and sentiment, tried from time to time to bridge the gap between the generations; but as career incentives were lacking, their successes were limited, and they left the universities for more promising alternatives. This helps explain the pattern of the stop-and-go nature of pedagogical reform in most of the colleges in the earliest decades of the nineteenth century, although it

[43] F. M. L. Thompson, *English Landed Society in the Nineteenth Century* (London, 1963), 86.
[44] Quiller Couch, *Reminiscences*, 317–18.
[45] 'This is one of the greatest curses of Cambridge: all the men whom you love and admire, all of any activity of mind, after staying here long enough to teach you to regret them, go abroad into the world and are lost to you for ever.' Mrs. Stair Douglas, *The Life and Selections from the Correspondence of William Whewell* (London, 1881), 24.

was precisely from such fits and starts that important experiments in teaching and teaching relationships occurred. Oriel College, for example, influenced Newman, even though he developed major disagreements with the other fellows. Relationships at King's College, Cambridge, were also unusually successful because the scholars and fellows were all Etonians, as the statutes required, and had known one another at school. To underline the broader differences between earlier and later periods, it is necessary to remember once again the pattern of club formation in the Victorian decades. There dons were closely involved in student games and a spectrum of activities that can be called extra-collegiate. Dons were instrumental in reviving student journalism and in founding musical and literary societies, beginning at both universities a tradition whereby fellows were the nominal heads of student societies. The late Georgian situation was quite the opposite. Clubs often met surreptitiously; dons regarded them suspiciously, disbanding societies or interfering with them where they could and usually separating themselves from the newly developing youth culture.[46] There is at least one recorded instance when the distancing was undertaken reluctantly. Two hundred Cambridge undergraduates wanted to organise an Auxiliary Bible Society. A delegation approached Isaac Milner of Queens' in late November 1811 to request his support. Sympathetic to the cause, indeed eager since he believed in the necessity for such a society and had corresponded with bishops and archbishops on the subject, he was nevertheless reluctant to join their efforts. He was 'fully aware of the danger of encouraging, or being thought to encourage, insubordination, by appearing as a leader in any plan which originated with undergraduates'. He cautioned the delegation to 'retire from the affair, and to place it entirely under the control of their superiors in the University'. Shortly thereafter the Lady Margaret professor of divinity published an address to the Cambridge Senate denouncing the Auxiliary Bible Society as harbouring Dissenters or members who were 'indiscriminately Churchmen' [e.g., evangelicals] since they distributed Bibles unaccompanied by the Book of Common Prayer, or notes and commentaries. In letters to friends Milner indicated how his sanctioning of the Bible Society in 'these delicate seasons' could easily be mistaken, but on the other hand he worried about being accused of timidity and excess caution in espousing a cause close to his heart. He had been called a Luther, but Luther 'was the most cautious man in the

---

[46] There is one example of interference that is not entirely negative. The fellows of Brasenose threatened to disband the Phoenix Club in the early 1820s unless it took steps to correct its highly snobbish entry policy.

world not to offend against order and good government. He acted precisely as I do, and that, on an occasion not very dissimilar.'[47]

The history of Oxbridge journalism provides further evidence of the formation of special student interests. While it is possible to trace the origins of student involvement in university publications to the middle of the eighteenth century, it is really only at the conclusion of the wars of the French Revolution that magazines of a distinctly undergraduate character began to appear. The tradition of university periodicals is held to commence with the appearance from January 1750 to July 1751 of *The Student, or the Oxford Monthly Miscellany*, which may very well have received undergraduate contributions. But the periodical itself was edited by the poet Christopher Smart, who was then a fellow of Pembroke College, Cambridge, received at least one piece from Dr Johnson, others from Thomas Warton the Younger and the playwright William Congreve and consisted of a mixture of belle lettrist materials and translations from the classics intended for a wider and older audience. It is not, however, until 1817 that we can discover a magazine whose overall tone is undergraduate. *The Oxonian*, possibly the work of a single student, appeared in three numbers, and two years later *The Undergraduate* was circulated and ran for six numbers.[48]

In the history of undergraduate journalism *The Undergraduate* plays a special role, for we know more about it thanks to the publication of John Henry Newman's autobiographical writings in the 1950s. The magazine was started by him and another student at Trinity College, Oxford, at the beginning of 1819 as a diversion from hard reading and as an outlet for talents not given adequate expression in the official studies of the university. The magazine was apparently well received by undergraduates in the university and enjoyed a brief popularity, when suddenly the cover of anonymity under which both editors took refuge was pulled away, and the enterprise folded. The anxious manner in which Newman explained the situation to his parents suggests that he was not comfortable working in the open. This was partly because of the rampant philistinism of other undergraduates, who still found it amusing to mock the reading man,[49] but partly also because Newman and his friend were casting stones at the dons. 'Do they really enjoy the sulky homage of the sneering Undergraduate', the young editors asked, 'or suppose, that as long as they require

[47] Mary Milner, *The Life of Isaac Milner* (London, 1842), 463–8.
[48] J. D. Symon, 'The Earlier Oxford Magazines', *The Oxford and Cambridge Review* (Lent Term, 1911), 39–57.
[49] *Autobiographical Writings of John Henry Newman*, ed. Henry Tristram (London and New York, 1956), 40–1.

reverence of arbitrary rule, the obedience of their temporary subjects can ever be extended into an affection for their persons?' The same article ended with a foolish threat: 'It will be well if this and other faults be amended quickly. A stronger pen than mine may otherwise be roused against them. Its energies repressed in one direction, may burst forth with double fury in another, and sweep away with a resistless force, both the obstacles of pride, and the arguments of folly.'[50]

It was with the Apostles that the gap between the university authorities and the students, between what was to be called 'don and man', became the most final. There were, it is true, connections between the society – located in Trinity College – and certain important young Trinity teachers, Julius Hare who was a college lecturer (and a better fellow than the rector he later became), and Connop Thirlwall, an assistant tutor. Nevertheless, it would be misleading to suggest that the Apostles possessed a strong identification with the teachers of Trinity. The inspiration, influences and objectives of the Apostles had little to do with either the college or the university. In fact, Hare arrived on the scene several years after the society was started, and during its formative years Thirlwall was in London reading law. Hare made a point of stressing 'that men of the world, men who act a prominent part in public life, feel little affection for their University . . . the University has in many cases done next to nothing for them'.[51] Both men reinforced influences that came to the Apostles from outside Cambridge; for these undergraduates were all of them Coleridgeans through F. D. Maurice, their moral and intellectual leader, and they connected themselves to the London intellectual world through friends, family and journalism.

The subjects discussed by the Apostles were intellectual and literary rather than academic. They made a special point, however, of broadening discussion beyond mathematics and classics, the principal Cambridge studies. They scorned the 'Stumpfs', the philistines of the day. Their special interests were poetry, politics and theology. They tended to be introspective, sickly and unworldly, precisely the qualities that infuriated the older generation of dons. They appear to have started as a spin-off club from the new debating union. Despite the overall seriousness of purpose of the Apostles, their discussions advanced by prepared argument and counter-brief, for which wit and mock combat were necessary. The playfulness underscored the youth worship in which they continually indulged and which is so conspicuous a feature of their early history. Through Romantic poetry, which was probably their chief interest, they

[50] *The Undergraduate* (Oxford, 1819), 37–8.   [51] Allen, *Apostles*, 11.

expressed themselves in the ideas and images of Rousseau's *Emile* and Wordsworth's *The Prelude*, and their tone and self-absorption made a great impression on family and friends. Although nearly all the Apostles became distinguished Victorians, biographers dwell on their youth and idealism, their anti-utilitarianism and semi-mystical yearnings. Readers are never allowed to forget the poignant, premature deaths of two of the most idealistic of them, Arthur Hallam and John Sterling, whose saint-hood is celebrated in two important Victorian literary productions, the first by Tennyson and the second by Carlyle. The abortive quixotic adventure of 1830 in support of Spanish liberals is always mentioned as proof of the Apostles' high-minded self-sacrifice. (A second Iberian expedition of Cantabridgians occurred nearly one hundred years later.)

It is true there was little in the educational content of the university that could inspire their interests or urge them toward a Byronic rescue of oppressed Mediterranean peoples. And this is nowhere more apparent than in what is surely the most conspicuous feature of their organisation, its mystery. The Society of Apostles was a secret club in its recruitment and proceedings, a decision of obvious importance in promoting its narrowly elitist purposes and for confirming the membership in a belief in its own intellectual and moral superiority. In another way, however, the code of secrecy and the hidden elections were essential to the survival of the society. The Apostles debated the admission of Dissenters and discussed the varieties of religious belief in a period in which the colleges regarded these questions as closed. (A literary society that met weekly at Oxford in the 1790s simply excluded all discussion of religious and political topics.)[52] And that they were closed is indicated not only by the case of William Frend of Jesus College, dismissed from his tutorship in 1788 and forced to leave Cambridge five years later for his radical politics, but by the example made of Shelley at University College, Oxford, for publishing an anony-mous pamphlet in 1811 – although it was not so much the anonymity of the pamphlet but its heretical content that offended authorities. Anonymity, however, inflamed college suspicions. That open debate or discussion of controversial subjects continued to be taboo is shown by the removal of Thirlwall's tutorship at Trinity College in 1834 because he advocated the end to subscription to the Thirty-nine Articles.

The Apostles was not the only student association to be suspected of subversion. Starting about 1790, when the first of the proto-debating or 'speaking' societies made an appearance, tutors and masters discouraged

[52] Fairer, 'Oxford', 803.

most attempts by students to organise in groups in order to argue questions of religion and politics. It is reported that the redoubtable Cyril Jackson, dean of Christ Church, forced George Canning, who was at the House from 1788 to 1791, to disband a debating society he had formed in the college because the toasts and speeches were thought to be reckless. But other evidence from 1808 indicates that Jackson vacillated, reinforcing the impression that some heads of colleges were feeling their way.[53] Also at Oxford in 1795 the vice-chancellor suppressed a student attempt to found a Society for Scientific and Literary Disquisition.[54] Did he see in the proposed organisation – which called its members Lunatics – a disconcerting echo of that celebrated Nonconformist association, the Birmingham Lunar Society? The quick-tempered, brilliant young Cambridge inventor and mathematician, Charles Babbage, mentions in his autobiography that the Analytical Society he and some friends established around 1812 to promote changes in the teaching of mathematics was 'much ridiculed by the Dons; and, not being put down, it was darkly hinted that we were young infidels, and that no good would come to us'.[55] The famous unions, which became one of the most celebrated features of university student life, began their existence precariously. After the close of the Napoleonic Wars the Cambridge Union was very nearly disbanded by university authorities, even though the majority were almost always pro-government on matters pertaining to politics and war.[56] The union had to adopt certain subterfuges in its proceedings in order to survive, most notably by pretending to debate only past issues. Macaulay, who entered the Cambridge Union in the early 1820s, traced the repressive attitude to the tory members of the university who had been attached to Pitt and Lord Liverpool (as a young whig would), but he correctly identified the source of the policy when he noted that the authorities 'had never been very much inclined to countenance the practice of political discussion among the undergraduates [and] set their faces against it more than ever at an epoch when the temper of the time increased the tendency of young men to run into extremes of partisanship'.[57] At Oxford the union was hunted from college to college as its members sought a permanent home for public discussion.

[53] Mallet, *Oxford*, III, 174; George Robert Chinnery Papers, Christ Church Library, 24 February 1808.
[54] Godley, *Oxford*, 141.
[55] Charles Babbage, *Passages from the Life of a Philosopher* (London, 1864), 29.
[56] *A Statement Regarding the Union* . . . (Cambridge, 1817), Cambridge University Library, Cam.c.817[7].
[57] George Otto Trevelyan, *The Life and Letters of Lord Macaulay*, I (Oxford, 1932), 74.

The failure of the senior dons to appreciate the benefits of free inquiry was singled out for special mention by Gladstone later in the century when he reflected on his experiences as a student. 'The temper which too much prevailed in academical circles', he said, 'was that liberty was regarded with jealousy and fear, something which could not wholly be dispensed with, but which was to be continually watched for fear of excesses.'[58] Yet we should not confuse a cranky intolerance for a policy of wholesale repression. The universities were no more consistent in ferreting out undesirable student societies in the early nineteenth century than they had been in enforcing the old disciplinary statutes in the previous one. Indecisiveness, half-heartedness and reluctance were the customary university responses of university authorities. A fear of offending high-born students whose parents could provide job patronage was probably a factor, and toadying continued well into the nineteenth century. In some instances, especially in the uncertain political atmosphere following the defeat of Napoleon, vice-chancellors may have been directed to take stronger action with students by government ministers.[59] Nevertheless, while the authorities in the ancient universities were in no sense tyrannical (Reginald Heber in 1818 thought Christ Church had exchanged ultra-oriental monarchy for oligarchy),[60] it is obvious they were doing nothing to encourage student enterprise and initiative where these seemed to imply independence. Perhaps this is the only consistent policy that can be found in any period of the unreformed universities. Moderators in the eighteenth-century Cambridge disputations were never pleased when students offered theses which seemed to violate Church doctrine, even when the disputant was Paley, who was prevented from arguing his utilitarian theories.[61]

This *leitmotiv* of suspicion and discouragement had an important effect on undergraduates of the early nineteenth century. Students of the Regency period like Babbage and his friends, or the members of the Apostles and unions, could not easily be put down by a warning or forbidding look. The unfriendly attitude of the dons only increased their desire to find friends and band together for mutual help; it put them squarely on their own resources and contributed to, if it did not create, the romantic narcissism and youth consciousness that were striking features of the history of the Apostles and so much a part of the tone of the period.

[58] Morley, *Gladstone*, 60.
[59] Hollis, *Oxford Union*, 14–15. Lord Sidmouth, the home secretary, is usually meant.
[60] *Life of Heber*, I, 498–9.
[61] W. W. Rouse Ball, *The Origin and History of the Mathematical Tripos* (Cambridge, 1880), 181.

Striking parallels exist between English and American student populations of the late eighteenth and early nineteenth centuries. Joseph F. Kett writes about the age-old fear of pedagogues that a mass of young people constitute a menace to society. However, like their English counterparts, American college authorities responded half-heartedly to pranks and rebellion and confused petty infractions with serious rioting. Rules and regulations of the most minute kind proliferated but were unenforceable, especially because (in sharp distinction to Oxford and Cambridge), most students boarded in town. Furthermore, college leaders were undermined in the administration of authority by the need to attract fair numbers of fee-paying students. Lay trustees worried about the loss of income that would follow from expulsions and suspensions.

The arrival of an older student towards the end of the eighteenth century, possibly even older on average than in the English universities, made matters worse since, as at Oxbridge, older students refused to obey regulations designed for much younger students. Kett mentions the growth of a distinct student consciousness and the development of a student estate ready to appeal above college authority to American conceptions of natural or human rights, ideas that were present in English universities after the American and French revolutions but hardly in the same degree. One other point offered by Kett deserves mention, the susceptibility of American students of the period of the religious Great Awakening to revivalist religion, an attraction that does not surprise psychologists like Erik Erikson, who find periods of historic upheaval particularly troublesome to 'adolescents' whose ego defences are still weak.[62]

NUMBERS

It might be conjectured that the trend toward association, and especially the self-discipline that students increasingly imposed upon themselves to guarantee some permanence to their clubs, would have mitigated the general level of wild behaviour which characterised undergraduate life in Hanoverian England, but the conjecture would be false. In several respects the problems confronting university authorities were more perplexing than a century earlier when it was apparent that an older student had come into residence and that simple habits were no longer valued. The restrictions imposed about the tenure of fellowships and the assignment of

---

[62] Joseph F. Kett, *Rites of Passage, Adolescence in America 1790 to the Present* (New York, 1977), 51–7, 62–3. Erikson makes another appearance in Chapter 6.

so many of them to those from specific counties or schools had long operated against teaching by reducing the pool of competent resident fellows who could teach and guide students. Yet the problem was greater in the reigns of the last two Georges than in the reigns of the first two. Simply put, there were many more undergraduates in residence in the first third of the nineteenth century than earlier. In 1800 enrolments in both universities suddenly increased. From 1800 to 1829 matriculations at Cambridge more than tripled, rising rapidly from 129 at the beginning of the century to 462 at the end of the third decade. In just the fourteen years from 1810 to 1824 matriculations more than doubled, and the curve is particularly steep from the end of the Napoleonic Wars. A similar if not quite identical phenomenon occurred at Oxford.[63]

Not only did matriculations increase, but the number of degrees awarded increased as well. Nearly three times as many Cambridge students received BAs in 1830 as received them in 1810. At Oxford there were about twice as many (in neither case, however, is the curve smooth).[64] A large increase in the number of degrees awarded meant that more students were remaining in residence for longer periods of time; and this in turn, combined with a higher median age at entry, provided Oxford and Cambridge with much older students than in the previous century when shorter residence was the rule. Furthermore, there is some evidence that a sizable percentage of young MA candidates were also present in the university, as the statutes, at least at Oxford, demanded a 'Master's Term' in residence. The presence of a substantial community of adults still under the traditional statutory restraints compounded the difficulties university authorities had to face, especially since no reform of the tutorial system had yet taken place.

The increasing numbers of students at Oxford and Cambridge put great pressure on existing rooms. The practice of 'chums' sharing rooms had gone out in the reign of Queen Anne as a consequence of the demand for more luxurious quarters, and this meant that existing facilities could not be stretched. The increases in enrolments affected the colleges differently depending upon their existing provision for accommodation. Reginald Heber found it a particular problem at Brasenose in 1801 and complained to his father that the college officials were not keeping their

---

[63] J. A. Venn, *Oxford and Cambridge Matriculations* (graph); Report of Syndicate appointed to consider what alterations it might be desirable to make in the present Distribution of the Fees ... Cambridge University Library, Cam.a.500.5[64]; J. R. Tanner, *The Historical Register of the University of Cambridge* (Cambridge, 1917), 990; *Journal of the Royal Statistical Society of London*, 5 (October 1842), 241. For Oxford see Stone, 'Student Body', Table I.

[64] *Journal of the Royal Statistical Society*, 240.

commitments to him. '[The] College is really overflowing.'[65] Caius, even with modest entries, could not keep up with demand.[66] At Trinity, Cambridge, the situation had long been desperate, forcing undergraduates into substandard housing or rooms in town, and in both universities a serious lodgings crisis existed in the early 1820s. While it is true that unused space existed in some smaller colleges – and of course All Souls which had no undergraduates was empty – there is no question but that the larger and more famous foundations were seriously affected. At Christ Church overcrowding was responsible for a riot.[67] At Cambridge the master and seniority of Trinity College recognised the need to restore 'the same degree of salutary *superintendence* and *discipline*, and the same undisturbed opportunities for study' as was presumed to have once existed, by laying the first stone of a new court late in the summer of 1823. Undergraduates were said to be wandering in the streets and living in unhealthy, expensive and scanty accommodations.[68]

More undergraduates residing in Oxford and Cambridge, both in colleges and digs, meant more undergraduates in the streets, more undergraduates attending public meetings, crowding the rivers and searching for amusements and diversions. There are numerous indications of widespread indiscipline, street brawling, the frequenting of taverns, visits to bawdy houses and an occasional political riot – some notable episodes took place at the time of Queen Caroline's divorce and later during the agitation for the great Reform Bill. A favourite occupation of the idle was still to wander the streets at night and knock out the lamps carried by innocent townspeople or to disrupt the studies of conscientious students. To counteract this mischief, Cambridge University tightened its discipline. Milner, who thought the spirit of insubordination was at work throughout the nation, cracked down in 1810 by expelling students for disturbing the peace. The niece of the master of University College stayed in the lodge in 1810–11 when she was a girl and remembered how difficult the undergraduates could be. One night they all turned out to hunt the fox beneath the window of the unpopular dean. An undergraduate dressed as a fox was released in the middle of a quadrangle, and his compatriots ran after him, barking, cracking whips, uttering loud halloos and blowing shrill whistles. The authorities finally located the 'fox', reading quietly in

---

[65] Bod.MS Eng. lett. c.204 (203).
[66] Brooke, *Gonville and Caius*, 208.
[67] W. R. Ward, *Victorian Oxford* (London, 1965), 54–5.
[68] Cambridge University Library, Cam.a.500.5[54].

his rooms, puzzled by the fuss.[69] This was an elaborate prank, but not especially serious. It was of the same order as 'rowing a fellow' as described in 1825. A party of roisterers would nail or screw up the oak on an unsuspecting undergraduate's door (usually a timid student) so that it could not be opened from the inside. Shavings dipped in oil taken from staircase lamps were then set on fire and the victim rudely awakened by shouts. Believing the entire staircase to be on fire, the student was frightened out of his wits and of course unable to escape from what he surmised was a burning trap.[70] A more serious indication of trouble came a decade later when Cambridge proclaimed a series of edicts, the first in 1823, and a larger number in 1825, to remind undergraduates that the giving of false names, firing guns indiscriminately and spending days at the race track were punishable university offences.[71] At both Oxford and Cambridge, authorities also were concerned about a growing student resentment against the wearing of proper academic dress.[72] While many students adopted club uniforms that set them apart from other students, as we have seen, refusing to wear the official university symbol of undergraduate status was of a different order. The first kind of dress was voluntary and self-chosen, but the second was imposed and a sign of university authority. The gown was always a quick way to recognise an undergraduate perhaps bent on mischief or out in the streets after dark.

Drinking certainly did not diminish. Drinking had always been prevalent. An upper-class man in 1767 tried to assure a Cambridge freshman 'that the custom of drinking is entirely exploded in polite company', but such soothing information lacked credibility since in the same breath the timid freshman was told not to be afraid of drinking because if the bucks knew they would make him drunk, 'and to make a freshman drunk is excellent fun to them'.[73] When he revisited Oxford in 1818, Heber was told that students were more diligent and orderly than formerly. He acknowledged that there were certain changes but was unconvinced that they drank less, and was certain that they hunted more.[74] A year earlier

---

[69] *Memoirs of a Highland Lady, the Autobiography of Elizabeth Grant*, ed. Lady Strachey (London, 1898), 128–9.

[70] Bernard Blackmantle [C. M. Westmacott], *The English Spy,* I (London, 1825), 158–9n.

[71] Cambridge University Library, Cam.a.500.5[48], [65–9].

[72] G. Newnham in *Our Memories: Shadows of Old Oxford* (May, 1889), 16; Cam.a.500.5[68].

[73] Brooke, *Gonville and Caius*, 181; Venn, *Early Collegiate Life*, 247–8. References to drinking are numerous. See W. B. Duffield, 'Cambridge a Hundred Years Ago', *The Cornhill Magazine,* 8 (March, 1900), 388; Blackmantle, *Spy*, I.

[74] *Life of Heber*, I, 498–9.

Newman wrote that 'if anyone should ask me what qualifications were necessary for Trinity College, I should say there was only one, Drink, drink, drink'.[75] Henry Gunning spent an astonishingly long life in Cambridge. He recalled that drinking was universal, and there are numerous references from the 1820s, 1830s and 1840s to prove that evenings spent over the bottle were common. The old trick of inducing timid freshmen to drink more than was good for them was tried right up to mid-century.

The frequency of drinking at Oxford and Cambridge is difficult to determine precisely because commentators vary in their opinions and estimates. William Barrow, who had delivered the Bampton lectures at Oxford in 1799, did not think drinking at the university was a problem. He wrote in 1802 and 1804.[76] An Oxford guide of 1830 insists that drinking to *excess* was no longer the practice,[77] which begs the question of when it had been the practice or how to define excess, or even whether the levels of alcoholic tolerance were the same. Very likely there were some periods in which drinking heavily was more common than in others and some colleges more noted for intemperance than others. If it were possible to quantify and graph the consumption of alcoholic beverages by under-graduates, the resulting curve might well be a jagged line, with no general rise or fall before 1850. Changes in the kind of beverages consumed are easier to discover. From the records of the Junior Common Room of Corpus Christi College, Oxford, the progress from Iberian wines like port, sherry and madeira, to French wines like claret (recorded in 1824) can be mapped, as can the introduction of spirits like gin and brandy (1826), whiskey (1829) and the always dangerous champagne (1828).[78] German wines were drunk in the 1830s, if the novels of the period can be trusted. Port remained a staple throughout, and ale was never neglected. Punch was popular in the 1820s and 1830s. Rather than diminish their intake of wines, undergraduates were extending the range of their drinking experiences. If debauchery resulting from drink was no longer the case, heavy drinking certainly continued. And the broadening of the alcoholic repertory allowed for some unprecedented and deadly combinations of drinks in the 1830s and 1840s.

[75] Newman, *Autobiographical Writings*, 32.
[76] William Barrow, *An Essay on Education* . . . 2nd ed., II (London, 1804), 343.
[77] The reference occurs on page 186 of a printed guide to Oxford published around 1830 and annotated by a Christ Church undergraduate of the same period. The guide is kept in the Balliol College Library.
[78] Sidgwick, 'The Junior Common Room', 89.

Long-term changes in the scheduling of meals allowed more opportunity for imbibing. In the reign of the later Stuarts dinner was taken at
noon or just before noon, leaving a full day for study. In the second half of
the eighteenth century, it became common in all Oxbridge colleges for
undergraduates to eat only two major meals per day, a large breakfast or
brunch in mid or late morning and a heavy dinner anywhere between
4 and 5 o'clock in the afternoon. The changes in dining habits effectively
reduced the working day for all but the most zealous students, who still
rose early and ate modestly. The rest regarded dinner as the end of the
academic day and looked forward to the commencement of a long evening
spent in wine-drinking and conversation. Drinking went hand in hand
with partying and with being a gracious, gentlemanly host and assumed its
modern place as a social lubricant and aid to sociability. Usually only posh
students such as the gentleman-commoners of Corpus Christi College,
Oxford, gave lavish entertainments in their rooms. Annoyed college
officials interfered in 1791.[79] Other eighteenth-century undergraduates
were accustomed to taking their ale in hall or carousing in the town.
University authorities had the impossible task of policing inns and taverns
where town and gown met and brawled. In an effort to control the traffic,
the Chancellor's Court at Oxford fined innkeepers who served undergraduates food and wine. Milner, when he presided over the Vice-
Chancellor's Court at Cambridge in 1810, was also worried about
undergraduates in taverns. Undergraduates also drank in the dining clubs
that were springing up, but in the Regency and afterwards the college
became a much more important locus for drinking. Taking wines after
dinner in someone's college rooms was routine until the rise of the undergraduate common room in the early decades of the nineteenth century
provided an alternative.

It is not possible to measure increases or decreases in the overall level
of student misconduct from the kinds of sources available to us. It is
also doubtful that lumping different categories of behaviour together for
statistical convenience is the best way to understand the problem of
discipline. It is wiser and more enlightening to pay attention to specific
kinds of offences, for there are in fact discernible changes in the way
students defied authority and broke regulations. There may have been, for
example, more promiscuous sexual conduct in the early 1820s. It is
noteworthy that a bill 'for the better preservation of the Peace and good
Order in the Universities of England' which became law in 1825 singled

---

[79] Thomas Fowler, *The History of Corpus Christi College with Lists of its Members* (Oxford,
1893), 296.

out for special mention prostitutes and night walkers.[80] The larger numbers of students in residence may have increased the traffic from ladies of the night. A problem that occupied the attention of legislators could not have been an insignificant university matter. The rivers were a special problem. There was a high number of altercations and brawls on the river, and there are even grounds for maintaining that this was a new pattern of difficulty. There had always been some form of violence on the Cam or Isis but usually only roughs had ventured out in the first place. It was not until 1815 or thereabouts that boating can be said to have become a popular activity (perhaps partly because of a change in the design of skiffs which made them more manoeuvrable and boating therefore less dangerous).[81] Boating was becoming respectable, and students sailed, rowed and went on excursions for pleasure and not in search of trouble.[82] Yet the river was a dangerous corridor. In the early nineteenth century the waterways through Oxford and Cambridge were crowded with commercial traffic. As undergraduates in greater numbers sailed, paddled and raced along the narrow channels challenging and bumping into one another, their boats also interfered with barges and irritated bargees. Furthermore, as most of the craft were rented from watermen, who were not averse to gouging, sufficient provocation existed on both sides. It is ironic that a recreation in itself harmless should have added to the perennial strain between town and gown.

It is possible to identify another change that also increased the tension and added yet another burden to the universities, namely student indebtedness. This was a long-standing problem associated with the spread of an ethic of high consumption among wealthier families and the use of private teachers to supplement college teaching. In the aftermath of the Jacobite uprising of 1745, Cambridge University drew up a long list of sumptuary and other regulations 'to restore discipline and dignity to University life' (a later editorial annotation to the list, however). Undergraduates were to wear clothes of a grave colour without frills. No one was to keep a servant or horse without permission from parents, guardians or heads of houses, nor were they allowed to receive credit at

---

[80] Parliamentary Papers 1825 (398) II, 639.

[81] This speculation is based on information contained in letters written in the 1830s by a Wadham College student. Maclaine MSS, 9 November 1838, and 30 January 1839, Bodleian, and in the letter from Chinnery to his mother, 4 March 1808, Christ Church Library.

[82] Boating is mentioned in passing by a number of sources, but see Oskar Teichman, *The Cambridge Undergraduate 100 Years Ago* (Cambridge, 1926), 14; Schneider, *Wordsworth's Cambridge Education*, 46.

local taverns and coffee houses for more than a pound.[83] College officials attempted to regulate student spending but apparently with only moderate success, if any. The new emphasis on clothes, furnishings, table-ware and entertainments tempted students into a pattern of expenditure suitable to the style of the new age. Clubmen, like the members of Brasenose Phoenix Club, believed it necessary to lay in a good cellar, and their account books show standing problems in meeting the bills of wine merchants. As the pattern of spending changed and many students catapulted into debt, a parade of tradesmen began marching through the colleges, and university officials attempted to enforce sumptuary legislation in the teeth of their own maxims regarding the liberality of a gentleman. Extravagance was partly the fault of youth, partly the fault of mismanagement and greatly the fault of pressure applied by peers and tradesmen. While the new clubs and societies vastly increased the opportunities for self-expression and widened the social–educational experience of undergraduates, they also immeasurably increased the pressure for conforming to newly developed codes and rules of dress and behaviour. Tradesmen too applied unfair pressure to gownsmen. They kept a sharp watch out for entering freshmen and were uncannily informed about social background and income. They were only too happy to take advantage of a young man's uncertainties about expectations and only too willing to allow long-term credit, being especially anxious to exploit a market which dried up in the summer (which was not the case in earlier decades when many undergraduates stayed on, although the numbers were small). It is likely that tradesmen received intelligence from college gyps and scouts who collaborated with them, probably for a percentage of the take, and that students may sometimes have been tricked into purchasing unwanted items. The colleges may have set spies to watch the spies. Jeremy Bentham was made Senior Commoner in 1763, and his responsibility was to report the faults of servants to the fellows.[84] A semi-fictional story written much later (1847) provides a variation on this theme possible only after the Oxford Movement: Hargrave, the new undergraduate, finds two gowns in his room. His scout,

> disinterested old Hidges, who does not like new-fangled ways, gives a hint of the arrival of a freshman to the hereditary college tailor, who joy-fully sends the academicals; but the junior Fellow and Tutor, the reducer of extracollegiate expenses, the economist outside of college, he has *his* tailor, who will do, and be, and suffer, all that is required of him with docility, and who cuts his garments according to Church principles, and who is civil and

[83] Wordsworth, 'Autobiography', 67–8.   [84] Sprigge, *Bentham*, 75.

cheap, and is 'recommended'; and hence a clash of gowns and caps; old High and Dry hereditary tailor conflicting with the new man of altar cloths, straight collars, and long skirts, patronised by Young Oxford.[85]

THE COLLEGES AWAKEN

Students spent most on food and drink. Time was on their hands, entertainments were few or prohibited, and sociability was the governing ethic of behaviour. The central importance of dining brought into prominence all the local purveyors of food, from fancy pastry chefs and other banquet specialists in the towns to their counterparts in the collegiate societies. College butlers, manciples and cooks profited hugely from the new patterns of consumption and welcomed an extraordinary windfall. Essentially middlemen and independent contractors who charged high prices for food to make a profit, their income was legendary. That they may have often miscalculated the quantity they could sell is suggested by the charges of debt brought against them in the Chancellor's Court of Oxford by town tradesmen. At Christ Church long-standing difficulties came into the open in the 1860s. At Cambridge butlers and cooks remained a source of unnecessary expense even in the twentieth century.[86] The shift to a professional style of business management and better accountability was one of the slowest changes in the history of the two senior universities and can only be explained by the long-standing association between Oxford and Cambridge and a higher income pool of students accustomed to a comfortable style of living.

Other college servants may have had more personal relationships with undergraduates, but they too contributed to the soaring social expenses of a university education. The gyps at Cambridge and scouts at Oxford became an extremely important part of the social and economic life of students in the period after 1780, taking over some of the duties once performed by the low-status sizars and servitors. These impecunious undergraduates were admitted to colleges with the understanding that they were to perform certain menial duties. Part public school fag, part college servant, sizars and servitors were emancipated and elevated into the ranks of students proper at the turn of the nineteenth century, leaving the domestic services of the colleges to be performed by the gyps, scouts and bedmakers.

[85] 'Chapters in the Life of an Undergraduate', *Oxford Protestant Magazine*, 1 (1847), 339.
[86] Rothblatt, *Dons*, 71. E. G. W. Bill and J. F. A. Mason, *Christ Church and Reform, 1850–1867* (Oxford, 1970), 132–6. Records of the Chancellor's Court are kept in the archives of Oxford University.

College servants do not write novels (although they appear in them and even provide protagonists), issue pamphlets, circulate flysheets or deliver sermons. They are in no position, therefore, to answer the calumny that has been flung at them by successive generations of undergraduates. 'A more rascally set of human beings cannot be imagined' is how they appear in one description, and 'they are generally a dirty, idle, thievish, impudent set' is how they are flattered in another.[87] They delight in deceiving innocent or foolish young men, egging them on continually to higher and higher forms of expense and luxury. 'La, sir, a gent like you wouldn't give a breakfast without a shoulder-of-lamb and a turkey. You must have a cider-cup and beer-cup at your lunch. It will never do to have ten gentlemen to wine, and only three dishes of dessert, for a gent like you, sir.'[88]

There is undoubtedly much truth in these character defamations, but we can obtain a more balanced view by considering their situation. Illiterate and low-born, college servants were thrown into a deferential society and like the slaves in Menander forced to rely on their wits for survival. They were either unpaid or in receipt of miserable wages from the colleges. They had little leisure and no security against misfortune until their self-help, friendly society movements began in the 1840s. As dependent on a seasonal market as tradesmen, they sought every opportunity to pull together an acceptable and even comfortable income. They were not adverse to payment in kind, taking samples from the sherry decanter in a student's room, trying out the candles, borrowing a few coals and feasting, like the sizars before them, on the remains of someone else's dinner. Directly and indirectly, servants pushed undergraduates toward more expensive living. But their most unfortunate contribution was to exacerbate the uneasy relations existing between the majority of undergraduates and the majority of dons. For the servants were caught between the gownsmen whom they served and the college authorities who were technically their employers, and one of their functions was to report on students for deans and tutors. Of course they assured their young masters that they would not (in the jargon of the 1820s) 'telegraph' the 'big wigs', but their double game was well understood. As it is impossible to serve two masters equally well, they were heartily despised and abused by undergraduates who nevertheless bribed them to conceal a nocturnal escapade beyond the college walls. Students and servants were trapped in an unhealthy symbiotic relationship. Neither benefited from it.

---

[87] *Anatomy of Oxford*, ed. Day Lewis and Charles Fenby (London, 1938), 308. *Oxford Academical Abuses Disclosed, by Some of the Initiated* (London, 1832), 18n.

[88] Lewis and Fenby, *Anatomy*, 308–9.

In the first part of the nineteenth century, vice-chancellors, proctors and masters of colleges tried sporadically to enforce the antiquated codes of behaviour and to prevent other peculiarities of student conduct but with no permanent success. The history of discipline at both universities is a study in alternating neglect and spurts of ineffectiveness, although it would be unfair to omit occasional successes. These did occur and with more regularity than is usually admitted. Even before the jump in matriculations raised new difficulties, and certainly during the period of increase, individual strong-willed masters and tutors were enforcing discipline. Sometimes the college gates were locked early, chapel attendance insisted upon (the practice varied widely according to college and period), proper dress demanded, particularly in hall. Mansel of Trinity insisted on knee breeches even though trousers had come into fashion,[89] and deans or censors took daily note of the card games and late suppers in college. Physicians as well as servants were used as spies – at least it appears that Christ Church so used them in the early nineteenth century for students living outside the college gates. As a check on malingering, only college-approved physicians were allowed to attend supposedly ailing undergraduates. Various other disciplinary measures were employed. Edicts, warnings, proclamations were issued, speeches were made in the Senate House and in Convocation, and there were a number of exemplary rustications (suspensions). Corpus Christi College, Oxford, revived rustication in 1797. Every now and then there were expulsions.[90]

But this was still a matter of trying to enforce an outmoded set of rules in the face of changing circumstances and to do that effectively would have required surveillance and policing on a scale for which there were no adequate resources. Servants of divided loyalty could hardly do the job. We cannot meaningfully speak of student self-restraint and internalised discipline until we come to the undergraduate who has been tamed at boarding school or has received minute attention at home and comes up to the university with a respect for teachers and academic authority. This change may be Georgian in origin, but it is Victorian in significance. A few undergraduates were raised in households that took seriously the Augustan idea of civilised conduct and others encountered conscientious headmasters in local grammar schools; but enough students

---

[89] D. A. Winstanley, *Unreformed Cambridge* (Cambridge, 1935), 205. There may have been some association of the new dress with whig reformism, and tories like Mansel objected to the symbolism. Wordsworth, 'Autobiography', 169.

[90] Fowler, *Corpus Christi College*, 289; Chinnery Papers, 4 and 5 March 1808.

at Oxford and Cambridge were still determined to hang the bell on the cat.

What is fascinating, however, is that despite the periodic attempts by officers of the universities to keep students from mischief and to punish offenders, there is at another level a genuine recognition of the new situation. From the second half of the eighteenth century right through the reports of the Royal Commissioners of the 1850s there appeared a new theme which is partly a rationalisation for deficiencies in the administration of university discipline but is also an effort to keep up with the times. It was the theme of the independent student who must not be treated as if he were merely a boy at school. The student is looked upon as having entered young manhood and as being at an age when his judgement and discretion were beginning to form. Too much regulation will suppress his initiative, hinder his development and delay a desired progress towards maturity. Here is the idea expressed in a metaphor memorable for its outrageous consistency:

> We want not men who are clipped and espaliered into any form which the whim of the gardener may dictate, or the narrow limits of his parterre require. Let our saplings take their full spread, and send forth their vigorous shoots in all the boldness and variety of nature. Their luxuriance must be pruned; their distortions rectified; the rust and canker and caterpillar of vice carefully kept from them: we must dig round them, and water them, and replenish the exhaustion of the soil by continual dressing.[91]

These remarks were made in the context of a defence of Oxford discipline against charges brought by Edinburgh-based writers, opening what was to become a lengthy quarrel between the proponents of Scottish and English university education. Since the attack was public, appearing in a new and important political-literary periodical, Oxford dons were forced to state their case to informed opinion and to circulate more widely their efforts to improve the state of student learning. The quarrel forced the more serious dons to review the basis upon which Oxford education was conducted.

The theory of education implied in these lines is important because it does not dwell solely on the responsibilities of the learner, or prescribe the proper course of study for him to follow or lecture him on deficiencies, but because it also requires a certain effort from the teacher. Growth will

---

[91] Edward Copleston, *Reply to the Calumnies of the Edinburgh Review against Oxford* (Oxford, 1810), 157.

occur as a matter of course, 'in all the boldness and variety of nature', but it will also occur indiscriminately or be liable to disease. The plant must be tended but special care must be taken to see that it looks natural. The landscaping metaphors replace a French garden with an English one.

Gardening imagery is not inappropriate to a discussion of educational questions in the early nineteenth century. Mechanistic language was being supplemented by organic images, and the idea of development was coming in to challenge some of the more static conventions of neoclassical thought, as well as to correct the mind-stuffing corollaries derived from *tabula rasa* epistemology. Nevertheless dons were by no means certain how much maintenance the garden required and how much supervision their new plant metaphors implied. There was some difference of opinion on how natural – that is, normal – it was for young men to game, brawl and whore, having once reached a particular stage of life. The difficulty of restraining them, however, lent plausibility to the new theory and gave it currency. Furthermore, into the new bottle a great deal of old wine could be poured: as the gentleman could never learn to be liberal unless he were allowed to squander his patrimony, an undergraduate could never grow to responsible adulthood unless he was given some latitude during a number of formative years. And there was a built-in safety valve in the theory: it promised that irregular conduct was self-correcting and would soon be outgrown.

How much Rousseau went into the making of the theory of the independent student can never be satisfactorily decided. A portrait painting in the Tate Gallery offers us a narrow opening for speculation. The philo-Rousseau Brooke Boothby, painted in 1780–1, is a man no longer young attempting to be dreamy, languid and natural. He clutches a volume with the name of the renegade Frenchman on its spine. The painting is definitely a period piece but no reliable test of the influence of *Emile*. There are hints in the last quarter of the eighteenth century of more permissive treatment of children. Charles James Fox was not able to order his son at Eton to cut his hair and pleaded with him instead.[92] Another, slightly later, writer was unhappy about the corrosive influences eating away at the customary authority relationships of boys and fathers. He could not decide whether the 'modern philosophy' was to blame – 'the fashionable doctrines of equality and independence, and the fashionable declamation against the usurpations of custom and prejudice' – or was itself the effect of new theories of child-rearing. Boys, he complained, were being indulged as never before. They were introduced to adult company

[92] Rosamund Bayne-Powell, *The English Child in the Eighteenth Century* (London, 1939), 2.

earlier, were permitted to hear worldly conversation before their minds were fit for it, were taught to drink wine, spend money, keep late hours and wander freely where once they would have been excluded. 'When boys are treated as men, the vices of men are naturally encouraged.' One result was to make it impossible for teachers to expect from pupils the reverence owed them by custom and station.[93]

The charge need not be taken literally to conclude that important changes were in fact occurring within the family structure of English society.[94] Dons were beginning to notice, although for the most part reluctantly, that undergraduates were arriving at the universities with different values and preparation than formerly. This was recognised as early as 1774. A Cambridge pamphlet of that year argued, with the usual exaggeration of pamphlets, that 'we educate our children, *even from their Cradles*, in a manner very different from former times – We now treat them like men, at an age, when formerly they had scarcely left their Nurseries . . . And we have long found, that we cannot govern our Youth here *now*, as Youth at their age *were wont* to be governed.'[95]

The writer, the wife of a don, offered a different perspective on the question of discipline. If old rules no longer sufficed, new ones needed to be devised, and if old methods no longer worked, new ones had to be tried. She was not talking about admonitions, rustications, compusory chapel, rules against the keeping of pets in college, walking across lawns or frequenting taverns. A different approach to a traditional problem of new proportions was being suggested. As undergraduates were in fact men in years, they ought to be disciplined positively by being invited to learn. 'We should have endeavoured, by every *possible incentive* to study, to have made them *ambitious* of acquiring every *manly attainment*.'[96] The sentiments expressed in this pamphlet occur at precisely the moment when a fundamental reform in the education offered at Cambridge was being proposed. The honours examination system began to assume its familiar pre-Victorian shape. Several decades later at Oxford, where the traditional degree examination system was moribund, systematic efforts were made to revive the principles of examining. In both institutions the new

---

[93] Barrow, *Essay*, II, 252–4, 195, 337.
[94] The implications of these for the universities are discussed in Chapter 6.
[95] *A Letter to the Author of an Observation on the Design of Establishing Annual Examinations at Cambridge* (Cambridge, 1774), 21, Cambridge University Library, Cam.c.774[5]. The author of this anonymously published pamphlet is very likely Mrs John Jebb, who entered the famous controversy over examinations in the 1770s on behalf of her husband. But even if her remarks on child raising are essentially polemical, it is interesting to have them so expressed.
[96] *Ibid.*

examination discipline (as it was called) was significantly related to the new type of student whose independence so baffled and confused the Georgian dons.

EXAMINATION RIDDLES

The development of 'modern' final degree examinations at Oxford and Cambridge has influenced the history of all other forms of selective and qualifying examinations in the United Kingdom, as well as the evolution of the British university system. Final honours schools at Oxford and the tripos examinations at Cambridge are famous throughout the world as model forms of meritocratic examining (see Chapter 4). Yet their precise origins remain obscure. Documents clearly specifying the reasons for their introduction, or motives linked to their introduction, are scarce even though the details of the examinations themselves are plentiful. The principal force behind the Oxford innovations was Cyril Jackson, who left orders that his personal papers were to be destroyed. Minutes of the meetings of the Hebdomadal Board are missing for the period from 1793 to 1800, with trivial exceptions.[97] The Cambridge situation is even more puzzling, since the progress of the tripos was a slow affair, occurring over many decades without as certain a benchmark as the Oxford Examination Statute of 1800. Recently John Gascoigne has suggested that once in existence the tripos could be used to defend Cambridge from charges that the university was a haven for crypto-Jacobites, although no one thought the junior university was as culpable a place of sedition as Oxford. The seriousness of the tripos and its connection to mathematics, the great symbol of progressive thought in the Age of Reason, might have been intended to show that Cambridge was in the business of education not politics.[98] If we cannot locate documents that solve the riddles of the meaning of the two honours examinations, at least we can show how an examination culture was forming in relation to larger political and religious concerns and how both examinations and historical changes were linked to the theme of the appearance of a new ideal-type undergraduate eager for distinction and distinctiveness.

Both universities had inherited a system of oral disputations and exercises, acts and opponencies leading to degrees. It was a curious

---

[97] V. H. H. Green, 'Reformers and Reform in the University', in Sutherland and Mitchell, 623 and 624.

[98] John Gascoigne, 'Mathematics and Meritocracy: The Emergence of the Cambridge Mathematical Tripos', *Social Studies of Science,* 14 (1984), 557–60.

carryover given the importance of writing and print to Protestant countries. We would expect to find written examinations in use, especially since, according to François Furet and Jacques Ozouf, the ability to write is one of the mainsprings of political and social authority. The masses, who have no such skill, cower before those who have the secret, magical gift.[99]

But although the advent of writing and printing gradually replaced an oral with a written culture, the former remained important for governing elites of aristocratic origin. Their lives were led in public. The ability to speak persuasively and effectively was considered necessary for the maintenance of political as well as social authority, and especially in a constitutional monarchy where a parliamentary system of government was dominant. Public speaking was therefore a major part of the education of a governing elite from the Renaissance onwards, when rhetorical models of classical origins became popular. Furthermore, the ability to converse was also part of the public life of aristocracies, especially with the coming of polite learning in the late seventeenth century. In recognition of this importance, Oxford added declamations to its degree exercises in 1662.

The advantages of an oral culture for English public life help explain why written examinations were resisted by many dons, why the new examinations culture was a mixture of oral and written exercises and why the long-run victory of written examinations at university levels was nevertheless complemented by the survival of public speaking and declamations at college levels. The eagerness with which undergraduates founded debating societies, with their metamorphoses into the famous unions, is further proof of the strength of the oral tradition.

Each of these forms of examining had different virtues and benefits, and each therefore had their own body of adherents. But the two forms were also antagonistic in a special way. The scholastic disputations served the oral culture, but written examinations, while they had certain advantages special to the universities, also served a meritocratic culture that was threatening to those who earned their places in society through birth and patronage. The battle between the two forms of examining, therefore, carried on until the newer, as suiting changing political circumstances, won out over the older.

In the meantime we find the oral, public culture flourishing in Cambridge and Oxford, especially the latter, where classical studies took pride of place as providing models for eloquence and masterly expression.

---

[99] François Furet and Jacques Ozouf, *Reading and Writing, Literacy in France from Calvin to Jules Ferry* (Cambridge, 1982), 305.

But mathematics had a part to play, being valued for the rigour and logic it lent to oral debate, to 'method and arrangement' in speech.[100] Sir Robert Peel, one of Jackson's protégés at Christ Church, exemplified the union of both classics and mathematics in his performance at the honours examination at Oxford. He received his degree in 1807 after achieving a double first. His favourite authors were Cicero, Quintilian and Homer, but he was specifically praised for his answers to an oral examination on *Robertson's Conic Sections*. And (it was after the fact) his facility in mathematics was held to be useful to the future financier.[101] But this justification was already pointing in a new direction.

Despite their intimate association with aristocratic culture, the inherited scholastic exercises have usually been denounced as farcical, elementary and inconsistent with the standards that ought to prevail in serious universities. Some students found any exercise challenging, partly because they were loungers but also because preparation for university work undertaken at school was uneven and unpredictable. But the better students were bored, and mercifully in some colleges they were allowed to skip lectures considered rudimentary.[102] More recent appraisals of university teaching provide a more confused or confusing pattern. While historians like Dame Lucy Sutherland have suggested that Oxford authorities enforced the taking of the scholastic tests, she also remarked that the administration of examinations was slipshod. No one failed the BA examination.[103] Professorial lectures at Oxford were not closely related to the examinations (nor were they so at Cambridge), but this is hardly as great an indictment as it appears. The irrelevance of the public lectures encouraged professors to lecture on new subjects like experimental science outside the scope of the first degree. These were even sometimes popular, but college teachers often refused to allow undergraduates to attend them on the grounds that time would be taken away from their own teaching. The same attitude prevailed at Cambridge. The college tutors opposed a far-reaching set of university examination proposals in 1773, fearful that their monopoly on teaching would be challenged. They were also concerned about introducing subjects not taught in the colleges.[104]

In the absence of a strong degree-based university curriculum, the

[100] *Sir Robert Peel*, ed. Charles Stuart Parker, I (London, 1891), 18.
[101] *Ibid.*, 19. For Oxford examinations see also L. S. Sutherland, 'Curriculum', in Sutherland and Mitchell, 469–85.
[102] P. Quarrie, 'The Christ Church Collection Books', in Sutherland and Mitchell, 522. Robert Southey's tutor, Thomas How, did not think his lectures would be useful and told the poet to find something better to do when he came up in 1792. Fairer, in Sutherland and Mitchell, 804.
[103] Sutherland, 'Curriculum', in Sutherland and Mitchell, 471ff, 475.
[104] *Ibid.*, 473; Winstanley, *Unreformed Cambridge*, 323–27.

Oxford colleges took up the slack. Student notebooks and the surviving 'collections' of readings and assessments at colleges like Christ Church record the range of readings and academic interests of undergraduates. One notebook from about 1744 contains extracts from reading, usually poetry, Latin and Greek, but also Clarendon's history of the great rebellion and Caesar's invasion of Britain. There are also comments on the excerpts, sometimes the student's but at other times the observations of someone else. A few lines of verse appear to be scribbled down, as well as mathematical propositions. There are lecture notes taken from Bradeley's course of mathematical lectures and experiments with space for nineteen lectures (the student appears to have missed only two of them). A final set of entries consists of recipes for horse purges.[105]

The colleges at both universities provided religious education, were somewhat flexible in their assignments, expected both oral and written declamations from students, ordinarily in Latin (these might be sent to parents) and offered lectures on special subjects. Some rich students tended to be idle despite the best efforts of college tutors to force them to study, as at Christ Church where from 1773 onwards they were required to do 'Collections'.[106]

There was enough being demanded to keep conscientious students sporadically busy, especially in the second half of the eighteenth century. Bentham prepared a declamation on the evils of drink in 1761 and wrote home to say that college scholars were examined for three days. He and other scholars were locked in hall from nine in the morning until dinner, and from dinner to prayers, where they had to do themes. He disputed in the Schools with another undergraduate in March 1762, being twice an opponent and once a respondent. '[It] is very uncomfortable work, as we stay an hour and a half or more in the cold; the Fees are ½ a Crown each time.' In the next year he disputed for the BA before a large, standing audience. He was up for nearly an hour, about twice as long as was customary.[107] Possibly the work was more physically than mentally gruelling. The thought is not far-fetched. Stamina, endurance, 'masculinity' were of possibly greater importance to a ruling class than developing brain power.

These instances of activity notwithstanding, the record of steady application is spotty. There were moments of intensity with lots of fallow periods, some indifference on the part of tutors and proctors, and a

---

[105] MS Top Oxon.e.379, Bodleian.
[106] Sutherland, 'Curriculum', in Sutherland and Mitchell, 476.
[107] Sprigge, *Bentham*, 55, 59, 71, 87.

relative absence of zeal, especially at Oxford since the Cambridge tripos was increasingly pointing towards competition with its order of merit rankings and rivalries between colleges for high places, even as early as 1763. This development has given rise to the sentiment that the object of both examinations was to 'raise and standardize performance'.[108] While this explanation may even make sense for certain historical periods besides our own, it is not necessarily a satisfactory interpretation of the reasons behind the earlier reforms. We cannot accept it without serious review. Surely the basic questions to be asked are why was it important to raise and standardise performance and what was to be gained by doing so?

The modern rationale for examinations is based on three distinct but interrelated assumptions: (1) that examinations discover and encourage merit or achievement; (2) that merit can be measured either comparatively through competition or absolutely; (3) that merit must be discovered, encouraged and measured because only by these means can talent be correctly allocated among existing occupations or career opportunities. The third point is absolutely central to the meritocratic ideal. It has given rise to a theory frequently employed by social historians that examinations principally benefit a group or class rising in status and income and searching for means of extending its social and economic opportunities. A reverse theory is sometimes used which states that examinations or educational innovations sometimes benefit a group or class confronted by declining social and economic opportunities and desirous of holding off impending calamity.

The three assumptions and several theories have a certain validity if carefully qualified when applied to the passage of the great civil service reforms of the mid-Victorian period. It makes a certain sense to speak of these reforms as embodying the principle of the career open to talent. But how far can the conventional explanation of the rise of the merit ideal be applied to the much earlier period when the Oxford examination system was in its infancy and the much older Cambridge tripos still in a state of development? To prove that the meritocratic ideal was the motive behind the reforms we would need to have a more solid grasp of certain historical variables. We would have to know, for example, the extent to which success in the Oxbridge examinations yielded definite valuable rewards and recognition both within the universities and outside of them. Gascoigne has shown a positive correlation between wranglers and appointments to college fellowships from the 1760s onwards, yet he

---

[108] A. V. Judges, 'The Evolution of Examinations', *The World Year Book of Education* (London, 1969), 23.

acknowledged that the rank order in the tripos was less significant outside Cambridge.[109] Even within the two universities a reward for excellence was not guaranteed (see Chapter 4). The idea of rewarding merit was certainly present, even in the later eighteenth century, but not the circumstances that made its concrete realisation possible. Very likely the closer we come to 1850 the more we may find that there is a rising curve of correlation between the honours student and recruitment to elite positions. But in 1800 or 1810 or 1825 this could not have been the case. The meritocratic ideal does not help us find the roots of the famous examination systems. The undergraduate in search of a career was far more interested in making contacts, in finding friends whose families wielded influence and patronage or were in a position to make powerful recommendations. A reputation for ability earned at the university might bring and no doubt did bring talent to the attention of those who could dispose of it; but merit had to be accommodated within the existing network of patrons and sponsors.

If it is not possible, given the evidence currently at hand, to connect the origins and growth of competitive examinations to changes in the occupational structure of English society in the later Georgian period, it is equally impossible to use the theories of rising or falling social mobility. There is no major new or old class or status group in the undergraduate population which is desirous of opening opportunites for itself or feels its position in the social structure threatened by changes in the society as a whole. That there were individuals who attempted to extend their career opportunities does not invalidate this point. If we use income rather than social class as the operative variable, interesting results might emerge as the two are not necessarily synonymous. But we are not yet in a position to offer generalisations based on detailed estimates of the family income of members of the undergraduate community, especially the changes in family circumstances that undoubtedly occurred.

Other explanations for the reasons behind the famous reforms must be sought. The problem should be approached in a different way, looking inward as well as outward. We must try to recapture the beliefs of the dons mainly responsible for the changes, explaining the motives and circumstances behind the examinations and especially the institutional and historical context in which they set roots and grew, to the extent that surviving evidence allows. We must then turn to the examinations themselves, showing how their internal characteristics yield further evidence for the reasons behind their revival. Finally we must return to the

[109] Gascoigne, 'Mathematics', 561.

undergraduates. They were after all the ones who were expected to sit the examinations and in fact did so, reluctantly at first but in rapidly increasing numbers. We shall find a highly mixed response on the part of students to examinations, not so much to their existence or to the necessity to take them, but to their finality. The old scholastic exercises only required students to pass, but the tripos and the Oxford honours schools ranked or classified candidates according to their performance on Judgement Day. Some students tried to discount failure. Others embraced victory with a shout. Still others were paralysed by the experience and thereby weakened such chances as they had through worry and ill-health.[110]

But for most students the conventional examination discipline rarely worked. The average number of students taking the Cambridge Senate House examinations was only 45 per year from 1767 to 1799 out of 114 BAs.[111] Clearly there was an abundance of leisure, although, as we have noticed, leisure provided the opportunity for the development of a new configuration of undergraduate activities. It now occurred to some members of the universities to tap that leisure in a different way. It was suggested that the Cambridge examination system be altered in order to force wealthy students to study. The suggestion was not adopted for a number of reasons. The man from whom the idea came was suspected of being a Unitarian – and in fact was. D. A. Winstanley, in explaining the conservative position, argues that the academic tories were not blindly anti-reform but 'feared for the peace and discipline of the University'.[112] Before dismissing this statement as specious, let us recall that Georgian students rioted for diversion and welcomed any controversy that could produce an exciting distraction. Even at the supposed solemnity of assizes, the gownsmen of Oxford created a great din, interrupting proceedings, and for some reason the judges failed to keep order.[113] Fear on the part of the dons was justified. But while acknowledging this, mention also must be made of their strong desire to prevent students from absorbing heretical ideas likely to disrupt the 'alliance' – to use Warburton's slippery anti-Erastian word – of Church and State to which the universities owed so much.

From the 1770s onward the governing authorities of England were challenged by a revival of Old Dissent. This was followed by the different challenge – military as well as ideological – of the bourgeois revolution in

[110] Chapter 4.   [111] Gascoigne, 'Mathematics', 552.
[112] Winstanley, *Unreformed Cambridge*, 315–16.
[113] Richard Lovell Edgworth, *Memoirs* (London, 1844), 58. The year was about 1761.

France, greeted with some enthusiasm by leading Nonconformists and an occasional freethinking peer or squire. In the early 1770s, because of the opening of the campaign by Dissenters for the removal of civil disabilities, the universities became embroiled in a major controversy to eliminate the oath of allegiance to the Church of England required of all undergraduates at some point in their careers. The movement to rescind subscription to the Thirty-nine Articles failed, but not before another university reform was proposed at Cambridge.

In the 1770s, at the time of the controversy over subscription, the Nonconformist threat to the 'alliance' was appreciated, but nevertheless there existed considerable sympathy for the protest against an oath of allegiance to the Church as by law established. Even the high steward as well as chancellor of Cambridge had supported efforts to revoke subscription. Sympathy was withdrawn when prominent Dissenting intellectuals welcomed the new republic in France. Quite suddenly the case for Roman Catholic relief, which had also started some decades earlier, acquired more favour. Not only did the prime minister William Pitt himself in the last decade of the century support Catholic emancipation, but the universities, especially Oxford, were very active on behalf of émigré priests, several of whom had come to reside in the town. In 1792 members of the university very generously contributed £500 to a fund to support the exiled clergy,[114] and many years later the testy rector of Lincoln College – to whom has been attributed the remark (or something like it), 'I suffer no one to be idle except myself' – denounced Nonconformists as a greater threat to education and morality than Roman Catholics.[115] This did not become the universal opinion, it must be added. The proposal to emancipate the English Catholics remained controversial in Oxford and Cambridge throughout the ensuing years.

The universities made the same connection between Dissent and Jacobinism that Burke did in his greatest rhetorical flights. They saw that the revolution in France was a demonstration of the power of ideas, of what one Church magazine called 'that reptile philosophy which would materialise and brutify the whole intellectual system'.[116] Caused by ideologues, men of education and learning, the French Revolution was an upheaval that threatened European security and aristocratic privilege on

---

[114] R. H. Cholmondeley, *The Heber Letters, 1783–1832* (London, 1950), 162–3.
[115] F. J. Haverfield, *Extracts from the 'Gentleman's Magazine' Relating to Oxford, 1731–1800* (Oxford 1890), 446; Edward Tatham, *An Address to the Members of the Hebdomadal Meeting* (22 June 1810), 23–6, esp. 25.
[116] J. M., 'On the Proposed Regulations in the University of Oxford', *British Magazine*, 1 (1800), 426.

more than one front and consequently had to be fought directly on those fronts. Undergraduates especially – so thought the dons – had to be protected because it was impossible to isolate them. In the turbulent environment of the 1790s everyone was exposed to French propaganda. There were scenes – tumultuous scenes – where orators, even distinguished politicians, stirred up undergraduates with panegyrics on Gallic liberty. In the later 1790s a crowd of students gathered on Castle Hill in Cambridge to hear the duke of Bedford, who '[In] a Brutus crop, in contrast with the full-bottomed wigs of the Seniors, and powdered locks of the Undergraduates of the University, stood up above the crowd, and made a long and vehement harangue in favour of those revolutionary measures which he had come there to advocate.' He was challenged by the Public Orator [of Cambridge] – 'A greater triumph over a demagogue assemblage was perhaps never achieved' – and the reward that Pitt preserved for the successful Mansel was the mastership of Trinity College.[117]

It is within this setting of challenge and tension that the Oxford New Examination Statute of 1800 must be set. It falls exactly in the period of a desperate military campaign in southern Europe, Pitt's second suspension of the Habeas Corpus Act as part of a counter-revolutionary policy and his measures placing the country on a wartime economy. The dons who were most instrumental in establishing the new examinations were those with the closest ties to Pitt's ministry, like the dean of Christ Church, Cyril Jackson, or other determined reforming heads like John Eveleigh, the provost of Oriel, and John Parsons, the master of Balliol, all described by memoirists as tories. (Parsons was suspicious of the newly formed junior common room at Balliol. He burned its rules and banned meetings.)[118] In his Bampton lectures for 1791 Eveleigh tried to counteract the mischief of 'an adventurous and sceptical philosophy' by refocusing undergraduate attention on orthodox theology.[119] The *British Magazine* immediately caught the connection between the examination reforms and affairs on the other side of the Channel. The French Revolution, wrote one of its contributors, was an international conspiracy which threatened morality

---

[117] Clement Carlyon, *Early Years and Late Reflections*, III (London, 1856), 50–1. Schoolboys were influenced by impassioned end-of-century ideas. Reginald Heber's father described his son's schoolfellows as responding to the 'prevailing Rage of the Times' and 'standing up for the *Rights of Boys*', adopting 'Tom Paine's principles and doctrines'. Apparently there had been a barring-out at Reginald's school that was put down by cutting off all supplies to the boys. 'So may all *rightful Monarchs* ever prevail against Levellers and Republicans the Pests of Society.' Bod.MS Eng. lett. c.204³. The date is 29 December 1792.

[118] Green, 'Reformers and Reform', 623.

[119] John Eveleigh, *Sermons Preached before the University of Oxford* (Oxford, 1794), 2–3.

and civilisation. It was promoted and advanced by educated men who nourished the ideas of revolution and prepared the attack on religion. It was important to understand, insisted the writer in what comes close to being a theory of the avant-garde, that the opinions of the philosophers spread everywhere throughout society. 'It is an observation of great truth, and as great importance, that the opinion of the learned part of a society will in time unavoidably become the general opinion. The present age has exhibited a melancholy example of its truth.' This being the case, it was necessary for the universities to decontaminate the fountains of learning (his image) and tighten their hold on undergraduates. The new examinations, the writer closed optimistically, will check the profligacy of idle young men and combat atheism by improving religious instruction.[120] William Barrow came to the same conclusion in 1802, believing that 'the rising generation' would 'learn to resist and refute the metaphysical subtleties, which have thrown half the nations of Europe into confusion' in the universities. At the same time and by the same means, they would learn patriotism and sound moral and religious conduct.[121]

The decision to introduce a new examination statute at Oxford was connected to the explosive international situation provoked by the renewal of war with the Directory and to the fear that the new independent student acknowledged in educational theory might embrace unsettling ideas. Dons had first attempted to discipline this type of student and then had finally resigned themselves to the situation when the events in France intervened. This produced a new working principle which was well represented in Edward Copleston's student-plant metaphor, that the undergraduate must not be indiscriminately trimmed but that his growth should also not be neglected. To the old catalogue of disciplinary restraints and punishments devised for schoolboys was added a new effort to promote ideas which would best allow the student to take his place as a leader and not a critic of society and its established institutions.

In the changing environment of 1800 it is not surprising to find that the great educational innovators were also the great disciplinarians. Jackson, when he was not disbanding incipient debating societies in Christ Church, was restraining students from drinking and gambling and trying to correct coarse manners. Eveleigh is credited by his supporters with having improved decorum at Oriel, for fellows as well as students. He is said to have started the Senior Common Room of Oriel on the road to its famed 'plain living and high thinking'. Parsons, besides the support he gave to university examinations, also reinvigorated the Balliol examination system

---

[120] *British Magazine*, 425.   [121] Barrow, *Essay*, II, 308.

and, like Eveleigh, firmly ruled the common room. All were interested in
serious scholarship and advanced proven fellows to responsible college
positions.[122] These men were not the first Oxbridge heads to realise the
disciplinary potential of examinations. Samuel Powell at St John's,
Cambridge, had embarked on what may seem a similar course in the
1770s. He required annual college examinations on one of the gospels or
acts (scholarship exams had existed since 1678) and awarded prizes out of
his own pocket. Yet Powell differed from the famous Oxford heads in one
important respect. He was concerned exclusively with the welfare of his
own college, jealousy protected its position against the university and
vigorously campaigned against the reforms proposed in the 1770s.[123]
Jackson, Eveleigh and Parsons attempted to improve the order and
standards of the entire university and promoted reforms in the university
as strenuously as they improved their own colleges. The relevant point
was made in 1799 by Edward Pearson, master of Sidney Sussex College.
College exercises were not a sufficient means for addressing the problems
of educational discipline because college exercises were not as public as
university based examinations.[124]

After 1800 the new discipline of Oxford examinations was conspicuous
everywhere. Honours schools was driving reform at the college level. Not
only were college tutors engaged in the task of preparing students for the
competition, but various kinds of other educational incentives were being
tried: cash, book prizes and medals. At St John's, Oxford, beginning in
1802, undergraduates had to be examined in hall before the president and
seniority every term, an innovation that became known as 'Collections'.
Book prizes began in the same college in 1811 as a reward for gaining high
honours in the degree examinations.[125] At Trinity College, Cambridge, an
entrance examination was started in 1810, although the examination was
not competitive and certain categories of students were exempted. Also at
Trinity some eight years later third-year students were required to take a
special examination. This meant that students at Trinity now had to take
an examination every year, for it had long been the practice to require
them of first- and second-year students.[126] At Cambridge in 1824 another
university examination was started for all second-year students and at the

[122] Godley, Oxford, 160. M. L. Banks, ed., Blundell's Worthies (London, 1904), 99. W. R. Ward, Victorian Oxford (London, 1965), 10–13; D. W. Rannie, Oriel College (London, 1900), 178; Green, 'Reformers and Reform', 624; DNB.
[123] Winstanley, Unreformed Cambridge, 316–20, 327–8, 330–1; DNB.
[124] Gascoigne, 'Mathematics', 557.
[125] W. C. Costin, The History of St. John's College, Oxford (Oxford, 1958), 245.
[126] Ball, Trinity Notes, 143.

same time a second tripos examination, this one in classics, began, although no one could read for classics without first doing mathematics. In the second half of the eighteenth century two chancellor's medals for Latin verse and an English essay existed at Oxford. In 1810 a third medal for a Latin essay was instituted. In 1817 the Craven Scholarship of the university was opened to competition, the money having previously been claimed by founder's kin. Copleston, one of the first of a new generation of university examiners, answered the criticisms of the Edinburgh reviewers in 1810 by outlining the Oxford programme of studies. At the beginning of the third year, students took a public examination allowing them to go on to the degree examinations. The Sophista Generalis consisted of elementary geometry and algebra, Aldrich's *Logic* and construing from Greek and Latin texts. After the third year, but no later than the end of the fourth, oral degree examinations were offered in *literae humaniores*, which consisted of Greek and Roman texts (the Greek Testament, Aristotle, Quintilian and a choice of Homer, Pindar, Aristophanes, Thucydides, Tacitus, Livy, Cicero and Juvenal), questions on doctrine and sacred history, rhetoric, ethics and logic. For some students a mathematical examination followed, mainly written. But after presenting what he called a 'formidable array of books and sciences', Copleston acknowledged that students of 'lower ability' but 'tolerably regular' in academic habits 'must be allowed to pass'.[127]

In both universities in the first third of the nineteenth century incentives to industry multiplied; miscellaneous exercises, themes, declamations were available, and various kinds of minor but not insignificant rewards for academic success became commonplace as efforts were made to improve the academic tone and reputation of the ancient universities. Indeed, rewards for success virtually accompanied the innovations. At Caius a fellow of the college named Francis Schuldham provided in his will for the gift of plate to the student excelling in the Senate House examinations, and this has remained a coveted prize.[128] Various opportunities still existed for evading serious academic work, and several colleges, King's College being one, held onto ancient privileges which excused their students from university examinations. But King's students went in for the examination anyhow, eager to gain the myrtle. By 1830 there could be no doubt that both universities had substantially improved their teaching. The presence of large numbers of evangelical students also led to an improvement in morals and conduct in some quarters. But if these developments were not generally reported in the press or widely

[127] Copleston, *Reply*, 138–44.   [128] Brooke, *Gonville and Caius*, 182.

advertised, it was because a culture of competitive examinations and the discipline accompanying it was not yet fully legitimate nor required of everyone. The 'old college system' seemed still to prevail. But another reason was that undergraduates, despite a new system of hurdles and barriers, seemed in some respects to be more independent than ever before and their behaviour more worrisome.

THE NEW EXERCISES

In order to understand the attitude of dons toward independent students, it is necessary to discuss the characteristics of the new exercises. The spread of an examining culture is in itself a landmark, but it is not sufficient to explain why the examinations developed in a particular direction. For that it is necessary for a moment to return to the scholastic disputations which both the tripos and *literae humaniores* ('greats') and mathematical examinations at Oxford eventually superseded. While the new examinations went off in an utterly different direction, they were in the beginning influenced by the disputations in several important ways.

The disputations were debates according to the rules of scholastic logic. The object was to find some fallacy in the argument of an opponent, some technicality by which he could be stymied. There was naturally some incidental testing of knowledge, since the syllogisms depended upon an acquaintance with traditional authorities, but it was the debate more than the knowledge that commanded interest. A debate implied a winner or a loser, and there was consequently an element of rivalry or sport in the old exercises. A debate also implied an audience. Hence the disputations were called public examinations, and the disputants were encouraged to perform. Winning the dispute was important, but winning in front of an audience, especially an animated audience, was exhilarating. A good wrangle excited curiosity and interest. Losing the debate was a public embarrassment, and the loser was exposed to the ridicule of observers according to the rules of shame typical of ruling classes that cannot afford public embarrassment.[129]

By the middle of the eighteenth century the disputations at both universities had deteriorated because students did not take them seriously, and the universities did not insist upon adequate preparation. The disputations themselves had become so formalised that answers could be

---

[129] Henry Latham, *On the Action of Examinations Considered as a Means of Selection* (Cambridge, 1877), 98ff, has some interesting remarks along these lines.

virtually rehearsed and all possible responses reduced to a few working formulas known as 'strings' and passed down from tutor to tutor, student to student. Even strings required some attention, however. As there were numerous undergraduates who did not even bother to rehearse, various kinds of cheating went on. The story circulated at Cambridge that one teacher devised a means of signalling answers to his pupil from the audience by the way he opened, buttoned, or threw back his coat.[130] Even if the story is spurious, it makes a point.

An early Oxford critic, John Napleton, fellow of Brasenose, appreciated the features of the disputation and advocated reviving the form in the 1770s. He was especially interested in the feature of open disputing. A debate in front of a group of fellow undergraduates and dons, he thought, enabled the university to encourage industry and expose indolence. The scholastic examinations were supposed to have accomplished this end, but at Oxford peer pressure operated to prevent undergraduates from competing. To do so was to risk being called vain and pedantic.[131] At Cambridge the charge was that moderators had corrupted the system by preventing matches between men of unequal ability or different habits of work.[132] What was required as an antidote to the endemic laziness of students was an appeal to lofty values such as public honour, or the threat of its opposite, public disgrace. The problem with Oxford's examinations, Napleton offered, was 'that they are become TOO private'.[133]

Napleton's thinking was perfectly in keeping with the ideology of high Georgian neoclassical culture with its emphasis on appearance, style and manner. For at least half a century writers, publicists and satirists had attempted to raise the level of social behaviour by emphasising the ideals of reputation, honour and virtue and by repeating constantly the favourite maxims and sentiments of great Roman moralists of the rhetorical tradition. The appeal of their writings lay in the connections that could be made between appearance and virtue and the ease with which the higher qualities praised in antiquity could be passed off as manners. Certainly style and a little Tully were useful in disguising the pervasive realities of Georgian social and political life, the world of connections, special arrangements, self-interest and nepotism.

Napleton's proposals were part of the reforming spirit of the 1770s that included the Feathers Tavern anti-subscription movement and

---

[130] *The Book of the Cambridge Review, 1879–1897* (Cambridge, 1898), 145.
[131] John Napleton, *Considerations on the Public Exercises for the First and Second Degrees in the University of Oxford* (1773), 24, 45–6, 12.
[132] Winstanley, *Unreformed Cambridge,* 45.
[133] Napleton, *Considerations,* 5.

examination controversy at Cambridge. They did not carry far in his own time, however; but when the new Oxford examinations were introduced, they were primarily *viva voce*. Although written parts were added a few years later, the examinations remained basically public and took place, as a critic of 1822 reported, before a large body of spectators.[134]

At Cambridge the old disputations lingered on side by side with the newer written Senate House mathematics examinations until 1839, with a good dispute occurring only every now and then. While by statute only the disputations were required for a BA, in actuality the tripos became indispensable as early as 1790. Even in 1763 the disputations were really no more than a sorting out procedure for the tripos to decide who was to compete for distinctions in the final round. Like the Oxford examinations, the tripos had been oral in the first decades of its existence. After 1770 all questions were dictated orally but answers had to be written down while examiners paused between questions so that students could finish their writing. Theoretically examiners were empowered to ask oral questions until 1827 when new regulations turned the tripos, both questions and answers, into a completely written examination.[135]

Gradually, but only gradually, the Oxford examinations followed the path of the tripos and became mainly written examinations. In the early 1830s the BA part of the examinations required five days of writing and only one day of *viva voce* examining. This change was partly the result of what a perceptive Victorian called the tendency for examiners to introduce modifications to suit their own convenience. 'Greats' was an examination in several classical subjects, and the range was far too extensive for most examiners, especially in the days of oral examining. It was easier to evaluate a written examination. That could be done privately or in consultation with other examiners, examination sources could be checked and marks and rankings assigned. The task was easier yet if the number of subjects examined was limited.[136]

There were other considerations, however, besides the internal development that pushed the Oxford and Cambridge examinations in a different direction from their origins. The first was the same reason that made dons suspicious of the new debating societies and junior common rooms, the desire to avoid controversy. This was a distinct departure from the spirit of the old disputations. A vigorous dispute was exactly what

---

[134] Thomas Vowler Short, *A Letter Addressed to the Very Reverend the Dean of Christ Church on the State of the Public Examinations in the University of Oxford* (Oxford, 1822), 16.

[135] Ball, *Mathematical Tripos*, 189–214, and *Cambridge Papers*, 252–316; D. A. Winstanley, *Early Victorian Cambridge* (Cambridge, 1955), 149–52.

[136] See Latham, *Examinations*, and also Ward, *Victorian Oxford*, 56–7.

spectators wished to hear. But in the first third of the nineteenth century dons were afraid that wrangles would occur over controversial political and religious questions. Napleton had concerned himself with this difficulty. He speculated that the disputations had been successful in past centuries because books were in short supply and knowledge was therefore uncertain. Students went to hear a dispute not only to experience vicariously the joys of open combat but also to learn. Napleton more than hinted that in his own time knowledge was no longer uncertain. All the essential answers to great philosophical and religious questions were known. Hence fresh answers were not to be expected, and controversy was unnecessary.[137]

Georgian sentiment on the question of original knowledge, while never rigid, nevertheless leaned in Napleton's direction. While there was great and confusing discussion concerning whether it was possible to be original, whether genius could exist without rules and whether rules followed nature, the general tendency in literary, artistic and academic circles was to regard knowledge as foreknown or received. Originality was not valued *per se* but had to depend upon imitation. Of classical origin, this artistic doctrine permitted considerable variety. As Sir Joshua Reynolds wrote, the highly disciplined mind could be safely allowed to play on the edges of fancy. But undergraduates, whose faculties had yet to be disciplined and whose activities were suspicious, could hardly claim this intellectual privilege. Even among scientists, until the first part of the nineteenth century, there was general agreement that absolute truth had been reached or was capable of being reached, even though here too it was possible to find differences of opinion on how real a mathematical theorem or proposition could be. Neoclassicism reinforced these general assumptions by the importance it attached to a few fundamental axioms of human behaviour and the respect paid ancient writers for having perceived universal principles operating in all areas of civilised endeavour. The net conclusion of Georgian thinking on the nature of knowledge was to regard it as more closed than open and to discourage students, especially in times of national and international disturbance, from too much speculation and free-thinking. William Hazlitt's essays of the early 1820s, wherein genius was defined as 'exclusive and self-willed, quaint and peculiar', and originality as 'the discovery of new and valuable truth', open a door, if not the very first door so to be opened, onto another and to us familiar world.[138]

[137] Napleton, *Considerations*, 17.
[138] Wiliam Hazlitt, *Selected Essays*, ed. J. R. Nabholtz (New York, 1970), 32, 38.

Copleston, who as a tutor at Oriel actively supported Eveleigh's reforms, unequivocally maintained that received knowledge alone constituted a university education. It was less important, he thought, to produce a few great minds 'exploring untrodden regions' than to turn out 'an annual supply of men, whose minds are . . . impressed with what we hold to be the soundest principles of policy and religion'. Copleston denied that he was adamantly opposed to discovery and experiment, but he did not think they were appropriate to a university (a point upon which Newman agreed). Once again calling upon his ample supply of agricultural images, he confidently proclaimed that 'experiments be tried, and repeatedly tried, [but] in some insignificant spot, some corner of the farm: but let us not risk the whole harvest of the year upon a doubtful project'. In religion there were no discoveries whatsoever to be made. 'The scheme of Revelation we think is closed, and we expect no new light on earth to break in upon us.'[139] Another Oxonian, although not a don, repeated these sentiments in a milder tone in 1810. Commenting upon the university curriculum, he observed that as there was little time at the university to teach anything but the rudiments of knowledge, it was important 'to teach, in the first place, those old and established principles that are beyond the reach of controversy'.[140] On this great educational question the opinions of Cambridge men were indistinguishable from those of Oxonians. Frederick Pollock, looking back from 1869 to his Cambridge experiences in 1806 when he was ranked first in the mathematics tripos as senior wrangler, thought that the Cambridge examinations had changed from what he knew as a student. 'I think a Cambridge education has for its object to make good members of society – not to extend science and make profound mathematicians.'[141] In 1821 an obscure, well-intentioned gentleman wrote to the vice-chancellor of Cambridge proposing to found two annual prizes to be awarded to two bachelors who passed the best examination in four works of religion and theology: the Bible, the Homilies of the Church of England, Bishop Pearson on the Creed and Burnet's abridgment of his own history of the Reformation. 'In fixing on the forementioned Books I have endeavoured to select such as are altogether unobjectionable.'[142] Henry Latham, in surveying the history of examinations in England, understood the dislike of questions that allowed interpretive answers when he noticed that ethics did not become a tripos

---

[139] Copleston, *Reply*, 150–2.
[140] Henry Home Drummond, *Observations Suggested by the Strictures of the Edinburgh Review upon Oxford . . .* (Edinburgh, 1810), 17.
[141] Ball, *Mathematical Tripos*, 113.
[142] Cambridge University Library, Cam.a.500.5[22].

subject in the first part of the nineteenth century because it left too much
room for varieties of opinion. In fact, early on the Senate House exercises
included examining on Locke and on William Paley's *Principles of Morals
and Political Philosophy*, but these texts disappeared, doubtless to avoid
raising uncomfortable questions.[143]

The desire to restrict the area of controversy that an examination might
provoke was one of the main reasons why the examinations ceased to
be oral and became written. Historians usually associate the growth of
written examinations with the preference for more rigorous and objective
examinations. In the written examination, especially if it is taken
anonymously, external considerations like personality and manner do not
influence the outcome. Nor is the examiner allowed to prefer candidates
from certain colleges or introduce pet topics without warning, as was
happening at Oxford in the 1820s.[144]

It should now be apparent why a conclusion such as the object of the
new examinations was to 'raise and standardize performance', if routinely
correct, is also insufficient. It should also be apparent that there is no
contradiction between the search for objectivity and the desire to reduce
controversy. The supporters of the examination system earnestly desired
to improve the standard of undergraduate achievement. The way to do so
was to devise a test of excellence immediately recognisable. The way to
achieve a more accurate and certain means of evaluating a student's work
was to narrow the range of likely disagreement and carefully define the
area of knowledge students were expected to know. The Senate House
examinations in particular became narrower, being basically geometry.
Their original relationship to Newtonian natural philosophy became
tenuous, and the educational aims of the examinations were more or less
equated with the spirit of the old oral disputations in logic and rhetoric.[145]
It is interesting to observe that once the decision was reached to make
the tripos into a single-subject examination, certain famous innovations
conveniently encouraged the trend. Technical changes permitting greater
precision of reasoning, like the new analytical mathematics at Cambridge,
were applicable only to written examinations. As Whewell much later

[143] Paley may have been used in colleges, however. Latham, *Examinations*, 127–8. John
Gascoigne, *Cambridge in the Age of the Enlightenment* (Cambridge, 1989), 272. Martha
Garland, *Cambridge before Darwin, The Ideal of a Liberal Education, 1800–1860* (Cambridge,
1980), nimbly describes the unitary or closed conception of truth assumed in the
Cambridge curriculum. The question is more problematically treated in Richard Yeo,
*Defining Science, William Whewell, Natural Knowledge and Public Debate in Early Victorian
Britain* (Cambridge, 1993), and further discussed in *Metascience*, 5 (1994).
[144] Short, *Letter*, 18n; Ward, *Victorian Oxford*, 58.
[145] Gascoigne, *Cambridge in the Age of the Enlightenment*, 273.

complained in the 1840s, the Continental notation was unsuited to oral examining.[146]

The switch from *viva voce* to written examinations can be accounted for in another way. Not only was a greater degree of fairness and accuracy possible in evaluating written answers, but the entire examination experience was positive rather than negative. In the written examination a student was examined only in what he knew, whereas in the *viva* his weaknesses were probed.

There is a last important reason why written examinations in time supplanted oral ones, and that is the sheer number of undergraduates presenting themselves for degree examinations. As matriculation levels rose and the examinations became a necessary trial for all ambitious students, the burden of examining increased. Whereas only a handful of Oxford students had to be examined orally in the first decade of the nineteenth century, several hundred came forward in the 1820s. Scheduling became a serious problem, and what had been the work of only a few days became the weary effort of many weeks. Written examinations were the solution to more than one difficulty.

The Oxbridge oral culture lived on in student debating and history societies in both the colleges and the universities as part of an expanding programme of university sponsored activities in the second half of the nineteenth century. But the examination system no longer carried the ideals associated with previous eras. This was the end result of a long-term epistemological shift where truth was no longer assumed to issue from public argument with the aid of various logical systems but was likely to be the outcome of solitary study and reflection more suited to an introspective and private phase in the history of civilisation.[147]

There is no conspiracy of dons at work, and no conspiracy theory intended by this analysis. It is not necessary to deny that there were forthright educational motives behind the examination system in order to affirm that the examinations also performed a disciplinary function and were strongly regarded as essential instruments of socialisation. Nor is it a question of mixed motives so much as entangled ones. Education was synonymous with discipline, indistinguishable from right conduct – not the first nor the last time in the history of teaching. 'Discipline' meant a process of instruction and study through which portions of the mind were stimulated and mental powers enhanced. It also bore a second meaning as

---

[146] William Whewell, *Of a Liberal Education* ... (London, 1850), Part I, 186.
[147] J. Yolton, 'Schoolmen, Logic and Philosophy', in Sutherland and Mitchell, 565–92, has stimulated this speculation.

restraint, regulation or punishment, both essential if the man was to be awakened in the youth. Throughout the second half of the eighteenth century reformers proposed educational changes in both universities with the problem of undergraduate indolence primarily in mind. Even John Jebb, the most politically radical of the reformers, spoke in conventional terms when he aimed his proposals mainly at the wealthiest students in Cambridge, by universal agreement the most idle. The Georgian academicians, living before the knowledge revolution of the next century, were satisfied if they could produce a particular sociomoral type whose behaviour could in some sense be guaranteed. This is the lesson that lies in the reading list Chatham sent his nephew, instructing him not to make additions to it. 'I propose to save you much time and trouble, by pointing out to you such books . . . as will carry you the shortest way to the things you must know to fit yourself for the business of the world, and give you the clearer knowledge of them, by keeping them unmixed with superfluous, vain, empty trash.'[148] With the coming of the French Revolution and the realisation that ideas had serious effects, the task of university education took on a greater urgency. Augustan universalistic ideals were reinvigorated and given an added boost by the pervasive neo-classical revival. The possibilities of examinations and other stimuli were seen in a new light.

So the evolution of the written examination suited the reasoning of the times. To simply associate that reasoning with the search for objectivity is to misunderstand the prevailing academic temper and to ignore the cultural assumptions and historical circumstances of the period.

At both universities the idea of a public examination before spectators or before examiners went out in the 1830s, and a parallel trend, objective, non-controversial examinations in written form, became the predominant mode of examining. This did not mean, however, that the idea of a public reward or a public shame completely disappeared as well. It merely took a new form. A different solution was found to the old problem of incentive. Students were no longer to be embarrassed in public, but neither was their fame or failure to be hidden under a bushel. The practice of printing the results of examinations and ranking students according to performance was a feature of the examinations almost from the start. Both universities adopted classes of performance, but Cambridge retained its earliest policy of listing the results of each examination in strict order of merit for all the world to read and know. Other triposes were established, but not all of them incorporated or retained an order of merit. The examinations

---

[148] *Letters Written by the Late Earl of Chatham*, 50–1.

acquired their famous reputation for being competitive, and gradually a system of marks was introduced to hasten the trend toward severe and accurate appraisal.[149]

Another point to consider in connection with changes in the form of examining at Oxford and Cambridge was the difficulty both universities experienced in trying to persuade students to take the new examinations. Napleton, who was writing at a time when the hard-working student was the butt and victim of other students, recognised the problem and suggested that examiners use variable standards in order not to humilate obviously mediocre students.[150] Apparently his standard of Fame was not a foolproof device for stimulating exertion. In the earliest days of the new examinations, it was recognised that many students would never achieve a very high standard of performance either because they were stupid or indolent by nature or because they were so well-connected and wealthy that virtue and reputation acquired through scholarship were of no consequence to them. Their careers were guaranteed and did not require academic success. For a long time it was known that most students could be made to study for only negative reasons – what was known in utilitarian thinking as self-interest. This idea was already present in Paley's Cambridge and deeply offended a sensitive Romantic like Wordsworth.[151] It also seemed to contradict the neoclassical idea of virtue being its own reward. Yet rewards and punishment were for dons the only realistic way of coping with the fact that most careers were still started by patronage, that founders' kin still had claims on certain emoluments and that most scholarships and fellowships were still restricted, although this does not mean they were entirely non-competitive.

A practical solution was devised to solve a problem that was otherwise beyond reach. Two different degree tracks were created for the two very different groups of undergraduates in the universities. The best or reading student would take an honours degree, and the weak or lazy student would study for an ordinary or poll degree, as would the occasional high-minded undergraduate who resented the narrow subject-concentration and ethos of expediency in the new examinations. At Cambridge the formal distinction between honours and an ordinary degree was introduced in 1828. At Oxford an honours category existed from the start. The usual method of distinguishing honours from passmen was to regard the

[149] Ball, *Mathematical Tripos*, 213.
[150] Napleton, *Considerations*, 29. For the same reason the *Gentleman's Magazine* of 1782 proposed private examinations for students 'having dull parts': Haverfield, *Extracts*, 430.
[151] The point of Schneider's book. See also A. W. Hare, *A Letter to George Martin, Esq.* (Oxford, 1814), 18.

lowest class as having taken a pass degree and to leave the names of these students off the printed list. Their public disgrace in the early years of the Oxford examinations took the form of not being mentioned. The distinctions between honours and ordinary students permitted examiners to concentrate on the better students and to make the degree examinations as difficult and objective as seemed necessary to wipe out old rankling reproaches.

THE RISE OF THE READING MAN

The developing tradition of the honours student joined with the trend toward sociability to produce yet another outstanding feature of the student life of the period, the reading and travel party. Circles of reading students organised to prepare for examinations, and famous friendships resulted. The reading set became one of the principal ways in which the late Georgian and early Victorian intelligentsia met and formed. The first of the reading and travel parties started at Cambridge around 1805, and we hear of the Oxford Cantabs by 1830.[152] Almost from the start the Cambridge students began the trend of going away to the Lakes or Scotland for study and companionship in more peaceful and what were regarded as more appropriate surroundings than the still rowdy universities. This was a new form of the Grand Tour, far less expensive, more romantic, a genuine retreat rather than mere retirement far away from the self-seeking and narrow-minded dons of the university. The Long Vacation and other breaks were spent away from the universities as studious undergraduates asserted their independence in yet another way by dissociating their academic studies from the places which required them. The new wandering student of the early nineteenth century would have pleased the writers of the picaresque tradition, especially an anglicised Scot like Tobias Smollett, who believed that it was just as educational to visit the remote corners of the islands as to tour Rome and Vicenza.

The improvements in communications, the better roads and especially the railroads of a later age made the travel and reading party still easier to arrange. And with the end of the Napoleonic Wars and the restoration of peace in Europe a Continental itinerary could be arranged. The new freedom meant more opportunity for learning and a greater range of personal experiences for the student. His eighteenth-century predecessor was far more confined, especially if his means and resources were limited.

[152] Wordsworth, 'Autobiography', 189.

Travel in his day was arduous and risky, the roads bad and highwaymen in wait. Vacation periods were therefore very often taken in college. Residence between terms was a good opportunity for concentrated study because the troublemakers usually left. One undergraduate wrote from Cambridge in 1767 that during the Long Vacation the 'Loungers' went down.[153] A decade or so later in the time of Wordsworth vacations were still periods of study and terms a time for an active social life.

The rise of the reading man, a change possible only because of the creation and progress of the new examinations, produced another legacy upon which the Victorians later capitalised, the elite theory of education. According to this theory, learning is largely the consequence of peer interaction. In general students learn more from each other than from their teachers. Sometimes the theory is a justification for a particular kind of student selection process and whatever instructional programme happens to exist. At most times those who cite the theory beg the question of just what it is that students are learning from each other. Whatever the value of the theory, it is important to remember that it originated in an Oxford and Cambridge in which students very often had a low opinion of their teachers. In the unreformed universities of Oxford and Cambridge students were usually contemptuous of the education on offer and frequently were bored or disapproved of their teachers. When the examinations offered a goal and reward for serious study, students devised their own means of preparation. They hired their own teachers, usually unemployed junior fellows or new BAs, and took them along as private tutors on the new travel parties. Lazy or dim students in the late eighteenth century frequently employed 'coaches' to help them stumble through their exercises or were supplied tutors by their parents, but now the routine was copied by better students anxious to do well. A new breed of sophists appeared within Oxford and Cambridge as one of the first consequences of the new examinations. Their presence, illegitimate from the university point of view, was in one sense a defiance of the old college system by undergraduates. The private teachers were a reminder that the official university was of only secondary pedagogical importance.

And yet despite the unmistakable irritation with their teachers that students of the period record, their attitude toward university discipline and suspicion was not outright defiance and hostility. Their feelings were mixed. Just as dons were both pleased and troubled by student independence – pleased by the new spirit of industry and troubled by the show of self-reliance – so students were of two minds about the universities they

153 Venn, *Early Collegiate Life*, 246; Godley, *Oxford*, 67.

attended. For if they chafed under the antiquated discipline of the universities, they also accepted the new and different discipline of the examinations. They clearly wanted recognition, and their parents were eager to see them succeed. An increasing number took their studies seriously and prepared earnestly. We can measure student commitment by the lengthening lists of successful honours candidates and by the greater use of private teachers in or out of term. We can derive some rough approximation of student interest in the university by noting the increasing use of college facilities for meetings and social occasions and the tendency for sporting associations to base their membership on the college and to take their names from the college. However independent the student was and no matter how defiant, he also had the deepest inclination to associate himself and his clubs with his college. In general, he wanted the college to be his special home, linked absolutely with the stages of his own growth towards maturity.

Students were not ambivalent about the university: they liked it. It was the dons about whom their feelings were mixed. They distinguished their teachers from the university itself, the dons from the institution, and thus it was possible for them to reject the first while accepting the second. In making this separation the late Georgian undergraduates were very different from their predecessors and successors. Wordsworth, for example, did what the Victorian students did, identified the institution with its teachers and regarded one as the embodiment of the other. But they were approving while he was disapproving. Neither St John's College nor Cambridge University was attractive to him. The university in any form was hateful, the wrong sort of people, the wrong sort of studies, and he preferred his beloved lakes and the serious, honest life of the northern counties where he had been happily at school. Years later he returned to Cambridge as one of its heroes.[154]

After the turn of the century, undergraduates began to regard the university as a unique place, and their relationship to it as special. The attachment they expressed can be correctly labelled romantic. Hitherto either an extension of the home or a boarding school from which to escape to a richer culture outside, the college was becoming a privileged sanctuary for the student, an arcadian retreat, 'his rooms . . . a sort of castle', the elated reminiscence of an Oxford undergraduate around 1800.[155] Newman, who was fortunate in having found a conscientious

[154] Robert Robson, 'Trinity College in the Age of Peel', in *Ideas and Institutions of Victorian Britain*, ed. Robert Robson (London, 1967), 326.
[155] Costin, *St John's College, Oxford*, 228.

college tutor in Thomas Vowler Short, was nevertheless unhappy with the advice he received from him and his other teachers; yet he loved Oxford with a haunting intensity. Macaulay never forgot the beauty of Trinity College and associated his years there with the portraits of Newton and Bacon, the sounds of the wonderful fountain and Neville's Court as it appeared under moonlight.[156] The magic of places and associations was having its intended effect.

The appearance and spread of a subjective aesthetic theory provides us with additional support for the hypothesis that a generation was being raised more permissively. Either because they were being encouraged to express their own views openly or because parents were unable to prevent them from doing so, students were coming to the universities in a questioning mood. In the second place, the new aesthetic theories explain why students were able to develop a sentimental attachment to Oxford and Cambridge irrespective of the frustrations actually encountered there. Continually in the early nineteenth century it is in terms of the aesthetics of associationism that Oxford and Cambridge were appreciated. It was remembered that these were ancient seats of learning, ancient places of fame in whose buildings theologians and doctors once sat and through whose grounds they strolled. The imagination was instructed to invest the ceremonies of the university with special meaning because tradition inspired them. And perhaps above all the university was beautiful and a university career emotionally satisfying because friends were to be found and youth – now in itself a unique experience – was spent there. A Regency history of Cambridge gives a good example of the uses of associationism. The author poses the question as to why a university botanical garden is impressive. His answer is that a garden may illustrate the principles of landscaping or offer agreeable scents and lovely plants, but a *university* botanical garden is the greater experience because it combines the pleasures of the senses with the joys of learning, 'and in reference to its more peculiar object, resembles the closet of a student, which comprehends the productions of genius in every climate. This is the more habitual feeling.'[157]

In recovering the responses of undergraduates to the beauty of the universities, in remembering the gardens which broke away from a Cartesian formality in the course of the eighteenth century, the moonlight in the courts, the ringing of chapel bells and the striking of a clock,

---

[156] Trevelyan, *Macaulay*, I, 69–70.
[157] George Dyer, *History of the University and Colleges of Cambridge*, I (London, 1814), 253–4, vi–viii.

especially at night when Archibald Alison, the leading theorist of associational aesthetics, said the sound was 'sublime' (sound without a visible source is intensified), we should also remember the poor student in a cold, dark attic room entered through a trapdoor. In books like Dyer's *History of the University and Colleges of Cambridge* he was asked to extend his imagination to take in the beautiful associations around him, to forget the inconveniences of his miserable quarters, the coarse treatment he received from the toughs on his staircase and the disapproving, dampening scowl of a tutor who preferred to end his career somewhere else.

PART AND PARCEL OF THE COLLEGE

Thomas Dibdin was at St John's College in the University of Oxford and took his degree in 1801. He boasted that students helped create the serious spirit that led to the new examinations at Oxford.[158] Dibdin is not ordinarily a reliable witness, but his boast contains some truth. Oxford students were indeed proud of an innovation which cut into their leisure and was partly intended to limit their independence. And although university-level written examinations eventually brought to an end the curricular freedom that students of an earlier century enjoyed, while this was happening undergraduates were becoming used to fabricating many aspects of their culture. The Oxbridge clubs, the debating societies, the intellectual and sporting associations, the expeditions, the strenuous exercises, the magazine essays and poems, the animated social life and convivial ethic all pointed in the same direction: toward a generation of young adults seeking distinctions, pursuing recognition, looking for public reputations and introducing into their university lives many of the social and intellectual ideas of their time, a time that was marked by disturbance on a national scale.

The extraordinary changes occurring in the organisation and routine of student life had the general effect of increasing group pressures in Oxbridge, thereby producing a situation wherein the necessity for peer approval reached new heights. The small population of the colleges, making anonymity hard, plus the withdrawal of dons and heads, encouraged this trend. One of the curious charges that Shelley (or Hogg for him) levelled at the Oxford dons was that the new examinations came too late in an undergraduate's career to allow him to enjoy the envy and admiration of his peers. No sooner had the undergraduate distinguished

---

[158] Godley, *Oxford*, 141.

himself than he was served his degree and told to leave.[159] The remark would be incomprehensible but for the history leading to it.

It is in the early nineteenth century that new student models or types emerge, new cult figures and legendary heroes admired for their prowess on the river, their brilliance in the unions, their stylish essays and prize poems, their surreptitious adventures among the demimonde, their capacity for drink or their ingenious challenges to donnish authority. Undergraduate heroes there had undoubtedly been before the nineteenth century – admired tripos winners, rakes on the loose – but there is nothing to approach the idealism and adulation that biographers bestow on the later generations. The opportunities for recognition in the eighteenth century do not begin to match those of the next; and the publicity accorded the distinguished undergraduate in the early days of George III cannot equal those available in the reign of his son. Nor was there a student subculture so varied in its range and activity, so influential, so self-conscious and anxious to write about itself, nor so identified with the idea of a university. So strong was the awakening becoming that it was increasingly possible for undergraduates to think that they and not their teachers were the essential university. 'They cannot expel *us*,' cries a peccant undergraduate in a quasi-fictional story set in the 1830s. 'We are a part and parcel of the College.'[160]

The new student and the new competitive examinations occurred together historically: one did not absolutely create the other, but each shaped some of the other's characteristics in a long period of mutual interaction. It is this continuing interaction and interrelationship that must receive emphasis. We must assess and credit the role of both students and dons in discovering new ways of combating the traditional university sin of sloth. As the students have just been given their due, we can now praise famous dons. Indirectly they encouraged a special student attachment to the university by insisting in their defence of the university against public criticism that Oxford and Cambridge were not schools and that undergraduates were not pupils under the rod. And it took some insight on the part of the masters and tutors to consider how they might build on student attachment to the fabric of the colleges, to their wish to take their pleasures indoors and to widen the educational possibilities of the universities, to broaden the education into the liberal education celebrated in Victorian literature. From the standpoint of institutional and cultural history, the changes taking place within the universities were

[159] Thomas Jefferson Hogg, *The Life of Percy Bysshe Shelley*, I (London, 1856), 259.
[160] *Passages in the Life of an Undergraduate, Edited by One of His Friends* (1847), 45.

striking cultural achievements. They did not just happen. The examinations did not merely slip into the unreformed universities. They were not simply a change in educational policy. They required whole ranges of adjustment in values and behaviour, the inculcation of self-discipline, for example, in a society whose governing elites were accustomed to free time and free schedules. In historical perspective the first third of the nineteenth century deserves a unique place in the history of the ancient universities.

Late Georgian Oxbridge possessed a character and tone entirely its own. It was the period of the independent student and the notion of a separate student estate and the period in which the idea of being young was accorded special value. Only the young could have certain types of experiences and certain kinds of feelings. Only the young were possessed of a special truth and a deeper sensitivity.

Late Georgian Oxbridge was also the period in which modern examinations supplanted, even while simultaneously influenced by, the oral culture of the generally despised disputations, but they were not yet self-consciously put to modern use. The period was one in which competition as a means of achieving recognition was accepted by students and incorporated into their activities, and upon this acceptance the new examining culture was built.

The first third of the nineteenth century was also the period in which dons and students openly parted, or to put it another way, in which students and teachers were conscious of their differences and uncomfortable in one another's presence. The strain they experienced was not simply the respect or awe with which a younger person regards his more learned senior, awakening in him a certain humility. Respect was low, awe rare, and teachers were not humble. Expectations were higher than earlier because the age was so different and students more sophisticated as well as older. We may offer one final reason for the mutual discomfort. Of all the changes that could have occurred in the educational system of Oxford and Cambridge, one did not. There was no radical change in the structure of teaching to accommodate the new student. Efforts were certainly being made by change-minded dons and by tutors such as Charles Lloyd at Christ Church, a proto-Tractarian who became professor of divinity and bishop of Oxford. He was lucky enough to have Peel as a student and managed, in his rough fashion, to have some influence on Newman. 'He brought me forward, made me known, spoke well of me, and gave me confidence in myself.'[161] From pockets of teaching such as this a later

[161] William J. Baker, *Beyond Port and Prejudice, Charles Lloyd of Oxford, 1784–1829* (Orono, ME, 1981), 211.

generation of dons drew the inspiration which, combined with shifts in public opinion, resulted in the reforms of the middle decades. But in the meantime the emergence of an examination culture produced what were the most conspicuous pedagogical features of pre-Victorian Oxbridge: a weak professoriate, a high degree of college autonomy, a large body of absentee fellows and an extensive network of private teaching. It should not be surprising, therefore, that the central purpose of the great reforms of 1850 to 1880 was to correct those deficiencies, in fact to undo some of the damage which arose paradoxically as a consequence of the most notable development in English higher education in over a century.

POSTSCRIPT

In 1952 the novelist E. M. Forster, a Kingsman at the turn of the century, gave a speech entitled 'Who Owns the College?' His answer was the Third Year. In the first year the undergraduate is unsure of his clothes. In the second an air of superiority and self-confidence prevails. But in the third year 'Without arrogance and with exultation, with occasional song and dance, I owned the place.' Although his kingdom would not last beyond the BA, Forster remarked that 'loyalty remained – in fact this is the only unforced loyalty I have ever experienced'.[162]

In pondering the question of the rise of the undergraduate, recognisable as such, remarks such as Forster's are enormously helpful. While there are many references to the beauty of the Oxford and Cambridge colleges and the pleasures of the universities in the sources before the last decades of the eighteenth century, even references to kindly old dons, conspicuously absent are statements that separate living in college from other kinds of formative experiences. As we have seen, there were innumerable other attractions available, and the return of the undergraduate to the college, if 'return' is correct, is a phenomenon of the last part of the reign of the Georgian kings. David Fairer notices the romance of Oxford starting to appear in literature towards the end of the eighteenth century. Writers are more concerned with nostalgia, the university providing a firmer base from which to indulge personal feelings. This he contrasts with the propensity to seek fame and fortune in the world so typical of poets and writers desperate for patrons in the age of Addison.[163]

John Coleridge, in reminiscing about his days with Thomas Arnold at

---

[162] Patrick Wilkinson, *Edward Morgan Forster, 1869–1970* (a memoir privately printed for King's College, Cambridge, 1970), 20–1.
[163] David Fairer, 'Oxford and the Literary World', in Sutherland and Mitchell, 779, 805.

Corpus Christi College, Oxford, concluded that the influence of friends and the college 'constitution and system' were much more than the world of dons.[164] This was the habitual attitude of the first undergraduates, recognisable as such. Hogg and Shelley may not have been absolutely prototypical, although perhaps archtypical. The undergraduate career of the poet Robert Southey shows similar signs of independence. He came up to Balliol in 1792 and found outlets for his libertarian idealism in writing. Two years later he left Oxford, announcing that he and Coleridge would establish a Pantisocratic society in America dedicated to tolerance and equality, values not high on the dons' agenda in the 1790s.[165] But there is one significant difference between Southey, Coleridge and Wordsworth and Shelley that makes Hogg's vindication of Shelley particularly apt. Hogg sounds all the right notes and captures the correct generational response. Shelley came to Oxford a confirmed whig or radical from a whig family. He saw no reason to hide those views from the academic tories. He regarded Oxford as his own personal patrimony, space in which to develop his own interests, dress as he liked (one observer thought he was simply slovenly), break such college rules as attending hall and wander off with Hogg in search of solitude and freedom, since for the most part he disliked his fellow students. The message of freedom proclaimed at the university was later magnificently announced in *Prometheus Unbound*. But the defiance he showed in word and deed should not blind us to the strong and deep attachment he felt towards his college. Peremptorily ordered away from its walls, he was thoroughly shaken. Hogg defended him. Had he been less sensitive, less impulsive, had he remained around for a day or two more the sentence of expulsion would have been rescinded. He was impetuous, but it was understandable. Rustication for a term or two would have been punishment enough for 'an ingenuous youth to whom a college-life was in all respects suitable, and indeed charming'. And now comes Hogg's denouement that explains what it meant to be the first undergraduate, recognisable as such. It meant the right to challenge but with impunity, the right to shock but not to be shocked. But even more so, it meant that the unique quality of the undergraduate was perfectly matched with the essential idea of a university, that a university was a place for being young, and that being young required self-exploration in an appropriate setting. 'Youth is happy, because it is blithe and healthful, and exempt from care; but it is doubly and trebly happy, since it is honest and fearless – honourable and disinterested.'[166] But youth cannot become

[164] Fowler, *Corpus Christi College*, 306.   [165] Fairer, 'Oxford', 804.
[166] Hogg, *Shelley*, I (London, 1858), 255–6, 328; Strachey, *Memoirs of a Highland Lady*, 129.

honest and fearless unless there is something to demonstrate against, and the environment has to provide just the right mixture of restraint and liberty. A generation of Romantic writers and critics raised Hogg's egregious sentiments of self-praise to the level of a new aesthetic. From immaturity a different art would arise, unspoiled and innocent.[167] The first of a genre of university novels would explore such themes. John Sterling's *Arthur Coningsby* (1833) and F. D. Maurice's *Eustace Conway* (1834) are about youthful idealism, rebellion and reconciliation. As for Shelley, he 'seemed to be one of those modest, studious, recluse persons for whose special behalf universities and colleges were founded and are maintained'.[168]

---

[167] Robert Rosenbloom on Philipp Otto Runge in *Transformations in Eighteenth-Century Art* (Princeton, 1967), 182, 182n.
[168] Hogg, *Shelley*, 254–7, 289.

CHAPTER FOUR

FAILURE

WHAT PRICE SUCCESS?

A university may have an idea, it may sometimes be a place for the teaching of universal knowledge, but it is also the arena in which young minds are probed, irritated, extended and weighed in the balance of life chances. Evaluation is painful and hard on the ego. Judgements translate all too readily into a string of numbers or letters indicating different levels of proficiency. If there is a single aspect of pedagogy that promotes anxiety and makes students petrified, it is exam-taking, especially and most acutely in the form of competitive examinations. The thought that there is only so much room at the top is chilling. Even success in academic studies can instil or widen an inherent sense of inadequacy. 'Success' is an elastic concept: after all, one may only be relatively successful. It is often afterwards, when memories of fright and anxiety have eased, that the mystery and surprise of place are strongly felt. The passage of years allows for many of the less agreeable aspects of the university's examination culture to diminish. Time permits the acquisition of skills and knowledge other than those emphasised by teachers, although a self-conscious liberal arts instructor will take credit for establishing the foundation upon which future success is built.

Examinations are justified in any number of ways: because they are a necessary means for social, occupational or economic advancement; because they are universal and therefore 'democratic' – all must submit to them; because they assist the learning process by pointing out deficiencies and indicating areas for improvement (in which case they need not be competitive); because they are a form of accountability, assuring parents or governments that money is not wasted; because they are a spur to ambition or because they function as rites of passage, or a series of such rites, trials that are necessary for advancing towards maturity. Precisely because they have become such a critical part of education, examination results are never free from suspicion, and they are frequently contested.[1]

University examinations have multiple functions. They certify professional competence. The university does not have a monopoly on certification; but the academic profession, as Harold Perkin has written, is the 'key profession', the one that supplies the others with its practitioners, and so its influence, its judgements, its methods of inquiry, its scientific outlook, help define professional conduct and values. Through participation in a network of interlocking associations, the university dispenses various forms of patronage, sponsors a large number of artistic and intellectual activities, sets the criteria for achievement in scholarship and science and distributes a great variety of prizes and awards. It bestows honours and prestige. And by offering opportunities for research, it makes the propagation and dissemination of original knowledge an on-going professional requirement subject to continual stringent peer review (although under different auspices in different countries). In so many areas of national life, the university is the motor that drives the modern system of competitive excellence. In Britain more than in America, universities virtually originated the systems of competitive and qualifying examinations in use throughout the professions, the civil service and the military.

A splendid performance at university is supposed to mean success afterwards. But the connection is tenuous. Not every university can promise graduates that a successful career automatically follows a laudable academic performance. In the United States, private elite institutions have the greatest chance of outfitting their graduates for success, insinuating them into alumni networks or providing them with degrees that are in effect strong letters of recommendation. National systems of education vary in their ability to 'charter' graduates. British universities are said to be more successful than those in the United States. Employers cannot expect to find 'standard' qualifications or solid proof of competitive excellence.[2] The widespread use of transfer as a means of furthering geographical as well as social mobility has also led to a depreciation in the value of most American first degrees, since only select colleges and universities can

---

[1] A polemic by Andrew J. Strenio, Jr, *The Testing Trap* (New York, 1981), maintains that testing and examining in the United States are conspiracies entered into by non-profit and for-profit corporations, publishers and consulting firms, that these industries are out of control and that claims of objectivity are false. One of his chapters is entitled 'Beating the System', and it is an essay on how to disguise a weak performance!

[2] John W. Meyer, 'The Charter: Conditions of Diffuse Socialization in Schools', in *Social Process and Social Structures: An Introduction to Sociology*, ed. W. Richard Scott (New York, 1970), 564–78.

really claim that degrees represent four years of competitive work in the institution itself.

Unable to charter their graduates, the more prestigious American universities and colleges have instead turned to chartering postgraduate students, taking advantage of the creation at the end of the nineteenth century of separate postgraduate schools or divisions sharing facilities with the rest of a campus but maintaining separate admissions standards under the control of departmental specialities. The first degree has acquired importance as a means of deciding who moves on into advanced education, and the graduate schools themselves have been successful in placing those holding advanced degrees into certain types of business and the professions, and particularly academia itself.

Despite the widespread absence of a chartering capability, the success of the great graduate schools, and the competition for entry to the best under-graduate programmes, have given rise to sentiments that the university's admission policies are discriminatory, the word in common use being 'elitist', which has lost its older and neutral meaning. The famous universities and colleges have been bitterly attacked during the last three decades for failing to admit large numbers of several minority groups. Policies redefining or adjusting what might be called a strict meritocratic position (even though historically rarely in use) were one outcome of the attacks. These are best known in the form of affirmative action guidelines and ethnic or racial set-asides for undergraduate and postgraduate admissions as well as hirings, promotions and retentions. At present there is a movement against certain aspects of affirmative action, if not the principle of helping an underserved population reach higher education, and this scenario will be played out in the remaining few years of the twentieth century's last decade.

In Britain the debate about university access has focused on the pivotal transition points in the nation's system of elite preparation. The movement from primary to secondary education, and from secondary to tertiary historically depended upon tracking and examinations. By the 1990s the eleven plus selection system determining entrance to secondary education had been abolished. The meritocratic, state-supported grammar schools were replaced with comprehensive high schools. Throughout the 1980s and 1990s government policy addressed the question of school-leaving examinations and credentials. Many of the examination requirements were changed. Tinkering continues, but with every change in the school-leaving examinations, and especially examinations that lead from the sixth forms to universities, higher education itself is forced to revise its entry requirements.

Changes are underway at the end of the twentieth century that may well alter the elite system of examining and marking that developed in Britain in the nineteenth century. But thus far the university retains some of its past authority as an arbiter of success and failure. The acquisition of that authority, principally represented by an examinations culture, is the subject of this chapter. In the preceding chapter the place of examinations in re-establishing university discipline was discussed in relation to an evolving student subculture. The plan here is to show how examinations helped Victorian civilisation redefine the definition of success inherited from the previous century, but also to explain how newer definitions of success were resisted throughout the nineteenth century. One form of assessment was not superseded by another. The two coexisted, and their simultaneous operation made a difficult situation yet more complicated and uncertain.

THE VICTORIAN GOSPEL OF SUCCESS: INCOMPLETE COMBUSTION

We are told that there was a gospel of success in Victorian Britain accompanying the rise of entrepreneurial capitalism, liberal individualism and the weakening of a national culture heavily influenced by aristocratic habits of work and taste. Thomas Carlyle, a testy and reliable opponent of Victorian materialism, sniffed the air and denounced the associated changes. In 1842 he asked rhetorically what the 'modern English soul' most dreaded and contemplated 'with entire despair'. Christians fear the tribunal of the Just Judge. Old Romans feared 'doing unworthily, doing unvirtuously'. So what is the English equivalent once we have got through Cants, Hearsays, Worships and so forth? 'With hesitation, with astonishment, I pronounce it to be: The terror of "Not succeeding", of not making money, fame, or some other figure in the world.'[3]

Success was discussed more positively by another resident of the mid-Victorian pantheon of influential or noisy personalities. The writer of the most popular success book of the period was Samuel Smiles, whose publication of 1859 called *Self-Help* sold some 150,000 copies in the thirty years following its initial appearance but 20,000 in its first year alone, a very successful sale for edifying Victorian reading. An anonymous author in the *Cornhill Magazine* (but actually a civil servant in the India Office, military historian and former artillery officer with service in Bengal, Sir John William Kaye), writing at about the same time, wholly agreed with Smiles that success was a desirable and worthy goal, that is to say, he

[3] Thomas Carlyle, *Past and Present* (London and New York, 1947), 140.

disagreed with Carlyle on the value to be accorded to success as an end. 'I have a great opinion of successful men', he declared, 'and I am not ashamed to confess it'. Some years ago, he continued, it was the fashion to scorn or revile success as an offence 'or at best a pretentious humbug'. Fortunately, 'a healthier social philosophy is now enthroned amongst us'.[4]

Walter Houghton, who cited Kaye in outlining the Victorian Gospel of Success in his highly useful work of some four decades ago, announced the victory of a 'naked creed of success' that had become eminently respectable by 1860. Yet we miss an important qualification in all of the customary arguments about ambition if we fail to notice the clothing that covers up the 'naked creed of success'. Smiles, for example, was clear on the point that particular personal traits were essential for becoming successful, notably 'purpose, and above all energy are the measure of character, and a man of character will succeed'. (John Mill agreed. Energy could be misapplied but was always preferable to indolence.)[5] It was not the results of striving that mattered, said Smiles, but striving in and for itself. Kaye, while welcoming the 'healthier social philosophy . . . now enthroned amongst us', ended up excising from success precisely the elements required to make it function as an instrument for promoting work, encouraging achievement and building into Victorian culture a principle of forward movement. Success was not to be measured 'comparatively'. It could not be gained through competition. It was an absolute and a moral standard, a form of individual accounting measured by self-denial rather than by socially directed goals. Kaye disagreed with Smiles. Mutual help not self-help was the key to success.[6]

In both Smiles and Kaye care was taken to avoid falling into the utilitarian trap of making a system of values subservient to an unworthy end. Success was important, and one must pursue it, never fogetting, says Kaye, 'the Market-place or the Council-house', but the pursuit was really intended to inculcate a set of ethical qualities or traits, 'that type of manhood, which most nearly approaches the divine, by reason of its creative energy'.[7] In these writers, then, we have the perfect formula for dealing with failure. If it is not the results of striving that matter but the striving in and for itself, the writer of advice books has nothing to fear. He boldly identifies the most likely route to success; he holds out the carrot of status and material comfort. But he also cautions, as did Kaye, against

---

[4] Walter Houghton, *The Victorian Frame of Mind* (New Haven, 1957), 194.
[5] *Ibid.*, 191, 117; John Stuart Mill, *On Liberty* (Harmondsworth, 1984), 124 and 135, who also asserted that few outlets for energy existed apart from business.
[6] [William Kaye], 'Success', *The Cornhill Magazine*, 2 (December 1860), 729–41, esp. 733.
[7] Houghton, *Victorian Frame of Mind*, 194–5.

immoral temptations and underhand negotiations, and he covers his tracks by deeming outcome less significant than process.[8] But none of this is surprising. Cultures must invariably be contradictory where values are applied, so to speak, and threaten other interests and ambitions. (And wherever moralists draw fine lines, the striver will surely cross them.)

The debate over success in mid-Victorian Britain was not a debate between a majority and a minority position. On the contrary, opposition to newer values concerning competition as the basis of success was formidable. It was represented by surviving attitudes concerning measurements of personal worth as well as newly developing ethical systems derived from Christian socialism, Broad Church nationalism, idealist philosophy and tory democracy, all of which carried anti-utilitarian messages. But liberal individualism was also deplored. Cooperative schemes of bonding were suggested as essential alternatives to save the nation from descending into an unending series of struggles for influence and authority.

No party disputed the need for a certain amount of ambition, for striving, for energy, for the existence of incentives to stir worthy motives and invite greater exertion. Mid-Victorian civilisation was industrial, urban and imperial. Sloughing off was no help. The question was how to stimulate honourable ambition without at the same time giving encouragement to what were seen as baser instincts. No one wanted a purely liberal ethic of free market entrepreneurship where competition operated on an abstract impersonal level of blinding ambition, so that all other claims for support or encouragement were ignored.

The problem was more abstract or philosophical than practical. Intellectuals debated the implications of selfish philosophies, but individuals made pragmatic accommodations, as did institutions like universities. It is rarely the case that one set of social values instantly replaces another. Writing about the advent of free markets, Karl Polyani once noted that the practice of the marketplace must inevitably depart from the theory of it.[9] No culture can retain in pure form the unmitigated assumptions of the world of classical economics. Market discipline is too harsh. No culture is either equipped or prepared to cope with the consequences of a theory of human striving which makes as much use of the threat of failure as the promise of success. Furthermore, circumstances and contingencies interfere with model mechanisms of supply and demand. Accordingly, says Polyani, the backing off from strict market

[8] [Kaye], 'Success', 733.
[9] Karl Polyani, *The Great Transformation* (New York, 1944), 192–219.

discipline came early, almost immediately. The first signs of strategic retreat occurred in the banking system when capitalists manipulated the money supply instead of relying upon the market's self-regulating mechanisms.[10] The historian T. S. Ashton, looking at another part of the growth of a market economy, noticed how readily manufacturers resorted to oligopoly.[11]

It is the tension implicit in the Victorian success ethic as much as the reaction to which it gave rise that is fascinating. The Victorian ethic of success was highly ambivalent. The public and the chattering classes of the day divided on how best to create a society balanced in moral and material aims. Ambition was necessary, but it had to be honourable and not rationalised as winning at any price. Playing the game in manly fashion was how the public schools took up the challenge; the way in which the game was played and not victory itself was the process leading to improved character.[12]

NO-FAULT FAILURE

Now let us ask how the ancient universities dealt with the same issues. We can begin with a model of how success was recognised or encouraged for much of the eighteenth century. In general, success was defined in relation to character. Individuals were judged according to a conventional range of traits describing how well they got along with others. English views about the importance of developing character were consistent with mainline traditions of liberal education from the sophists of Attica to the courtiers of Florence and Urbino. It was understood that ambition had a number of consequences, some more desirable than others. Negatively, ambition fostered jealousy, and jealousy was a powerful and socially destructive passion, difficult to control. The right kind of upbringing, social setting or education could improve character. Study 'Men and Manners' the Georgians said. Observe conduct, reduce that conduct to universal rules and principles and make career calculations accordingly.

---

[10] *Ibid.*, 194.

[11] T. S. Ashton, *The Industrial Revolution 1760–1830* (London, 1957), 127.

[12] Victorian conceptions of manly, manliness and masculine were many and varied, depending upon context and speaker. It encompassed physical as well as moral and mental traits, but all seemed to be grounded on determination, even singlemindedness. A recent addition to the literature is Peter H. Hansen, 'Albert Smith, the Alpine Club, and the Invention of Mountaineering in Mid-Victorian Britain', *Journal of British Studies*, 34 (July 1995), 312. See also the essays in *Manliness and Morality, Middle-Class Masculinity in Britain and America, 1800–1940*, ed. J.A. Mangan and James Walvin (Manchester, 1987).

That is one major reason why so little stress was placed on the curriculum. Traits such as sociability, reasonableness, good temper, liberality and generosity were difficult to inculcate through the kinds of exercises required of undergraduates. But even in the relaxed eighteenth century a complete disregard for the official teachings of the universities was embarrassing, so the existing curriculum was defended in a number of different ways. Classsical literature provided examples of good and bad character, as well as principles of decision-making. Theology provided moral lessons. Mathematics improved reasoning skills, but could also be linked to religion through natural theology. Oral examinations provided a needed instruction in the arts of public speaking. The 'unofficial curriculum', composed of subjects like modern languages or certain kinds of physical science supplied at market prices, was justified in a different way, as suiting individual needs. Since the unofficial curriculum lay outside the regular examining system and was voluntary only, the question of success and failure did not arise.

There was another way to measure character. A lack of success was not so much a personal failing as the fault of the system of networking within which ambition operated. Where connections failed, where one believed himself chosen but lived to experience rejection (for another was preferred in his place), bitter disappointment followed. But, the fault, dear Brutus, was in the stars. 'Character' had not failed. The system had failed, and others were to blame.[13]

To be competitive simply for its own sake, or to have a competitive nature, was far too threatening to others, one of those 'appetites' or imbalances described in classical literature. A Cambridge observer put it this way in 1814: suppose 'A' was worthy and studied hard, but 'B' lounged and hunted. If, at the time of college-level examinations,

> 'A' forgets to contract his knowledge, till he reduce himself to the scale of his learned associate, how will every individual in the College, scarcely excepting the tutors themselves, exclaim against his pride, pedantry, and want of feeling. For ten years after he will be pointed out as the man, who, when no real good would be gained by it, was examined in twenty authors,

[13] These disappointments and their contexts show up readily in the Introduction to *The Journal of the Reverend William Bagshaw Stevens*, ed. Georgina Galbraith (Oxford, 1965). The exhilaration with which Samuel Johnson was able to reject Lord Chesterfield's offer of financial patronage is very much to the point. His answer to the noble lord was almost gleeful but certainly facetious as he explained that when he was needy he had been disregarded. Now that he had triumphed in an alternative system of a flourishing market for literature, he could be disdainful of handouts. James Boswell, *Life of Johnson* (London, 1966), 184–8. The year was 1754.

for the purpose of gratifying his vanity, and of triumphing over the ignorance of a friend.[14]

In this educational model, ambition presented a problem. If too openly displayed, it was considered to be a form of aggression, but it was acceptable when disguised as 'emulation'. Education was consequently a process of instruction through which undergraduates learned how to copy good examples and proper models. Students were expected to show a command and understanding of time-tested ideas and texts. Classical traditions of education (in which the theory and practice of a liberal education were so firmly anchored) emphasised socio-moral rather than intellectual qualities as the ends of education: virtue, high-mindedness, self-sacrifice, wisdom, nobility, humility, courage, and so on – qualities that could be imitated or were within the reach of all. Failure to adopt the best examples of conduct was attributable to wilful choice, reprehensible no doubt, but a defect of character, not an inherent lack of ability, not a final judgement, and therefore not likely to permanently damage *amour-propre*.[15] These assumptions were not altogether discarded by a generation of early Victorians at Oxford and Cambridge. In fact, to some extent they supported them with arguments from the philosophy of Design. The world was the result of a divine act of creation, all knowledge was known and could be discovered but could not be manufactured. Innovation, creativity, originality – the qualities so admired in our own academic world – were looked upon with suspicion as tempting and disruptive.

Talent and personal merit were never disregarded as qualifications for recognition and promotion, but they needed to be confirmed in some reliable fashion, captured within the system of patronage, sponsorship and nomination that guaranteed, or was expected to guarantee, chains of loyalty and political and moral reliability. The redoubtable Cyril Jackson was expert at moving talent through the existing system of sponsorship. He stressed a work ethic remarkable for his time, and he used Oxford's new Examination Statute of 1800, for which he was partly responsible, as a means of recognising merit worthy of supporting. Robet Peel and George Canning were among his protégés.[16]

Jackson's use of Oxford's historic examinations discipline to stimulate

---

[14] A. W. Hare, *On the Proposed Inclusion of New College in University Examinations* (Oxford, 1814), 23.

[15] For further remarks along such lines, see Sheldon Rothblatt, 'Federal Universities and Multi-Campus Systems', in *Scottish Universities, Distinctiveness and Diversity*, ed. Jennifer Carter and Donald Withrington (Edinburgh, 1992), 164–87.

[16] W. R. Ward, *Victorian Oxford* (London, 1965), 10–12.

even greater exertion was not an espousal of a newer meritocratic ethic. It was an interim step perhaps, but the students whose careers he advanced had already been tested in the older elite selection system. Canning is a perfect example. He made a name for himself at Eton by editing a satirical magazine called the *Microcosm*, which, oddly enough, sold 700 copies by the tenth number, outside as well as inside the school. When in 1794 he met the royal couple on the terrace of Windsor Castle, they knew about his publication. At Christ Church, watched over by the dean, he gathered a prominent peer group around him that included the son of a future prime minister, the son of the archbishop of York, Charles James Fox's nephew, Lord Holland, and other representatives of important families. Vetted and prepared in this way, his removal to London upon going down was just more of the same.[17]

Ambition was acceptable if it was directed towards familiar, acceptable objectives, was modelled on an approved style and linked to reliable persons. Those without connections, were relatively poor and had weak career prospects were forced to improve their chances by distinguishing themselves in some visible manner. But they were faced with real dilemmas. In competing for prizes and honours, they could expect to be stigmatised by their peers as vain and unsociable creatures. When Newman was at college in 1817 he was insulted by his peers for conduct not befitting a gentleman simply because he studied too much. He was even threatened with bodily harm as a reward for his exertions.[18]

Undergraduates would also receive mixed signals from tutors and fellows, whose own views about success were divided. Urged to make a name for themselves, they would also be cautioned against vanity, boasting and self-seeking. Over-zealous dons, who were excited by competitive examinations because they were a kind of horse race on which bets were placed, did the cause of the underdog no real good. Language such as Joseph Romilly entered into his diary on 17 January 1834 – 'Our Champion Birks is beaten. Kelland of Queens is the Hero of the Day' (he became senior wrangler)[19] – only reinforced beliefs that examinations were inconsistent with true education and examination success only another form of bragging. What would happen to intellectual curiosity and independence of mind if only examinations mattered?

From this perspective it is instructive to contrast the famous Northcote–Trevelyan Report of 1854 with its only major predecessor, Henry Taylor's

---

[17] *The Letter-Journal of George Canning, 1793–1795,* ed. Peter Jupp (London, 1991), 6–7.
[18] Jan Morris, *The Oxford Book of Oxford* (Oxford, 1978), 182.
[19] *Romilly's Cambridge Diary, 1832–42,* ed. J. P. T. Bury (Cambridge, 1967), 45.

The Statesman, first published in 1836. While Northcote and Trevelyan wrote about the need to recruit and reward merit in the civil services, as determined competitively through examinations (implying that a new generation of inexperienced politicians required guidance from superior intellects), Taylor relegated native ability to secondary status. (Smiles had written similarly, pronouncing talent to be less important than purpose.) Imagination was to be avoided, independent thinking was unsuited to the exercise of authority, and the pupil was to be made to endure drudgery at an early age, earlier (so he claimed) than was usual.[20] These arguments continued to register late into the century. The man 'well qualified for practical duties' was not likely to be very good at passing examinations. He would certainly 'be beaten most egregiously in a *competitive* examination', yet that should not be the issue. 'After all, examination is recommended only as a means of testing probable merit in the absence of proved merit.' Any other use of it was '*doctrinaire* pedantry ... theory actually preferred to practice, probability to certainty, the presumption of capacity afforded by scholarship to the proved capacity ascertained by service'.[21] The distinguished barrister Sir Frederick Pollock, reflecting upon his tripos experience in 1806, wrote the equally distinguished mathematician Augustus De Morgan some sixty years later that he too believed that 'the most valuable qualities for practical life cannot be got at by examination – such as steadiness and perseverance'. Examinations have a place in judging fitness for tasks, but to use them to put someone into public office 'is ... a bad mode of preventing mere patronage'.[22]

In the older set of values a lid was placed over ambition. Equally significant, a floor was placed beneath it. The purpose of a university education was to guarantee success by preventing failure. As we move into the nineteenth century, the great new worry was that if competitive examinations became a means of determining worth, one man's failure would be required to promote another man's success. An Iron Law of

---

[20] Henry Taylor, *The Statesman* (Cambridge, 1957), 7, 19–20. This is not the place to enter into the historiography of the origins of civil service examinations in Britain, but I would agree with historians who argue that identifying the Report of 1854 with the idea of merit in the abstract does not do justice to the reasons behind the recommendations. Since any civil service examination at that time would be aligned with the Oxford and Cambridge system of examining, it is evident that only candidates with that background would qualify. The examinations were therefore not open to merit but merit as carefully prepared in a specific way. For a sharply argued analysis of this position, see Peter Gowan, 'The Origins of the Administrative Elite', *New Left Review*, 162 (March–April 1987), 4–34.

[21] Arthur Helps, 'Thoughts upon Government', *The Quarterly Review*, 133 (1872), 246–7.

[22] Walter William Rouse Ball, *The Origin and History of the Mathematical Tripos* (Cambridge, 1880), 113.

Success was developing comparable to the classical economics theory of an Iron Law of Wages. There was only so much success available at any one time. We could also call it Malthusian. Someone might have to suffer for the sake of another.

THE CULTURE OF PLUCK

Competitive examinations had penetrated the universities as default settings. Their purpose was to safeguard the nation's elite entrusted to the care of the ancient colleges, preserving 'their minds untainted by the visionary novelties and frantick doctrines, which modern philosophy has generated in such mischievous profusion, and propagated with such unprecedented zeal and success'.[23] It crept in through the back door, along with a mixture of other rewards and incentives: college prizes, first- and second-year examinations, declamations in hall, essay contests and book awards.

One result was predictable. The level of recorded instances of student anxiety over the outcome of various university trials and hurdles rose. Nevertheless, we must imagine that any test of ability is liable to raise some alarm, even in less competitive periods. In 1767 a Cambridge under-graduate already in residence wrote to a friend contemplating residence that he had nothing to fear from the examination to which he would be subjected upon arriving (usually no more than diagnostic). It was, he counselled, nothing else than 'a mere matter of form'. 'My Tutor', he continued,

> when I first went to him, only desired me to construe an ode in Horace, a few lines in the beginning of a Satire in Juvenal, not more than three sentences in one of Cicero's Orations, and as many verses out of the Greek Testament. A Homer indeed was produced; but as it had a Latin version quite uncovered, which, if there had been occasion, I might with one single glance of my eye have had recourse to, it hardly deserves to be mentioned. The examination by the Master and Dean was still more easy than the Tutor's.[24]

Even the trivial acts and opponencies, the leftover medieval disputations that were still around at both universities in the second half of the eighteenth century, must have raised blood pressure levels, otherwise

---

[23] William Barrow, *An Essay on Education* . . . , 2nd ed., II (London, 1804), 308. See also Chapter 3.
[24] John Venn, *Early Collegiate Life* (Cambridge, 1913), 243–4.

cheating would not have existed. But cheating was, as cheating usually is, a desperate measure; it was necessary only because preparation was normally deferred until the eleventh hour.

Reports of serious fright begin to increase as we move towards the end of the eighteenth century. The Cambridge mathematical tripos generated more concern than the scholastic disputations. Isaac Milner, who was a sizar of Queens' College, Cambridge, in the 1770s and later became Lucasian Professor, president of Queens' and vice-chancellor in the rotation of heads of houses, confessed to the historian Thomas Babington Macaulay in 1820 that he worried continually about success when he was an undergraduate and about his prospects for the tripos. His academic record was actually extraordinary. He had been senior wrangler in the tripos and First Smith's Prizeman and was so 'superior to all his competitors, that the Moderators put the word Incomparabilis after his name'. Yet he recalled that 'he had been in a very desponding mood, and had feared, till the result was known, that he had completely failed'.[25] As for Macaulay himself, he was 'gulfed'; in the patois of the day, that meant he failed to qualify as a wrangler in the mathematical tripos. Under Cambridge rules, he could not then compete for Chancellor's medals, the highpoint of a classical career. The family discussed how to break the news to his father. Arriving home (a winter household had been established at Brighton), he was told by his mother to 'go at once to his father, and get it over'.[26]

Another famous prelate, Charles James Blomfield, bishop of London, who came up to Cambridge in 1804, taxed himself to the point where his bodily health suffered. A light burning late in the rooms of the undergraduate opposite invariably spurred him on to greater exertions. It was only afterwards that he learned that his neighbour burned the midnight oil for the sake of chess not books. A nervous spasm left his digestive system weakened for years, and 'he could not ride on horseback without having to dismount at the slightest alarm, and cling for support to a tree or railing, until the nervous tremor had passed off'.[27]

When honours schools was established at Oxford after 1800, the regulations prescribed that even wealthy entrants enrolling as gentleman-commoners were required to take the examinations. Since a similar regulation did not exist at Cambridge for those allowed to matriculate in the category of nobleman, one wealthy undergraduate, described by a

[25] Mary Milner, *The Life of Isaac Milner* (London, 1842), 707.
[26] George Otto Trevelyan, *The Life and Letters of Lord Macaulay,* I (Oxford, 1932), 78.
[27] Alfred Blomfield, *A Memoir of Charles James Blomfield,* 2nd ed. (London, 1864), 3–8.

correspondent as 'not . . . very brilliant, and extremely nervous', was deliberately sent to Cambridge.[28]

In the same period, but at Oxford, Henry Addington knocked himself dizzy with overwork by following his 'natural predilection for abstruse and laborious studies' before his 'intellectual powers . . . reached maturity' – at least his father attributed 'poor Harry's bad health and depression' to that cause.[29] A young Robert Peel, fun-loving and given to practical jokes, nevertheless worked himself into near hysteria over final honours schools. In the year before his examinations he claimed to have 'read eighteen hours in the day and night'. Lacking sleep and exercise, he contemplated bowing out of the competition, but a 'father, whose ambition, though ardent, had never deviated from the path of honour, and who owed . . . everything to steadiness and perseverance', calmed him down. On the eve of his legendary double triumph in classics and mathematics, the first in Oxford's history, Peel enjoyed a strenuous game of tennis.[30] Other Oxford contemporaries were not necessarily so self-possessed. A serious Reginald Heber wrote home at fascinating length about the competition for honours in Oxford, leaving us with a picture of intercollegiate rivalry whipped to a frenzy by zealous tutors, and undergraduates virtually passing out from panic:

> I have delayed writing till now, in order to give you an account of Winfield's success in the public examination for honours which concluded yesterday evening. He has gained the second rank, – and might I think have stood still higher, as none of his Competitors were anything very extra-ordinary, had he been at all collected. – But in fact all the four candidates were so terribly frightened that they could scarcely speak. Winfield was the most affected, and was led out into the air three times to prevent his fainting, – Mr. Barry, the man who got the first honours, dropt down in a fit through fatigue and apprehension, in the very school, at the close of the first days [*sic*] examination. – It is certainly a most formidable ordeal, but I hope if ever I appear as a Candidate, my nerves will prove firmer than what I have just seen. – So much for this dreadful tribunal, though I ought to mention that I shall have I believe some very formidable antagonists for next year, as the Christchurch Tutors are feeding up four of their best scholars for the purpose.[31]

[28] Corpus Christi College, Oxford, B/14/5/3 (6 September 1816).
[29] George Pellew, *The Life and Correspondence of the Right Hon. Henry Addington, First Viscount Sidmouth*, II (London, 1847), 389.
[30] *Sir Robert Peel*, ed. Charles Stuart Parker, I (London, 1891), 16, 18, 21–2. I am grateful to Dr Harry Judge of Oxford University for suggesting Peel.
[31] Bod. MS Eng. Lett. c.204 (264).

A few years later Reginald writes that he is going in for one of the prize poem competitions and 'will keep my embryo prize poems in secret, as I shall not wish it even to be suspected'.[32]

We can see that the competitive spirit is taking over. Not only are undergraduates discussing the tribulations of exam-taking with parents, they are also on the lookout for espionage agents searching the colleges for precious ideas useful for boosting their own chances for success in one of the many prize competitions becoming available.

From an undergraduate at Wadham College in the late 1830s we collect more evidence about the 'dreadful tribunal' that by Queen Victoria's reign had become a fixture of Oxford's academic landscape. William Osborne Maclaine, the oldest son of a Gloucestershire squire, reported to his mother that 'Thursday was a day pregnant with fate, an immense number of accidents happened here.' Among them, a certain Gordon at Worcester College decided to cut his throat 'because he was afraid of being plucked in Little-go' (a preliminary examination).[33] We can be relieved. Gordon survived, but the remainder of the letter is worth recording for the hints it provides concerning the attitude of dons towards the ordeal to which many of their charges were submitting. One of the Worcester dons, a man named Bullock, went along to check out the young man presumably on the point of death, arriving at his rooms just as the surgeon was sewing up his injured throat. But why not let Maclaine tell the story?

> Just as he entered the room the attendant let go Gordon's head so being very faint from loss of blood he let it fall on his breast. At this Bullock was greatly pleased mistaking it for an obeisance to him. Afterwards during the operation Gordon in his half insensible state uttered a faint scream or two. – Now Bullock is not a remarkably pompous man for his tribe, but however when he went into the common room that evening he made this speech – 'Hm! I do not think Gordon is in imminent danger, for I myself heard him emit a vocal sound and was pleased to perceive that he still knew how to respect *me*.'[34]

---

[32] *Ibid.* (256).

[33] Bodleian Library, Maclaine MSS, 22 February 1840. From page 195 of the *Oxford University Guide* of about 1833, Balliol College Library: 'The term *Plucked* is derived from the circumstances of the two Proctors, the moment a member's name is called by the Vice Chancellor when conferring the B.A. gown upon him, passing down the Hall on each side in order to give any tradesman or other person, who may have any complaint to prefer against the man whose name is so called, an opportunity of declaring his complaint – The Proctor's notice is attracted by *Plucking* his sleeve as he passes along – whereupon he reports to the Vice Chancellor who punishes the gentleman by refusing him his Degree.' The word then transfers to examinations.

[34] *Ibid.*

This may be perceived as a needlessly extreme reaction to examinations, but that is exactly the point. The mid-Victorian imperial manner of fearlessly braving danger had not yet developed as part of the emotional equipment of those who were born to lead. Reactions were emotional, and fears were openly expressed by parents and children alike.

That the reading man of the late eighteenth or early nineteenth century perceived himself to live in an anxious environment is not to be doubted. Letters and biographies describe the different kinds of contests in detail and indicate worry about failing or just general apprehension. Self-possession on the eve of combat was critical. Jitters during the night could be fatal, but sometimes the degree candidate was a victim of sheer bad luck. One Frederick Lowten Spinks spent a bad night because a sudden hurricane blew broken chimney pieces into his rooms at Madalene College, Cambridge, just as he went to bed. Unnerved, he went home and did not show up for his degree examinations scheduled for the next morning, 7 January 1839. He received a BA the following year.[35]

Some parents took upon themselves responsibility for keeping up the grind when sons faltered or showed signs of opting out. 'I feel myself rather anxious and ambitious for Your signalizing Yourself, and exhibiting your Learning & Genius the ensuing Act, when many of Your Friends will be happy to hear and applaud You . . . [Shake] off the Enchantress Sloth and rise to Excellence, and honour.'[36] Many years later we hear from Cambridge that 'academical honours would be less than nothing to me were it not for my father's wishes' – the sorrowful cry of Arthur Hallam in 1830.[37] Other parents, troubled about the possible ill effects of exams preparation, tried to ease rather than apply pressure, sometimes receiving reassurance that the strain was manageable or that due precautions were being taken by students and tutors alike. 'You need not trouble yourself with thinking that I shall not get through eventually, because the Tutors of my college would never have given me their permission to go up *before* my time if they had not thought me fully competent to pass,' writes Maclaine soothingly.[38] But his parents were actually divided in their own minds about examinations, wishing him to make good academic progress while at the same time avoiding an emotional breakdown. He now had to write to explain why he was not coming up before his time, trying to convince his mother that a delay in the

[35] *Romilly*, 161.
[36] Reginald Heber, father, to Richard Heber, son (20 February 1793), Bod. MS Eng. lett. c.204 (9–10).
[37] John Morley, *The Life of William Ewart Gladstone*, I (London, 1903), 66.
[38] Maclaine, 17 May 1840.

taking of a college examination was not a sign of academic difficulties. Her anxiety must have been keen because the pestered undergraduate insisted that postponing college exercises was not regarded as a sign of disgrace. Furthermore, it seemed as if all of Wiltshire had been apprised of his situation, and the entire county was on edge! Why, he writes, do the neighbours have to be kept abreast of the dates of his examination? 'It will be thought nothing of or be forgotten, and nobody in our neighbourhood need be a bit the wiser do you say nothing about it, or make light of it . . . So set poor Daddy's mind at rest and tell him he need not engage Mr. Darville [a private tutor] yet.'[39] These scraps of exchanges over what might seem like a trivial issue suggest an emotional involvement with a son's academic career, and with the psychological dimensions of exam-taking quite inconsistent with a portrait of the gentry as distant parents eager to fob off their adolescent children on surrogate dons.

Elsewhere in the highly useful Maclaine correspondence there are references to students who have been 'plucked' – one the second son of a colonel at University College who failed the Little-go twice ('I wonder what are *his* future prospects?') – and another, also a repeat ('he is of a poor family and had a curacy of 100 pounds a year waiting him').[40] Of a certain Bowden, late of Wadham, he reported that he was a 'slow man'[,] that is to say he was never remarkable for learning, or *talents* of an opposite[?] character'.[41] He mentioned that 'our friend failed' the translation from English to Latin paper in the Little-go[42] and promised to provide his mother with a 'full treatise on the various modes of reading, not reading, passing, plucks, classed'.[43]

Some successes were really only apparent. Maclaine mentioned an undergraduate who took a pass not an honours degree – 'nothing to boast of'.[44] But happier news was announced. 'Shute of this College passed his Little go . . . with great éclat: which is the more creditable to him as more men are plucked than passed now through the great strictness of the Examiners this year.'[45] A year later he mentioned that he attended some fifteen lectures per week (!) but had somehow found time to take a 'fast' student under his wing and will endeavour 'to make something of him'.[46] He described the curious case of his friend Davy, the eldest son of a knight, who went up for his final examinations in his fourteenth term rather than keeping the statutory sixteen. Davy invoked a little-used privilege of rank,

[39] *Idem*, 14 May 1840. [40] *Idem*, 15 November 1837.
[41] *Idem*, 9 March 1838. [42] *Idem*, 9 March 1838.
[43] *Idem*, 5 November 1838. [44] *Idem*, 26 October 1837.
[45] *Idem*, 4 March 1838. [46] *Idem*, 12 February 1839.

and his bold gesture paid off. He 'did it just to show the Balliol men that
he was somebody'.[47]

Examinations and other forms of 'discipline' were a dominant concern
of college authorities in the decades prior to 1850, an additional responsibility added to the list of duties required of college teachers who stood
in loco parentis to undergraduates. The new devices for spurring
achievement, the inducements held out for hard work, deeply penetrated
the student subculture, shaping it, defining its boundaries, creating new
rituals to mark the decisive moments in the undergraduate career. They
certainly threatened collegiality, the bonding relationships and internal
networking so important to the idea of a college. A world of student slang
sprang up, based on the examination experience, a *lingua franca*
functioning as initiation rite and as a mechanism for defining the
parameters of the student world. The language was the language of
contest and drawn from sports and games by the class of students least
adept at examinations. Metaphors from cricket, hunting, wrestling,
boxing were appropriated to new uses; but unlike sports (at least amateur
sports where winning was not everything), the undergraduate slang of the
early Victorian period expressed a mood of defeat. Many new words for
failing or not succeeding were in vogue: to 'floor', 'ground', 'gravel', 'gulf'
(to deliberately avoid the final round of the mathematical tripos), 'knock
down', 'plough', 'pluck', 'post', 'spin' or 'throw' down. A few of them –
'floor', 'ground' – could be applied to students who triumphed over their
examiners, but the relative absence of words to denote success shows us
where the emphasis lay.[48] There were new words for cheating – like
'cab' from 'cabbage', tailor's slang for pilfering;[49] and phrases that today
we might call 'survival strategies': 'cram', 'grind', to be 'coached' (i.e.,
driven), to 'ride hobbies' (i.e., make extensive use of translations in
preparing answers). An Aristotelian squib circulated around Oxford in
the mid-1830s gave advice on how to fail examinations. Certain to be
'plucked' were those who read many books and those who read few, those
who knew many pretty girls and those who knew only one, those who
attended dog fights and those who wore white gloves while shooting, those
who ate too much or broke lamps in the street. The list concluded with 'He
that thinketh he will be plucked' and 'he that thinketh not he will be
plucked'.[50] In short, 'plucking' is the fate that must befall every under-

[47] *Idem*, 17 May 1840.
[48] Morris Marples, *University Slang* (London, 1950), 5.
[49] *Ibid.*, 49.
[50] Edward Caswall, 'A New Art – Teaching how to be Plucked', in Morris, *Oxford Book of Oxford*, 215.

graduate. It cannot be averted or avoided, for no one can satisfy ruthless and relentless examiners armed with the most formidable weapon the university could employ against unprotected undergraduates now attacked on two flanks, the second assault being the unceasing advice, exhortation and reproval arriving frequently from home. Failure but not success can almost be guaranteed. The picture is one of a community of young persons threatened by a gerontocracy and forced into a life of academic crime - finding ways to mitigate the experience of examinations and college competitions, or to justify poor performance – as a form of legitimate self-defence.

By the mid-1860s new slang suggests that the culture of competition is winning. Words like to 'score off' or to 'notch' are in vogue to signify a triumph (generally a temporary one, as if to suggest that competition never ceases). Once again the slang derived from games where points were obtained, 'scored' or 'notched', from an adversary.[51] Learning to cope with a stressful academic environment was a major feature of early Victorian student life for all but the most indifferent. Success, or at least a pass, provided some relief. 'The Seventh heaven of Mahomet was a joke to the blissful state of idleness in wch [sic] I reveled, having no bugbear of a "*Pluck* hanging over my head".'[52]

On 19 March 1848, Richard Wilton described the Little-go examinations in his college. The examinations lasted from 8 a.m. until 11 a.m. After a break, examining resumed at noon and went on for three more hours. The results were announced at 10 p.m. on the same day. 'A little before ten the men turn out of their rooms into the court to hear the fate of their companions. If he is through, immediately begins the most boisterous cheering; on the other hand[,] a pluck is received with melancholy silence.' Evidently it was also the custom at St Catharine's College, Cambridge, for the undergraduates to 'mew' when a student completed his degree, which Wilton did, taking a first in mathematics.[53]

Some failures slunk away in disgrace, but others began to participate in a counter-revolution that was actually an appeal to inherited ideals of self-worth and a refusal to accept the view that examinations were a true indication of merit. They put a bold face on their supposed humiliations and made light of them, even forcing their peers into an open display of support. In a number of cases the undergraduates resisted the effort by the

[51] 'Oxford Slang', *Macmillan's Magazine*, 21 (November 1869), 71.
[52] Written on the endpapers of a 'Guide with annotations to Oxford University compiled c. 1833 by a privileged undergraduate of Christ Church who took his degree as allowed for privilege u.g.'s in two years', Balliol College Library.
[53] Mary Blamire Young, *Richard Wilton, A Forgotten Victorian* (London, 1967), 65–6, 93.

dreadful tribunal judges to single out one of their members as a warning and rallied behind him. He was, after all, an example of the possible fate awaiting them all. The older aristocratic notion of public shame was employed but in reverse as public acclaim. They were two sides of the same coin. There can be no disgrace if the community refuses to acknowledge disgrace, and what appears to be failure is actually, by the operations of a reverse code of values, a form of success. This is the charivari syndrome, turning the world upside down. In one account, several unfortunate Oxonians, floored in Smalls (another name for Little-go), nevertheless presided over raucous celebrations. When these events were reported home by letter, it was explained that college practice was to honour all remarkable occurrences, whether fortunate or unfortunate.[54] Even the idlers were drawn in. True to their instincts as sporting men, if they did not study themselves, they could at least bet on the favourites. In another and different situation, a student who had laboured mightily with little hope of success actually achieved a breakthrough. A 'slow man', with nine years of residence in Oxford, boasting of six 'plucks' and 'driven' by four 'coaches', finally made it through his examinations. The news arrived during dinner in Hall, and loud cheers followed, shaking the 'pictures of the old worthies hung all round, as I have seldom heard'.[55] A wild celebration ensued. The episode admits of a number of interpretations. After so many attempts, merely succeeding warranted a victory celebration. But a clamorous marking of the occasion also drew attention to the student's arduous passage, reminding everyone present of how much support the slow and fast alike required from friends and how much money had to be given to private tutors by parents in order to haul a simpleton or wastrel through the unavoidable ordeal. If rituals are required to turn tragedy into comedy, and to placate the Muse of Tragedy with a classic *komos* of dance and song led by the lords of misrule, the undergraduates created them.[56]

If an effort was often made to turn failure into success, so too do we find instances in which success is made to appear failure. We have the morning

[54] Maclaine, 20 October 1838.
[55] Young, *Richard Wilton*, 30.
[56] It would be interesting to compile a list of the rituals or traditions students created in order to defeat or ameliorate the harsh judgements that examinations bestow upon candidates, but more importantly, to oppose the deleterious effect that examinations have on group cohesion. Student solidarity rituals take different forms. After about 1970 graduate students in history at the University of California at Berkeley formed support groups to accompany doctoral candidates to their oral qualifying examinations and to greet and cheer them at the end of the two- to three-hour ordeal. The show of solidarity was, to the best of my knowledge, unprecedented at Berkeley.

shadow of a new culture, perhaps Romantic, certainly introspective. No amount of ostensible success is ever satisfying. There is always another prize to be won or lost. A nagging sense of inadequacy haunts the performer, robbing him of his triumphs. There is a Nemesis in the environment – another competitor, but actually himself. As far back as the 1790s a future bishop of Calcutta, Thomas Fanshawe Middleton, left Cambridge bemoaning the circumstances that prevented him from gaining the Chancellor's Medal or scoring higher than Fourth Senior Optime in the mathematics tripos. More than once he felt like quitting. His competition was Edward Maltby, another future bishop, who swept all before him. All his life Middleton bitterly regretted that he had not achieved higher distinction at Cambridge, and he seemed to believe that harder study would have gained the elusive prizes.[57] In a later period Fitzjames Stephen, Leslie Stephen's illustrious older brother, was tipped as a high flyer and received the midnight knock at his door that announced his selection to the secret undergraduate society of Cambridge Apostles. As Apostles were expected to speak out at meetings, and as Fitzjames was reticent, even this high distinction came to naught – in his own mind at least. Admired by his peers, he nevertheless failed to get either a scholarship or fellowship at Trinity and took the news very hard, as did his father. Sir James's feelings on these occasions were highly ambivalent. He confessed to his disappointed 'parental ambition', deplored the 'demoralizing sense of failure' inflicted on young men 'not fitted for early success'. To Fitzjames he recommended regular prayer. Fitzjames was of course devastated. 'He had a more or less dim foreboding of the difficulties which were to meet him in the world at large.'[58] Leslie Stephen himself became thoroughly disenchanted with the competitive culture of mid-Victorian Cambridge, even while he contributed to its making, and resigned his fellowship in a famous episode.[59]

Although advancement by strict academic merit had not replaced networking as formerly understood, by the 1820s or 1830s it had become an important means of attracting the attention of influential persons in government and Church; and while success in examinations was not yet the sole criterion by which college fellowships were assigned, there too merit as more narrowly measured was being recognised. Earnest parents

[57] Clement Carlyon, *Early Years and Late Reflections*, I (London, 1856), 9–10, and II (London, 1856), 281.
[58] Leslie Stephen, *The Life of Sir James Fitzjames Stephen* (London, 1895), 106, 110–12.
[59] Noël Gilroy Annan, *Leslie Stephen, His Thought and Character in Relation to his Time* (Cambridge, MA, 1971), Chapter 1. A revised edition appears under the title *Leslie Stephen, The Godless Victorian* (New York, 1984).

and their serious-minded undergraduates worried about how a weak performance at university might affect both career prospects and the family's reputation in the vicinity, but, as already suggested, the zeal with which a student might participate in the developing culture of examinations created another kind of distress. It was possible that protracted study and burning the midnight oil might lead to a withdrawal from the social whirl of college life, an arena of conviviality in which character was tested according to conventional standards of sociability.[60] The person who isolates himself from the world may be advertising himself as unsuited for leadership roles. How then to balance the two opposed conceptions of achieving success, one that required active participation in the clubs and activities of peers, another that necessitated isolation and solitary application?

SYMPTOMS OF DISTRESS

Cyril Jackson deplored the habit of lounging that was so prevalent in the ancient universities of England. He continually stressed the necessity for strenuous work. In 1810 he told his former pupil, the rising young politician Robert Peel, to continue the regimen of application acquired in the House. 'Work very hard and unremittingly. Work . . . like a tiger, or like a dragon, if dragons work more and harder than tigers . . . Don't be afraid of killing yourself.'[61] Richard Wilton did almost that. In 1847 he told his parents that he had gone in for the Skrine Scholarship examination in his Cambridge college. 'The suspense, excitement and excessive labour of three days [*sic*] examination, joined with the late hours I was obliged to keep preparing it, left me . . . very unwell.' The outcome was nevertheless successful.[62]

Jackson's attitude was not typical of Oxford and Cambridge dons, although it was precisely the kind of attitude emerging with the new examinations culture. It was absurd to believe that without such prodding the student estate would take the new competitions seriously as there remained conventional reasons for sloughing off. Yet the intense kind of preparation required for passing the honours examinations, even the less intense preparation required for taking the pass examinations, plus the multiplication of college prizes, awards and examinations, gave rise to

---

[60] See Sheldon Rothblatt, *Tradition and Change in English Liberal Education, An Essay in History and Culture* (London, 1976), Chapter 7.

[61] Parker, *Peel*, 29.

[62] Young, *Richard Wilton*, 55.

fears that personal health was likely to be affected, reinforcing older surviving attitudes. One good reason that indolence was so much tolerated in late Georgian Oxbridge – besides the difficulty of getting bloods and hearties to slog – was the fear of damage to young lives through overwork. It would be a disservice to society to ruin the health of future leaders, or of the elite in general. Tennyson's father admitted that he had a positive distaste for hard work when at St John's, Cambridge. Excelling, he informed his own father, required 'such continual application and exertion, as would neither suit my health, time, nor inclination. The anxiety I should suffer and the deprivation of better knowledge, could only be compensated by the hope of an uncertain and at best a transitory honour.'[63] Something ventured but nothing much gained.

Indeed. In the older or inherited theory of a liberal education, extended periods of study were disparaged as both unsociable and likely to produce the psychosomatic illness that since Elizabethan times had gone under the designation of 'melancholy'. Low spirits, hypochondria, hysteria, the spleen and vapours were much discussed in the eighteenth century and publicised in George Chapman's work of 1733, *The English Malady*. In the Victorian era it was common to refer to many different symptoms of profound malaise as 'shattered nerves'. Sexual worries, effeminacy (a special concern occurring with the Anglo-Catholicism of the Oxford Movement),[64] fears about family bankruptcies (common enough in an era of partnerships and family-owned businesses), problems of religious orientation and concerns about grace and redemption were among frequently listed anxieties. Somatic symptoms included lethargy, impotence, weight loss and horrible headaches.[65] Low personal esteem often surfaced as a sign of emotional disturbance.

Overwork was the common explanation for most signs of instability. Some of the anxiety about working too hard may have arisen precisely because families were transmitting their own fears to children at university, warning about possible difficulties that may not have yet arisen or taking student complaints out of context. Frequent letter writing has the virtue of maintaining close connections over distance, but like a diary it is also a medium that allows for the recording of daily minutiae. What may be troubling at dawn has frequently disappeared by dusk. The increasing emphasis on the importance of a child's environment (discussed

[63] Edward Miller, 'St John's', in *The Victoria History of the County of Cambridge and the Isle of Ely*, ed. John Roach, III (London, 1959), 442.
[64] David Newsome, *Godliness and Good Learning* (London, 1961), 208–9.
[65] Janet Oppenheim, *'Shattered Nerves', Doctors, Patients and Depression in Victorian England* (New York, 1991), 3–5, 13–14, 157, 167–9, 196, 226–7.

more fully in a later chapter) indicates closer parental supervision over the emotional and bodily condition of children and adolescents. Where familial relations were close and emotional, the tendency would be for parents to encourage children to identify irritations and strain, or for mothers and fathers to suspect their presence from a hundred signs (including silence), infecting or reinfecting young persons with their own fears and suppositions. Evidence of short-term psychosomatic difficulty exists, and in some instances the problems extended well into maturity.[66]

A young man who entered Christ Church in 1808, George Robert Chinnery, received weekly and bi-weekly bulletins from his overly protective mother on how to manage his health and care for his body. No detail escaped her attention, from drinking to jumping ditches and riding hacks, which she initially forbade in the strongest terms. There were good grounds. Horseback riding was always risky since the animal could easily stumble and fall. Riding in a wheeled vehicle was equally dangerous. If the wheel came off, or the horse fell, the passenger could be crushed. The House bullies teased Chinnery mercilessly. Was he expecting a hobby horse from home? His mother was alarmed by his headaches – 'at your age . . . a most unnatural thing' – and he popped squill pills to prevent colds and sore throats.[67] Of course Maclaine from time to time had to reassure his own mother that he was in solid health, in fact, 'stronger and better than I have felt for some time back'.[68] As we might expect in close families, there was an almost fanatical eagerness to report sniffs and coughs; but once reported, they were likely to be a recurrent subject longer than a dutiful, now chastened son had bargained for.

The sources reflect an on-going preoccupation with the handicaps of university residence and intensive studying on young men. When the volatile Apostle 'Jacky' Kemble was at Cambridge in the 1820s, his

---

[66] The phenomenon is doubtless European as well as English. Theodore Zeldin, *France 1848–1945*, II (Oxford, 1977), 825–41, has a fascinating discussion of anxiety in Victorian France. Fear of failure and of not passing examinations enters the picture there as well, and mental health, raised to a high level of consciousness by the popularisation of medical knowledge, became, as in England, a continual topic of conversation or latent worry. Some of Balzac's views on the connection between excess energy and illness resemble those of Victorian writers. For reflections on anxiety and fear as intrinsic parts of early modern European culture see William J. Bouwsma, 'Anxiety and the Formation of Early Modern Culture', in *After the Reformation: Essays in Honour of J. H. Hexter*, ed. Barbara C. Malament (Philadelphia, 1980). The ingredients of the new malaise were: changing conceptions of time, the conditions of urban life, death and redemption. Anxiety was 'managed' by new psychic and intellectual control mechanisms.

[67] Chinnery Papers, Christ Church Library, 19 January 1808, 28 January 1808, 16 February 1808, 4 June 1808, 27 October 1808.

[68] Maclaine, 17 May 1840.

younger sister expressed the fear that 'excitement' would injure his health[69] – the kind of excitement, incidentally, associated with the enthusiasms of the Romantic movement.

Every aspect of schooling or university life was, at one time or the other, a worry for some parent; swimming, for example. Heber took easily to water when boarding with a clergyman at Neasden in the 1790s; but his tutor, afraid of parental reaction, limited his dips to ten minutes at a time. He also sent progress reports on appetite and complexion to Reginald's parents.[70] An increase in water-related activity at Oxford and Cambridge in the first two decades of the nineteenth century had much to do with the fear of drowning. The river had customarily been a hangout for roughs, and the defective design of recreational craft produced frequent capsizings. Maclaine had promised his mother that he would not row; but in a letter of 1838 he asked to be released from his vow on the grounds that boats were safer now and rowing was a sure means of improving his health.[71]

Biographies of famous Victorians, whether at Oxbridge or not, report the notorious migraine headaches and nervous disorders that afflicted them: A. C. Benson, J. A. Symonds, John Ruskin, Joseph Lister, Arnold Toynbee and Charles Darwin all suffered from some form of depression or another at university, or just after going down. J. S. Mill and George Eliot did not go to university, but managed to become depressed without that experience.[72] Eliot was troubled by her unorthodoxy of thought and action. Mill has recorded for posterity his problems with James Mill and the arid abstractions of palaeo-utilitarianism. Darwin, according to a recent, not wholly convincing account, was similarly shaken by the ramifications of his own thinking.[73] He went down from Christ's College, Cambridge, without taking a degree. Ill health, nervous agitation, neuralgia and headaches were the order of the day for young people who nevertheless, as a very old William Ewart Gladstone recalled of several of his contemporaries, managed to live to an uncommonly old age.[74] Judging from his diaries, Gladstone himself showed signs of psychic discomfort as a boy and young man. When at Eton he carefully monitored the

[69] Peter Allen, *The Cambridge Apostles, the Early Years* (Cambridge, 1978), 98.
[70] Bod. MS Eng. lett. c. 204 (313, 317).
[71] Maclaine, 26 October 1837, 9 November 1838.
[72] Oppenheim, *'Shattered Nerves'*, 166.
[73] See Ralph Colp, Jr, *To Be an Invalid, the Illness of Charles Darwin* (Chicago and London, 1977).
[74] Charles Robert Leslie Fletcher, *Mr. Gladstone at Oxford [1890]* (London and New York, 1908), 33.

appearance and severity of his headaches, which may have abated when he came to Oxford. When they occurred during his undergraduate years, they were usually associated with career anxieties. In 1831 he vowed to work ten or eleven hours per day, health permitting, and at one point he read so hard that his eyes and head were painfully affected. 'He declared that the bodily fatigue, the mental fatigue, and the anxiety as to the results, made reading for a class a thing not to be undergone more than once in a lifetime.'[75] Some parents shopped for less competitive colleges in which to place their frail sons. Sir James Stephen sent his eldest son Fitzjames to Trinity College, Cambridge, but he sent Leslie to Trinity Hall, believing him to be in less robust health. Leslie's spectacular improvement through a regimen of sustained physical exercise is nearly legendary, leading one to suspect that part of his problem was growing up in the home of a member of the intellectual aristocracy. A Cambridge contemporary of Leslie, Richard Wilton, suffered frequent attacks of neuralgia while at home, partly caused, no doubt, by a late adolescent switchover from chapel to Church. There might well have been something to the claim made by the kindly Professor Corrie of St Catharine's that college life would restore his condition.[76]

BODILY HEALTH

While fear that overwork might lead to a serious collapse was common, there exist many concrete reasons for parental concern over the health of sons away at college. The physical conditions at university were not of the best. Poor and primitive forms of lighting made study hard on the eyes, and the coming of winter invariably lengthened the use of artifical light. The record of famous literary figures who went blind or impaired their vision by reading and writing long hours into the night is familiar to us, and was familiar then. Rudimentary health practices were not observed. The standard diet was appalling: heavy on protein and rich sauces, with fresh fruits and vegetables in short supply. Undergraduates rose late and had pantagruelian breakfasts. The consumption of alcohol was heavy, although varying in type and quantity according to drinking fads. Gout and obesity afflicted the older dons, and everyone suffered from hangovers. There were many headaches and stomachaches, especially among the naive freshers whom upper classmen loved to tempt with drink. Rooms in or out of college could be dank. Undergraduates worried

---

[75] *The Gladstone Diaries*, ed. M. R. D. Foot, I (Oxford, 1968), 339; Morley, *Gladstone*, 76.
[76] Young, *Richard Wilton*, 52.

about having acceptable quarters. Heating arrangements were unsatisfactory, especially for sizars, servitors and other students of straitened means since coal was an additional expense in the days before changes were introduced in the methods of computing battels (bills). Sanitation could be rudimentary. Bathing was infrequent. At Caius College in 1850 no water was laid on in the rooms, and the privies were located near the pumps.[77] Fire was a constant hazard and hence a continual worry, and when it occurred undergraduates and 'big wigs' lined up side by side in the bucket brigades. Recreational facilities were not readily available, although the development of collegiate sports and the widespread habit of taking long afternoon walks burned off excess calories and counteracted the effects of self-indulgence. Field sports and riding were expensive, however, as was boating, and also liable to produce injuries. Finally, just to cap this review of the hazards to health that existed in late Georgian Oxford and Cambridge, we need only mention the dreaded and costly epidemics of the nineteenth century – cholera, typhoid, typhus and the brief return of smallpox – as well as the omnipresent threat of influenza and other respiratory illnesses not readily amenable to such treatments as then provided. Disease spreads quickly in congested environments.

Muscular development and bodily health were favourite topics, especially when the consequences of living in the expanding cities of the nineteenth century were discussed. Air and water pollution made cities hazardous places indeed. Rushing off to the Swiss mountains in summer or to the Mediterranean in winter were remedies much in fashion in the mid-Victorian period.[78] One of the arguments circulating at the time of the founding of University College, London, was that an unhealthy metropolis was a poor situation for a new college.[79] When Fitzjames Stephen was preparing for Cambridge by studying at King's College, London, which then, and for sometimes afterwards, also functioned as a college preparatory school, he noticed that London boys were of inferior physique compared to public school boys (he had spent several miserable years at Eton). He was therefore surprised by the fact that they were so industrious, and he thought the answer lay in their upbringing as sons of London business and professional men.[80] Was this an implicit criticism of his own upbringing?

The connection between health and academic work, especially competitive examinations, became more conspicuous as the century

[77] Venn, *Early Collegiate Life*, 273.   [78] Oppenheim, *'Shattered Nerves'*, 130.
[79] Hugh Hale Bellot, *University College, London, 1826–1926* (London, 1929), 62–3.
[80] Stephen, *Sir James Fitzjames Stephen*, 86–7.

progressed. They seem almost directly proportional to one another. The Oxbridge examination system became more strenuous. Written work replaced vivas; examining was less open-ended, the questions more technical and greater emphasis was placed on speed and endurance. The mathematical tripos of 1836 was possibly the first one in which all the papers were actually closely marked. Earlier examiners and moderators tended to rely on impression.[81] Serious preparation for final schools now involved disciplined use of the 'Long Vac', reading parties and the extensive use of private coaches. Examinations anxiety was exactly what a marginal class of university teachers needed to bring in the extra income, or even the basic income, required to marry and maintain gentlemanly standards of living. (The thought that directly, but more likely indirectly, they encouraged students to worry about academic success is mischievous but possibly relevant.) Accounts of breaking down while studying hard are a standard part of the reminiscences of the 1840s and 1850s. Francis Galton virtually collapsed in his third year at Cambridge. 'My head is very uncertain so that I can scarcely read at all', he wrote to his father in 1842. '[However], I find that I am not at all solitary in that respect. Of the year above me the *first three men* in their College examinations are all going out in the poll, the first two from bad health and the third . . . from finding that he could not continue reading as he used to do without risking it.' He adds:

> It is quite melancholy too to see the men who stood high in the College, but did not get scholarships this year in May; they seem most of them quite broken spirited . . . I feel more convinced every day that if there is a thing more to be repressed than another it is certainly the system of competition for the satisfaction enjoyed by the gainers is very far from counter-balancing the pain it produces among the others.[82]

Is it perverse to suggest that it was precisely Galton's failure to cope with the Cambridge tripos that made him put so much more emphasis on inherited genetic traits than on achievement?

An American at Trinity in the 1840s, Charles Bristed, has left us with excellent acounts of the pressure-cooker environment in which the reading man lived. For many the preliminary examinations at Cambridge and Oxford were turning points, having some of the characteristics of a matriculation examination. But differential calculus alone took a number of students out of contention. Bristed himself became ill and found

[81] W. W. Rouse Ball, *Cambridge Papers* (London, 1918), 298–9.
[82] Karl Pearson, *The Life, Letters and Labours of Francis Galton*, I (Cambridge, 1914), 170–1.

himself unable to cope with the cycle of examinations and competitions. He was mortified:

> The dancer with a sprained ancle [*sic*], the horseman with his bridle hand disabled, the rower with a broken oar, the epicure condemned by his physician to hospital diet – are all to be pitied for their tantalizing plight; but none of them so deserving of commiseration as a young man eager for the acquisition of knowledge, with everything around tempting him to it, and every one about him engaged in the pursuit, yet forced by the instinct of self-preservation to be systematically idle and lie back like a boat aground, seeing others float by him.[83]

The last point is the key to reading the paragraph.

MANLINESS

It is not fanciful to regard the Victorian habit of stressing manly and masculine conduct as a psychological means of strengthening resistance to the various kinds of anxieties arising in nineteenth-century society. '[The] over-worked mind in an under-worked body' is how the great Victorian and Regius Professor at Cambridge John Robert Seeley put the problem in 1849.[84] The whole system of competitive selection threatened the well-being and health of young adults. Medical practitioners were provided with a windfall. Their numbers and the numbers of urban medical schools were greatly expanded, creating a large body of medical students eager for opportunities to display their training. Anticipatory socialisation was quite strong among medical students, who, more than any other body of career-minded students in London, had a firm sense of fellowship and sociability. Medical men were the most active of the professionals of the early nineteenth century, forming the largest single group of specialists in old and new professional societies and scientific organisations.[85]

Faculty psychology, the most famous learning theory of the nineteenth century, was a particular menace. The theory stressed the need to increase brain power through serious mental stimulation and exercise. Learning was therefore a form of gymnastics, requiring excellent coordination and top physical condition. A single-minded coach whipping up his protégé's

---

[83] Charles Astor Bristed, *Five Years in an English University* (New York, 1852), 103–4.
[84] 'College Life. The Ideal Student', *London University College Magazine* (1849), 334–5.
[85] E. W. Beal, 'Students' Clubs and Societies', *The London Student* (June 1868), 147. Jules Romains, *Dr. Knock*, and Thomas Mann, *The Magic Mountain*, remind us that the supply of medical services may well lead demand. A sick but curable society is a great boon to profession building.

memory and endurance would very likely destroy cerebral balance by undue stimulation of one or more cortical functions to the detriment of others. It is easy to see why Bristed's lament, however melodramatic, rings true for the period and why illness was the great pervasive fear of the reading man. 'Slanged' and 'driven' by high-priced 'coaches', forgoing exercise, suffering from headaches, worrying about colds and the possibility of accidents, knowing all the while that there would be no second chance in schools or the tripos and with no opportunity for the Macaulays of the future to bounce back from a failed honours performance, the serious mid-Victorian undergraduate was very often a bundle of nerves.

The corrective to mental exertion was clearly a sound body:

> It is, perhaps, to this neglect of physical exercise that we find amongst students so frequent a tendency towards discontent, unhappiness, inaction, and reverie, – displaying itself in a premature contempt for real life, and disgust at the beaten tracks of men, – a tendency which in England has been called Byronism, and in Germany Wertherism.[86]

This was Samuel Smiles again, a leading authority on energy, expressing conventional reservations about the effect of excessive study on moral habits and character. '[Stomachs] weak as blotting-paper, – hearts indicating fatty degeneration – unused, pithless hands, calveless legs and limp bodies' – not a pretty picture of young manhood in flower![87] Out too came the old leering enemy of the scholar and student, melancholia, *furor*, partially legitimised by Plato, Aristotle and Renaissance intellectuals as one source of creativity, but now, after the narcissistic indulgence of the Romantic movement, showing its true colours.

Bruce Haley has written about aspects of the nineteenth-century health movement in his study, *The Healthy Body and Victorian Culture*, which helps explain such Cambridge fads of the 1840s as standing up while studying as a means of promoting stamina[88] (and preventing an undergraduate from falling asleep at his post). We can contrast this association between job performance and health with earlier – let us say, turn of the century – manifestations of concern over the condition of the body. In both instances an interest in muscular development is evident, but in 1800 there was still intermixed with it a leftover aristocratic posing, for deportment

---

[86] Samuel Smiles, *Self-Help* (Boston, 1866), 310.
[87] *Ibid.*
[88] Bristed, *Five Years*, 104. But the practice may have been in vogue earlier, for Chinnery's mother thought he sat too much and sent him a high writing table. Chinnery Papers, 28 January 1808.

as well as strength, for style as much as performance. Thus Chinnery's mother, fearful that he might tumble while riding, did not express similar reservations about fencing, and along with every other piece of advice she eagerly provided her hard-pressed son, also told him how to move his legs so 'that your outward actions may at all times bespeak the gentleness and politeness of a well-bred gentleman'.[89] (Poor Chinnery appears to have been in the unenviable position of Lord Chesterfield's illegitimate son, so beleaguered with counsel from his distant yet overbearing father that he was sure to humiliate himself in public not once but often.)

For the later decades the interest in bearing and demeanour lessened. The courtier gave way to the muscular Christian. Exercise was an antidote to brain work. Organised sports and physical conditioning became more widespread and popular, not just in relation to examinations but in response to all anxiety generating changes. Exercise of a rugged kind was pursued in an effort to counteract the effeminacy of Byronism. Smiles was very clear on the issue: success required endurance and strength. The lawyer, for one, needed a good thorax![90] Tramping, alpine climbing, rugger, cricket and so on were the means to health. The deepest moral purposes underlay these physical activities, even crazes. Exercise was the path to that celebrated 'manliness' by which Victorians battled against the constant urge to indulge in spleen, fretting, restlessness and torpor. It was the means they chose to combat the fear that their energy was flagging, that luxury would produce a loss of ambition and that in time the English would become a lost and degenerate race, brutish again, as the thin crust of civilisation broke and flaked.

Inevitably there were critics of the health movement, warnings that it had gone too far the other way. Modern technology, pleaded one opponent, eliminates the need for a 'regiment of Polyphemuses'.[91] Mental vigour did not rely exclusively upon muscular development. But the ideal was actually the golden mean, 'the sound mind in a sound body' which the Victorians with their interest in things Grecian revived for their own purposes. The two were intimately related, as Haley demonstrates, and the man broken in body would inevitably be broken in mind too. In order to avoid the one, it was necessary to avoid the other. So play, recreation, games were not reactions to schooling and more academic discipline, but went hand in hand with them. Headmasters pushed games, making

---

[89] Chinnery Papers, 19 January 1808, 15 February 1808, 2 February 1809.
[90] Smiles, *Self-Help*, 315.
[91] Henry Fearon, *Mental Vigour: its Attainment Impeded by Errors in Education* (London, 1859), 6.

certain that all pupils in one way or another experienced the competition of the playing fields, the success of the players also redounding to the glory of the school.[92] The study of the effect of examinations on mental health was not incompatible with a greater emphasis on it and eventually led to psychometry and the more precise measurement of achievement. Resting and relaxing, instead of being alternatives to work, were regarded as vital to ambition, as Seeley inimitably put it, 'the secret both of energy and endurance, because play is food' and re-creates the man.[93]

What help did the undergraduate of the earlier nineteenth century have when experiencing strain, whether its sources lay in religion, in the choice of career, in parental or personal ambition, peer pressure or causes either obscure or too alarming to admit? The question is natural, given a university world which was increasingly exposed to a success ethic, to incentives for hard work, to competition as a means of selection – sometimes *pour le sport* to combat the boredom and isolation of small-town life and gossip[94] – and to public shame and humiliation as mechanisms for encouraging ambition. Furthermore, in every decade undergraduates could hear about the debates among medical authorities on the causes of hypochondria, learn the latest theories pertaining to nervous disorder and the effects of exertion on bodily health.

Relief, however, was not readily forthcoming except where special ties were developing between undergraduates and dons just several years their seniors, the tiny circles of friendships being created by a reawakened religious intensity, by the graduates of reading parties, by the Apostles, by proponents of pastoral teaching like Newman and by the would-be reformers of another generation. These were significant and would cumulatively construct a movement for educational improvement from within, first at college and later at university level. But institutionally the Oxford and Cambridge of the first half of the nineteenth century did not provide the extensive student support services today deemed essential for coping with anxiety, whether or not of academic origin. Correspondence from early decades shows parental understanding mixed with exhortation and prompting. Private and college tutors were occasionally approached

---

[92] James A. Mangan, *Athleticism in the Victorian and Edwardian Public School: The Emergence and Consolidation of an Educational Ideology* (Cambridge and New York, 1981).

[93] John Robert Seeley, 'Recreation', *The London Student* (July 1868), 207.

[94] Savants, Seeley noticed, were carried away by the excitement of undergraduate competitions. 'It makes them feel young again to assist as trainers, backers, and umpires to the young people'. Seeley, 'A Plea for More Universities', *The London Student* (April 1868), 9. The regeneration theme is encountered repeatedly. See Sheldon Rothblatt, *The Revolution of the Dons* (London and New York, 1968, reissued Cambridge, 1981), 246–7.

by parents with requests for assistance. Sympathetic friends could be found but not guaranteed in what was still mainly an insensitive student subculture. In general, making friends in college was a problem, as the sources indicate. Older dons, especially in the earlier decades where the senior members were expected to be aloof and pompous symbols of rectitude and authority, were unpredictable. Some were kindly, others quirky. Younger dons, if they remained in Oxford and Cambridge during the tenure of their fellowships, were probably distracted by neurasthenic difficulties of their own arising from career uncertainties and the shortage of suitable women. The question does not really admit of a full answer now. All that may be hazarded is that the junior members of the university did not have automatic recourse to alert and discerning guides or reliable information on the causes and nature of stress. Reluctant as well to talk openly about certain topics upon which taboos were laid, they doubtless lived in conditions of far greater anxiety that we have hitherto suspected, but which every fresh biography or new cache of letters reveals, confessing to it wherever possible or sublimating and disguising their fears and learning to live with worry as best they could.

THE REWARDS FOR SUCCESS

The ancient universities were equipped to provide certain kinds of rewards for worthy candidates, but these were not necessarily granted on a basis of measurable merit. Some 600 clerical livings under control of Oxford and Cambridge colleges were filled in order of seniority by date of appointment to fellowships. Fellowships themselves were not necessarily 'open' to competition, but were also tied by college statutes to certain categories of person, geographical location or school. Scholarships were similarly restricted. Yet there were innumerable and complicated exceptions. At Christ Church, for example, only four of a hundred (or 101) studentships ('students' at the House could be bachelors as well as under-graduates) could be described as closed (although exhibitions could be restricted).[95] But on what basis were the majority of studentships granted if so few of them were closed? Lesser scholarships (exhibitions, bursaries, demyships) were given on a basis of need – there were a few exceptions – reflecting the commitment of the ancient universities to a class of students, generally of 'limited means', whose career ambitions led to clerical preferment.

At a number of colleges, the scholarship and fellowship systems were

[95] E. G. W. Bill and J. F. A. Mason, *Christ Church and Reform, 1850–1867* (Oxford, 1970), 11–13.

interconnected. An undergraduate holding a scholarship was eligible in due course for a college fellowship, and his ranking in the tripos was irrelevant. This was certainly the case at King's College where the scholars, all Etonians, could move on to fellowships without even taking a first degree. Brasenose fellowships were highly in-grown. Of twenty fellows in 1770, only two came from outside. Eighteen fellows had been in the college, fourteen of them scholars and four others commoners.[96] At Magdalen College, Oxford, scholars succeeded to fellowships almost as a matter of course. Balliol went outside college between 1783 and 1800 to elect six fellows from a broader pool of candidates, yet in the middle of the nineteenth century no less a figure than the renowned Mark Pattison thought that examinations had little effect on election to fellowships in that college.[97] Most colleges at Oxford appear to have favoured their own undergraduates. Isaac Milner at Cambridge supported this policy. He vehemently protested in a letter to William Wilberforce in 1801 that the only reason he once went out of college to find a fellow (such appointments were in his gift) was that in-house candidates had been 'Jacobins or infidels'. He selected a fifth wrangler.

Those who had not managed to find a place in the queue leading from scholarship to fellowship were tempted to take the easy way to a degree by avoiding honours and going out in the poll. Fitzjames Stephen was one of them. Failing to win a scholarship at the end of his second or third year, and therefore deprived of a chance to compete for a fellowship, he reasoned that he should avoid the strain of further competition. However, he stayed the course.

Yet at Trinity College, Cambridge, the principle of competition appears to have been winning, and Trinity generally set the intellectual example at Cambridge, at least after 1800. The overwrought scholarship competition in that college led to an out-migration of undergraduates to smaller Cambridge colleges where neither the scholarship examinations nor the tripos were required for election and fellowships were awarded on a more flexible basis.[98] There is a possible correlation between this trend and a sharp decline in the numbers of scholars at Trinity from Westminster School elected to fellowships in the college. In the first half of the eighteenth century, 62 out of 187 Westminster scholars became fellows. In

[96] W. T. Coxhill, 'Brasenose College in the Time of Principal Ralph Camley, 1770–1777' (Oxford B.Litt. thesis, 1946), 31.

[97] Bill and Mason, *Christ Church*, 15.

[98] D. A. Winstanley, *Unreformed Cambridge* (Cambridge, 1935), 228; H. A. Wilson, *Magdalen College* (London, 1899), 222; Milner, *Life of Milner*, 243, 344; H. W. Carless Davis, *Balliol College* (London, 1899), 274.

the second half, only 30 of 180 gained the prize. In the first half of the next century, the numbers plummeted. Of 170 Westminster scholars, only four received fellowships.[99]

Trinity had a separate oral fellowship examination at the end of the eighteenth century. This suggests that the Senate House examinations may have been relevant but not decisive. Another deduction is that because the mathematical tripos had been converted into a written examination, the senior fellows still wanted some evidence of rhetorical facility, an important part of the older oral culture. John Venn noted that the earliest mention of the tripos in the awarding of any prize at Caius was in 1803.[100] Writing about Oxford, A. D. Godley noted that most fellows in the eighteenth century were elected after some kind of a test or examination (presumably after close awards were taken into consideration). No examination papers or details of such examinations survive, and Godley suspects that 'interest' also operated.[101]

Oriel College, Oxford, like Trinity College, Cambridge, also had a special fellowship examination, and Newman was able to take advantage of it since he received only a common pass on the undergraduate terminal examinations. The indomitable Edward Copleston, provost of Oriel from 1814 to 1828 and afterwards bishop of Llandaff, defended the practice of separating honours examinations from fellowship selection, even though the 'quackery of the Schools' (as the aggrieved put it) had been partly his doing. In a letter of 1843 he stated that 'Every election to a fellowship which tends to discourage the narrow and almost the technical routine of public examinations, I consider as an important triumph.'[102] He recalled that Newman 'was not even a good classical scholar, yet in mind and powers of composition, and in taste and knowledge, he was decidedly superior to some competitors, who were a class above him in the Schools'.[103] The Coplestonian tradition as established at Oriel specified that fellowships were to be 'given in conscious independence of academic conventions, and in disbelief in the finality of the verdict of the schools'.[104] Newman said that he was humbled by his failure in schools and punished (pride?). His brother Francis did brilliantly: a double first at Worcester in 1826, followed by a fellowship at Balliol.[105] Newman was not the only

[99] Ball, *Cambridge Papers*, 67.
[100] John Venn, *Grace Book Delta* (Cambridge, 1910), ixn.
[101] A. D. Godley, *Oxford in the Eighteenth Century* (London and New York, 1908), 87.
[102] *Autobiographical Writings of John Henry Newman*, ed. Henry Tristram (London and New York, 1956), 64.
[103] *Ibid.* [104] D. W. Rannie, *Oriel College* (London, 1900), 169.
[105] William Robbins, *The Newman Brothers* (Cambridge, MA, 1966), 15–16.

Oriel great who failed to gain a first class. Hurrell Froude, Thomas Mozley and Richard Whately were others. Arthur Hugh Clough was another.[106] Matthew Arnold, also an Oriel fellow and a carrier of the Coplestonian tradition, took only a second. John Duke Coleridge, the great-nephew of the poet and a fellow of Exeter in the 1840s, went out in the poll. He had a distinguished career none the less, rising to lord chief justice.

At King's College the scholars could proceed BA without taking the tripos until 1853, but they competed for classical awards and prizes and obviously attained fellowships in their own college and undoubtedly elsewhere. Some evidence exists that several may have taken the tripos.[107] Thomas Macaulay at Trinity College was gulfed and still obtained a fellowship at his college in the 1820s. He was elated. At the other university and the other Trinity College, a fellowship as late as 1845 could be obtained with only a second class in *literae humaniores*, since that is where Edward Augustus Freeman, the historian and future Regius Professor, was placed.

Anomalies of every kind abound. The studentships at Christ Church, somewhere between scholarships and fellowships and available in quantity to undergraduates, were awarded by nomination of the Dean and Chapter in rotation. No founder's kin or claims of locality were relevant. Before merit examinations were instituted in 1854, the House defended its ancient procedures to the Oxford Royal Commission by claiming that its pool of candidates was far wider than existed at other colleges. 'Mere intellectual merit', the Dean and Chapter maintained, should not prevail over need. They then went on to explain how donors had provided for the education of the needy, who doubtless were mediocre ('the mass of mankind are of average ability') but deserving. The Senior Censor drove the point home by writing to Christ Church's distinguished alumnus, William Gladstone, that 'We have no right, to expect all first rate men.'[108] The era of twentieth-century mass education has given new life to these sentiments.

An 1847 appeal by a failed candidate to the Visitor of Lincoln College, Oxford, indicates how thorny is the problem of trying to pinpoint a clear definition of merit in the award of fellowships. The distressed party had been beaten out in the race but cried 'foul'. He maintained that the college statutes allowed for 'moral qualifications and propriety of conduct' as a

---

[106] W. Tuckwell, *Pre-Tractarian Oxford, a Reminiscence of the Oriel 'Noetics'* (London, 1909), 22.
[107] Venn, *Grace Book Delta*, xxi–xxiii.
[108] Bill and Mason, *Christ Church*, 13–15.

condition of appointment as well as intellectual qualifications. Nevertheless, he was eligible on the latter grounds as well. He had 'passed all his University Examinations without failure, and obtained a third class' in Schools, 'which was probably a higher degree of attainments than was ever contemplated by the Founder himself'. Yet the college had elected two fellows without even his level of distinction. One had taken a fourth class, and the other had not received any classical honours at all. He next argued that he should have been given a separate examination to strengthen the basis upon which a decision was made, and finally he closed by stating that the elections were not based on merit at all but on 'interests'.[109]

One reason why the unreformed colleges were sometimes reluctant to select fellows from prize-winners was their size. A difficult personality could divide a small college, forcing the fellows to go outside to the Visitor for a solution. Copleston hinted at such when writing to Peel in 1845 recommending a candidate for a canonry at St Paul's. It was easier for all parties if appointees were capable of 'liberal and cordial concurrence in all plans'.[110] Perhaps this helps explain why very large colleges such as Trinity at Cambridge were usually in the forefront when advancing the claims of merit. A cranky success would not be too difficult to control.

Only gradually did the newer and narrower measurement of merit win, and sooner at some colleges than others. Sometimes it was very narrow indeed. The Oxford University Royal Commissioners actually criticised the university in 1850 for ignoring students who read mathematics. The 'Greats' men monopolised the academic prizes. The Commissioners also thought that the range of required classical authors had narrowed.[111]

The influence of degree examination results on the award of fellowships has not been systematically studied. However, some recent evidence shows a correlation between success in the honours examinations and the award of fellowships for some periods. John Gascoigne finds that senior wranglers in particular were being appointed to college fellowships from 1753 (when the designation senior wrangler was first officially used) to 1810. During the 1750s, 51 per cent of all wranglers became fellows. Afterwards, the numbers usually rose, increasing to 66 per cent in the next decade, 74 per cent in the 1770s, 78 per cent in the 1790s. A dip and jump followed so that the numbers reached 81 per cent in the first decade of the

[109] Copy of Appeal of Mr F. F. F. Aldred against the Election of Mr Andrew, sent to the Visitor, the Bishop of Lincoln (n.d. but 1847), Lincoln College Strongroom (Library).
[110] British Library Add. MSS 40561, f. 319 (6 March 1845).
[111] Charles Edward Mallet, *A History of the University of Oxford*, III (London, 1927), 308.

nineteenth century. In 1789 one wrangler became master of St John's, but outside the university the reputation of the wranglers made little impact until the nineteenth century,[112] which is what we should expect from an unsettled examination system. William Lubenow, in a forthcoming book on the Cambridge Apostles, calculates that the numbers of Apostles with first-class honours elected to college fellowships increased in the course of the nineteenth century. In the 1830s, 20 per cent of the Apostles received top honours, and virtually all received fellowships. Nearly half received firsts in the next decade, and 39 per cent went on to become fellows. In the 1840s, 57 per cent of the Apostles obtained firsts, 43 per cent of them obtaining fellowships. The pattern holds up well through the 1870s: 85 per cent firsts, 70 per cent of them leading to fellowships.

A break occurs in the 1880s and afterwards. The likelihood of a first obtaining a fellowship remains high, but the percentage is dropping from 64 to 50 to 43 per cent; and finally, in the four years before the outbreak of war in 1914, to 14 per cent. The overall record from 1860 to 1914 is still very good: 77 per cent of the Apostles took firsts, and 57 per cent of these were elected to fellowships.[113] As a footnote it needs to be said that the quality of those selected for membership in the famous secret society did not fall off. The general competition increased. Many excellent students of ability equal to that of the Apostles could not be elected to a society limited to a dozen undergraduates at any one time.

THE ADVENT OF THE 'FIRST CLASS MAN'

Examination results became the means for defining a successful university experience. Indeed, in the form of the Oxford and Cambridge final honours schools and tripos, academic distinction was regarded as the epitome of all success, to shine with even more lustre as career success inevitably followed. The belief in university examinations as the principal means for identifying talent is a species of what social scientists call 'primordialism'. This describes a fundamental attachment to a group that is not necessarily based on common interest or affection but nevertheless possesses a nearly unaccountable strength. It is a first premise or starting point for commitment, and from it arise other attachments and

---

[112] John Gascoigne, 'Mathematics and Meritocracy: the Emergence of the Cambridge Mathematical Tripos', *Social Studies of Science*, 14 (1984), 561; Miller, 'St John's', 442.

[113] William Lubenow has very generously allowed me to use his figures, which are taken from Chapter 2 of his forthcoming book (Cambridge), *The Cambridge Apostles, 1820–1914: Liberalism, Imagination and Friendship in the British Intellectual Aristocracy*.

legitimising principles.[114] Even before honours became the necessary route to fame, its potential as a primordial sign of extraordinary talent was being trumpeted. 'In England', *The Christian Remembrancer* explained in 1826, eulogising the death of a distinguished prelate who had triumphed at university,

> a man's college-reputation, if he has been pre-eminent in literature or science, accompanies him into the world . . . That he was senior wrangler at Cambridge, is still held honourable to Copley, now that he is Lord Chancellor of England; that he was a first-class man in literature and science, is still remembered to the glory of Peel, after he has shown himself to the world, one of her consummate statesmen . . . [In] our English universities, men contend with men – as distinction is difficult, so is ambition high, and success glorious, in the rivalries of the flower of the English youth. That great acquirements must be theirs who stand pre-eminent in scholarship or science, at Oxford or Cambridge, is certain.[115]

We have no firm idea of how many 'first-class men' or high seconds fell short of achieving place and reputation in British society. We also have no solid basis on which to calculate how many lower seconds, or third- and fourth-class minds rose to eminence or reasonable success after university. We are also uncertain whether career success in each instance was the result of a further surge of effort in a chosen or assigned occupation or whether older support systems remained in place. The evidence suggests a combination of both. Two investigators hypothesise that career success may also be related to age and longevity, and the well-fed and looked-after members of a privileged set of classes have clear advantages in this regard. The same authors have analysed the educational and career patterns of Wykehamists starting with the generation born in the 1820s. There is some correlation between obtaining firsts or scholarships at Oxford and Cambridge and subsequent employment, and some evidence that those most willing to compete did so because of social or financial need. However, the Winchester elite whose career patterns they discuss were not really significantly less privileged than the other members of their cohorts. The overall results, as the authors admit, are not decisive.[116]

Even though taking honours was the highpoint of an Oxford and

[114] For a detailed and stimulating exposition, see Neil Smelser, *Social Paralysis and Social Change, British Working-Class Education in the Nineteenth Century* (Berkeley and Los Angeles, 1991), Chapter 3.

[115] Obituary notice of Reginald Heber, bishop of Calcutta, in *The Christian Remembrancer* (November 1826), 618.

[116] T. J. H. Bishop and Rupert Wilkinson, *Winchester and the Public School Elite, a Statistical Analysis* (London, 1967), 133, 156, 160, 161, 196.

Cambridge undergraduate career in the second half of the nineteenth century, a large number of students took only ordinary degrees, and a substantial group did not take degrees of any kind. From 1851 to 1906 one third of all Cambridge students took only pass degrees, and one quarter went down without proceeding BA.[117] Other calculations put the percentage of BAs to freshmen at 55–71 between 1800 and 1900, indicating a dropout rate as high in some eras as about half of all matriculated students. From 1850 to 1900, using the same calculations, 25–30 per cent of Oxford matriculants went down empty-handed.[118]

The situations at the two universities were comparable. Very large numbers of students resisted the fierce grind. They were nevertheless made to undergo a variety of collegiate exercises, but they did so quite mechanically. Those who stayed on for a degree by going out in the poll did only a minimal amount of work. We might expect them to have been the sons of wealthy parents with good career prospects or social connections, but one impression gained from the sources suggests this was not necessarily the case. Students from low income families with poor life chances also chose not to go in for a degree or honours, and many of the hardest working students, from Peel to Gladstone and beyond, were well financed and connected. Some families were probing the rewards system for opportunities to advance the fortunes of unpromising children. Finding both old and new pressures too great, or not worth the competitive effort, they negotiated a strategic retreat. Other families watched with delight as their talented sons swept every honour and dignity before them, even though money and connections existed to place them in good careers, and welcomed the contributions to family reputation provided by the new academic rewards system.

Self-confidence is a critical byproduct of merit-based systems of success. The assumption that a first-class degree meant a first-class mind able to undertake any subsequent assignment is a Victorian myth, but in the deeper and effective meaning of the word as self-validating evidence of a culture's fundamental beliefs. Hence the first-class mind was supposed to entertain few qualms about exercising judgement and leadership. The headstrong and opinionated headmasters, businessmen, imperial leaders and Victorian adventurers whose idiosyncrasies and peculiar bravado appear everywhere in biography and literature provide innumerable examples of an exaggerated sense of self-worth.

---

[117] Rothblatt, *Dons*, 185n.
[118] Lawrence Stone, 'The Size and Composition of the Oxford Student Body 1580–1909', in *The University in Society*, ed. L. Stone, I (Princeton, 1974), 95.

But self-confidence is also a byproduct of elite or highly select educational systems that do not recognise merit as measured by competition. We have seen how primordial was the culture of the ancient universities, how hesitant were the dons to replace their earlier version of merit with a newer form since their traditional conception of leadership would be undermined. Every possible objection to competition as a winnowing out process was raised – illness, effeminacy, vanity, pedantry, unfairness, denaturing, unsociability. The new examination systems, while seen as a spur to industry, were not intended to replace character formation with another kind of educational goal. That this happened in spite of such wishes is embedded in the logic of the new 'discipline' at Oxford and Cambridge, but the actual result until the second half of the nineteenth century was the creation of two separate merit tracks, one reflecting older concerns about the quality of the whole person, the other moving in the direction of a far more impersonal measurement of ability. Divided college opinion over what kind of person should receive scholarships and fellowships is an excellent indication of the resulting confusion, as is the uncertainty on the part of students whether to engage in the examination grind or take an easier path. In society at large both views were also available for the good reason that liberal individualism raised too many fears about the consequences of a success ethic insufficiently anchored by social constraints and altruism. That is why the cultivation of friends, taking time out to dine, making certain that posting up a ledger in the counting house was not an all-consuming passion, remained invaluable means of acquiring recognition, status and prosperity. '[Every] year convinces me more and more that social intercourse, of the right kind, is a material aid to success.'[119] Here is the authentic voice of the courtier tradition which the Victorians never quite forgot. Many observers remarked upon the need to have strong legal and social disciplinary structures to keep self-regard in check. Mill's *On Liberty* is a protest against these in the name of the new freedoms of the nineteenth century.[120]

In reality, nineteenth-century Britain developed numerous different paths to the top; but the myth of a first-class mind equipped to travel anywhere was widely accepted. It helped furnish Oxford and Cambridge with more undergraduates than had ever before matriculated. However, while examinations became an important means of selection, neither university developed a formal admissions system until the twentieth

---

[119] Quoted in Houghton, *Victorian Frame of Mind*, 195.
[120] And especially in regard to his affair with Harriet Taylor. For social and legal disciplines, see the chapters by these names in W. L. Burn, *The Age of Equipoise* (London, 1964).

century, leaving decisions on access to the separate colleges, another mode
of contributing to a two-track selection system. Ralph H. Turner has
called such tracks 'contest mobility' and 'sponsored mobility'. He uses
these concepts to contrast basic features of American and English culture;
but as historical circumstances are rarely either/or but simultaneous, it is
more accurate to see each form of support as coexisting. The operative
variables are time and degree. Contest mobility did not automatically
replace sponsorship at Oxford and Cambridge, or in nineteenth-century
Britain, but was regarded as an alternative means of bringing promising
talent to the attention of those who controlled the instruments of nomi-
nations and appointments. Much remained before competition could be
regarded as a superior form of discerning merit and rewarding achievement. A further step required mechanisms for stirring up ambition and
motivating students in a world where patronage prevailed.

Henry Latham, author of a leading book on competitive examinations,
concluded that the battle to give priority to first-class degree holders
had been essentially won by 1877.[121] The Oxbridge model of using examinations to identify and even more to verify competence was followed in
public and grammar schools, in military academies, in the system of local
examinations and in the various branches of the civil services, excepting
the Department of Education and the Foreign Office. Different career
phases became linked together by the same examinations, and the
flexibility that Copleston and others defended diminished. Towards
the end of the century, however, under the influence of new ideas of
scholarship emanating from Germany, fellowship dissertations became
important as a rival to competitive examinations for choosing the scholars
and teachers of the next generation.

TWO CULTURES, AND EVEN A THIRD

The slow incorporation of a competitive success ethic into the ancient
universities began approximately after 1790. A precise correspondence
with market economics – a standing temptation – is difficult to make since
the ancient universities were tangential in spirit and geography to the
energy centres of British industrialism, their loyalties overwhelmingly
fixed on the assumptions of the old regime. The changes in examination
discipline were separate from any of the larger transformations associated
with liberal individualism. Their simultaneous appearance was

---

[121] Henry Latham, *On the Action of Examinations Considered as a Means of Selection* (Cambridge,
1877), 428.

coincidental. Yet when Northcote and Trevelyan signalled the need to use universities to create an administrative class that would be able to restrain, temper and educate the political classes that were 'temporarily set above them' (in the words of the famous Report), a meritocratic ethic based on contest was in place, the result of a special history internal to the two senior universities, partitioned off in so many ways from the growth of industrial, liberal culture.

We must return to the theme that where there is success, there will inevitably be failure of some kind, even though personal connections continued to matter. Psychological failure was feared from the outset, the loss of self-confidence so essential to those who were destined for status and position. And this did indeed happen. A diminution in self-worth occurred, a feeling of having disappointed one's family followed by anger at the inherent unfairness of existing systems of assessment. We have the appearance of a new ideal-type personality. He is a hybrid. From Georgian ideas about self-possession, he has learned how to avoid confusing his true character with superficial symbols of success. From Victorian ideas about the need to test one's strength against trials, he has learned to face the potential humiliation of defeat by bravely accepting the challenge of a new form of humiliation. He has willingly risked his moral and physical health and has emerged from the experience hardened and superior because he has learned to rise above it. He has not been corrupted by the material standards of success, and he has not bowed down in the House of Rimmon or anyone else's house. This is Leslie Stephen's allusion, and the best illustration of it belongs to Stephen's eulogy of Henry Salisbury Hughes, a younger and forgotten brother of the renowned author of the Tom Brown books. Here it is:

> Long years ago I knew a young man at college; he was so far from being intellectually eminent that he had great difficulty in passing his examinations; he died from the effects of an accident within a very short time after leaving the university, and hardly any one would now remember his name. He had not the smallest impression that there was anything remarkable about himself, and looked up to his teachers and his more brilliant companions with a loyal admiration which would have made him wonder that they should ever take notice of him. And yet I often thought then, and I believe, in looking back, that I thought rightly, that he was of more real use to his contemporaries than any one of the persons to whose influence they would most naturally refer as having affected their development. The secret was a very simple one. Without any specific intellectual capacity, he somehow represented a beautiful moral type. He possessed the 'simple faith miscalled simplicity', and was so absolutely unselfish, so conspicuously pure

in his whole life and conduct, so unsuspicious of evil in others, so sweet and loyal in his nature, that to know him was to have before one's eyes an embodiment of some of the most lovable and really admirable qualities that a human being can possess . . . Young men were not always immaculate in those days; I don't know that they are now; some of them probably were vicious in conduct, and might be cynical in the views which they openly expressed. But whatever might be their failings, they were at the age when all but the depraved – that is, I hope and believe, all but a very small minority – were capable of being deeply impressed by this concrete example. They might affect to ridicule, but it was impossible that even the ridicule should not be of the kindly sort, blended and tempered with something that was more like awe – profounded respect, at least, for the beauty of soul that underlay the humble exterior . . . He would have been unfeignedly surprised to hear, what I most sincerely believe to have been the truth, that his tutor owed incomparably more to his living exemplification of what is meant by a character of unblemished purity and simplicity, than he owed to the tutor, whose respectable platitudes he received with unaffected humility.[122]

George Malcolm Young would possibly have called Salisbury Hughes a Victorian 'middle brow', one upon whom the solid but not profound culture of the nineteenth century would have laid hold, a man of earnest faith and modesty wedged in between the relaxed values of Oxbridge at its most unreformed and the new avant-garde intellectualism of the Edwardian period, contemptuous, angry and narcissistic.[123]

Leslie Stephen's 1895 portrait of Hughes is sad, in keeping with the tone of the occasion on which it was drawn, a sermon in chapel on 'Retrospective Benefactors'. But no one can mistake the defensive tone, the implication that in the modern world good and noble men will come and go unnoticed. Leslie Stephen himself certainly felt that way at Cambridge, as both Frederic Maitland and Lord Annan have elaborated.[124] The portrait of Hughes is also of a piece with those ideal-type gentlemen who appear in the writings of Newman and Matthew Arnold, hurt, isolated and turning the other cheek to the slanders of the modern world, to mechanical or market determinations of worth. The Byronism which Samuel Smiles deplored hung on nevertheless, as in Arnold's belief late in life, when he if not his sons could claim a high degree of public acceptance, that 'inner freedom' was still preferable to outer success.[125] Famous

---

[122] Frederic Maitland, *The Life and Letters of Sir Leslie Stephen* (London, 1906), 70.
[123] G. M. Young, 'The New Cortegiano', in *Victorian Essays* (London, 1962), 211.
[124] Maitland, *Leslie Stephen;* Annan, *Leslie Stephen.*
[125] Park Honan, *Matthew Arnold: A Life* (London, 1981), 380.

Victorians repeatedly returned to the theme that Oxford and Cambridge had betrayed their high purpose by an unseemly attachment to narrow forms of determining capacity. The universities singled out the wrong values for praise and made potential successes into failures. Seeley could not stay off the topic of examinations, especially honours examinations, to which he was adamantly opposed. The 'use' of examinations, he wrote, was not to estimate merit, but to detect demerit. 'The object of examinations . . . is to pluck.'[126]

This is by now a familiar complaint, a shout of anguish sent up whenever the pressure of competition is thought unbearable or the grounds for judging success hollow and corrupt. Later the Victorian sages would find unexpected allies in their depiction of the universities as betrayers of culture in the proponents of German *wissenschaftliche Methoden* who found the British preoccupation with examining detrimental to genuine scholarship. This was in fact Seeley's exact point.

The protest is still alive, although it may assume peculiar forms. It springs up from time to time in defiance against the dehumanising characteristics of modern bureaucratic and technocratic life. Thus in America today there is a school of 'non-cognitive education', whose goal is the imparting of moral and personality traits that will directly influence proficiency, instead of what is now common, the inculcating of skills that have character as a by-product. Agreement or disagreement with Arnold, Newman, Seeley, Stephen or other prominent Victorian voices is not the point of this discussion. The point is to show how in the course of time the universities reformed themselves and were reformed, and incorporated into that reform was a conception of merit separate and distinct from older inherited versions. Proof of the rejection of the past was proudly assigned to a series of honours examinations, becoming more numerous in number in the second half of the nineteenth century, and praised as absolutely beyond reproach as an objective measure of worth. The respect and prestige accorded the two senior universities of England, their continuing function as the principal university educators of an administrative, professional and literary elite, and their influence over other parts of the educational and examining systems of England, even Scotland, guaranteed a firm place for terminal examinations, blind marking, unseen questions and external examining in the educational experience of ambitious and go-ahead young men and women and their families.

[126] Seeley, 'A Plea', 5.

THE RAMIFICATIONS OF AN EXAMINATION CULTURE

The long-term shift brought with it a network of associated changes. A reordering of university priorities was necessary, affecting the calendar for scheduling and marking examinations. Students and tutors were now bent on a common task. Procedures for selecting and rotating examiners needed to be worked out, as well as compensation for additional service. Examination papers had to be chosen and set. This required meetings of faculty boards and committees and the continual airing of opinions regarding the merit of particular pedagogical approaches. Textbooks and other reading and studying matter relevant to the syllabus were prepared and published. Guides, advice, the exchange of information, hints, ponies, undergraduate backchat – all of this became a much more important aspect of a university experience than ever before. Innovations designed to improve the objectivity of the examination process led to increased specialisation and the multiplication of examining specialties. A broadly based curriculum was thought to be too general and insufficiently rigorous. This was an aspect of the heated debate between Scottish and English versions of liberal learning in the Victorian era.

More work was now available for tutors and especially for a large and important class of private coaches and crammers, some of whom also held college posts. Disgruntled opponents of the changes, especially those opposed to replacing oral by written examinations, pointed to the earlier days when cramming was less in evidence. Throughout the century dons, tutors and graduates amused one another with lengthy, witty disquisitions on the evils or virtues of one kind of examination experience over another, one set of papers over another, one set of texts rather than another. In 1883 'Anthropos Lincolniensis' was happy to conclude that as now constituted *literae humaniores* or Greats was clearly the work of a committee. 'No one man could have been fool enough to put together the various elements of the examination . . . it required the combined folly of a number of fools, each wishing to air his own hobby.'[127]

The advent of an examinations culture featuring days of judgement also had a major impact on the division of teaching responsibilities within the universities. Examinations strengthened the colleges and weakened the teaching function of professors. Reorganising their tutorial systems to support terminal examinations, the colleges tightened their hold on their student populations, and professors, especially in newer science subjects as yet without an examinations referent, complained bitterly about low

[127] *The Oxford Magazine* (16 May 1883).

attendance at lectures. It was argued that the numbers of students attending professorial lectures dropped by half at Oxford in the 1830s, and some lectures (it was asserted) would have stopped altogether if colleges like Balliol and Christ Church had not made attendance a college requirement. A crisis ensued as to what the proper role of a professor actually was in an English university.[128] The issue continued to bother Oxford (as well as Cambridge) and was taken up in the 1850s and 1860s when the ancient universities underwent the statutory reorganisation that has been the centre of most historical attention, careful consideration being given to financial issues in which professorial remuneration figured. But the fights between tutors and professors were more pronounced and protracted at Oxford than at Cambridge, possibly because the colleges were even stronger.

Once established, the further development of the honours examinations system proceeded 'logically' along largely internal lines, each refinement, addition or alteration following upon one another in order to solve problems arising from the innovation itself. Once begun, the process of internal repair and replacement never ceased. The examinations grew in rigour, the rigour based on academic specialism; and whereas paradoxically the scholars and scientists of the second half of the nineteenth century believed that examinations were the wrong means for teaching undergraduates how to acquire knowledge, academic specialisation became one driving force behind the continual evolution of final schools and tripos. One newer and very popular tripos, Natural Sciences, illustrates the phases perfectly. When first established at mid-century, the natural sciences were considered to be a species of liberal study. Twenty years later the issue was the level of appropriate specialisation, but a vestigial interest in general or liberal education still existed. By the turn of the century none of the traditional concerns was paramount. The central issue was science itself, its depth, research capabilities and soundness as an education.[129]

Here again national comparisons are useful. Specialisation and professionalisation drove the American undergraduate curriculum too, and in certain fields to an even greater extent than in Britain.[130] But the absence of final degree examinations meant that differing ideas about undergraduate education would continue to coexist in the same institution

---

128 Ward, *Victorian Oxford*, 108.
129 Roy MacLeod *et al.*, *Days of Judgement, Science, Examinations and the Organization of Knowledge in Late-Victorian England* (Driffield, N. Humberside, 1982), 206–7.
130 The argument of Reba Soffer with respect to history. See her book, *Discipline and Power: The University, History and the Making of an English Elite, 1870–1930* (Stanford, 1994).

and even within separate departments. Some instructors, heavily influenced by developments in disciplinary subfields, introduced undergraduates to the 'latest findings' in a particular area of inquiry. Others, adopting the attitude that political science, for example, really should be taught as 'civics', preferred to emphasise broad themes and perspectives. The specialists were forced by circumstances to create separate graduate programmes for higher degrees. The American undergraduate curriculum was then caught between the schools below, sending up students with varying levels of proficiency and very often in need of remedial instruction, and the graduate schools above, pushing specialism down onto the bachelor's degree. This created the particular bifurcations of the American undergraduate curriculum. A Judgement Day could not emerge.

Perhaps, unintentionally, the professionalisation of academic life in Britain was a further legitimatisation of the conclusion that a first-class degree deserved special attention afterwards as signifying a first-class man. The arrival of a solid meritocratic culture meant that the university's characterisation of success as fair and uncontestable now rested on a number of axioms. The first was that the experience of an honours degree was decisive. Intellectual development had reached its highest point, and no further mental progress would occur. Further training but not education was possible, even necessary for entry into the professions, although such examinations as might be required for professional careers should be qualifying not competitive. The second axiom was that the severity of the examination process, its physical as well as cerebral demands, could only be undergone when the student was young and making the transition from adolescence to maturity. Age 22 should be the cutoff point.[131] Talent had to be recognised early. Only in youth was the mind supple enough to be receptive to external guidance but also unencumbered enough to be free. If the right moments were missed, the talent would never properly develop. Taken later in life, examinations produced a counter-effect, discouraging 'spontaneity and independence of judgement'.[132] Talent manifested itself as quickness of mind, memory, a gift for aphorism and stylish response, or, in Oxbridge patois, a talented student was 'clever'. We can see why Victorian critics of the honours examinations believed these qualities were unsuited to 'practical' tasks, but they might have agreed that the examinations required and tested stamina, and that young people were healthy enough to endure a gruelling regimen. The emphasis on young minds, however, has had to be overcome

---

[131] Latham, *Examinations*, 405.   [132] *Ibid.*

in our century when universities are no longer the sole possession of late adolescents.

A third axiom was that the examination experience, precisely because it was so demanding, was unsuited for women. A post-1860s generation of women dons and students had to struggle against this attitude. At Newnham College, Eleanor Balfour produced statistics confirming her belief that strenuous examinations were not deleterious to the health of women undergraduates. She might have ironically observed that it was not long before her own time that examinations were thought inimical to the health of young men, whose history of courage and fortitude at the ancient universities leaves much to be desired.

This is all interesting enough, another instance of moving from status to contract (as Sir Henry Maine described it in his classic Victorian work of the difference between ancient and modern cultures), from worth defined in personal terms, allowing for errors and growing up, to assessments based on impersonal, universalistic criteria. The old college system encouraged favouritism, bias and toadying. It automatically gave advantages to birth and influence. As such it was unsuited to a time when external considerations were no longer as widely acceptable as earlier. But that the English honours examinations never actually became the only means for locating oneself in a satisfactory career is explained by the coexistence of a leftover rival system of assessment based on a fear of anonymity. An examination that is 'objective' or 'value-free' requires no other certification beyond itself. The candidate's success is implicated in the examination system; he, later she, is equated with the outcome. Strictly speaking, a prospective employee who can show proof of a first, at worst a high second, needs no other validation. But the suspicion may well remain that, despite a splendid performance before the dreaded tribunal of honours examiners, the candidate is otherwise unknown. Is he virtuous, reliable, agreeable? Does he possess the personal qualities that guarantee leadership? Can he set an example for others to follow, especially at moments of crisis and despair? Can he rally the troops? Does the examination, for all its rigour and requirements of time management and self-discipline, really provide the tests of maturity and discernment that are the ultimate signs of elite preparation? Perhaps – the thought did arise – the examination results conceal more than they reveal. The candidate may not be the brilliant, spontaneous and lively first-class mind that the mythos of the examinations culture promises. He may only be an honest slogger whose lack of general curiosity and all-around abilities are perfectly suited to a specialised examination but no more. The very severity of the examination and its narrow focus were from this perspective main drawbacks.

Hence the older system of attempting to discern character never vanished, receiving new life in the form of the personal interview, where, in face-to-face discussion, the give and take qualities respected by the Victorians were more apparent, and Oxbridge candidates were able to assert their superiority over the graduates of the Scottish universities, London or the civic universities.

The new culture of examinations did not exactly triumph, winning out in all particulars against courtier ideals, just as the marketplace did not necessarily triumph over the principles of state economic intervention. Each form of assessment had its own institutional home within the collegiate university. Terminal examinations belonged to the university, but initially the colleges had played a larger direct role in selecting examiners, whose partialities towards candidates from their own colleges were all too evident. It was also greatly feared that if college fellows took on the responsibilities of examiners within the colleges themselves, college friendships would disintegrate.[133] Placing the examinations in the university, separating them from teaching and allowing blind marking, preserved the colleges, left them free to maintain their other functions and to make room for Newman's *genius loci*. A college was more than a place where undergraduates were plucked for the sake of plucking.

---

[133] Hare, *New College*, 21.

CHAPTER FIVE

HISTORICAL AND COMPARATIVE REMARKS ON THE 'FEDERAL PRINCIPLE' IN HIGHER EDUCATION

PROLEGOMENA: VANISHING IDENTITIES

Universities today arrive packaged in every conceivable shape and style. We should not be surprised. In its long and impressive history as a distinct institution within western civilisation, the university has never assumed a single form or followed a single pattern, nor, despite undeniable similarities in organisation and curriculum, has one university been a carbon copy of another. National differences of organisation, mission and curriculum have been plentiful; and within nations themselves numerous forms have coexisted.

This remains the situation, and if anything the variety of types has multiplied even more in the hospitable environments of our own century. In Austria and Germany many 'universities' of that designation are relatively specialised institutions, *wirtschaftsuniversitäten* or *technische universitäten*. Austria established a University of Mining at Leoben and a University of Educational Services at Klagenfurt. In the 1990s more than half of all French universities offered programmes of study confined to a limited range of specialties.[1] In the fomer Soviet bloc, exclusively focused universities were established in conformity with communist government policy to concentrate on applied subjects. A University of Economics was established in Hungary in 1948, followed in the next year by a University of Heavy Industries and two years later by a University of Chemical Industry. In Stockholm, Lyngley (near Copenhagen), Paris, Lausanne, Zurich, Berlin, Vienna, London and Cambridge, Massachusetts, high-prestige engineering establishments have long flourished. They do not carry the hallowed name 'university', but this has not been a drawback. It may in fact have become a reverse form of snobbery. In any case, within

---

[1] Guy Neave and Richard Edelstein, 'The Research Training System in France: A Microstudy of Three Academic Disciplines', in *The Research Foundations of Graduate Education*, ed. Burton R. Clark (Berkeley and Los Angeles, 1993), 218, also 197 *passim*.

these establishments certain forms of social science or even humanities teaching are carried on, so that the institutions simulate parts of the curricula of institutions that do abide by the designation 'university'.

The bifurcation of universities into those of narrow focus and those with comprehensive and ever-growing missions is a reality, defying attempts to pinpoint their identities. The familiar Carnegie classification scheme is widely used in the United States to differentiate institutions according to their primary emphases – research, liberal arts, doctoral degrees but not research, research but not all forms of professional education. This may be as useful a taxonomy as can be expected in today's environment of mixed institutions. One sub-set of American institutions, the 'New American College' (see Chapter 2), is still in the process of establishing an identity. Academic leaders in this sector are wondering whether the absence of a firm identity may not in fact bestow unnoticed blessings. Clarity of mission may be important in certain environments but not in others.

Why are efforts at identification necessary, if at all? Does it truly matter whether an institution of education and learning is called a university, a college, an academy, an institute or a school of advanced studies when no clear 'idea' any longer attaches to any of these designations?

Logically names should be less important in *étatist* than in market-related systems, or important only for the civil servants whose task requires them to make distinctions for distributing revenue. But when institutions struggle in the open market, competing for attention, students, professors, endowments and operating expenses, brand name familiarity is important. One of several good reasons why intercollegiate sports flourish in the United States is the publicity that big game competition receives in the mass media, enhancing the reputation of a university simply through name recognition. In the market a university or college needs a 'saga', a roll call of epic names, a list of blue ribbons won or nearly gained. Where the State or states have assumed responsibility for institutional support and planning – setting enrolment targets, more or less defining the curriculum, apportioning disciplines between institutions, establishing research priorities, specifying teaching salaries and the conditions for tenure, accounting for student aid – a clear identity or institutional image would seem to be less significant. The State has defined supply and constrained or directed demand, taking these calculations away from the institution itself. In such circumstances, a *genius loci* is also less important. The territory of the university, the grounds upon which it stands, cannot be symbolically or actually useful as a component of the education on offer. Bureaucrats cannot be concerned with the aesthetic dimensions of undergraduate education. They are little interested in 'heritage' and neither are multi-campus 'systems' (apart from individual constituent campuses).[2] Furthermore, as remarked in an earlier chapter, today's technology linked international world of invisible colleges takes no special heed of *terra firma* except as a professional *pied à terre*.

Yet the architectural heritage of wholly state-supported universities cannot be completely ignored when prestige is being measured. Universities in Sweden like Lund and Uppsala take great pride in their historic buildings and grounds, past associations and achievements. It would be absurd to suggest that such Uppsala treasures as the Aula Magna (although at most only a century old) and the fabulous anatomy theatre that paraphrases Padua are not appreciated, or that the street façades and inner courts of Bologna do not tease the imagination and provide welcoming niches for tutelary spirits. The now accessible Humboldt University in Berlin, with its spacious boulevard axis and superb legacy of Schinkel buildings and bridges, assuredly retains a capacity to summon up the German university's place in the development of modern science and critical scholarship (as well as the power of the House of Brandenburg). All these historic assets are available to be used; but whether they need to be used and how they are to be used are the issues.

The dichotomies outlined for State and market may be too distinct for the ragged institutional edges of the 1990s. The American higher education situation has long been muddled. Classifications such as those of Carnegie are meant to bring a certain element of order to the field and to help institutions compete in their own league. But today the European statist inheritance is equally confused. Market ideas in the multiple forms of 'privatisation' compete and overlap with bureaucratic proposals for solving the immense problems of access and quality associated with mass education. The European Union, with its own ever-shifting objectives and priorities, adds another level of disorder. Possible governance alternatives range from a loosening of external controls in the French system (how much is in question) to new forms of institutional autonomy as yet in the making at places like the Chalmers Institute of Technology in Göteborg, Sweden. Privatisation entails a greater use of lay or mixed boards of trustees and stronger top-down management, a departure in countries like Britain from faculty, senate and collegiate decision-making. But there is no single model dominating discussion today.

---

[2] Clark Kerr, *Higher Education Cannot Escape History, Issues for the Twenty-first Century* (Albany, NY, 1994), 48.

Boundaries are blurred in 1990s Britain to an extent unique in the history of British higher education. The abolition of the legal and hence funding distinction between polytechnics and universities (the 'binary line') has hastened the process of upward institutional drift. An emerging if still inchoate sector of further education colleges maintains that a certain number of its course offerings should be recognised as degree level. Why, ask some further education leaders, should any limits be placed on institutional self-development? And Gareth Williams, as well as other analysts, takes up the point, explaining that an imposed standard can be narrow and stifling. Furthermore (as American examples testify), parts of a single institution, like sections of a symphony orchestra, may be superior to other parts.[3] Wherever blurring does exist, universities and colleges sometimes strive for coherent and distinct missions and traits in order to attract attention.

The British situation, as is the case in most Continental examples, is interesting precisely because the government has not really allowed higher education institutions to use the market or 'private sector' to define themselves. Politicians promise, but uncertainty about the effect of market pricing mechanisms on access and demand for university openings, as well as a reluctance on the part of civil servants to lose control over a great national resource, leave strong bureaucratic controls in place (as I write, the further education sector has just been absorbed by the Department of Employment, which certainly suggests a policy emphasis) through the principal mechanism of a number of university and college funding councils. But the most fascinating control measures established during the Thatcher revolution of the 1980s and continuing into the 1990s are a new use of an old idea, namely, that bodies intermediate between single universities and the government should be assigned responsibility for guaranteeing the quality of academic activity within their spheres of influence. But Victorian agencies entrusted with the task were truly intermediate, whereas present-day creations, funding and quality councils, are much more responsible to government.

The measures undertaken by such bodies fall under the headings of research and teaching exercises. They represent efforts to restrain competition and curb the rising costs resulting from the removal in the 1990s of legal distinctions such as the binary line. A legacy of the Lionel Robbins expanionist era of the 1960s, the binary line divided universities from polytechnics. The disapppearance of an invidious distinction left the

---

[3] Gareth Williams, 'The Missing Bottom Line', in *Standards and Criteria in Higher Education*, ed. Graeme C. Moodie (Guildford, Surrey, 1986), 31–4.

State with no clear means of differentiating the unit of resource. The introduction of frequent audits and assessments for teaching, research and programme was meant to repair the deficiency. Assessments and evaluations are wittily parodied in the columns of Laurie Taylor for the *Times Higher Education Supplement*, but they cannot be said to amuse the large communities of teachers and researchers whose time they occupy and whose success is heavily dependent upon the published lucubrations of a new horde of Visitors and Examiners.

At one level the final decade of the twentieth century is one of revolutionary, far-reaching and unpredictable change in the structure, governance and partnership of British universities and colleges with the State, the result of a liberated mass demand for education quite without historical precedent in the islands. Nearly discarded in the process has been the precious label 'university', carefully guarded over a century and a half, once reserved for a particular type of institution (hard to define even then) and now much more freely available. But the ironies of history generally prevail. The momentous events of the past two decades have led to a continuous debate, and a spate of publications, over 'standards' and 'quality' quite unprecedented in British university history. The debates range from American notions of quality as particularistic and relative, to British beliefs in precisely the opposite. The debates are arresting in at least two ways. They illustrate the emergence of an accelerated movement to mass access higher education, a sort of Trotsky law of combined development speeding up a process that took a century or more to accomplish in the United States. They also show the survival of Victorian beliefs in a higher, even an absolute standard of measurement. Since absolute definitions of quality are hard to identify and even harder to apply, the debates are mainly concerned with the process of measurement, with the mechanisms of evaluation more than the substance of education. Is this inevitable?

THE 'FEDERAL PRINCIPLE'

The idea that institutions have or ought to have an essential idea began to attract attention more or less at the same time as the inauguration of a device for determining the quality of a university education. That device was the 'federal principle' but it can also be called the 'Cambridge principle', as we shall see. The federal principle refers to the habit or practice of grouping separately governing units, normally for teaching, around a core administrative organisation. In the historiography of British universities, the federal principle receives only scattered and incomplete references. It is taken for granted as simply another in a sequence of transformations of the system of British higher education in the course of the nineteenth century. Its special history, in so far as it can be said to have a history, is more or less merged into mainline developments, or what is taken to be the orthodox situation. It is certainly true that the greater number of universities of the past were unitary not federated. They possessed their own governing centre, or more properly centres in the case of European universities, since rectors and vice-chancellors had limited powers in relation to the authority of faculties or senates. In the United States, because lay ownership of universities occurred before the appearance of academic occupations, central university governance (management?) was the stronger.

The federal principle is normally associated with political constitutions and refers to unions of states or nations, empires for example that are composed of kingdoms but also republics or federations such as Canada, Australia, the United States, Switzerland and Germany. The historical experience of Britain has actually taken the country in a different direction, towards centralisation rather than federation, or what in the 1960s was discussed under the heading of 'devolution'. The kingdom of Scotland was brought into union with Britain at the beginning of the eighteenth century, Ireland a hundred years later. In both instances hitherto independent national parliaments were dissolved and local representation transferred to the centre at Westminster. But the culture of Victorian Britain was rather more openly plural, that is 'liberal', than the culture of preceding centuries, and federal solutions came under discussion because they combined unlike units in a common structure to achieve a harmony of interests: initiative could be paired with restraint, flexibility with regulation, independence with responsibility. Assuredly we would expect a liberal like John Stuart Mill to say something in praise of federation, and he does, if not fulsomely. He writes in *Representative Government* that 'Identity of central government is compatible with many different degrees of centralisation, not only administrative, but even legislative.'[4] Other Victorians discussed political federation as the middle ground between national government and government by confederation. The key element was the representation of the people. In a national government, people were directly represented through the vote. In a confederation, only separate governments were represented. A federation was a compromise (and here the American model was being thought of), since both people and separate governments were represented. The

---

[4] John Stuart Mill, *Representative Government* (London and New York, 1951), 507.

historian E. A. Freeman expressed the solution this way: in a perfect federation, each member of the Union is independent in matters which concern it alone, but all members are subject to a common power in matters that concern the whole body collectively.[5]

These words usefully introduce the topic of federated universities. In the world of universities, the principle of federation has a riveting history, even a longer one than might be supposed by examining only modern liberal cultures. It is medieval, as indeed it should be, for the notion of power shared or distributed between centre and periphery belongs to the middle ages, never so well expressed as in the idea of a 'liberty' where the king's writ does not run.

The particular medieval inheritance relevant to the discussion is the collegiate university, which Sir John Robert Seeley, no foreigner to paradox, once called 'that inscrutable puzzle of the relation between the college and the university'.[6] The collegiate university has sometimes been called the 'Merton idea' because Merton College, Oxford, was the first of the colleges to house undergraduates. Some historians, however, would give pride of place to the King's Hall, which evolved into King's College, Cambridge.[7] The discussion appears to depend upon how a college is defined and governed, the nature of its educational mission, and the source of its finance, but these important details need not detain us now. What is fairly certain is that the collegiate university came into its own in the sixteenth century and has a great deal to do with the English Reformation. The royal court and its officials found the college to be a more reliable unit of student discipline and overall authority than the university, easier to manage and to control and hence easier to endow and direct. Universities in England had been weaker at the centre than their southern European counterparts anyhow, and so the move towards a collegiate structure was logical and perhaps natural. The college, because it was an endowed institution, was able to supplant outlying student halls and hostels which relied more upon the market; and as an endowed institution it was also private, having its own fabric, separate admissions policies and separate sources of student financial aid. In time the college was also able to invent its own curriculum, which was sometimes markedly different from that of the university to which it was connected. In some instances – the King's College in Cambridge, for example – students could receive first degrees

[5] F. P. Labilliere, *Federal Britain; or, Unity and Federation of the Empire* (London, 1894), 64n, 84, 94n.
[6] Sir John Robert Seeley, 'A Midland University', *Fortnightly Review*, n.s. 42 (1887), 704.
[7] A. B. Cobban, *The King's Hall within the University of Cambridge in the Later Middle Ages* (Cambridge, 1969).

without sitting the university's Senate House degree examinations until the reforms of the middle of the nineteenth century.

Legally, a college was not a university. The term *collegium* denoted a guild, a combination or corporation, usually self-governing, under a constitution whose provisions might vary, and only late in history does the word primarily suggest an educational body – it could also be a school such as Eton or Winchester or Carmel (founded in the twentieth century).[8] Whatever its legal position, in less technical language a college was by the nineteenth century regarded as a 'private' body and autonomous, although limited in authority by its statutes. By contrast, a university was a 'public entity', even a national one.[9] An MP for Oxford University accordingly argued the case for his university in 1854 to protect the colleges from the inquiries of royal commissioners. Parliament could legislate for a university but colleges should only receive such attention as essential to their self-reform. Enabling legislation was consequently acceptable, as well as certain forms of compulsion to free the governing bodies from stringent oaths.[10] Although the Oxbridge colleges had virtually acquired all of the first-degree teaching functions once associated with their universities, the latter retained one crucial prerogative. Only public bodies could give degrees, could certify that a particular course of studies had been satisfactorily completed, and could therefore directly and indirectly bestow upon graduates certain privileges associated with degrees, such as the right to vote in Convocation or Senate or similar body. Other benefits were not exactly rights but became in time dependent upon degrees. The colleges regarded them as essential for holding clerical livings in their gift or obtaining college fellowships. Anglican bishops required degrees as a condition of taking holy orders. Professional societies like the Royal College of Physicians only admitted Oxbridge degreeholders to fellowships. Degrees were not a licence to practise medicine. In 1827 less than 100 licentiates of the Royal College of Physicians had university degrees out of some 300 licentiates and another 300 county doctors without licence. Only a half dozen of the 6000 members of the Royal College of Surgeons had degrees.[11]

Degrees had certain historical uses in arenas of activity connected to the

---

[8] James Williams, *The Law of the Universities* (London, 1910), 4–6.
[9] *Substance of the Speech of Sir Charles Wetherell before the Lords of the Privy Council on the Subject of Incorporating the London University* (London, 1834), 23.
[10] Discussion on the Second Reading of the Oxford University Bill, Parliamentary Papers, House of Commons, cxxxii (7 April 1854), col. 674.
[11] Arthur Percival Newton, *The Universities and the Educational Systems of the British Empire* (London, 1924), 15–16.

interdependence of guild-like corporations. Clerical preferment depended upon degrees, but degree advantages in a more broadly conceived labour market were negligible. This situation persisted throughout the eighteenth century and for the first forty years or so of the next century.

Expansion in the size and character of professional occupations boosted the demand for degrees. Degrees and admissions are correlated. In the US, mass access and mass student transfer affect graduation rates, and their improvement, especially for low-income students, is a continuing concern. In Britain high entry standards have produced limited access to 'universities' until virtually the present (although the segment itself expanded), but they have also led to the most favourable graduation to admissions ratio anywhere in higher education. Wastage rates have been nearly insignificant in the university sector. Graduation is therefore more or less guaranteed by matriculation. Seen in another way, the efficiency of British universities as measured by graduations per member staff is the highest in the world.[12]

But this has been a twentieth-century development. In Newman's youth, entrance rather than exit, selection rather than certification, matriculation rather than graduation, really mattered, and this was for many decades as true of newer nineteenth-century establishments such as the Queen's University in Ireland as it was of ancient foundations.[13] The importance attached to matriculation corresponds to the distinction between 'contest mobility' and 'sponsored mobility'.[14] In the American case, admission to all but the most exclusive colleges and universities is relatively easy but graduation harder. Progress towards the degree is what counts, and the undergraduate must continually prove his worth by beginning each module of study as if it were the commencement of an utterly new experience. Education is a continuous process of nervous adjustment to unfamiliar locations and ordeals, but especially where transfer occurs. Attendance can be erratic, dropout rates high and graduation rates unpredictable.

The American first degree has a certain amount of value for determining admission to advanced and professional studies. Its worth in the marketplace, however, is less reliable. Where mobility is sponsored, admission to an institution of high selectivity is critical, since social

[12] Sinclair Goodlad, *The Quest for Quality, Sixteen Forms of Heresy in Higher Education* (Buckingham, 1995), 7.
[13] Eric Ashby, *Universities: British, Indian, African* (London, 1966), 36.
[14] Ralph Turner, 'Modes of Social Ascent through Education: Sponsored and Contest Mobility', in *Education, Economy and Society*, ed. A. H. Halsey et al. (New York, 1961), 121–39.

standing, if not exactly career success, is thereby almost instantly assured.

The 'devaluation' of a degree in the early nineteenth century for all but those whose livelihood depended upon it was implicitly justified by theories of liberal education. It was an ancient idea that a gentleman should not be overly proficient, or as the old apothegm had it, a gentleman should learn to play the flute, but not too well. Gentlemen should never allow a skill or a competence to take precedence in their minds and actions over character, which was a representation of the whole person. There was always the danger that an interest in competence would lead to a certain imbalance of character, to self-consciousness without self-confidence, and if this happened the rounded view of men and manners that a good liberal education provided would be impaired. It therefore followed that a gentleman had an obligation to resist any external attempt to alienate his personality, such as competitive examinations. In America a similar attitude has been labelled the 'Gentleman C' syndrome. It refers to the same reluctance on the part of privileged individuals whose career chances are more or less assured to submit themselves to the potential indignities of an examining and ranking system.[15]

COLLEGE AND UNIVERSITY

The natural educational home of gentlemanly values was the college not the university, and in its prime the collegiate periphery was stronger than the university centre. The only 'hold' of the centre on the periphery was the importance attached to degree-taking, and in time it was virtually the only control of the whole over its parts. With some exceptions, Oxford and Cambridge colleges became rich in relation to their teaching responsibilities, many handsomely endowed, founded and refounded by generous patrons, and from the sixteenth century onwards increasingly attended by sons expecting handsome fortunes from wealthy families not averse to paying high fees for residence, board and instruction. The student standard of living went up, setting a pace that lesser incomes could not match and jeopardising the financial position of undergraduates with only modest resources. Exhibitions and other college emoluments of eleemosynary purpose were correspondingly important and a significant educational lifeline for the younger sons of gentry and the offspring of clergy. We have already seen in an earlier chapter how resistant some

---

[15] See Sheldon Rothblatt, 'The Limbs of Osiris', in *The European and American University since 1800*, ed. Sheldon Rothblatt and Björn Wittrock (Cambridge, 1993).

resident members of the ancient universities were to competition as a means of deciding merit. In the older view, merit meant those who were meritorious, that is, those who were entitled by background to special consideration.

Universities were poor. They attracted few endowments. These were largely confined to professors, readers and some buildings. The historic strength of the university had been its professional schools, but the importance of the common over the canon law meant that in time the English university would lose out to new and successful schools that could do the work of a secular society. Medicine at Oxford and Cambridge declined as well (although there is debate about the extent of the decline), and the story of the subsequent success of the Scottish universities in this regard, especially Georgian Edinburgh which drew from all over Europe, is sufficiently familiar not to require retelling.

The college was an identifiable institution. It had a fellowship; it had a Rule; it had a common way of life. It was a substitute for home. The colleges collectively were strong and relatively autonomous, each more concerned with the authority that might be exercised by an outside Visitor named in the statutes than by a vice-chancellor, whose term in office was limited in any case by rotation. The university retained certain police powers respecting undergraduates, but colleges supplied the proctors, and individual tutors and deans normally preferred to handle the task of meting out discipline themselves rather than handing undergraduates over to the court of the vice-chancellor. So the centre declined still more, its basic function being to set degree examinations for reluctant and scarce candidates.

On the basis of a fundamental disjunction between the two parts of the collegiate university, there arose several consequences for the future history of university development in all parts of the United Kingdom. The first was that the essence of a university in England was the experience of college, and the essence of a college was the private relationships and friendships that were formed within it – examinations, degrees and all other such means of self-promotion being crass, illiberal and denaturing. The second was that a university was impersonal, distant and vaguely administrative: its task was to collect fees, publish calendars, set examinations, award degrees and support a small number of scholars – we might even call them 'researchers' but at least 'practitioners' – whose activities were secondary. The primary responsibility of a collegiate university was superintending the young and making them moral and responsible subjects of Crown, Church and Nation. In neutral language, this is an elite function since educationally it ranges far beyond competence. Elite sentiment was expressed repeatedly in private and official correspondence, memoranda, public pronouncements, magazine articles and testimony before government commissions of inquiry.

THE RISE OF THE CENTRE

We might very well adopt nineteenth-century language and refer to unreformed Oxford and Cambridge as confederations rather than federations, since it was the colleges, through the machinery of a Caput or Hebdomadal Board consisting of heads of colleges and a rotating vice-chancellor drawn from the colleges that dominated and weakened the central administration of the system. We must expect that in the nature of things two bodies occupying the same space will contend for its mastery (if equal, the result is stalemate). Therefore, one narrative thread in the history of Victorian Oxford and Cambridge was the attempt made by the centre to regain authority from the periphery by strengthening the only leverage universities possessed, namely examining and degree-giving powers. In the case of Cambridge the attempt began as a byproduct of the introduction of a new type of final examination in the obscurity of the middle of the eighteenth century. With Oxford it occurred more precisely in 1800 with the establishment of honours schools. Gradually these innovations took hold, followed by other innovations and refinements in the mode of examining and preparing undergraduates for examinations as explained in earlier chapters. Two groups now sought degrees through the medium of openly competitive examinations. The first were Dissenters, who hoped to capitalise upon their victories in the movement to reform the national electoral franchise. These triumphs notwithstanding, they failed to disrupt the ties of the Church of England to Oxford and Cambridge. In 1834 the House of Lords, where the ecclesiastical interest was entrenched, refused to dispense with religious tests. Subscription to the Thirty-nine Articles of the Church of England was required at matriculation at Oxford and at graduation at Cambridge, which meant that the occasional Nonconformists who might enrol at Cambridge were certain to go down without a degree. But the social humiliation to which they were subjected during residence was itself sufficient to deter matriculation. Subscription as a requirement for the first degree disappeared in the 1850s, but not until the 1870s was oath-taking eliminated for proceeding to MA since this degree carried with it the right to vote on university policy.

The next group to attempt re-establishing the balance within the Oxbridge confederations also chose the degree as an issue. Anglican in religious persuasion or willing to practise occasional conformity, they were more successful. Let us call them Lord Annan's 'intellectual aristocracy'.[16] While Dissenters concentrated their attack on the requirements for matriculation and residence, the next group pursued the lucrative emoluments available in the colleges to improve their chances for graduation. The prohibitive costs of university residence made the financing of a university education the most important issue for under-graduates from comfortable but not luxurious homes, and it was therefore necessary to pry loose scholarships, exhibitions, bursaries and demys, as well as fellowships, from such restrictions as founders' kin, school and geography. The studentships at Christ Church were already open, although to nomination rather than competition in the strictest sense, and they were defended on the grounds of their accessibility to ordinary undergraduates or graduates. The strategy adopted in the fight to open awards to general competition was to accuse colleges of mismanaging their endowments. As colleges were private societies free to dispose of income in accordance with statute, virtually the only effective charge that could be brought against them was that the heads and fellows had disregarded the intentions of benefactors. Since nepotism, favouritism and 'interest' were not demonstrably illegal, it was difficult for accusers to pry open the oysters to get at the pearls.

After the famous reforms of the 1850s and 1860s, what had been a confederation at Oxford and Cambridge became something closer to a federation. The centres were strengthened by the addition of new chairs, readerships and lectureships; the creation of new honours degree programmes produced boards of studies outside college control and new loci of teaching in the form of laboratories and intercollegiate lectures. Higher demand for degrees generally strengthened the examining system.

Correspondingly, the colleges were technically weakened by these changes, although not at first when the examination system was still in a process of development. They lost their curricular flexibility, a point usually under-appreciated by historians, their capacity to introduce teaching and subjects without regard for external examinations (as happened in the eighteenth century).[17] Eventually they more or less lost the option to farm undergraduates out to private coaches, a notable feature of the pre-1850 universities, yet their prestige as educational institutions was elevated. The colleges retained control over the critical functions of

[16] Noël Gilroy Annan, 'The Intellectual Aristocracy', in *Studies in Social History,* ed. J. H. Plumb (London, 1955), 241–87.
[17] See, for example, Dame Lucy Sutherland, *The University of Oxford in the Eighteenth Century, A Reconsideration* (1973).

admissions and the award of scholarships and fellowships, as well as the right to appoint to clerical livings in their gift. The colleges retained and vastly improved their hold on ideas of a humanistic or liberal education appropriate to the notion of the gentleman and consequently became the models for that kind of education throughout the English-speaking world. Once the central university had reasserted its hold over the degree, which represented the utilitarian and inferior idea of 'mere' competence or proficiency, the colleges were free to maintain that they and they alone represented the antithetical and higher idea of the unity of knowledge, the Hellenic-Renaissance ideal of the whole, the complete, the rounded personality.

A DIVISION OF LABOUR

Differentiation by function was a prime aspect of nineteenth-century institutional history generally. Cabinet, Commons, Lords, Crown and the civil service separated into branches, not for purposes of checks and balances as in the American constitution but as a consequence of greater political and administrative activity. Placemen who sat across the division between Commons and civil service yielded gradually to an expert class ('expert' not in the sense of specialised training but in the sense of being educated for public responsibility). The Lords ceased to control the Commons through the manipulation of interest groups. Political parties gave greater definition to Cabinets, hitherto patchwork alliances between rivals; and Cabinets, technically servants of the Crown, became in due course executive committees independent of the sovereign. The emergence of a prime minister who was more than *primus inter pares* awaited the birth of the next century.[18] Attempts were also made with varying degrees of success to separate the electoral system from the influence of landlords and proprietors, although more towards the end of the century than at the beginning when landlord influence was actually wanted. Differentiation was the tendency, and the operative word truly is 'tendency'. At no point in the nineteenth century did the kind of partitioning just described result in high definition institutions.

Yet the division of labour and responsibilities was perhaps greater than it had been in centuries, or at least clearer, certainly in the universities and colleges. Universities examined: that was mechanical, utilitarian. Colleges taught: that was nurturing. A college had to provide for the *eruditio*

---

[18] Lord Balfour? See John P. Mackintosh, *The British Cabinet*, 2nd ed. (London, 1968), 314.

of young men, and it had some of the characteristics of a school or *gymnasium*. Colleges educated for living, the 'common vocations of life'. Universities were concerned with mental training, skills, career preparation, 'the higher demands of science', *universitas literarum* and (later) research.[19] One kind of institution hearkened back to an organic order of relationships and communities. The other belonged to the same universe of energy that had built machines and factories. It was instrumental. The division of functions was never absolutely perfect within the ancient universities. To take only one simple fact, the examiners were drawn from colleges and therefore carried with them some of that ethos. But blind marking reduced some of the remaining ambiguity, as did the conduct of vivas by committee. In the twentieth century the external examiner became a bedrock feature of all quality systems, going beyond the Oxbridge conception of extra-collegiate but intra-collegiate examiners by drawing them from other universities. The polarities were sufficiently pronounced to inspire argument and debate as professors fought for one conception of a university and tutors for another.

The separation of teaching from examining within a federal university constitution can also be called the 'Cambridge principle'. Although that separation was implicit in the collegiate structure and existed before the tripos supplanted the older scholastic disputations, the newer honours examinations were destined to become the strongest cause of the division and a model for other institutions to follow. Therefore it should not be altogether suprising that the Privy Council, in the text of the royal charter of 1836 establishing the examining University of London, the first of the new federal universities of Britain, referred to a 'Board of Examiners ... to perform all the functions of the examiners in the Senate House of Cambridge'. It should not be news to learn that the new governing body of the University of London drew as many as ten of its founding fellows from Trinity College, the nineteenth-century intellectual leader of the Cambridge colleges (and to this day the best endowed of all UK educational institutions).[20]

---

[19] *Journal of the Proceedings of a Convention of Literary and Scientific Gentlemen, Held in the Common Council Chamber of the City of New York, October 1830* (New York, 1831), 247. The founders of what became New York University were greatly interested in the new London University.

[20] W. H. Allchin, *An Account of the Reconstruction of the University of London*, Part 1 (London, 1905), 21–3; Negley Harte, *The University of London, 1836–1986* (London, 1986), 86; Ted Tapper and Brian Salter, *Oxford, Cambridge and the Changing Idea of the University: The Challenge to Donnish Domination* (Ballmoor, Bucks, 1992), 98.

The federal principle, centre and periphery, the separation of functions and the academic division of labour, was Cambridge's gift to British higher education generally. In the course of the nineteenth century the Cambridge example also influenced the Scottish universities, for the honours degree was introduced into Scotland in 1858.[21]

The very notion of a federated, examining, non-teaching institution bearing the title 'university' in a British historical context is perplexing. It only makes sense when the separation of teaching and examining are viewed as quintessentially European, as found, for instance, in the State-administered examinations of France and Germany. Yet there was no actual precedent in England, Scotland or Ireland for a university that merely examined. The word 'university' always implied teaching of some kind, or scholarship. In addition, no extended discussion of examining procedures appears to have taken place during the debates and arguments over the founding of the first or 1828 London University, really a university college with an attached medical schoool, at most only an oblique reference to external examiners. The formation of an examining, degree-granting university without teaching is an anomaly.

While Cambridge was identified by the Privy Council as the source of their solution for the London University, the junior of the two ancient universities was never itself contemplated as a model for any federal arrangement. Durham, with colleges, founded in the early 1830s, was modelled on Oxford, and parts of its financial settlement on Christ Church, but Durham floundered and continued to flounder for decades, too expensive for the needs of the mining and industrial north. For a brief moment in the 1830s its students read for the new London degree while Durham awaited degree-conferring authority from the Privy Council. After Durham no statesman, industrialist, university reformer, professional or significant intellectual figure believed that Oxford and Cambridge ought to be emulated. Few would have wanted to do so in any event, if only to preserve the reputation of Oxford and Cambridge. But, as a practical measure, the costs for establishing collegiate universities ruled them out of serious contention as a model for new universities. The Oxbridge colleges had proliferated but only over a long period of time, and the financial history of any number of the colleges was spotty and unreassuring.

Collegiate universities did not really exist outside England. The University of Aberdeen had not yet become a dual collegiate institution:

[21] Ashby, *Universities*, 26.

Marischal College and King's College retained separate identities. St Andrews had two self-governing colleges, and each specialised. St Mary's taught theology, United College offered an arts curriculum. In Ireland Trinity College, Dublin, was supposed to have developed as a collegiate university when founded in the sixteenth century but failed to do so. Irish penury was undoubtedly one reason.

The available and realistic model for a new university in London in the 1820s was Edinburgh or Glasgow. The Scottish universities were non-residential, hence less expensive for students, they took in part-time, non-degree students, forced professors to woo undergraduates by tying fees to attendance (at least in part) and, although parts of a regenting or tutorial system remained, used the cheaper lecture system of teaching. Degrees were not in themselves as important as accessibility. The founders of the 1828 London University had a clear working example close at hand (and Scotland was re-exported from London to become the foundation of the three Queen's colleges of Belfast in the mid-1840s). Recent German foundations like Berlin and Bonn were also considered, although how seriously and deeply is difficult to imagine, and the leaders of the movement to create a metropolitan university had further acquainted themselves with plans for the establishment of a university in Virginia, which itself in many ways reflected Scottish ideals of teaching and access. Yet suitable as the Scottish model was for the first London University, it was rejected for the second or examining university. The federal principle reigned in its place and became so attractive that until Birmingham successfully challenged the principle in 1903, it dominated all nineteenth-century discussions about the place, mission and structure of new universities in Ireland, Wales, the English provinces, the colonies and the empire. We are presented with a number of historical riddles.

THE COMPROMISE OF 1836

The exact origins of the compromise of 1836 are obscure. Little by little pieces of the puzzle are coming together.[22] The problem of reconstructing the entire story arises from the absence of critical documents. There appear to be few relevant Privy Council records, no Cabinet notes – or none that have come to light – and the debates in Hansard give only the merest hint of the play of interests and circumstances. Historians have found useful hints in diaries and private papers. One hint, suggesting that

[22] Harte, *University of London*, and F. M. G. Willson, *Our Minerva, the Men and Politics of the University of London 1836–1858* (London, 1995), are recent, indispensable books.

discussions about a new kind of examining university was widespread, occurs in a letter from Charles Lloyd, bishop of Oxford and Sir Robert Peel's tutor at Oxford. Writing to him in 1828 about the constitution of King's College, the second university college to be founded in London, Lloyd pondered whether undergraduates completing four years of study could be given testimonials allowing them to sit the Oxford degree examinations, 'and if they pass . . . [be] given an A.B. degree'.[23] The letter is not otherwise illuminating. The *London Medical Gazette* also proposed the formation of a federation in 1828 as a means of resolving the issue of how many new institutions could be chartered.[24] In 1833 the idea of an independent board of degree examiners was broached by physicians and surgeons as part of a general public debate on medical standards.[25] In any event, the direction of the compromise of 1836 is clear. An unheard of independent body with degree-granting authority was created and assigned the title 'university', which at law meant that the word could not be used by the two existing teaching colleges. The new 'University of London' or even 'Royal University of London' ('Royal' was dropped almost immediately)[26] could devise examinations, appoint examiners and award degrees to successful candidates. Examiners were to be entirely or mainly drawn from a body of distinguished scientists, academics, professional men and public figures who had no necessary teaching connection with either King's College or the first London University now renamed University College. The new examining institution was staffed by a tiny number of officials subsidised by the State when necessary. Its premises were maintained by the Department of Works.

The University of London was a *de facto* arm of the State. It was a 'public' institution, and the two colleges were 'private'. The distinction was fully in keeping with the public/private dichotomy that had evolved in connection with the collegiate institutions of Oxford and Cambridge and more recently applied to Durham. As private foundations the colleges could impose religious tests as a requirement for admission (King's did so), charge fees for teaching and services and establish a curriculum independent of the university's, in which case the courses of study would not be proof of preparation for degree examinations. Both university colleges were proprietary companies in origin, and it was widely believed, especially of University College, that if left alone they would attempt to

[23] Charles Lloyd to Sir Robert Peel (10 November 1828), Sir Robert Peel Manuscripts, BL Add. MSS, No. 40343, vol. clxiii, f. 307.
[24] Willson, *Our Minerva*, 7.
[25] H. Hale Bellot, *University College London 1826–1926* (London, 1929), 236–7, 246.
[26] Willson, *Our Minerva*, 3.

improve their market position by lowering classroom standards in an effort to attract students and increase fees. The point keeps recurring as new information comes to hand.[27] The solution, therefore, was to completely detach the university from teaching and make it solely responsible for the degree, while insulating the colleges themselves from cruder educational aims. This was the customary division of responsibility between universities and colleges in any case. Colleges could keep their special historical legacy by offering (if they so chose) a 'higher' humanistic form of education.

The founders of University College had hoped to avoid a fight over degrees, possibly believing that they could appropriate the title 'university' without claiming degree-granting authority. 'University' appeared to be the favoured title since it was being used in connection with new foundations overseas. As an Anglican institution King's College wanted the same degree privileges as other Anglican institutions. Even a college like Trinity College, Dublin, could award degrees, perhaps because it was founded to be a university but never became one. So degrees and title were linked in everyone's mind. A furore was unavoidable.

Looking backwards, the historian should be astonished by the events of the 1830s. The compromise of 1836 was ingenious. It seems almost predestined. But stating the problem in this way, even calling it a 'compromise', does not do justice to what was a rambling, fumbling solution without historical precedent yet not, under the circumstances, illogical. For the present its exact origins must remain unknown. Whatever clues we have about its genesis derive from the overall political and educational context of the 1820s and 1830s, our understanding of what was happening in the kingdom generally.

The second quarter of the nineteenth century was an important period for university history in many ways. Discussion about new teaching institutions – and three of them were founded – urban universities, examining systems, higher education for Dissenters and the circumstances of Scottish universities and colleges were rife. In 1826, in fact, the first of the nineteenth-century royal commissions on higher education was created to deal with structural and statutory bottlenecks in the Scottish universities, with special attention directed to the quality of their teaching, examinations, degrees and graduation rates. The honours degree examinations at both Oxford and Cambridge were still in a process of evolution, still giving rise to controversies, anxieties and misgivings, and their legitimacy within the two universities was hardly beyond question.

[27] *Ibid.*, 8.

Examinations had not yet acquired their ultimate function as arbiters of success and failure. For many supporters of examinations they were probably only prizes, of the same nature as other Oxford and Cambridge awards for declamations, Latin translations and poetry submissions, exercises useful for distilling discipline and encouraging work but more in the order of rewards for proper academic behaviour. A prize was not a 'qualification' nor a durable platform on which to build a career.

So the air was full of argument and challenge, and unsettled or not, the Cambridge or federal principle triumphed. The centre maintained the standard and protected the quality of the degree, and it did this in the name of the public – in fact in the name of the State – and in accordance with a rationale that the famous liberal politican and Cabinet minister, Robert Lowe, made much of two decades later, namely that the duty of the State in higher education was not to assist institutions financially but to control and regulate their examinations.[28] Successful institutions could then receive payment by results. But if the Cambridge principle triumphed, it did so more thoroughly than in its own home, for there at least examiners were teachers in their capacity as dons. The separation was more rigidly observed in the case of London than in later federations, where professors were not barred from external examining.

THE MEANING OF 1836

The federal principle solved certain difficulties. The first was the problem of how to handle degrees. The second was how to cope with plural values in the higher education system, the problem that Raymond Williams once addressed in a long discussion about the culture concept in English history. In the 1820s pluralism in higher education meant utilitarian rather than collegiate conceptions of learning, the notion of 'accountability', an exclusively secular curriculum and a diminished role for the Church of England. The educational rationale, a number of historians have said, seemed to follow the advice laid down in Jeremy Bentham's *Chrestomathia*. This is unfair, but in keeping with the accusations that opponents of the first London University favoured. It is true that utilitarian considerations such as efficiency (costs), curricular utility and secular teaching all found a place in the new institution, but once underway the curriculum was not fundamentally different from what could be found in existing English or Scottish universities, consisting of classical and modern subjects and professional courses. Most of the

---

[28] Thomas Lloyd Humberstone, *University Reform in London* (London, 1926), 46.

problems associated with pluralism surfaced immediately when the founders of the first London University announced that their university was non-denominational. Indeed, since the founders were drawn from every religious group in London – Anglican, Nonconformist, Roman Catholic and Jewish (although a tiny community, its support proved critical) – no other possibility existed.

The departure from accepted English practice led to the immediate creation of a second institution in London known as King's College. One college was 'godless' and was satirised in a student publication as a 'metropolitan pest-house'.[29] The other met the requirements of the historic identification of an English college with religious teaching and observance. The 'godless' institution audaciously called itself a 'university' and was attacked for arrogating to itself a title to which it could make no historic or legal claim since it had never been chartered by the Crown in Council or the Crown in Parliament. (The older Scottish universities acquired their charters from the papacy, later confirmed by Crown or by Act of Scots or still later by Parliament.) But was such authority actually required for assuming the title 'university' if no degrees were involved? Must a university even provide degrees? The law regarding the granting of titles was wholly unclear, but a title which is vigorously disputed must have some value or wider resonance even in the absence of contemporary explanations. Opponents of the first London University argued casuistically that the legal power to grant degrees was 'incident' to the title, and the title was 'incident' to the largely ecclesiastical uses to which degrees were put.[30] The paucity of legal precedents often enough left attackers dependent upon shallow wit and implicit appeals to the prejudices of listeners. Sir Robert Inglis, the member of Parliament from Oxford University, made much sport of London as a 'joint stock company university' in reference to the financing of the new institution in his speeches before the House of Commons in the 1820s. Later on in 1835 Sir Charles Wetherell, also representing the opposition of Oxford, amused the Lords of Council with similar gratuitous remarks.

The derision, however, was keenly felt. In response to the criticism that the London University was not an educational institution but simply a business company, the uneasy founding proprietors limited the return on their investment and imposed restrictions on the sale of stock. Yet we can surmise that the establishment of the university as a business enterprise had legal advantages. If chartered, endowed or registered as a charity, the

[29] *First Book for the Instruction of Students in the King's College London* (London, 183?), 8.
[30] For which see *Substance of the Speech of Sir Charles Wetherell, passim.*

London University would most likely have fallen under the jurisdiction of Church and State and such administrative instruments as the recently created body of charity commissioners. It needed another legal identity on which to rest its desire for independence.

The problem of degrees could not be avoided, even though the backers, and especially the great Henry Brougham, the steam engine that drove the steam engine university, made a point of saying in Parliament that the godless institution was not concerned about degrees. Everyone knew that he was playing for time. The Dissenters wanted degrees. They had talked about creating a university of their own to replace the moribund Nonconformist academies of the eighteenth century, and suggestions were made about placing one somewhere in the north of England. In 1835 Henry Warburton, a great advocate of the first London University, and now regarded as a key figure in its early development, spoke in Parliament about the possibility of creating a university for Dissenters with separate examiners for quality control, and the question of how and where to educate non-Anglicans had certainly been reviewed in the Privy Council. On 27 May 1835, the London University applied for a charter.[31] Despite the fuzziness of the law regarding the title and power of the word 'university' and the weak arguments against them, and despite the support of whig ministers (who relied on Dissenting votes) and the House of Commons, the precious title was lost. The Church party prevailed in the House of Lords. However, credit for the defeat must also be given to the fierce opposition of the hospital-based London doctors, eager to prevent competition from the infidel college and its showpiece medical school.

Defeat led directly to the curious solution of 1836. Lord Melbourne (a Cambridge man), who was prime minister and therefore on the Council, had suggested that the special connection between Dissenters and the London University be underplayed in the new draft statutes: 'I would omit the words which I have underlined in the preamble and in the first enacting clause. There is no need to point so precisely to its being a measure for the benefit of the Dissenters.'[32] But as a 'college' could still be created just for Dissenters (and other non-Anglicans), it was necessary to establish another institution that guaranteed wider access while protecting the degree and the degree standard. There was another reason for the

---

[31] Willson, *Our Minerva*, 2, 308–9; for Warburton's speech, see Parliamentary Papers, House of Commons Debates (26 March 1835), col. 289.

[32] For Melbourne, see W. M. Torrens, *Memoirs of the Right Honourable William, Second Viscount Melbourne*, II (London, 1878), 158.

solution of 1836. Unless teaching was separated from examining, professors, paid like Scottish professors from student fees, would almost assuredly use degrees to attract students, exchanging quality in the class-room for a full house. The Scottish universities had been severely criticised for the level of their teaching. It was necessary to insure professors against their own greed by removing all temptation. A federation could do this; otherwise, Prince Albert was reported to have said somewhat later, colleges become inefficient, mere 'nests of jobbery and sectarianism'.[33]

Yet another difficulty was resolved in 1836: whosoever controlled the examinations, in so far as they were valued, also controlled the curriculum. This was as true of Cambridge as of London. Indeed, Cambridge was the prime illustration. The vigorous system of private teaching or coaching that grew up at the ancient societies in the first half of the nineteenth century was sufficient proof of this, as it engaged the energies of the best teachers and the best students in the most efficient cramming system that the nineteenth century had yet known. The consequences were not exactly unforeseen. From the first day of the establishment of the honours degree at Oxford (the Cambridge tripos had evolved almost imperceptibly), opponents had argued that a system of examinations, and especially written examinations, would eventually drive the entire educational system, leading to a loss of flexibility in matters of curriculum and to a narrow and constricting definition of excellence or merit. Only certain kinds of achievement would be recognised as reaching an acceptable or high standard. It was a conservative argument, in part meant to protect the gentlemen who by upbringing and ethic would not compete, might fail and would in any case be especially humiliated when losing to their social inferiors. University College, London, had no social class to protect. On the contrary, it needed to open its doors as widely as possible in order to attract the middling classes of the capital, 'small comfortable trading fortunes'. The spiritual founder of University College, the Scottish poet Thomas Campbell, said that he wished to draw from families living within two miles of the institution.[34] Residence had to be dispensed with, the degree mattered, utilitarian education counted. The first warden of University College minced no words about this. He unabashedly compared his institution to a great engine akin to the one invented by Watt.[35] John Henry Newman was so appalled by the establishment of

[33] Ashby, *Universities*, 31.
[34] Cyrus Redding, *Literary Reminiscences and Memoirs of Thomas Campbell*, II (London, 1860), 11.
[35] Chester W. New, *The Life of Henry Brougham to 1830* (Oxford, 1961), 383.

the University of London that in letters to *The Times* in 1841 signed 'Catholicus' he began to develop the argument that eventually issued in the great discourses.[36] The defence of the traditional 'idea of a university' consequently arose almost directly from the creation of the nineteenth century's first new university.

THE NATIONAL ROLE OF THE FEDERAL PRINCIPLE AFTER 1836

The legislation of 1836 required students reading for degrees to present certificates of attendance at recognised schools and college lectures before sitting examinations, but, as amended by legislation in 1858, the London examinations were thrown open to anyone wishing to take them, and London became the first British open university. The external degree was created. Students could sit examinations at other colleges or at local centres. Medical students were an exception; they were still required to take courses. Examinees educated privately were on the same footing as those who had taken formal degree courses. Degree access was accordingly widened, and the chasm between examining and teaching also grew larger. Thus appeared that special British invention, the external student. As the decades progressed (or waned), external students considerably outnumbered internal students, and the nineteenth century closed with movements to restore the balance by creating for London either a separate teaching university – it was proposed to call it the Albert University – or by amending the constitution of 1858. In 1898 institutions affiliated as 'schools of the university' were subject to visitations, and London also claimed the right of approval of anyone wishing to be an 'appointed teacher' of the University. Other instructors not so appointed could still be 'recognised', and it was possible for their students to sit internal examinations, at least in some cases.[37] The reorganisation of 1900 established a new federal University of London for internal students. The 1836 Examining Board was nevertheless retained for external degree candidates.[38]

Of particular importance was the use of Cambridge or federal principles to maintain a common standard of degree achievement across

[36] James Wieland, 'John Henry Newman, "The Tamworth Reading Room": Towards *The Idea of a University*', *Downside Review*, 103 (1986), 128.
[37] Harold and Pamela Silver, 'The Escaping Answer', in Moodie, *Standards and Criteria*, 12.
[38] Rowland B. Eustace, 'Gold, Silver, Copper: Standards of First Degrees', in *Quality and Access in Higher Education, Comparing Britain and the United States*, ed. Robert Berdahl *et al.* (Ballmoor, Bucks, 1991), 31.

the great diversity of Victorian Britain. At least one of the principal supporters of the original University of London admitted in Parliament that a London degree was at first likely to be of lower quality than an Oxford or Cambridge and perhaps a Scottish degree, 'but grant the power and the Professors would naturally feel anxious so to exert themselves in the cause of education as to bring respect to the degrees conferred by the institution'.[39] In other words, degrees first and standards later; but Victorian Britain would have none of it. The rule was to become standards first, degrees later.

The federal principle – teaching colleges joined to a centre empowered to award degrees – travelled well in the nineteenth century, but the severity of the London model was mitigated. The Queen's University in Ireland, for example, was set up in the 1840s. It had three branch university colleges in three different cities, Cork, Galway and Belfast (although examinations had to be taken in Dublin, considered a 'neutral location'). Residence (as in Scotland) was not required for a degree – the expense would have been counter-productive – but students presenting themselves for examination had to prove that they had been taught in one of the constituent colleges, the policy in London before 1858. No religious tests were required for students, and teaching, again as in Scotland, was by lecture. Tests would have been difficult in any case, where Anglicans, Presbyterians and Roman Catholics uneasily coexisted. A proposal to construct a federal university based on Trinity College, the sole college of the University of Dublin, was abandoned in the face of Anglican opposition. In 1882 the Queen's University was dissolved just as a new federation, the Royal University of Ireland, came into being, which, however, followed the London scheme of 1858 and dispensed with certificates of attendance as too expensive. After many additional years of controversy resulting from the particular features of religious conflict in Ireland, another plan was adopted in 1906 which abolished the Royal University and created a federal institution on the Welsh model, another federation to be called the National University of Ireland which resembled the old Queen's University more than it did the Royal one.[40] The

---

[39] The speech of Dr Lushington, in Parliamentary Papers, House of Commons Debates (26 March 1835), cols. 285–6.
   A central examinations board was introduced into Belgium in 1835, but its tenure was apparently brief. See Johanna Roelevink, 'Curriculum and Practice in University Teaching in the Low Countries and England 1800–1850', in *Studia Historica Gandensia*, 279, ed. John M. Fletcher and Hilde de Ridder-Symoens (Ghent University, 1994), 96.
[40] T. W. Moody, 'The Irish University Question in the Nineteenth Century', *History*, 43 (1958), 90–109.

federation of 1880 that became the Victoria University, consisting of university colleges in Manchester, Liverpool and Leeds, was also established on this basis, that is, combining examining with required attendance at colleges.

The charter of the University of the Principality of Wales was sealed at the end of 1893. Three university colleges had been established in Wales in the later nineteenth century. Since only one of them, Cardiff, could be said to exist in an urban environment, a federal rather than a unitary solution appeared to be more practical. The distances between colleges and the expense of travel would have made a centrally located single national University of Wales a hardship for the majority of Welsh families, and the limited resources of the Principality appeared to rule out fully autonomous and separate foundations. A variation on a common theme was introduced. Examining and teaching were actually combined in the Welsh federal system, and teachers were even allowed some freedom in designing their own courses. They could also act as internal examiners, but in all cases the final arbiter was the body of external examiners.[41] In 1905 Wales was called 'the last asylum of the federal system in Great Britain'.[42]

By the seventh decade of the last century the belief in some form of federation as the best way to ease fledgling, or as Lord Bryce would derisively call them several decades later, 'Lilliputian Universities',[43] into the higher education system was so firmly established in Britain that it was fully expected that a new university must first be founded as a college and then federated, either with an existing union or with a new one. Federation, it was said, was an 'inevitable' stage.[44] 'It is curious', wrote one contemporary, 'to find how obstinately there remained fixed in the minds of some of those concerned, a faith in the University College, or something

J. Gwynn Williams, *The University College of North Wales: Foundations 1884–1927* (Cardiff, 1985); D. Emrys Evans, *The University of Wales: A Historical Sketch* (Cardiff, 1953); W. Cadwaladr Davies and W. Lewis Jones, *The University of Wales and its Constituent Colleges* (London, 1905).

Gwynn Williams, *North Wales*, 117; see also 115. At one point in the 1890s the designation 'the Albert University' was suggested for Wales. Although provisionally accepted by the Charter committee, the name was soon discarded. Thus two nineteenth-century attempts to create a fitting memorial to the worthy prince who championed higher education came to nought.

In 1995 the Cardiff Institute of Higher Education and Gwent College were added to the existing six constituent colleges, one of which, Bangor, had previously swallowed a normal college. *Times Higher Education Supplement* (14 April 1995).

Don Carleton, *A University for Bristol* (Bristol, 1934), 13.

Edward Fiddes, *Chapters in the History of Owens College and of Manchester University 1851–1914* (Manchester, 1937), 106; Sir Adolphus William Ward, *Collected Papers*, V (Cambridge, 1921), 225.

not very different, as the supreme goal of achievement – the best, at all events, that was open to them.'[45]

The lay and academic leadership of university colleges usually accepted the reasoning behind the federal principle since their institutions were highly vulnerable to fluctuations in student demand, upon whose fees their survival rested. But the leadership of Owens College in Manchester was an exception to the general rule. Off to a shaky start when founded in 1851, Owens prepared students for the London degree and was formally affiliated in 1858. Two decades later the college felt sufficiently pleased with its improved market position to amalgamate with the Royal Manchester School of Medicine and in 1877 applied for a royal charter. It appears as if the Privy Council approved the application in 1880, believing that the college's trial period was now ended. But opposition from university colleges in neighbouring regions led immediately to federation. Liverpool and Leeds greatly feared that the success of Owens was detrimental to their own fortunes. Federation provided a compromise. For several years Owens was the sole college in the federation, although in anticipation of improvements in staff, students and resources, Liverpool and Leeds were allowed to send representatives to the federation's governing body.[46]

While throughout the nineteenth century substantial disagreement occurred in virtually all areas of education, there also remained a strong feeling that a university must discriminate in what or how it taught, and that unless its authority operated through the curriculum, standards would be adversely affected. Sir Henry Enfield Roscoe, the renowned Manchester chemist and Owens College professor, said that if a university could not, for one reason or another, prevent the establishment of a new curriculum, it was not under obligation to allow a new entrant an old and historic degree. He related in his autobiography that the protection of the arts degree was assured in the Victoria University when in 1881 a bachelor of science track was created especially for engineers.[47] (The same tactic of separating degree tracks to protect the BA degree was used in elite American universities in the nineteenth century.) Such sentiments have a continuous history. Much nearer to our own day the principal of the College of Technology in Birmingham explained that federation or affiliation of technical colleges to universities usually leads the former to

[45] Edward Jamie Somerset, *The Birth of a University* (Oxford, 1934), 5.
[46] David R. Jones, *The Origins of Civic Universities, Manchester, Leeds and Liverpool* (London, 1988), 54, 62–164.
[47] *The Life and Experiences of Sir Henry Enfield Roscoe by Himself* (London, 1906), 186.

change their character and mission so as to avoid the reproach of 'sub-university work'. He mentioned part-time courses as a specific casualty of union.[48]

In the 1880s schemes of federation were extremely popular. The Victoria University was spoken of with pride as a federation of the north, and it was subsequently proposed that a University of the Midlands be created, then a University of the East Midlands and a University of the West Midlands, or a federation based on Leeds, but more probably Birmingham. A Western University was mentioned and would be more or less mentioned again. For a moment, too, with visions of federated examining universities popping up all over England, it was even possible to think of the University of London as a University of South-east England. When Liverpool and Manchester left the Victoria University in 1902, representatives from the Yorkshire College in Leeds, the remaining member of the triumvirate, proposed federating with the university college in Sheffield or establishing another grouping that would be a county University of Yorkshire.[49] In 1915 plans for a university in Exeter were being contemplated, and it was suggested that a federation be established under the name of the University of South-west England, consisting of an arts and sciences college in the cathedral city, a marine biology and technical education college at Plymouth, a school of mines at Camborne in the centre of Cornish mining, three teacher-training colleges and a newly founded agricultural college. An alternative view was that Bristol should form the heart of a federation for Devon and Cornwall.[50] In 1917 the possibility of establishing a university for Leicester was discussed. One suggestion was that it should take the shape of a federal University for the East Midlands, to be called that, or as an alternative, the 'University of Mercia' after the Anglo-Saxon kingdom. The constituent parts might be a combination of the university colleges of Leicester and Nottingham, an existing agricultural college and the engineering institution of Loughborough, or – and this was a new idea – a union of specialised faculties rather than university colleges. Discussions about such a university continued right into the 1940s. While it was never created, *Whitaker's Almanack* insisted on listing an 'East Midlands University (in process of formation)'.[51] In fact, none of these federation dreams ever came into being.

[48] P. F. R. Venables, *Technical Education* (London, 1956), 496.
[49] Arthur W. Chapman, *The Story of a Modern University of Sheffield* (London, 1955), 178.
[50] B. W. Clapp, *The University of Exeter: a History* (Exeter, 1982), 48–9.
[51] Jack Simmons, *New University* (Leicester, 1959), 62, 64, 96.

The enthusiasm for federal systems appeared to wane, and no genuinely new federations on a Victorian scaffolding were erected in the twentieth century. But some are being discussed, if under different sponsorship. The notion of a University of the Highlands and the Islands in Scotland is being floated as a consortium of research institutions and twelve further education colleges, with possible linkages to such student exchange programmes as the European Union's SOCRATES, the successor to ERASMUS. This is basically a distance learning project.[52] The University of Ulster in Belfast has branches but is not a federation.

Yet there was also no rush on the part of the government or a new intermediate body, the University Grants Committee set up after the First World War, to nurture a new generation of unitary universities. Keele, first known as the University College of North Staffordshire, was set up after the Second World War and in an unusual move was given degree-granting powers, but the college had to be 'sponsored' by a number of other universities as a guarantee of its legitimacy.[53] Not until the University of Birmingham became the prototype of a special kind of British institution, followed by Sussex sixty years later, did the instant degree-granting university, well-known to that republic across the Atlantic, make an appearance. Instead, there was a reversion to a familiar pattern of controlling degrees. Local teacher-training institutions, technical colleges, design schools and arts faculties were allowed to form themselves into university colleges incorporated under articles of association granted by the Board of Trade. They were given the option of following the regulations for matriculation and examination of the original federal university, London. Southampton, Exeter and Leicester were all required to remain in this mould.

The federal principle was repeatedly modified in different circumstances, experimented with and adjusted. It was never dogmatically applied in a single form, except for the belief in the singular value of independent examiners. And therein lies its historical importance. As long as such sentiments were translated into actual policies, certain alternatives were automatically ruled out, notably those that were connected to market

[52] *Times Higher Education Supplement* (3 November 1995).
[53] The story is told in Michael Shattock, *The UGC and the Management of British Universities* (Ballmoor, Bucks, 1994), 54–6. The Committee of Vice Chancellors and Principals opposed granting university status to the University College of North Staffordshire on the grounds that it deviated too much from the norm. Opposition was overcome for strongly political reasons. Stoke was a Labour stronghold, and a Labour government was in office. The sponsorship of Oxford, Birmingham and Manchester also helped, and there was genuine postwar support for curricular experiments. See also Sir James Mountford, *Keele, An Historical Critique* (London, 1972).

or consumer initiatives. These had been suspect from the moment that the enterprising London professional and business representatives floated stock to create an educational company. It is not too far-fetched to see the federal principle taking rise from that moment as a government policy strategy. Scholars who have called the system of external degrees 'the most momentous step ever taken in the history of the English universities'[54] are surely correct, which makes the history of 1836 an even more alluring candidate for historical investigation.

THE CHANGING IDEA OF A UNIVERSITY AND THE RETURN OF THE UNITARY MODEL

Joseph Chamberlain helped interrupt the process of federation making towards the end of the century when he suddenly announced that instead of bowing to custom and allowing Mason College in Birmingham to federate as a university college, he would instead seek a royal charter for an independent university. His surprised collaborators were utterly convinced that the Privy Council would reject a proposal for a unitary civic university. Universities cut from whole cloth were unheard of. Chamberlain may not have arrived at his decision overnight. Engrossed in the 1890s with plans for a great British overseas federation of colonies and dependencies, he may at first have been thinking about a union of local colleges and institutions sharing a common core of instruction.[55] But his mind once set, he triumphed in 1903. His successful resistance was the first serious challenge to the federal principle since its inception. (The challenge was especially daring because Birmingham was designed as a suburban campus with a central tower as landmark much like many American campuses of the same period. In fact, there appears to have been American influence.) The new University of Birmingham, the first of the English redbrick universities, proceeded to demonstrate that it was not a Lilliputian university. It immediately absorbed an existing medical school and developed a School of Commerce, a clear sign of its freedom. The model for Birmingham was not the English federal university but the Scottish unitary university, the model that at one time had most promised to influence the course of higher education history in nineteenth-century Britain but had been supplanted in one respect by a different conception born of a different national experience. Eager to avoid federation by

54 Cited in Silver and Silver, 'The Escaping Answer', 12.
55 See Julian Amery, *The Life of Joseph Chamberlain*, IV (London, 1901–3), 211–12; and Elsie E. Gulley, *Joseph Chamberlain and English Social Politics* (New York, 1926), 125–6.

leaving itself open to charges of lowering standards, Birmingham immediately incorporated the principle of external examining into its charter.[56]

But there is a new element in the story of what the title of a university means. Inevitably a change in the idea of a university could also produce a serious challenge to the federal principle, and that idea had been making the rounds since at least the 1870s. A subcommittee reporting to the Annual Committee of London University's Convocation in 1877–8 had recognised the importance of 'the advancement of knowledge as an object of national interest', but the Senate, which was the governing body of the University and represented the examiners, unsurprisingly preferred the old commitments.[57]

The argument that universities were founded for research was very clearly introjected in the Birmingham case. Chamberlain was undoubtedly influenced by Edward Sonnenschein, a graduate of University College, Oxford, a classical scholar of national and international reputation and professor of Greek and Latin at Mason College. Sonnenschein's first thoughts about a university for Birmingham were actually federal in character, although in novel form. In 1896 he proposed the establishment of a University of the Midlands, to be composed of professors from university colleges in Bristol, Nottingham and Birmingham. They were also to hold appointments in colleges. As university professors, they were researchers, but as college staff they prepared students for examinations. This was not an elegant solution, as Chamberlain recognised, but the idea of a research mission greatly appealed to him, and he saw that it was better fulfilled by a unitary than a federal structure. By 1897 he had firmly decided on a civic university that would incorporate postgraduate instruction, the ideal of the advancement of learning, autonomous or powerful faculties and professorships with security of tenure to provide opportunities for long-term research (Mason College had put staff under terminal but renewable contracts).[58] The influential and active Lord Haldane was sympathetic to the position. He specialised in appeals before the Privy Council and the House of Lords and was fast becoming an important leader in British higher education, having been educated at both Edinburgh and Göttingen. He believed that federated colleges were intellectual colonies that deprived professors of

[56] Eustace, 'Gold, Silver, Copper', 36.
[57] Allchin, *Reconstruction*, 21–3. Campbell, in considering the duties of chairholders, had ruled out 'authorship', that is research, and in this regard is a fair representative of educated thinking (see Bellot, *University College London*, 51.)
[58] Somerset, *Birth of a University*, 7–8.

Lehrfreiheit, but he fell back upon federalism wherever he saw no clear alternative.[59]

The new position was this: colleges teach, and teaching can be made 'accountable' through the machinery of external examinations, but original inquiry does not flourish under such conditions. In fact, examinations hinder the work of the investigator, since the process of imaginative discovery requires qualities of intelligence and independence that cannot be standardised. The real and fundamental purpose of a university is not teaching and examining as commonly understood: it is the advancement of knowledge and the promotion of learning and research at their highest levels. A very high degree of institutional autonomy is essential to this type of university, and this cannot be realised wherever teaching is dissociated from research and subjected to the requirements of a syllabus under outside control (precisely the French situation in 1995, or the situation obtaining in the eastern European soviet academy/institute structure). Therefore the historic association between college and university must be broken and replaced by an organisation consistent with new values, such as faculties or departments rather than colleges, unitary institutions rather than federations and academic senates that embody the views of researchers, professors or teachers. Governing councils should consist of similar types, rather than the external representatives of Crown, State, the great professions and even professors from 'rival' institutions – the combination introduced when the federal system was created in its Victorian phase.

Encouraged by Birmingham, Liverpool decided on a similar course, and the government of the day agreed (at Lord Haldane's suggestion) to allow the matter to come before the Privy Council instead of appointing a Royal Commission to conduct inquiries.[60] So in 1902 Liverpool's prayer to leave the most famous of federations, the Victoria University, was discussed in Council. As Liverpool went, so assuredly would Manchester, the seat of the Victoria University itself, leaving only Yorkshire College at Leeds and its affiliated schools. This in fact happened, but to forestall that eventuality, representatives from Leeds invoked a classic argument for federations, namely, that they made a higher educational standard possible. Federation offered 'a much better guarantee of breadth of view and freedom from local or individual prejudices'.[61]

Behind this apparently clear statement lay the many assumptions about the nature of higher education in regard to national purposes, about the differences between colleges and universities and about the relationship

[59] Carleton, *Bristol*, 15.   [60] *Ibid.*, 17.   [61] PRO PC8/605 (27 October 1902), 5.

between teaching and examining that had developed in the course of the nineteenth century in connection with the evolution of British universities, their reform, and their gradual movement to an important place in the State. The unitary conception of a university was successfully embodied in the Scottish universities, but even a new Scottish University College like Dundee (1883) ended up preparing its students for the London University examinations when it might have collaborated with St Andrews.[62] The Scottish single university had not served as a model for Ireland or Wales. After a strong start, it had been bypassed in London and rejected at Durham, but it was now resurrected for Birmingham, which, however, had begun life as a technical college. Federation was triumphant, although in 1902, as a last-ditch measure to save the Victoria Federation, the suggestion was made that departures from some common examining practices might be possible.[63] A stronger argument for any lingering sentiment about starting life as a unitary foundation could generally be dispelled in the final decades of the nineteenth century by shaking the American example in the faces of unitary enthusiasts. A 'crowd of inefficient degree-giving institutions' would mean the end of the higher quality and superior education given in British universities.[64] There were Anglophiles on the opposite shore who cheered and American Germanophiles who joined them, puzzled by what their countrymen considered higher education but which they knew to be no different from what occurred in *gymnasia*.

The two escapees from the Victoria University were in fact guilty of the charges made by accusers. They did want stronger unitary universities precisely because they wished to put their services at the disposal of great provincial cities. The different regions and cities had different industries, different civic histories and objectives, and no federation had yet proved flexible enough to satisfy all local needs.[65] Newman had said that a university must engage in the teaching of universal knowledge. Put another way, borrowing the distant vocabulary of the medieval university, a university was a *studium generale* not a *studium particulare*: it was a place that drew students from many localities not from one.[66] Its task was to

---

[62] Robert D. Anderson, *Education and Opportunity in Victorian Scotland*, Schools and Universities (Oxford, 1983), 82.

[63] PRO PC8/605 (27 October 1902), 32.

[64] Fiddes, *Owens College*, 103. The inadequacies of American higher education (and German!) were argued in a submission to the Lords in Council in 1902 by Thomas Fowler, President of Corpus Christi College, Oxford. See PRO PC8/605 (27 October 1902), 35.

[65] PRO PC8/605 (27 October 1902), I, 11–14, 61–2.

[66] The conversion of redbricks to *studia generale* has in fact occurred in the twentieth century, as provincial universities now draw students primarily from distances greater than thirty miles. This notion in modern form has a place in the American higher education system as

impart breadth to a curriculum and large-minded views to narrow-minded students. But what the provincial cities were requesting at the turn of the century was the right to promote specialised knowledge relevant to their geographical circumstances. An examining university constrained that right.

THE SEARCH FOR STANDARDS REVISITED

The State represented culture and the best that had been thought and said in the world. This was Matthew Arnold's famous refrain. Arnold also supported federations as a means of keeping down the number of competing universities.[67] Competition was part of philistine culture. The State must regulate examinations, Robert Lowe had said, and the State had chosen to do this in the case of higher education by creating examining universities to which colleges could affiliate. Federations on the post-London model, it was true, were a step below the State, a mitigated substitute for it, but they still represented the principle of degree accountability to an examining centre. How, in the absence of federations, could a high and uniform national standard of achievement be maintained across the higher education sector generally? At issue were not only the quality of degrees, but the quality of teaching (as validated by degree results), as well as admission standards since the effects of degree examinations were continually driven downwards. If federations dissolved, was there another method available for assuring an acceptable standard? Could this desideratum be achieved by creating a system of external examining applicable to solitary universities?

This solution, typical by the end of the twentieth century, was proposed in the 1902 Privy Council discussion. In view of the fact that the external

well as the British. The elite private sector of American colleges and universities prides itself on the geographical diversity of its students and partly measures its prestige by national appeal. Admissions officers are instructed to choose undergraduates competitively according to regional spread. Localism and local control are widely considered to be the marks of an inferior institution, or an inferior department or programme within a larger organisation. Since even the leading American public universities do not possess such freedom, being state and not national institutions, they do not expect their undergraduates to reproduce the academic results of the famous private universities. However, postgraduate programmes usually have greater flexibility in admissions, and selection is undertaken with a national market in mind. The reputation of state universities is therefore based on the quality of their graduate research and professional degrees rather than on their undergraduate colleges and schools. For some interesting remarks on the history of localism and nationalism in American colleges and universities, see Christopher Jencks and David Riesman, *The Academic Revolution* (New York, 1968), 155–96, 380–2.

[67] Fiddes, *Owens College*, 76.

examining system outlasted most applications of the Victorian federal principle as a means of quality control in British universities, it is interesting to look back at 1902 to see how the suggestion was taken. The proponents of federation were hardly convinced. External examiners taken from outside a federation were not as reliable as a body of resident and 'permanent examiners'[68] because ... ? We need to fill in the sentiments missing from Council records: because external examiners had no commitment to a unitary institution and did not really care about its quality, being drawn from competitor institutions, whereas the examiners attached to the examining core of a federal university had a vested interest in the overall welfare of the institution and its subsidiaries. We know today that the opposite tendency is more likely: that external examiners may ratchet the standards too high for any number of personal or competitive reasons.

Other arguments on behalf of the federal principle were less vague or ideological and more practical and contextual. Not all the Victorian cities could manage or find resources at a satisfactory level to finance unitary institutions. Federation enabled precarious institutions like the Yorkshire College in Leeds to draw upon the assistance of wealthier partners and to extend their catchment areas, provided geography and the expense of travel imposed no barriers for students. Yet this possibility was actually difficult in the case of the London colleges. The solution of 1836 may have been a 'compromise' but a compromise that favoured a university system driven by degree examinations. The colleges, technically independent, were hindered in their efforts to raise revenue for operating expenses. The federal system did not encourage much collegiate *esprit de corps* or produce strong alumni support associations. Writing to Roscoe in September 1876, Professor Sir Benjamin Brodie, the discoverer of graphitic acid, noted that 'University College and King's College have by no means been successful, except in their schools [secondary schools], and I fear have no inclination to support the upward movement of others.'[69] Throughout the nineteenth century the two colleges experienced periodic budgetary crises, especially after they lost the right to compel students to attend courses in order to obtain degrees. A lucrative source of income was thereby withdrawn. The flow of fees was towards the centre which collected money for examination-taking. More than once King's College was bailed out through the generosity of the liveried companies of the City. The income problem was one of the causes behind the later ninetenth-century movement to found a new federation to be called the

---

[68] PRO PC8/605 (27 October 1992), 10, 29. [69] Roscoe, *Life and Experiences*, 182.

Albert University, a university for the internal student, a university that would emphasise teaching and would be empowered to collect and, still better, to retain tuition fees.

Still the belief prevailed that cost-effective teaching and accountability were best handled in a federal system, and a number of different schemes were tried in the hope of finding satisfactory solutions. Wherever systems of a *national* character were established, as in Ireland and Wales, the less expensive London model of 1858 was reconsidered. In Ireland, as observed, opinion oscillated. Both revenue schemes were tried, and in the debates over the Welsh university the option of employing 1858 in aid of the adult education movement was pushed by one of the parties.[70]

A problem that federalism was expected to address arose as a consequence of the small size of the applicant pool. The Balfour Education Act did not come into effect until 1902, and secondary education did not become compulsory for some years after. Even so, the school-leaving age remained low until late in the twentieth century. Throughout the nineteenth century the new university colleges were hampered in their educational efforts by the disappointing number of qualified applicants, and often – this was certainly true of University College and King's College – college preparatory schools had to be established to ensure a supply of competent undergraduates. The Oxbridge colleges had experienced this difficulty until the reforms in the elite schools and the creation of Victorian public schools produced a reliable clientele; and once these changes were in place, the ancient foundations could proceed with their nineteenth-century agenda of raising standards, which entailed eliminating remedial education, attacking the problem of private coaching, introducing new subjects and extending the variety of honours degrees. Changes in secondary education invariably affect the quality of undergraduate teaching. The emergence of the A-level examination as another gold standard parallels the history of federalism and external examining in their later phases. It and similar examinations on the Continent are among the most important dimensions of the success of elite university education in Europe. Their absence is accordingly one of the most significant reasons why American colleges and universities offer so many different levels of quality however measured.

The public school model was also introduced into Scotland, but the kingdom had its own historic system of lower education which was upgraded in the course of the century. The new university colleges of England, which drew many of their staff from the ancient colleges, aspired

[70] Gwynn Williams, *North Wales*, 113.

to the Oxbridge standard but had no reliable upper secondary school sector to draw from comparable to the great public schools and the leading reformed grammar schools. In fact, the university colleges of the Victorian period, including the pioneering foundations of London, often served as feeder institutions to Oxford and Cambridge, much as the Scottish universities did (it was said that entrants to Marischal College in Aberdeen were only 12 years of age in the 1820s!).[71] The standard of university preparatory education was so low in Wales that it was sometimes unhappily predicted, even as late as 1885, that the Welsh university colleges 'were doomed for a quarter of a century to serve as preparatory schools for the degrees of the University of London'.[72] The temptation to recruit underprepared students was always present, but the federal principle at least provided a higher standard of aspiration: 'In a Federal University the standard of the best becomes the standard for all.'[73] Federation also made possible the existence of honours degrees, an even higher standard. Honours degrees could not easily be offered in small universities since the numbers of aspirants were few, but within a federation sufficient candidates could be found to allow for the multiplication of honours courses. It was even said of Oxford that the quality of honours degrees was partly a function of the size of the candidate pool, and some degrees were therefore clearly superior to others.[74] It is interesting to notice that during the 1902 deliberations of the Privy Council on the Victoria Federation that secondary school teachers, such as those in the West Riding of Yorkshire Secondary Schools Association, were sufficiently exercised about the tendency for non-federated colleges to revert to secondary school status to suggest that a lower age limit be imposed on entrance to universities, lest competition ruin the Victoria University and honours degrees vanish. It was feared that the disappearance of honours degrees would cause universities and colleges to simply raid the schools wholesale and thereby lower the standards of admission.[75] The bottom would influence the top. The purpose of examining universities was to prevent this from happening.

---

[71] Anderson, *Education and Opportunity*, 29.   [72] Gwynn Williams, *North Wales*, 112.

[73] PRO PC8/605 (27 October 1902), 10.

[74] PRO PC8/605 (27 October 1902), 29. In 1993 Oxford allowed itself to be scrutinised by an external body for the first time. The Higher Education Quality Council noted in its audit how many variations in style and standard existed in the marking of scripts and award of degree classes. The Council's report also criticised Oxford for defining courses almost exclusively in terms of examination papers. Oxford's reply (quite properly) was that the tutorial system provided other kinds of student assessments. *Times Higher Education Supplement* (24 September 1993), 2.

[75] PRO PC8/605 (27 October 1902), 73.

The question of standards was intimately connected to the problem of institutional competition, and those who defended federation before the Lords in Council in 1902 wished to protect new and struggling institutions from the full play of market forces by employing the federal principle on their behalf. The centre was to be strong enough to deter the periphery from temptation unworthy of an institution entitled to call itself a 'university'. Doubtless compromises were necessary. Victorian Parliaments were still committed to liberal principles, but a regulatory State was also in the making. It can be argued that, under the influence of aristocratic leadership, the principle of intervention into society and the economy had never actually been abandoned. The persistent survival of sentiments favouring a gold standard of degree attainment can be associated with this 'metropolitan' culture, and yet the Britannic State was never as *dirigiste* as the Gallic State. Walking a tightrope seemed to be the only possible result. In 1892 the *Quarterly Review* favoured 'compromise', defining it as 'mutual concession and helpfulness, a willingness to give and to take', while adding the commonplace clincher, 'and a common subordination to some recognized central authority'.[76] After more than half a century the idea of a federal principle of some kind was hard to relinquish.

A TALE OF MANY CITIES

The tale of federalism is also a tale of cities, and it is therefore necessary to return for a moment to the process of urbanisation that is one of the great themes of nineteenth-century civilisation. The federal university system was first established to regulate the educational ambitions of Londoners and was then introduced into the great provincial centres, where it actually served regions. But even the Royal University of London was not really a municipal institution. No official city control over any part of the university system existed. Also, metropolitan London lacked an integrated government. London was a collection of parish and later (to adopt the New York terminology) borough governments. The conception of London as a special kind of urban area called a 'metropolis' first emerged in the early Victorian period,[77] but there was no London County Council to actually represent the idea of a greater London. The LCC was not created until the very end of the Victorian age and only then was there a 'municipality' that could be tapped for support. Possibly that is why the London School of Economics, founded in 1895, is a London-related

---

[76] *Quarterly Review*, 174 (1892), 252.
[77] Anthony Sutcliffe, *Metropolis 1890–1940* (Chicago, 1984), 67, 256n.

institution far more than the university which grants its degrees. Its founders were greatly concerned about urban problems of poverty, health, education and social mobility, and the Fabians among them, at least Sidney Webb, were closely associated with the evolution of London's municipal government. Its most recent chronicler, Lord Dahrendorf, stresses the importance of London to the School, but he also defines 'London' very broadly as a world city, attracting students and teachers to LSE from innumerable international locations. 'LSE has made a major contribution to combating one of the plagues of the twentieth century,' he writes, 'the plague of narrow and often aggressive nationalism'.[78] It is not idle to speculate that London University's difficulties in finding a separate city government with which to identify had something to do with its financial problems and its characterisation in 1903 by H. G. Wells as a headless, flaccid institution, or in his colourful biological language, 'an acephalous invertebrate'.[79]

In the absence of an identifiable city with which the University of London could negotiate, discuss, appeal for assistance and morale-boosting, it made sense for the examining centre of the University of London to cast its net as widely as possible and draw external degree candidates from everywhere in the kingdom. The educational imperial-ism of the university followed the lead of the capital itself, which increasingly dominated the cultural, economic and political life of the nation. London was what geographers call a 'primate' city, exercising a disproportionate influence over the country as a whole through its network of monopolies. This process of aggrandisement began in the late seventeenth or early eighteenth century and was powerful enough to force a brain drain out of Scotland. The build-up of population in the south-east in proximity to the capital, and the disparities in wealth and prosperity that distinguished the southern from the northern portions of England, have possibly never been more pronounced than today, but the attractions of London in relation to the provinces were also very evident in the last half of Victoria's reign. The enlarged reach of the capital adversely affected the great urban communities of the midlands and the north, whose birth and growth were directly connected to industrial civilisation as London's had never been. Every major advance in transportation and communication – railways with their hub in London, a national press with editorial offices in the capital – drew attention and income away from the

[78] Ralf Dahrendorf, *LSE, A History of the London School of Economics and Political Science, 1895–1995* (Oxford, 1995), 519.
[79] Harte, *University of London*, 24.

periphery to the centre. The growth of provincial suburbs, the popularity of public boarding schools, the decline of interest in local affairs which accompanied the assumption of greater control over municipalities by Whitehall (as when the Local Government Board was established as a Department of State in 1871) and the tendency for younger potential leaders to use London as an outlet for their ambition left management of the cities to older and less affluent residents. Attempts by the once isolated but vigorous communities to gain or retain their independence were handicapped.[80]

London was all things to all people, but the industrial cities were in some sense company towns possessing a certain coherence and identity. Civic pride should have been a natural result. Indeed, in the work of important philanthropists like John Owens, who founded Owens College in Manchester, we notice the effects of a positive civic attachment, and the same can always be said of Joseph Chamberlain. However, the partiality towards federating university colleges in some sense deprived the fine provincial communities of the symbolic advantages carried by the idea of a university. Lord Haldane told an audience at Leicester in 1923 that 'a city gets its true stature when along with its great churches it has its great university',[81] and this was certainly the late nineteenth-century view. All great European cities had universities, but not all great English cities had universities. Federation created this situation by drawing attention away from peripheries to centres. London attracted the external degree student away from the Victoria University. Manchester, the seat of the Victoria University, drew attention away from Leeds and Liverpool and completely dominated that federation. The residents of these cities – so it was argued – were consequently deprived of an incentive for charitable giving; and as the nineteenth century closed we find the State taking its first tentative steps towards support of what in origin had been private foundations, expressions of local pride and manifestations of the Victorian belief in the efficacy of self-help. Small grants to civic university colleges began in 1889, to medical schools in 1911. State support to Scotland never actually ceased.

THE FEDERAL PRINCIPLE IN THE TWENTIETH CENTURY

The federal principle strengthened secular and lay tendencies and paved the way for greater State involvement in the functioning of universities.

---

[80] Donald Read, *The English Provinces, 1760–1960: a Study in Influence* (London, 1964), 232–61.
[81] Simmons, *New University*, 91.

Since controversy today concentrates on the 'unintended centralisation' of Conservative party policies in the 1980s,[82] it is necessary to stress relevant Victorian administrative inventions. While providing an arena for participation by local interests, federalism also imposed constraints; and by claiming exclusive control over degree examinations (except where entrenched interests were particularly strong), federations in effect nationalised degrees, protecting them from the likely intrusion of particularism.

When the nineteenth century began, the English universities were regarded as national assets but not necessarily national institutions. Their affiliation was closer to Church than to State, certainly closer than to nation-state, but State and Church were intertwined. During the period of franchise reform from 1828 to 1832, the constitutional notion of a confessional State (as it is now often termed because of the work of J. C. D. Clark[83]) was greatly modified. An Anglican political constitution was largely transformed into a Christian one with the admission of Roman Catholics and Dissenters to the electoral system. Several decades of debate at Oxford and Cambridge, but especially at Oxford, then ensued over the meaning of a Protestant (rather than a Church of England) university. The debate was moved forward by Broad Church arguments for comprehension, anticipated in some cases by non-latitudinarians.[84] Some Churchmen correctly foresaw the eventual emergence of a non-denominational university; indeed, they did not have to look far since University College, London, was to hand. But the process of secularisation of the ancient universities would not be complete until the early twentieth century when the 'external university', the non-resident MAs, lost their historical right to block certain kinds of legislation. Overwhelmingly clergy, they tied Oxford and Cambridge to a particular community of religious interests through their voting rights in university legislatures. The admission of Jews into both Houses of Parliament after mid-century disrupted even a Christian conception of the State, and this issue much more than the triumph of liberal principles of toleration was paramount according to David Feldman. It was an issue that bothered Jews in the

---

[82] The phrase appears in Mrs. Thatcher's memoirs. *Times Higher Education Supplement* (20 October 1995).

[83] As in such works as *English Society, 1688–1832: Ideology, Social Structure and Political Practice During the Ancien Regime (Cambridge, 1985)*.

[84] For some interesting accounts of political theology in this period, see H. C. G. Matthew, 'Noetics, Tractarians, and the Reform of the University of Oxford in the Nineteenth Century', *History of Universities*, IX (Oxford, 1990), 195–225; and Richard Shannon, 'John Robert Seeley and the Idea of a National Church', in *Ideas and Institutions of Victorian Britain*, ed. Robert Robson (London, 1967), 236–67.

same way. If accorded citizenship in a religiously neutral nation-state, would Jewish self-government through its system of courts, synagogues, welfare agencies and educational institutions survive?[85] One solution for the Church of England was the revival of its own legislature, Convocation, and this was duly accomplished, although the Crown in Parliament never actually relinquished its supremacy. By the end of the century books could be written about the 'nationalisation' of the universities wherein the operative definition was the absence of any religious connection. This was a negative definition and consequently only the first step towards the erection of a positive identification of universities with governments, the university in service to England rather than to the Church of England, now just another of many constituencies.

Scottish university history contributed signally to this transformation. The association between the Presbyterian Church and Scottish universities had been important but the relationship between Church and State was much freer than in England. Students, for one thing, were not required to subscribe. The Scottish Disruption of 1843, creating two Presbyterian churches, ended whatever quasi-monopoly existed. The Free Church, in fact, was disappointed by the liberality of the older Church since its tolerance for schismatics stood in the path of their own conception of a university dominated by evangelical teaching. Free Church adherents were welcome to teach in the existing universities.[86]

But if Scotland's Church/State connection was weak, its University/State connection was unusually strong, extending well back in time, and no one north of the Tweed was particularly anxious to end it.[87] The Scottish idea of a university had always featured a strong and intimate relationship with Scottish culture and with Scotland as a nation, so much so that Scottish universities had long shown a willingness to join around some kind of Scottish national federal model featuring the interchange of students. Scotland's democratic self-conceptions allowed for the existence of romantic myths such as an idealisation of 'the social harmony of the older society . . . and the sentimental world of the kailyard, the parish school, the village dominie and the lad o' pairts'.[88] However, the federal concept would not have replaced a system of unitary universities, nor

---

[85] David Feldman, *Englishmen and Jews, Social Relations and Political Culture 1840–1914* (New Haven and London, 1994), 47–9, 73, 136.

[86] Donald J. Withrington, 'Adrift Among the Reefs of Conflicting Ideals? Education and the Free Church, 1843–55', in *Scotland in the Age of the Disruption*, ed. Stewart J. Brown and Michael Fry (Edinburgh, 1993), 79–97.

[87] Anderson, *Education and Opportunity*, 358–61.

[88] *Ibid.*, 26.

did the Scots ever approve of the English idea of separate examining centres.[89]

By the beginning of the present century the secularisation and laicisation of Oxford and Cambridge, the development of an imperial mission for the University of London and the adoption of a research or applied research mission in all universities created a 'drift' towards a higher education policy based on the notion of a university as a national asset.[90] Overseas rivalries and the critical work of British chemists, metallurgists, physicists, cryptographers and other academic specialists during the First World War strengthened this perspective.[91] Universities were necessary instruments for achieving national political and economic, even military, objectives.

The policy question was how to finance this view and develop methods of accounting for its success while at the same time maintaining the gold

[89] Robert Anderson of the University of Edinburgh has very graciously responded to my inquiries into federalism in Scotland by informing me by letter (5 January 1987) that 'the Universities (Scotland) Act of 1858 had a clause allowing for a National University of Scotland, of which the existing universities would become colleges. This was put in by Gladstone, presumably on the Irish model. But it was not a popular idea . . . However, it could be argued that the system set up by the 1858 Act, and continued in 1889, came as near to federalism as was compatible with the existence of independent universities: curricula, degree regulations, entrance standards etc. were all regulated by statutory Ordinances which could not be changed without the consent of all four universities. This system was only really dismantled in 1966. In the nineteenth century, though few went as far as Gladstone, nearly all academics took it for granted that national uniformity within Scotland was a good thing, and were prepared to accept severe constraints on their autonomy.'

Martin Harris of the University of Manchester kindly furnished me with information concerning a 1980s' consortium of further education colleges and programmes in the Manchester area called the 'Manchester Open College Federation'. The governing body appears to be drawn from representatives of all post-secondary institutions and authorities in the greater Manchester area, with the addition of the Open University. Over 90 per cent of the federation's budget is provided by the Manchester Education Committee but allocated by the Continuing Education Department of the local education authority. However, the federation itself is given some responsibility in distributing those parts of the budget that do not go into salaries, and decisions on the content, structure and design of particular courses appear to be in the hands of peer groups broken down by faculty. It is difficult for an offshore observer without first-hand knowledge of the system to decide how much flexibility of curriculum design and assessment actually exists. On the face of it these complex arrangements represent a considerable departure from the kind of federal systems created in the last century and suggest fresh thinking on the possibilites of combination, especially where variations on the modular system are incorporated. Quite possibly we are seeing convergences between British and American models of federation.

[90] Sheldon Rothblatt and Martin Trow, 'Government Policies and Higher Education: a Comparison of Britain and the United States from about 1630 to 1860', in *Social Research and Social Reform: Essays in Honour of A. H. Halsey,* ed. Colin Crouch and Anthony Heath (Oxford, 1992), 173–216.

[91] See Michael Sanderson, *The Universities and British Industry 1850–1970* (London, 1972), Chapter 8.

standard of excellence that had been so important in Victorian university history. Institutions could no longer be expected to live of their own. A new funding mechanism was required, and this was duly established in 1919 as the University Grants Committee (UGC), initially a subcommittee of the Treasury. This funding model has travelled well and has appeared in parts of the empire and Commonwealth as well as in post-Mandate Israel.

The UGC was another intermediate institution standing between government and the universities, but as its latest biographer notes, throughout its more than half century of important existence the committee was controlled by the university community itself through direct membership. Most of its chairs had been vice-chancellors and highly sympathetic to the historical aims of universities. The UGC served those aims long and faithfully, helping to define the cohesiveness and unanimity of outlook within the academic community from which it also drew. The universities were regarded as a 'club' with exclusive membership. Outsiders were admitted only after long and cautious review. The UGC protected the Victorian definition of a 'university' by such practical measures as supporting requests for elite staffing ratios and by advancing criteria for excellence based on considerations of autonomy (e.g., the proportion of lay to academic influence, type of curriculum, amount of debt). Drawing its inspiration from a past era of meritocratic selection, the UGC was not particularly eager to embrace the consequences of mass higher education. Members of the Committee were not interested in continuing education until the 1980s, they were reluctant to be involved with distance learning in the form of the Open University and were not inclined to recognise technical institutions as universities unless, like the Imperial College, they were part of a federation. They disliked the influence of lay councils and preferred the authority of academic senates. The medium of support was the quinquennial block grant which allowed single universities considerable latitude in allocating resources internally according to institutional desires and priorities. As an advisory body, the UGC could not make decisions unilaterally. Its famous strength and prestige ultimately derived from a broad consensus within the Cabinet, the civil service and another academic body, the Committee of Vice Chancellors and Principals, on the privileges that ought to accompany institutions bearing the cherished title 'university'.[92] In its golden years the UGC was the envy of Americans, whose public-sector universities appeared to be far more subject to political interference and certainly

---

[92] Shattock, *The UGC*, Chapters 3 and 8.

vulnerable to waves of populism and market discipline and also did not enjoy (in most cases) the insulation that a five-year budgetary cycle provided.

Here was a distinct carryover from the past century guarding the label 'university' from possible misuse and at the same time defining the prerogatives that through history and policy had become attached to that label by nobbling alternative ways of defining mission and role.[93]

The further expansion of higher education and the increasing acceptance on the part of politicians, civil servants and some academic leaders of a large body of unmet demand for higher education led to a reconsideration of the role of the UGC and its commitment to the status quo. Furthermore, comparisons between Britain and other European countries, not to mention the United States, turned up unfavourable statistics concerning the percentage of pupils going on from school to higher education (although the value of the statistics depended upon shaky estimates of the comparability of national systems). While some growth occurred in the years immediately following the Second World War, the critical decade was the 1960s, overseen, if that is the word, by the policy recommendations laid down in the Robbins Report.

Robbins has since been variously interpreted as the kindling of the torch of a new era or as the dying embers of an old. The latter seems more plausible, for the Robbins Report followed time-honoured assumptions about universities. Robbins was very sensitive to the charge that the acknowledged high quality of British universities would be severely compromised if the door to the university club were thrown wide open to all applicants. A few institutions had proven themselves. They were Colleges of Advanced Technology, and a number of them were allowed membership. But the question remained how to treat the rest of the poly-technics and technical schools and colleges that were demanding greater resources and more prestige and were in many cases eager to exit from local control. They too were important for enhancing educational opportunities throughout the kingdom and needed some element of encouragement. But Robbins was firm in denying to them the one thing

---

[93] The case of the trials and tribulations in the late 1960s of the proposed private University of Buckingham is usually cited in support of the thesis. Sir Alan Peacock describes the ordeal of a university college 'kowtowing to some parent institution . . . as if a new institution must consist of untested and untried academics who have sprung up from holes in the ground' in 'Buckingham's Fight for Independence', *Economic Affairs*, 6 (February–March 1986), 22–5; and in 'The Trials of Setting Up in the University Business & the Funding Problems', *Conversazione* (La Trobe University, 1989). Sir Alan approves of external examiners, however (page 13 of 'Trials').

needful. The Victorian ghost continued to haunt the banquet and shake its chains as the question of the degree, its meaning and its accessibility, arose once again.

The Victorian answer to degree-giving was still in effect when the Robbins committee reported. Students enrolled in institutions empowered to award less-prestigious diplomas could take degrees if they were prepared to read for external degrees given by neighbouring universities.[94] But their home institutions were humiliated by this conventional solution, believing themselves worthy of the sacred gift. The civic university colleges of the nineteenth century had thoroughly committed themselves to external degree-seeking, using the examination results to boost their reputations and attract students, but some thought the price was now too high. Yet as students entering polytechnics often did not have the requisite A-level grades to gain a place at a university, there appeared to be some justification to the policy of denying polytechnics degree-giving authority. One of the distinguishing features of a university was still meritocratic entry standards.[95]

Still, governments were now sensitive to the accusation of discriminating against students whose upbringing and schooling handicapped their chances for upward educational mobility. The degree still possessed scarcity value in Britain, and diploma candidates often accepted the view of themselves as less academically gifted than degree students. To rectify this situation, Robbins recommended the establishment of a two-tier higher education, or binary system, one composed of autonomous degree-granting institutions, the other of polytechnics. In a switchover from Victorian terminology where universities were 'public', implying a wider responsibility, the polytechnics were now to be called 'public'. Universities were 'private', not technically but in spirit, meaning that they enjoyed much more institutional autonomy. Polytechnics were not granted the privilege of awarding degrees. The solution adopted there was to call upon the useful and patient federal principle for assistance. A new examining body at the centre of a loosely structured federation called the Council for National Academic Awards (CNAA) was devised.

The CNAA itself is evidence of the continuing value placed upon the idea of a national or at least a central measure of quality. Statute 9 (1) of the CNAA states that degrees and other awards 'are consistent in standard and are comparable in standard with awards granted and conferred

[94] Guy Neave, *Patterns of Equality, The Influence of New Structures in European Higher Education upon the Equality of Educational Opportunity* (Windsor, 1976), 86.
[95] *Ibid.*

throughout higher education in the United Kingdom including the universities'.[96] The council assumed the part taken by London and the federal principle in the nineteenth century as the representative of the State or the public's interest in quality and standards. The polytechnics and large teacher-training establishments, such as Jordanhill in Glasgow, had to seek degree course approval from the central body, certainly for all full-time courses, after having first received course validation from the Secretary of State for Education. (Jordanhill has since been incorporated into Glasgow University.) Her Majesty's Inspectorate, established in the nineteenth century to maintain a watchful eye on the condition of schools, was also given a role in maintaining the quality of the polytechnic sector which it never possessed in the case of independent, degree-granting universities.[97]

Over its short history the CNAA developed a comprehensive set of policies in fulfilling its mandate. Institutions were granted more flexibility through the notion of a 'partnership in validation', which led to the establishment of an in-house 'validation specialist', suspected by colleagues of receiving favours and advantages. Other discontents also surfaced, since a little freedom is a dangerous thing and always stimulates a desire for more.[98]

Although the point is rarely resurrected in post-Robbins discussions, the Robbins Report was quite definite about the need to insulate higher education from market pressures, most particularly in the case of student demand as represented by institutional transfer. The relevant passages were embedded in circumlocutions, but the general position appeared to be extremely cautious at best about how far to extend the privileges of student movement from institution to institution. In the report transfer was supported 'when this is appropriate' to the student's 'intellectual attainments and educational needs. We attach great importance to this.' Yet this and similar espousals of student needs were mentioned only in passing in the context of a discussion about the inevitability of institutional differences in prestige, financing and standards. Nowhere in the body of the report is the issue discussed in systematic fashion. No specific recommendations concerning transfer occur in the list of recom-mendations concluding the report beyond the suggestion that some

---

[96] Graeme C. Moodie, 'Institutional Government, Quality and Access in the United Kingdom', in Berdahl *et al.*, 82.

[97] Her Majesty's Inspectorate has now been abolished for higher education.

[98] Harold Silver, '"Assessment" and Effect, Experiences with the Council for National Academic Awards', in *Changing Contexts of Quality Assessment, Recent Trends in West European Higher Education,* ed. Don F. Westerheijden *et al.* (Utrecht, 1994), 253–62.

students in 'area colleges' ought to be eligible for advanced courses in other similar colleges, or allowed, at the postgraduate stage, to move into universities or polytechnics. This last point does not really refer to transfer as commonly understood. Elsewhere there were references to 'a minority of students' for whom transfer to a university might be appropriate, but readers were assured that eligible transfers were always likely to be 'small'. Robbins never referred to the mechanisms by which transfer might operate, but the report had harsh words for American means for facilitating transfer, such as the system of course credits. There was a passing allusion to the 'worst excesses' of that system (but not to its merits). In fact, the phrase is used twice.[99]

External degree and course control as the most effective means of enforcing standards of teaching and student work in the 'public', that is non-university, sector according to present usage, was continually challenged by the affected institutions. They found themselves in the same position with respect to internal growth and development, especially in relation to market demand, as the Victorian university colleges. Yet such pressure had achieved only limited recognition in the past, although from another perspective a loosening of central controls had been occurring into the 1970s and 1980s. One analyst found CNAA degrees 'more liberal in their demands compared with university external degree courses'.[100] Conceivably internal pressure from more or less federated institutions in central bodies like CNAA would in time have widened degree possibilities, with some polytechnics attempting to escape into the freedom of the 'university', even allowed to drift in that direction after publication of the Lindop Report of 1985. Yet this latest manifestation of federal control principles at work was quite suddenly ended when it was announced at the beginning of the 1990s by the government in power that the Robbins binary line would be dissolved. Polytechnics eager to change their names to universities would now at long last have that opportunity.[101]

The disappearance of the binary line, but the maintenance of a different line separating a college sector of 'further education' institutions from higher education proper entailed new funding arrangements yet again.

[99] Report of the Committee appointed by the Prime Minister under the Chairmanship of Lord Robbins, 1961–1963 (October 1963), Cmnd. 2154, pages 38, 306, 307, 338, 424, 432, Appendix v, 179.

[100] Neave, *Patterns of Equality*, 86.

[101] On the CNAA I have been greatly enlightened by R. A. Barnett's paper, 'The Maintenance of Quality in the Public Sector of United Kingdom Higher Education', which was prepared for the Anglo-American Seminar on Quality in Higher Education held at Templeton College, Oxford University, 19–21 December 1986.

The two separate funding councils created to finance and as it turned out manage the universities and the polytechnics were now combined into one Higher Education Funding Council, and afterwards the 'national' regions of the United Kingdom were granted their own funding councils. These new bodies were distinct in every respect from the old UGC. They were staffed by civil servants who, unlike their Victorian and Edwardian forebears, did not identify with the academic aims and values of the old university culture. The idea of a university meant little to them. In its final years the UGC had ceased to be a subcommittee of the Treasury. It had been transferred to the Department of Education and Science, losing in the process the quasi-independence that had made it a 'buffer' (in the well-worn notion) between the universities and the State.

New issues had arisen. First was the global inflation of the mid-1970s, which had led Labour governments to consider how to economise in higher education. One casualty of history was the quinquennial grant.[102] Second was the beginnings of a mass access higher education system, increasing with intensity throughout the 1980s. Since such pressures also involved reshaping the system of university admissions, numerous changes were introduced into the historic school-leaving examinations and certificates. These occurred so often and so rapidly that it is hard for the historian to understand how both schools and pupils could have accommodated to standards that were continually revised. The only way such accommodation could be made was to have reasonably flexible admissions standards and to allow considerable variations on a theme. No institution was unaffected by these developments, and even at Oxford and Cambridge, still at the top of the university league standings, the colleges agreed to cooperate more than compete in offering places to under-graduates.

In many respects events seemed to spin out of control. Demand for admission to higher education increased because of a number of inter-connected factors, one certainly being radical changes in labour markets making degrees and qualifications even more important, and another being the role of the European Union in promoting conceptions of democratic access and opportunity to higher education. The British State had played its part in removing the barriers that dampened or directed demand, but it was soon discovered that the elimination of what were termed 'artificial' educational barriers within the higher education sector

---

[102] Graeme C. Moodie, 'The Debates about Quality in Higher Education', paper presented to the Anglo-American Seminar on Quality in Higher Education, Templeton College, Oxford (December 1986), 3, 5.

had resulted in an alarming problem. How was this vastly enlarged sector of higher education to be paid for if the title 'university' still carried with it certain funding assumptions based on elite staffing ratios and expensive research missions? Little thought apparently had been given to the question of whether the polytechnics, known mainly for teaching, were equipped for important research assignments.

The solution that emerged was to use the new funding councils to establish elaborate criteria and formulas for measuring excellence through the use of quality councils. The principle of external assessment through examinations had served as a regulating device since the nineteenth century and very early twentieth century. Peer review had entered – indeed, it is a guild principle – and institutional self-review was encouraged, but the actual financial health of an institution in so far as it was in receipt of substantial public funding was determined by outside granting and evaluating agencies that participating academic reviewers served. There was also the view that peer approval was useful in allocating awards but did little to eliminate mediocrity.[103]

The story of audit and assessment exercises sponsored by funding councils – audit to determine the processes and procedures by which an academic programme is constructed and administered, assessment to grade the quality of teaching and research as measured by announced bureaucratic criteria – is raging as never before at the close of a millennium. The outcome of audit and assessment exercises is closely watched and anticipated with trepidation. To an outsider, the kingdom seems obsessed with evaluations of every kind, and many quality assessment councils appear to be in existence, some established by professional bodies, others dealing with business and vocational education. There are also numerous subcommittees collecting data from the universities from which a rank order of excellence in teaching or research is compiled.[104] The mathematical tripos's order of merit appears to have returned with all of its past severity and strict numerical tabulations. The exercises come too often and occupy too much valuable time, and recently critics have charged the government with increasing the frequency of university visits rather than reducing them as promised. The range of issues in dispute covers government intrusion into the internal affairs of universities, the subjection of teaching and research to mechanical measures of assessment, the divorce of teaching from research and the dissolution of trust between

[103] Moodie, 'Institutional Government', 80.
[104] Moodie, 'Debates about Quality', 13, thinks that professional associations are more interested in coverage of a curriculum than in the quality of teaching or the institution.

all parties, a situation that is affecting university morale and professional self-esteem. Supporters of government measures argue that the universities are evasive: they engage in 'scams' and 'games' and other mechanisms for coping with the external demands, making reported numbers and information unreliable.[105]

Other conditions leading to the emergence of government instruments of assessment in the form of quality councils, namely, the anarchic conditions of mass higher education paired with political conclusions about what the role of universities should be in enhancing national well-being, have produced additional questions about the historic role of the system of external examining. That role had been broadening away from a nineteenth-century emphasis on guaranteeing disciplinary excellence in examinations to functions that duplicate those of assessment exercises. The external examiner is now also expected to audit examination procedures, play some part in course development, protect the interests of students during and before examinations, provide comparisons between institutions and also to function as a consultant, a role, it has been noted, that leads to conflicts of interest. The multiplication of modular-type courses in newer or recently upgraded institutions has also placed a heavier strain on the external examiner system which was once used exclusively for maintaining the standards of final degree examinations.[106]

With so much at stake, it is only to be expected that the government and universities should be exchanging angry words over how audits and assessments are conducted and the criteria to be used for assuring the public that universities are efficient and productive, however misapplied those entrepreneurial conceptions might be to institutions whose historical purposes and values are so different from industry. It is also only to be expected that the universities and their representatives would prefer to

---

[105] The *Times Higher Education Supplement* has carried accounts of the running battle between the Higher Education Quality Council and the Committee of Vice Chancellors and Principals, as well as other disagreements and discontent. See, *inter alia*, the issues for 24 September 1993, 19 May 1995, 23 June 1995 (the article by Leslie Wagner, director of Leeds Metropolitan University) and 21 July 1995. For an acute offshore analysis, see Martin Trow, 'Managerialism and the Academic Profession: The Case of England', *Studies of Higher Education and Research* (Council for Studies of Higher Education, Stockholm, Sweden, 1993), 4. Institutions receiving weak evaluations, especially where rewards and punishments occur, will always quarrel with the evidence and the process and often with good reason since the criteria used can be questionable. Another typical response is to rephrase the conclusion to produce a more favourable outcome. This has occurred with the National Research Council rankings of American graduate research universities in 1995. Institutions that were dropped out of the top ten have instead boasted of their inclusion in the top twenty.

[106] *Times Higher Education Supplement* (23 June 1995), an account of the report by Harold Silver of the Open University's quality support centre.

rely upon peer review and the professional standards prevailing in the disciplines and fields of study for an accurate assessment of institutional strengths and weaknesses. Therefore the insistence of many members of the Committee of Vice Chancellors and Principals in May 1995 on higher education's control over the assessment and audit process is certainly in keeping with the preference for in-house peer evaluation. Sharp differences notwithstanding, there is persistent agreement on two very large principles, the belief that a national standard of attainment is desirable, if in some instances watered down to be national guidelines or broad operating procedures, and the utility of outside sources of evaluation to assure the public that quality concerns are being addressed. In 1986 the Committee of Vice Chancellors and Principals stated that 'degree qualifications from different institutions [should] approach as nearly as possible to common standards'.[107] Some nine years later the chairman of the Committee of Vice Chancellors and Principals once again proposed that a uniform policy of quality assessment be adopted for the entire United Kingdom, that only one agency should be assigned the responsibility, an independent outside body to which the funding councils would contract the tasks of audit and assessment. The universities would simultaneously conduct rigorous self-evaluation.[108] In 1995 the Liberal Democratic Party declared that it too favoured establishing a quality control council outside government, as well as a national credit accumulation and transfer scheme.[109] How such advocacy would fare if the party achieved power is another question.

Presumably such proposals would permit a considerable amount of institutional diversity, the professed aim of contemporary mass higher education systems, but the debates still indicate confusion over the issue of finding a 'standard' means of encouraging 'initiative' while maintaining 'quality'. All discussants seem to believe that an external agency can achieve all these objectives. In 1995 the director of Leeds Metropolitan University put the issue in this way: everyone accepts 'the absolute necessity for external accountability. It is the nature and form of such accountability which is at issue.' Most proposals, he continued, aim at a combination of 'internally-organised peer review including external oversight of an independent body'.[110]

[107] Eustace, 'Gold, Silver, Copper', 31.
[108] *Times Higher Education Supplement* (21 July 1995). A national standard was emphasised because of the creation of regional quality control units.
[109] *Times Higher Education Supplement* (22 September 1995).
[110] *Times Higher Education Supplement* (23 June 1995).

THE FEDERAL PRINCIPLE IN AMERICAN HIGHER EDUCATION

The nation without a federal political constitution, the one that resisted devolution, has a continuous history of employing the federal principle in the service of higher education, principally to guarantee that degree standards be uniformly maintained across a given sector. But it was soon realised that standards placed at the top of a system effectively drove the system itself, determining course structures, content, the regulation of student work and even student admissions. Since the quality of entrant bore an obvious relation to the success rate in passing examinations, universities, polytechnics and colleges all retained a basic interest in attracting achievement-minded undergraduates. Inevitably, therefore, the schools themselves were drawn into the national preoccupation with gold (or silver) standards.[111] Whether or not the maintenance of common standards of achievement and assessment has always been successful – and the historian must agree with one sceptical view[112] – it is the desire for it that matters. Measuring the actual gold standard of academic outcomes in the long duration of a nation's history is impossible, but the effects of having one are much easier to describe. The desire has been responsible for the creation and continuation of an impressive array of centralised machinery and institutional management procedures with major budgetary consequences. Over 150 years, royal commissions, privy councils, government ministries and advisory bodies, not to mention the higher education community itself, its representatives and conjoint bodies, have been engrossed in the task of finding first-rate minds, recognising those minds by the outcome of their examinations.[113]

One effect of the reorganisation of higher education in Britain in the last fifteen years – 'British higher education has undergone a more profound reorientation than any other system in industrial societies'[114] – has been to draw increased international attention to comparisons between national systems. Having consistently disparaged the greatly uneven admissions, course-credit and degree standards in American colleges and universities, British commentators, staggering under the weight of a massive intrusion of government into virtually every aspect of academic institutional and professional life, have started to decipher the mysteries of American higher education, putting into systematic perspective the quirks, the

---

[111] Eustace, 'Gold, Silver, Copper', 29–41.
[112] I.e., Tony Becher as quoted in Eustace, 32.
[113] See Eustace, 'Gold, Silver, Copper', and Moodie, 'Institutional Government', 75–85.
[114] Trow, 'Managerialism', 2.

strengths, the weaknesses, the governing assumptions and rationale of the Republic's provision for education. American system or systems of higher education are no more static than any other country's provision for guaranteeing access to career and positional goods, but there are continuities. They are by no means reassuring when viewed from British perspectives, but at least some greater understanding of how mass education systems operate within the paradoxes and contradictions of market economies has emerged.

The country without a federal constitution found a fascinating use for federal ideas and drifted towards a higher education policy dependent upon them. The country with a federal constitution also employed federal ideas in expanding the provision for higher education, but the difference in their use could not have been greater. The mere existence of a solar system of bodies rotating around a heliocentric authority does not reveal how centre and periphery interact. Whereas in Britain the key element in a university's federal constitution became the centre, in America it was usually the periphery. This being the astonishing (in comparison with Britain's) outcome, some explanation is required.

A cardinal concern of British federalism was the likely downward effect on standards that would occur under conditions of free institutional competition. American institutions are conventionally regarded as welcoming competition, even at elite levels where British fears of declining controls were always greatest. We can go back at least to George Ticknor, the president of Harvard, to find evidence for what was a characteristic American attitude. In the 1820s he was faced with a financial and educational crisis when, after a series of highly disruptive student events (a feature of American colleges since colonial times),[115] the lower house of the Massachusetts General Court withdrew its annual subsidy. Ticknor was committed to academic reform even before these unfortunate events. He concluded that the standard of admissions and intellectual attainment was low, student workloads meagre and teaching greatly in need of a jolt. He immediately thought about introducing ideas from other places. He was inspired by German examples (he had been amongst the first generation of Americans to study in Germany) but also by the educative work going on in the training of engineers and scientists at the military academy of West Point. He was also attracted to Thomas Jefferson's plan for the new state University of Virginia. Jefferson actually offered Ticknor a chair. He refused but was impressed with the exquisite

---

[115] Joseph F. Kett, *Rites of Passage, Adolescence in America, 1790 to the Present* (New York, 1977), 51ff.

campus, the palladian and neoclassical architecture and many of the educational ideas, although these inclined more towards the practical than he would have preferred. However, he thoroughly welcomed Virginia's initiative in education, believing that a rivalry – for students, for teachers – would be salutary for lifting Harvard out of its academic doldrums.[116]

In England, Oxford and Cambridge were the established institutions against which any competitor needed to struggle. Harvard, a seventeenth-century foundation derived from Emmanuel College, Cambridge, found itself overmatched repeatedly in its history. Its leaders, instead of decrying the competition, used it again and again to obtain leverage against rivals and not merely to survive but to survive as an example of excellence. In 1873 another innovative Harvard president, Charles W. Eliot, wrote to the head of the University of California at Berkeley deploring what he called an 'utterly unrepublican and unAmerican frame of . . . mind', the issue being public demand for government money in every conceivable kind of project. 'As to national university or agricultural school subsidies, they are only special and not very important symptoms of a deep-seated disease.'[117] In the American educational environment no protective mechanisms existed for preserving established institutions from market forces, but few were sought.

Yet it would be a serious error to conclude that even in the absence of protective mechanisms educational rivals were always welcomed or that fears similar to those expressed in Britain (or England) never existed across the Atlantic, or that attempts to safeguard elite functions were not made or repeatedly made. American educational leaders may, like Ticknor, have found important uses for rivalries in upgrading teaching and programmes, but they have simultaneously worried how high perform-ance standards could be preserved, and especially when confronting popular demand.[118] The rapid proliferation of academies, colleges, institutes and universities in nineteenth-century America often produced a reaction on the part of established foundations not unlike that of Oxford's response to the establishment of the godless institution in Gower Street. The Yale Report of 1828 included a warning about inferior institutions so market-obsessed that they would freely abandon the old college curriculum and allow academic standards to fall in an effort to attract trade. Some forty years later Yale was still fretting about the effects

[116] David Tyack, *George Ticknor and the Boston Brahmins* (Cambridge, MA, 1967), 99–104.
[117] Fabian Franklin, *The Life of Daniel Coit Gilman* (New York, 1910), 356. I am indebted to Carroll Brentano for this reference.
[118] Clark Kerr makes this a central point in his collection *Higher Education Cannot Escape History*. See the discussion of equality versus merit, 39–79.

of unscrupulous competition on the quality of university education. Its president, Noah Porter, insisted that

> colleges are not in a proper sense, rivals or competitors for the public patronage or favor . . . They ought not to be stranged from one another through petty jealousies, or superciliously to ignore each other's existence or influence . . . Least of all should a college or any other school of learning, play the demagogue, by adjusting its principles of education or its methods of teaching to any real or supposed fluctuation of the public taste which it knows to be capricious, and presumes may be temporary.[119]

Porter, following the lead of the famous president of Princeton University, James McCosh, suggested the creation of an American version of 'the Dublin and London Universities', combining the 'several colleges of a State or of a vicinage . . . as subordinate members of a common university' which would be 'solely an examining and degree-giving body'.[120]

The irreverent *Blackwoods' Magazine* joined in from across the water, bringing up the question of the label 'university' and informing readers that 'Americans take a strange delight in high-sounding names, and often satisfy themselves for the want of the thing, by the assumption of a name.'[121] So much for the brazen academies and seminaries of the 1830s aspiring to the prestige of the best intellectual products of western civilisation.

Expressions of sympathy for the belief in the ruinous effects of unregulated academic competition do not cease with the representatives of old and illustrious elite colonial foundations. The General Conference of the Methodist Episcopal Church expressed concern in 1860 about the competition for students between institutions, mentioning the 'undue multiplication of literary institutions, especially those of higher grade'.[122] If we jump ahead to the twentieth century to look for a moment at what is probably the best known of the American federal systems, the University of California, we also find sentiments in favour of restricting the expansionist aims of new institutions. Until the later 1920s the University of California, whose foundations go back to the 1860s, was a single-campus institution situated on the hills of Berkeley on the eastern side of San Francisco Bay. 'Branches' existed, but these were specialised schools such as the agricultural station situated some 80 miles away near the state's

---

[119] Noah Porter, *The American Colleges and the American Public* (New York, 1969), 250–1.
[120] *Ibid.*, 257.
[121] Tyack, *Ticknor*, 105. The author was probably an American.
[122] Daniel Sammis Sanford, Jr, *Inter-Institutional Agreements in Higher Education* (New York, 1934), 10n.

capital or the medical school in neighbouring San Francisco. In 1927 an institution which began life as a normal school in southern California was recognised as a general campus under the name of the University of California at Los Angeles (UCLA), but constitutionally it remained a branch of the Berkeley campus under the same president, who jealously guarded the conception of a unitary university. President Robert Gordon Sproul can be described as Victorian in this sense, that he believed in the primary importance of established centres of academic excellence in safeguarding admissions and teaching standards and degree quality. He feared that new universities would dilute the value of the product, especially because their initial vulnerability would lead them to court local business and political interests whose academic values and credentials were wholly unreliable. Sproul did not like (in his own happy choice of words) 'local prides and prejudices'. While president of the University of California he obstructed all efforts by UCLA to establish its independence and allowed it to be headed only by a provost responsible to him until its first chancellor was appointed in 1952.[123] The director of the sometime normal school, Ernest C. Moore, had always looked forward to a merger of Berkeley and Los Angeles under a unified governing body. At the same time, he too expressed his dislike for competition amongst educational institutions. Some kind of federal system might be a good solution to the problem of allowing for self-development without yielding to the surrounding pressures for vocational and utilitarian instruction. Responding to the commonplace opinion that it would be impossible to keep a university in a populous and prosperous region like Los Angeles enclosed within a federal system, Moore remarked that those who even raise the question 'think of institutions only as they have known them; they have not asked of themselves what they must become'.[124]

Moore's preference for federal systems because they appeared to be an excellent middle ground between local prides and prejudices and the great purposes of universities was fully realised in the 1960s with the California State Legislature's adoption of the extraordinary Master Plan for Higher Education, creating three federal systems in California, in effect a trinary system demarcated by separate admission standards, faculty responsibilities, funding formulas and salary differentials. By the end of the 1960s the University of California federal system had grown to nine campuses,

[123] Eugene C. Lee, 'The Origins of the Chancellorship, The Buried Report of 1948', in *Chapters in the History of the University of California*, 3, ed. Carroll Brentano and Sheldon Rothblatt (Center for Studies in Higher Education, University of California, Berkeley, 1995).
[124] William Warren Ferrier, *Origin and Development of the University of California* (Berkeley, 1930), 542.

each under its own chancellor, but the one San Francisco campus was entirely devoted to the health sciences. While each of the campuses was responsible for research and professional education, the president's office still retained some control over outlying marine research stations or astronomical laboratories and the critical functions of the outreach agricultural programme so important to the state's economy. Attention was paid to the question of how to uniformly protect academic standards. A single faculty academic senate was created with 'divisions' on each campus. Stated degree and admission requirements were similar. A common salary schedule was adopted.

This much appears to be in the spirit of the history of federalism in Britain; and California has often been described as having established the least American of American state higher education systems, eager to establish itself on the same level as the great private universities of the United States and equally eager therefore to prevent 'mission creep' and upward academic drift in a second tier of California public universities called the State University and College system. The university has been particularly concerned with maintaining a monopoly over graduate research and professional degrees, especially the doctorate, as the real 'gold standard' of American higher education.[125] A third sector of two-year community colleges presents no competitive difficulties. A fourth or independent sector of universities and colleges is not unified. It lies outside the trinary system altogether and possesses the autonomy that private education enjoys in the United States.

Yet while aspects of the history of the federal principle are evident in the development of systems like the University of California, it is equally interesting to consider the features that British and American institutions do not or no longer share. No effort was made to impose a common degree standard on the constituent campuses and no system of external examining was ever in place, although within a single state and system it would have been possible to construct one. The modular system of cumulative course-credits simply ruled out this solution, and professors continued to reign in the classroom as absolute monarchs. Here was a clear instance of how only one feature in the great number of features that animate universities affected an entire system of teaching. Shift to a consideration of final degree examinations, and the story might have been different, but the 'module' is a fundamental aspect of an American's right to an education and cannot be discarded. The gradual adoption of

---

[125] As noted by Eustace, 'Gold, Silver, Copper', 37.

modular-style courses in the United Kingdom has, as already noted, had an impact on the functioning of the system of external examining. If a full-scale modular system combining teaching and examining on the American plan were to be adopted by all United Kingdom institutions, the external examiner would have to be placed on a protected species list.

Admissions was a second area where federalism attempted to intrude, but the nature of American secondary education and campus independence (backed up by strong alumni associations and regional interests) meant that at best only a uniform policy of minimal expectations could be adopted. The campuses were largely free to build on that platform and to respond to their own perceived needs and desires. This was especially the case when affirmative action policies were adopted in the 1970s.

But the possibility of imposing maximum or even optimum standards of admission throughout the multicampus system was hampered, indeed prevented by student transfer, another cherished educational right in the United States, and the California Master Plan guaranteed that right. Transfer rendered any effort by campuses to control their own degrees as lessons in futility, and the best that could be achieved were high standards relative to other systems of separate institutions. Transfer within British universities, or between binary and trinary sectors, was always problematical, in part because degree programmes were often if not invariably three years in length; but a prejudice against students who invade with bags of credits earned elsewhere remains deep. While there is some 'articulation' between institutions today, it is rudimentary. In the early nineteenth century only a handful of undergraduates 'migrated' (that was the term) between the ancient universities. The Scottish system, which envisaged a national standard of degrees and curriculum, never really developed a full programme of student exchanges.

The centre's part in maintaining academic standards in America was quite perfunctory in theory as well as in practice. The centre at the University of California had no monitoring staff and no provision for audit and assessment (in British terms) apart from the academic senate, a part-time association of professorial representatives from the campuses. With only a shadow non-academic support staff, the professors served on a large number of committees charged with a considerable range of different responsibilities. However, all real decision-making or implementing authority lay in the hands of campus chancellors according to the hierarchical principle of executive governance in the United States and in contrast to the committee principle of governance in Britain dominant up through the 1980s. The centre's principal duties were 'coordination', budgeting and planning and the maintenance of good working relations with secondary feeder schools, the state governor and legislator and the outside world in general. One major purpose of federalism in an American context was strengthening the bargaining position of public-sector universities against state government.[126]

Any federal system must by the facts of its very existence undergo periodic struggles for domination between the centre and the parts. Such has been the history of federalism in the United Kingdom and such within systems such as the University of California, but the outcome of these struggles in the University of California, the offloading or the regaining of central responsibilities, has not been very profound in realigning the fundamental priorities of academics, which are departmental control over research, teaching and professional education. In these respects American universities remain 'bottom-up' organisations, although a closer analysis would reveal ambiguities.

It is difficult to generalise about any nation's system of higher education, especially one so mammoth as America's. Still, some functions assumed by strong centres in Europe may be safely ruled out as a primary American concern. Maintaining a high uniform standard of teaching or examining has not been a goal and separating teaching from examining has never been seriously contemplated. Perhaps it has been necessary in certain states to introduce one or two required courses – American history and institutions at the University of California comes to mind – but this has been a state requirement, a vestigial reminder of a former belief in the importance of 'civics' as preparation for citizenship. Otherwise teaching belongs to senates (barely), departments and, even more, to the individual teachers.

It is hard to find lasting examples of a federation that is formed for the main purpose of restricting the spread of higher education as Noah Porter wished. It is more often the case that ailing institutions will be merged or absorbed into larger, more secure organisations. The Rhode Island School of Design allied itself with Brown University, the Institute of Paper Chemistry associated with Lawrence College, the California College of Pharmacy was absorbed into the University of California, and Columbia University in Manhattan absorbed most of the theological seminaries in the boroughs.[127] Three campuses joined together in North Carolina to form one multi-campus university in 1931 for the express purpose of

---

[126] Clark Kerr's Foreword to Eugene C. Lee and Frank M. Bowen, *Managing Multicampus Systems* (San Francisco, Washington and London, 1975), x. On page 148 the authors refer to 'inappropriate centralization at the expense of desirable campus authority'.

[127] Frederick Rudolph, *The American College and University, a History* (New York, 1962), 344,

economy. There is some distant correspondence in these examples with the old Victorian federations that sheltered fledgling university colleges (although not if they were on the point of expiry) but not with the policy of the University Grants Committee to keep institutions off the grants list unless they met threshold criteria. Centripetal forces in higher education tended more towards the affiliation or grouping of institutions together for the administrative convenience of state governments faced with a bewildering plethora of very different kinds of post-secondary institutions each pressing its claims on the public purse.

Several of the very earliest American university federations were so diffuse in membership and functions that in the absence of detailed information it is puzzling to know why they were cobbled together in the first place. It is also the case that the word 'university' was never protected and could pop up at almost any time. 'University' was used as early as 1775 in connection with a proposed 'American University in the province of New York'. The reference does not indicate whether the university was unitary or federal, but soon afterwards 'university' was being applied to an administrative network of preparatory and collegiate bodies in southern states like Georgia and Kentucky. Other early American federations include the entity provided for in Michigan's constitution of 1835. A superintendent of public instruction with authority over all phases of education was created. Since in its earliest years the University of California was greatly influenced by Michigan models, the idea of a single system of public education extending from the earliest years of schooling to the first degree at university was floated but not acted upon in California. Another statewide educational board was invented by North Dakota in 1889, and the Mormon State of Utah in 1851 established one that was competent to create new branches of a state university. Some American federations appear to be *ad hoc* efforts at administrative rationalisation, attempts to keep the messy universe of American higher education in some kind of respectable order.[128] Many were created by states, but another group sprang from institutional initiative and negotiation. These represented a pooling of resources in the interests of survival, much like the mergers that occurred between private colleges, as when in the mid-1850s, to give only one example, the Pennsylvania institutions of Franklin College, located at Lancaster, and Marshall

---

[128] Jürgen Herbst, *From Crisis to Crisis: American College Government 1636–1819* (Cambridge, 1982), 160; J. C. Moffitt, 'Pioneer University', *School and Society*, 72 (1950), 389; Eugene C. Lee and Frank M. Bowen, *The Multicampus University* (New York, 1971), 68–79; Rudolph, *American College*, 344–9.

College, situated at Mercersberg, joined together to form the new
university of Franklin and Marshall, still very much alive. In remarking
on this consolidation, a contemporary noted that 'Hitherto the tendency
has been to multiply colleges and to isolate them, with the consequence
that numerous ill-endowed and scattered colleges survived where larger
and better-provided-for establishments ought to flourish. Colleges must
combine', he said, and 'prepare the way for the open University which, like
the universities of London and France, may be merely an organic center
for purposes of supervision'.[129] 'Merely an organic center for purposes of
supervision' would scarcely appear to be an adequate description of the
British examining university, but our observer may be pardoned for
viewing the transatlantic situation through characteristically American
lenses.

The mergers, affiliations and unions, combinations of women's and
men's colleges, technical schools and universities, some private, some public, have not in the United States typically produced universities that are
offspring of the educational innovations associated with the Senate House
and Burlington House examinations. The revolutionary University of
California at Santa Cruz, whose collegiate structure has received more
close attention from analysts and novelists than any single American
institution founded in the last thirty years, never adopted the principle of
the separation of examining and teaching. The campus remains fundamentally modular, apart from 'foundation' courses in several of the
eight colleges. But the future of even this modest trial, wholly in keeping
with the tradition of American liberal arts college 'core' curricula, is
shaky.

The founders of Santa Cruz were influenced by the Oxbridge collegiate
structure and by some of the British collegiate experiments of the Robbins
era, but another source was the 1920s federated Claremont college system
of southern California. President James A. Blaisdell of Pomona College
dreamt of a 'group of institutions divided into small colleges – somewhat
of the Oxford type . . . In this way I would hope to preserve the inestimable
personal values of the small college while securing the facilities of the
great university. Such a development would be a new and wonderful
contribution to American education.' He may also have had in mind
separating examining from teaching, but by 1930 disappointment was
clearly setting in. A separate graduate division had been created, draining
away commitment to undergraduate instruction, and each of the colleges

---

[129] The Right Reverend Alonzo Potter, 'Consolidation and other Modifications of American
Colleges', *American Journal of Education*, 1 (1856), 472.

retained its separate and distinct identity. The federation had no regulatory centre. Furthermore, the mood and spirit of a collegiate university were absent. 'In America', Blaisdell ruefully noted, 'the word "college" has commonly come to signify merely the group of buildings where the tools of study are housed.' The ghost of Newman, he could have added, would never be found whimpering upon the grave thereof. Blaisdell himself wanted buildings 'such as shall give the impression of an interesting, stimulating and inspiring life'.[130]

The relative absence of centralised administrative structures designed for quality control, the weak historical efforts at institutional differentiation to protect the standard of teaching, is captured in American English, often so impatient of fine distinctions. There exists in American diction an inclination to blur the meanings of words. 'School', 'college' and 'university' are used interchangeably. This habit had appeared by the 1820s and irritated the professors who produced the Yale Report. 'Seminary', 'college', 'academy' and 'university' were used as synonyms, hence the Yale Report insisted on a proper definition of 'college'. None of the words possessed the highly selective meanings they have in Britain, with 'university' historically and legally protected by royal charter. Not that the contrast everywhere was so sharp. Scotland (or at least historic Scotland) also confused 'college' and 'university', which, given the extraordinary influence Scotland had over the American colonial college, explains the transfer. (The American phrase 'public school' to denote a tax-supported secondary institution may also derive from Scotland where, as in Glasgow, the words can be discerned on school buildings.[131]) It has already been stated that the word *collegium* could be and was applied to a school, and 'school' of course also meant and still means a discipline or faculty within a university. Harvard University called itself a 'school or colledge' in the seventeenth century. Yale University, founded in 1700, referred to itself as a 'collegiate school' for a short period of time, and others called it an 'academy'.[132] But while the conflating of designations is historical and therefore pardonable, Americans retained the ambiguities and overlapping meanings and Britons did not, except where, as in the case of certain public schools, the

[130] William W. Clary, *The Claremont Colleges, a History of the Development of the Claremont Plan Group* (Claremont University Center, CA, 1970), 1–29, 288. Wilson Lyon, 'English Precedents in the Associated Colleges at Claremont', *Association of American Colleges Bulletin*, 34 (1948), 270–5.
[131] Or at least on one, shown to me by James A. Mangan.
[132] James Bryce, *The American Commonwealth*, II (New York, 1923), 712.

word 'college' could not possibly be misunderstood (just as the distinction between colleger and oppidan at Eton is clear and apparent).[133]

In the first half of the nineteenth century, schools, colleges and universities in England, Scotland, Ireland and America overlapped in function, and the distinction in level and quality between the various kinds of institution was not yet in every instance fully recognised. The founders of what became University College, London, were, to begin with, uncertain whether they wished to establish a university, a college or even a school on the model of the High School of Edinburgh.[134] By the end of the century that sorting-out had been achieved in Britain. The utility of the federal principle was proven. In America, by contrast, despite the creation of the common secondary school and the invention of the graduate school in the second part of the nineteenth century and other manifestations of institutional differentiation, language continued to express the older encroaching meanings. The blurring of distinctions was in fact necessary in a democratic polity where equal opportunity was a belief if not always a reality and where all kinds of very different educational establishments acquired or simply appropriated the right to award degrees. There was much less concern with protecting the examinations standard than with providing the public with a great range and variety of educational institutions, leaving it to the market or to voluntary accrediting agencies rather than to the State or a special corporation to determine the value of degrees. The 'habit of granting degrees grew up naturally and most imperceptibly', said Lord Bryce, and he was surely correct.[135]

One consequence has been highly variable standards of academic quality; and while in Victorian Britain similar variations existed, a national concern for the degree standard emerged at the exact same moment as the first of the new universities was founded. Since a similar course was not followed in the United States – because a similar course could *not* be followed in the United States – American higher education has not on the whole been able to 'charter' its institutions and guarantee the social standing of its graduates and the occupational worth of its

---

[133] Some residual meanings to descriptive institutional labels have remained in America, although it can never be predicted how and where they will be used. The University of California opposed giving the title 'university' to the state college system, presumably because a university had doctoral and research functions, but UC lost. In the private sector the words university and college have been chosen at will.

[134] Bellot, *University College London*, 48.

[135] Bryce, *American Commonwealth*, 712. See also Rothblatt and Trow, 'Government Policies', 173–216.

degrees.[136] Further tests are therefore required, such as entrance or 'diagnostic' examinations for graduate and professional schools administered by independent bodies such as the Educational Testing Service in Princeton.

Two types of American federalism are presently in existence. The first, referred to as segmental, groups together campuses with similar missions: for example, the University of California, the California State University and College system or the University of Illinois. The second is denoted 'comprehensive'. The individual institutions often bear little resemblance to one another even though they are neighbours in one system. The system can include two-year community colleges as well as research universities with professional schools. A notable example is the State University of New York (SUNY). In 1971 the state of Texas supported at least thirty-seven public sector universities under as many as fifteen different governing boards, six of which controlled systems. Single systems with a single governing board existed in about one third of the states.[137]

The multiplicity of institutions and objectives in America has given rise to an interest in a special kind of federalism that one leading sociologist has called 'agencies of coordination and authority',[138] either at the centre of multi-campus conglomerates or at the top of a given state's pyramid of instruction. It has been calculated that in 1988 some twenty-three states had formed coordinating boards, most of which were single boards with authority – how defined is difficult to say – over public institutions. Another twenty-three states had 'coordinating-board structures' consisting of a state agency of varying authority squeezed in between campus or system boards of trustees and governors and legislators. The remaining four had some kind of weak planning agency. The authority wielded by these bodies is impossible to summarise. Some are merely advisory, others highly interventionist, or they can prepare the way for legislative action. Some have substantial line authority, others have none.[139] At present there is some fear that state governments are inclined to interfere more and more with the running of the massive systems of public instruction that are their fiscal responsibility. This is especially noticeable in the primary and secondary sectors, where quality is perceived

---

[136] John W. Meyer, 'The Charter: Conditions of Diffuse Socialization in Schools', in *Social Process and Social Structures: An Introduction to Sociology* , ed. W. R. Scott (New York, 1970).

[137] Lee and Bowen, *The Multicampus University*, Chapters 2 and 3.

[138] Neil J. Smelser, 'Growth, Structural Change, and Conflict in California Public Higher Education, 1950–1970', in *Education in California,* ed. Neil J. Smelser and Gabriel Almond (Berkeley, 1974), 12.

[139] Information from a draft essay by Eugene C. Lee.

to be (and is) in fact a major and also a standing American problem; but the higher education sectors cannot be presumed free of the threat of external legislative and gubernatorial attention, such a threat being implicit in the social contract to which state-supported institutions are party.

Although most agencies of coordination are ordinarily limited in the exercise of authority, there is at least one major interesting exception. In the 1960s the state of New Jersey established a coordinating Board located within a state-level Department of Higher Education. The Board grew into a highly regulatory bureaucracy employing as many as 300 staff, administered innumerable regulations and allocated large sums of money to the state's higher education institutions. The Board tangled repeatedly with the trustees of those institutions and was accused by them of being dilatory, unimaginative, punitive and intrusive, mixing coordination with system and campus governance. A change of governors in 1994 and the appointment of a task force led to the dismantling of a disliked state bureaucracy and its replacement by more traditional methods of decentralised decision-making.[140]

Visitors to the United States who have evaluation as their special interest generally ask about the role of the eight regional accrediting agencies in maintaining standards of quality. These are voluntary bodies financed from member contributions, although the states may also contribute. Seemingly these agencies perform functions similar to those of audit and assessment teams in present-day Britain. Teams of academics volunteer to spend a few days visiting another institution and evaluating its programme, so accrediting agencies adopt some of the characteristics of peer review (but peers can also have political agendas, and this occurred in at least one region in 1994). But no absolute academic standard is used for judging the success of an institution. The accrediting agencies are usually only concerned with minimal standards and generally in relation to the stated goals and resources of the institution. Goals that are not consistent with the institution's resource base would be grounds for criticism or the withdrawal of accreditation, without which the institution's credit-unit courses would be unacceptable elsewhere. A frail institution would fear the possible loss of a valued privilege, but stronger or elite institutions are less concerned about the findings of regional accrediting agencies which, in any case, have no authority over research and do not assess the quality of departments as measured by output. Research assessments are made

[140] Darryl G. Greer and Paul R. Shelly, 'A State of Change', *Trusteeship*, 3 (July–August 1995), 16–18.

internally at institutional levels, but every decade or so national voluntary bodies like the National Research Council produce rankings. The weakness of accrediting agencies has led to a recent proposal to shift their duties to a more powerful national body. Given the current ideological and political divisions within higher education, no guarantee of objectivity exists. The creation of such a body is therefore far from assured.

The manifest function of American multi-campus federations is to legitimate a great variety of activities more than to establish common standards or procedures beyond a useful minimum. The latent function of American federations is essentially the opposite of the federal principle as employed in the United Kingdom. Public-sector American universities and colleges most fear the intrusion of outsiders, legislators and governors into core functions: teaching, research and curriculum, admissions to undergraduate and graduate or professional programmes and the hiring, promotion and retention of faculty. The latent function of federations is therefore to protect member campuses from outside interference and to ward off the effects of externally mandated policy decisions through negotiation, ambiguity and bureaucratic obfuscation, American forms of 'scams' and 'games'. The large staffs available to system heads in organisations like the University of California are a useful means of check-mating state bureaucracies. The American rationale for federation is perfectly explained by two Californians in a March 1989 report on the University of London commissioned by the vice-chancellor. The report lists the virtues of federation as central planning and, definitely if more quietly expressed, the capacity of a well-focused centre to help the constituent colleges, schools and hospitals resist the manipulations and pressures of Whitehall and the funding councils.[141] Instead of being the channel through which external assessment enters the university, it is a stopcock for regulating the flow.

A SUMMING UP

British and American concerns about mass access education, quality maintenance and the preservation of elite functions are not dissimilar, but each nation has devised different methods for achieving what might be

[141] Eugene C. Lee and Frank M. Bowen, *The University of London; an American Perspective* (Working Paper 89–3, Institute of Governmental Studies, University of California, Berkeley, March 1989). The authors list 'quality control' among the general missions of multi-campus universities, but they almost immediately temper this object with another and opposite goal more American than British – 'the promotion of differential dimensions of quality'.

considered common goals. Each nation has also had different preoccupations and obsessions. The application of the federal principle in the two societies has a special history and divergent aims. Pragmatism governed the choice of methods used to advance educational goals in the United States. George Ticknor's outburst in 1824 is as good a quotation as any in this regard. 'I care not three straws about any of the *theories* from Plato and Quintilian down to Rousseau. Show me what has been *done*, and I am ready to believe and trust and imitate.'[142] He believed in multiple or pluralistic solutions, a plethora of innovations from which borrowings could be chosen. Federation sputtered along in America, but it did not prevent unitary institutions from forming. Federation was a means of allowing for their almost instantaneous creation under the sponsorship of a benign centre. They could arise wondrously in a single night like an Aladdin's enchanted palace, as Lord Macaulay's sister said of the first, the unfederated London University.[143] Federation in America assumed many forms and did not really become a conspicuous figure in the carpet until large amounts of state and Washington money began to pass into universities for research, or into universities and colleges for language-training or student aid in the period after the Second World War. Furthermore, American federal systems did not adopt the Cambridge principle and did not have behind them the force of a national conception of what a university degree must stand for, did not aim at creating a national 'academic culture' and have generally been more tolerant of growth at the periphery than have federations on the eastern side of the Atlantic.

Federation emerged in Britain at the outset of the movement for expansion in higher education. It became a device for curbing the ambition of Lilliputian universities by holding them to university college status. The belief that a central body was necessary to protect the degree standard against localism, the open market, self-interest and particularism was, as Robert Lowe's remark establishes, also an opportunity for the Victorian State to discover a role for itself. Historians have for many years argued about the significance of State intervention in nineteenth-century Britain and have conspicuously disagreed about the origins of bureaucratic institutions. In fact, the role that Lowe desired for the Victorian Liberal State was precisely the role that it could easily undertake. It cost very little to regulate examinations. The small clerical and administrative staff retained by the University of London was paid out of examination and degree fees. The Treasury received the surplus, if any, and paid out

---

[142] Tyack, *Ticknor*, 100.   [143] Harte, *University of London*, 63.

subsidies as required. The State did not have an obligation to educate its citizens and subjects. That was a matter of individual choice and individual means, and Victorian Britain provided the nation with a great variety of endowed, private and proprietary sources of education. But the State did have an obligation to guide and regulate; and if Robert Lowe's words to this effect lack the metaphysical reach of those of his contemporary, Matthew Arnold, there is a level at which they are in agreement. The State recognised the best standard. The State encouraged aspirants to reach it.

The conception of a standard, however 'essential', and the idea of a university appear together historically. The first was the chosen instrument for realising the second. Whereas leading Victorians divided on the wisdom of using examinations as the standard, the fear of the market dictated this solution as the easiest to implement. As the business of a university was the dissemination of learning, examinations made sense. Furthermore, in an age when mathematics, classics (literary studies) and theology were the main teaching subjects of universities, examinations were all the more obvious instruments for achieving quality. With only a few subjects in need of testing, examiners were plentiful.

An absolute standard of quality is an idea. However, in reality there are only variable standards. Nineteenth-century sources often mention that the standard for the external student was lower than for the internal student, or that one federation had lower standards than another, or that none of the federations could ever be the equal of Oxford and Cambridge, with their pick of the applicant pool, superior resources and historical prestige.[144] But this is all relative, relative to what one would find in another country, and the value of comparison and contrast is precisely that it provides us with a measure of the aspirations of a culture as well as the institutional solutions to its fundamental problems.

Higher education and higher education systems are institutional manifestations of national cultures. This statement should not be read as an affirmation of the commonplace observation that all institutions merely 'reflect' social conditions. The interaction is rarely straightforward. The exact institutional structures that social and cultural behaviour produces cannot be easily predicted. One does not 'reproduce' the other, yet there

---

[144] Variations in external examining and practical questions concerning the maintenance of comparable national standards are discussed in a number of recent studies, but see especially Harold Silver *et al.*, *The External Examiner System: Possible Futures* (Report commissioned by the Higher Education Quality Countil, May 1995). As Britain's higher education system continues to expand and differentiate, worries generated by an historic fidelity to the Cambridge principle are bound to produce acute anxiety over academic standards.

are correlations. It may therefore be hazarded that the federal principle in Britain was exactly what 1836 represented in the history of the University of London, a compromise that reminds us of other compromises in other areas of Victorian society. It was a compromise between centre and periphery, a point midway between French centralism in higher education and American decentralism, a George Romney portrait of Emma, Lady Hamilton as Nature – the restraint of the grand manner moving towards the freedom of Romanticism. It was a compromise between a belief in the importance of individual competition and a fear of the wasteful consequences of institutional rivalry. Federation balanced private and public interest, enabling universities to maintain a working distinction between college work and university standards.

Federation was also a compromise between liberal values and the idea of an Establishment. Liberal values are in theory and should in practice be antithetical to the idea of an Establishment, but Victorian Britain was never a thoroughly liberal culture, although it may have been a strongly liberal State, wary of collecting voter taxes and equally wary of spending them, believing in the importance of civil society, self-help and voluntarism, reluctant to protect businesses from market competition, worried that trade union principles would result in restraint of trade. It was liberal in higher education in so far as it recognised some of the advantages of decentralisation, of devolution, of local initiative. It was liberal in devising a method for education on the cheap: federations were considered less expensive than unitary establishments because duplication was prevented, and federations were therefore a form of popular education, arising historically in the same period as mechanics' institutes, adult education and monitorial systems. It has long been pointed out that a number of the founders of the London University were also advocates of education for the masses. Federation was a liberal idea in so far as it joined the ideas of dissimilarity and combination. In federations, religious differences could be accommodated within the same structure, as in the case of London, as in the case of Toronto, and as in the case of Oxford and Cambridge, whose collegiate organisation had no difficulty in absorbing the new mid-nineteenth-century Anglican foundations of Keble and Selwyn at just that moment when the other colleges had discarded religious exclusion.

But the federal principle also incorporated values from that second or other Victorian Britain representing the 'metropolitan culture'. Centralised governing institutions had been strengthened by a land-owning aristocracy. Georgian ideals of Taste lingered on into the next century. The idea of an Establishment still had a future and was carried forward by an 'intellectual aristocracy'. Chaos at the periphery was unacceptable. The values associated with pluralism could always expect a hard fight from those who held firmly to a belief in the best that had been thought and said in the world.

INTERLUDE: GENERAL INTRODUCTION
TO CHAPTERS SIX AND SEVEN

In writings about the history of British education, supply is easier to discern than demand. The actions of market providers – schools, colleges and universities, but also parliaments, cabinets, prominent politicians, civil servants and leading academics – leap from the pages of the past to provide a fairly obvious account of the facts at major turning points. Demand, especially if it is mass demand, is more difficult to explain. The indicators are harder to interpret. In crude fashion, enrolments are at least one tangible measure of the existence of market pressures. The causes of a sudden rise or fall may not be readily explicable, but the consequences have measurable effects on such variables as space use and the quality of facilities, size of teaching and support staffs, institutional income or curricular diversity. Student numbers affect housing, the provision for recreation, commercial activity and transportation. A 'critical mass' of students influences teaching relationships. Several of these variables are also affected by supply irrespective of demand, since curricula, to take only one example, can be altered even if there is no increase in numbers or shift of interests within existing markets. Staff augmentation can similarly occur without apparent increases in demand.

The demand for education is volatile. Innumerable historical examples are available of private sector initiatives that failed to achieve a solid fiscal footing in the long run or experienced serious short-term downturns. Some three-quarters of a hundred Dissenting academies of eighteenth-century England were more or less moribund by the early nineteenth century. The demise of the academies cannot be wholly attributed to public suspicion that teachers were crypto-jacobins during the French Revolution. The academies faced competition from private-venture schools preparing students for entry-level market skills. They were desperately dependent upon fees and probably lowered their standards to attract paying customers, whose interests were limited in any case. They could not provide the individual instruction in vogue at the time nor maintain satisfactory levels of internal discipline.

Manchester College, a descendant of the once-illustrious Warrington Academy, is a major exception. Its remarkably chequered history offers many clues to its survival. Throughout the nineteenth century Manchester College continually shifted its educational goals and loyalties, sometimes appealing to the families of wealthy Dissenters, at other times catering mainly to Unitarians, occasionally offering boarding facilities or arranging for private tutors. Its clientele to begin with were drawn from wealthy merchant or landed classes. Later the college tried to recruit from industrial and professional families. However, it never had more than thirty-one students in any given year. Changing location was another survival strategy. The college moved from the north to London in the hopes of building a stronger support base in the kingdom's leading population centre. After the 1840s, Manchester's curriculum was influenced by the London examinations. Students continued to read for the London degrees until 1967 when, having long since again relocated, this time to Oxford, the college found a home at last and was listed in the Oxford University Handbook.[1] Longevity was purchased at the price of identity. Staying alive in chameleon fashion, Manchester College was unable to make effective use of its heritage or develop the kind of institutional 'saga' that was so important a factor in the history of American colleges.

Many of the newer university colleges of the nineteenth century were close to collapse when they failed to recruit enough qualified students to maintain an ambitious programme of studies. The numbers of full-time students at Owens College fell so low in the 1860s and 1870s that adequate staff could not be retained. The response of the authorities, correct as it turned out, was to turn towards niche marketing by offering high-demand evening classes and special courses for schoolmasters.[2] King's College, London, was in precarious straits throughout the nineteenth century since fee income left substantial shortfalls in operating expenses. Even during rapid enrolment growth at Oxford and Cambridge in the early nineteenth century, with an increasing number of fee-paying undergraduates in attendance, some colleges remained tiny and financially undernourished. In the United States several hundred private and proprietary institutions went under in the last century, unable to attract sufficient students or gifts to establish a viable programme of studies.

---

[1] Barbara Smith, ed., *Truth, Liberty, Religion, Essays Celebrating Two Hundred Years of Manchester College* (Oxford, 1986), xvii, 9, 33, 37, 51, 53, 57, 67, 88, 250–1. Newman's brother Francis was at one time professor of classics at Manchester College.
[2] D. J. Palmer, *The Rise of English Studies* (London, 1965), 56–7.

Precisely because the demand for education is historically mercurial, academics everywhere understandably prefer more reliable sources of income, especially those that allow full guild control over the conditions of teaching or research. Given a choice, academics prefer endowments. Coleridge understood the preference perfectly well. A 'class' as well as an institution could have an 'idea'. He created a special class of scholars which he called a 'clerisy', whose essential task was to pursue knowledge without fear of encroachment from the outside. The theory of a protected stratum of intellectuals, endowed to preserve culture, has retained a certain allure right to the present. *Vide* Hermann Hesse, *The Glass Bead Game*. (Coleridge was a better littérateur than economist. Endowments need to be invested, and investments need markets.)

University scientists and scholars are not customarily comfortable with any economic theory that regards professional services merely as commodities purchased through the pricing mechanisms of a market. The 'expert' does not suffer purchasers gladly. For centuries education and knowledge were considered to be sacred since they contained an 'objective system of truths' and needed to be sheltered from the mutabilities and corruptions of a profane universe.[3] Since State churches in Europe normally possessed a monopoly on higher education, a class of priestly elites was insulated from pricing discipline. Supply was therefore able to lead demand. Competition from other providers of education was effectively minimised, and guild professionalism maintained its authority.

In Britain, Oxford, Cambridge and the Scottish universities had long enjoyed an association with Church and Crown which, despite a history of political interference, notably in appointments to professorial chairs and attempts to influence curricula, was glamourised in the nineteenth century when market alternatives began to appear. The pattern was as much European as British. The highest prestige for any university was always reserved for institutions that could maintain an identification with grander national and political responsibilities and in so doing draw students and faculty from the widest available talent pools, slotting graduates back into occupations enjoying excellent reputations. This was as true for the United States with its strong democratic inheritance of mass education and land grant service universities as for Europe.

But the new partnership between nation-state and university, superseding that of Church and University, required the better part of a century to achieve. First came the disentanglement from State Churches, achieved in Scotland by the Disruption in the 1840s that divided Presbyterians and

---

[3] Florian Znaniecki, *The Social Role of the Man of Knowledge* (New York, 1968), 163.

in England by the reform-minded royal commissioners investigating the teaching and finances of Oxford and Cambridge in the 1850s and 1860s. While this was occurring, the State was building a different relationship with a newer higher education sector, represented at first by the federation based on London. Few observers supposed that a systematic, far-reaching policy of State intrusion was in the making. The changes were rather in the character of a 'drift' towards an expanded State role.[4]

The British State was actually reluctant to assume the responsibility of being the principal purchaser of university services. This was not even a serious consideration during the Oxford and Cambridge reform period of 1850–70. The role of the State was limited to helping colleges remove many of the legal barriers that interfered with a flexible and efficient use of available endowment income. Universities were teaching institutions, as Newman said, and most academics still agreed, so vast new sources of income were not required. Only the academic tories resisted State action, seeing in the royal commissioners, backed by administrative assistants, parliaments and cabinets, all with unlimited access to the media, as potential intruders into university autonomy.

Advocates of the mid-Victorian 'endowment of knowledge' movement to strengthen research within universities, eager to attract new money, nevertheless did not initially call upon the State for special support. Their goal was diverting existing income and endowments from the tutorial towards the professorial side of instruction, since, in the words of polemicists, the money had been intended to support scholarship and research but had been 'usurped for other purposes'.[5] The State itself was a 'reluctant patron'[6] and only agreed to higher education subsidies when no other alternative seemed likely.

New foundations were established continually throughout the nineteenth century by private donors, although these were mainly technical or university colleges. Yet financial difficulties handicapped most of the new institutions of the nineteenth century, and historians are not always clear about the reasons for the relative absence of steady private support. Was it the system of taxation? But taxes were not a major burden in an age of liberal economics. Was it a fear of risk, a reluctance to finance institutions that might succumb to bankruptcy? The history of Dissenting

[4] For a fuller discussion, see Sheldon Rothblatt and Martin Trow, 'Government Policies and Higher Education: A Comparison of Britain and the United States, 1630–1860', in *Social Research and Social Reform*, ed. Colin Crouch and Anthony Heath (Oxford, 1992), 173–216.
[5] C. E. Appleton, 'Economic Aspects of the Endowment of Research', *The Fortnightly Review*, n.s. 16 (1874), 519–36, esp. 530.
[6] Peter Alter, *The Reluctant Patron, Science and the State in Britain, 1850–1920* (Oxford, 1987).

academies was well known. The establishment of the first London University was almost a direct consequence of the demise of the famous eighteenth-century alternatives for non-Anglicans. In any case, British investors in general were known to be cautious with capital, preferring secure, low-interest returns to high-interest investments. Were there insufficient incentives? But the age of the Victorians was full of philanthropical contributions of every kind. Public statues, plaques, libraries, public lectures, hospitals commemorating generous donors are plentiful. Did the action of the State, at times liberal but at other times intrusive, constrain markets and frighten potential benefactors? The University of London's most recent historian leans towards this explanation, stating that the policy of direct government control over the examining and degree system arising as a consequence of the arrangements of 1836 was an inhibiting factor.[7]

Because we know that the State emerged in the twentieth-century as the principal financial support of all British universities, it is indeed logical to suppose that this direction was all along intended, or rather, inevitable and even desirable, given reluctant market support. This may well be true; but historians should nevertheless be intrigued by other attempted outcomes and arrangements, if only to get the story right.[8] There was in fact a long history of market experimentation in England, as already suggested, when universities and colleges tested consumer interest. Consumer behaviour with respect to education goes back well into the eighteenth century.

The purpose of the discussions in the next two chapters is not to replace one kind of historiography with another in order to justify one set of policies rather than another. The purpose is much simpler: to provide the largely missing half. Since the supply side of education has received the most attention, it is sensible to look at demand as also a factor in the making of university history. It is useful to provide some account of how that demand was negotiated, met or resisted, and to offer some explanation for the ensuing consequences. The stories to be presented could probably be rescripted and told differently, but the point is to notice how the narrative line shifts when viewed from a different angle, when demand not supply is isolated as the leading variable, when consumers not government are assumed to be the principal buyers of education. If there

---

[7] Negley Harte, *The University of London 1836–1986* (London, 1986), 177.
[8] For further remarks along these lines see the review essay by Sheldon Rothblatt, 'Supply and Demand: The "Two Histories" of English Education', *History of Education Quarterly*, 28 (Winter, 1988), 627–44.

is any notable bias in the narrative, it is towards the wayward quality of human experience and its richness and infinite variety.

Two case studies follow. The first exemplifies the effect of market pressures on the unreformed colleges of Oxford and Cambridge, pressures that originated from within university-bound families. The second illuminates the circumstances that led the first London University away from many of its initial intentions, resulting in a new and indeed revolutionary idea of a university.

In both examples, 'demand' is represented by local influences, obligations or accommodations. 'Localism' at Oxford and Cambridge means a system of preferential scholarships, eleemosynary awards and fellowships ('studentships' at Christ Church) favouring founders' kin, particular counties and schools and undergraduates seeking clerical preferment, in effect, a limited or niche market. But 'local' in this context also means parental efforts to influence college admissions, teaching and examining. Parents were invited to intervene because of the absence of a clear-cut, university-wide admissions policy, the inherent flexibility of college teaching and a willingness on the part of college leaders to make special and private arrangements for study. In other words, guild control over the conditions of university entrance and study was weaker than later, a fact that also explains why the history of examinations was so necessary for the success of academic professionalism. The haphazard character of pre-university schooling cannot be overlooked as another reason for guild instability. Linkages connecting upper secondary education with the universities were far less secure than after the middle of the nineteenth century. For guild control to be re-established, a more rigid system of articulation had to be constructed. In this regard, the reform and rise of the public schools, where so many good histories are available, can never be overestimated.

The importance of the federal principle in elaborating a new form of university structure has already been discussed. The example that follows in Chapter 7 parallels the Oxbridge story in explaining how the University of London was also freed from a preoccupation with local interests and drifted towards a State alliance that effectively replaced multiple buyers with a single source of support. The final stages of rationalising the British higher education system occurred in the twentieth century but with a twist, for what we have seen in our age is a struggle for guild independence from the State and not necessarily from consumers, for a full market principle has yet to be established. Whether it will develop is a matter for speculation and not for history.

The shift from local to national was parallel to larger changes in British political history, surely interrelated if not precisely correlated. After the franchise reform of 1832, Parliament and Cabinet became stronger, the House of Commons more independent of the House of Lords, and national party politics developed to a point where organised constituency voting could underpin the authority of the executive side of the constitution. Local interests no longer predominated. The 'independent MP', pushing private bills through the legislature on behalf of the unreformed boroughs and counties, ceased to be a fractious force in Parliament by 1867. The condition of cities – slums, housing, health, transportation, drinking, proverty – were central as much as local interests. The transfer of authority from the localities to the centralities, a slow but steady process, enhanced the influence of a nation-minded corps of elites and provided them with an institutional base largely under their management. That is the familiar story of the university meritocracy.

CHAPTER SIX

SUPPLY AND DEMAND IN THE WRITING
OF UNIVERSITY HISTORY SINCE ABOUT 1790
I. 'THE AWKWARD INTERVAL'

BRINGING A MIND OUT OF THE CLOD

We begin with a fundamental historical problem briefly exposed in the chapter describing the new undergraduate culture of unreformed Oxford and Cambridge. That culture was made possible by a number of confusing transformations in the emotional relationships between the members of families from which the senior universities recruited their students. While we understand that upbringing affects subsequent conduct, precision in such matters evades us. Amongst the more bewildering subjects in the writing of social history, none ranks higher than trying to understand child development in relation to parenting, sibling relationships and the interpenetration of family with other socialising institutions, such as schools, churches, neighbourhoods and voluntary organisations. They are bewildering because the sources of family history are multi-varied and contradictory. Our own understanding of how families function as primary institutions is rent by inconsistencies and controversies, making a sober, consensual analysis quite daunting. The subject was and remains critical because upbringing followed by peer associations has an obvious relevance to present-day social policies respecting abortion, divorce, child abuse, juvenile crime, schooling, teaching and preparation for entry into the labour market, to name only the larger questions currently at issue in most contemporary societies.

The subject is truly vexed. Existing theories about family history, when scrutinised carefully, have not generally stood the test of scholarly review. Dramatic reinventions of childhood in particular centuries are less apparent to some observers than to others. Parental attitudes towards the use of physical punishment may not have shifted spectacularly from one era to another. Techniques of upbringing may not be as radically different as several historians have assumed.[1] There are many considerations, but a trio of them may suffice for present purposes. First is the absence of agreement on cognitive development in relation to the biology of coming of age. What stages of mental or emotional growth can we identify and how are they to be correlated with age and bodily changes? How independent a variable is puberty? The precise interaction between nature and nurture divides scientists today. Evidence for leaning one way or the other can be found to suit every ideological predisposition.[2] Second is an equally perplexing effort to generalise about the effects of specific socialising environments on the formation of the attitudes and values of the young, especially when we introduce distinctions such as class (or tribe, clan and kinship group), ethnicity, religion, sex, historical period and nation or country. A third difficulty derives from having to take notice of transformations in attitudes towards parenting or changes in conceptions of the elemental 'nature' of children, whether, for example, they are naturally good or basically wicked or just a lump of clay at the origin of life (Jeremy Bentham opined that it was the Divine intention to bring a mind out of the clod).

During the last thirty years, in a worthy attempt to identify the successive levels of maturation, historians have struggled with such notions as 'childhood' and 'adolescence', and the results have been so opaque, varying so much across time and country that comparisons are impossible.[3] If adolescence is formed and named by culture, and puberty a biological phenomenon largely controlled or explained by culture, then coming of age cannot be a single experience occurring everywhere in the same manner or at the same time. Recent historiography has correctly supplied us with radically different periods for the 'discovery' of adolescence. French writers favour the late eighteenth century, and American historians prefer the late nineteenth century or slightly later. Histories of Britain have selected both the later eighteenth century and the late Victorian or Edwardian periods as critical transformations in conceptions of the child, the adolescent or the youth. The case for the Georgian era is plausible, but arguments for the later century are also credible. In both eras, change is most evident in the middle levels of

---

[1] Significant points are made in the comprehensive discussion by Linda A. Pollock, *Forgotten Children, Parent-Child Relations from 1500–1900* (Cambridge, 1983).

[2] *The Times Higher Education Supplement* (15 March 1996), 15.

[3] See Philippe Ariès, *Centuries of Childhood* (London, 1962); John Gillis, *Youth and History* (New York, 1974); John Springhall, *Coming of Age, Adolescence in Britain, 1860–1960* (Dublin, 1986); Paula S. Fass, *The Damned and the Beautiful, American Youth in the 1920s* (New York, 1977).

society. The utility and the morality of corporal punishment was questioned, children's books, toys, clothes and games proliferated, separate bedrooms were popular, and handbooks on psychology were widely disseminated – in our century imported from Germany, France and America. Original sin lost much of its terror, but a religious upbringing was still valued. Innocence was regarded as an essential attribute of childhood. New entertainments contained themes about youth. In the Edwardian period, James Barrie's play about permanent adolescence, *Peter Pan* (1904) and the Christmas pantomime (hitherto only deemed appropriate for lower-class adults) received widespread attention. Play lost its connection with original sin in the eighteenth century, and a hundred years later the Montessori kindergarten was continuing the search for creative ideas about the use of children's time. 'The child is a new discovery', wrote a Harley Street pediatrician in 1910, and occupies a separate stage of growth requiring special attention.[4]

Granted that each nation's understanding of the adolescent condition may well be historically unique, how are we to reconcile radically similar shifts a century apart within a single nation, both purporting to be fundamental historical transformations?

One answer is that historians are simply mistaken in their reconstructions and are reading the data wrong. But another and quite possible explanation is that certain cultural states, if once invented, can be reinvented, especially if the first development has been interrupted. Arguments for proto-industrialism in sevententh-century Europe fall into this category. Events resembling those of a later century exist but fail to 'take off' into sustained industrial development. Might this have happened to what is called the 'discovery of the child' or the discovery of adolescence in the eighteenth century?

Another explanation is that the first manifestations of a set of interconnected social and cultural values touch only a small number of families, but the second reach many more from different social strata. It is only our inexact social categorising that creates the confusion. There is also the possibility that we have looked at only one category of change. Clothing fads, hairstyles, popular recreations, mating patterns, challenges to parental authority may appear together in more than one historical period, raising worries about teenage behaviour that seem to be identical, but we have failed to notice the existence of other variables that transform our understanding of what might have happened. The same phenomena,

---

[4] Jose Harris, *Private Lives, Public Spirit, a Social History of Britain, 1870–1914* (Oxford, 1993), 86–8.

apparently reappearing at a later point, may have quite different institutional implications. As we shall see, a child's formal education became an issue of great concern to parents in the eighteenth century, but in 1790, unlike 1870, 1890 or 1914, mass education did not exist (nor did mass transit), and *ad hoc* arrangements largely prevailed. Teenage behaviour in the context of one is likely to have a different meaning when seen in the context of the other.

The strength of restraining institutions is also critical. Erik Erikson has made this point effectively. In writing about the Reformation, he observes that most cultures suspect adolescence to be a troubling phase (biologically?), when ego dangers are substantial and need to be anticipated or diverted by a variety of ceremonial or symbolic rites anchoring a young person firmly to heritage. But this is more easily accomplished in ordinary than extraordinary times. Periods of acute religious change weaken ego defences and increase the vulnerability of immature persons to extreme claims and promises.[5] Joseph Kett makes a similar point in writing about college age populations in the United States, noting how prone they were to enthusiastic religions in the Great Awakening.[6]

Another difficulty derives from trying to connect generalisations arising from the findings of individual psychology, notions such as latency periods devised by Anna Freud or liminality (transitions) and other formulations of cyclical transfer points, to demographic information properly disaggregated to reflect specific family structures. A similar problem exists when we try to fit older metaphors and lexicons of upbringing into heuristic categories of present-day origin, as, for example, the ancient taxonomy of the seven ages of man. So the combined task is staggering, and it is no wonder that qualitative approaches to the history of childhood, resting on period piece conceptions, are resorted to more readily than quantitative methods.

We are nearly reduced to a trite reflection, that parents or surrogate parents are concerned about how children are likely to fit into society and how family relationships will function when separation from the home takes place. But even such an unobjectionable statement, when put into precise historical contexts, helps us speculate about such evidence that does exist for understanding how the comfortable classes of the later eighteenth century struggled to make sense of contradictory information and

---

[5] Erik Erickson, *Young Man Luther* (New York, 1962), 43, 114, 134.
[6] Joseph F. Kett, *Rites of Passage, Adolescence in America, 1790 to the Present* (New York, 1977), 62–3.

hypotheses concerning mental and moral development for the purpose of guaranteeing a safe, or at least a reasonably secure future for their heirs. Two essential points can be made at the outset. The first is that education was understandably central to any strategy for success, and the second is that evidence for parental uncertainty about prevailing educational alternatives was reflected in an interesting and unexpected instrumental use of available schooling options. So the approach adopted here is primarily institutional and cultural, the family's relationship to other institutions with a stake in upbringing and the changes in overall culture, the process of self-control of which Norbert Elias has written, that are typically associated with aspects of the Ages of Reason and Illumination.[7]

DEFINING THE LIFE CYCLE

We can now start with a summary of the character of undergraduate life in the late eighteenth and early nineteenth centuries as discussed in an earlier chapter and work backwards to the family. Critics, moralists and some academics greatly feared the strength of an undergraduate peer culture thoroughly dominated by an unprecedented hedonism manifested by a far more interesting and diverse world of recreation, comfort and intellectual interests than had existed before. Parents – how many can never be precisely gauged – tended to agree. The evidence for their concern comes from correspondence, from Polonius-like talk on the wisdom of choosing companions of suitable moral character and from expressions of concern about negligence and waste. To allow a young man his head was to stand by helplessly while dissipation took its predictable toll on health, led to moral deterioration and resulted in a miserable and embarrassing academic performance. Deviant behaviour could easily plunge a family into debt and shame.

Admonitions abounded, but they were mitigated by a clear conflict of interest. In the same breath, a son was advised to be sociable and to avoid giving offence and to be thick with companions in a position to advance his prospects. To be overly scrupulous was to jeopardise the life chances of

---

[7] Pollock, *Forgotten Children*, 269, seems to agree that emphases varied in the eighteenth century. 'Training' a child became especially important. 'Both mothers and fathers approached parenthood with apprehension and trepidation, worrying whether or not their modes of child care were correct and whether they were sufficiently competent to rear their children.' The 'civilising process' can be discussed under any number of headings, but for now let us settle on the extraordinary preoccupation with normative rules of conduct underlying any society identified as enlightened. See the history of manners as sketched in Norbert Elias, *The Civilizing Process* (New York, 1978).

sons dependent upon the potential patronage of aristocratic heirs. A hierarchical society preached deference to social superiors and condescension
to inferiors. The dons themselves were trapped in similar dilemmas,
needing careers outside the universities that required toadying and the
culling of favours.

The personal discomforts caused by special pleading produced a third-
party culture where potentially embarrassing face-to-face relationships
could be avoided by employing friendly intermediaries, messengers who
relayed the terms of social negotiation and were expected to soften the
realities that were the subject of long-distance exchanges, at the same time
preserving the personal ties that formed the basis of the late Georgian
'vertical' opportunity structure described by Harold Perkin.[8] Some form
of face-saving illusion is necessary to the functioning of all cultural
systems, whether in the Bali described by Clifford Geertz or the Britain
of George III.[9] The systems can function only if the contradictions are
concealed.

One of the outstanding structural peculiarities of the public schools and
the old college system at Oxford and Cambridge was the absence of
any systematic or consistent application of rules and discipline. Certain
colleges might acquire a reputation for leniency, others for a stricter
discipline; some were known to favour the scholars, others to be partial to
the wealthy, and parents tried to find out where their children might
receive the best reception. Everywhere, in any case, exceptions and
exemptions abounded, either for categories of student – the wealthy who
did not have to keep the usual number of terms for a degree, or were
excused from examinations – or for individuals. The introduction of a new
examinations discipline, the beginnings of meritocratic measurement, the
religious pluralism that most masters of colleges disliked, the suspicions
that followed all undergraduate efforts to establish a strong student
subculture, coexisted with an attitude of laxity. Students received mixed
signals on how to behave. There was a certain haphazard quality to the
daily life of pupils and students, which is why so many reminiscences paint
a picture of arbitrary behaviour and vacillation in the enforcement of rules
and regulations. Steering one's way through the university labyrinth
occupied much student energy and invited parental comment.

Cultural contradictions cannot be fully contained where they embody
opposite sets of values. While academic success, for example, did not

[8] Harold Perkin, *The Origins of Modern English Society, 1780–1880* (London, 1972), 17–62.
[9] Clifford Geertz, 'Deep Play: Notes on the Balinese Cock Fight', in *The Interpretation of Cultures* (New York, 1973) 412–54.

guarantee a good career, it could attract a certain amount of attention. Boys excelling at school, acquiring what was called 'literary distinction', undoubtedly pleased their parents. But literary distinction, the ability to declaim well and to turn a fine Latin phrase, coexisted with an almost abandoned juvenile life in the boarding schools of the later decades of the eighteenth century. Schoolboy theft, lying and continual brawling and bullying were so prevalent in the better-known schools of the period that parents debated twice before sending their sons to them. Yet here too there was a rational explanation for a cruel regimen for those parents who believed in the exposure of infant leaders to the pains and humiliations of places like the Long Chamber at Eton. Boys were hardened in such environments, their resistance to childhood diseases improved (a vain hope). They were taught courage and fortitude, learned to endure nightmarish conditions and would grow up to form a leadership elite. Seen in this light, punishment at school sometimes (although not usually) received wholehearted parental approval, especially from the great aristocracy. Returning to his London residence after an Eton schoolboy rebellion in 1768, Lord Roos was taken out for the evening by his father, the marquis of Granby. He was told that he would visit the theatre that evening for his own pleasure 'and tomorrow shall return to Mr Foster and be flogged for mine'.[10]

Undergraduate patterns of response were greatly shaped, if not precisely shaped, by prior experiences at home or school. Undergraduates who came from a great public school had longer exposure to the terrors supporting the politics of aristocracy, but, as we shall notice, even the great boarding schools of the Georgian period were not wholly masters of their fate. Other undergraduates entered the universities from different locations where parental supervision appears to be more in evidence, but the difference may be only one of degree. It is extremely difficult to prove that the great families treated their children fundamentally differently from lesser ones. It is likely that in the eighteenth century the child-centred family took hold among the families of the great peers of the realm and the country gentry and clergy, as well as among urban professional and business families. These encompassed a broad range of income and status levels; but it was from these comfortable ranks that the Georgian university principally recruited.

Recent writings on the history of the family have concentrated on the growth of child-centred relationships and of a more child-centred society

---

[10] Cited in M. V. Wallbank, 'Eighteenth Century Public Schools and Education', *History of Education*, 8 (March, 1979), 9.

generally, but no change is wholly without precedent. At least one scholar finds the child-centred home to be typical of town life starting with the late medieval period, where households (to include servants and kin) were smaller than those of the aristocracy.[11] Another historian suggests that working-class families of the later eighteenth century provided an example of close-knit family relations, intensified by limited household space, and that the example of a 'moderately affectionate and caring' family spread upwards, encountering a downward moving trend towards greater kindness towards children.[12] Quite possibly the smaller family is an urban phenomenon, although the interpenetration of city and country culture in the eighteenth century, *rus in urbe* and *urbs in ruri*, makes the distinction less decisive. The growth of London, its Season and other ravishments, the centralisation of legal, political and publishing functions, brought the gentry and aristocracy and the numerous class of ladies and gentlemen into contact with city culture. The Grand Tour brought the urban styles of the Continent directly into the homes of aristocracy and substantial gentry, and other households benefited from the spread of consumerism. We are left with uncertainties about exact causes but not about the existence of a phenomenon.

A caveat: the phrase 'child-centred' is in danger of overuse and does not adequately convey the subtlety of complex historical developments. As here used it is intended to draw attention to family investment in a broadly-conceived notion of welfare and positive incentives for children. With regard to formal education, the term 'child-centred' is usually taken to mean that a curriculum is adapted to the learning capacity and pace of the child. The learner is not forced to submit to rigid schedules and hackneyed pedagogical methods.[13] In this meaning it would be difficult to find many examples of pupil-oriented educational practices in England or elsewhere at almost any time. But the great and important exception was tutorial instruction. The tutor, working closely with the pupil, usually in a household setting, devoted his attention exclusively to the child, making adjustments in learning as circumstances required but also, it needs to be added, with the regulatory approval of parents. A tutorial approach to teaching is not fully pupil-centred if it is tied to a set syllabus and structured according to a definite calendar. It is a more closely supervised approach to achieving the stated ends of a particular programme of

---

[11] See Leah Sinanoglou Marcus, *Childhood and Cultural Despair, a Theme and Variations in Seventeenth-Century Literature* (Pittsburgh, 1978), 30, 33, 37–8.

[12] F. M. L. Thompson, *The Rise of Respectable Society, A Social History of Victorian Britain, 1830–1900* (Cambridge, MA, 1988), 128–30.

[13] Cf. John Passmore, *The Philosophy of Teaching* (Cambridge, MA, 1980), 23–4.

studies, with the advantage that one-to-one teaching relationships allow for the incorporation of other, less academic considerations.[14]

Evidence for alterations in patterns of upbringing has been adduced from the proliferation of a special literature for children, both didactic and for pleasure, from the diversification of the toy market, to include educational games and from the gradual disappearance of symbolic acts of deference, such as kneeling and standing in the presence of adults. Formal addresses such as 'sir' and 'madam' were being replaced by 'papa' and 'mama'.[15] A probable increase in the use of contraceptives points to a view of marriage as incorporating love and affection and of the household as the place for encouraging close and warm relationships. With this went an emphasis on the special nature of the primary family itself, which developed strategies for partitioning itself off from some of the routines and intermixing of everyday life. Servants were kept more at bay instead of weaving in and out of family life as had been the case earlier, a situation that led many educational writers (following the lead of John Locke) to dwell on the bad habits children acquired from menials and domestics. (This may partly account for some of the problems students encountered with servants in the colleges, whose presence there was institutionalised as part of *in loco parentis*.) The invention of the bell-rope and the bell-pull made it possible to confine servants to their quarters until needed, instead of permitting them to lounge and watch in hall. The architecture of new country houses incorporated a growing interest in privacy and informality. Bedrooms were put exclusively upstairs, and the custom of receiving visitors in a private dressing room or sleeping quarters, as nicely portrayed in *Der Rosenkavalier,* died out. From the 1790s onwards more asymmetric houses were built, rambling, irregular *cottages ornées* communicating a sense of playfulness and informality.[16]

Although demographers do not wholly agree on the relative increases of birth and death rates, there may well have been a comparative decline in infant and child mortality rates amongst the better off, making possible a larger investment of love in children. Maternal affection especially

---

[14] It has been cursorily suggested – e.g., David Wardle, *English Popular Education, 1780–1970* (Cambridge, 1970), 89–90 – that in a casual and almost evolutionary fashion several eighteenth-century private schools drifted towards a child-related approach; but it is certain that this was primarily a much later development.

[15] Rosamunde Bayne-Powell, *The English Child in the Eighteenth Century* (London, 1939), 3.

[16] See such writings as Neil Mckendrick *et al.*, *The Birth of a Consumer Society* (Bloomington, IN, 1982); J. H. Plumb, 'The New World of Children in Eighteenth-Century England', *Past and Present*, 67 (May, 1975), 64–95; and Mark Girouard, *Life in the English Country House* (London and New Haven, 1978), 219–30.

appears evident, with a higher degree of personal supervision exercised by mothers over children.

Visual evidence has received an unusual amount of attention from scholars. A plethora of paintings about the British family and the child's place within it survives. These mainly depict the genteel, professional and commercial classes, but references to the rural and urban poor also exist. Both in quantity and theme Georgian family portraits or scenes of children at play seem to be a break with mainstream traditions of domestic art, although Dutch and a few French and Italian forerunners supply a minimal amount of continuity. Before the eighteenth century paintings of European domestic relations were normally anecdotal or depicted the Holy Family, cupids, dynastic families boasting of wealth and status. But in the eighteenth century the child becomes a central interest, and not only the child but particular children, individualised and singled out, existing as both a general category – the child – or as an actual person. A third reading of the paintings suggests they are about 'childhood', a stage of life with a significance all its own. These are too numerous and striking to be overlooked.

Paintings and drawings show childhood as spontaneous, lively, emotional and exploratory and as a period in which children come to terms with their development. Parental warmth, tenderness and sentimentality are evident; brothers and sisters play together. Children ride hobby horses, chase butterflies and read or are read to. Walking is shown, and exercise for health is a theme, pointing us towards a concern that shows up in biography, letter-writing and advice books. Georgian art is invariably preachy. We can expect painterly warnings about inappropriate conduct. George Morland's *A Visit to the Child at Nurse* (c. 1788) contrasts the bonding between a child and a wetnurse with his hesitant, even fearful reaction to a little-known biological mother. She comes for a visit so perfectly attired that the viewer can only wonder about the consequences of a burp.

We cannot know precisely whether such visual evidence is artistic licence and advocacy (a role entirely consistent with market economics), nor how paintings proclaiming the advent of the 'new child' were read by viewers and buyers. Were paintings reflecting actual circumstances? They may have represented the yearnings of adults for an imagined simpler or happier youth, which partially explains the heavy sentimentality evident in every genre. Irrespective of income levels, the coarse treatment of children did not disappear in the Georgian century, nor for that matter did it vanish in the next one. Corporal punishment was not discarded. We can assume from our own awakening knowledge that child abuse was common, beggarly children certainly were. But the overall impression gleaned from paintings, child-rearing manuals, letters and educational innovations is that the second half of the eighteenth century was indeed an age of family experiment, however much the experiments actually led to permanent changes.[17]

But what is also likely, in fact certain, is that reflections about the value of freedom, spontaneity and greater latitude in upbringing produced a counter-tendency, not, to be sure, towards cruelty and rigidity but towards more imaginative restraints. Moralists were quick to claim that parental authority had been compromised by a greater permissiveness in speech and conduct. Children were too outspoken, disrespectful and spoiled. The greater latitude of conduct now accorded them was believed to promote habits of indiscipline and insubordination, and it was a short mental step from these symptoms to the diagnosis that 'French levity' was at work in the body social. From there it was but another short step to conclude that the breakdown in family authority would lead to conditions of political anarchy such as existed in France or the failure of nerve that had led to the loss of the American colonies. The simple cure was to advocate more discipline and more watchfulness in raising children.

From the later eighteenth century onwards there is evidence to support the simultaneous existence of two contrary positions. The first was a belief in the importance of allowing children greater initiative as the best preparation for coping with a world of competing demands and pressures, and the other was an equally firm recommendation for greater constraint. Parents were caught between dual positions, both of which appeared to be sensible and necessary.

The difficulty was choosing between them, but the foremost difficulty was determining when children were to be completely released from the home in order to enter a wider world where ambition and initiative mattered. At what point in the life cycle ought the full break from parental authority occur? Or were full breaks necessary? Perhaps gradual, controlled weaning was better.[18]

The initial step was to define the life cycle itself, a period of growth and

---

[17] James Christen Steward, *The New Child, British Art and the Origins of Modern Childhood, 1730–1830* (Berkeley and Seattle, 1995), 11, 16–27, 211. See also Hugh Cunningham, *Children and Childhood in Western Society since 1500* (London, 1995), 61–77.

[18] I am informed by Karen Zilberstein that life-cycle theories such as developed by eighteenth-century writers were based on expectations regarding boys. Since boys needed to become men and assume leadership responsibilities in society, their upbringing was discussed in terms of eventual independence and separation from the family. The boarding-school model made these assumptions even more explicit. 'Independence' was not expected of girls.

development through which children passed in order to reach a safe state of adulthood. Teachers had been doing this for centuries, aided by conceptions such as the seven ages of man where the third, covering the period from 15 to 25, was regarded as dangerous. The Tudor schoolmaster Roger Ascham adjusted the figures to read from 17 to 27, a period 'most slipperie to stay well in'.[19] Comenius divided schooling into a quartet of six-year segments, each with a different sensory or cognitive bias. John Locke, repeatedly 'revived' in the eighteenth century, talked about the 'middle period' extending from ages 15 to 21 where children were headstrong and uncontrollable. Rousseau had a scheme which made the child a savage until age 12. A pre-adolescent period lasted for three more years, distinguished by an increase in bodily strength and an interest in practical matters. Adolescence extended from 15 to marriage at 25, during which conscience and other moral, intellectual or sensual development occurred.[20]

Eighteenth-century commentators spoke vaguely of 'youth' and even more vaguely, as did Blackstone, of the awkward interval from childhood to age 21.[21] Outside of the elite world an effort to connect a stage of growth with a specific age occurred in the factory legislation of the early nineteenth century, but for the same reason that 21 was regarded as maturity at common law, namely, that the law cannot afford to be vague for very long where questions of inheritance and citizenship enter. Except for the legal age of majority long set in western culture at 21, all other age categories were speculative and arbitrary, the result of personal observation and experiences translated into assumptions and theories about upbringing. The category designated 'youth' was especially broad, applying to anyone from a child to a university undergraduate.[22] It could

---

[19] Susan Brigden, 'Youth and the English Reformation', *Past and Present*, 95 (May, 1982), 37–67.

[20] C. M. Fleming, *Adolescence* (London, 1963), 34–44, 118–23.

[21] Vicesimus Knox, *Liberal Education; or, a Practical Treatise on the Methods of Acquiring Useful and Polite Learning,* II, 11th ed. (London, 1795), 220.

[22] Patricia Meyer Spacks, 'The Dangerous Age', *Eighteenth-Century Studies*, 11 (Summer, 1978), 418. The use of the word 'pupil' to describe Oxford and Cambridge undergraduates appears to be another instance of a word so broadly employed that no specific condition can be imputed to it. We can hold out the possibility, in light of the argument developed in this chapter, that college tutors regarded their charges as essentially immature, but the habit has persisted to our own day. It is also probable that the word was used in reference to the personal nature of tutorial teaching. A 'pupil' belonged to a teacher; an undergraduate was a category, as was a student.

Nineteenth-century American academics were as befuddled by the problem of correlating age and maturity as their English predecessors. Eliot of Harvard thought that character was formed by age 21 and university work could commence. The Yale Report assumed age 14. President McCosh of Princeton alighted on the number 16. Part of the difficulty was defining a university, which in America as in Scotland catered largely to boys. Hugh Hawkins, *Between Harvard and America* (New York, 1972), 106.

afford to be so because the ramifications were a matter of culture not law and politics.

William Cobbett, indefatigable writer, unrepentant radical, anti-Semite and undying foe of septennial parliaments, was still using vague categories of growth as late as 1830. His book of advice on child-rearing incorporated all the stereotyped positions of his day. He divided the life cycle into three parts. The first was babyhood or infancy. The second, lasting from 14 to nearly 20, was called 'youth', and the third and final stage was entitled 'young man'. The 'youths' are offered copybook advice on dress, friends, sobriety, gluttony and living on one's own. Resting at least eight hours is important, so is rising early, avoiding the 'slop-kettle' (tea and coffee) and enjoying sports of the field because they are pursued in daytime and take place away from the town with its wicked habits and immoral amusements. There is a disquisition on the pox, biting and mastication, good food and air followed by other salutary counsel. Cobbett offered a few words on education: grammar, composition, geography, how to study history and the necessity to avoid reading mock-epic romances and 'the historical plays of the punning and smutty Shakespeare'.[23] He insisted that a happy life could not follow from a careless upbringing, but this was conventional wisdom in 1830 and said much earlier by the Cambridge utilitarian, William Paley. He wrote in the former century that a 'parent has, in no case, a right to destroy his child's happiness' in the context of a meandering discussion on the moral foundations of duty in civil society.[24]

Correlations between age, phases of growth, segments of schooling and instructional content remain a cardinal preoccupation of modern societies, with continual institutional attempts to group and separate students by age. Many of the older ideas about cognitive development are still present. Memory is situated in childhood, weakening at puberty. Abstract reasoning is assigned to adolescence, ages 11 to 14. Mechanical, artistic or commercial abilities are put into that same time frame. Some of the early twentieth-century theorists maintained that as an economic instinct appears around age 13, compulsory schooling need not last beyond 14. Some recent theories have played down the role of puberty as a factor in the ability of children to memorise and reason.

This remains a vast subject where angels and researchers should fear to tread. It includes the thorny history of intelligence testing, physiological

---

[23] William Cobbett, *Advice to Young Men and to Young Women* (Oxford, 1980), *passim*.
[24] William Paley, *The Principles of Moral and Political Philosophy*, 5th ed. (Dublin, 1793), 246 *passim*, 248.

and cognitive distinctions between the sexes that some researchers notice, as well as differences attributable to distinct personal or group experiences. The point of this paragraph, however, is not to demonstrate how primitive and inept were eighteenth-century opinions about the best way to raise children but to show how continuous is the concern and how significant are the ramifications. If we, with sophisticated clinical experiments and scientific data for defining and measuring development, cannot agree on stages and correlations, it is useless to expect parents and schoolmasters of the Georgian period to be closer to the mark. Yet one present-day finding is relevant. Testing and observation have shown great variations in the individual differences of adolescents of the same age, along with the over-lapping of age and sex groups.[25] This working conclusion seems to fit very well with the pragmatic patterns of schooling followed by parents of a much earlier era.

Cognitive and epistemological states of growth notwithstanding, there were always simpler reasons for dividing a child's exposure to the world into phases. One was the savagery of schools, where older boys trampled upon the younger. It has been suggested that the origins of the English preparatory school can be traced to parental desires to protect children from bullies. Thomas Arnold did not want boys under 12 at Rugby mixing with the teenagers. He and other headmasters of the 1820s managed to create second schools on the same endowed foundations. We have already noticed how parents worried that a work ethic would under-mine their children's stamina, but much more worrisome was the fear of infant and childhood diseases. Underlying Enlightenment and post-Enlightenment optimism about achieving a high state of civilised conduct were the brute facts of disease, permanent injury, deformity and death, and fears about their frequency were continually transmitted to school-masters and sons, who knew the risks from their personal childhood histories. Preparatory and private schools, the former making an initial appearance in the early nineteenth century, were ravaged by scarlet fever, diphtheria, measles and whooping cough. To provide a more salubrious location for young children, schools were located or relocated in seaside resorts, the Malvern hills or open areas of the north of England. An epidemic could close a school down and devastate the fortunes of an entrepreneurial schoolmaster. That is one principal reason, according to Leinster-Mackay, why the preparatory movement took off so late, not really until after 1870 when medical advances could truly make a

[25] Fleming, *Adolescence*, 243.

difference in the health of a teaching environment.[26] In the meantime, parents exercised the numerous schooling options available to them.

The 'dangerous years'[27] being lengthy, the period of weaning was likewise protracted. It was necessary to specify a proper diet of edifying reading for children: sermons, stories of petty Greek tyrants and debauched Roman emperors, a gallery of rogues, scoundrels, criminals and the lesser knaves and fools who generally beset the innocent and well-meaning picaroon in the course of mock-heroic novels. Novel reading was not quite respectable, but since novels would in any case be read, they might as well be didactic. The consequences of vice and self-indulgence could be read in endless accounts of death through dissipation or the majesty of the law, or the loss of a family fortune and the birth of an unwanted child, or through the theme of the prodigal son, whose misadventures and lack of filial piety resulted in the premature death of a devoted father. The continuous reiteration of the need for discipline and self-regulation, for the encouragement of virtue, temperance and religion, for care in the choice of companions, for the conquest of irregular appetite and the maintenance of a good reputation served a purpose, however tedious these pieties sound today and doubtless sounded then.

A FLEXIBLE EDUCATIONAL MARKET

Against this background of confused advice and circumstances, we can now situate some of the contradictory educational patterns encountered in the last decades of the eighteenth century and around the turn of the century. Whatever formal arrangements parents felt required to make for the education of their children, and especially their sons (but the education of girls was also a serious matter), they never quite relinquished their own role as moral superintendents and guides. Children were not to be handed over to schoolmasters or tutors without assurances that the task of steering them through the dangerous years would be undertaken seriously. There were poor choices, but as soon as the inadequacies were made evident, children were transferred to other surrogates. What is conspicuous about the pattern of schooling is the variety of expediencies, the continual shuttling of children between options, often leaving them with little opportunity for rooting themselves in a specific location, developing habits of self-reliance or acquiring a circle of friends. Yet some children

[26] Donald Leinster-Mackay, *The Rise of the English Prep School* (London and Philadelphia, 1984), 12, 121–6.
[27] The phrase used by Patricia Meyer Spacks in 'The Dangerous Age'.

flourished under such arrangements, pleased not to be under the endless domination of a tryannical schoolmaster. It was an entrepreneurial period for primary and secondary education, with numerous market opportunities for enterprising and small-minded schoolmasters, usually but not invariably clergy, for whom alternative careers were not necessarily available in an age of pluralism and sponsorship. Unbeneficed priests moved into a lucrative private education market, but so did parish clerical pluralists. They established new schools, either for day boys, boarders or both, or, if already teaching in a local grammar school, they increased the boarding side of the school, making it into a separate establishment and taking on pupils in a private arrangement. Even public schools were affected. Pupil overflow at Eton was guided into private houses run independently of the school.[28] Clergy not normally engaged in teaching also took private pupils, sometimes instructing them as day boys but in other instances boarding them in the new and larger parsonages which are the surviving symbols of their enhanced status. Young priests without preferment or curates and assistant vicars hired themselves out as home tutors. 'Pupillisers' and crammers were plentiful.[29]

For parents an unparalleled opportunity for shopping led to a wide range of options: some combination of home tutorial instruction, a local or distant private school, a nearby grammar or public boarding school with day-boy sides. From the sources it is often impossible to define a 'school', which might be just a half dozen pupils gathered in some spot. Rectory 'schools' in the early nineteenth century were frequently of this nature.[30] The period was one of great flux in education. Some well-known grammar and public schools rose and fell in popularity, or changed their social class character. Some private schools were successful, but except for a few they tended to die out fairly quickly. The Nonconformists established a chain of famous academies, but these were not in the business of preparing youths for Oxford and Cambridge, which was the destination of many of the families being discussed.

A typical pattern in Leicestershire from the 1780s onwards is described by Zena Crook and Brian Simon. William Gardiner, the son of a hosier, was sent to a dame school when only two (a 'dame' could be male). He

[28] Malcolm Seaborne, 'The Architecture of the Victorian Public School', in *The Victorian Public School,* ed. Brian Simon and Ian Bradley (Dublin, 1975), 177–86.
[29] Joan Simon, 'Private Classical Schools in Eighteenth-Century England: a Critique of Hans', *History of Education,* 8 (1979), 179–91; also Brian Simon, 'Local Grammar Schools, 1780–1880', in *Education in Leicestershire 1540–1940,* ed. Brian Simon (Leicester, 1968), 130–55.
[30] Leinster-Mackay, *English Prep School,* 77.

stayed for five years (a long period actually) and passed over to another day school where he learned writing and rundimentary arithmetic. On one occasion he unsuccessfully tried to find a teacher for trigonometry and algebra. Family friends seem to have provided supplementary assistance. A language teacher was located; he started Latin but ended with French.[31]

Edward Gibbon's autobiography provides a remarkable if exaggerated account of how parents, or particular circumstances – the death of a parent, change of address or occupation and health – affected the pattern of instruction. After the frailties of his earliest years – lethargies and fevers, 'a consumptive and dropsical habit', nerves, an eye infection and the bite of a dog suspected of rabies – he was sent at age 7 to a neighbourhood day school in Putney, where he had a 'domestic tutor'. At nine he was transferred to a boarding school at Kingston-upon-Thames and told by his mother that he was 'going into the world, and must learn to think and act for yourself'. There he endured the rod, the despotism of older pupils and the 'rude familiarity of equals'. After two years, his mother died, and her place was taken by a devoted and loving aunt. She, to make ends meet, converted a large house into a boarding annex for Westminster School, which Gibbon attended by day in fits and starts, his illnesses resuming. For the next few years he was moved from location to location and taught by a number of different teachers in different private schools, ending up at Esher in Surrey in the year 1752. He lived with a clergyman who instructed him in classics, but preferred spending his days indulging the pleasures of London. A succession of other teachers and schools followed until suddenly his father broke this arrangement of desultory schooling by a 'singular and desperate measure' and carried him off to Magdalen College, Oxford, before he finished his fifteenth year. 'I arrived at Oxford with a stock of erudition that might have puzzled a doctor, and a degree of ignorance of which a schoolboy would have been ashamed.'[32]

The education proposed in 1790 by the warden of Winchester College for Lord Addington's eldest son provides another good example of the typical pattern of schooling in operation even for the child of a noble family who might have been entered at a public school when reaching age 11. First the boy was sent to Ealing where he was put under the care of his father's old master, Dr Goodenough, later bishop of Carlisle. He was next trundled off to Winchester when the warden suggested his own household for tutoring (but not necessarily by the warden himself). Entry to the

[31] Zena Crook and Brian Simon, 'Private Schools in Leicester and the County 1780–1840', in Simon, *Education in Leicestershire, 1540–1940*, 107–8.
[32] Edward Gibbon, *Memoirs of My Life* (Harmondsworth, 1984), 61–73.

college school would follow when the boy was ready for it. But entering the school did not mean that private tutorial instruction would cease, for some subjects were not offered in the school. At the age of 12 the son was to be given a close companion, a tutor in holy orders who was also 'a gentleman and a scholar to be with him as much as possible. I know the evils arising to young men of that age from associating with servants in their hours of recreation.'[33] Despite these expensive arrangements, he was removed from the school at age 16 because his progress was too rapid. '[It] was thought he had raised himself too high in the school for his age.' He was then sent to reside with the bishop of Gloucester, and in 1803 he went up to Oxford and Christ Church.[34]

Another instance of the mixed pattern of schooling can be gathered from the useful reminiscences of Thomas Mozley born in 1806. He took holy orders and was a leader writer for *The Times*. He also married Cardinal Newman's sister Harriet Elizabeth in 1836. Considered too delicate for boarding school or for the rough and tumble of private establishments, he was sent at the age of 5 to day school in Gainsborough, Lincoln, where several ladies gave instruction. When nearly 12 years of age and residing with his family now in Derby, Thomas went to the private school of the Reverend Mr Edward Higginson, who did not scruple to hide his Unitarian sympathies. 'The school was a necessity of existence, not a pleasure, and he scamped it', wrote Mozley of the supremely undistinguished schoolmaster. (The alternative local grammar school in Derby was then run by an old clerical pluralist and was in a sorry state, as was nearby Repton, later a famous public school.) Higginson had about a dozen boarders from the county, but he allowed Mozley to be taken on as a day boy. At the school he was under orders 'to associate as little with the other day boys as we could help, that is, with certain exceptions. But we were also made fully aware that boys of a lower caste were more likely to be black sheep than professionals or country lads.' From private school he passed on to Charterhouse, at that date still situated in London, and finally he went on to Oriel College, taking a BA in 1828 and becoming a fellow of the college in the next year. His brother James followed a different educational trajectory. He was sent to a local grammar school in Lincoln and then studied with a private tutor who had been an exhibitioner at Brasenose.[35]

---

[33] F. M. L. Thompson, *English Landed Society in the Nineteenth Century* (London, 1963), 85.

[34] *Ibid.*; George Pellew, *The Life and Correspondence of the Right Hon. Henry Addington, First Viscount Sidmouth*, II (London, 1847), 385–7.

[35] Thomas Mozley, *Reminiscences Chiefly of Towns, Villages and Schools*, I (London, 1885), 243–6, 283, 287–9.

The father of John Keble, one of the leaders of the Oxford Movement, kept his son happily at home in the Fairford family parsonage in Gloucestershire until he reached age 15 in 1807, when he matriculated at Corpus Christi College. Young John frittered away his time but surprised companions with a double first when he reached the age of 18.[36]

These examples of the different routes by which university could be reached may well puzzle the inquirer. They are so disconnected, the outcome so uncertain. Much truth exists in the observation that education was not so much regularly acquired as picked up.[37] Missing are all of the elements of institutional interfacing and regularity typical of periods many decades later and especially after the 1860s and 1870s. Parents appear to be hesitant, confused about the next step on the educational ladder, worried about the fate of their offspring away from the parental nest. They are anything but indifferent about what happens outside the home. Letters to headmasters express concerns about health – dancing might be good exercise[38] – social mixing or the range of instruction available at a given school. Parents shop for the appropriate environment for their children and are willing to pay for it. Private, grammar and public schools are compared at the various stages of a child's education, but the stages themselves seem arbitrary. If the school's provision for close supervision is inadequate, schoolmasters or parents specify additional tutorial superintendence.

The preference for some kind of personal instruction goes back to the beginnings of the history of elite education, but its antiquity is of less importance than its purpose. Eighteenth-century parents held firmly to the view that a tutor's functions extended to the education of the whole person, must encompass nurturing and upbringing, moral as well as mental instruction, the physical as well as the intellectual person. To mould the character of the child required authority over him, and so the theory arose that in order to perform this task adequately, a tutor needed to stand as a parent to the child. Within the household itself, however, conflicts were certain to arise over the division of responsibility between actual and surrogate parenting. The tutor was always in danger of being reduced to the status of a domestic, a likelihood that provided some of the impetus behind the private school movement where the tutor could put some distance between himself and employers[39] without, however,

---

[36] Marvin R. O'Connell, *The Oxford Conspirators, A History of the Oxford Movement, 1833–1845* (London and Toronto, 1969), 91.

[37] Crook and Simon, 'Private Schools', 108.

[38] Bod. MS Eng. lett. c.204 (292).

[39] George Chapman, *A Treatise on Education,* 4th ed. (London, 1790), 40–7.

completely abandoning the more intimate relationship typical of household pedagogy.

Advice on schooling continued to be highly subjective well into the
nineteenth century. No clear-cut pattern had yet emerged, and the fitting
of specific ages to particular educational experiences remained a preoccupation. Robert Peel wrote to his old Christ Church tutor, Charles Lloyd
(translated to the see of Oxford in 1827) about educating his young
children and received the following seemingly precise instructions, the
rational basis of which remains a mystery. 'My idea is, that a boy ought not
to go to a *private* school earlier than six, nor later than eight years old – nor
to a public school earlier than eleven, nor later than thirteen [precisely the
opposite of what might be supposed].' In preparation, Lloyd suggested
engaging a young clergyman to take lodgings in the neighbourhood. The
children would be sent to him each morning, but why he was not to come
to the house is unstated.[40] Was Lloyd protecting the young cleric's
independence, since once in the employer's household he could be
mistaken for a servant?

PARENTS AND COLLEGES

What is fascinating about these examples is not the common use of tutors
to provide primary or supplemental instruction while the child was a
'youth' but the extension of the practice throughout the period of the
awkward interval. As far back as the earliest eighteenth century (and very
likely earlier), private tutors accompanied pupils to college as household
representatives and resided within the college walls.[41] The long reach of
parents continued on throughout the century as mothers and fathers
struggled to maintain a familial presence in their son's new and dangerous
life. Almost all noblemen and gentlemen of fortune had private tutors, a
controversialist wrote from Cambridge in 1774, almost always appointed
by parents or guardians or at their request.[42] Critics like Vicesimus Knox,
headmaster of Tonbridge School, thought this was an absolute necessity in
the 1770s. A 'private tutor of character' had to be engaged (if affordable)
'to inspect his pupil not only in the hours of study, but also amusement'.
Overseeing finances was an additional responsibility. '[A] faithful tutor,
who will thus condescend to watch the moral conduct of his pupil will be

[40] British Library Add. MS 40343, ff. 297–8.
[41] A. D. Godley, *Oxford in the Eighteenth Century* (London and New York, 1908), 55.
[42] *A Letter to the Author of an Observation on the Design of Establishing Annual Examinations at
    Cambridge* (?1774), 15. The author is probably the wife of the Cambridge don, John Jebb.

far more desirable than a man of genius and learning, who will only attend to literary improvement.'[43] A cheerful Reginald Heber wrote on the eve of his entry to Brasenose College in 1800 that he was to have a private tutor. 'It is, I believe, principally a contrivance to keep me out of drinking parties, and to give me the advantage of reading to another person instead of to myself.'[44] Mr Smith (or Smythe) proved to be a successful private tutor who sent Reginald's father reports of his son's progress, attitude and disposition.[45]

The correspondence with parents and third parties maintained by John Cooke during his long tenure as president of Corpus Christi College is an invaluable source for understanding how the irregular patterns of schooling affected teaching. Cooke continually received requests from parents or their factors for tutors of suitable character and attainments. Occasionally he was asked whether the college's senior tutor himself was available for extra work. Cooke appears to have regarded such requests as entirely proper. A parent writing in 1785 heard that a private tutor should be employed in the Long Vac. French could be studied, useful in 'polite circles'.[46] On one occasion Cooke replied to a mother anxious about her dull son that a private tutor was useful for guaranteeing that a pupil was diligent and well-conducted because he would 'require from him a daily specimen of his progress and improvement'. The mother speculated that only relevant studies should be undertaken, such as English composition, history and geography, possibly public lectures could be attended in law, natural and experimental philosophy.[47] In 1812 a Magdalen demy, after a flirtation with Roman Catholicsm that left family and college distraught, requested a private tutor 'as the best means of making up for lost time'. The clergyman chosen to attend the repentant student was described as a safe companion, a steady guide, a close observer, 'in the best acceptation of the Term, to be what Russell was at Corpus, & William Scott of University College, in my day'.[48] A father in Lincolnshire, regretting that no exhibition was available for his son at Corpus, was leaning towards Worcester, but only if a certain uncommonly clever and able tutor remained.[49]

Some years earlier Cooke had heard from Provost Eveleigh of Oriel

---

[43] Knox, *Liberal Education*, II, 87–8.
[44] Amelia Shipley Heber, *The Life of Reginald Heber*, I (London, 1830), 20.
[45] Bod. MSS Eng. lett. c.204 (201), 26 May 1801.
[46] Corpus Christi College (henceforth CCC) B/14/51 (6 June 1785).
[47] CCC B/14/51 (28 April 1789).
[48] Magdalen College Oxford MS 465, H. Waldo-Sibthorpe to Martin Routh (1 April 1812).
[49] Magdalen College MS 475 (V), f. 20 (30 June 1813).

about a 19-year-old who hoped to enter Corpus as a gentleman-commoner. His education was sadly neglected because of ill health and a 'disinclination in his parents to permit him, as an only child, to go far from them'. His conduct, however, was modest, and he was 'manageable'. Eveleigh hoped that one of the Corpus tutors would take him on in a private capacity and 'thus be better acquainted with his attainments & abilities, & will know what he may expect from him in public or in company with others'.[50] In 1810 he heard from a father who wished 'to procure a private Tutorship for the time . . . [my son] is obliged to reside at Corpus. – My principal objects in this are to give him a stimulus to his studies, & that he may gain some proficiency in that line of life, to which he is in future destined.'[51] Seven years later Cooke considered a request from a parent for the name of a tutor who would inculcate 'Church of England Principles, Loyal Sentiments, the manners of a Gentleman & the cultivating of his heart as well as his mind'.[52] In 1818, in explaining the college accounts of her son to Lady Berkeley, he remarked soothingly that the extra amounts for private tuition were 'not unusual'..For 'Gentlemen of Mr. Berkeley's expectations in Life, and Situation to [have] . . . some young men of the College [selected] to attend & assist him in his private hours of reading, independent of the general Collegiate charges of Public Instruction', was perfectly routine.[53]

We have long known that there was a flourishing traffic in private instruction at the ancient universities and especially in subjects that neither professors nor college lecturers were required by statute to provide, but official tutors also practised on the side, as it were, and provided supplemental instruction for payment. Newman, in his quarrel with Provost Hawkins over pupilmongering, argued that coaching was necessary for honours. 'Oriel men ceased to take high honours, when the Tutors ceased to take private pupils.'[54] Remedial teaching was an especially vital function. The colleges admitted fee-paying pensioners and commoners nearly at will, and they were often ill-prepared for university-level work. In 1808 Cooke informed one inquirer that a comprehension of school classics and a certain facility in composition were prerequisite to entry as a gentleman-commoner, yet he does not appear to have bothered overly much about the accomplishments of prospective matriculands.

It is clear that authorities at both universities encouraged the use of private teachers as a temporary solution to the shortage of suitable

50 CCC B/14/5/3 (1 September 1806).   51 CCC B/14/5/2 (1 February 1810).
52 CCC B/14/5/3 (5 April 1817).   53 CCC B/14/5/3 (May 1818).
54 Oriel College, Library, Newman to Hawkins, 29 April 1830.

teaching positions within colleges. It was also a way of soothing the nerves
of tremulous parents worried about a son's development when away
from home. Also, since many undergraduates left after a year or two, an
exclusive concern with main-line teaching leading to a degree was not
altogether necessary. In such a situation private instruction was in great
demand, a product to be purchased by the consumer for his own uses and
satisfaction.

But private teaching was acceptable only as long as it supplemented the
existing programme of studies or provided a service not otherwise readily
available in a college. Problems were certain to arise if the attractions of
private teaching interfered with the normal state of college business. This
actually began to happen at Cambridge in the last decades of the
eighteenth century. The establishment of the mathematical tripos was an
unexpected windfall for underemployed fellows in search of income. It led
to a great increase in the numbers of coaches preparing students for the
Senate House examinations. But by employing coaches, degree-bound
students were being forced to pay twice for their university education,
and this was troubling to parents and college leaders alike. Cambridge
authorities attempted to stifle the trade in 1777 and 1781. They were
unsuccessful because of the growing importance of the tripos and the
failure of colleges to anticipate the demand for appropriate teaching.[55]

Admission to college was an understandable concern of parents,
especially where a specific college was preferred. No study of Oxbridge
admissions has ever been undertaken that clarifies how decisions were
made. We do not know who or which category of entrant was refused
admission or what the grounds of refusal were. We cannot be absolutely
certain how resistant to parental pressure the numerous small societies of
Oxford and Cambridge actually were. As with so many other features
of the unreformed colleges, we can surmise that customs and practices
varied greatly by college and period, that fee-paying undergraduates
found entry fairly easy, if not always at a college of choice, and that
foundationers experienced a variety of tests, with considerable discretion
remaining to the colleges within the framework of close awards and
college patronage.

From the college's perspective, an admissions interview could be
critical, especially in the case of scholarships which so often led directly to
fellowships. Summoning a scholarship candidate to college afforded
the society a chance to form an immediate impression of the potential

[55] John Gascoigne, 'Mathematics and Meritocracy: The Emergence of the Cambridge
Mathematical Tripos', *Social Studies of Science*, 14 (1984), 555.

undergraduate's character and behaviour and gave the fellows an opportunity to see how he might comport himself once in residence. Colleges had an obvious self-interest in making their initial selection of scholars reasonably careful. Once chosen, a young man was likely to be around for many years; it was important to ascertain whether or not he would join the ranks of the idle.

College statutes usually limited the number of scholarship holders who could be carried on the foundation, or restricted the entry of high-paying fellow-commoners, gentleman-commoners and noblemen. Advance planning was therefore required to ascertain whether vacancies would be available down the line. Families might also need time to prepare a son for departure from home. The final two years or so of schooling could be carefully scheduled and 'ego dangers' avoided.

In 1784 Cooke heard from a Somerset parent with a 14-year-old son who was too young to be entered for a Somerset close scholarship. The parent was actually a former fellow of Corpus. His son had been educated in Somerset with a concentration on translations but for the last seven months had been learning composition at Exeter Grammar. Cooke did not think age 14 was a bar; but years later in 1802 he agreed with a parent from Wells who proposed keeping his son at school for another year (or having him tutored) so that he could better compete for an award at another college.[56] In 1790 a parent asked for deferred admission so that his son could continue to reside with his old schoolmaster. He would gain additional instruction, but, equally important, he would become 'steadier' and therefore join a 'larger circle' when he did come up.[57]

Cooke kept a personal memorandum book, 'my private Booke' as he referred to it, in which he entered the names of prospective gentleman-commoners in the event of vacancies since only six places at Corpus were reserved for them by statute. Third-party intervention came into play. On 2 October 1802 a letter arrived from a tutor in Hackney who described a young man under his tutelage as heir to a considerable estate. His parents being dead, his 'guardian is anxious that he should be entered at a College where he might form good connections'. Though not much of a scholar, 'his rank in life requires a good introduction'. The clincher, given the notorious collegiate behaviour of sons of the rich, was that the young man was a 'docile, regular, & well disposed youth'. To establish his own credentials, the Hackney tutor mentioned that he was acquainted with a member of the president's family and once taught a pupil known to him.[58]

---

[56] CCC B/14/5/2 (7 July 1802).
[57] CCC B/14/51 (16 August 1784) and (13 April 1790).   [58] CCC B/14/5/2 (2 October 1802).

Personal recommendations were necessary for a number of obvious reasons, but one of them was to receive some prior intelligence of the nature of an undergraduate's preparation in an age where standardisation was far off. The bishop of Rochester wrote in 1817 on behalf of two young men seeking entry as gentleman-commoners. The first was the son of a Worcestershire gentleman, but the second was his own nephew. Cooke replied that the first could not be accommodated when he wanted to come, but the nephew would be admitted early in 1819 as requested, 'and, by your consent, [I] will enter the name in my private Booke; which from the lively sense we all entertain of your Lordship's late kindness to us, I doubt not will be considered by the College as a Solemn engagement to be performed in whatever hands the appointment may then be lodged' (a reference to Cooke's advanced age).[59] The Reverend Mr Bradford wrote concerning an Irish gentleman who sought room for his son in the gentlemen-commoners' building for Michaelmas Term 1819. 'I know that you are very select in your Society at Corpus & do not admit every Young Man who offers himself.' The founders provided few places. All being filled, Cooke promised to enter 'his name in my private book for succeeding in the first vacancy after my present engagements are fulfilled'. He added: 'More I cannot do.'[60]

The numerous admissions categories, awards structures and legal entanglements of the unreformed colleges as to undergraduate eligibility created a thicket of exemptions, strategies and special programmes of study. Parental anxieties, whether expressed directly to college authorities or through third parties, are continually evident: the right college, the right friends, the right prospects, the best chance for obtaining recognition or a secure habitat – these considerations permeate college correspondence from the end of the eighteenth century through the Napoleonic wars. Some undergraduates came to Oxford and Cambridge without an intention to pursue the principal studies of the universities. Cooke even assured a parent in 1789 that classical literature was not the only means of forming gentlemen and men of real worth.[61] A former tutor of Magdalen College recalled that when he was a tutor there was a formal entrance examination, 'and so it was when I matriculated at University. Nobody was refused, whatever might be the character of his ignorance.'[62] For students carried on the foundations and those eligible for eleemosynary awards – scholars, 'students' (Christ Church), Bible and choral scholars,

[59] CCC B/14/5/3 (17 July 1817).   [60] CCC B/14/5/3 (2 May and 5 May 1818).
[61] CCC (28 April 1789).
[62] Francis A. Faber to Martin Routh, Magdalen College MS 474, f. 86 (n.d.).

exhibitioners, sizars, servitors and those eligible for bursaries and demyships – the process of admission was both more stringent or constrained by the terms of the endowment. The procedure varied. At King's College, the provost himself admitted the scholars, who by statute were all Etonians. No commoners were admitted. At Corpus, as the president explained to an inquirer in 1821, 'The statutes do not describe any particular mode of examination.'[63] However, the custom was for seven fellows and the president to examine candidates by themselves, asking questions based on texts used in the grammar and public schools, a procedure possibly biased against the many private schools without university connections, or at least one (successful) candidate so thought.[64] (If true, we have an explanation for why parents sometimes rotated their children to an established school in search of last-minute, sixth-form-style cramming.) Unseen translations were also required, but the emphasis was on prose and verse Latin composition, and these were indeed emphasised in the greatest of the public schools.[65]

In 1808 Cooke told a correspondent that the scholarship examination was 'very strict', and in another letter he tried to explain to a parent that the president could not possibly dictate to the electors. Yet in 1803 he may have committed himself to the award of a scholarship or exhibition (probably the latter) to the son of a clergyman in desperate straits without requiring an examination. The text of the letter, however, is ambiguous.[66]

The successful formula for attempting to influence admissions decisions from the outside was some combination of the following: respectable family (or relatives of former college members), numerous children, moderate income, intention to pursue a clerical career, special circumstances (illness or misfortune). Here is Thomas Arnold, who had been an undergraduate at Corpus, writing in 1819 about the son of 'a great Friend of mine . . . heir to a considerable Property tho' his present Income is very moderate, and any thing which would assist him in the Education of his children, five in Number, would be of great consequence to him'. The son was disqualified by place of birth (London) from most of the Foundations in Oxford. Cooke's reply was that he hoped he would live long enough to assist this worthy family.[67]

Another third-party intervention occurred in 1808 when a parish priest wrote to the president on behalf of his curate's son, who was at Tiverton

[63] CCC B/14/51 (28 April 1789).   [64] CCC B/14/5/2 (14 September 1803).
[65] Wallbank, 'Public Schools', 13.
[66] CCC B/14/5/3 (5 January 1808); B/14/5/2 (14 December 1803).
[67] CCC B/14/5/3 (24 June 1819 and 28 June 1819).

School in Devon. Alas, the youth was no match for a Winchester competitor in the scholarship race, but he could manage at college with only an exhibition. Cooke answered that while no vacancies existed at present, he would add the candidate's name to his waiting list, just after 'two names ... who as old members of the College I sh'd be glad to oblige in their turn'.[68] The two declined the offer, and the worthy Tiverton youth received his exhibition some months later. In 1821, however, Cooke found himself unable to accommodate a similar request, refusing to consider a young man some two to three years away from admission because of a shortage of rooms in college.

Similar patterns of third-party advocacy appear in the correspondence of yet another venerable college head, the courteous yet forceful and remarkably ancient Martin Routh, who was president of Magdalen from 1791 to 1854. A clergyman's son sought admission to Magdalen, his credentials unknown because he had been at school in the north for the past four years. Could the college give the intermediary a 'Hint as to ... [the] State of Things'. The request is followed by an apology, a hope that an inquiry will not be taken amiss. 'The anxiety of Fathers and Mothers sometimes gives their Requests the appearance of Selfishness and Intrusion; and we must pardon them if we can.'[69] In 1810 Routh heard from a member of the college that Dr Storer of Nottingham had a son, 'exemplarily moral & respectable, qualities which cannot be made known to the electors in a classical examination, but which would influence them in making their choice'. Since the son was a candidate for the demyship, 'I hope it will not be deemed presumptuous in me to put you in possession of this information.'[70]

Of the four exhibitions at Corpus, two were in the gift of the president and two disposed of jointly with the bursar. 'There will be an opening next year', Cooke answered a correspondent in 1817, 'but it is promised to a friend of the College Bursar'.[71]

And so the style continues, right up through the first half of the nineteenth century: requests to take account of special circumstances in the granting of awards, reminders of worthy moral character and excellent family, descriptions of schooling and preparation. In 1843 Routh, now a veritable Methuselah, was informed about the youngest son of a very poor but very worthy clerical friend who desired to be a chorister. The clergyman, socially well-connected, 'has brought up seven children upon two hundred a year – his nephew the present Earl will do nothing

[68] CCC B/14/5/3 (22 August 1808). [69] Magdalen College MS 475 (V), f.20 (26 May 1793).
[70] Magdalen College MS 474, f.22 (21 May 1801). [71] CCC B/14/5/3 (20 November 1817).

for him'. The story has a happy ending. The pathetic Mr. Erskine's son was made a chorister but refused the award when Gladstone offered him something better.[72]

While colleges might sometimes hide behind statutes, which specified numbers and types of entry, they could not always hide behind the 'objective' criteria of competitive entry. Nor did they always wish to, for they thought of themselves as elitist but not meritocratic. The universities had to remain accessible to those who by origins and destination could make use of them. This was the main consideration.

A highly flexible college admissions policy, one that allowed for personal considerations and was amenable to advance planning, was exactly suited to a child-rearing philosophy that was more concerned with overall development than with hothouse forcing. If a child appeared ready for university, or if surrogate parenting could be guaranteed, he might be released from the home early, but otherwise it was best to let the child stretch out the years of the awkward interval. Intellectual precocity in fact had to be watched, for the earlier the child was released from home, the more parents experienced doubts about companions and judgement.

It was not that eighteenth-century parents regarded precocity as unnatural. *Tabula rasa* epistemology declared the opposite. Since the mind was almost immediately formed at birth, it was perfectly normal to expect quick results from a carefully constructed educational scheme. We hear no outcry over premature learning comparable to what a late Victorian might utter. A century of scientific discussion, a belief in stages of growth, social as well as intellectual, and the virtual confinement of instruction to the formal classroom would produce firmer – one is almost inclined to say 'dogmatic' – views on the nature of the life cycle. 'The biological truth cannot be too often repeated that, the higher the order of the creature, the slower, as a rule, is its progress towards maturity, and . . . any attempt to hasten adolescence is a sin against nature, often ending in mental atrophy, and even more serious physical and moral consequences.'[73] These are Victorian, even Darwinian, fears generated by the movement of the public schools to a central place in elite education, worries about the close action of the boys upon one another and the adverse effects of intimacy and sexual aggression. The casual, free-wheeling, uncoordinated, wild guessing about the nature of youth typical of an earlier period is missing. To be sure, epistolary and picaresque novels of the eighteenth century continually raised the issue of sexual transgressions, and such a worry

---

[72] Magdalen College MS 472 (9 January 1843 and 16 February 1843).
[73] H. B. Gray, *The Public Schools and the Empire* (London, 1913), 212.

was probably in the minds of parents of modest circumstances; but the educational problem in 1800 was not so much physiological development as health and the child's lack of experience in the ways of the world. A 'Mama's child' was the subject of correspondence in 1796. The family was wealthy, the son was educated at Hackney School 'under the immediate eye of his parents'. Would Corpus please avoid giving him a damp ground floor room?[74]

Fitting in safely in every sense: this was the principal reason for the odd pattern of schooling, for picking and choosing experiences, for rotating the child around according to his presumed educational needs and for trying to assure a smooth transition from a period of schooling into college. Perhaps that is a major reason why the median age of entry to universities rose about a year in the eighteenth century, and the percentage of 16-year-olds plumetted. The closer in age of the youth to the upward limit of the awkward interval, the greater the chance he would escape the threats and lurking evils of the dangerous years. This was at least a hope, but a parent could never be certain exactly when the endpoint was reached since the period of being a 'youth' was so protracted. A tutor at Brasenose received a third-party plea in 1828 for help in teaching an undergraduate how to select acquaintances and guide his habits as 'the Means of forming the future Man'.[75]

Fictional tales of the period amplified parental fears by drawing the portrait of an honest, simple, God-fearing family whose son proves to be a wastrel and dissolute. Once at university he becomes self-conscious about his clothes, his hair, his inferior social status. He runs up huge debts, and his tutor, instead of providing a model of restraint, encourages the youth in further dissipation. But maybe the worst has been avoided. At least orthodoxy is not in jeopardy. 'Nobody can accuse you of unitarianism, arianism, or any other *ism* but epicurism, puppyism, and jockeyism.'[76] The needed insurance was the willingness of the colleges to cooperate in a system of close surveillance involving private tutors, who might be unengaged fellows but all the more useful for that, and the much-despised college servants, bedmakers foremost.

---

[74] CCC B/14/51 (18 June ?1796). Substandard accommodation was always a difficulty. A student at Wadham in 1839 wrote to his mother about one 'Conybeare [who] is put into rooms worse than the black hole, or a Venetian under-water prison cell . . . where there is no fire place, and even the bed is damp. The dean will give him no redress.' Bodleian Library, Maclaine MSS, 26 November 1839.

[75] Brasenose College B4C.1 (3 November 1828).

[76] Vicesimus Knox, *Winter Evenings; or, Lucubrations on Life and Letters*, 3rd ed., I (London, 1795), 300–13.

LIBERTY?

Undergraduates, on the other hand, regarded college entry as the essential transition from parental regulation to freedom. And we can examine this response from several perspectives, beginning with the history of corporal punishment, a highly significant yet confusing symbol of age status. The unreformed statutes of colleges were based on the supposition that under-graduates were mainly or essentially schoolboys, irrespective of their actual ages. Physical punishment was statutorily permitted at Oxford even if undergraduates were 18 or even 20 years of age since they were still in the awkward interval. At Cambridge the statutes of Caius College permitted birching for undergraduates under 18, while at Trinity College undergraduates were eligible to receive the rod on Thursday nights in the presence of all junior members of the college.[77] Possibly 18 was chosen as the dividing line between youth and maturity because the average age at entry was lower until the eighteenth century. The colleges were accustomed to matriculands who were boys not men.

To put corporal punishment into a larger context as part of the life cycle, we need for a moment to go back in time to the middle ages. 'Among the personifications of the Seven Arts which adorn the front of Chartres Cathedral', writes Hastings Rashdall, 'grammar alone carries the rod'.[78] Where whippings occured at medieval Oxford colleges, Queen's and Magdalen for example, they were administered to pupils who were either receiving instruction considered to be of grammar school level or attending such schools associated with colleges. It was the very young who were struck.[79]

This practice was nearly reversed (or just extended) in the early modern period. Older students were now candidates for physical edification, as the revised college statutes indicate. 'The sixteenth century was the flogging age *par excellence*', wrote Rashdall.[80] He connected the increase in corporal punishment with the rise of colleges to a central place in the universities. The creation of scholarships associated with particular foundations not unnaturally produced a desire to protect endowments against youthful misuse of them; and the difficulty of selectively enforcing a code of conduct led to a uniform set of disciplinary regulations for scholars and commoners who began to invade the societies. The more substantial scale,

---

[77] W. A. Pantin, *Oxford Life in Oxford Archives* (Oxford, 1972), 62; George Peacock, *Observations on the Statutes of the University of Cambridge* (London, 1841), 3n and 4n.
[78] Hastings Rashdall, *The Universities of Europe in the Middle Ages*, III (Oxford, 1936), 358, 358n.
[79] *Ibid.*, 370–1.
[80] *Ibid.*, 362, 371.

construction and accommodations of the colleges made discipline easier to effect than in the decrepit halls or boarding houses set amidst teeming city streets. The building of collegiate gardens and courts provided internal recreation space that reduced the necessity for students to wander off, an essential historical prerequisite, in any case, for summoning the guardians of place to college. Collegiate espionage was now encouraged.[81] It is also possible that the increase in corporal punishment for older adolescents was related to the great influx of sons from noble and gentry families and the beginning of the syndrome of high living, lavish entertainment and the pursuit of secular interests that accompanied the importation of courtly values from the Continent. It may well have been felt that young men not conspicuously intended for clerical occupations and lacking this incentive for self-restraint might require a different form of discipline than commonly employed. However that may be, the result of the early modern transformation of the social values of the colleges had a profound effect on the relations between teacher and taught. The gap perforce widened.

Yet no undergraduate was actually flogged at Oxford and Cambridge in the late Enlightenment. 'Impositions' (additional written assignments), 'gating' (restriction to college) and 'rustication' (temporary suspension) were more humane substitutes. (In a celebrated remark, Dr Johnson disagreed. Punishment ought to be immediate, swift and terminal, otherwise the victim was continually visited with remorse and guilt. Michel Foucault agreed.) The ultimate sanction was the threat of expulsion, severance from the community responsible for conducting youth through the final phase of the adolescent youth cycle. He was then returned to the humiliation of domestic obedience. Corporal punishment, even arbitrary corporal punishment, was a function of schools. Mozley recalled a nervous schoolmaster who was never fully clothed without a stick twitching in his hand. It was his unfortunate duty to thrash non-stop, either for some petty infraction – a mistake in addition, a grammatical slip – or for the principle itself. Mozley was led to reflect that 'The cane is personal . . . It becomes part of the man; it is his sting, his tusk, his horn . . . A schoolmaster is lost without his ferule.'[82] What might be put down to sadism, frustration and even to self-defence, given the appetite of

---

[81] *Ibid.*, 364–6.
[82] Mozley, *Reminiscences*, I, 288. Dr Johnson approved of the rod because (like hanging) it was decisive, a self-contained act, over and done with. Other mechanisms for discipline such as guilt, ambition and emulation had undesirable lasting effects and 'lay the foundation of lasting mischief'. James Boswell, *The Journal of a Tour to the Hebrides* (Boston, 1965), 177. First published 1785.

wealthy boys for destruction,[83] Philippe Ariès explains as a shift from the principle of punishment as corrective discipline to a rite of passage, a method of instilling self-control which is the cultural state separating boyhood from manhood.[84] If he is correct, entrance to a college and matriculation at the university were indeed dividing lines for the student formerly at school, the signal for his movement to a new state of independence and self-reliance, the lifting of a former condition of nonage, servitude and degradation.[85]

Certainly the new-found pleasure of a room of one's own added to the sense of liberation. The negotiation of unfamiliar territory is part of the ritual of passing from one life stage to another.[86] While the domestic circle of country and urban professional families drew emotionally closer, as reflected architecturally in larger private quarters and less public space for visitors and entertaining, the great boarding schools were frozen into an earlier and wholly different conception of socialisation. Typically, instruction took place in two very large schoolrooms, an upper and a lower school. Boys sat in groups and worked individually in pairs, while masters surveyed the vast chamber from strategically located high desks. This arrangement of space inhibited lecturing or catechetical teaching. Boys were instead summoned forward to recite or construe where they could be publicly shamed. Dining and sleeping arrangements were similarly

---

[83] Examples are legion and appear in the standard works on public schools as well as in biographies. The practice of 'barring out', mentioned by Samuel Johnson in his *Life of Addison*, continued throughout the eighteenth century. Boys would take over school buildings and barricade themselves within. Rugby pupils blew off a door with a petard in 1797, and soldiers were called in to subdue them. Several years earlier Wykehamists armed with missiles and swords captured the school and hoisted the red cap of liberty. Winchester blew up again in 1818, and troops were needed. At Harrow in 1805 the boys violently demonstrated over a decision not to appoint the second master to a headship. A trail of gunpowder laid down in a passage through which the new master was to pass was considered the work of Lord Byron. A second outbreak occurred in 1808. Eton had a rebellion in 1768 and a famous one in 1818. These were but the more explosive manifestations of schoolboy potential for violence. Parents were all familiar with routine bullying, tossings in blankets, sexual abuse, exposure of very young boys to inclement conditions, marrings of the flesh, assaults on farmers and shopkeepers, the terrorising of stagecoach passengers. John Chandos, *Boys at School* (London, 1984), provides examples and an interesting, if odd, defence. See also W. L. Burn, *The Age of Equipoise* (London, 1964), 66–7; Mozley, *Reminiscences*, I, 399; Edward C. Mack, *Public Schools and British Opinion, 1780–1860* (London, 1938) and house histories of schools.

[84] Ariès, *Childhood*, 265.

[85] As sixth-form education became standard in English schooling in the nineteenth century, the emancipation of pupils from dependency began when the older or senior boys were detached from juniors and given the right to apply corporal punishment. Thomas Arnold at Rugby was one of the first headmasters to appreciate the uses of surrogate authority in this way, drawing the older boys into his inner circle of governance.

[86] Thomas A. Leemon, *The Rites of Passage in a Student Culture* (New York, 1972).

communal, with little privacy or self-government by boys but ample opportunity for them to inflict harm upon one another.[87] The university's provision of freedom for boarding-school pupils and for those whose pattern of preparatory education had been different, less school-bound and more individual, was symbolised by the Cambridge matriculation ceremony. It was a rite of passage ending one stage of personal development and commencing another. After the division of term, or on the following day, the Registrary gave public notice of the time. Proctors wore their hoods squared. The persons to be matriculated wrote their names in the Registrary's book and appeared in the Senate House. A copy of the Matriculation Oath in Latin being given to each, a fellow-commoner was chosen to go first. A grace in Latin was subjoined. The senior proctor then administered the oath to other fellow-commoners, and they in turn were followed by pensioners and sizars in that order. Noblemen underwent a different procedure marking their higher social standing.[88]

The separate space, the public location, gowns, the authority of university officials and some three lines of a special language recalling the university's particular past were compressed into a few solemn moments. Together they possessed what one modern author has called the effective simplicity of ritual. Great meaning is instantly and unambiguously captured and communicated.[89] The confused and weighty process of destroying the past, of breaking from the home and renouncing childhood while anticipating a future of independence, learning how to handle expenses and apportioning time between learning and play was concentrated in a brief, colourful act of ritual deliverance, followed by the peculiar advantages of college residence.

Such, at least, is suggested by the joyous outcries of undergraduates released from home or school irrespective of age. At age 15 Gibbon announced that he was suddenly raised from a boy to a man. Removed from Magdalen by his father for flirting with Roman Catholicism, he was dispatched to Protestant Lausanne and put under strict regulation. The process of emancipation was reversed, and he was 'degraded to the dependence of a school-boy'.[90] Remarked an undergraduate of a later period, 'Just emancipated from the slavery of birch at Harrow, I was

[87] Seaborne, 'Architecture', 178–9.
[88] Adam Wall, *The Ceremonies Observed in the Senate-House of the University of Cambridge, with the forms of proceeding to all degrees, the manner of electing officers, tables of fees, etc.* (1798). A new edition by Henry Gunning (Cambridge, 1828), 61.
[89] Paul Fussell, *The Great War and Modern Memory* (New York, 1977), 131.
[90] Gibbon, *Memoirs*, 93.

plunging into the unrestrained liberty of college life.'[91] George Colman the Younger came up to Christ Church from Westminster in 1780 at age 18. His first act was to embrace the symbols of emancipation and flout authority. '[The] hand of Time was forestall'd by the fingers of the Barber: and an english [*sic*] stripling, with his hair flowing over his shoulders, was, in the course of half an hour, metamorphosed into a man, by means of powder, pomatum, the comb, the curling irons, and a bit of black ribbon to make a pigtail.' As Colman knew, university statutes specified a more sober aspect, but no one called him down for tonsorial extravagance. 'No character is more jealous of the "Dignity of Man"', he added, 'than a lad who has just escaped from School-birch to College discipline'.[92] At the end of 1837 a Wadham undergraduate wrote to his parents that 'T'is pleasant to think I am no longer a school-boy. I shall be able to hold up my head and waltz with good grace at Mrs. Tonge's.'[93] Advice books picked up the same theme in the next decade.

> You have passed now, by a journey from home to the university, at one step, from boyhood to manhood. You were an Eton boy, you are now an Oxford man . . . You have committed your last *freak*; for freaks will now be follies, and your follies will be grave errors in judgment, or something worse.[94]

Many parents, suggested another writer, did not understand that undergraduates of 19 or 20 were no longer schoolboys. 'John is no longer Jackey but a gentleman – no more a Master but a Mister.'[95] And on the same note from another corner of advice just a few years later: 'Men at the University will not submit to be snubbed and "floored", like boys at school.' Perhaps not, but suppose they fail to understand the higher calling of their situation? Then we fall back upon a trusted alternative, the 'friendly advice and correction of a Private Tutor'.[96]

There was also the unfriendly advice and correction of an elder brother. In the 1840s Richard Wilton at Cambridge received an angry letter from his clergyman brother, Edward, seven years his senior, admonishing him for his air of self-satisfaction, superiority and attention-getting. He contrasted his younger brother's passage through university with his own

[91] Clement Carlyon, *Early Years and Late Reflections*, III (London, 1856), 28.
[92] L. M. Quiller-Couch, *Reminiscences of Oxford by Oxford Men* (Oxford, 1892), 168–70.
[93] Wadham College, Maclaine MSS (9 December 1837).
[94] Charles Clarke, *Letters to an Undergraduate of Oxford* (London, 1848), 1–2.
[95] [John M. F. Wright], *Alma Mater*, II (London, 1827), 140.
[96] D. J. Vaughan (of Trinity College, Cambridge), *A Few Words about Private Tuition* (Cambridge, 1852), 8. Emancipation from school as allowing an advance into manhood is mentioned in *The Oxford University Magazine* (1834), 101, and *The Public Right to the Universities, by a University Man* (London, 1851), 25.

career struggles. 'I pursued a solitary and unaided course, and I needed all the *helps forward* [*sic*] I could gather from my own resources.' His younger brother, on the other hand, yet 'barely twelve months escaped from what the law deems infancy', guided by 'tutors and governors . . . [and] almost entirely dependent on his father for subsistence', had an easy ride. He urged modesty and simplicity, reminded Richard that his 'own unaided energy would never have raised you from the obscurity to which you were destined', and pounded home the lesson in this way: 'a *man!* . . . I hold that no one deserves the name of man who does not support himself and household and who does not contribute something to the common stock, whether that contribution be material or intellectual.'[97]

Many college dons and former fellows repeated the conventional wisdom that a university experience was decisive for reaching maturity. But at the same moment fears of what the sudden transition might entail also led to expressions of hesitation, qualification and warning. You only 'fancy' yourself a '*Man*', yet another advice book of 1848 admonishes an undergraduate (much in the spirit of Edward Wilton), but you are only 'conventionally and by courtesy a *Man*', and the essential modifier follows: 'that is a youth, *adolescens,* an inchoate and promissory man'.[98]

Combatting the effects of a university environment filled with the signs and emblems of privilege and inferiority could not be simple. Costume was an instant rating system. Gowns at the ancient colleges reflected the *Stände* of a rank order society, although wealth was virtually as important as birth in determining university status. Fellow-commoners at Cambridge and gentlemen-commoners at Oxford bought their signs of social superiority. But Colman's dress, or Shelley's appearance, were not reflections of social hierarchies but expressions of personal, even defiant taste. For some time college authorities had expressed their irritation at breakaway costuming, but controversy broke out afresh during some half-dozen years after 1812 at Trinity College, Cambridge. The master and seniors tried to prevent undergraduates from substituting the wearing of trousers for breeches in hall or chapel, but trousers won out.[99]

In truth, the rite of passage for all but the wealthiest students was illusory or confused. The arithmetic of servants to call upon, dress, university slang and association with the fast set of bucks and pickles added up to a promise that a new life was beginning and the awkward

[97] Mary Blamire Young, *Richard Wilton, A Forgotten Victorian* (London, 1967), 74.
[98] Charles Daman, *Ten Letters Introductory to College Residence, by a Tutor* (Oxford, 1828), 7.
[99] Robert Robson, 'Trinity College in the Age of Peel', in *Ideas and Institutions of Victorian Britain*, ed. Robert Robson (London, 1967), 328.

interval coming to an end. It was supposed to be the start of an adventure defined by trust and emancipation, yet innumerable ambivalences about the meaning of freedom remained. Constraints on upbringing rooted in the assumptions of a prior century lingered on, captured in the assumptions of growth psychology that insisted upon the impossible task of defining the stages of a life cycle. Families of leisure and income found means for prolonging dependency until the upward edge of the awkward interval was reached, unless, as in the case of parents who brought their 15-year-olds to university, no other alternative seemed so useful for reaching the end of a phase in the life cycle. The point is that they retained their options and reserved the right to be the final authority on all matters pertaining to the upbringing and education of children.

Since life-cycle phases had become entangled with institutional considerations and rites of passage, they could not be readily disregarded, nor can we say that institutional interfacings with culture are ever easy to disconnect when complex systems of financing, teaching, legal considerations and career preparation result from them. Yet in the early nineteenth century other possiblities were glimpsed that provided individual if not institutional solutions to the problem of the life cycle. Newman, for example, consistent with his understanding of experience and growth, replaced a mechanical or legal compartmentalisation of growth with a more problematical view of human development. In 1822, the year he was elected to a fellowship at Oriel, he turned 21 and confided to his diary that he could no longer call himself a boy. 'Today I am of age. It is an awful crisis.' Yet thinking his way through the meaning of the legal beginning of maturity, he noted that the words 'being of age' falsely conveyed the idea of a 'sudden and unknown change'. The reality was 'slow and silent progress'.[100] Reflection on its meaning was far more important than liberation from a state of subjection. However much he deplored the self-interest philosophy of his age, Newman's reflections on liberty are closer to the ethics of Victorian liberal individualism than to Enlightenment precepts of freedom. Instead of promising liberty, maturity entailed additional responsibilities. This was a solution that Thomas Arnold was applying at Rugby School at exactly the same time, converting the senior boys into moral examples for the younger to follow.

The system of university discipline was divided between insisting on liberty as a prerequisite to maturity and regarding pupils as 'not entirely

[100] Maisie Ward, *Young Mr. Newman* (London, 1948), 65. Later Newman considered university residence to be a transition period. See Fergal McGrath, *Newman's University, Idea and Reality* (London, 1951), 339.

set free from the leading-strings of the school', as a Corpus contemporary of Thomas Arnold remembered.[101] Many of the learning techniques employed at school were still in use: *viva voce* renderings and translations where precision was insisted upon, question and answer sessions in lecture – the oral, public culture of the eighteenth century. The college 'constitution' as contemporaries might term it contained restrictions and requirements, duties and responsibilities, time-tables and assignments peculiar to itself, and it was becoming more constraining not less, more subtle surely. The new ideal form of guidance was enunciated at the turn of the century in an epitaph placed in the ante-chapel of Trinity College, Cambridge, to honour a sometime tutor:

> The wild unbroken boy he led, not drove,
> And changed coercion for paternal love.
> By mildness won, youth found resistance vain,
> Bound in a silken, yet a snapless chain.[102]

Kindly but firm, understanding but unyielding, generous but within limits. This sounds 'modern' and familiar, but it lacks a nuance. The view is from the tutor. He notices that youths want to break away. He agrees that they must, otherwise how can self-reliance be learnt during conditions of widespread changes in religious feeling, politics and family life? But he will be steadfast and alert. However, what if the tutor himself is subject to the same temptations and pressures as students and also wishes to break away? How can a necessary university discipline be maintained when all parties, those in authority and those subject to it, are chafing at the bit? A busier culture was distracting teachers, who then sent double messages to already perplexed students. Heber noticed an important change in the habits of dons when he visited Oxford in 1818. He concluded that the tutors at Brasenose in his day were different from their predecessors. The 'old boys' never left the place, while the new generation 'pass their whole vacations on the continent, are geologists, systemongers, and I know not what'.[103]

Newman, as a high-minded don, reflected on his obligations not his liberties, but he was older and special. Just as parents had been unwilling to relinquish full control over children, so the dons, new and old, were reluctant to release undergraduates from their watchful care. If there were new freedoms, there were also new impositions and thresholds. Later in the nineteenth century, in the 1860s in fact, an intrigued and

---

[101] Thomas Fowler, *The History of Corpus Christi College* (Oxford, 1893), 307.
[102] Robson, 'Trinity College', 323. [103] Heber, *Life of Heber*, I, 498–9.

distinguished French visitor noticed a fundamental contradiction in the way pupils and undergraduates were treated in English schools and universities. Judging from the perspective of the *lycée,* he admitted that French boys were pleached and pollarded like the trees of Versailles, whereas English schoolboys were shaped like the natural growth of a landscaped garden. He was impressed by the casual air of English boys and their freedom to roam the town. 'It is curious to see babies of twelve raised to the dignities of manhood', commented Hippolyte Taine. But when he turned to the condition of undergraduates, he was equally surprised by a set of reverse discoveries. The English undergraduate was less free than his French counterpart and less insouciant than the English schoolboy. The routine of chapel, hall, scheduled tutorials, lectures and curfews more properly belonged to the world of the schoolboy. These paradoxes pleased Taine. The schoolboy was being eased into the responsibilities of manhood, which required independence, while the undergraduate was being instructed in the benefits of self-reliance, which entailed restraint.[104]

Taine's observations of Harrow and Oxford occurred after mid-century in the exciting years of reform. Much of what he witnessed was a distinctly later development of English education. But his essential point should not be lost sight of, for it applies equally well to the earlier period. Students were still in limbo between boyhood and maturity; the combination described in the 1840s by a Christ Church undergraduate was 'an immense deal of formality and etiquette mixed with the manners of a school'. He drew the only conclusion possible from such a mix: 'it is hard to conduct yourself decently'.[105] While the threat of the school cane had lifted, the dignities of manhood had not been granted. The dons still stood *in loco parentis.* Some were clearly behind the times. Daniel Wilson, who tutored at St Edmund Hall, Oxford, in the first decade of the nineteenth century, later becoming bishop of Calcutta, was stiff and donnish and insisted that students wear the bands that used to decorate the undergraduate gown. He was consequently known as 'Bands Wilson'.[106] An undergraduate was still *in statu pupillari.* He was expected to doff his cap to senior members of the university, an archaic act no longer being demanded in the home as deference to paternal authority.[107]

[104] Hippolyte Taine, *Notes on England, 1860–1870* (London, 1957), 104.

[105] Lord Dufferin to Lord De Ros from Christ Church (n.d.). Public Record office of Northern Ireland, Belfast.

[106] William Tuckwell, *Pre-Tractarian Oxford, A Reminiscence of the Oriel 'Noetics'* (London, 1909), 1–10.

[107] Knox, *Liberal Education,* II, 199.

The symbolic handing over of the son to the college by relatives had long been ambiguous. Samuel Johnson's father went with him to Oxford, 'anxiously' we are informed, and met his tutor.[108] Richard Cumberland came up to Trinity College, Cambridge, in 1747 accompanied by his father who 'put me under the care of the Rev. Dr Morgan, an old friend of our family and a Senior Fellow of that Society'.[109] Reginald Heber was accompanied by both parents.[110] Newman was personally escorted to Oxford by a clerical friend, who made inquiries for vacancies at Exeter and Trinity.[111] These actions could be interpreted either way as a very specific transition from home to surrogate home, or as the ending of the period of close parental care; but in no instance did the promised weaning occur as expected.[112] In Lord Byron's case there was no ambiguity. Educated at home, Aberdeen Grammar School, private schools and Harrow, he weaned himself. Rebellious, without a father and estranged from his mother, 'an hysterical Scotch heiress', he went up to Cambridge alone in 1805, commenced a 'continued *routine* of Dissipation' – dinners, claret, London – and chained his tame bear in Trinity Great Court.[113]

We encounter repeated ironies. For both English and American under-graduates, 'college' was (is?) a regressive as much as an emancipatory undertaking. In so far as undergraduate education is regarded as an 'experience', part of a finite but still extended period of self-exploration, it is a late phase of adolescence. Protections are still required: the protections of the guardians of place who retain control of the mysteries of their domains. Students who do not have 'college' as an experience – those in distance learning, part-time attendees, commuters – forgo the special isolation and thrills of ritual separation whose end comes with the ceremonies of graduation (although the trials begin again with entry upon postgraduate study). But they are free in a more absolute meaning, with-out the baggage of rituals, spatial constraints and emotional entanglements with peers. They also do not have recurrent memories of bygone

---

[108] James Boswell, *Life of Johnson,* ed. Christopher Hibbert (Harmondsworth, 1981), 43–4. The anxiety might have been attributable to class differences.

[109] D. A. Winstanley, *The University of Cambridge in the Eighteenth Century* (Cambridge, 1922), 6.

[110] Heber, *Life of Heber,* I, 23.

[111] John Henry Newman, *The Letters and Diaries,* ed. Ian Ker and Thomas Gornall, I (London, 1978), 28n–29n.

[112] The pattern of mixing adult freedoms with close supervision is also apparent in the history of Oxford and Cambridge women's colleges. While women students, from well-understood Victorian fears, were considered particularly vulnerable, a similar if not identical pattern had been set for men students in the earlier period (as noted in Chapter 5).

[113] *Dictionary of National Biography; 'In My Hot Youth', Byron's Letters and Journals,* I, *1798–1810,* ed. Leslie A. Marchand (London, 1973), 124, 135.

university experiences. To the extent that 'college' is part of a saga that forces undergradutes to identify with Alma Mater and retain an affection for her in after years, the memories of being young are prolonged, extended throughout life and revived again and again through old boy and old girl events, alumni reunions, retreats and camp outings, fund-raising occasions, campus visiting days and, in America, a continual round of social events, lectures by presidents and professors and other means of maintaining loyalties and affections across the generations. Adolescent behaviour – cheering at social and sporting events, forgetting one's age on college-linked occasions – summon up recollections of a carefree but actually tension-filled period of growing up. American fraternities and sororities, full of rites of passage of their own, intensify feelings of nostalgia and self-absorption. '[Its] affiliations are supposed to transcend differences in age, facilitating an exclusionary bonding that makes all the brothers into honorary adolescents.' The author of this remark is surely right, and he goes on to say that the American university can be regarded as a giant sandbox for extending adolescence, with 'sex and booze, many trends and a few ideas'.[114] Put in another way, however, the gift of 'college' is eternal youth.

These general reflections need to be anchored in specific chronologies. It took some decades for the colleges of Oxford and Cambridge to develop a myth of the golden age of undergraduates. While undergraduates, recognisable as such, were eager to locate such an age, college authorities were always uncertain about the benefits of freedom. Student stereotypes of the don highlighted a forced gravity, the absence of spontaneity and the association of authority with premature aging. Innumerable recorded instances of genuine affection between senior and junior, admiration and gratitude survive. Excitement could break into college life at any time, living legends like Wordsworth invited back to college to inspire terrific conversations.[115] But a leaden stereotype persisted none the less until the 1850s and 1860s when new stereotypes of 'Young Oxford' or 'Young Cambridge' described a different, more light-hearted ambience, the triumph of youthfulness as it were, expressed academically in a wider curriculum, positive regard for the 'reading man', varied career possibilities and departures in teaching at university and college levels.[116] The changes of the earlier periods had come more slowly; old and new

---

[114] Herbert N. Schneidau, 'On Being the Right Age for Theory, Notes of a Fellow Traveler', in *Arizona Quarterly*, 50 (Spring, 1994), 5.

[115] Robson, 'Trinity College', 326–7.

[116] See Sheldon Rothblatt, *The Revolution of the Dons: Cambridge and Society in Victorian England* (London and New York, 1968, reissued Cambridge, 1981), Chapters 6 and 7.

commingled. Those of the later period were compressed and lay thick upon the ground. They were more visible and mutually reinforcing.

What emerges from a consideration of the interactions between home, schooling, student cultures and university in a 'long duration' is a contest for a dominant role in defining the stages of growth and development associated with growing up. It is a narrative, with the tensions of a narrative, about those who supplied education and those who purchased it. The universities offered their customary wares, but diversified their product line in response to consumer demand, allowing parents to select teachers and employ the mechanisms of third-party intervention to create special conditions for their children. Parents were knowledgeable shoppers, gathering the necessary intelligence for making decisions. To the extent that openings in the market could be exploited or turned to their advantage, parents negotiated, retaining as much influence over their offspring as could be obtained under shifting circumstances. Since the market is the arena in which negotiations take place, and since the process of negotiation is unpredictable and the outcome of bargaining uncertain, the resulting pattern was spasmodic.

It was not a pattern that university leaders necessarily enjoyed. Private instruction paid for directly by parents threatened their control of education even as it provided employment for fellows. As the traffic of undergraduates increased, dons were faced with the prospect of endless inquiries about places and awards, and a newer generation would not have the patience of a John Cooke sifting through competing claims. Cyril Jackson anticipated the future. He was one of the least tolerant of the dons of his generation and regarded the anxieties of parents as a needless challenge to his judgement and the authority of his college.

But the busybody parent and family representatives in the form of third parties would continue to annoy dons until an academic guild culture based on its own internal professional career interests could form. The strength of home attachments and substitute parenting, represented by disagreements over the authority to be relinquished to dons *in loco parentis*, helps explain the sporadic efforts to reform teaching that appeared in various colleges in the first four decades of the nineteenth century, the complaints and criticisms voiced about the old college system that mounted steadily until public opinion formed. Not all the critics were equally remarkable as teachers or scholars. Some were really quite mediocre but suspected that teaching and disciplinary arrangements could be improved. Some – their ideas have been mentioned – regretted such reforms as did take place, notably around the examinations system. Newman was far more radical (and iconoclastic) than his own reform-tolerant provost. The new dons, scarcely older than the under-graduates whom they taught, were aware of the possibilities for shaping character associated with the emergence of the 'first undergraduates, rec-ognizable as such', but their efforts could be suspected of personal motive and gain, either to attract disciples, interfere with areas of moral concern best left to parents or as opportunities to take advantage of the willingness of parents to pay for extra teaching. Consequently the market had to be resisted as an unnecessary and unwanted intrusion on the right of educational experts to determine the overall conditions of teaching, learning and examining.

Seen but hardly appreciated from the university end, demand also had a positive side. Market response made the transition from demand to supply possible. It was precisely the dramatically increasing outside pressure for an Oxford and Cambridge education, first in the early nineteenth century, then again in the 1860s, that made it ultimately possible for the colleges to be selective, just as it was the over-supply of places in many colleges of the earlier periods that gave parents an advantage.

But what of the awkward interval, the theories and speculation, the 'myths of youth and the adult imagination' that had so enlivened discussion about child-rearing in the former century?[117] Upbringing, as previously hinted, needed to be made scientific, or at least 'professional', the subject of technical discussion by experts and institutionalised into a system of feeder schools where properly alerted schoolmasters promised to guard the boys at school and sublimate their energies into busy, productive activity. That system was more or less in place by 1850. Now the royal commissioners could commence their work.

[117] Paricia Meyer Spacks, *The Adolescent Idea, Myths of Youth and the Adult Imagination* (London, 1981).

SUPPLY AND DEMAND IN THE WRITING
OF UNIVERSITY HISTORY SINCE ABOUT 1790
2. THE MARKET AND THE
UNIVERSITY OF LONDON

A METROPOLITAN PESTHOUSE

The history of the invisible hand of the market in relation to English universities is also illuminated by analysing the foundations and subsequent evolution of the University of London and its colleges.

Three particular themes or threads run through the course of the following discussion. The first is the relationship of the London University to its specific urban environment at the time of its founding, meaning the relationship of the university to an actual or potential local market for students, resources and services. The second is its relationship to other preexisting educational institutions against which, inevitably, it was compared and measured. And the third is the position of the new university with respect to certain special features of Britain's urban and national cultural history.

Conceived in 1826, the London University was only the third university to be created in England, although smaller Scotland had five, two of which, Marischal and King's College, were university colleges later united as Aberdeen University in the middle of the nineteenth century. London was not established as a rival to Oxford and Cambridge, whose curriculum and socially exclusive intake had long been under attack, but as a university serving a different market. It could not be convincingly argued that London's establishment was necessary because of the decline of Oxford and Cambridge. The fortunes of the ancient universities were actually on the rise at the time of London's founding. Matriculations were up, and the 'new discipline' was in place if not yet fully evolved. But the ancient universities remained socially exclusive. They were sufficiently protected by the Established Church of England to retain most of their religious restrictions for another thirty years. Expenses had risen in the eighteenth century owing to private tuition and a higher level of conspicuous consumption. The excluded had to look elsewhere.

The London University was founded in a period when urban populations were expanding throughout the island, as they were in western Europe generally, when towns were improving their political influence in England by threatening gentry control of county franchises and when the besetting problems of cities – housing, expansion of the built-up areas, sanitation, poverty, crime, popular education – were under continual review.[1] Cities were moving to the forefront of social policy in many countries, and it was only natural that they should become the home of educational experiments. City-based universities were appearing in Germany and in the United States, and the only major question for England was not whether a new university should be founded, but where and of what type. The population of the relatively new manufacturing districts of the midlands and the north was soaring as the principal cities absorbed neighbouring towns and villages, drew labour from the surrounding countryside and experienced the effects of a higher birth rate. Birmingham underwent an increase from 71,000 in 1801 to 102,000 in 1821. Ten years later growth had reached 144,000. Manchester grew even more rapidly. Starting at a little more than Birmingham in 1801, the city swelled to 182,000 inhabitants after thirty years. Sheffield at 42,000 in 1801, was well over 100,000 by 1841. Liverpool surpassed Bristol as a port to stretch from 82,000 at the beginning of the century to a remarkable 202,000 in 1831, still growing at 286,000 ten years later.[2] And so it went. The resources for establishing a provincial university of some kind were probably available, but selection of London was more appropriate since only the capital was the home of numerous interests whose combined strength could be effective against the Anglican university monopoly. London was the only city whose prestige could give a university in its midst something of the importance attached to Oxford and Cambridge.

Furthermore, London itself was changing. Its population increased by at least three-quarters of a million in the first three decades of the nineteenth century, and at no point in the first fifty years did the decadal rate of growth fall below 17 per cent.[3] Spectacular building programmes associated with the Regency and reign of George IV dramatised the

---

[1] Andrew Lees, *Cities Perceived: Urban Society in European and American Thought, 1820–1940* (New York, 1985), Chapter 2.
[2] Population data from B. R. Mitchell with Phyllis Deane, *Abstract of British Historical Statistics* (Cambridge, 1962), 24–5.
[3] *Ibid.*, 19.

increases. Residents of the vast and fragmented capital were beginning to think of themselves collectively as having a common identity and purpose, of being part of a great city of unprecedented scale. The disparate and hitherto separate and even isolated nodes of the capital – its financial district or 'City', its royal enclave, West End fashionable streets, developing inner suburbs and older commuter villages – were just starting to be regarded as a greater London or 'metropolis'.[4] Supporters of a new university believed that London Town had now reached a stage of development where it needed and could maintain an institution of higher education. It was more than once observed that the capital was the only major European city without one, an anomaly in view of London's size and world importance in finance, shipping and representative government.

The first London University was a small institution of some thirty professorial chairs situated in Gower Street, that was really only a university college except that it possessed an associated medical school. Many of the chairs were the nuclei of what much later became academic departments. Chairs in the biological sciences were grouped together to form the medical 'school' or 'department', which almost immediately sought a suitable location for a teaching hospital.

The university was founded as a non-sectarian proprietary company. No reason is customarily offered as to why the founders avoided placing their institution into trust as a non-profit foundation, but one reason might have been to avoid jurisdiction by the Ecclesiastical Commissioners and the Church of England which had responsibility for charitable societies. The company was initially supported by the proceeds from the public sale of shares in a joint-stock company but a cap of 4 per cent was put on the returns to shareholders in order to counter the reproach that profit and not education was the true object of the new foundation.[5] There was an additional risk. Since limited-liability firms were illegal, shareholders in proprietary companies were individually responsible for all debts. Unlike

[4] Historically, a metropolis was an archiepiscopal see, a capital city usually, or the centre of some important activity. The word was used in the 1780s to describe a monster, but the more neutral meaning to indicate a conurbation appeared in the 1820s and 1830s. One of the 'founders' of the University of London called the capital 'our gigantic metropolis'. Thomas Lloyd Humberstone, *University Reform in London* (London, 1926), 25. See also H. J. Dyos, 'Greater and Greater London: Notes on Metropolis and Provinces in the Nineteenth and Twentieth Centuries', in *Britain and the Netherlands,* ed. J. S. Bromley and E. H. Kossman (The Hague, 1971), 93; Anthony Sutcliffe, *Metropolis 1890–1940* (Chicago, 1984), 67, 256n; Raymond Williams, *The Country and the City* (London, 1973), 146.
[5] However, no interest was ever paid on the shares. Hugh Hale Bellott, *University College, London, 1826–1926* (London, 1929), 305.

Oxford and Cambridge or the Scottish universities, the new university in London did not possess degree-granting authority, which could only be conferred by royal charter, an uncertain prospect for a non-sectarian foundation at a time when all universities were historically if not legally connected to religious establishments, whether north or south of the River Tweed, and tied to them by golden strands of patronage and mutual advantage.

Access and cost were the two most unambiguous policies of University College. Ambitious, the founders talked about attracting some two thousand full- and part-time students from London's diverse and comfortable but not necessarily affluent population. London families certainly could not afford the third or more of their annual incomes required for residence in costly Oxford and Cambridge.[6] In the language of the day, the university's constituency was to be the 'middling classes' (or 'middling orders' or 'middling rich') whom the poet Thomas Campbell, perhaps the university's first publicist, identified as 'small, comfortable trading fortunes', the large indeterminate group that stretched from skilled workers, shopkeepers and clerks in commercial houses to *rentiers*, business and professional men but did not include the 'higher orders' of great barristers, the upper officers of the armed services, leading medical practitioners and the landed and financial aristocracy and clergy. Today we might call the middling classes a middle-income group. They were a politically active and influential body in the rather unsettled social climate of early nineteenth-century London.[7]

Religiously, some of the original shareholders were evangelical or latitudinarian Anglicans who could foresee the benefits to their children of a low-cost alternative to the ancient universities. However, the expected pool consisted primarily of families of Dissenting or Nonconforming Protestants and secondarily of others, such as freethinking intellectuals, the small numbers of Roman Catholics, whose political emancipation

---

[6] *Ibid.*, 51; and Donald Olsen, Introduction to David Owen, *The Government of Victorian London, 1855–1889: The Metropolitan Board of Works, the Vestries and the City Corporation* (Cambridge, MA, 1982), 3. Total costs at Oxford and Cambridge were habitually estimated at between £250 and £300 per annum, and it was claimed that attendance at London University would cut these figures by two-thirds. Cyrus Redding, *Literary Reminiscences and Memoirs of Thomas Campbell*, II (London, 1860), 12. George B. Jeffery, *The Unity of Knowledge: Some Reflections on the Universities of Cambridge and London* (Cambridge, 1950), 10, says that there were 600 full-time students at University College in its first year, but attendance had dropped considerably by 1835 if William Tooke's remarks to the House of Commons, 20 May 1835, col. 281, are correct.

[7] Bellot, *University College*, 47–8; R. S. Neale, *Class and Ideology in the Nineteenth Century* (London, 1972), 30.

occurred at the end of the 1820s, and the even smaller numbers of Jews, who remained unemancipated for several decades more. As a representative of the tiny Jewish community, the City financier Isaac Goldsmid, a friend of Henry Brougham, the brilliant parliamentarian most responsible for securing support for the upstart institution, was particularly effective in bringing coalitions together and keeping alive the principle of a non-sectarian university.[8]

The Dissenters were not a unified body. Some had close effective economic and political ties to the governing elites, while others were marginalised intellectuals; but in so far as there was a distinct culture of Dissent, as inherited from the political awakening of the late eighteenth century, it tended to be individualistic, market-oriented, utilitarian, 'rational' in the Enlightenment meaning of the word and consequently secular or at least non-sectarian and tolerant.[9] A small Unitarian element – Socinians who had alarmed the ancient universities in the later eighteenth century – reinforced these preferences. In the eighteenth century the educational needs of Dissenters had been met by Dissenting academies that offered an education roughly parallel to that of Scottish universities (and like them serving a lower age group). Their intellectual interests had also led them to create a famous urban network of 'Lit and Phil' (Literary and Philosophical) societies. But the great age of the academies was virtually over when discussions about a city university began, and interest shifted from the model of the academy, which was essentially a *Hochschule* for pupils of secondary school age, to the model of the university where a wider range of subjects could be taught and professional, especially medical, training obtained.

There were several schemes afoot in the 1820s for a non-denominational university. Besides the London University, a plan was sketched out in 1826 for a university in the north, quite possibly in highly populated Liverpool, to which denominational colleges could be subordinated.[10] A shadowy 'federal principle' may have been involved, but the scheme is too vague for

---

[8] Bellot, *University College*, 29–30; Chester New, *Life of Henry Brougham to 1830* (Oxford, 1961), 360.

[9] John Seed, 'Gentleman Dissenters: The Social and Political Meanings of Rational Dissent in the 1770s and 1780s', *Historical Journal*, 28 (June 1985), 299–325. Dissent grew rapidly between 1770 and 1810. The Wesleyans increased fivefold and the Baptists fourfold. The size of the Dissenting community has been estimated at about 312,00 in 1810, 437,000 in 1820 and 600,000 in 1830, and its growth in numbers can be correlated with its enhanced political influence. See Robert Currie, Alan Gilbert and Lee Horslay, *Churches and Churchgoers* (Oxford, 1977), 23–5.

[10] N. R. Tempest, 'An Early Scheme for an Undenominational University', *Universities Review*, 32 (February 1960), 45–9.

us to deduce any such tendency. It is possible that for many proponents of a new university the issue was not necessarily a university of and for the metropolis of London, not a 'Cockney University' as the tory writers of the satirical journal *John Bull* scoffed, but a national university for Dissenters in some convenient and appropriate location. It can therefore be surmised that a potential 'national' mission was hidden in the history of the London University's first decade even as the founders set about to create an urban institution in the capital. The poet, Thomas Campbell, who had talked up the idea of a London university, once stated that he did not want a 'mere Dissenters' University',[11] but some sentiment in favour of such an institution remained.

The question of whether a new university should be for Dissenters or whether it should be secular figured in the earliest discussions. A majority of the Christian supporters of the London University would have preferred some religious teaching, but the nature of the political alliance prevented such a policy. The new foundation, like Thomas Jefferson's University of Virginia (founded in 1819), was consequently called an 'infidel' or 'godless' university and joked about in a student publication as a 'metropolitan pesthouse'.[12]

The founding coalition was even more mixed politically than religiously. It included radicals of the left – Benthamites and upper-working-class reformers like Francis Place – who were joined to liberal aristocratic whigs and Scottish democrats. It included single-issue groups, such as evangelical Anglicans, generally conservative and philanthropically high-minded or humanitarian, who, if they were in the forefront of movements to suppress public vice, were also active in the campaign to abolish the slave trade throughout the empire. Socially, all of the participants, secular as well as religious, comprised a good cross-section of London's population and can be accurately described as embodying the spirit and energy of the metropolis.

No single body represented the government of the capital for there was none. Despite some attempts to rationalise London's administration, a large number of separate local authorities remained in existence, no less than thirty-eight in the year 1855, and consolidation did not occur until the last decade of the century when the first of a number of metropolitan

---

[11] William Beattie, *Life and Letters of Thomas Campbell*, 2nd ed., II (London, 1850), 411.

[12] *First Book for the Instruction of Students in the King's College London* (London, 183?), 8. For Virginia, see Jennings Wagoner, 'Constraint and Variety in Virginia Higher Education', *History of Education Quarterly*, 25 (Spring–Summer, 1985), 184; and 'Honor and Dishonor at Mr. Jefferson's University', *History of Education Quarterly*, 26 (Summer, 1986), 157.

jurisdictions was created.[13] There was consequently no centre for a new university to affix itself to, no cushion to fall back upon, no identifiable municipality which could serve as a source of support and encouragement for a young institution facing the uncertainties of the market, the competition of the organised medical profession and the hostility of the bishops and Oxbridge clerical Establishment. By the same token, the new institution was theoretically 'free' from such external interference once it could establish a working relationship with a viable market. Yet there was one political ally. The Court of Common Council of the autonomous City of London very demonstrably took the side of the new university during the battle over the granting of a royal charter in the 1830s. The City, which has retained its independence to this day, had a history of supporting higher education efforts dating as far back as the late seventeenth century when proposals for a university first circulated, and in the nineteenth century the City retained some endowments collected for that purpose and used them to underwrite public lectures. Later in the century great liveried companies representing the City's merchant community – the clothworkers, for example, or the drapers – were strong benefactors of the London colleges at shaky financial moments.[14]

No urban type of university existed in England. The closest native models were Scottish, particularly the sixteenth-century foundations of the 'College of Edinburgh' and Marischal College in Aberdeen. Edinburgh itself was modelled on the Protestant academy in Geneva with which many Scots had been associated. The ties between college and municipality at Edinburgh were so close that what was to become the university was often referred to as the Town College. The city powers of Edinburgh even authorised the college to grant degrees (before an Act of Parliament was passed in 1621). However, by the nineteenth century the Scottish universities did not regard themselves in any sense as municipal or civic universities. They identified with the northern kingdom, with its history and with Scottish culture generally, with a Presbyterian inheritance, Enlightenment traditions of thought and a certain conception of humanist education which travelled well, having crossed the Atlantic and implanted itself in the colonial colleges of America. They thought of themselves as a system or group of universities, even, it might be suggested, a State system. Long before State aid to higher education began in England, they were in receipt of regular royal or parliamentary grants.

[13] Francis Sheppard, 'London and the Nation in the Nineteenth Century', *Transactions of the Royal Historical Society*, 5th ser., 35 (1985), 60.
[14] Gordon Heulin, *King's College London, 1828–1978* (London, 1978), 29, 42.

Furthermore, they contemplated having a certain element of student transfer among themselves. The medical schools of the Scottish universities had distinguished courses in the eighteenth century, attracting students from other parts of the kingdom and earning in this respect a national and even European reputation still very viable in the early decades of the nineteenth century.[15]

From Scottish universities the new university colleges of London took a great deal. They borrowed a set of far-ranging mechanisms for achieving relatively open access: a curriculum responsive to market demand and amenable to change; flexible programmes of study including part-time; a low-cost system of professorial lecturing; non-residential instruction; and a particular spirit of general and professional education concentrated more on the well-educated student of a service culture than on the potential social, political and religious leader of society that was the conventional English assumption of the purpose of a university education. A university should produce 'useful men', Professor George Jardine of Glasgow had once stated, not 'great men', and Jardine was greatly admired by Campbell.[16] The Scottish model convinced the leaders of the movement to found a new university that a non-residential institution could be successful in the capital.

Those leaders, it has often been remarked, were themselves largely Scottish or had been educated in Scotland, men such as Brougham and Campbell, prominent evangelicals such as the Macaulays or intellectuals such as James Mill. One of the leading Dissenters, F. A. Cox, the Baptist minister at Hackney Academy, was a Scottish graduate. Liberal whigs with an anti-establishment bent such as Lord John Russell had spent some time at Edinburgh, home of the great polemical journal *The Edinburgh Review*, which had launched a famous attack on the education offered at Oxford and Cambridge in the first decade of the new century, and Scotland was the source of the revolution in economic thought which made possible a market view of education. It has often been pointed out that Scots predominated among the first selections of London University's professors. In the words of a detractor, the University of London was,

[15] For the Scottish universities, see Paul Robertson, 'Scottish Universities and Industry, 1860–1914', *Scottish Economic and Social History*, 4 (1984), 53; Douglas Sloan, *The Scottish Enlightenment and the American College Ideal* (New York, 1971), 19–28; Robert D. Anderson, *Education and Opportunity in Victorian Scotland, Schools and Universities* (Oxford, 1983).
[16] Redding, *Thomas Campbell*, 19–21. My colleague Gunther Barth has suggested that the aim of producing 'useful men' is particularly urban.

The conception of an inexpensive, non-residential unitary university featuring compensation for professors pegged to attendance rather than the English idea of an expensive residential collegiate university with tutorial instruction was unquestionably the inspiration of Scottish universities, but foreign models were also considered – the German universities, as represented by the two new foundations of Bonn and Berlin, and an American state institution, the University of Virginia, which was founded in 1819 but opened its doors in 1826. Campbell had twice visited Germany to study its university structure, and the plans for Virginia were well known in London because the Rockfish Gap Report was being flogged around the capital in an effort to attract teaching talent to the Old Dominion. However, foreign models did not really provide the fledgling institution with a workable urban model. That would have been difficult, for Virginia was not an urban university, and the German universities were far more closely tied to State objectives than to a service mission for cities. The city of Berlin, in any case, surprised visitors by its lack of urbanity and depressing architecture.[23] At best foreign models only reinforced certain directions in London's early history – the system of professorial lecturing supported partly or wholly out of fees, for example, and some freedom of student choice in selecting courses. These were probably most useful as part of the public relations effort undertaken to attract backers to the scheme.

An urban theme is apparent in the curriculum of the London University, but most obviously in the professional divisions. It has often been remarked that cities foster a division of labour and generate a demand for specialised services.[24] Rapidly growing cities encounter problems that require some element of expert knowledge, although problem-solving methods will inevitably vary according to time and place. In the case of late-Regency and early-Victorian London, it was the state of the capital's sanitation and physical condition generally that led the founders to promote the foundation of a medical department. The university's trump card from the first was medical education, which supporters hoped could be improved by the addition of scientific instruction to what by tradition was clinical training based on the hospital ward. The opening of the medical school at University College was in fact the official opening of the university. Possibly no other feature of the curriculum caused the

[23] Charles E. McClelland, '"To Live for Science": Ideals and Realities at the University of Berlin', in *The University and the City, from Medieval Origins to the Present*, ed. Thomas Bender (Oxford and New York, 1988), 185.
[24] George Simmel, *On Individuality and Social Forms* (Chicago and London, 1971), 325–37, esp. 337.

pre- or post-1836 University of London more difficulty than medicine. Rivalries with existing teaching hospitals and medical royal societies continually hampered efforts at reorganisation and accounted for a number of the structural peculiarities of London that remain to this day. The medical profession caused the university as much trouble as the Established Church during the 1830s controversies over the granting of a royal charter empowering the institution to grant degrees.

King's College also had a medical school, but the college surpassed University College as a source of innovation when a department of civil engineering was established in 1838. Engineering, too, was thought to be a crucial way of addressing the problems of urban sanitation and of controlling the spread of disease and epidemics, such as the dreaded cholera which returned to the kingdom in the early 1830s. Sanitary engineering was a pet solution of the Benthamite fellow-traveller, Edwin Chadwick, who, during his tenure on the sanitary commission in 1839 and 1844, and on the board of health from 1848 to 1854, shared responsibility for introducing the system of drains that emptied household and street wastes into the Thames, contributing to the spread of water-borne diseases since the Thames was one source of London's drinking water. No progress could be made in this area until the discovery of the germ theory of disease transmission. Civil engineers were less in demand for industrial purposes because the scale of enterprise in the lower Thames Valley was largely handicraft. Approximately 80 per cent of London's manufacturing establishments employed four workers or fewer as late as 1851, in contrast to the very large factories of the company towns to the north. Small workshops were scattered throughout the metropolis, with heavy concentrations in the eastern and north-eastern districts. The capital did not take the lead in the great transportation revolution that rapidly covered the kingdom with a system of railroads. That honour belonged to places like Stockton, Darlington, Liverpool and Manchester, but by the 1850s London was indisputably the hub of the kingdom's communications network,[25] and railroads were well able to absorb the engineering skills being certified by the new university.

The anticipation of a demand for skills and education is as important in determining the presence of market mechanisms as the actual measurable demand itself. The introduction of a new commodity does not depend upon the clear existence of consumer pressure but upon how producers read market signals. Risk-taking is essential to entrepreneurial innovation, and efforts to reduce risk lead to the adoption of strategies

[25] Sheppard, 'London and the Nation', 56–7.

such as advertising and the production of pilot products as a first step in stimulating and widening demand. Curricular innovation within universities often – probably most often – leads demand, and many subject innovations, especially in exotic languages or similar rare specialties, may never develop anything approximating a market extensive enough to cover the costs of teaching. An entrepreneurial university, like a publishing house, needs a market leader to subsidise a highly diversified curriculum.

The absence of a ready market for most educational products did not mean that the principles of an open market were ignored by the first two university colleges. Neither of them were ever certain that students were available for all of their courses, but the governing councils behaved as if sufficient numbers would in time develop. The one area where the existence of a particular market was assumed to exist was in medicine, or professional education, so that one leading strategy was to persuade parents and students that many different subjects were relevant to a professional career. The utilitarian intellectuals backing the new institution in Gower Street particularly approved of 'useful' education, as did the representatives of rational Dissent; and science and applied science received their blessings, as we might expect, since these subjects were connected to professional education and regarded as progressive. Both university colleges also provided a general or arts course. These were not easy to characterise as urban-related, and yet the rationale specifying them as such was employed. Borrowed from the late-Enlightenment Scottish universities and the old Dissenting academics, the liberal arts curriculum was made 'relevant' by stressing the importance of modern subjects such as English language and literature or modern history, foreign languages, logic and moral philosophy that were claimed to be directly useful either for careers in international trade or for understanding the suppositions of contemporary cultures.

Quite probably we should not expect radical departures in every respect whenever a new university curriculum is announced, nor should we suppose that new urban institutions will automatically reject conventional courses of study merely because their clientele are city dwellers whose needs are presumed special to their urban circumstances. Universities by their very nature as depositories of learning are loathe to break completely with past practice, nor are they always able to do so, whether they are land-grant institutions in American states or new universities in Britain and its empire. Their faculty have normally been educated conventionally and owe some loyalty to the basic disciplines that stand as the foundations of any curriculum, no matter how innovative. The existing knowledge base is therefore ipso facto constraining. Furthermore, there is usually a certain expectation on the part of potential users that while departures from convention may be desirable, a university should not completely abandon the traditions that have given it strength, prestige and above all legitimacy. There is always the additional likelihood that newer uses will be found for older fields of learning. These reflections account for the presence of traditional subjects such as Latin and Greek in the subject offerings of the godless institution. Classical learning not only remained in the curriculum; it actually predominated in the first two years of the four-year general course at University College.[26]

As important as the actual curriculum, at least in London's case, was the spirit in which the professors were to approach teaching. Here we can certainly identify an urban influence or connection. In the first place the professional curriculum partly drove the general curriculum. An obvious case was medicine, which required the colleges to invest resources in the teaching of the biological and physical sciences, and another was engineering, which required mathematics. But other subjects also fulfilled some of the aims of the backers. Political economy, a favourite of London's utilitarians, was thought to be essential for the training of civil servants, and a chair of Hindustani established at University College could be justified as preparation for bureaucratic positions in the East India Company, the public monopoly located in the metropolis and chartered by the government for the administration of British-controlled areas of the Indian subcontinent. Both James Mill, a backer of the London University, and his son John Stuart Mill, worked in the company's London office. Jurisprudence and mathematics were claimed to be useful for such widely differing but not unrelated activities as commerce, foreign affairs and law.[27]

Utility was also emphasised at the rival institution in the Strand, but with a notable exception: the teaching of English language and literature. At University College, English was taught conventionally, that is, with the same broad goals as classical languages. Grammar, composition and the structure of literature were stressed in order to strengthen the powers of written and oral expression useful in any public or business career. Language teaching had followed this pattern for centuries, although in

---

[26] James Henderson Burns, *Jeremy Bentham and University College* (London, 1962), 10.

[27] Liberal or general education, it has been pointed out, survives in urban-based universities despite a heavy demand for basic skills and vocational education because urban environments require highly developed arts of communication, negotiation and mediation. See Park R. Kolbe, *Urban Influences on Higher Education in England and the United States* (New York, 1928), 123–4.

some historical periods logic and dialectic rather than composition and declamation were more important.

At King's College in the Strand the purposes were different. Literature rather than language was at the centre of attention. Individual authors were scrutinised and studied in association with the development of modern history. The originators of this pioneering approach were the poet Robert Southey, who was offered but declined a chair, and F. D. Maurice, the inspirer of the Apostles and sometime president of Gladstone's Oxford essay society. Maurice connected England's special national virtues, discernible in its literature, to the middle class and commercial success. At the same time, fearing that his London students would be too eager to embrace the narrower aspects of that inheritance, he taught duty and responsibility and respect for national purpose as reflected in literature and history. His aims were those of the Broad Church movement in which he was a major figure: self-sacrifice, community, a sense of the larger whole. To underscore the importance of this approach, the English course was made a regular part of the full-time curriculum, whereas at the rival college it remained optional.[28]

In Gower Street the message of material gain and career was not similarly restrained. The founding of the first London University was part of the same popular or mass education movement that had produced the monitorial system advocated by the educators Lancaster and Bell, the mechanics' institutes and the Society for the Diffusion of Popular Knowledge, all of which, as a practical necessity, accepted cost cutting as a first step and utility as a second. But cheap education and 'merely' useful knowledge were poor education and by their very nature supremely self-serving unless leavened with a higher purpose – such, at least, were the public accusations of critics.

The accusations had a point or two in their favour. The educational theory behind all popular education was more or less the same: the Lockean/Utilitarian assumption of empty mind spaces which had only to be 'furnished' or 'stocked' with information by a process of associating ideas. A complicated epistemological theory, refined over the course of a century, was vulgarised into a crude method of mind cramming, and the teacher to whom Maurice had assigned an elevated role had often to be content with lesser employment.

The teaching of English at the first two constituent colleges of the University of London illustrated the effect a particular urban environment could have on pedagogy, but, as the examples show, there was no necessary

---

[28] Bacon, 'English Literature', 600–12.

slavish relationship between the two. Other variables and influences entered the picture, and all that can be confidently said – and it may be saying a great deal – is that the urban context forced the colleges or individual professors to consider or reconsider seriously the grander or larger objectives of their teaching.

An urban preoccupation or concern was and continued to be important for both of the new colleges. It is certainly reflected in the relatively early provision made for educating young women. The more open life of the city, its multifarious influences and the greater accessibility of schools in urban as opposed to rural settings created a demand for the further education of women and gave to University College the distinction of being one of the leaders in the nineteenth-century movement for coeducation. As early as 1832 women were admitted to lectures on electricity. Thirty years later several London-based women's associations demanded and received a special course of thirteen lectures on animal physiology that attracted 113 women. Between 1869 and 1878 changes were introduced that allowed University College to become the pioneering coeducational institution in the kingdom.[29]

At King's in the 1850s an annual course of lectures on the physical condition of the poor was instituted to aid clergy working in city parishes. '[Little] progress can be made in the attempt to persuade men to be Christians', reads an entry in the council minutes, 'so long as their physical condition is degraded below the level of humanity'.[30] (Did this imply a 'mission' to the Jews of the East End, whom proselytisers attempted to woo throughout the second half of the nineteenth century with little success?[31]) In the Department of General Literature and Science a professorship of the 'Principles and Practice of Commerce' was reinstituted in 1852 when the chair was given to the famous statistician Leone Levi, who agreed to give a course of evening lectures on commercial and banking law 'which has attracted a large class, including the chief Managers of the principal banking firms'.[32]

As the century progressed and the city's economic infrastructure underwent change, both institutions agreed to assist London-based industrial enterprises. The earliest contributions were in chemistry. Largely technical at first, of a low level and oriented to the needs of

[29] Negley Harte, *The Admission of Women to University College London: A Centenary Lecture* (London, 1979), 5.
[30] *King's College London Calendar* (1850–1), 22–3.
[31] Todd M. Endelman, *Radical Assimilation in English Jewish History, 1656–1945* (Bloomington, 1990), Chapter 5.
[32] *K. C. Calendar*, (1856–7), 40.

London manufacturers in the food, soap, glass and cement industries, contributions after the 1880s became increasingly part of a major applied science and research effort second to none in the kingdom. Sir William Ramsay at University College was a consultant to the British Radium Corporation in London and was involved in the beginnings of what became the great chemical firm of Courtauld's located in Kew. The establishment of the Imperial College of Technology in 1907 greatly extended the University of London's capacity for high-level technology in such fields as electrical engineering, gas, industrial dyestuffs and petroleum. By 1914 the university was actively involved in agriculture and aeronautics but not marine engineering, navigation and nautical astronomy despite the capital's Thameside location.[33]

However, the new research undertakings were not necessarily restricted to London markets, especially toward the end of the century. Secret work was performed for the national steel industry, as well as for government, and London professors had connections to firms in places like Huddersfield, Warrington and Manchester. The historian who has done the most to advance our understanding of the relationships between British industry and universities has stated that the ties between researchers in the University of London and manufacturers located in the capital were actually not as strong as those between civic universities and their cities, especially in the north. He lays the proximate blame at the feet of local industrialists rather than the university and the ultimate blame on the nature of the metropolis. 'London', he concludes, 'was too large to generate a cohesive movement of loyal support to its own university.'[34]

UPWARD ACADEMIC DRIFT?

Today higher education institutions are defined as urban if their location is in a city, if their student body is recruited locally, if improved access is a policy objective, if professional or specialised programmes of study are featured and if the institution repeatedly shows itself sensitive to urban social and economic problems.[35] By all of these criteria both University and King's College were urban in conception and commitment. The first two

[33] Michael Sanderson, *The Universities and British Industry, 1850–1970* (London, 1972), 106–20.
[34] *Ibid.*, 118. Sanderson, 'The Professor as Industrial Consultant: Oliver Arnold and the British Steel Industry, 1900–1914', *Economic History Review*, 31 (November, 1978), 585–600.
[35] Title XI of the United States Higher Education Act of 1980. See Henry R. Winkler, 'Higher Education in an Urban Context', in *Preparation for Life? The Paradox of Education in the Late Twentieth Century*, ed. Joan N. Burstyn (Lewes and Philadelphia, 1986), 58–76.

university colleges of the University of London were remarkable examples of the new social forces at work in England in the third and fourth decades of the nineteenth century. The early educational policies adopted by both were strongly oriented to the local market and were in this respect, as in so many others, conscious departures from the historic model offered by the ancient universities. Yet we must be prepared for a paradox. Despite these undeniable facts, the subsequent development of the University of London is a history of academic drift, of movement away from what appeared to be a primary local market orientation towards a wider set of objectives. To capture this movement, we must recall that underlying the earliest speculations concerning the expansion of higher education in England was the question of a 'national' university mission for Dissenters whose political strength and numbers actually lay outside London. As long as there was some hope that the connections between Oxford and Cambridge and the Church of England could be relaxed, the matter of a national university was secondary. But its great constitutional victories of 1828 to 1832 notwithstanding, the Dissenting community failed in its efforts to use Parliament to remove subscription to the Thirty-nine Articles of the Church as a virtual condition of attendance at the ancient universities. The House of Lords, where the bishops sat, could not be brought around, and the ancient foundations were able to hold tightly fast to their monopoly despite strong Commons support for the integration of Dissenters. Failure reopened interest in the possibility of a national university for Dissenters in some other location, but the non-sectarian direction of University College had already been set.

The question of a national university for Dissenters and others brought up the related issue of whether the new institution would be empowered to grant degrees. The degree problem had been shelved in the 1820s because Brougham, anxious to see the new enterprise launched, wanted to avoid unnecessary controversy. Everyone knew, however, that the issue would reappear. Of little use to the landed aristocracy whose sons attended Oxford and Cambridge, since their careers and fortunes were otherwise ensured, degrees were valued by Dissenters and others in need of a certification of competence. Degrees were also necessary for fellowships in the royal medical societies, although this privilege could only be bestowed upon Oxbridge graduates.

The degree in Britain was protected from market forces. As such it was presumed to be relatively free of precisely the kind of local pressures to which the new self-styled 'university' was responding. It could not be created virtually at will as in the American case but represented, no matter how imperfectly, a standard of learning and especially 'discipline'.

It was a privilege bestowed by the centre and specified in the grant of a royal charter obtained by prayer to the Crown in Council.

The Privy Council was divided on the issue of a London University degree, but the House of Commons was strongly in favour and voted a memorial to the Crown. Many members of the government also supported the new institution, but in the complicated and protracted process of deliberation, which covered the years from 1831 to 1836, the Church lobby was able to rally its supporters. The education offered by the new institution was faulty and suspect, opponents said. The standard was lower and would be driven still lower by a helpless dependence on consumer preference. This could be shown in the first instance by the absence of theological instruction. But there was also no teaching of religious ethics as part of moral philosophy, no required attendance at chapel and no reference whatsoever to even the most broadly defined Christian heritage. At stake, therefore, was a particular definition or conception of university education in England: that it had, via history and law, a close and inextricable connection with the Church of England, and that the Crown, to which the Privy Council was advisory, was bound to that law and was itself part of the Church of England, the head and supreme governor, in fact, and could not, however well disposed to the new University of London, contradict itself. The bachelor's degree carried certain privileges largely related to ecclesiastical purposes, and to grant these to graduates of a 'metropolitan pest-house' was unthinkable.[36]

Since no nondenominational university had ever been founded in Britain before the 1820s, the law governing the title 'university' was unclear. The issue had simply never arisen, but in a period of intense religious rivalries and evangelical and High Church revival, an attempt was made by the Church party to attach a narrow and precise legal definition to a vague historical word. Happily, the Church found an unlikely but invaluable ally in the opposition of the organised medical profession, whose strength and resources lay in the capital. The teaching hospitals and royal medical societies did not want control over the education of doctors shifted to a new institution, and to give the London University power to award degrees, including medical degrees, meant the potential loss of medical recruits for themselves.[37]

---

[36] For the Establishment argument, see Sir Charles Wetherell, *Substance of the Speech of Sir Charles Wetherell before the Lords of the Privy Council on the Subject of Incorporating the London University* (London, 1834).

[37] Bellot, *University College*, 236–7.

Learning was inseparable from discipline, and the standards of both had to be maintained. Universities in Britain existed to teach undergraduates (medical students were usually undergraduates as well), and undergraduates, whether at English or at Scottish universities, were under the tutelage of teachers concerned with their moral superintendence. The new University of London was more than godless. It had (so opponents claimed) shamefully abandoned students to the extreme dangers of London streets and temptations of the nearby West End theatres. These charges were irritating, especially in light of the notorious conduct of Oxbridge sporting hearties, and they were countered by arguments pointing out the virtues of home residence. Yet supporters of the audacious London University were sensitive to the accusation that they were no more than a licensed business offering a mechanical or utilitarian education indifferent to the moral development of the whole person – a particular view of liberal education that had come to be closely associated with residential forms of higher education. The first warden of London University himself made a compromising analogy when he (proudly) informed Brougham in 1828 that the new institution in Gower Street was 'a great machine . . . Your pleasure would be something like Watts' when he first saw the steady majestic motion of a great engine.'[38] This unfortunate image was used at a time when the mechanistic language of the eighteenth-century Enlightenment was being replaced by organic metaphors of nurturing, growth and development. A university education was supposed to form and shape character and inculcate a sense of high responsibility to society. It was not, as Maurice would inform his students at King's College, an instrument for selfishly advancing one's social and economic position in society.

There followed the famous solution of 1836 discussed in an earlier chapter. The new 'royal university' was denominated a 'public' institution, but the original foundations were to remain 'private', as were Oxford and Cambridge colleges. Private bodies could impose religious tests or make any other disciplinary arrangements for students, and therefore King's College could keep religious tests for its students (which it did, but for only full-time students). University College could retain its secular status, but in the act of preparing students for degrees the infidel college would not have control over the university curriculum and standards.

University College was unhappy but bowed to the inevitable. The new constitution did not altogether suit King's College either. No religious

---

[38] New, *Henry Brougham*, 383.

instruction was necessary to pass the London University's examinations, and degrees were not awarded in divinity. For several years King's boycotted the university's examinations altogether, finally submitting to the market in the form of student pressure.[39]

The solution of 1836 divided responsibility for teaching and examining between two very different kinds of institutions – colleges and university – but a connection was maintained through the stipulation that candidates for degrees show proof of attendance at lectures in officially recognised 'affiliated' institutions. In 1850 new colleges in the empire were allowed to affiliate, but in 1858 the whole idea of a formal affiliation was dropped, with the sole exception of candidates for medical degrees. The university was now permitted to grant degrees to anyone who had successfully taken and passed its examinations. It no longer mattered whether candidates had actually attended lectures at King's and University colleges. It no longer mattered whether candidates had been tutored at recognised or affiliated institutions. They could be taught privately, attend cramming sessions, sign up for courses in new civic colleges such as Owens College, attend extramural courses or be tutored in remote imperial territories. They could sit examinations with only the equivalent of a sixth-form school preparation. None of this was of consequence in deciding who could take the London University degree examinations, and at this stage London was the world's first Open University.

Thus initial steps were taken toward granting the degree to 'external students' so important in the twentieth century. To begin with there were neither internal nor external students, only students, but with the reforms of the early twentieth century an internal teaching staff was created, and the distinction could now be made. But external degree candidates remained extremely important and actually outnumbered those who were reading for an 'internal degree'.[40] By the end of the nineteenth century the

---

[39] Heulin, *King's College London*, 15. The religious issue as a national issue is well illustrated by Thomas Arnold's latitudinarianism. He was outraged by the compromise of 1836. 'There is no difficulty', he angrily wrote from Rugby School in 1837, 'with Dissenters of any denomination', but 'are we really for the sake of a few Jews, who may like to have a Degree in Arts, – or for the sake of one or two Mahomedans, who may possibly have the same wish, or for the sake of English unbelievers . . . – are we to destroy our only chance of our being even either useful or respected as an Institution of national education?' Arthur Penryhn Stanley, *The Life and Correspondence of Thomas Arnold*, 9th ed., II (London, 1868), 9, 82, 85.

[40] Technically, the Act of 1836 made all degrees external, but a *de facto* distinction could be drawn between degrees awarded to students in attendance at London colleges or schools and those who were taught in the provinces and overseas. Careful statistics are difficult to gather, but according to one calculation for the years 1889, 1890 and 1891, a total of 138 first degrees were awarded to students from London institutions, 240 to students from national institutions and 552 to candidates from elsewhere. Therefore, approximately 15 per cent took

external-degree function of the university was so pronounced that a bill in Parliament to strengthen the position of resident teachers was opposed on the grounds that it would 'Londonise' what was a university for the empire.[41]

The division of labour between a set of teaching institutions and a central administrative body represented a brilliant compromise among deeply opposed religious, professional and social interests, between entrenched institutions and upstarts. It was a compromise between a local and a national conception of a university's responsibility to society, since it appears plausible that the strict separation of centre and periphery was intended to forestall some of the implications of a free market for higher education. Created by shareholders, weakly endowed and driven by fees, the godless institution in Gower Street was highly vulnerable. The founders were willing to offer part-time courses, evening classes and remedial education to attract the occasional and, as we now say, the 'mature' student and to make still other adjustments to the requirements of the urban London market. Charges that standards would be sacrificed in an effort to attract students were not totally disingenuous, as even parliamentary supporters of University College were willing to admit.[42] To prevent downward drift in the quality of the degree, the architects of the compromise of 1836 took examining out of the hands of professors and deprived them of a role in setting the highest standards of academic achievement.

It was a considerable exaggeration to suggest by comparison that the academic standard at the Oxbridge colleges was particularly noteworthy when only a small number of their undergraduates in the 1820s and 1830s showed an inclination to compete for BA distinction, but the number of degree candidates was unquestionably growing, and students sitting the honours degree examinations were attracting attention and praise. Had the 'new discipline' not taken hold at Oxford and Cambridge, it is doubtful whether opponents of the first London University would have been able to make their case.

While the precise requirements of 1836 were not altogether satisfactory

---

what may be called 'internal' first degrees. Humberstone, *University Reform*, 67. In 1903, when a formal distinction between inside and outside degrees was made, there were 912 external candidates for all degrees compared to 160 internal candidates. Royal Commission on University Education in London (1911), Appendix to Second Report, 240.

[41] Humberstone, *University Reform*, 70.

[42] Dr Lushington in Parliamentary Papers, House of Commons Debates (26 March 1835), cols. 285–6. A hint that King's did not perform university-level work in the arts and divinity courses appears in the *King's College London Calendar for 1846*, 12.

for King's College, the compromise fulfilled some of its earlier aspirations. King's had been searching for ways of embracing a national mission and mitigating its relationship to the local open market. It is true that in much of its curriculum and in its establishment of departments of medicine and engineering the college in the Strand had followed the lead of University College in appealing to a London constituency. It had similarly made provision for part-time students, but at the same time it had endeavoured to follow the example of the two senior English universities and attach itself to the Establishment. In order to attract the patronage of the court of King George IV (with some minor success), it had named itself after the monarch and obtained a royal charter of incorporation in 1829, although without the right to grant degrees. From the start it had connected itself to the Church of England. The principal was to be in holy orders; professors, with a few exceptions, were expected to be members of the Established Church; and outside ecclesiastical leaders were part of the structure of governance. The college's loyalties were caught between a market and an elite conception of education, which is where King's remained for the rest of the century.[43]

The creation of a second and different University of London was a solution to the problem of quality control, as it was at the same time a compromise between rival conceptions of a university education. The two colleges, or any other affiliated institutions, remained free to establish their own working relationships with the local market, to include admissions, the level of fees, staffing and non-degree courses; but in so far as they wished their undergraduates to obtain degrees, they had to submit their teaching to an impartial audit in the form of external examinations. A meritocratic top pressed down on a mass-market base to allow access while controlling the output of graduates, leading to protracted disputes between the colleges and the university, between the professors who wanted to teach (or conduct research) in their own way and a body of outside examiners who were primarily interested in guaranteeing the degree standard and the uniform quality of undergraduate teaching and who captured the high moral ground since they had no pecuniary interest in the success of candidates.

Through the machinery of degree examinations, the new royal institution insulated new university colleges from the pressures for open access and easy degrees. It could also be said that while it protected

---

[43] Martin Trow defines elite education in 'Problems in the Transition from Elite to Mass Education', *Policies for Higher Education,* General Report of the Organisation for Economic Co-operation and Development (Paris, 1974), 55–101, esp. 80–1.

institutions, it also prevented them from adopting policies aimed at improving market position and competing with one another for students and resources. Administrative costs for the examining university were minimal. Staffs were small and overheads low. This was an important political objective of mid-Victorian liberalism, which favoured cheap forms of administration and high consumer choice, but at the same time accepted a minimal regulatory role for the State in such matters as education, the protection of minors in industry and the adulteration of food. The constitution of 1858 had been adopted because the University of London found itself without the resources to determine whether certificates of attendance in affiliated institutions were genuine and reflected a serious level of instruction.[44] It was simply more practical and economical to affirm the principle of minimal governmental interference by controlling examinations, which could be made as stringent as desired. Indeed, after 1858 the examination noticeably stiffened, and in the 1860s nearly half the candidates for degrees were failed.[45]

From the middle of the nineteenth century until the last decades, when a noisy campaign was waged for what was called a 'teaching university' in the capital, the University of London had a confused relationship with the metropolitan area that had been its original home. A 'Cockney University' it may have been from the start but a wider mission was hinted at. An early statement looked forward to a time when the university's draw would be world-wide. Lord Auckland, who had been the first president of the council of the original University of London, predicted that his institution would become imperial, that colonial students would journey to London to study in Gower Street.[46] It is in the middle years of the nineteenth century that the sources first begin to mention actual imperial responsibilities. The council of King's College referred to the need for civil engineers to build railways 'in the various dependencies of the British Crown, particularly in the East Indies, in Canada, and in Australia', and fully expected King's students to seek such opportunities, recalling in their service 'at home and abroad, the sound religious principles, as well as the

---

[44] Negley Harte, *The University of London 1836–1986* (London, 1986), 74, credits Thomas Spring Rice, Chancellor of the Exchequer, with playing the leading part in creating the University of London of 1836 but provides no account of his precise role or the genesis of his ideas. Judging by a hilarious obituary notice in *The Times* for 9 February 1866, 10, the Irish-born politician had few admirers, but new work is uncovering his role in many important educational enterprises. See Ian D. C. Newbould, 'The Whigs, the Church, and Education, 1839', *Journal of British Studies*, 26 (July, 1987), 333.

[45] Harte, *University of London*, 106.

[46] Arthur Percival Newton, *The Universities and the Educational Systems of the British Empire* (London, 1924), 18; Bellot, *University College*, 48.

science, the industrious habits, and the practical skill which they have learnt within the walls'.[47]

Having thus begun as an experiment in higher education to establish a new university called 'metropolitan', London University rapidly acquired a national mission and almost concurrently an imperial one. Local ties and services were certainly maintained, as already enumerated, but the London University was not a 'municipal' institution as sixteenth-century Edinburgh had been a Town College, responsible to a well-defined local authority and incorporating Renaissance and Reformation theories of public responsibility. It was not even a 'civic' one, to draw a further distinction between universities that are municipal and maintained by local authorities and those that are independent but in a more general way represent the principal interests of specific urban regions. Although London is sometimes called a civic university, credit for being Britain's first such institution must go to Birmingham. Given the association between a university and the nation that existed in the 1830s and beyond, given the nature of the capital – its patchwork system of internal governance; its increasing economic, political and cultural domination of the kingdom; and its position as (to use a geographer's phrase) a 'primate' city – civic status would have been far too limiting.

For many the supersession of the original university by a different conception was perfectly consistent with the character of the metropolis as the centre of a proud island kingdom and as a global city or, as so many of its inhabitants were pleased to say, the 'Metropolis of the world'.[48] But others phrased it differently. Less pleased, the principal of King's College said in 1888 that the University of London was not a university and was not of London.[49]

LONDON: THE UNIQUE CITY

London was a great city, possessing the population, the human and capital resources, the communications infrastructure, the cultural institutions and the grandeur and style that great cities possess, but it was also a special kind of urban creation. To appreciate that dimension of its history and to grasp its importance for understanding the place of the London University in nineteenth-century Britain, we need to view the metropolis's

---

[47] *K. C. Calendar* (1856–7), 41.

[48] *Spectator*, 18 (18 June 1898), 851. London's nineteenth-century domination over English provincial cities is illuminatingly discussed in Donald Read, *The English Provinces, 1769–1960: A Study in Influence* (London, 1964), 232–61.

[49] Harte, *University of London*, 120.

morphology and cultural traits from another, a broader, and, to begin with, a comparative and offshore perspective.

London has often struck Continental visitors as the least European of great cities. A classic work by a Danish architect and city planner approvingly calls London unique because of its human scale, represented principally by its special morphology of a central core of Georgian squares, low-rise prospect and endless suburban villages separated by green spaces.[50] The latter features have also led some critics to call the metropolis anti-urban. A second Continental observer provides us with one typical elaboration of this view. The Englishman, he says, 'has no feeling for the beauty of the town . . . [He] has no scruples about destroying monuments of architecture, but is up in arms as soon as anyone proposes to fell a tree.'[51] The real love of the English is the garden, the landscaped square, the park: space use historically associated with the stately home, the cathedral town, the hamlet, the country cottage, the village green, the churchyard overgrown with grass and wildflowers, common land, lovers' lanes and hedgerows filled with game and song-birds. The English prefer low-rise buildings and detached or semi-detached houses – in a word, the suburb, particularly and especially that great Victorian creation, the garden suburb, which crossed the Atlantic and appeared at such places as Forest Hills. London is the anti-city because the suburb is what matters, the periphery and not the centre. The two interpenetrate in a carefully defined manner. The periphery is the private and separate world of home and family. The centre is the public world of work, competition and strain. The animation of city streets is a fact of daylight. At night one nurses the soul in the isolation of the suburb.[52]

Historically it was not always this way. In the eighteenth century, men of letters, critics, Grub Street journalists, people of fashion and habitués of the theatres regarded London as the embodiment of civilisation or civility. There was a darker side – the mob, the idle and debauched, the stews and rookeries, the thieving and physical squalor – but even these drawbacks contributed to the unique thrill and adventure that was a city. The concentration of population and resources, elegant structures, pace and

---

[50] Steen Eiler Rasmussen, *London: The Unique City* (London, 1948).

[51] Paul Cohen-Portheim, *England, the Unknown Isle* (New York, 1931), 87–8.

[52] For the Victorian suburb, see Williams, *Country and City*, 47; D. A. Reeder, 'A Theatre of Suburbs: Some Patterns of Development in West London, 1801–1911', in *The Study of Urban History,* ed. H. J. Dyos (London, 1968); Dyos, *Victorian Suburb* (Leicester, 1973); Donald J. Olsen, *The Growth of Victorian London* (London, 1976), and 'Victorian London: Specialization, Segregation and Privacy', *Victorian Studies*, 17 (March 1974), 265–78; Alan A. Jackson, *Semi-Detached London* (London, 1973); and Nicholas Taylor, *The Village in the City* (London, 1973).

perpetual novelty stimulated conversation, broadened one's understanding of human affairs and the human condition and extended the
range and possibilities of personal achievement. A city and London
especially were places that excited the imagination and heightened
perceptions, and some nineteenth-century commentators, still under
this spell, even applied to the capital the word *sublime*, normally reserved
for natural and supernatural phenomena.[53] A great city was the
Enlightenment itself, a source of hopeful ideas about human potential and
material progress. It followed that a city did not necessarily require a
university because the city itself was a university, at least according to
littérateurs such as Joseph Addison, the Oxford graduate, for whom a
superior education was acquired in the corner of a London coffee house
affording an outlook upon the vibrant, laughing town.

These sentiments did not vanish in the next century, nor have they
vanished today. They still exist everywhere as part of the mental baggage
citizens carry with them into daily life. However, against the view that
London was urbane and civilised there arose a different opinion in the
nineteenth century, namely, that a city had the defects of its merits. If it
was a source of lively invention, it did not necessarily respect tradition and
custom. If it was a source of ambitious experiment, it deprecated the old
ways. The desire to embrace the very latest in news and fashion inclined
the successful to ignore the unsuccessful, as did competition for the city's
considerable resources. It was easy enough, in a community of large
numbers of strangers, to feel lost or marginal, handicapped or disadvan-
taged. Sublime for some in the eighteenth century, London became
pandemonium for others in the nineteenth century, an infernal city
or Babylon. 'Even Dickens', writes Richard Shannon, 'the first major
imaginative writer to accept the unavoidable reality of the city, never
reconciled himself to it as the primary source of moral energy.'[54]

From the 1860s on, when the underground and overground railways
began to transport Londoners farther out into the pastoral regions of the
greater metropolitan environment, London was sharply transformed
from a city that had once been strongly influenced by Italian Renaissance
ideas of central town planning to a city ringed and interpenetrated by
suburban villas and gardens. The financial district closed down at night.
Centrally located flats, of which a few were built at mid-century, were

[53] Nicholas Taylor, 'The Awful Sublimity of the Victorian City', in *The Victorian City: Images
and Realities,* ed. H. J. Dyos and Michael Wolff, II (London and Boston, 1973). See also
Sheldon Rothblatt, 'Nineteenth-Century London,' in *People and Communities in the Western
World,* ed. Gene Brucker (Homewood, IL, 1979), 199–206.

[54] Richard Shannon, *The Crisis of Imperialism, 1865–1915* (St Albans, 1976), 270.

occupied only by *boulevardiers*, bachelors and others suspected of loose morals. No respectable family lived in the centre. The slums spread and were shut off from the more fortunately situated residential areas. Neither the city nor its more fashionable population continued to orient itself to the street, as they were inclined to do when the fine public squares of the preceding century were laid out and as Paris and Vienna still did.

The Victorians (and Edwardians) preferred cities that evoked villa and countryside; and most of nineteenth-century London, as well as provincial factory cities and seaports, drifted toward a suburban configuration. The result was many Londons rolled into one. There was the London of fogs, crime and terrifying slums stretching from Aldgate eastward along the Thames and northward into Middlesex. There was the London of the two historic 'cities', the City of Westminster, royal and glamorous (but once also the home of the radical Utilitarians who helped in the establishment of University College), and the City of London, the greatest capital market in the world. There was the London of the garden suburbs, country villages in the city, plantations of fine and pleasant houses such as Regent's Park and Swiss Cottage or Bedford Park, or modest but desirable districts like Camberwell south of the river, the new home of the lower middle class, especially clerks from London's expanding office economy.

A CAPITAL UNIVERSITY

The new University of London corresponded more to the ideals of the older eighteenth-century city than to the nineteenth. The equation of cities with civilisation in Enlightenment Europe, the public conception of city life that led to the proliferation of open squares and public gathering places, the orientation to the street and the feeling that the Town was a source of social and intellectual emancipation were closer to the vision of an interconnected university and city held by the founders of the infidel university than later Victorian views. The neoclassical façade of University College, designed by the same architect who was building the British Museum, at once declared its affiliation with the grand tradition and demanded a prominent place in the cityscape. (King's was laid out as a set of palladian terraces forming a cloister approached through an arch. The site constraints were serious, but the difference in orientation to the street and invocation of the 'gothic' universe of reference was significant.) By one of history's ironies, the university was founded at precisely the moment when the pressures and problems of city life were beginning to attract considerable critical attention, when the Romantic exaltation of village and field was influential and when the flight to the suburbs was about to commence. Raymond Williams called this major reorientation in the topographical sensibility of the English a 'rentier's or dormitory dream'.[55] A different view of the ideal university was emerging and found its home in the reviving fortunes of Oxford and Cambridge, whose residential colleges and tutors *in loco parentis* more closely approximated suburban aspirations than did the aims of the new colleges in the geographical centre of the capital. The revival of Oxford and Cambridge, the mid-century 'Young Oxford' and 'Young Cambridge' spirit that accompanied the reform movement, and the ensuing golden age of the colleges corresponded exactly to the suburban juxtaposition of beauty, young manhood or womanhood, innocence and segregation, the private and the personal. The ideal university was situated among giant horse-chestnut trees and fields of asphodel, and in quiet cloisters were heard the sound of chapel bells through the soft nights of summer. But here is the authentic mid-Victorian voice itself, declaiming the Romantic mythos of Oxford to a House of Commons assembled to consider reform legislation:

> Could anyone who looked back to a place, which, despite of regrets for time mis-spent, and opportunities wasted, was endeared to him by a thousand recollections, – could any one who had formerly paced the High Street and the Long Walk, who carried with him the memory of his first responsi-bilities in life, of his early struggles, perhaps of his early successes, – could any one who still cherished, as one of his greatest privileges, the friendships first formed and cemented within some college quadrangle, – could any one influenced by these feelings and these recollections fail to have taken a deep interest in a measure vitally affecting that great institution?[56]

It is all here: the special freedom of youth to choose and to choose wrongly; the process of exchanging immaturity for responsible manhood; the associations of notable streets and byways; the friendships caught and made and enforced by special enclosures; and even the despised exam-inations which provide opportunities for success as well as failure. The whole is an adventure with its temptations and dangers – is there any other way to learn? – but ultimately rich in feelings and recollections that abide and influence.[57]

[55] Williams, *Country and City*, 47, 297. The suburban perspective imposed on the tradition of rustic painting is discussed in Ann Bermingham, *Landscape and Ideology: The English Rustic Tradition, 1740–1860* (Berkeley, CA, 1986).

[56] G. E. Vernon, Discussion on the Second Reading of the Oxford University Bill, Parlia-mentary Papers, House of Commons, cxxxii (7 April 1854), col. 715.

[57] Kolbe, *Urban Influences*, 127, speaks of an impairment of the aesthetic sense as one of the drawbacks of urban-based education: '[Youth] of the college age is particularly susceptible

The ideal university, then, did not lie in London districts such as Bloomsbury, where University College and its medical school were to be found, or in South Kensington, where the Imperial College was to have its home, although Egham, where in the 1880s Thomas Holloway had used the immense profits from the sale of quack medicines to build a storybook French chateau as a college for women, was pleasantly suburban and had real possibilities. The genuine article lay much farther afield, well beyond the edges of London's northernmost suburbs, across the ridges of hills where Roman soldiers had marched and past country churches, in the busy market towns that still embody one of the most alluring dreams in the repertory of universities. For the moment we can capture the essence of that dream by saying that it is (or was) fundamentally anti-urban as urban was understood in the nineteenth century.[58] It rejected the laboratory of experiment that is the city, as well as the urban assumption that socialising the young is the joint responsibility of many institutions. It took its inspiration from tradition and from an ancient belief in the importance of educating young people to be 'whole', not professional. As good a symbolic statement of the separation of city and university, of town and gown, as one might imagine took place in 1858 when the mayor of Oxford was no longer required to take an annual oath to keep 'the liberties and customs of the University . . . for the quietness and weal of this University, and of this town also, or city'. On the day of the mayor's feast to celebrate the removal of an ancient burden, the university proctors do not patrol the streets, except to quell a student riot.[59]

The Victorian debate on higher education, therefore, was also connected to an on-going larger cultural debate on the merits of the city and the country and whether cities could even provide the kind of nurturing environment from which strong and self-confident personalities came forth. Something of the flavour of that debate is preserved in these well-known remarks about two undergraduates who attended University College in the 1840s:

to beauty of surroundings . . . The memories of a college life spent among beautiful surroundings form an intangible treasure which is not the least of the benefits of higher education.' Whether true or not, the idea has had a profound effect upon campus planning in the United States as discussed in Chapter 2.

[58] I am aware that for earlier centuries different criteria were used, and Oxford City was indeed urban, as small towns were 'cities' and returned 'citizens' to Parliament if they had a cathedral.

[59] L. H. Dudley Buxton and Strickland Gibson, *Oxford University Ceremonies* (Oxford, 1935), 154–5.

It is sometimes said that it needs the quiet of a country town, remote from the capital, to foster the love of genuine study in young men. But of this at least I am sure: that Gower Street, and Oxford Street, and the New Road, and the dreary chain of squares from Euston to Bloomsbury, were the scenes of discussions as eager and as abstract as ever were the sedate cloisters or the flowery river meadows of Cambridge or Oxford.[60]

This is Richard Holt Hutton recounting the day that he and Walter Bagehot, the renowned editor of *The Economist*, were lost in philosophic argument and therefore unable to locate Regent Street after many hours of wandering. The anecdote is intended to illustrate the exciting early days of the University of London and to suggest the positive effect on learning that a city can have. The exchange of intellectual ideas takes place on a public street, not in a protective enclave. The environment is neither beautiful nor evocative: the streets, simply a list taken from a map, have no wider frame or reference, and inner London squares are unappealing, only a 'dreary chain . . . from Euston to Bloomsbury'. The physical setting is contrasted with other kinds of 'scenes' where eager and abstract discussion occurs in order to reinforce the point that place is irrelevant. The *genius loci* is deliberately banished but suggested in the conventional equation of a 'scene' with attractive and romantic topography. And a final comparison is made between 'sedate cloisters' and city energy where conversation occurs during the long stretches of walking that city thoroughfares allow.

The anecdote is a eulogy of intellectual life and the power of ideas and debate, and these, it may be argued, are particularly characteristic of a great city. They derive from the dynamism of the city, its open and inquisitive character, and its abstract or distancing nature. The Oxbridge idyll, however, was not about distancing but about intimacy. It was more than the life of the mind. It was also about friendships, tradition, associations and loyalties, about the very fact of being young and hopeful. The English idea of a university was that it was cloistered and self-contained, its own milieu. When Durham University was founded in the early 1830s, virtually on the heels of the London University, it was located in a cathedral town on a bluff overlooking a delightful English river. All the correct historical associations were present. (Durham's lack of success despite these advantages is another story.)

Youth was presumed to be responsive to the symbols of association,

[60] *The Works of Walter Bagehot*, ed. Forrest Morgan, I (Hartford, CT, 1891), xxvii–viii.

tradition and beauty celebrated in Victorian neo-historicism. In the London University there was to be

> no melodramatic pageantry, no ancient ceremonial, no silver mace, no gowns either black or red, no hoods either of fur or of satin, no public orator to make speeches which nobody hears, no oaths sworn only to be broken. Nobody thought of emulating the cloisters, the organs, the painted glass, the withered mummies, the busts of great men, and the pictures of naked women, which attract visitors from every part of the Island to the banks of Isis and Cam.

But the same sardonic writer, a talented and confident graduate of Trinity College, Cambridge, converted to London's cause, was prepared to sweep away the romantic cobwebs concealing the truth that 'Young academicians venture to get drunk within a few yards of the grave of Newton, and to commit solecisms, though the awful eye of Erasmus frowns upon them from the canvas.'[61] Nevertheless, just as the metropolis was a 'Grete Wen' to detractors like the rural apologist William Cobbett, who in a famous image of the 1820s compared it to a swollen, suppurating, repulsive blemish on the face of England, meaning also that it was a tissue of unhappy and indissolubly connected social relationships, so was it stated that the university founded there was unsuitable for educating the young.[62] Urban attachments in Victorian England were not as strong as pastoral ones and could not be similarly sentimentalised. In short, '[a] Metropolitan University, whose students live at home or in lodgings, cannot under any conceivable arrangements offer an exact equivalent of camaraderie, "studious cloisters pale" and "the elms which shaded Newton or Milton"', wrote *The Quarterly Review* in 1887.[63]

Walking about London, Bagehot and Holt found the squares and streets of Bloomsbury second to none as places for animated intellectual talk, but on another occasion Bagehot defined the process of a university education differently and with a different emphasis as the 'impact of young thought upon young thought, of fresh thought on fresh thought, of hot thought on hot thought',[64] words that describe the close friendships and school-like environment of isolated English (or American) colleges, not universities open to the world. They are also words that do not

[61] [Thomas Babington Macaulay], 'Thoughts on the Advancement of Academical Education in England', *Edinburgh Review*, 43 (1826), 316, 324.

[62] Cobbett was not the first writer to use the word 'wen' in relation to London. Williams, *Country and City*, 146.

[63] *Quarterly Review* (January, 1887), 57–8.

[64] Bagehot, *Works*, xcii–xciii.

correspond to the sophistication and cosmopolitanism associated with cities but to the inexperience that confuses thinking with discovery. During the University of London reorganisation controversy of the 1890s, a writer for the *Spectator* was led to praise private American universities such as Harvard for retaining the kind of aesthetic environment long considered essential for educating young people while adopting a research function. Without lawns, rivers and quadrangles, without a 'campus', without separate space, there was no such thing as a university.[65]

Against this history and in relation to it, the first University of London had undertaken a formidable assignment. A university for the capital had been discussed since the seventeenth century but had never been achieved. Once achieved, it had encountered two types of opposition: the clerical and religious establishment, in alliance with the entrenched interests of the older liberal professions, accustomed to privileges and monopolies; and the equally effective and widespread sentiment that cities were inherently threatening and competitive, dangerous to mental and bodily health alike.[66] The history of nineteenth-century London University, therefore, is the history of a new type of institution attempting to discover a mission for itself unique and special enough to avoid unflattering comparisons to Oxford and Cambridge.

That search was full of unexpected twists and turns, many of them outside the control of the first University of London but a logical or at least understandable result of the larger cultural and institutional history of England. Once the title 'university' was taken from a privately funded college and delivered to an agency of the State – restored, that is, to the 'public' sphere where by tradition and dubiously by law universities belonged – it could be predicted that a change of mission and ethos would follow. 'Public' educational institutions had wider responsibilities than private ones. Such was certainly the history of those historic grammar schools that had once been the source of local pride and initiative but had gone 'public' in the eighteenth century, expanding their intake to regions well outside their original catchment areas. Such was to be the history of those early- and mid-nineteenth century proprietary schools that metamorphosed into great Victorian boarding schools in their own right, proud of their role in producing political and military leaders for the

[65] *Spectator*, 18 (12 February 1898), 231.
[66] See Bruce Haley, *The Healthy Body and Victorian Culture* (Cambridge, MA, 1978). In his diary Shephard Taylor describes the violence and dangers of London during his days as a King's medical student in the 1860s. He attended about three or four public hangings, repulsed the advances of prostitutes and was several times the victim of pickpockets. He mentions a number of grisly murders, one of them the garrotting of a fellow student.

empire.[67] Here certainly was a conjunction of purposes. Glamour was always available in an imperial dimension. Lord Rosebery, the sometime Liberal foreign secretary, opined in 1903 that the London University should stand to the British empire as the great technological institution in Berlin, the Charlottenburg, stood to the German empire.[68] For that purpose, for professional education, for scientific research, for the study of tropical medicine and exotic languages, for the development of the applied social sciences, if not for a traditional English undergraduate education, the new university was perfectly situated. It was a capital university in the heart of empire. What else could be expected?

AT HOME

It has been said that great universities do not make much difference to capital cities.[69] The university in a metropolis is no more obvious than great courts of law, than organs of government, than the headquarters of global corporations, than the intellectual and artistic life that may in fact go on without it. The university is no more visible than other giant edifices. The sudden vision of Magdalen Tower in the High or the fantastic appearance of screen, porter's lodge and chapel of the college in the King's Parade at Cambridge best achieve their theatrical effect without competition. Imagine an eighteenth-century *capriccio* of Oxbridge colleges painted in London settings. What would be the impact? The charmingly irresistible collegiate courts and spires would no more dominate the metropolis than does the London law school of Lincoln's Inn which resembles them. Perhaps in 1828 there was a chance. The capital was still advancing. The great public buildings, hotels, banks and insurance companies were yet to be built. Even so, the effect of University College's handsome front was limited. There was no campus of walks, gardens and meadows and no soaring campanile. As the century moved along, the University of London's fiefdoms were not concentrated in a single spot or neighbourhood but scattered throughout the capital, absorbed by it and coterminous with it. Sir William Beveridge understood the difficulty when in 1928 he called for a new central administration

[67] For which see J. A. Mangan, *The Games Ethic and Imperialism* (Harmondsworth, 1986).
[68] Humberstone, *University Reform*, 168.
[69] Cohen-Portheim, *England*, 95. A similar thought has occurred to Daniel Bell. In *The Reforming of General Education* (New York, 1966), 3–4, he writes: 'In its traditions and public character, Columbia has ambitiously sought to be the great university in the great city, though never wholly succeeding to that task. (What single institution can dominate this city?)'

building that would replace the Imperial Institute in South Kensington that was the university's headquarters from 1900 to 1936, itself a replacement for the original Burlington House. It was an imposing enough building in mass, but evidently not imposing enough. The University of London needed a clearer statement of its relation to the metropolis:

> The University of London is at once civic and national and international, federal and collegiate, though not residential, a poor man's University in a city of boundless wealth . . . The central symbol of the Bloomsbury site can not fittingly look like an imitation of any other University; it must not be a replica from the middle ages. It should be something that . . . can only be at home in London.[70]

A tutelary spirit inhabits buildings that are replicas of the middle ages, hidden among the surprises of irregularity. London has its share of twisted alleys, concealed walks and unannounced vistas, its picturesque moments, but what is required of an imperial university is not a series of low-rise sheltered spaces but a strong and loud symbol of authority and domination. When completed, the Senate House was the tallest building in London.[71] It is not so today. Most assuredly it is not a replica of the middle ages. It is not a college masquerading as a Cotswold village. Unlike such historical possibilities, it has worn badly. In fact, it has not worn at all, having been called 'one of Mussolini's monstrosities. Worse still, it has been accused of serving as the model for George Orwell's dreaded Ministry of Truth.'[72] Whether it is 'at home' in London is for the observer to decide, unless nobbled by the mischievous suggestion that in a great city no building, as no person, is truly ever at home.

HERETICAL THOUGHTS: LONDON, THE PARADIGMATIC MULTIVERSITY

Seven royal charters were issued to London between 1836 and 1878. In 1900 new statutes expanded the size of the Senate, the faculties, provided for new degrees in engineering, economics and theology. Colleges and schools of independent origin were made official parts of the university or were admitted to particular faculties – for example, arts and science for Royal Holloway College, science for the Royal College of Science,

---

[70] Sir William Beveridge, *The Physical Relation of a University to a City* (16 November 1928), 16.
[71] Harte, *University of London*, 219.
[72] Ralf Dahrendorf, *LSE, A History of the London School of Economics and Political Science 1895–1995* (Oxford, 1995), 193.

engineering for the Central Technical College, economics for the London School of Economics and Political Science. Various denominational schools were aligned with the faculty of theology, medical schools went to the faculty of medicine.[73]

Some teachers were appointed by the Senate and others received 'recognised' status. The inns of court refused to affiliate and chose to stay out of the examinations maelstrom for which the university was famous. More schools were subsequently acquired, absorbed, and autonomous extramural functions were also captured. The whole was imposing on a map. The university occupied a catchment area with a 20-mile radius, well beyond Campbell's heady plans for a 2-mile reach, which is why Bloomsbury was more important a site for a headquarters than peripheral South Kensington.

This was hardly the end of London's experiments in system-building, but one detail from the new arrangements cannot be omitted. There was a pressing need to simplify the patchwork financing in existence since 1836 and changed somewhat in 1884, a mixture of annual parliamentary grants and payment in kind from the Treasury, which, however, hoped to reimburse itself from examination fees. It was time to adopt the principle, extended to the federated universities outside London, of direct grant funding. This occurred in 1901. The new London County Council was willing to contribute £10,000 per annum. Gifts, hitherto discouraged by an antiquated system of financing (or so it was argued), started to arrive. Fund-raising for medicine was attempted, was partially successful, but ran aground on old animosities. The medical schools remained difficult to deal with.

By 1910 London had 4000 internal students and was the largest university in Britain by far, and the fourth or fifth largest in the world. Yet to outsiders it remained a curious institution, without idea or place. The American observer Abraham Flexner, writing comparatively about universities in the late 1920s, still thought that London did not qualify for the designation 'university'. Even Columbia and Chicago with their 'excesses and absurdities' came closer to the ideal than London. But what were the objections? After all, the American idea of a university was modified beyond all historical recognition. Flexner's answer was that whatever the nature of a university, its core was an 'organism, vitalised, not by administrative means, but by ideas and ideals, with a corporate life'.[74]

---

[73] The facts for this section and what follows are taken from Harte, *University of London*, 164ff.
[74] *Ibid.*, 164.

The journey of the University of London from its first appearance as a university college to and through the twentieth century is as interesting a story of university history as can be found anywhere. Starting with a clear idea of an urban, market-directed institution serving a specific clientele, the university had become a sprawling conglomerate similar to the capital and empire and dominated by the professors and their professional interests. But what is this university really? Why not assign to it the neologism that Americans would give to their own sprawling multi-campus systems with similarly invisible central administrations largely separate from teaching, research and professional service, and therefore helpless to fashion the legacies and rituals that give meaning to sites and ideas? The examining function apart (and this may be in the process of disintegration in the 1990s), the resemblances are striking. London is a multiversity, the world's first. Is that why from time to time, confused by the riot of competing forms of institutional growth encountered in a country that could not escape the market principle and troubled by wildly fluctuating variations in student achievement standards, Americans thought that the University of London might well serve as *their* model?[75]

But these, as announced, are heretical thoughts.

---

[75] See Chapter 5, p. 284. The attraction was diversity combined with degree control from the top.

   A 'convention of literary and scientific gentlemen' meeting in New York City in October 1830 voted to gather information on University College and King's College to use in contemplating a model for their own proposed New York University. The date rules out an interest in the plan of 1836. What caught the attention of the convention was 'useful instruction, at a reasonable rate, primarily for young men of the middle classes'. Theodore Francis Jones, ed., *New York University, 1832–1932* (New York, 1933), 6. Also *Journal of the Proceedings of a Convention of Literary and Scientific Gentlemen, Held in the Common Council Chamber of the City of New York* (October 1830) (New York, 1831).

CHAPTER EIGHT

ALTERNATIVES
I. ON THE IMPORTANCE OF BEING UNATTACHED

HERMIT CRABS

Some scenarios of the future may be compared to the surrealistic picture of the university as a shell into which homeless hermit crabs crawl seeking temporary shelter and affiliation. Some are gypsy scholars in high demand. A second set is composed of employees seeking part-time, contractual work in a secondary labour market, unionised perhaps on an industrial, conflict model. The third group appears consisting of large support staffs and non-professorial researchers, sometimes professional, sometimes semi-professional and at other times skilled or unskilled labour. And then of course there are students of every type, building various forms of association with the university, some lasting and senti-mental, others routinely utilitarian. Most students today are 'mature'. They are busy with jobs and families. Many take their education at a distance, others journey to 'subway colleges'. Newman had a vision of such a world of hesitant university attachments. He could hardly have imagined the varieties of communities and non-communities emerging by the end of another century. For him, the university was such an enclosed and singular institution that a humble snapdragon, struggling to root itself in stone, was enough to stimulate memory and suggest experiences.

The university as a shell is a wild and irresponsible metaphor, but it vividly captures aspects of today's higher education world. The phenom-enon of entrance and exit is highly pronounced in America. It is becoming so elsewhere, or is already so advanced, as in Austria and Italy, that tracking the record of students has become a problem and even a scandal.[1] Academics exchange institutional locations for career and other reasons (tenure, family, environment), but simple exit is not required for loyalties to weaken. Emotional detachment is possible, the result of various

---

[1] Information from Hans Pechar, Institut für Interdisziplanare Forschung und Fortbildung, Vienna.

tendencies. One is the increasing pressure for efficiency or productivity, producing new forms of accountability and assessment. Another is the attractions of a fuller involvement with a much wider range of outside activities. Members of the guilds become unwilling employees or voluntary entrepreneurs. Yet another is the gravitational pull of invisible colleges where membership is voluntary and some degree of guild authority remains.

Mercurial and multifaceted, the history of universities is the history of roles and types of academics shifting and changing in accordance if not precisely in syncopation with altered responsibilites and career lines, with structural changes in schooling, child-rearing and student cultures. But a break with the past is never wholly final. Discontinuities compete with continuities, and the weighting of the two in relation to one another depends upon the judgement of historians.[2] Role confusion is probably the rule. The career of the legal scholar and pioneer anthropologist, Henry Maine, illustrates how one Victorian academic nervously prowled through existing markets in order to use his talent during an unsettled period in the history of the ancient universities.[3] Yet the variety of alternatives available today, made possible by systems of highly differentiated institutional missions, suggests even greater uncertainty. The liberal arts teacher, the researcher, the academic physician, lawyer or engineer, the musician or sculptor, the journalist or the adjunct professor who moves between government, business and the university hold different views on teaching and research, on the time properly allotted to each, on the criteria for success, on remuneration and authority.[4] For some the correct ideal for internal bonding is the *Gemeinschaft*, organic, familial, self-absorbed. For others the model is the *Gesellschaft*, where working arrangements are looser and more dependent upon the principles of exchange and contract.[5]

---

[2] I opted for discontinuities in *Tradition and Change in English Liberal Education, An Essay in History and Culture* (London and Boston, 1976).

[3] Sheldon Rothblatt, review of George Feaver, *From Status to Contract: a Biography of Sir Henry Maine, 1822–1888* (New York, 1970), *Journal of Modern History*, 43 (March 1971), 158.

[4] Elaborated at length with customary insight by Burton R. Clark, *The Academic Life, Small Worlds, Different Worlds* (The Carnegie Foundation for the Advancement of Teaching, 1987).

[5] The distinctions of Ferdinand Tönnies, *Community and Society* (East Lansing, MI, 1957), 33–6, 64–5, 71. Ralf Dahrendorf, *LSE, A History of the London School of Economics and Political Science 1895–1995* (Oxford, 1995), 360, calls the Cambridge college a *Gemeinschaft* and LSE a *Gesellschaft*, but the former too shows signs of disintegrating into the less real, more imagined form of association under the impact of changing career opportunities and the pressure to secure non-governmental sources of funding. More and more essential decisions affecting colleges are being taken outside colleges according to the account in Ted Tapper and Brian Salter, *Oxford, Cambridge and the Changing Idea of the University*

And for yet others there are simply multiple reference groups, with role adjustments made accordingly.

Career definitions and expectations cannot be uniform in an era of greatly distinct institutions. The *wirtschaftsuniversität*, the *högskola*, the *grande école*, the liberal arts college (secular and church-related), the multiversity and the multi-campus system, the eastern European academy with its institutes have overlapping features but also a different ethos, governing and funding structures, career lines and wide variations in teaching and research assignments. The tensions are apparent when composites are created, as in Sweden in the 1970s when researchers and non-researchers were joined together in the same teaching departments with unhappy consequences. Discussions concerning the amalgamation of teacher-training colleges with university departments of education in Australian universities produced similar difficulties in the 1980s.[6]

For the purpose of understanding some forms of role change, we can for a moment create a typology of academic roles. The conception of the academic as 'don' fits with the idea of a college as a place nurturing the young. In English, Scottish and American traditions, the college mission includes citizenship training. The professional career belongs more to the service idea of a university. Teaching is related to professional labour markets. Research as an academic career belongs to the idea of a university as a place for the pursuit of learning, but the real difficulty has always been in deciding how that learning was to be used, whether it should be self-referencing or applied to specific social or technical tasks. If the latter, then the question of priorities instantly arises, as well as the problem of who pays for research and the terms of negotiation. Even more difficult questions of how to produce and organise knowledge, how to encourage particular intellectual lines of endeavour and reward practitioners appear when universities become comprehensive, broadening their range of expected undertakings.One obvious solution to the problem of reconciling multiple functions is to assign specific missions to single institutions, to place undergraduate instruction in one kind of institution, professional training in another and research in yet another. The attraction of such solutions – practitioner-run professional schools in England, the specialised academies or universities of the former soviet

(Ballmoor, Bucks, 1992). The emergence at Cambridge of a huge sector of part-time, short-course students, some 11,000 at the end of 1995 or nearly as many as full-time students, certainly represents a dramatic shift away from traditional conceptions of a collegiate university. *Cam: the University of Cambridge Alumni Magazine* (Michaelmas, 1995).

6 See *Institutional Amalgamations in Higher Education, Process and Outcome in Five Countries*, ed. Grant Harman and V. Lynn Meek (University of New England, 1988).

system, the French tripartite division of professional schools, universities and research organisations – is easy to appreciate. The distinctions are rational, and they inhibit the emergence of such ambiguities as exist in the United States where the multiversity model prevails. Yet the trend appears to be away from strict division by mission towards the multi-purpose institution with weak boundary protection, and the merit claimed for such organisation is that the rapid movement of society requires forms of higher education that are fluid and adaptable.

What therefore is the role of an academic under conditions of acute change: scholar, researcher, don, *clerc* (*à la* Julien Benda), specialist, expert, critic of society or its loyal servant? Should the university passively 'reproduce' the values it finds outside – aristocratic, meritocratic, bourgeois, popular, or all of these? Or better, is the university, in its current fragmented state, even able to choose among competing options, adopting some and rejecting others? That appears highly doubtful, as does the possibility that it can sustain itself as a largely autonomous body, with its own internal private life, machinery of self-government, norms and regulations, what Clark Kerr calls its 'heritage' and without which pride and quality – Newman's 'integrity' or wholeness – are impossible.[7] 'Independence', said Edward Gibbon, 'was the first of earthly blessings'.[8] How did he express his own good luck? The famous response is supposed to make us squirm. 'The tears of a son are seldom lasting . . . [It] is a melancholy truth, that my father's death . . . was the only event that could save me from a hopeless life of obscurity and indigence.'[9]

THE CLERISY

In defining academic roles, Coleridge again is a central personality. It was not universities that he had in mind in describing the functions of a 'clerisy', but his formulations answered academic fears about the possible transfer of higher education authority in England from Church to State to consumer sovereignty. Coleridge is said to have first employed the word in 1821, but it entered literary circulation only after the publication of his influential work, *On the Constitution of Church and State* in 1830. His sources were probably the German *Clerisei* from the late Latin *Clericia*. Coleridge visited Göttingen in 1798 and sympathised with the unhappy

---

[7] Clark Kerr, *Higher Education Cannot Escape History, Issues for the Twenty-First Century* (Albany, NY, 1994), Part 2.
[8] Edward Gibbon, *Memoirs of My Life* (Harmondsworth, 1984), 158.
[9] *Ibid.*, 154.

Frühromantiker. Earlier he had been attracted to Enlightenment ideas, Unitarianism and other radical politics and dreamt of universal brotherhood. He turned conservative, at the same time reacting to the 'commercial spirit' of his time, a reaction that became part of the history of the idea of a university. He concluded his journey by seeking local or intimate attachments. The Pantisocratic scheme was one alternative. The plan for a clerisy was another.[10]

The history of the clerisy parallels that of the idea of a university. Clerisy writers were eager to combat the full implications of the notion of a marketplace of ideas, since in their opinion the bad ideas would drive out the good. They were sceptical of the ultimate benefit achievable through mechanisms of supply and demand, for they began to appreciate, standing somewhere at the beginning of this development, that culture was a consumer artifact, and its purchase could be manipulated. Ideas could be 'sold' like any commodity if the buying public or public opinion was persuaded of its value. Adam Smith had said as much. Philosophy or speculation, he wrote, was a trade or occupation like any other, 'subdivided into a great number of different branches . . . each individual becoming more expert'.[11]

From Coleridge the clerisy notion passed into the mainstream of nineteenth-century English intellectual life, to be appropriated in part or whole by a large number of distinguished writers. The clerisy theorists are often identified as Thomas Carlyle, John Henry Newman, Matthew Arnold and J. S. Mill, but the list grows much longer when we admit several variations on the theme, so that F. D. Maurice and Charles Kingsley, John Robert Seeley and T. H. Green, Henry Sidgwick and many lesser dons and clergymen of the later nineteenth century also qualify. The numerous differences and even contradictions in the writings of these men make identifying the essential clerisy idea somewhat awkward, but a working typology of sorts can be constructed from their secondary agreements.

The heart of the clerisy approach, as first outlined by Coleridge, was the endowment of an educated class in order to ensure its survival in a market economy. The model but not in the strictest sense, as the word clerisy itself suggests, was the English clerical or religious establishment, which Coleridge called a National Church whose 'idea' was 'to secure and

---

[10] Samuel Taylor Coleridge, *On the Constitution of the Church and State*, ed. John Colmer (Princeton, 1976), 46n; Marilyn Butler, *Rebels and Reactionaries, English Literature and its Background 1760–1830* (Oxford, 1982), 74–5, 77–9. 82, 87, 89, 91, 126.

[11] Adam Smith, *The Wealth of Nations*, I (London and New York, 1957), 10.

improve that civilization, without which the nation could be neither permanent nor progressive'.[12] He also used the word 'cultivation' to distinguish between moral values and material ('civilized') values and composed the famous dictum that 'a nation can never be too cultivated, but may easily become an over-civilized race'.[13] Coleridge derived the 'idea' of the clerisy from the historical experience of the Church of England in national education. Certain institutions, resembling the National Church – in later thinkers (as already suggested) the universities would be seen as a new Establishment – were to provide a home for learned men who would distribute their learning through a local network recalling the parish system of Church governance.

If this was an effort to protect a republic of the mind from the market, from the swings of public opinion, it was also an attempt to avoid the German solution of transforming *Gelehrten* into civil servants. Only Matthew Arnold among the main clerisy intellectuals was *étatist* or *dirigiste*, believing in a State that metaphysically embodied the best part of its citizenry. But if Arnold stood largely alone as a theorist of the benevolence of the State, a significant number of Oxbridge dons of his generation welcomed and actively encouraged government interference into the affairs of the universities as a practical step in their reform. Their counterparts in other English as well as Scottish universities also preferred Whitehall's intervention (except for the special circumstances of the first London University). The danger of protection from above was mainly grasped by the academic tories of the 1850s, who defended collegiate independence against the royal commissioners.

If the mid-Victorian clerisy believed in the power of the State to create ideal conditions for intellectual work, they were also liberals in regard to one important facet of their existence. They were concerned about the rights of minorities since that is what they came to regard themselves as being. And if they advocated the endowment of learning and preferential treatment for men of ideas, it was to shore up a vulnerable position, easily overwhelmed (so they thought) by public opinion.

We should remember that the clerisy idea took shape in the second third of the nineteenth century when aristocratic social and political leadership was seriously challenged by great extra-parliamentary organisations such as the Anti-Corn Law League, when reform of the franchise was a subject of continual national discussion, and when there

---

[12] Coleridge, *Constitution*, 44.

[13] *Ibid.*, 49. Thus narrowing the meaning of 'civilisation' from its eighteenth-century use, where it was closer to 'civility', a term to denote a higher form of personal conduct.

was talk of disestablishing the Church of England. This carried with it the alarming implication that a second Reformation was possible, a massive expropriation of ecclesiastical property. In this connection we should also recall the extraordinary increase in the non-Anglican portion of the English population which, in conjunction with electoral reform in a country where the Church Settlement was Erastian, threatened (or so it seemed to Church and State proponents) for a time to put the State into the hands of a powerfully organised, single-interest lobby group.

The clerisy ideal presupposed a fiduciary agreement with the State. (Coleridge shifted constantly between broad and narrow definitions of the State, sometimes making it coterminous with civil society, sometimes limiting it to politics.) This was a form of trusteeship established by social contract, wherein the services of a learned stratum were exchanged for endowments. The guarantee that such an arrangement did not deteriorate into the type of hated vested interest so much a target of radicals in Coleridge's lifetime was the ideal philosophy which brought the clerisy into existence to begin with. The idea of the clerisy was a constant, but its institutional form was a variable, amenable to alteration as circumstances required.[14]

In exchange for material support the members of the clerisy agreed to remain loyal to civil society and the State. Although they might be critical – how else to carry out Coleridge's commitment to 'progress'? – they promised to respect the permanent foundations upon which English security was built. Since they constituted a National Church, how could they be divided against themselves? Endowed, they had no reason to be alienated; maintained at public expense, they forfeited the independence that came from being unattached. Here then is one source of the essential conserving impulse of the clerisy, their preference for reform over revolution, as noticed by Lord Annan in his seminal essay on the English intellectual aristocracy.[15]

Two decades ago one writer described the clerisy as an unattached stratum.[16] But Coleridge's theory actually makes them into an attached class. An abbreviated statement of their role produces the following features:

    1. A holistic conception of society with a corresponding dislike of

---

[14] *Ibid.*, 8.

[15] Nöel G. Annan, 'The intellectual aristocracy', in *Studies in Social History*, ed. J. H. Plumb (London, 1955).

[16] Ben Knights, *The Idea of the Clerisy in the Nineteenth Century* (Cambridge, 1978), 31. The author seems to prefer a more embittered and radical group, but to pose questions and answers his way takes the subject out of history altogether.

particularism, sectarianism or cultural pluralism. The drift consequently is to speak in terms of the 'nation' or to favour comprehensive goals such as those of the Broad Church. At times this shades into a mitigated platonism where society is viewed in functional terms, each level of it having a suitable function. 'Duties' and 'responsibilities' are therefore favourite words.

2. The clerisy tend to view themselves as 'classless'. The clerisy are what Karl Mannheim, in *Ideology and Utopia*, called a 'stratum' or mediating group that exists between the spaces of a horizontally stratified society. In origin the Victorian clerisy were drawn mainly from the clerical and professional sectors of society. The word 'professional' begins to circulate from the 1840s onwards to describe the responsibilities of educated people. The clerisy thought of themselves as 'professional'.

3. A playing down of religious ritual and theology, since these were so divisive in the early Victorian period, defining evangelical and High Church positions, and an emphasis instead on the historical dimensions of Christianity, underscoring the human, rational evolutionary and relativistic dimensions of religious belief. From here it was an easy slide into secularised forms of faith or metonyms such as 'the religion of humanity'.

4. Insistence on the overriding importance of literacy and education in raising the levels of cultivation and civilisation. Within education, a preference for literature and art, for these were (given the legacy of Georgian didacticism) regarded as best able to address the pressing moral and social questions generated by a society in change. Art must offer guidance to a world in confusion, illuminate the dilemmas of choice, provide some standard for decision-making, elevate feelings, induce compassion and inculcate a sense of humanity.[17]

5. A propensity to see problems as socio-moral rather than political, or as spiritual rather than material, thus opposing a kind of leftover Swiftian toryism to an on-going whiggish politics of interest. With this goes a fear of majoritarian politics. In general the clerisy tends to be apolitical. Political authority (collectively the clerisy have none) is applied through public administration rather than politics.

---

[17] George Watson, *The English Ideology* (London, 1973), 136, argues that Matthew Arnold takes these ideas to their extreme. 'The Arnoldian critic . . . aspires to intellectual and even moral authority over governments: not just as a citizen . . . but as an expert, and his claim to the expert's status is somehow thought to be based on his knowledge of literature and a burning conviction that such knowledge is a talisman to the whole world of human commitment.'

THE UNATTACHED INTELLECTUAL: TWO ELIOTS

In a curious paper, whose provenance is unclear, the poet T. S. Eliot decided in 1944 to lay out some of the strategic elements of the clerisy position. He mixed terms such as clerics (doubtless thinking of Julien Benda's *clercs*) and clerisy, intelligentsia and men of letters with another layer of 'emotives'. The origins of all these groups lay somewhere in the broad reaches of the middle classes and its 'imperceptible subdivisions'. The confusion of terms is instructive. Eliot, unlike Coleridge, did not assign his clerisy to a sheltering institution. Any occupation would suffice, and it is reasonable to suppose that he was thinking of himself and several of his unglamorous sources of support. The university was only one of several locations in which a cleric might find himself. '[The] question is the degree to which his paid activities support or interfere with his preferred clerical interests.'

In Eliot's analysis, the clerics are not exactly outsiders but mingle with and are part of any society's occupational structure; and, like anyone else, they must cope with exigencies of making a living. It is useful for the task of thinking if some clerics have independent sources of income, but there is danger in being too isolated from public pressures, just as there are dangers in being too closely identified with specific publics. Nor do clerics appear to have any special wisdom or culture by virtue of their self-appointed role as serious thinkers. Some, the emotives, are in fact 'feeble or irrational'. Some – Eliot calls them 'clerical small fry'– are an intelligentsia; and for this group he has little respect. They express their 'discontent in subversive moments, and in Cairo and such places, [by] overturning trams'.

The principal function of the clerics or clerisy is to 'originate dominant ideas' and 'alter the sensibility of its time', but 'originate' is not to be taken literally. The clerisy draws its ideas and inspirations from the general culture, or from what is already 'in the air'. Loosely assembled, it can be denominated an elite, but it can expect no particular privileges and has no automatic right to be heard. It is an unprotected species.[18]

Robert Anderson remarks that the clerisy ideal did not ever have a solid footing in Scotland. James Lorimer, a Victorian Edinburgh lawyer and law professor, was one of the exceptions, going so far as to identify Coleridge's clerisy with the learned class of the university. He disseminated his views at the time of vigorous discussion about the future of

---

[18] T. S. Eliot, 'On the Place and Function of the Clerisy', in Roger Kojecky, *T. S. Eliot's Social Criticism* (London, 1971), 240–8.

Scottish universities taking place in the 1850s and attracted lively and largely negative comment. The clerisy ideal was a distinctly foreign import, too exclusive and alien to Scottish conceptions of an openly accessible university serving all the needs, practical or otherwise, of the Scottish public.[19]

The task of assisting us in exploring the theme of intellectuals in relation to universities, strange as the choice may at first appear, can next be assigned to that other Eliot, the novelist, literary critic, translator and editor, George Eliot. She herself was certainly not an academic, did not aspire to teach in a university (and was in any case, as a woman, barred from such employment until the 1860s) and did not speak directly to the issues of university reform in her own day, although in later life she enjoyed a great reputation among university undergraduates. George Eliot's life and circumstances, her thought, writings and associations provide us with a very special opportunity to explore a particular problem. What role could educated men and women play in society if they did not enjoy the protections of a university? What authority could they claim, and how could they claim it, if they were comets, free to describe their own orbits, rather than fixed stars in a constellation of regulated galaxies? Suppose attached and secure positions in a university were unavailable? How might we imagine the consequences?

George Eliot offers us an alternative to platonic-guardian theories of moral and intellectual responsibility. In self-flattery, one is immediately tempted to regard her as an academic intellectual in any case, like the clerisy concerned with high moral ideas concerning human relationships. She was certainly deeply attracted to abstract thought. From an early age she zealously absorbed the leading philosophical ideas of her day: phrenology, German history and aesthetics, developmental biology and philosophies of system such as Saint-Simonianism, Comtism and, closer to home, utilitarianism. Her letters are essays on the importance of ideas in illuminating the human condition, especially in times of acute change, and her novels employ characters who may be described as intellectuals – Felix Holt, for example, or Mordecai, Casaubon and Lydgate – or characters attracted to them for their qualities of mind.

George Eliot did not write – she could not possibly have written – a *Künstlerroman*, a novel about the making of an intellectual. Such a feat would have been in advance of history. A writer born a few years after the exile of Napoleon (as she was) would not have regarded an intellectual as

---

[19] Robert D. Anderson, 'Institutionalization and Social Adaptation: Scottish Universities in the Nineteenth Century', *Università in Europa* (Messina, 1995), 461.

a separate occupational species. An intellectual was anyone interested in the wider problems of existence. He could be a clergyman, a physician or (although rarely) a scholar. Her scholar, however, the wretchedly inadequate Casaubon (who may or may not have been patterned on Oxford's Mark Pattison[20]) does not provide us with much hope. George Eliot could also picture the intellectual as an artisan, a member of the rural working classes, but this too conforms to the generalisation that in the England of her day no single occupation was charged with the special task of generating or disseminating ideas.

There is still no occupation actually denominated 'intellectual', no chance that such a designation would appear in the Registrar General's list of job classifications. There is no separate social 'class' composed of intellectuals,[21] nor, if we believe that groups in present-day industrial democratic societies are distributed more according to status than class, are there single-status groups appropriately termed 'intellectuals'. Occupation, role errand, family and institutional affiliation are by no means mutually exclusive. To be in the theatre of the world is to play many parts, even simultaneously.[22]

There is no occupation called 'intellectual', but it is certainly true that one leading difference between the mid-nineteenth century and the late twentieth century is the amount of endless discussion concerning intellectuals, who they are and what their special traits and qualities might be. But, remarks A. H. Halsey, if the subject of intellectuals has been endlessly discussed, 'It has settled nothing.'[23] Quite true; but an industry has been created. Literature, programmatic statements and manifestos abound.

If we attempt to place intellectuals in the social structure, at least in England and America, we do so by attaching them to supporting institutions, most frequently universities, for the university as it has

---

[20] The favourite, but there are also the scholarly Robert William Mackay or R. H. Brabant, the father of a friend. He was a physician who once treated Coleridge, read German and got up German theology. He knew Strauss. Gordon S. Haight, *George Eliot: A Biography* (Oxford, 1968), 47. Henry Halford Vaughan, an Oxford professor, has not been named as a prototype, but possessed the same paralysing megalomania. See E. G. W. Bill, *University Reform in Nineteenth-Century Oxford, A Study of Henry Halford Vaughan, 1811–1885* (Oxford, 1973); John Sparrow, *Mark Pattison and the Idea of a University* (Cambridge, 1967), 9–18; and Gordon S. Haight, *George Eliot's Originals and Contemporaries, Essays in Victorian Literary History and Biography*, ed. Hugh Witemeyer (Ann Arbor, MI, 1992), 18, 36.

[21] A. H. Halsey, 'In a Class of Their Own?', *The Times Higher Education Supplement* (28 January 1983), 13.

[22] Robert K. Merton, 'Insiders and Outsiders: a Chapter in the Sociology of Knowledge', *American Journal of Sociology*, 78 (1972), 22.

[23] Halsey, 'In a Class of Their Own?'.

changed in the past century seems to provide greater scope for intellectual work than do other major alternatives, such as churches, governments, trade unions and the media. Probably it is more certain today than in the past – though hardly fully certain – that the plural world of the contemporary research university is the natural home of intellectuals, those people whom Daniel Bell once rather flatteringly described as 'the custodians of critical and creative thinking about the normative problems of their society'.[24] But enter Halsey once again. What universities house, he says, are 'the specialisms of the highly educated' – brain work associated with computer programming, teacher training, accounting, high-energy physics, quandry ethics and urban demography. It is a nice question whether such a variety of specialists is best described as 'custodians of critical and creative thinking'. This indeed is the burden of the accusations brought by those who prefer that professors be 'thinkers' and 'intellectuals' rather than professional experts.[25]

Whatever the association between intellectuals and universities, the equation is only possible in the last hundred years. It is a change that occurs after George Eliot and has recently been sketched out by T. W. Heyck.[26] In her day there was substantial disagreement on the question of whether institutional support for writers and thinkers was at all desirable. George Eliot herself inclined to the view that it was preferable to be 'unattached', for independence was impossible wherever group norms prevailed, or where negotiation and compromise were essential means for obtaining material support, which in turn opened up channels for the intrusion of extra-institutional opinion and influence. Such sentiments are in line with the European tradition of thinking most notably associated with Benda but including Benedetto Croce and the British Labour Party cabinet minister, now deceased, Richard Crossman.[27]

In the corpus comprising the sociology of knowledge, a number of theories emphasise the central importance of institutional distancing and consequently the corresponding value or condition of marginality. The intellectual must be a 'stranger', separated from society, family, class or culture by choice or circumstances. In her writings, correspondence and

---

[24] Quoted in Halsey, *ibid.*

[25] John Hall, 'The Curious Case of the English Intelligentsia', *British Journal of Sociology*, 30 (September 1979), 291–306, maintains that the mid-Victorian 'lights of liberalism' (in Arnold's phrase) were an intelligentsia that in time lost their 'free-floating' quality and succumbed to the 'genteel culture of the professional ethic'.

[26] T. W. Heyck, *The Transformation of Intellectual Life in Victorian England* (London, 1982).

[27] For Crossman see the recent piece by Robert Dare, 'Instinct and Organization: Intellectuals and British Labour after 1931', *The Historical Journal*, 26 (1983), 678.

actions, George Eliot often behaved as an outsider. She was, for one thing,
self-consciously 'provincial', on the 'periphery' of social and intellectual
life to employ Edward Shil's useful word.[28] Equally important, and
equally obvious, she was a woman, and for her time bold and unconventional in her personal conduct. Only in isolated circles, in the
environment of the salon, as one example, in radical Nonconformist
networks of the 1790s, to give another, was it admitted that hard thinking
was a matter of mind not gender. In so far as the exploration of ideas and
value systems requires some degree of rational detachment, some sense
of distance from the objects observed, George Eliot's position as an
unconventional woman in Victorian England helped supply this.

THE 'INTELLECTUAL'

Thus far the word 'intellectual' has been used to describe special social
roles in a society composed of occupational status groups rather than
classes. Ambiguity has surrounded the designation from the outset. There
is some disagreement over the date 'intellectual' as a noun first appeared in
England; but such evidence as exists favours a late nineteenth-century
circulation. George Eliot herself used the plural version 'intellectuals' as
early in 1852, which suggests that in either singular or plural form the
word was known before Clemenceau assigned it to the Dreyfusards in
France – the usual starting-point for the history of the word. George Eliot
referred to a meeting at the home of John Chapman, publisher of the
Westminster Review, which she helped edit from 1851 to 1853, as an
'assemblage of intellectuals'.[29] They included immensely successful
novelists like Charles Dickens and Wilkie Collins, the mathematician
Charles Babbage, thinkers like Herbert Spencer, naturalists such as
Richard Owen, other literary figures, editors, lexicographers and
illustrators – in other words, an assortment of educated and well-known
Victorians not easily categorised as to political beliefs, intellectual predisposition, role or mission except perhaps faintly 'radical', some of them
breathing in Nonconformity or the stale air of Utilitarianism, the initial
bent of the *Westminster Review*. We have only this hint of George Eliot's
use of the word 'intellectuals'; but in context it seems to be more general
and embracing than particular and exclusive, in this respect much like
Enlightenment French words such as *savant* and *érudit*.

Raymond Williams points out that the plural form 'intellectuals' was

---

[28] Edward Shils, *Center and Periphery* (Chicago, 1975), Part 1.
[29] Haight, *George Eliot,* 110; Heyck, *The Transformation of Intellectual Life,* 17.

used as early as 1813 by Lord Byron in a 'faintly pejorative' sense; but most historians, literary critics and sociologists are normally satisfied with a pedigree that suggests 'intellectuals' descended in no clearly discernible fashion from Russian collective nouns of the 1860s like 'intelligentsia', generally thought to derive from the Latin for 'intelligence' or 'mind', conceivably from the German 'Intelligenz'. The Russian 'intelligent' was an educated person characterised by an independent position toward the masses or the imperial court.[30] Thus employed, the word does not correspond to George Eliot's reference to an 'assemblage of intellectuals', nor does her phrase suggest that single-minded commitment of the Dreyfusards. Her use of the plural form is less overtly political, although in her novels political implications of a broad nature can be derived indirectly.

GEORGE ELIOT AS A MEMBER OF THE CLERISY

When set against the neologism 'clerisy', George Eliot's views appear to make a fair match. In her letters and novels she was deeply troubled by the disruptive consequences of egoism and self-regarding acts, by the universal practice of seeking status, money, power, position or pleasure at the expense of others. She seemed to favour collectivity over self, community over family. She constantly referred to the necessity of duty in a world of selfish acts. She deplored class or sectarian conflict, and she emphatically denied that injustice could be removed by overturning the social structure. Her principal working-class spokesman, Felix Holt, is a William Cobbett-like tory radical. That is, he looks backwards for social and political solutions, especially as political solutions and loyalties in his day could be bought like any other consumer good. Politics was part of the problem of modern society, not its solution.

Also like the clerisy, George Eliot advocated a religion of humanity. She was, in fact, in the forefront of this development, having translated the relevant works of German scholarship during her intellectual apprenticeship. She believed in the importance of education and thought that women especially would not cease to be 'silly novelists' or show-off bluestockings until they were as decently educated as men – a feminist concern

---

[30] Nicholas V. Riasanovsky, 'Notes on the Emergence and Nature of the Russian Intelligentsia', in *Art and Culture in Nineteenth-Century Russia*, ed. Theofanis George Stavron (Bloomington, 1983), 3–4; Raymond Williams, 'Intellectual', *Keywords* (New York, 1976), 141. See also Daniel Bell, *The Reforming of General Education* (New York, 1966), 307, and Irving Howe, review of Jonathan Frankel, *Prophecy and Politics: Socialism, Nationalism and the Russian Jews, 1862–1917*, *New York Review of Books* (15 July 1982), 31.

extending back at least to Mary Wollstonecraft who died in the 1790s. As she was an artist, she naturally regarded literature as the proper vehicle for elevating sentiment and illustrating the dilemmas of the human condition. And she shared with the clerisy a predisposition to see all of society as 'whole', as interconnected, all problems as interrelated, all events and outcomes as mutually interdependent, so that what affected one person would inevitably affect another. This total, comprehensive view of social relationships, covering high as well as low, and encompassing the ordinary events of everyday life - 'That element of tragedy which lies in the very fact of frequency'[31] - is sometimes said to make her unique among English novelists. Finally, she shared as well a mediating conception of the artist, so akin to the role assumed by Mannheim's stratum. When eventually she had worked through the philosophies, social sciences and pseudo-sciences of her youth, she decided that her own normative philosophical and aesthetic position was something she called 'merliorism' - a middle term, her husband J. W. Cross noted, somewhere between optimism and pessimism. Her goals were modest: gradual improvement of the masses, a helping hand, attachment to home and hearth. 'Few are born to do the great work of the world, but all are born to this.'[32]

Eliot's belief corresponds well with the many symbols of family figures in her novels, the helpful, hovering, wise avuncular personalities ingeniously identified in an essay by Ulrich Knoepflmacher.[33] She even specifically extended this idea to the woman as cerebral midwife, as when in an essay of 1854 she wrote that Madame de Sable 'seconded a man's wit with understanding - one of the best offices which womanly intellect has rendered to the advancement of culture; and the absence of originality made her all the more receptive towards the originality of others'.[34]

In many fundamental ways, then, George Eliot's conception of the artist and intellectual parallels that of the mid-Victorian clerisy model, although she did not actually use the word. Were we to leave the matter here it could be conveniently concluded that she was in all but name a member of this intellectually minded community, a fellow traveller certainly, and every bit as much as Coleridge, Carlyle, Arnold and John Mill distressed by the disruption to social and personal values caused by the twin movement of

---

[31] G. Eliot, *Middlemarch* (London, 1953), Book II, Chapter 20, p. 207.

[32] J. W. Cross, *George Eliot's Life as Related in Her Letters and Journals*, III (New York, 1885), 309–10.

[33] U. C. Knoepflmacher, '*Middlemarch:* an Avuncular View', *Nineteenth-Century Fiction*, 30 (June 1975), 53–81.

[34] *Essays of George Eliot*, ed. Thomas Pinney (New York, 1963), 74.

industrialism and democracy. But actually in the strictist sense she never was a candidate for the clerisy, for she remained 'unattached'. From the start of her career she was thrown into the market in order to secure a living, as neither her small inherited competence nor the earnings of her long-standing lover, G. H. Lewes (especially in view of his own family expenses) guaranteed a comfortable life. Unlike the clerisy, which was always in search of a structurally secure, constitutionally guaranteed, institutionally based position in English life (or, in Mill's case, some special privilege for the educated, such as plural voting), she accepted the necessity of coping with consumers and was prepared to quarrel with publishers, those great tyrannical interpreters of market demand. After initial disagreements over *Scenes of Clerical Life*, she was fortunate in winning Blackwood's early support, and the two settled into a satisfactory working arrangement. Looking back upon her life as an unattached intellectual, she wrote to Harriet Beecher Stowe in 1876 that she was 'happily independent in material things, and felt no temptation to accommodate my writing to any standard except that of trying to do my best in what seemed to me most needful to be done'.[35]

It turned out well – speaking now of her material success despite her unorthodox conduct. She flouted the conventions in her long illicit union with Lewes, her bohemian friendships with Thornton Hunt and Chapman, her agnosticism and her willingness to experiment in fiction. It is very doubtful if the successes she wanted could have occurred if she had been an attached intellectual. It is whimsical to conjure up the vision of George Eliot on a recurrent grant and subsidised out of the public purse in Victorian England.

Yet it is also true that public recognition did not come quickly and that for many years she and Lewes lived on the margins of respectability, taking flight abroad whenever her novels appeared. She could not cope emotionally with the possible criticism. Over and over again one sees her tipping towards alienation; but she determinedly resisted, psychologically disguising her personal feelings by equating them with a more abstract social crisis.[36] The path she did not take, the freedom she did not use, the restraints she put upon her own life and thought are fascinating. The positivist, freethinker and daring translator of daring German works, who from time to time paused to announce in her writings a new programme

---

[35] Cross, *Life*, III, 212–13.
[36] That is, rationalise a private crisis into an impersonal one – a form of psychic reassurance noted by historians and sociologists who write about the psychological dimensions of extreme alienation.

for art which would not indulge the reader, the rationalist who proclaimed that the proper use of intellect was 'the free search for truth' – this bold and unconventional Victorian woman ended by casting doubt upon the value of ideas in and for themselves, questioned the role of a man or woman of ideas, took issue with the clerisy belief in leadership by intellectuals and in the whole notion of them as the protectors and guarantors of continuity. No one in particular guarded the precious legacies derived from the past, for all were charged with that responsibility.

George Eliot delivered a preemptive strike against the theory of the avant-garde. No more than Matthew Arnold did she care for doing as one likes or for the free swing of this and that. She emphatically believed in the need for self-restraint in art. We have her statement in a discussion of Goethe's *Wilhelm Meister* that the 'sphere of the artist has its limit somewhere', and her opinion that if Goethe respected the boundaries, Balzac – 'the most wonderful writer of fiction the world has ever seen' – did not.[37] The difference between the two turns on their use of what might be termed negative examples of human nature. Goethe, according to George Eliot, used them properly, in a fashion calculated to 'call forth our best sympathies'. But Balzac 'drags us by his magic force through scene after scene of unmitigated vice, till the effect of walking among this human carrion is a moral nausea'.[38] The most hideous passions, she explained, were fit subjects for art only if they served as the 'background for some divine deed of tenderness or heroism, and so the novelist may place before us every aspect of human life where there is some trait of love, or endurance, or helplessness to call forth our best sympathies'.[39] And in her devastating criticism of the well-known evangelical preacher, Dr Cumming, she nevertheless agreed that art like religion must have moral purpose. Her theory of the aesthetic underscored 'that . . . tendency towards good in human nature . . . which no creed can utterly counteract, and which ensures the ultimate triumph of that tendency over all dogmatic perversions'.[40] Our 'best sympathies' she regarded as inherent not conditioned; but in so far as they were a 'tendency' rather than a certainty, requiring a meliorist, avuncular intervention. Arthur Donnithorne and Gwendolyn Harlech are characters whose better selves are momentarily obscured by self-regarding actions; but taught by example or adversity, their innate tendency to good emerges.

Thus stated or simplified, George Eliot's view of the limits of art depends upon that Calvinist or evangelical emphasis on an internal

---

[37] *Essays of George Eliot*, 146.   [38] *Ibid.*
[39] *Ibid.*   [40] *Ibid.*, 189.

struggle between virtuous and vicious behaviour which she absorbed at a private boarding school in Coventry and never abandoned. It is partly romanticised into a version of the divided self – as is typical of her time – and it is not distant, as a psychological phenomenon, from the personal experience of many of the clerisy intellectuals, who also underwent the sensation of schizoid regeneration. George Eliot's view of this cycle of division and reunion, of lapse and redemption, however, differs rather profoundly from that of her distinguished contemporaries. Whereas they tended to blame society for their personal sense of loss, and proceeded from there to elaborate institutional solutions, she – and this was quite remarkable in view of her highly developed understanding of the primary bonding institutions of society – rejected them. Family, Church, government and village cannot be relied upon to promote the natural human tendency towards good, nor can classes and groups. There are honourable men of religion, even if dispassionate, and dishonourable men of religion, even if passionate, but no church or chapel capable of guaranteeing right conduct. There are idealistic workers and brutalised workers, but not an inherently noble working-class. And there are men of ideas steady in their adherence to the highest aims of mankind, but not a class of thinkers whom she would invest with the responsibility for promoting them. In fact, in George Eliot's novelistic world the primary institutions have virtually forfeited their bonding function and pose a threat to right conduct. Commercial self-interest has infiltrated village and community, religion is often narrow and canting,[41] family relationships are built on lies and are easily broken apart by misunderstanding and stubborn pride. The law serves sinister interests, and politics is a disguise for ambition and material recompense. Her abandonment of positivism fits this overall pattern. When, in retrospect, she saluted the St Simonians and Comte, it was in the spirit of a chastened former lover, sorrowful, perhaps respectful but assuredly disengaged. French positivism had contributed to her understanding of the changing nature of ideas and institutions and had strengthened her capacity to generalise about social phenomena. Before Darwin, Gallic thinking had introduced her to an evolutionary way of viewing time. Mill had similarly benefited and similarly withdrawn. But Comtism was only partly a heuristic means for probing the relationship between institutions and ideas: it was also a monumental theoretical effort

---

[41] Except where, as in the autumnal portrait of the rector, Mr Irwine, we have a representative of the old high and dry Church, relaxed, undogmatic and gracious, more concerned with 'men's characters than interest in their opinion'. G. Eliot, *Adam Bede* (London, 1977), 68. Irwine has emancipated himself from institutional constraints. He humanises social problems by making them personal.

at institutional reconstruction, directive and managerial in the typical French mode, Cartesian in its completeness and very much a product of Gallic logic. Was it 'human'? Particular? Historical? In time its abandonment by Eliot was predictable.

Mary Ann Evans, the young George Eliot, had been deeply attracted to ideas and men of intellect. As was only natural for someone born in 1819, she learned to think of intellect and feeling as opposed. The phrenological theories then fashionable encouraged this conventional, romantic distinction, even enclosing it within what for a time seemed like scientific proof. The theory of the cortical localisation of functions placed thought and feeling in separate portions of the brain as specialised mental powers. Mary Ann Evans, surrounded and accepted by fascinating, even glamorous figures like the Brays, Hennells and Chapmans, very much conscious of the traditional division between men's work and women's work, delighted in the opportunity to exercise her intellect. I am 'liberated from the wretched giant's bed of dogmas', she wrote when only twenty-four, and two years later she said that 'I every day seem more and more to value thought rather than feeling.'[42] The pursuit of ideas and her friendship with unconventional people opened her eyes to radically new perspectives on society, history and morality; but they also led to a break with her own family, an outcome that grievously upset her. Partly for this reason, she made herself see the other end of the problem. One day she would celebrate her liberation from doctrinal error and the next she would talk about 'the truth of feeling as the only universal bond of union'. In this same letter of 1843 she warned that 'It is the quackery of infidelity to suppose that it has a nostrum for all mankind, and to say to all and singular, "Swallow my opinions and you shall be whole."'[43] As she grew older and tried to make sense of what she sometimes thought was an unintelligible world, her view of the supremacy of rational thought to feeling altered, although she never really believed that one could replace the other.

She was unusually consistent throughout life in resisting the temptation to intellectualise experience and, in the form of the social novel, to entrust only to intellectuals the responsibility for offering solutions to social dilemmas. Her meliorists are drawn from all walks of life, and men of ideas are no more praiseworthy in her writings than others. In fact, one could argue that they are more likely to appear confused or wrong-headed, more apt to mistake ideas for solutions or to be satisfied with logical self-indulgence than those who make no claim to the unique

[42] Cross, *Life*, I (Edinburgh, 1885), 95.   [43] *Ibid.*, 99.

privileges of intellectual life. Her particular enemy became and remained dogmatism and narrowness in thinking, and rationalists were as likely to display these qualities as simpler folk. 'Freethinkers are scarcely wider than the orthodoxy', she wrote in 1859, 'they all want to see themselves and their own opinions held up as the true and the lovely. I have had heart-cutting experiences that *opinions* are a poor cement between human souls.'[44] Some years later she wrote again to the same effect. 'We must not take every great physicist – or other "ist" – for an apostle, but be ready to suspect him of some crudity concerning relations that lie outside his special studies.'[45] Felix Holt has much to learn about the relationship of ideas to actions, Lydgate must be made to understand the amount of self-interest in his pursuit of science and Mr Brooke is weak and quixotic. In fact, anywhere in the novels where ideas are substituted for a direct under-standing of suffering, their limitations are unequivocally exposed. Even where, in her writings, men of ideas appear to triumph, it is for special, larger reasons that have little to do with the sheer exercise of reason. Thus Mordecai in *Daniel Deronda* may be said to be an intellectual whose explication of a body of ideas provides Deronda with the solution to his identity problem, but Mordecai represents the strain of messianic yearning in Jewish prophetic theology. It is passionate, evocative and not part of a logical system of reasoning, nor does it conform to rationalist theories of knowledge. It is selfless and mysterious and points the seeker in the direction of his natural community, but a community based on a dream. Therein, however, lies its strength.

George Eliot's departure from the clerisy programme is nowhere more apparent than in her view of the place of the individual in modern society. *Au fond*, much of clerisy thinking was anti-individualistic, hence the fear of anarchy, the insistence upon order, tradition, continuity and standards, on history and a comprehensive Broad Church. Hence too the organic or holistic ideal, which, when the historical conditions were right, easily migrated towards centralised and collectivised solutions to national and social problems, towards T. H. Green's fusion of liberalism and Hegelianism, for example, or towards the Welfare State, towards nationalism or towards the militant ethic of the late Victorian public school. Once it became apparent that the State would not be captured by Nonconformity and that through the mechanism of a new civil service meritocracy, recruited from a regenerated Oxford and Cambridge, a class of platonic guardians, proconsuls, intellectual patricians and mandarins would be assigned to a fixed place in the English constitution, the clerisy

[44] Cross, *Life*, II (Edinburgh, 1885), 95.   [45] *Ibid.*, III, 182, 237–8.

search for an Establishment was no longer so urgent since universities were to hand.

Despite so much else she held in common with the clerisy, this was not George Eliot's way. Whatever her inner yearnings towards the collective, towards a *Gemeinschaft*, the community of a departed past (which she understood as mythos), she rejected systems and remained faithful to mid-Victorian liberal individualism. In fact, she tried to shore it up by demonstrating how personal problems could only be solved individually. It was part of her famed Realism to demonstrate that when institutional life-support systems collapse, relationships must be negotiated on a new basis, and that basis will always be personal.[46]

It is true that her vision of humanity was not exactly in keeping with the ethos of an age of progress. John Holloway is quite right. There is a fatalistic or deterministic philosophy of the universe underpinning much if not all of George Eliot's thinking, a sense of the tragic, of personal flaws that will eventually bring down their possessors, of mistakes that cannot be rectified, of second chances that will never come.[47] She deplored professions of sincerity that were not founded upon honest inner struggle, and she detested moral conversion on the cheap, especially if it came in a sudden flash of illumination. Wisdom, if it came at all, came cumulatively, working its way gradually through the 'slow entire of Victorian time' (to appropriate a conceit of John Fowles). Probably this is the way her famous seventeenth chapter in *Adam Bede* and other similar statements on Realism should be read, not as an aesthetic doctrine rigidly adhered to but as a means of underlining the fact that struggle leading to wisdom was inherently tragic. This is not the individualism of optimistic self-help or of *homo economicus*, but it is also not inconsistent with evangelical Christianity, with individuals working out for themselves the problem of redemption. Ready-made formulas could not be substituted for daily trial and error. The egregious Dr Cumming, she says, 'dwells on salvation as a scheme rather than as an experience'.[48] No inner sense of religious joy or sorrow was possible under such circumstances. Nor is her individualism compromised by a determinism incorporating Nemesis or coincidence, for

---

[46] Raymond Williams, *The Country and the City* (London, 1973), 180.

[47] John Holloway, *The Victorian Sage* (New York, 1965), 124–6. There is an ambiguity in this valuable discussion, however. At one point Holloway refers to irreversible laws governing morality in Eliot's fiction, but shortly thereafter he says that feelings determine morality. What needs to be clarified is the connection between feelings and laws in a determined universe. In any case, George Eliot's position on the role of fate in human affairs is hardly absolute since the meliorative element is so pronounced.

[48] *Essays of George Eliot*, 162.

this paradox too had been worked out theologically in the Christian ethics of free will. Calamity was no excuse for making the wrong moral choices. Morality itself was not to be confused with utilitarian ethics, with making right conduct dependent upon the approval of others. Cross was right in seeing her mind as essentially religious. In George Eliot's system of ethics material success came a long way behind spiritual or moral success; and meliorism, at least, could mitigate suffering even if it could not prevent it.

THE IMPORTANCE OF BEING UNATTACHED

The habit of being at the 'centre', a sense of possessing influence, prestige and perhaps power, is probably the most important source of the strength of the clerisy ideal in Victorian England. George Eliot did not possess that sense. She was decidedly at the periphery and not the centre. No part of her life took place in the Establishment, and this was not merely because as a woman she was denied access to the public schools and Oxbridge and prevented from entering the priesthood. Of course this was all too evident, but whether the pattern of her thinking related to gender, both by her choice of ideas or her denials, can be debated by others. Her own roots lay deep in the provincial culture of the western Midlands and northern Wales, in 'Stonyshire' and 'Loamshire', where new manufacturing towns and old farming communities existed conjointly. If she could not idealise the provinces, she could still express her 'love for our old-fashioned provincial life'.[49] This love for the periphery also partly accounts for her interest in Continental cities like Weimar, which despite its princely status was (she said) old, homely and comfortable. Her first circle of intellectual friends was not drawn from the Establishment, but was composed of those typical, self-made, educated manufacturers, business and professional men who had sometimes turned up in the old late Georgian Dissenting academies, who spread literary and philosophical societies around the Midlands and the north – not *arrivistes* at all, but dynamic men and women, intellectually curious, widely read in science and philosophy and in the arts of manufactures, Enlightenment people in their tastes and breadth of interests. From them George Eliot drew her initial acquaintance with Utilitarian philosophy and *laissez-faire* economics, positivist history and German scholarship, and not from the Oxbridge clerisy, where these ideas were often later imports, or the preoccupations of isolated bachelor dons and not to become the common property of university undergraduates until the 1860s. To be sure, there was a London

[49] Cross, *Life*, III, 66.

tie, the years with the Chapmans and life in the suburbs. But George Eliot was never comfortable at the centre. Part of this was her awkward arrangement with Lewes, which prevented her from being accepted into the common round of social life. But part of it was her own sense of being a provincial, and contemporaries played this up. Her 'rival', Mrs Lynn Linton, called her 'under-bred and provincial; and I was repelled by the unformed manner rather than attracted by the learning. She held her hands and arms kangaroo fashion; was badly dressed; had an unwashed, unbrushed, unkempt look altogether.'[50] This was partly but not altogether spite, for even many years later, in the 1870s, George Gosse, seeing Lewes and George Eliot from afar, thought that the 'solemnity of her face and the frivolity of her headgear had something pathetic and provincial about it'.[51] If she did not feel comfortable in London, she also had no experience of that other 'centre', the country house social world of the important gentry, one pole of what Sir Lewis Namier has termed the 'amphibious' existence of English nobility. As she noted *à propos* of *Daniel Deronda*, the scenes between the aristocrat Grandcourt and his hanger-on Lush were not based on direct experience.[52] Years later she would know some parts of the centre, for her friendship with Mark Pattison took her down to Lincoln College, Oxford, and her interest in women's higher education to Girton College, Cambridge, and she enjoyed the luxury of being popular with the new type of undergraduate who began to reside in the universities from the 1860s onwards. But her formative years were passed in the provinces and in the strong self-consciousness of having come from the periphery. For the clerisy it was quite the opposite. Being at the centre, they poorly understood the periphery, and the transforming energy that radiated outwards from the industrial cities of England distressed more than it elated them. They could never understand it; and for a number of them, such as the Cambridge-educated literary critic Sir Walter Alexander Raleigh, who taught at Liverpool and Glasgow before taking a chair at Oxford, the civic universities were a form of exile.

To the end of her life George Eliot carried with her the individualism of the Victorian provinces, and because of this she experienced both the

---

[50] Margharita Laski, *George Eliot and Her World* (London, 1978), 36.

[51] *Ibid.*, 97. See also page 46 for Laski's continued reference to the coarse element in George Eliot's (and Lewes's) conduct.

[52] Cross, *Life*, III, 200. Williams, *The Country and the City*, 178–81, takes off from this point to make George Eliot the founder of the country house genre of English fiction, i.e. symptomatic of the shift in the English novel from the 'known' to the 'knowable' community – the community that has to be explained and interpreted because it is no longer part of the received national experience.

advantage of being unattached and the vulnerability of the isolated worker. The former expressed itself as moral responsibility for one's actions, no matter how doggedly pursued by fate; the latter as meliorism and mediation, as sympathy for others since suffering was the common lot. In this respect, the source of her outlook on life was profoundly unlike that of the clerisy intelligentsia; although in so much else, particularly the determination to preserve and not destroy, to challenge but not hate and finally to conform rather than revolt, she was just as English as they.

The point has been made with respect to Continental typologies of the intellectual that intellectuals do not have to be estranged or alienated from their society or culture in order to appropriate the label. Detachment or independence is not synonymous with extreme marginality. Intellectuals can be, to use a technical phrase, 'cognitive insiders', whose criticism of their society is 'axionormative'. That is, they are 'strangers from within'. Their criticism affirms or upholds prevailing values or is undertaken in the spirit of what the intellectual judges to be a society's own best standards.[53] Matthew Arnold's marvellous rhythm, 'the best that has been thought and said' in the world, catches at this hook.

George Eliot the social moralist appears to fit this model. She was, as has been noted, a 'stranger from within'. But the special characteristics of mid-Victorian society should make us pause before applying Continental models of intellectuals too rigorously. There were two Victorian Englands, two cultures, the centre and the periphery, the metropolitan and the liberal cultures or the aristocratic and the Dissenting. In relation to the second in each pairing, George Eliot was not really a stranger or cognitive insider except as her personal behaviour when younger brought her into conflict with social conventions. That second culture was the theoretical anarchy of Victorian liberalism. George Eliot did not believe in the efficacy of political intervention, did not believe that social problems were amenable to State planning. She did not really trust the power of the mind to comprehend and solve or even institutionalise solutions. Nor could she ever imagine herself as part of a vanguard of intellectuals whose especial mission it was to push thought into radically new areas of comprehension, what G. M. Young deplored as the terrorism of the higher culture.[54] She could not, as the American novelist Mary McCarthy impatiently noted, do what Continental contemporaries did, think the

---

[53] Paul R. Mendes-Flohr, 'The Study of the Jewish Intellectual: Some Methodological Proposals', in *Essays in Modern Jewish History*, ed. Francis Malino and Phyllis Cohen Albert (London, 1982), 156–7.

[54] G. M. Young, 'The New Cortegiano', in *Victorian Essays* (London, 1962), 210.

unthinkable, turn rationalism against itself and imagine a world in which all relationships and values were upside down. Unlike Dostoevsky, she could not create a fictional world in which crime was committed and justified in the name of humanity.[55] Nor can her most pathetic and inadequate characters approach the hallucinatory and paranoid features of Kafka's protagonists, although Grandcourt, it must be admitted, is virtually a portrait of evil. Nevertheless, for the English liberals of her generation, social problems were never seen to be so desperate as to require desperate solutions. The English did not have to worry about national unification as did Germans and Italians, dictatorship and revolution as did the French, Czarist savagery and serfdom as did Russians, Austrian and eastern European anti-semitism, issues that were more than controversial and more than social 'problems' calling for royal commissions, parliamentary debate, policy decisions, public awareness. These were issues destined to bring out the darkest and most violent side of nationalism and human nature. For a sense of the horror that lies at the bottom of the human experience, the English had to await the coming of Joseph Conrad and the moral dilemmas of English imperialism (the horror of which Charles Dickens wrote was *bizarrerie*).

To a large extent it is simply true, and even a truism, that, as Gertrude Himmelfarb sardonically reflected in an essay of some thirty years ago, English intellectuals generally were not deserving of the word.[56] Perhaps, after all, George Eliot's marginality was minimal.[57] Her role was not to transform the world through thought, not even to fundamentally dissent from it, but to single out for praise those native moral values that had been essential to England's cultural evolution, to reaffirm them as a standard. Even her emphasis on the importance of feelings rather than reason is conventional and mild when compared to the submerged forces of

[55] Mary McCarthy, 'Ideas of the Novel: Dostoevsky's *The Possessed*, *The London Review of Books* (17 April 1980), 14–16.
[56] Gertrude Himmelfarb, 'Mr. Stephen and Mr. Ramsay: the Victorian as Intellectual', *The Twentieth Century*, 152 (December, 1952), 525.
[57] An 'outsider' and an 'insider', at one and the same time thus avoiding the extremes of both. The advantages of this interaction are explained with a different objective in mind by Merton, 'Insiders and Outsiders', 36–8. Lynn Hunt, *Politics, Culture and Class in the French Revolution* (Berkeley, 1984), 184–219, discusses 'marginality' as a positive condition, a combination of geographical and social positions that allows new men to take advantage of new opportunities. So Everett Hagen in an analysis of English entrepreneurs in the formative phase of the industrial revolution attributes innovation to marginal families such as Lowland Scots, English Dissenters and lesser gentry or other landowners. *On the Theory of Social Change* (Homewood, IL, 1962), 292–302. In these examples marginal men and women are not really strangers. They have 'need autonomy', and their societies offer outlets for such need.

intellect and the unconscious summoned up by European writers, a Hoffmann, to pick an early example, a Sorel to use a later one. George Eliot's feelings were guided and controlled by an inherited system of religious ethics which assumed that the emotional life was intrinsically good and could be trusted. From time to time it needed awakening, especially when reason or self-interest predominated.

GEORGE ELIOT AS A WOMAN OF LETTERS

No, 'intellectual' is not quite right, even as an anachronism. If the example does not appear to be merely semantic, we can elicit another generic label from those available to us from the age of the Victorians. George Eliot should be situated in the mainstream of English intellectual history as a 'critic' or 'man of letters'; and this designation has the merit of drawing us closer to another nineteenth-century conception of an academic role.

The pedigree of the man of letters extends into the eighteenth century and no further. His existence was made possible by the commercial and financial revolution that produced an impersonal market as an alternative to royal and aristocratic patronage. Gradually the writer, especially the London-based writer, was transformed from political hack and pamphleteer in the service of politicians into a 'critick'. Georgian writers detached themselves from royal and aristocratic patrons to woo a varied public consisting of connoisseurs, antiquarians and common readers. This made possible a change in role, first undertaken, according to Dr Samuel Johnson's reluctant admission, by the Queen Anne essayist and playwright, Joseph Addison, but only fully realised in Johnson's own career.[58] The writer became an independent observer of events, parties and personalities, what Johnson called, with an eye on Frenchmen like Boileau, an *Arbiter elegantiarum*. The programme was what in our own time Norbert Elias refers to as the 'civilizing process'.[59] Here the intellectual task was to carry on (and out) a revolution in manners, an improvement of personal conduct in everyday life. The conception of role that accompanied this programme was not that of the intellectual as cognitive insider, or as dissenter, adversary or political partisan. Quite the contrary: free of the necessity to serve a specific master, the critic became the agent of civilisation, the upholder of Taste, Reason and Nature. The function of art was to elevate conduct in accordance with the highest received standards of behaviour. The medium was satire and wit, for the

[58] See Samuel Johnson, 'Life of Addison', in *Lives of the Poets*.
[59] Norbert Elias, *The Civilizing Process* (New York, 1978).

general view of life in the eighteenth century was hedonistic rather than tragic. Literature played on the margins of entertainment, was often confused with pleasure until the political novel appeared in the 1790s.

An alternative mission emerged in the nineteenth century. The unattached artist intellectual, who hitherto adopted the historical task of sustaining the march of civilisation, now became as much interested in self as society, in private as in public behaviour, and in experiment as much as imitation. Some writers put forward the view that art suffered unless free of regulation and convention. This familiar Romantic theme does not have to be pursued much further just now. The overview is merely intended to indicate that George Eliot could choose between two intellectual conceptions of the independent thinker: the critic or man of letters who was 'scientifick' (to use Dr Johnson's word), who judged according to universal, which also means received standards, the best that has been thought and said in the world; and the artist, who put his private vision of humanity first. Some crossing of borders inevitably occurred, some confusion of mission and roles. But the usual compromise was a Humean bargain, a social contract, wherein the independent thinker led two lives, a private one for himself as a liberated artist and another for the public as a responsible critic or man of letters. Thus Francis Jeffrey, the first of the new generation of nineteenth-century critics, drew a 'veil round the furtive individual pleasures of literature in the name of universally accepted standards'.[60]

The historical and sociological sketch is necessary for a clearer under-standing of George Eliot's self-conception. She began her career as a critic, as a woman of letters and translator, as someone whose job it was to disseminate and interpret information for what she called in 1854 'that very indeterminate abstraction "the public"'.[61] Her medium of communi-cation was in the first instance, as mention of Francis Jeffrey indicates, the high journalism of the great Victorian periodicals, the *Edinburgh Review*, the *Quarterly Review, Blackwood's,* the *Westminster Review*, the *Fortnightly*, the *Cornhill, Macmillan's* and so on. The first generation of them were highly partisan politically – whig, tory or radical – but some leavening occurred in the mid-Victorian period to provide a fairly common standard of reviewing and reporting for the important Victorian middlebrow culture.[62]

Also like the critic and like another great Victorian provincial, her friend Herbert Spencer (their lifelong relationship was not without

---

[60] John Gross, *The Rise and Fall of the Man of Letters* (Harmondsworth, 1973), 14.
[61] *Essays of George Eliot*, 60.   [62] Young, 'The New Cortegiano', 210–11.

difficulties), George Eliot held no conscious or firm conception or role which related intellectual function to social structure.[63] No more than the man of letters did Spencer and Eliot believe that social position, achieved or ascribed, or even acquired knowledge automatically implied specific role responsibilities. If culture was more important than class, so community was more important than role.

George Eliot had been unconventional in her private life, but as she grew older and famous her personal behaviour and social beliefs came closer together. The artist-intellectual rebel within her yielded in open society to the attitudes and values traditionally associated with the critic. She believed in both of them, but the public one had always adhered, if not slavishly, to the rules of good taste and respected the proper boundaries of art.

[63] For Spencer, see J. D. Y. Peel, *Herbert Spencer* (New York, 1971), 183, 191.

CHAPTER NINE

ALTERNATIVES
2. BORN TO HAVE NO REST

INTRODUCTION

The clerisy and the man (or woman) of letters were two possible roles for academics discussed in the nineteenth century, each implying different strategies and paths towards independence. A third career alternative, that of the professional academic, developed in connection with the Scottish universities and the first University of London and was achieved at Oxford and Cambridge after the period of reform. This alternative derived from guild (or to use A. H. Halsey's word, *syndicat*) traditions of institutional self-management characterised by control of the conditions of recruitment and training and domination of relevant markets. The history of the guild ideal runs parallel to the history of universities, and by the beginning of the present century professionalism became the singlemost important career model for university based professors and lecturers.

Once described as the 'forgotten middle class',[1] professions have been the subject of intense interest in the last few decades primarily because of the transition undergone by modern societies from manufacturing to service. Fatigue arising from attempts to explain all historical change in the language of social class is another reason. The majority of scholars agree that there is no single model of professional development, that variations on the theme occur within nations as well as between them, nor is there any one professional occupation that serves as the archetype for all the others.[2] In France and Germany the State has been the decisive influence in defining professions (in Germany academics have civil service status), in America it has been the university and in England the guilds

---

[1] Harold Perkin, *The Origins of Modern English Society, 1780–1880* (London, 1969), Chapter 7.

[2] However, Bruce Kimball, *The 'True Professional Ideal' in America, a History* (Cambridge, MA, 1992), divides the history of professionalism in the US into discrete chronological periods, each with its own professional 'architectonic' and model profession.

of practitioners.[3] With regard to academic professionalism, twentieth-century developments in Britain, notably State centralisation, the growth in importance of research and expansion first of the provision for elite education, second for mass education, have led to conditions of steadier parliamentary interference and bureaucratic steering in all parts of the higher education system. Academic professionalism in today's Britain is therefore no longer the envied model for self-government that it was before 1945. Several recent analyses conclude that 'donnish dominion' has declined throughout higher education, affecting even the most elite institutions.[4] In the United States, academic self-government derives from the delegation of responsibilities by boards of trustees to faculties; but if faculties in America have had less formal and legal autonomy than their British counterparts, the action of the State (or states) has been more diffuse, more subject to electoral and consumer pressures, and the resulting exercise of political authority with respect to universities has been typically spasmodic and inconsistent.

Many forms of academic professionalism are associated with the history of academic disciplines as self-referencing bodies of knowledge, but all are based on the principle of mastering the materials, methods and conceptions of a given field of inquiry as defined by a particular community of scholars (the starting point for Thomas Kuhn's discussions of intellectual paradigms). The 'liberal professions' – law, medicine, architecture and so on – however, share authority with State licensing agencies, the relative influence of each depending upon the composition and mandate of the agency in question. Domination of markets, another common tendency of professions, is doubtless important; but for practitioners to acquire and retain a dominant occupational position, another element is required, a code of disinterested service without which professions are no different from any other occupation and professional men and women no more entitled to respect or admiration than other salary earners. Harold Perkin observes that the success of a profession is measured by the degree to which its legitimating principles of

---

[3] Michael Burrage, 'From Practice to School-based Professional Education: Patterns of Conflict and Accommodation in England, France and the United States', in *The European and American University since 1800, Historical and Sociological Essays,* ed. Sheldon Rothblatt and Björn Wittrock (Cambridge, 1993), 142–87; Charles E. McClelland, *The German Experience of Professionalization* (Cambridge, 1991).

[4] A. H. Halsey, *Decline of Donnish Dominion* (Oxford, 1992); and Ted Tapper and Brian Salter, *Oxford, Cambridge and the Changing Idea of the University: the Challenge to Donnish Domination* (Ballmoor, Bucks, 1992). Their remedies, actual or implied, are however nearly opposite.

disinterested service receive wide public acceptance.[5] Sceptics remark that
professionals are as fundamentally self-interested as any other market-
reliant group and no more deserving of special recognition than others
who labour and profess. As we reach the end of the twentieth century,
deprofessionalisation has commenced in Britain and America, most
notably in school-teaching where classroom independence is minimal.
But even the leading model of a profession in the United States, that of
medicine, is experiencing a wrenching transformation. Cost-cutting (and
profit-making) have created circumstances in which formerly independent practitioners succumb or threaten to succumb to the direction of
insurance companies and health maintenance organisations which dictate
the conditions of employment. The international academic community
is also uneasy. Security of academic tenure has been abolished for new
academic entrants in Britain. Tenure faces an uncertain future in
America. Efforts to regain market position have led some academic
specialities into adopting entrepreneurial styles, and, as is well understood,
the vaunted mobility of American academics has long been connected to
market pricing. But when intellectual and professional occupations are
closely associated with the buying and selling of commodities, there is
danger that they will lose the two qualities that have consistently defined
their attempts to achieve independence. Samuel Haber calls them 'honour
and authority', and both are related to the fiduciary responsibilies that
professions claim to uphold. Because of the intimate historical connection
between professions and universities, which includes the association
between guild ideals and the idea of a university, the loss of a validating
principle by the first leads to the same loss in the second.

Thomas Bender has looked at academic professional responsibility and
its ethical code in another way, one that draws from the tradition of
civic humanism. Its object is to encourage citizens to participate in the
institutions of free government, to understand those institutions and to
contribute to their maintenance and vitality. It appears that he has in mind
a composite conception of an academic role, one that combines college
and university roles, liberal and professional education. His paragon is
John Dewey. He notes that the first American graduate schools
prepared students for careers relevant to city life, such as public service and
journalism or other activities that could lead to improvements in political
practice. But the professors abandoned the culture of the city and
replaced it with narrower career interests. The university, enlarged

---

[5] Harold Perkin, *The Rise of Professional Society, England since 1880* (London, 1981); Joseph
Ben-David, *The Scientist's Role in Society* (Engelwood Cliffs, NJ, 1971), 180.

and self-absorbing, became more interesting than the town. Bender is thinking principally of metropolises like New York City,[6] for elsewhere in the United States, especially in small towns, universities and colleges have been major providers of entertainment and the arts. But admittedly culture and politics are not the same.

Writing from a personal perspective, Lord Dahrendorf recounts the history of the London School of Economics as the story of a continuing tension over two other academic ideals, the scholar or 'ascetic' in pursuit of value-free knowledge, and the second, overlapping Bender's example, is the activist, eager to provide society with a template for social improvement.[7] The activist role is instrumental and task-oriented. Its aim is to alter social conditions – schools, poverty, housing, energy use, transportation, health – in accordance with some plan for a good life. Once social amelioration becomes the goal, political ideology must inevitably enter. It is hardly surprising that at the LSE some professors were attracted to authoritarian solutions, while others preferred to rely on the operation of free markets.[8]

We have noticed that George Eliot discharged her moral responsibility to society largely through literature and criticism, preserving her independence in the process by remaining unattached to any supporting institution. For the man of letters generally, for the type also represented by Leslie Stephen, the university was not the best location from which to comment on the standards essential to the preservation of high culture.[9] Yet in the twentieth century the university's mission has broadened to the point where such concerns have become professionalised (if they exist at all) and are incorporated into the several fields of academic inquiry, where, precisely because of an activist ethic, they are controversial. The issue of whether knowledge is ever value-free, whether professionalism is tantamount to expertise and whether, as a consequence of specialised training, the pronouncements of academics warrant unusual respect is being fiercely debated both within and outside the academy. At stake is the historical issue of whether academics, as 'attached' men and women of knowledge, are entitled to the shelter provided by one of society's cardinal institutions.

As an illustration of the university's search for independence, the first of

[6] Thomas Bender, *Intellect and Public Life, Essays on the Social History of Academic Intellectuals in the United States* (Baltimore and London, 1993), xii–xiv, 6–9, 130, 136–7, 140, 144.
[7] Ralf Dahrendorf, *LSE, A History of the London School of Economics and Political Science 1895–1995* (Oxford, 1995), 128, 421–2, 515.
[8] E.g., Harold Laski versus Lionel Robbins.
[9] Noël Annan, *Leslie Stephen, the Godless Victorian* (New York, 1984), Chapter 1.

earthly blessings, we can take up the issue of the growth of academic
professionalism with special reference to scientists. Their case is particularly interesting because science, apart from mathematics or natural
philosophy, was not as vital to the liberal arts tradition of university college
teaching as language, literary, theological or philosophical studies before
the nineteenth century. Its institutional basis in America and England, if
less so in Scotland, lay largely outside universities in academies, botanical
gardens, observatories, government agencies, hospitals or museums. An
historical aim for scientists was gaining a foothold in the support structure
provided by universities, acquiring occupational security and respectability and using the growing prestige of universities to establish a
commanding position for science in the world of learning. Before Darwin,
science was reasonably popular, especially where linked to theological
paradigms concerning the age of the earth, the origins of species and the
descent of man, but science needed to establish its freedom from religious
entanglements, as well as from natural philosophy, by developing its own
enclosures of thought. The ultimate success of this historical endeavour is
not solely the result of the efforts of scientists. It owes just as much to the
development of modern industry and the requirements for waging war in
an increasingly sophisticated and destructive weapons environment. The
embrace of the modern State cannot be overestimated. Yet it is also
instructive to identify the strategies adopted by scientists to improve their
social standing, enhance the importance of their disciplines and achieve
professional integrity. In time the sciences, and perhaps the physical
sciences, became the paradigmatic academic disciplines against which all
the others were viewed. All fields of study were required to be 'scientific'
in some obvious way and to adopt the language and values of research
in order to develop measurable criteria for evaluating academic success.
Science and scientists established the parameters of the university's
relationship to government, the economy and society. Their object was to
restore guild control over the conditions of employment, but their very
success created the conditions for even greater vulnerability. Paradoxically, what was now at stake was the essence of professional culture itself.[10]

We can begin the narrative with the apparition that has stalked English
intellectual life since the eighteenth century and reappears at critical points
in university history, namely the market, which always seemed to beckon
threateningly along the road towards professional self-realisation.

---

[10] George Marsden would add the 'soul' of the university, the advent of new unacknowledged
orthodoxies. See his *The Soul of the American University, from Protestant Establishment to
Established Nonbelief* (Oxford, 1994), 422–4.

THE EFFECT OF THE MARKET ON INTELLECTUAL LIFE
IN BRITAIN

The theory of the market was developed in the late seventeenth and early eighteenth century and is closely associated with Britain's peculiar economic environment: her island position, climate zone, lack of arable land for a growing population and limited access to surplus bullion. From an early date, slowly and virtually without being conscious of it, Britain replaced a protectionist economy with one dependent upon trade balances. The result was the creation of a vigorous commercial and financial community – the 'monied interest' – located in the City of London, a representative selection of foreign trading interests nearby in another district and a habit of acquisition frankly pointed towards the open market. This development was abetted by an influential section of landed aristocrats who, for quite independent reasons, had taken control of local and national government and needed capital markets in order to solve certain taxing difficulties. Thus commenced a collaboration of propertied and trading interests, and as national income grew, so did other linked characteristics of a market economy. The British aristocracy, grown wealthy on the profits of land, office and City investments, were heavy consumers. Aristocracies tend towards conspicuous consumption in any case.

In the early eighteenth century the open market began to challenge patronage as a means of providing a livelihood for writers, artists and thinkers. Given the existing variety of publics, a certain amount of vulgarisation took place, but marketing initiatives also produced radical departures in art and thought. A summary includes the social novel, a form of literature denounced at the time as 'romantick', that is, frivolous because it was popular; the British School of Painting featuring portraiture, since buyers wished to be commemorated; English as distinguished from Italian language opera; connoisseurship, the collecting of objects of all kinds for pleasure and as a hobby and writings pertaining to collecting. Gardening created an immense industry of growers, nurseries, landscapers, builders of garden ornaments and tools, collectors of seeds and plants from the world's exotic zones.[11]

The public, declared Gibbon, is seldom wrong,[12] but he was a well-received author, and many other writers and artists had also learned how

[11] Sheldon Rothblatt, *Tradition and Change in English Liberal Education, An Essay in History and Culture* (London and Boston, 1981), Chapter 7.
[12] Edward Gibbon, *Memoirs of My Life* (Harmondsworth, 1984), 163.

to please consumers. Finding slack in the market, some Georgian authors and artists saw an opportunity to elevate public taste. The novel became didactic, even while it had to be humorous. Painting became neoclassical by adopting the technique George Santayana called the 'idealization of the familiar', wherein heroic, epic, religious and historical models were used to enlarge the perspectives of sitters. Even the foolish gothic novel of the late eighteenth century – usually the story of a late adolescent woman undergoing a series of improbable adventures – was an attempt to heighten sensibility and even to introduce an element of religious feeling or 'awe' into works meant essentially for titillation.

Only a broad definition or category of science can possibly encompass the varieties of intellectual activities occurring in an unsettled economic and social environment. Intellectual elements mixed with popular interests. Science was a model for Scottish social science, esteemed throughout Europe. The greatest animal painter of the age, George Stubbs, was something of an anatomist. Provincial literary and philosophical societies disseminated scientific ideas but also gadgets to town gentlemen. Science was often merely a hobby or amusement. The century was filled with charlatans, *jongleurs*, millenarians and assorted enthusiasts who hid behind the mask of natural philosophy and enthralled audiences with sensational electrical spectacles that came close to resembling superstitions the Enlightenment had been eager to dispel.[13] John Heilbron has suggested to me that this motley group might be called purveyors of science. They were particularly numerous and earned their keep as popular lecturers, instrument makers, writers of best-selling texts, busily creating a mass market for scientific and technical information and for scientific products. Compilers of almanacs did a thriving business. Tiberio Cavallo (born in Naples) and William Nicholson were particularly successful writers of popular scientific texts.[14]

Another group, composed of members of the learned societies or holding professorships, experimentalists with institutional affiliations and a demonstrated interest in advancing science, can be called doers of science. The doers of science preferred employment with some security or stability. Their homes were institutions like the Royal Society and teaching academies (really upper secondary schools) established by non-Anglican Protestants. But the doers of science were occasionally also to be

[13] Simon Schaffer, 'Natural Philosophy and Public Spectacle in the Eighteenth Century', *History of Science*, 21 (March, 1983), 31–2.
[14] John L. Heilbron, *Elements of Early Modern Physics* (Berkeley and Los Angeles, 1982), 157–8.

found in the open market alongside the purveyors of science, sometimes driven there by necessity.

Pressure for useful knowledge was indeed a feature of the Age of Illumination. Applied mathematicians found jobs in government, as did surveyors and cartographers. Several applications benefited from theoretical work. The lightning rod was the result of the investigations of eighteenth-century experimentalists. The improvement of windmills and the design of ships' hulls owed a great deal to the calculations of mathematicians.[15] There are indeterminate areas, such as the invention of James Watt's steam engine, the premier machine of the industrial revolution, which a few authorities have tried to attribute to Joseph Black's theory of latent heat. Several scholars have argued that a lively interest in applying theory to the industrial arts was emerging in Scotland, the northern English provinces and southern Ireland at the end of the eighteenth century. The members of the very short-lived Academy of Physics at Edinburgh carried out research on soda, and University of Glasgow professors studied bleaching and other industrial processes. The evidence does not suggest great utility as a result of these researches, however, many of which were classificatory and therefore only a first step, if a necessary step, in the study of natural phenomena.[16]

The Royal Institution, a new turn-of-the-century science association that gave a chair to the distinguished Humphry Davy, supported work in agriculture and tanning. The Royal Institution is an interesting example because it is one of the very few instances of an institutionalised response to an actual demand for applied science. Its distant origins lay in an earlier philanthropic organisation founded to pacify the rural poor at a time of mounting disorder in the English countryside. It was the specific creation of a group of aristocratic landlords who were anxious to improve crop yields and animal breeding. Although Davy's prolific investigations, which he released publicly as lectures and subsequently published, did not actually lead to any practical changes, his benefactors were apparently pleased by his efforts to solve technical problems. Davy called himself a campaigner for science. He often treated science as a commodity and was quick to employ utilitarian reasons on behalf of science when he needed money. His patrons allowed him to build a large voltaic pile, for example, when he contended beforehand that soil fertility directly benefited from

---

[15] These examples have been given to me by Heilbron.

[16] Arthur Donovan, 'British Chemistry and the Concept of Science in the Eighteenth Century', *Albion*, 7 (Summer, 1975), 131–144; and G. N. Cantor, 'The Academy of Physics at Edinburgh, 1797–1800', *Social Studies of Science*, 5 (May, 1975), 109–34.

electricity.[17] These efforts did not go very far in connecting pure science with industrial development; but they do suggest a respectable start and were possibly important for separating science from natural philosophy.[18]

Compared to Continental science in the seventeenth and eighteenth centuries, British science had a meagre support base. The Church of England provided no direct institutional support comparable to the assistance given inquirers by the Society of Jesus, the leading patron of physical and mathematical science in the seventeenth century. Nor did British societies or academies dedicated to the advancement, improvement or cultivation of science like the Royal Society provide as many career positions in the eighteenth century as did those in Protestant Germany. A certain amount of significant intellectual work in experimental physics was carried out by professors in Oxford and Cambridge and in the Scottish universities, but their role was essentially the traditional one of teaching or professing rather than research or free inquiry. Few purveyors, practitioners or doers of science derived their primary source of income from basic science or received a salary or stipend from a scientific institution or position. They did science on the side, as it were, and pursued other occupations. Only a few exceptional Enlightenment experimentalists like Christian von Wolff were in great demand throughout Europe and could offer their services to the highest bidders.[19]

There were no finely drawn communities in control of scientific knowledge and information, and that is the point. The intellectual and occupation distinctions between scientists, natural philosophers and instrument makers were gossamer, leading to attempts to resolve status ambiguities, as the career of Alessandro Volta in Italy also demonstrates.[20] But the stature and occupational standing of scientists had long been nebulous. As commonly observed, the word 'scientist' itself is an English neologism of the 1830s and 1840s, quite possibly coined by more than one person but certainly attributable to the eminent Cambridge University philosopher, William Whewell. It was by no means eagerly seized upon. The word dragged on for decades unappreciated, the butt, in fact, of much humour and invective. It was denounced for being a formation from incorrect Latin or a Latin-Greek hybrid. British writers particularly enjoyed calling 'scientist' an Americanism (as they called anything they disliked an Americanism), as unpleasant a word, said the great Professor

---

[17] Morris Berman, 'The Early Years of the Royal Institution, 1799–1810: A Re-evaluation', *Science Studies*, 2 (1972), 205–40.
[18] *Ibid.*   [19] Heilbron, *Physics*, 35–6, 112–13, 146–7.
[20] Information provided by Giuliano Pancaldi of the University of Bologna.

Thomas Huxley, as 'electrocution', which was, in fact, American. 'Scientist' was not accepted in either country until the nineteenth century was nearly over.[21] Even the word 'science' was undifferentiated before the nineteenth century, being interchangeable with 'philosophy'.

In France there was similar confusion. *Le scientiste* applied only to the followers of the nineteenth-century school of scientific materialism. *Un scientifique* was not commonly used until the twentieth century. The favourite old regime workhorse word was *savant*, which pulled in meanings from *érudit*, but it had no specific occupational reference. Those who wrote scientific texts in France (and in Britain) were known by the catchall designation of man of letters.[22]

From the perspective of quality, or lasting contributions to science or to science as a collective activity, the development of a market for intellectual products had mixed results. Considerable diversification of mental and artistic endeavour occurred, but there was also work that was unimaginative, shoddy, cynical and silly. Market pressures resulted in plagiarism (a widely circulated word in the eighteenth century) and other forms of unacknowledged borrowing. Competition led to conduct that was morally suspicious, actions that were regarded as reprehensible, sometimes because they were unprecedented. Changes in taste created cyclical variations in demand. For example, the market for lectures on experimental physics was better in London in the early decades of the eighteenth century than some thirty or forty years later. Despite high admission fees, it was better in the English provinces in the second half of the eighteenth century than in the London of the same period.[23] For the average independent researcher, the greatest drawback of the market was its unpredictability.

THE UNIVERSITY AS A PLACE FOR SCIENCE

The university was potentially a possible source of support for science. The universities in some European countries, the Netherlands for example, managed to incorporate a research mission into their institutions.[24] But the open question for Britain was whether the university itself could remain

---

[21] Sydney Ross, 'Scientist: the Story of a Word', *Annals of Science*, 18 (June, 1962), 65–85; Howard S. Miller, *Dollars for Research: Science and its Patrons in Nineteenth-Century America* (Seattle and London, 1970), vii.

[22] Ross, 'Scientist', 73n; Roger Hahn, 'Scientific Research as an Occupation in Eighteenth-Century Paris', *Minerva*, 13 (Winter, 1975), 503.

[23] Heilbron, *Physics*, 154.

[24] *Ibid.*, Chapter 2.

independent of the market. The answer was clearly dependent upon the university's sources of support, as establishment of new universities like London was to illustrate. But even the Oxford and Cambridge colleges, many but not all of which enjoyed substantial endowments, relied heavily upon fee income to support expansion in student numbers, as occurred in the early nineteenth century. All the colleges showed how vulnerable they were to particular user pressures for admission and specific courses of instruction. The Scottish universities, open to all and underpinned by a widespread system of parish schools, suffered from lower standards, at least from an English perspective. The professors had to make continual adjustments in their teaching to take cognizance of student deficiencies. This was a concern addressed by the royal commission investigating Scottish universities in the 1820s.

In the course of the nineteenth century, the doing of science became increasingly expensive. Equipping labs, hiring assistants, maintaining buildings and outfitting expeditions could not be done cheaply. When science was an unpaid or less capital-intensive activity, when a Darwin could equip himself and sail off on the *Beagle*, support for science was not a serious issue. Nor was it a problem when science was viewed as a form of liberal instruction or annexed to theology, or when, in universities, professors regarded their proper role as the dissemination but not the advancement of knowledge. Costs were of course relative. In the mathematical fields the work was essentially abstract. Even in chemistry, metallurgy and agriculture, the expense was minuscule compared to what is required today.

Apart from the expenses of science, the question of whether scientists themselves were under pressure to earn a living, as in the previous century, opens up a secondary level of inquiry. Were scientists increasingly recruited from lower-income groups, as in the case of early and middle Georgian writers?[25] There are hints (but also rumours arising from Oxbridge snobbery) that distinguished mathematical graduates of Cambridge University from about 1830 to 1860 were of lesser social standing. But proof is elusive; and at any rate, most of the Cambridge honours students or 'wranglers' did not pursue science careers because mathematics was regarded as an excellent means of acquiring a liberal education.[26]

The expansion of medical opportunities in the nineteenth century

---

[25] Raymond Williams, *The Long Revolution* (London and New York, 1961), 234–7. Recruitment shifts upward again after 1830 in conformity with expansion of the upper middle class.
[26] A subject of special interest to Harvey W. Becher of Northern Arizona State University, Flagstaff.

provides clues about the growth of new academic specialities and their professionalisation. Doctors deserve to be recognised as the strongest moving force in the institutionalisation of science in the first half of the nineteenth century.[27] An expanding market for services, driven by the sanitary requirements of an urbanising society (where doctors faced competition from engineers who held rival epidemiological theories), consumer interest in standards of personal health and rising income and educational levels provided physicians and allied practitioners with a chance to enhance their prospects. New hospitals and clinics were established in provincial areas. Doctors were among the major forces behind the foundation of University College and King's College, London, and the singlemost important lobby and pressure group in the University of London's earliest years.[28] Medical men were the dominant group in a scheme to establish a Royal College of Chemistry in 1845. When clinical medicine returned to the ancient English universities, from which it had been virtually absent for well over a century, it became the means for the entry of new scientific specialities, such as physiology, bacteriology, medical physics and organic chemistry.

But medical specialists were not necessarily scientists. Some combined practice with original inquiry, others preferred one or the other. For certain purposes a university affiliation might be useful, for others less so. But once confidence in diagnosis and treatment were established, the profession could flourish. This was partly achieved by raising academic and training standards, partly by employing the licensing power of the State to eliminate the rivalry of quacks and bogus medical men who had flourished in an unregulated market and partly through key discoveries like the germ theory of disease that came late in the century. American physicians could rarely or hardly rely upon the protections of central or state governments, receptive to other and rival claims, and learned instead to sell themselves to different publics with astonishing success in the long run. The first step was recognising the particular qualities of the American consumer. The second was providing a superior product, and the third was consistency in setting the kind of ethical example that appealed to an individualist, Protestant culture.[29]

---

[27] Sheldon Rothblatt, 'The Diversification of Higher Education in England', in *The Transformation of Higher Learning, 1860–1930*, ed. Konrad H. Jarausch (Stuttgart and Chicago, 1983), 135–6.

[28] F. M. G. Willson, *Our Minerva, the Men and Politics of the University of London 1836–1858* (London, 1995), 18–25, 65, 138, 225, 269–76.

[29] Samuel Haber, *The Quest for Authority and Honour in the American Professions, 1750–1900* (Chicago, 1991), ix, 16, 184, 295, 356.

In the Victorian period there was a robust effort on the part of many other science-related specialities to encourage outside support on a medical model. The activities of professors in the new universities in the great provincial cities and the metropolis were notable in this regard. Civic universities could not depend upon an established elite for support, and their early histories provide plentiful examples of linkages between the heads of departments and local business. Important changes in the structure of enterprise facilitated cooperation. The older textile industries which had given Britain her industrial supremacy were limited-capital ventures with simple or craft technical requirements. The new products of the imperial period were science-based industries such as rubber and petroleum, the internal combustion engine, the pneumatic tyre, electro-communications, synthetic dyes and electric power and traction. These required some greater degree of correspondence between pure and applied research. Furthermore, the new large-scale industries based on chemical technology required more technically trained executives, which the older family-run and limited partnership firms did not. Michael Sanderson's investigations into the relations between the university and business sectors in the last hundred years provides us with a detailed account of the role played by university based scientists in British industrial development. His research is an important corrective to the widely believed argument that the contacts were minimal and insignificant. He has uncovered documents that reveal that University of London professors carried out secret research for the British steel industry, and he has suggested there may have been more such agreements.[30]

Some professors turned to industry – we do not know how many, but this solution does not appear to have provided sufficient opportunities for more purely theoretical work. Yet in the period between the great wars signs appeared indicating that the alliances struck between London, redbrick and British industry were temporary and beginning to break down. The new leading sectors of British industry were very large and in a position to consider establishing their own research laboratories, reverting to an older British attitude that industry was better served by scientists directly employed in the works than by outside specialists possessing a greater degree of independence and perhaps freer to challenge priorities set by the firm.

Efforts to generate market interest in science, and especially applied

[30] Michael Sanderson, *The Universities and British Industry 1870–1970* (London, 1972); and 'The Professor as Industrial Consultant: Oliver Arnold and the British Steel Industry, 1900–1914', *The Economic History Review*, 31 (1978), 585–600.

science, are characteristic of the second half of the nineteenth century. Yet an inherent suspicion of the market never really disappeared. As Haber argues, professional men drew their values from a world of production, services and personal relationships that antedated the spread of capitalist ideologies. The market experience of the eighteenth century had left a legacy of warnings about the quality of science when doers of science were without independent resources. Continuing fears about the conversion of intellectual domains of thought into commodities, reinforced by Coleridgean arguments for the need for an endowed class of thinkers, enhanced the view that the best science was pure and disinterested. Furthermore, centuries of royal charters and aristocratic government had accustomed the arts and sciences to receiving patronage from the centre. Victorian writers and academics were troubled by 'public opinion', regarding it as inimical to their best interests. At the same time, some scientists and scholars expressed reservations about drawing too close to a third alternative, the State, fearing the consequences of heavy dependence upon such a potent source of research support.

Reform of the ancient English and Scottish universities, the expansion of the higher education sector to include the English provinces, Wales and Ireland and improvements in secondary education, if mainly private, eliminated reservations about the university as an effective sponsor of intellectual work, as well as applied science. New physical laboratories at Cambridge and Manchester provided a chance to recruit higher-level engineering and medical students. Their fees could support teaching; and while teaching was undoubtedly time-consuming and not exactly what research-minded scientists wished, it allowed more opportunity for purely theoretical work than did business contracts.[31] In telescoping the process by which science found a home in universities, we should avoid minimising the battles that unorthodox subjects faced when seeking entry into the curriculum. Academic disciplines have an imperialistic dimension, especially if over time they become vested interests enjoying institutional benefits. Nevertheless, by the end of the nineteenth century science and technology alike were both esconced within universities, competing for resources in some instances, engaging in battles of the books in others, enduring slights in some cases, creating laboratory alternatives to existing programmes of studies but in general establishing themselves as major participants in all forms of higher education, from liberal to technical. Better-prepared university entrants allowed for greater

[31] Romualdas Sviedrys, 'Physical Laboratories in Britain', *Historical Studies in the Physical Sciences*, 7 (1976), 435, and information from Heilbron.

specialisation in the curriculum. The university world had been won over, and a place for science found.

Up to the period of the American Civil War, there were few institutional homes for the doing of science considered as research rather than as liberal education. In the Yale University curriculum, the teaching of science consumed only about 20 per cent of the total pedagogical effort. As in the case of Cambridge University before 1850, science was justified in two ways: first, as a form of liberal education, a way of disciplining the mind;[32] and second, as part of the tradition of natural theology inherited from the Enlightenment. American professors of science no less than British ones were expected to be gentlemen, to be cultivated, to be liberal and not servile, broad but not specialised.[33]

At the beginning of the second half of the nineteenth century, the quality of American colleges and universities was much closer to that of the Scottish universities or the new civic university colleges than to Oxford and Cambridge. The distinction between higher and lower forms of education was uncertain. The 'common school' movement had not yet taken off, and students were moving from school to university without the standard of preparation becoming the norm in Europe. Still, the expanding public university sector was an obvious science location, but by no means did the individual states provide adequate support for pure work. They saw their main task as providing sums for teaching, especially in a period of rapidly rising matriculations. Furthermore, it was not certain that American universities could provide an alternative home for intellectually advanced work of any kind. American academics envied the gentlemanly standing of English counterparts and admired German intellectual life – some 10,000 studied in German universities in the nineteenth century.[34] They despaired of American populism and hucksterism. Efforts to raise American popular taste by bringing universities and colleges up to European levels were certain to be frustrated if higher education could not be insulated from the cruder demands of a vigorous and undiscriminating market demand. If dependent upon consumer taste,

---

[32] A nineteenth-century shift, nevertheless, from earlier versions of liberal education which were more ethological in nature.

[33] Daniel J. Kevles, *The Physicists* (New York, 1978), 21, 26.

[34] Konrad Jarausch, 'American Students in Germany, 1815–1914: The Structure of German and U.S. Matriculants at Göttingen University', in *German Influences on Education in the United States to 1917,* ed. Henry Geitz *et al.* (Cambridge, 1995), 195.

mental products would become far more responsive to whims, fads and utilitarian ambitions than to the wishes of academic guilds. Whole areas of institutional life under the guidance of the professors would be affected. The traditional arts curriculum would be replaced by subjects with more practical use, and standards would be lowered as universities and colleges concentrated on student intake to meet operating costs. Here were the same anxieties as appeared in Britain, but no federal or Cambridge principle emerged to counteract the perceived difficulties. New universities continued to arise proclaiming a belief in consumer sovereignty, especially during the 1860s when the land grant university movement began. Regarded by elite institutions as occupying the periphery, market-oriented colleges and universities in America responded by boasting of their unique flexibility and by welcoming (or pretending to welcome) the open market for the opportunities it provided for the exercise of imagination and initiative. They accepted challenges in a Robinson Crusoe mood of exhilaration at the prospect of new territories waiting to be mapped. They accepted forthright the basic premises of the European and American Enlightenments that a dynamic society required a correspondingly dynamic educational system. If the established institutions behaved defensively with respect to changing patterns of demand, then the 'periphery' had to assume leadership. Such was the reasoning. Such was the outcome.[35]

Nevertheless, although the applied mission was foremost in the establishment of state universities, at the same time an opening was provided for basic science, since physics, mathematics and chemistry were certainly needed in even the most pronounced technical fields. In some institutions, therefore, technology provided another avenue into the university for research science, although traditional subjects like mathematics, as the British example of Cambridge shows, were also a means of entry into the physical sciences.

Working closely with lay boards of trustees, American university presidents were often instrumental in determining whether science activity received encouragement. James McCosh, a Scot who brought British ideas of liberal education with him to the congenial environment of Princeton, was unsympathetic, but Charles W. Eliot at Harvard and

---

[35] Even within the periphery, however, some departments emulate elite practices and come into conflict with administrators who see their first duty as service to the consumer. Conversely, within elite universities, professional schools may be more responsive to the market than the traditional or 'autonomous' disciplines, possibly because they have a well-defined clientèle in mind. (My thoughts on such questions have been greatly aided by discussion with Martin Trow.)

Daniel C. Gilman at the new private university of Johns Hopkins were intensely interested in folding science into the university curriculum. Gilman, incidentally, had pushed science while leading the University of California at Berkeley, but he could not convince potential supporters of its value. Farming interests were predominant and very practical-minded in California. In the 'heroic age' of university building in the second half of the nineteenth century, American presidents enjoyed powers of innovation and financing unavailable to British vice-chancellors, whose authority was constrained by guild traditions. In the new universities of the English provinces, academic senates rapidly took effective control of the institutions away from vice-chancellors and lay trustees.

Professors, it was decided, had marketable products. Boards of trustees and presidents saw an opportunity to use them to bring added income and prestige to their institutions, which in turn attracted more income and more prestige. Individual states encouraged their publicly supported institutions to be competitive, so that multiple sources of revenue would flow into the university. Political leaders in the states participated in this process by instructing representatives in Congress to obtain lucrative contracts and awards from federal agencies. Since the professors developed the intellectual products, it was logical to establish central government funding policies that rewarded individual initiative and entrepreneurial energy. A practice of awarding external grants directly to individual applicants or teams grew up, strengthening the role of professor as principal investigator. This was the system, and the reasoning, that eventually led to a golden age for science, especially physical science, in the decades following the Second World War.

Outside the universities there had been no immediate demand for pure scientists in the rapidly industrialising economy of the post-Civil War period. In the physical sciences a disparity had already grown up between young physicists who were excited by brilliant work in Europe on the atom, radioactivity and quantum physics, and the business sector which had no room for them. Just as in Britain, however, the changing structure of business and the chemical revolution produced opportunities for the employment of engineers, chemists and physicists. Openings appeared in Western Electric, the manufacturing subsidiary of the American Telegraph and Telephone Company, in DuPont, the giant chemical firm, in the petroleum industry and at General Electric. Even so, stockholders and management in the new chemical industries were not always quick to see the advantages of expenditure on research that did not initially appear productive. Up to the First World War there was still a discernible gulf between the research scientist and industry. Divisions opened up between those scientists who were willing to work according to the schedules and requirements of industry and those who laid hold of older traditions and wanted research to be disinterested and pure, preferring, therefore, appointments where those values were acknowledged.

The decisive point in the history of the institutionalisation of Anglo-American science was reached in war. The impact of world wars, defence and imperial expansion in bringing government and science together is of such magnitude that it can hardly be disputed. Awkward as the truth may appear to be, war did more to provide the institutional backing for modern science than any other single development. This is hardly a surprise, but it requires some discussion none the less. Although the main interest of government was applied science, war provided opportunities for the most varied kinds of basic research: contracts for consulting, directly funded projects, the expansion of government-owned research laboratories and government support for universities. As funding arrangements were worked out, especially in the United States, the more limited or precise government objectives adopted at the outset were exceeded or widened.

The history of government involvement with science goes back, in the case of Britain, to the late seventeenth century when imperial interests were pursued largely at the expense of the Dutch, French and Spanish. The most notable collaboration between government and science occurred as a consequence of the founding of the Royal Society, which offered advice on navigation, the steam engine and gunnery. The received opinion is that the Society turned away from applied science and from an active association with the various branches of government. Marie Boas Hall has forced a reconsideration. Taking another look at the Society's Council minutes, she has discovered a considerable variety of links between the Society and government ministries when Britain was engaged in a momentous struggle with Napoleonic France. The ties beween the two continued on well past this period. The Board of Ordnance sought advice on gunpowder and cartridges, the Navy Office on copper sheeting and lightning conductors, the Customs Office on the fumigation of bales of cloth. The Treasury consulted the Society on the establishment of overseas observatories, and the government sought assistance on the construction of what became the Victoria Embankment along the Thames. In the middle of the nineteenth century the government decided to broaden its interest by providing a meagre £1000 per annum for the

promotion of science generally. The Royal Society was asked to adminis-
ter the fund, which went for the support of individual research or for specific investigations.[36]

These examples show us the multiple ways in which government
recognised science in the first half of the nineteenth century. There
was even more direct government involvement with scientific work than
is usually realised. The government supported tidal, ordnance and
geological surveys. It sponsored research into illuminants and lens systems
for lighthouses, an obvious interest for a nation that in 1850 controlled
42 per cent of the world's maritime trade.[37] It had scientific posts at the
Assay Office of the Royal Mint, the Observatory at Greenwich and
the Botanical Gardens at Kew. The Medical Department of the Privy
Council underwrote various kinds of scientific projects. The Inland
Revenue and Excise Department sponsored research into hydrography,
munitions and astronomy. Geological support was channelled through
the Museum of Economic Geology which was associated with the
Commissioners of Woods and Forests, as was the Mining Records Office.
In 1851 a School of Mines and Science Applied to the Arts was established.
The Board of Agriculture provided grants from the 1890s onwards
and was followed by a Development Commission for Agriculture and
Fisheries. Teacher-training grants stimulated an increase in science and
mathematics teachers.[38]

The Victorian State honoured certain historic arrangements but was
usually reluctant to embark on what appeared to be new directions.
Despite the pre-existing alliances between applied science and government, each fresh scientific venture had to be renegotiated and Cabinet or
civil service reluctance overcome. An excellent case is the establishment of
the National Physical Laboratory around 1900. The idea for the project
took wing in a period of great imperial economic and military rivalry. For
some decades prominent scientists had been asking for the creation of a
national laboratory that could undertake research for industry. There was
disagreement among them, however, as to whether the primary mission of

[36] Marie Boas Hall, 'Public Science in Britain: the Role of the Royal Society', *Isis*, 72 (1981),
627–9.
[37] Roy M. MacLeod, 'Science and Government in Victorian England: Lighthouse Illumination
and the Board of Trade, 1866–1886', *Isis*, 60 (Spring, 1969), 7.
[38] Roy M. Macleod, 'Science and the Treasury: Principles, Personalities and Policies,
1870–1885', in *The Patronage of Science in the Nineteenth Century*, ed. G. L. E. Turner
(Leyden, 1976); Roy M. Macleod, 'Resources of Science in Victorian England: The Endowment of Science Movement, 1868–1900', in *Science and Society, 1600–1900*, ed. Peter Mathias
(Cambridge, 1972), 11–66; W. H. Brock, 'The Spectrum of Science Patronage', in Turner,
ibid.

the laboratory should be pragmatic, whether it should content itself with testing electrical equipment or analysing chemical compounds and metals, or whether it should be pointed towards basic research. A number of leading scientists believed that only the universities should be entrusted with basic research. In any case, the British government saw no need for an industrial laboratory, at least not beyond a certain point. The marvellous explanation of the prime minister, Lord Salisbury, was that 'research into the secrets of nature affords a horizon to which there is no end or bound'.[39]

Scientists found considerable indifference to basic science in the senior levels of Whitehall, especially at the Treasury, which was required to furnish a modest annual grant towards operating expenses. The mandarins thought the laboratory should be user-supported and in the long run totally self-reliant. Some support for the laboratory from outside was in fact forthcoming. Fees doubled in the period before the First World War, and small private donations rounded out the budget. Testing was also undertaken for the Admiralty and the War Office. But government interest only really picked up when the laboratory began to undertake aeronautics research, which had clear military application. Treasury grants for this work increased strikingly as war approached.[40] Until the newly founded Department of Science and Industrial Research took over management of the laboratory in 1918, the Royal Society negotiated with the Treasury for the annual grant. The new arrangements solved the funding problem but continued to raise some fear that science had acquired a new master.[41]

The First World War increased the amount of government assistance to science. A number of prominent British academics still complained that government was slow to take advantage of the skills and talents of university scientists. There were some egregious and tragic blunders. A notable one was the death of the extraordinary physicist, H. G. J. Moseley, who enlisted in the army only to die at Gallipoli, and similar stupidities continued on even to 1917.[42] Valuable discoveries, such as Chaim

[39] Russell Moseley, 'The Origins and Early Years of the National Physical Laboratory: A Chapter in the Pre-history of British Science Policy', *Minerva*, 16 (Summer, 1978), 227.

[40] *Ibid.*, 249–50.

[41] *Ibid.*, 245.

[42] None of the First World War belligerents had a monopoly on idiocy. Science students, young researchers and professors from France and Germany also rushed to the front or were mobilised. They served in a variety of combat roles, from infantry to the technical services. Casualties were horrific. It took a year or more for the several governments to understand the effect of such wastage on the war effort. (Information from an unpublished paper by John Heilbron, 'Physicists in World War I'.)

Weizmann's process for the manufacture of acetone, essential for naval gunnery, were overlooked until 1916. This was of a piece, however, with the government's failure to mobilise the industrial effort until a year into the war when the shortage of shells led to a crisis. The turning point came with the establishment of a Ministry of Munitions in 1915 which called upon the universities for direct assistance in fighting the war. University scientists discovered new methods of creating explosives and battlefield gases, developed the gas mask, created new medical drugs, improved the properties of optical glass, essential for gunsights, rangefinders and periscopes (a German and Swiss monopoly before the war) and worked on aircraft and the hydrophone for detecting enemy submarines. The list of inventions is too vast for summary. Suffice it to say that innovation went on in every discernible scientific field, and the universities at Cardiff and Liverpool even undertook the manufacture of military hardware.[43]

Sanderson, whose treatment of the theme of war work is highly illuminating, maintains that the ties between university science and industry, which were strengthened during the years of the First World War, proved to be lasting, and he gives several examples of continuing cooperation. However that may be, it is certain from the record that scientists suspected that the new alliances both with industry and government might prove too limited. In May 1915 the Royal Society initiated government talks which eventually produced two important innovations with long-lasting consequences for the support of twentieth-century British science. The first was the creation of the University Grants Committee, to place the funding of the university sector on a regular basis. The second was the Department of Scientific and Industrial Research, to further a wider connection between science and industry. It is perhaps worth noting that the Department still fell short of what distinguished academics like the Nobel Prize winner J. J. Thomson, then president of the Royal Society, and the famous economist, Alfred Marshall, wanted, which was a science and industry office at ministry level.

Between the wars the Department of Scientific and Industrial Research found that many industries were simply uninterested in the benefits of applied science. When coaxing and encouragement failed, the Department established its own laboratories and offered assistance to industry. A given industry was asked to form a trade or research association which would then apply to the Department for assistance in solving specific industry-related problems, but this plan for creating a smooth working relationship between industry and government was inherently faulty.

[43] Sanderson, *Industry*, 232 and Chapter 8.

Many firms not only failed to perceive the direct benefit of such arrangements, they also sensed an erosion of their competitive market position if the results of research were shared widely within the industry. Large-scale firms especially, as they were able to afford their own laboratories, remained aloof. By contrast, since a university's income was mainly applied to teaching, as had always been true, university requests for research funds from the Department through a network of associated research councils tended to increase. By 1964 (and probably long before) when it was disbanded following new arrangements for funding basic research and postgraduate training, the Department had shifted its function from a government body with responsibilities to industry to one with exceptionally strong commitments to university research.[44]

In America no organisation comparable to the Department of Scientific and Industrial Research was created to stimulate scientific and technological research even after the mobilising efforts required to manage a global war. Instead of a single agency for disbursing tax money to science, the funding of research products was spread among a number of different departments of state and research councils. America remained committed to a liberal political philosophy of divided authority long after it was rejected in Britain. American scientists did not find the absence of a central bureaucratic focus necessarily a handicap. They prospered in an environment where plural sources of support were available and political representatives, unhampered by party loyalties, exercised influence as lordlings over committee fiefdoms. Projects rejected by one agency could be welcomed by another. Individual congressmen serving on key appropriations committees could be separately lobbied, cajoled, flattered and persuaded. Where political power is widely shared, the search for research funds may be time-consuming, but, in the American experience, the effort was successful. This conclusion hardly suggests that it will always remain so.

While decentralisation remains a particularly American preference, there are some crude similarities with the United Kingdom. In the US as in the UK, government, whether local or central, was understandably more interested in applied science and technology than in basic science. In the nineteenth century the federal government had concerned itself with exploring and developing the vast interior natural resources of the continent. The government supported a weather service, a naval observatory, coast and geodetic surveys, ordnance facilities, a Bureau of Standards and agricultural improvement stations. These in turn provided

[44] Ian Varcoe, *Organizing for Science in Britain* (Oxford, 1974), 80–1.

jobs for chemists, agronomists, meteorologists, metallurgists, mathematicians, physicists, astronomers and mining and hydraulic engineers. At the turn of the century, when America was rapidly urbanising, the federal government began to supply technical assistance to manufacturing. All of these efforts are closely parallel to the kind of science support provided by British governments of the same period.

And just like their British counterparts, American scientists had long disagreed on the effects of a closer link with government. The issue had been debated by the American Association for the Advancement of Science in the 1880s. As in the British case, the relative paucity of opportunities for the doing of science in industry ultimately threw the leading scientists towards the universities (at least in physics), and from the universities they approached government. It was believed, not without justification, that as government must pursue the common welfare, it could be persuaded to take the widest possible view of the utility of science. However, there were always scientists in Britain and America, and often the leaders, who were willing to extol the merits of science for the practical benefit of society. How much they believed in their own rhetoric is a matter of judgement. However, it may at least be suggested that the issue was not always the utility of science but the terms on which support would be demanded – and the degree of control to be exercised from outside the scientific community on the project itself, on the use of postdocs and their training, on the hiring of staff, on the construction of laboratories, on methods and techniques of investigation, on matters that the working scientist wanted to retain as a matter of professional discretion. These were no less than the classic elements and concerns of guild association: not support at any cost but support in conjunction with the benefits of a service ethic that neither government nor markets was expected to define. The constraints on guild conduct were substantial but self-imposed and comprised a moral code designed to assure users that the service being proffered was well beyond rudimentary self-interest.

Members of the American Association for the Advancement of Science discussed the desirability of a closer involvement with government, but members of the National Academy of Sciences, founded during the Civil War, actively sought it. During the First World War the Academy established another body, called the National Research Council, which was essentially an advisory body occupying a position not unlike that held by the Royal Society. Later a National Academy of Engineering was founded in confederation with the Academy, partly to assuage the anger of technologists who had not been invited to join the original Academy.

After half a century, the number of different scientific bodies providing advice to the federal government can only be described as staggering. The president and Pentagon have science advisory councils, the army and navy have theirs, the Environmental Protection Agency, the Department of Transportation, the Department of Labour all sponsor science projects conducted in universities. There are quasi-governmental agencies like the Atomic Energy Commission, the National Science Foundation, the National Aeronautics and Space Agency and the National Institutes of Health, which support projects in their own laboratories or fund them in universities. Together these form a decentralised set of institutions, in accordance with American pluralism, with support less concentrated than in the research councils of European countries. Possibly the differences are only a question of degree, since science support in today's United Kingdom is also dispensed from numerous public or quasi-public bodies. Yet the differences in the political system of each nation remain profound. The executive in the American constitution cannot retain as close a control over the numerous agencies of government as can a British Cabinet backed by a majority party. However, the changing configuration of European science support in the 1990s as a result of the European Union cannot be overlooked as a future determinant of science policy.

PEER AND PROJECT REVIEW SYSTEMS

In his valuable book, Daniel Greenberg has noted that government support for science in America is based on two principles, that of peer review and that of the project.[45] Peer review actually owes a great deal to the private philanthropic foundations which developed this form of assessment in the period before the Second World War. Its origins in some form may even be traceable to the nineteenth century, or perhaps further back to the earliest days of the Royal Society.

The project system derives from the war itself. As part of project costs, universities were granted the right to charge high overheads for administering grants given to principal investigators. For some years the project system was really a device for channelling assistance into the higher education sector when Congress was unwilling to provide universities with any other kind of assistance. In the 1980s overhead costs became a major bone of contention, partly because of public pressure to reduce government spending. How universities used and reported their overhead became a subject of government inquiry. Individual investigators complained that campus administrations had sequestered grants (sometimes called 'opportunity funds') intended for them and their supporting departments, spreading them around the campus to subsidise activities not provided for in line-item budgets. Other issues did not involve the use and mismanagement of overheads. Large sums granted to certain academic fields and certain individuals created disparities in income and status between the disciplines. Summer income, postgraduate fellowships and postdoctoral appointments were more readily available in science and technical fields, or in some applied social science areas. Degree candidates in other disciplines struggled to make ends meet, spent considerable time in teaching and postponed completing their degrees (although this was not the only reason for delay).

The project system, combined with peer review and the influence of the key advisory committees and elite science associations, also created disparities between institutions, exciting jealousies and giving rise to charges of favouritism and unfair treatment. The counter argument was that research money should go to the best talent and the best organised research units, but any explanation based on merit will always be regarded by someone else as an excuse for privilege.

In both Britain and America many scientists turned away from the private sector of the economy when that sector proved, initially, to be resistant to the allures of applied science. Government and the universities were the principal alternatives, therefore, but the universities, fulfilling their historic role of teaching and preparation for the liberal professions, could not provide the resources necessary for twentieth-century science. Ultimately science turned to government, and the experience of the wars, followed by global military tension between East and West, expanded and reconstructed the relationship. The peer review system in America, the project system, the establishment of an imposing network of advisory bodies in government, quasi-public funding agencies like the National Science Foundation, the creation of central elite associations, comprise a formidable if hardly invincible system of scientific influence in the United States. They represent the culmination of a drive for professional recognition that began a century ago when science began to sell itself to prospective buyers, and when scientists, like other men of ideas, slowly but steadily learned how to publicise their virtues. A similar process was discernible in Britain.

SCIENCE AS A PROFESSION

Energetic but lacking both a shared intellectual purpose and a common institutional identity, scientists of earlier centuries were not in a position to combine. The absence of a clear conception of science as an occupation, however, did not prevent voluntary umbrella associations from arising. These, beginning in the seventeenth century, continued to be founded right into the nineteenth century. As noted, they marketed scientific services and provided a limited amount of direct support for research. Nevertheless, scientists could not have improved their support base in more recent periods if they had not successfully learned how to bring influence to bear on modern government. Scientists were able to do this because, like other professional groups that arose in the nineteenth century, they specialised, concentrated their energies on a clear scientific mission, systematically broadened their institutional means of support and learned how to transform existing associations into reliable lobby groups. They produced leaders, spokesmen and *ad hoc* committees, all of which, by their very existence, lent credence to the claim that scientists did in fact comprise a community with a single purpose. Scientists also substantially improved their claim to speak as professional experts. Since for centuries the expert status of scientists was in doubt, or at least ambiguous, this is a point worth further discussion, but to illustrate the point it is not necessary to provide examples from earlier than the middle of the nineteenth century.

One of the first steps taken in the direction of professionalism was the drawing of clear lines between career research scientists and the general run of practitioners and dabblers who had for so long populated the scientific universe. Joseph Henry, America's leading physicist in the middle of the nineteenth century, announced in 1846 that 'We are overrun in this country with charlatanism. Our newspapers are filled with puffs of Quackery and every man who can burn phosphorus in oxygen and exhibit a few experiments to a class of young ladies is called a man of science.'[46] In the next few years the emerging scientific researchers competed against the representatives of the tradition of the man of letters for control of the Smithsonian Institution (the gift of a British philanthropist). After much Congressional lobbying and shrewd political in-fighting, they succeeded in capturing the Smithsonian for the specialist.[47] In 1874 the research scientists in the American Association for the Advancement of Science assumed the leadership in an organisation which, like the British Association for the Advancement of Science, founded in the 1830s, was composed of amateurs, 'cultivators', technicians, gentlemen of science and all others who had an interest in scientific work whether or not their

---

[46] Miller, *Dollars for Research*, 7.   [47] *Ibid.*, 15–23.

careers depended upon it. The amateur or lay members were banished to
the periphery. Henceforth only those who were called fellows could hold
office, and most fellows were career scientists.[48] In Britain the lay element
within the Royal Society declined after 1881 as the career scientists
tightened their control over that celebrated institution.[49] In sum, a
distinction that had been blurred over in centuries past was made precise,
and associations that had once represented many interests now
represented fewer, reflecting developments within science itself where
specialisation was winning. Some scientists were now 'mere' practitioners,
and others were serious, that is, professional. Their lives were dedicated to
science, and their stake in it was greater because they were paid.

A case might be made for the opposite. The unpaid – the 'amateur' –
should be regarded as having the stronger commitment to science for he
requires no incentive other than his love for the subject. The amateur
delights (*dilettare*) in his work. No doubt there is some truth in this
paradox, but the fact remains that necessity is a primary driving force in
human affairs. The dilettante, sufficient unto himself, does not possess
the sense of urgency or desire for immortality that organises and
institutionalises thought, that brings into existence acolytes and potential
followers variously called apprentices, interns, pupils, clerks and
probationers. Or, as Max Weber phrased it, the dilettante does not know
how to estimate and exploit even his most excellent ideas.[50]

Academic professionalism coincided with the expansion of higher
education opportunities in the last decades of the nineteenth century. New
institutions were arising rapidly. New institutions are generally more
amenable to change than older ones. The story of the University of
London is a case in point, as are the English provincial universities, but the
American university structure following the Civil War was particularly
open or at least in the process of removing such constraints on innovation
as earlier may have existed. New academic disciplines did not face the
hurdles imposed on the Continent by a system of chairholder control over
faculties, institutes and departments. (Joseph Ben-David has explained
how young German researchers needed to migrate in search of

---

[48] Kevles, *Physicists*, 41–2. Separatist feeling had emerged even at the time of the founding of
the British Association for the Advancement of Science. '[It] would be desirable', wrote
Whewell, 'in some way to avoid the crowd of lay members whose names stand on the lists of
the Royal Society.' The inclusionists won, however, at least initially. See A. D. Orange, 'The
British Association for the Advancement of Science: The Provincial Background', *Science
Studies*, 1 (1971), 315–29, esp. 326.

[49] D. S. L. Cardwell, *The Organization of Science in England* (London, 1957), 176.

[50] Max Weber, 'Science as a Vocation', in *From Max Weber*, ed. and trans. H. H. Gerth and
C. Wright Mills (London, 1970), 136.

opportunities for innovation.[51]) Furthermore, no federal system on the model of London existed. New subjects and subdisciplines did not have to contend with a supra-departmental examining system, whether on the unitary or federal university model.

Nevertheless, British universities enjoyed one advantage over American ones with respect to the advance of specialism. Once a new subject was established within a university, it could proceed along lines of further specialisation with relative ease. Students usually read only one subject (or in Scotland several) while at university. In America, the spread of the course module both facilitated and inhibited the progress of specialisation. The module made course innovation easy, providing individual researchers with freedoms that could hardly be imagined in Europe. It was also simple for university presidents to support particular subjects, because in doing so they encountered fewer vested interests. Professional subspecialisation could proceed exactly as described by Roger Geiger: some subjects 'led predominantly by knowledge growth, some by community formation, and others by university sponsorship'.[52] Yet the very success of modularity in America gave rise to a reaction in favour of broader rather than specialised curricula. Science teachers might have their majors as well as captive audiences wherever breadth requirements were introduced, but they also had to share undergraduates with many other departments and disciplines. Further specialisation in the United States was not possible without the inauguration of separate graduate schools. Do American forms of general education make the nation more hospitable to pure science? It is impossible to know. But there is no doubt that general education has generated student audiences for science lecturers.

In today's Britain, Treasury control over the civil service and greater centralisation usually mean that British scientists have fewer options than American ones,[53] but generally speaking it is accurate to conclude that up to the 1990s at least scientists in both countries are the beneficiaries of the governmental support systems which they have sought, even when hesitant, for a century or more.

The State in western democracies today is a very different institution

[51] Joseph Ben-David, *Scientific Growth,* ed. Gad Freudenthal (Berkeley and Los Angeles, 1991), 116–17.
[52] Roger L. Geiger, *To Advance Knowledge, the Growth of American Research Universities, 1900–1940* (New York, 1986), 20.
[53] For a role similar to the Treasury's now being assumed by the Office of Management and Budget in Washington, see James Everett Katz, *Presidential Politics and Science Policy* (New York and London, 1978), 66–83.

442   *Alternatives: 2. Born to have no rest*

from what it was in previous centuries. It is far more formidable and arguably more competent, but it is also subject to plural pressures from below. Recent changes in American politics illustrate the confusion that can result and its effects on the practice of pure science. The continuing disintegration of party loyalty in a country with a long history of relatively weak political parties has produced a vacuum filled by single-issue pressure groups: the environmental lobby, the oil lobby, the women's movement, the animal rights movement, the campaign against the misuse of medicinal drugs, and so on. Each has its own priorities for the use of tax monies. Each has a public position on the uses to which science should be put and on how university laboratories ought to be managed, regulated and staffed. Furthermore, several controversial issues, usually involving nuclear, biological, environmental and human or animal subjects research, understandably engage the emotions of scientists as well as laymen. The resulting division of expert opinion has inevitably weakened public confidence in the judgement of scientists, many of whom are suspected of narrow self-interest and contempt for the public anyway on issues ranging from disputes over the credit for discoveries, the falsification or careless use of evidence, the withholding of embarrassing research findings to medical malpractice.

Ironically, given current public discontent with the professions, one other source of difficulty for institutionalised science, especially university based science, is the spread of professionalism into areas of government from which it has hitherto been absent. The very success of the American higher education system has contributed to a remarkable increase in the number of young college graduates employed by congressmen, senators and assemblymen at state and national levels. Consequently elected representatives have a better grasp of issues and complexities, or perhaps it is better said, tend to rely for advice and information on their staffs as much as on outside experts. College graduates, especially recent ones, have a certain amount of inside information on how educational institutions function, at least with respect to matters that concern them, and their perceived dissatisfactions are easily communicated to political incumbents. (The British MP has nothing remotely approaching this enormous and quite unprecedented staff support expansion. A small step in that direction was undertaken in the 1980s by the use of a parliamentary system of standing or select committees on a congressional model but with limited results.[54])

---

[54] Geoffrey Smith and Nelson W. Polsby, *British Government and its Discontents* (New York, 1981), 126–34.

The setting of science priorities in America from outside the guild has also been affected by what some analysts have called the emergence of the 'power presidency'. The interest of the executive branch in science matters goes back a long way, but it is essentially an outgrowth of the Progressive Era with its emphasis on social reconstruction and government regulation of the economy. During the 1920s and 1930s, however, physical scientists did not succeed in gaining a firm footing in the White House. Social scientists in the 1930s had more influence in Roosevelt-era New Deal programmes. But since the Second World War presidents have been very much concerned with science and applied science; and, according to one analyst, have acquired a much stronger role in science policy-making.[55] The growth of a huge system of defence contracting and funding for at least 4000 Research and Development installations has provided an opportunity for the executive branch to exercise greater management of these sectors through its constitutional authority over the granting of contracts. The executive branch has also acquired some of the glamour that for centuries surrounded the princely courts of Europe where hangers-on lingered in expectation of rewards and recognition, pensions, honours, privileges and favours. Leading scientists instinctively gravitate towards the centre, welcoming appointments as science advisers. It is perfectly in keeping with the authority vested in the president to choose congenial advisers, but it has been suggested that the selection of advisers is often based on political or ideological expediency. Issues that lie on the border between science policy and social policy – abortions, for example, or the teaching of Darwinian theory in state-supported schools, issues on which there is currently a serious division of national or religious opinion – especially lend themselves to political exploitation. It has also been suggested that several presidents have openly espoused science pro-grammes which they have no intention of establishing or keeping merely to improve their public image.[56]

SCIENCE AS AN OPEN COMMUNITY

Western scientists certainly appear to subscribe to the proposition that freedom of scientific interchange is essential to the progress of science. 'Scientific communication is traditionally open and international in character', affirmed a National Academy of Sciences panel inquiring into the problems of technology transfer in the 1980s (the Corson Report).

---

[55] Katz, *Presidential Politics*, for most of what follows.   [56] *Ibid.*, 215.

'Scientific advance depends on worldwide access to all the prior findings in a field – and, often, in seemingly unrelated fields – and on systematic critical review of findings by the world scientific community.' The panel then considered the question of national security, concluding that controls on technology transfer should be imposed only as a very last resort, even if risks were involved, and that universities in particular should rarely be subject to restrictions.[57]

A number of separate but interrelated issues have to be considered. The first is the actual degree to which scientists, practitioners, *savants* and so on have been willing to share the results of their inquiries. The second is the degree to which, therefore, they have regarded themselves as part of a family, a common culture or a network of learned men and women devoted to a single purpose. The third is their dislike of secrecy, even self-imposed secrecy, and their resistance to attempts to impose it upon them so that research results cannot be widely shared.

As expected, the historical picture is contradictory. It is very difficult to estimate the extent to which science has been what John Ziman calls public knowledge or has formed itself into invisible colleges.[58] For earlier centuries a vast amount of information on the formation of international networks lies hidden in private correspondence. Some of it has been made public, such as that of Martin Mersenne and Henry Oldenburg, but much remains to be found. It is also difficult to measure the amount of science kept secret in earlier centuries, either because of the threat of persecution in the Counter-Reformation, or the fear of offending powerful patrons or because of rivalries and jealousies engendered by the race for fame. Personal quirks and special circumstances abound, as in the case of the alchemists, who were secretive about their work. Many of Newton's writings had to be pried from him, though that may have been more the result of uncertainty on his part than a desire to withhold information. His mystical beliefs were also likely to upset representatives of the Church of England. The great seventeenth-century experimentalist, Robert Hooke, wrote down some of his findings in anagram form and deposited them in the Royal Society to shake off competitors and establish priority of discovery.[59] In the nineteenth century the famous geologist, Charles Lyell,

---

[57] *Scientific Communication and National Security*, a report prepared by the Panel on Scientific Communication and National Security, Committee on Science, Engineering and Public Policy, National Academy of Sciences (1982), 2, 48–51. The panel's guidelines for deciding when restrictions on university research are warranted have not been easy to interpret, however. See *New York Times* (26 June 1983), EY9.

[58] John Ziman, *Public Knowledge, the Social Dimension of Science* (Cambridge, 1968).

[59] Information from Hahn and Heilbron.

systematically misled the public on the implications of his theories concerning the Noachian Deluge, since the issue was tempestuous. Eager to appease benefactors and achieve public acclaim, he coaxed into history a view of himself as a man of the utmost probity.[60] As a story of professional rivalry, the desire for prestige, the temporary withholding of critical information in order to ensure priority of publication, we have no book so frank as *The Double Helix*, which is invaluable as an account of some of the contradictions created by the institutionalisation of science at present.

We have already noticed that secret research on metals was carried out by London University scientists before the First World War on contract to the steel industry. War itself, it goes without saying, makes the survival of normative values difficult. When the nation is imperilled, the usual reservations are suspended, but for how long afterwards? The scale of preparation for modern war and the weaponry employed during conflict places a special burden on scientists. It brings into consideration the issue of classified research. American scientists associated with the National Research Council broke with the military after the First World War precisely because of the secrecy issue.[61] However, is such conduct typical of academic scientists? What does the 'idea of a university' tell us about nationalism and the university? Newman himself thought of his new university in Ireland as Irish but only because it was Roman Catholic. Strong national feeling has interfered with international scientific cooperation in the past and is not absent today. The First World War virtually destroyed the international community of science as represented by the International Association of Academies, an organisation consisting of twenty-one national academies, fourteen of them in belligerent nations, four of them in Germany alone. The International Research Council, which was founded after the war as a successor to the International Association of Academies, changing its name in 1931 to the International Council of Scientific Unions, was heavily politicised, national interests continually dominating discussions and programmes. Long before the First World War, literary, archaeological, philosophical and geological academies, either of national origin operating abroad or of international constitution, were showing the same effects of patriotic zeal. Many academicians, whether scientists or not, simply accepted their role as instruments of national policy. Their partisanship was no more

[60] Roy Porter, 'Charles Lyell: The Public and Private Faces of Science', *Janus* (1982), 29–50.
[61] Kevles, *Physicists*, 148.

sophisticated than the crudest jingoism from the classic period of imperialism.[62]

Can science or any academic speciality resist the call to arms when the nation is imperilled or when national 'interest' is invoked? The questions are hardly new. As long ago as the 1830s, the brilliant English mathematician, Charles Babbage, a great propagandist for the importance of research, talked about a race between nations for scientific achievement. It was Sir Norman Lockyer, the distinguished astronomer, who in the early 1900s asked that British universities be mobilised for imperial struggle with Germany. Two British universities were to be built for every German one, he said, making an explicit comparison between universities and British naval policy.

Yet even in national emergencies serious differences of opinion have existed on whether strategic information ought to be released. Atomic scientists in the United States decided to withhold publication of information that might aid Germany's ambition for world conquest when several scientists gradually realised that the discovery of the chain reaction in nuclear fission could result in the development of a terrifying weapon. Leo Szilard, driven out of Hungary by the Nazis, was working on fission with a team of Columbia University physicists in the late 1930s. His imagination foresaw the creation of atomic weapons, and he appealed to leading nuclear physicists, younger researchers and journal editors to refrain from publishing any information that might be useful to Germany. Many of the principal scientists in Britain and the United States, refusing to believe that danger was imminent, were disturbed by Szilard's demand for a conspiracy of silence, which a number of them regarded as absolutely antithetical to science. Others went so far as to suspect him of private motives, none flattering. The American government saw no case for secrecy, but Szilard prevailed. The result was a setback for German atomic development and a corresponding gain for American science.[63]

How does secrecy in general affect the scientist's code of professional ethics? It can be argued that even short-term secrecy has an adverse affect on professional relationships. Peer and project review processes are definitely influenced, for how can hidden work be evaluated, and if hidden work cannot be subjected to open criticism, how can quality be assured? Trust disintegrates rapidly in an environment of secrecy, as even the Szilard episode shows. Existing rivalries are exacerbated, new ones

---

[62] Brigitte Schröder, 'Caractéristiques des relations scientifiques internationales, 1870–1914', *Cahiers d'histoire mondiale,* 10 (1966), 161–77.

[63] Spencer R. Weart, 'Scientists with a Secret', *Physics Today* (February, 1976), 23–30.

created. Secrecy affects the industrial scientist in another way, since firms are required to declare a profit. In an empirical study, Kenneth Prandy has shown how scientists and engineers employed in industry are caught between labour market conceptions of an employee and professional ideals of status. The interesting question is why scientists who are clearly dependent upon employers retain professional ideals, since they weaken job protections, such as class loyalties and collective bargaining.[64] Income, honours, prizes and recognition are, it is certain, important elements in any occupation, but the central animating value of scientific professional life is distinction of mind as recognised by those most qualified to judge. Employers have the power to reduce income and terminate employment. Professions have the power to deny or diminish esteem. Each sanction emanates from a different body of values.

Secrecy upsets working relationships based on the team and the research unit. While prototypical instances may be cited, the team is a relatively new form of scientific endeavour, virtually unknown in the earliest days of modern science when the scientist worked more or less alone and kept his own counsel. It would be a nice test, indeed, to determine how successful science and applied science have been without the cross-fertilisation that occurs within the research team, without the confirmation and verification necessary for high-level work. Of course whole teams can and do work together secretly. What are the consequences of such arrangements in what may gingerly be called normal times?

Since in America and Britain the universities have a great share in fundamental research, greater than in Germany and France where research has been placed into extra-university institutes and programmes under mainly government auspices, secrecy is a persistent problem for university based physical scientists. Are foreign graduate students to be given access to classified projects, or barred from teaching that involves issues of technology transfer? So troubling is the question of classified research in the contemporary university that one hears suggestions of moving research laboratories into other kinds of institutions where academic scruples may not weigh quite so heavily, or, as a first step, dissociating federally supported laboratories from university management. These proposed solutions are hardly simple. To take only an obvious point, the scientific elite in the United States tends to be concentrated in or near the leading research universities. Diverting public money

[64] Kenneth Prandy, *Professional Employees, a Study of Scientists and Engineers* (London, 1965), 176–8.

from university to federally owned and managed laboratories may solve an administrative or ethical problem, but it hardly begins to address the question of the quality of scientific research.[65]

It would not, in any case, solve all ethical problems. As said before, scientists may at certain times for purposes of institutional necessity behave as if they were a single community, but at other times the cracks and divisions show. How the individual scientist accepts the restrictions brought about by secrecy imposed from the outside depends upon a number of considerations. It depends upon how theoretical or applied is the research undertaken and therefore how close to the actual production of destructive weapons. It also depends upon the science speciality, the need for costly equipment, the size of the research team and the degree to which support derives from defence contracts. Doubtless many scientists would prefer to carry on their work untroubled by such academic and perhaps for them irrelevant intrusions.

'Public knowledge' as an ideal faces additional challenges at the moment in America through the combined pressures of a new phase of international economic competition – other nations feel this as well – and the financial stringency affecting so many American research universities. The expenses of research universities are fixed, equipment needs to be upgraded, the imposition of new missions leads to new financial burdens. Government support has not kept pace in either Britain or America, if for different reasons, and all universities, public, private or 'privatised', have intensified their appeals to non-governmental sources. In genetic engineering and biomedical research some professors have actually formed corporations and companies, a matter of concern to Americans (although not to Europeans for some reason) because of conflict of interest issues. Consulting activities lead to similar problems and controversial attempts by administration and academic senates to define the normal work week, place limits on the receipt of outside income and revise regulations regarding outside employment.[66] Yet temptations continually arise. 'Privatising' in Britain (and elsewhere in Europe) and the search for income characteristic of American colleges and universities are likely to

---

[65] Some writers have even suggested that teaching, professional education and research functions are not comfortably integrated in most systems of mass higher education, or at best only integrated in isolated parts of a given institution. They suggest that the natural home for scientific research is not necessarily the modern university and that for developing countries especially a parting of the ways would be beneficial to both. See the discussion in Simon Schwartzman, 'The Focus On Scientific Activity', in *Perspectives on Higher Education, Eight Disciplinary and Comparative Views*, ed. Burton R. Clark (Berkeley and Los Angeles, 1984).

[66] A heated issue before the Berkeley Division of the Academic Senate in 1995.

produce awkward episodes such as occurred in 1981 and 1982 when a wealthy industrialist named Edwin C. Whitehead concluded an arrangement with the Massachusetts Institute of Technology (MIT) unique in the history of American higher education. The Whitehead Institute for Biomedical Research was approved by the MIT administration; and although opposition to the alliance was bitter and vociferous, the MIT faculty supported the agreement (with some reservations) by a ratio of eight to one in a straw vote despite fears that Whitehead's business interests would lead him to favour research with commercial application. The administration approved of the Institute connection because it increased MIT's biology faculty by one-third, provided more operating funds and a huge endowment (when Whitehead died) and put their institution into the forefront of bio-engineering research.[67]

The ramifications of current trends favouring wealth-generating technologies or research on social issues with medical and environmental implications, or the privatisation of universities and technological institutes in some countries, cannot be wholly anticipated. Conventional polarities – pure versus applied science, guild versus market control of intellectual products – are breaking down as the organisation of science shifts even more heavily towards team research with built-in sunset clauses specifying project termination dates. From the research scientist's point of view, the issue remains adequate support for pure science; but there will always be (there always have been) scientists who believe that even massive intrusions of public money will first serve other interests. After the First World War the British mathematician, Hyman Levy, stated that government support of science had a much greater impact on the growth of science as a profession than on basic research.[68] Similar arguments are raised in connection with the National Aeronautics Space Administration and space exploration generally, the pure science advocates expressing disappointment with the expenditure of public money when prestige and political considerations are present.

Historically, however, the boundaries between pure and applied science and technology have been imprecise. Significant cross-fertilisation has occurred, and it is difficult in practice to disentangle 'R' from 'D' or 'D' from 'R' in a research and development budget despite one conclusion that

---

[67] See *Science*, 214 (23 October 1981), 416–17, and *Nature*, 294 (26 November 1981), 297. Dorothy Zinberg of the Center for Science and International Affairs at Harvard University very kindly sent me information on the establishment of the Whitehead Institute for Biomedical Research.

[68] Roy and Kay Macleod, 'The Contradictions of Professionalism: Scientists, Trade Unionism and the First World War', *Social Studies of Science*, 9 (1979), 2.

in the United States 'R' comprises no more than 10 per cent of the whole. It is maintained that the difference between basic and applied science depends less upon the actual research assignment than on such elusive factors as the motivation of the researcher. At the same time it is grudgingly conceded that the relationship between pure science and utility is problematical and is perhaps clearest only during the educational process undergone by technologists, who are usually trained in basic science. The conventional wisdom is that technology builds upon itself.[69]

ORIGINALITY

Contradictions and dilemmas inherent in the system of rewards and incentives created by science have continuously produced awkward instances of conduct inconsistent with the belief in open communication. Robert Merton places them under the heading of 'ambivalences', and he notes that the social institutions of science are malintegrated.[70] The structure of modern knowledge rests on a late nineteenth-century premise that originality is the leading characteristic of the most advanced and esteemed work, but discovery was not always accorded the special distinction it enjoys today. In the writings of eighteenth-century humanists like Jonathan Swift and Samuel Johnson, scientists were viewed as madmen eager to control the processes of nature. In the nineteenth century discovery in science and scholarship was regarded as inappropriate for the education of undergraduates, who would be disturbed by wild conclusions or misled into the narrow paths of specialism. Small achievements, it was asserted, would be magnified out of all reasonable proportion, and the resulting puffery of self would damage academic working relationships. In America there were fears that research might adversely affect the partnership between the university and alumni, whose identification with alma mater derived from the memory of happy college days of games, theatricals, beer parties and eccentric professors. These were not foolish arguments. They emanated from a

[69] Greenberg, *Pure Science*, 31–2. It is often impossible to distinguish between the categories. A Pentagon listing of basic research projects included 'self-contained munitions', 'electro-optic counter-measures', 'low speed takeoff and landing' (*New York Times*, 26 June 1983). Yet no one disagrees that development leads research. In Sweden R&D in industry means only about 3 per cent for 'R'. Svante Lindqvist in *Science, Technology and Society in the Time of Alfred Nobel*, ed. Carl Gustaf Bernhard, Elisabeth Crawford and Per Sörbom, Nobel Symposium 52 (17–22 August 1981), 300–1.
[70] Robert Merton, *Sociological Ambivalence and Other Essays* (New York, 1976), 32–65.

particular conception of the university and of knowledge, and they were related to very specific educational objectives. Since then a very different kind of intellectual world has developed with a different set of values.

In order to be appreciated in this new world, the scientist had to be original, yet what was originality? How was it to be weighed, measured, assessed? At what stage could it be recognised? When should one publish? The question led to the notion of premature publication, to waiting 'until all the evidence was in', but what if rivals declined to wait? How were the accusations of postgraduate students that professors appropriated their work to be adjudicated? And who should receive primary credit in a collaborative effort? How was unintentional plagiarism to be handled? What about the issue of simultaneous discovery, difficult enough, and priority of discovery? These have been problems for scientists since at least Galileo. As questions involving professional ethics, they became more pressing because of the issue of originality, the expansion of research opportunities and the proliferation of rewards for success.

Merton cites a marvellous passage from the life of Freud which states the dilemma of originality acutely and ironically. Reading a work on Michelangelo published by an Englishman in 1863, Freud was startled to find therein certain observations which he supposed original to himself. He found himself 'anticipated' – surely the most remarkable euphemism in the researcher's vocabulary. Distressed, he consoled himself with two rationalisations. The first was that no matter who published first, he himself had made the observation independently. The second was that his own discovery was now 'confirmed'.[71] Any research scientist or scholar experiences the same mixture of fright and reassurance in attempting both psychologically and professionally to cope with the internal conflict between a personal desire for esteem and a sense of belonging to a city-state of common intentions, in straddling the gulf between self-interest and disinterest.[72]

---

[71] *Ibid.*, 42.

[72] Science makes discoveries. Are these qualitatively similar to those which historians, literary critics, linguists or economists make? The building-block characteristics of science which make incremental discovery so central – perhaps thereby increasing the professional pressure on young researchers – may not really be matched in the social sciences and humanities. Fear of the 'scoop' certainly exists outside the sciences. But other factors strongly enter into the evaluation of non-scientific work: rhetorical questions of composition, art, communication; broad humane questions of vision, wisdom, a grasp of the whole. These are not, of course, absent from scientific work, but are they so paramount?

WHITHER?

Science is a branch of knowledge. It is also an intellectual product. It is an end in itself. It is also useful. Scientists may distrust markets, or grudgingly accept them, sometimes preferring the State as buyer, but they require markets in order to function, as do universities and the guilds of practitioners. The resulting entanglements, as well as those arising from other causes, political or cultural, produce the mixtures of anxieties, self-seeking and idealism rife in these voyages around Newman. No institution can ever remain free of entanglements in any serious sense. Nostalgia for a golden age of independence is unwarranted, but so is simple-minded optimism, although both, being present in the historical record, are legitimate subjects for investigation.

In every instance of historical change there are losses and gains, but how they are to be selected and assessed is a matter of judgement. 'Idea', so necessary for Newman, and 'place', so fascinating a part of the history of universities – 'the question of the *site* is the very first that comes into consideration, when a *Studium Generale* is contemplated, for that site should be a liberal and noble one'[73] – are less essential to those who see history as a narrative of privilege or to those whose vision of the future includes cyberspace but not snapdragons. The College Invisible, home to some of the most creative collaborative work in science and scholarship, is antithetical to the College Visible, home to the nurturing experiences associated with coming of age. Standardised, national examinations, hotly debated in Britain yesterday and today but weakly advocated in the United States, are at once the enemy of innovation and self-discovery and the path to advancement by merit. And guild ideals, the fiduciary responsibilities that secure honour and authority for practitioners, how are they to be viewed? As apologies for collective advantage or as a genuine code of ethics, a self-denying ordinance really, by which practitioners pledge themselves to uphold the rules of evidence and acknowledge the limitations of disciplines and competence? Such dilemmas are continual and cannot be resolved. However, failure to acknowledge them openly and sensitively will, as is already evident, severely compromise the autonomy of the guild-university, which must always be more than a collection of individuals, since knowledge acquisition is itself a joint undertaking.[74]

---

[73] John Henry Newman, *Historical Sketches*, III (London, 1881), 24.
[74] I am, I suppose, less confident than Edward Shils about the internal strength of science's devotion to the pursuit of truth and excellence, as portrayed, for example, in his *The Torment*

The university arrives at the end of another century caught between two uncompromising polarities apparent in these chapters. The first is the on-going stimulus to differentiate and divide into specialised activities or arrangements, intellectual domains and career patterns in response to multiple and unavoidable pressures, as already present in consumer-minded, competitive Scotland and America in the eighteenth century.[75] But the second is exactly the opposite and is partly but not wholly a reaction to the first. It is the tendency for universities to shed their distinguishing traits and whatever legacies they may respect and converge on common types.[76] In either case, what do we gain or lose?

For many centuries universities have exercised a disconcerting aesthetic and moral hold upon the imagination of European and American societies. University histories are full of promise, full of disappointments, but always, like the open ovals of seventeenth-century astronomers, pointing beyond themselves. The result resembles the one described by Thucydides as he pondered the essence of his native Attica. Athens, reflected the exiled narrator, was born to have no rest. It would also give none to others.

---

of Secrecy (New York, 1956). He underplayed, I believe, the internal vulnerability of institutionalised intellectual life. But I obviously agree that without ideals and an appeal to the best parts of a tradition, the enterprise is forsaken. The scientist's responsibility to society, professional ethics and the role of the public in deciding which projects should be funded are discussed at length in Keith M. Wulff, *Regulation of Scientific Inquiry* (Washington DC, 1979). See also Michael Burrage, 'Why Do Professions Behave the Way They Do', in *Societies Made Up of History*, ed. Ragnar Björk and Karl Molin (Edsbruk, 1996), 131–46.

[75] Donald J. Withrington. 'The Scottish Universities: Living Traditions? Old Problems Renewed?', in *The Scottish Government Yearbook 1992*, ed. Lindsay Paterson and David McCrone (Edinburgh, 1992), 132.

[76] Or as Burton R. Clark puts it: 'Most perilous are the sectors where open access and the search for clientele has turned purpose into all things for all people.' The end result is deprofessionalisation. See *The Academic Life, Small Worlds, Different Worlds* (Carnegie Foundation for the Advancement of Teaching, 1987), 273.

INDEX